Lecture Notes in Computer Science 10894

Commenced Publication in 1973
Founding and Former Series Editors:
Gerhard Goos, Juris Hartmanis, and Jan van Leeuwen

More information about this series at http://www.springer.com/series/7409

Domenico Prattichizzo · Hiroyuki Shinoda
Hong Z. Tan · Emanuele Ruffaldi
Antonio Frisoli (Eds.)

Haptics: Science, Technology, and Applications

11th International Conference, EuroHaptics 2018
Pisa, Italy, June 13–16, 2018
Proceedings, Part II

 Springer

Editors
Domenico Prattichizzo
University of Siena
Siena
Italy

Hiroyuki Shinoda
University of Tokyo
Tokyo
Japan

Hong Z. Tan
Purdue University
West Lafayette, IN
USA

Emanuele Ruffaldi
Scuola Superiore Sant'Anna
Pisa
Italy

and

MMI s.p.a.
Pisa
Italy

Antonio Frisoli
Scuola Superiore Sant'Anna
Pisa
Italy

ISSN 0302-9743   ISSN 1611-3349 (electronic)
Lecture Notes in Computer Science
ISBN 978-3-319-93398-6   ISBN 978-3-319-93399-3 (eBook)
https://doi.org/10.1007/978-3-319-93399-3

Library of Congress Control Number: 2018946626

LNCS Sublibrary: SL3 – Information Systems and Applications, incl. Internet/Web, and HCI

Printed on acid-free paper

This Springer imprint is published by the registered company Springer International Publishing AG
part of Springer Nature
The registered company address is: Gewerbestrasse 11, 6330 Cham, Switzerland

Preface

This volume contain the proceedings of the EuroHaptics 2018 conference, which was held in Pisa, Italy, during June 13–16, 2018. EuroHaptics is a major international conference on haptics and touch-enabled computer applications and is the primary European meeting for researchers in this field.

Eurohaptics 2018 covered all aspects of haptics, including neuroscience, psychophysics, perception, engineering, computing, interactions, virtual reality, and the arts. The papers address the recent advancements in haptics organized by three topic areas: haptics science, technology, and applications. We received a total of 138 submissions for the full-paper category. The contributions were from 24 countries: 41% from Europe, 45% from Asia, 12% from the Americas, and 2% from Oceania. The review process led to 95 of these being accepted for publication thanks to the great effort of the 43 members of the Program Committee and 270 external reviewers. These papers were presented at the conference either as oral presentations (40) or as poster presentations (55). In the proceedings, the two types of presentations are both published as regular papers with no distinction between them in terms of paper length. Furthermore, 48 hands-on demos were exhibited and 61 work-in-progress papers were presented.

The proceedings are organized in two volumes: the first covering "Haptic Science," and the second covering the other two topics of "Haptic Technology and Applications."

We thank the four distinguished keynote speakers from academia and leading industries who provided their insights and vision on current and future directions of haptic research: Mel Slater (University of Barcelona and University College of London), Hiroyasu Iwata (Waseda University), Freddy Abnousi (Facebook), and Shumin Zhai (Google).

We are thankful to the organizations that supported and sponsored the event: academia (Scuola Superiore Sant'Anna), industrial gold sponsors (Lofelt, BHCT and Moog), silver sponsors (Boreas, Bps Polytec Haption, Ultrahaptics, ForceDimension, Immersion, 3Dsystem, Hapt2U and EPCOS AG), and the industrial bronze sponsors (Tactile Labs, Disney Research, Facebook Reality Lab and Tanvas). We thank also Springer for sponsoring the Best Paper Award.

Finally, we thank all the speakers and paper contributors, associate editors, members of the Organizing Committee, and reviewers without whom the event could not have taken place. This scientific gathering has proven again the vibrant and multidisciplinary community of haptics.

June 2018

Domenico Prattichizzo
Hiroyuki Shinoda
Hong Z. Tan
Emanuele Ruffaldi
Antonio Frisoli

Organization

General Chair

Antonio Frisoli   Scuola Superiore Sant'Anna, Italy

Program Co-chairs

Domenico Prattichizzo   University of Siena, Italy
Hiroyuki Shinoda   University of Tokyo, Japan
Hong Z. Tan   Purdue University, USA

Publication Chair

Emanuele Ruffaldi   Scuola Superiore Sant'Anna & MMI s.p.a., Italy

Finance Chair

Claudio Loconsole   Polytechnic University of Bari, Italy

Industry and Sponsorship Co-chairs

Carlo Alberto Avizzano   Scuola Superiore Sant'Anna, Italy
Manuel Ferre   Universidad Politécnica de Madrid, Spain

Publicity and Media Co-chairs

Claudio Loconsole   Polytechnic University of Bari, Italy
Ildar Farkhatdinov   Imperial College London, UK

Workshops and Tutorial Co-chairs

Vincent Hayward   Pierre et Marie Curie University, France
Jee-Hwan Ryu   Korea University of Technology and Education,
                                  South Korea

Poster Co-chairs

Hirouyki Kajimoto   University of Electro-Communications Tokyo, Japan
Marc Ernst   Ulm University, Germany

Demo Chair

Massimiliano Solazzi   Scuola Superiore Sant'Anna, Italy

Awards Committee Co-chairs

Massimo Bergamasco   Scuola Superiore Sant'Anna, Italy
Antonio Bicchi   University of Pisa, Italy

Student Volunteers Co-chairs

Daniele Leonardis   Scuola Superiore Sant'Anna, Italy
Matteo Bianchi   University of Pisa, Italy

Local Arrangements Co-chairs

Daniele Leonardis   Scuola Superiore Sant'Anna, Italy
Michele Barsotti   Scuola Superiore Sant'Anna, Italy
Claudio Loconsole   Polytechnic University of Bari, Italy
Massimiliano Solazzi   Scuola Superiore Sant'Anna, Italy

Advisory Committee

Ed Colgate   Northwestern University, USA
Jan Van Erp   University of Twente, The Netherlands
Yasuyoshi Yokokohji   Kobe University, Japan
Seungmoon Choi   Pohang University of Science and Technology,
                               South Korea
Hong Z. Tan   Purdue University, USA

Program Committee

Haptic Science

Andrea Bianchi   KAIST, South Korea
Matteo Bianchi   University of Pisa, Italy
Heather Culbertson   University of Southern California, USA
Massimiliano Di Luca   University of Birmingham, UK
Marc Ernst   Ulm University, Germany
Jessica Hartcher   TU Delft, The Netherlands
Astrid Kappers   VU University, The Netherlands
Scinob Kuroki   NTT Communication Science Laboratories, Japan
Masashi Nakatani   Keio University, Japan
Shogo Okamoto   The Nagoya University, Japan
Kyle B. Reed   University of South Florida, USA
Oliver Schneider   Hasso Plattner Institute, Germany
Jan van Erp   University of Twente, The Netherlands

Qi Wang   Columbia University, USA
Junji Watanabe   NTT Communication Science Laboratories, Japan

Haptic Technology

Kaspar Althoefer   King's College London, UK
Seungmoon Choi   POSTECH, South Korea
Brent Gillespie   University of Michigan, USA
Hiroyuki Kajimoto   University of Electro-Communications, Japan
Vincent Lévesque   École de technologie supérieure, Canada
Claudio Loconsole   Polytechnic University of Bari, Italy
Monica Malvezzi   University of Siena, Italy
Leonardo Meli   University of Siena, Italy
Kouta Minamizawa   Keio University, Japan
Marcia K. O'Malley   Rice University, USA
Claudio Pacchierotti   CNRS, France
Evren Samur   Boğaziçi University, Turkey
Massimiliano Solazzi   Scuola Superiore Sant'Anna, Italy
Michael Wiertlewski   CNRS, France

Haptic Applications

David Abbink   Delft University of Technology, The Netherlands
Cagatay Basdogan   Koc University, Turkey
Manuel Cruz   Immersion Corporation, Canada
Ildar Farkhatdinov   Queen Mary University of London, UK
Francesco Ferrise   Polytechnic of Milan, Italy
Rafael Morales Gonzàlez   Université Paris-Sud, France
Matthias Harders   ETH, Switzerland
Yang Jiao   Purdue University, USA
Ayse Kucukyilmaz   University of Lincoln, UK
Yoshihiro Kuroda   Osaka University, Japan
Yasutoshi Makino   University of Tokyo, Japan
Sabrina Panëels   CEA, France
Angelika Peer   Free University of Bolzano, Italy
Yoshihiro Tanaka   Nagoya Institute of Technology, Japan

Additional Reviewers

Miguel A. Otaduy   Kerem Altun
Anthony Aakre   Tomohiro Amemiya
Arsen Abdulali   Hideyuki Ando
Muhammad Abdullah   Ferran Argelaguet Sanz
Victor Adriel de Jesus Oliveira   Gabriel Arnold
Marco Aggravi   Yusuf Aydin
Ioannis Agriomallos   Mehmet Ayyildiz
Baris Akgun   Stephanie Badde

Priscilla Balestrucci
Yuki Ban
Giacinto Barresi Barresi
Michele Barsotti
Edoardo Battaglia
Gabriel Baud-bovy
Lynne Bernstein
Amir Berrezag
Joao Bimbo
Serena Bochereau
Henri Boessenkool
R. Brent Gillespie Gillespie
Jack Brooks
Paul Bucci
Domenico Buongiorno
Felan Carlo Garcia
Selem Charfi
Aashish Chaudhary Chaudhary
Francesco Chinello
Youngjun Cho
Vivian Chu
Simone Ciotti
Gabriel Cirio
Roberto Conti
Jeremy Cooperstock
Sabine Coquillart
Steven Cutlip
Benoit Delhaye
Yoshinori Dobashi
Yanick Douven
Knut Drewing
Lucile Dupin
Basil Duvernoy
Brygida Dzidek
Ulrich Eck
J. Edward Colgate
Mohamad Eid
Khaled Elgeneidy
Ildar Farkhatdinov
Feng Feng
Manuel Ferre
Davide Filingeri
Sean Follmer
Camille Fradet
Rebecca Friesen
Qiushi Fu

Shogo Fukushima
Masahiro Furukawa
Massimiliano Gabardi
Simone Gallo
Gowrishankar Ganesh
Igor Gaponov
Paolo Gasparello
Michele Gattullo
Chiara Gaudeni
Nirit Gavish
Theodoros Georgiou
Anne Giersch
Marcello Giordano
Frederic Giraud
Florian Gosselin
Danny Grant
Burak Guclu
David Gueorguiev
Kaiwen Guo
Abhishek Gupta
Taku Hachisu
Abdelwahab Hamam
Jaehyun Han
Ping-Hsuan Han
Nobuhisa Hanamitsu
M. Harders
Vanessa Harrar
Keisuke Hasegawa
Shoichi Hasegawa
Yuki Hashimoto
Christian Hatzfeld
Hirohiko Hayakawa
Lauren Hayes
Vincent Hayward
Niels Henze
Kosuke Higashi
Hsin-Ni Ho
Van Ho
Sang Ho Yoon
Elif Hocaoglu
Mehdi Hojatmadani
Raymond Holt
Charles Hudin
Thomas Hulin
Ke Huo
Irfan Hussain

Inwook Hwang
Chung Hyuk Park
Dong Hyun Jeong
Gholamreza Ilkhani
Yasuyuki Inoue
Hiroki Ishizuka
Ali Israr
William Jantscher
Seungwoo Je
Seokhee Jeon
Lynette Jones
Hernisa Kacorri
Jari Kangas
Fumihiro Kato
Takahiro Kawabe
Oguz Kayhan
Arvid Keemink
Gerard Kim
Hwan Kim
Sang-Youn Kim
Seokyeol Kim
Seung-Chan Kim
Yeongmi Kim
Ryo Kitada Kitada
Masashi Konyo
Rossitza Kotelova
Yuichi Kurita
Kiuk Kyung
Roshan L. Peiris
Roberta L. Klatzky
Hojin Lee
Philippe Lefevre
Arnaud Lelevé
Fabrizio Leo
Daniele Leonardis
Teng Li
Minas Liarokapis
Justin Lieber
Tommaso Lisini Baldi
Daniel Lobo
Pedro Lopes
Céphise Louison
JH Low
Granit Luzhnica
Juan M. Gandarias
Tonja-Katrin Machulla

Charlotte Magnusson
Maud Marchal
Kazumichi Matsumiya
Craig McDonald
Jared Medina
Martin Meier
Claudio Melchiorri
Mariacarla Memeo
Anna Metzger
David Meyer
Ekrem Misimi
Alessandro Moscatelli
Christos Mousas
Joe Mullenbach
Hikaru Nagano
Dhanya Nair
Kei Nakatsuma
Takuji Narumi
Ilana Nisky
Yohan Noh
Ian Oakley
Matjaz Ogrinc
Masahiro Ohka
Ata Otaran
Nizar Ouarti
Gunhyuk Park
Jaeyoung Park
Volkan Patoğlu
Ugo Pattacini
Sean Perkins
Michael Peshkin
Myrthe Plaisier
Jonathan Platkiewicz
Henning Pohl
Maria Pozzi
Roope Raisamo
Anuradha Ranasinghe
Jussi Rantala
Mohammad Reza Haji Samadi
Alessandro Ridolfi
Charles Rodenkirch
Emanuele Ruffaldi
Shah Rukh Humayoun
Alex Russomanno
Jin Ryong Kim
Jee-Hwan Ryu

Contents – Part II

Haptic Technology

Haptic Applications

Contents – Part I

Haptic Technology

Weight Estimation of Lifted Object from Body Motions Using Neural Network

Tomoki Oji[1(✉)], Yasutoshi Makino[1,2], and Hiroyuki Shinoda[1]

[1] Graduate School of Information Science and Technology,
The University of Tokyo, 7-3-1 Hongo, Bunkyo-ku, Tokyo, Japan
oji@hapis.k.u-tokyo.ac.jp,
{yasutoshi_makino,hiroyuki_shinoda}@k.u-tokyo.ac.jp
[2] JST PRESTO, Tokyo, Japan

Abstract. In this paper, we propose a method based on machine learning, which estimates the mass of an object from a body motion performed to lift it. In the field of behavior recognition and prediction, some previous studies had focused on estimating the current or future state of a person from his/her motion. In contrast, this research estimates the information of an object in contact with a person. Using this method, we can obtain a rough estimate of an object's mass without using a weighing machine. Such a measurement system will be useful in several applications, for example, for estimating the excess weight of baggage before checking-in at the airport. We believe that this system can also be used for the evaluation of haptic illusions such as the size–weight illusion. The proposed system detects human-body joints as the input dataset for machine learning. We created a neural network that estimated an object's mass in real-time, u/sing data from a single person for training. The experimental results showed that the proposed system could estimate an object's mass more accurately than human senses.

Keyword: Machine learning

1 Introduction

In this research, we propose a method to estimate the mass of an object from the measured body motion of lifting it. As shown in Fig. 1, when we lift a heavy object, the body movements change according to the mass of the object. Imagine a pantomime. It is possible to trick the audience into believing that a light bag has suddenly become heavy, by performing the "heavy" action accurately. Therefore, we can consider that the mass information of an object can be estimated by measuring the body motion of lifting it and judging using a machine-learning scheme. This paper tries to confirm this hypothesis.

In our system, we first record a person's motions while lifting an object, using a depth sensor (Kinect V2, Microsoft Corp.). Next, we extract the body-joint

© Springer International Publishing AG, part of Springer Nature 2018
D. Prattichizzo et al. (Eds.): EuroHaptics 2018, LNCS 10894, pp. 3–13, 2018.
https://doi.org/10.1007/978-3-319-93399-3_1

positions using its API, which become the input data for regression machine learning. The learning is performed using the motion sequence of body joints for one second as the input and the object mass as the correct value.

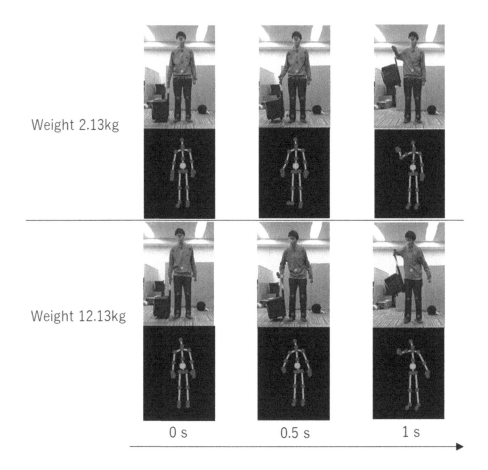

Fig. 1. Lifting motion with different weights

Several studies that combine body motion and machine learning had been conducted in the past. For example, many studies were done in the field of behavior recognition and prediction, using a motion dataset called Human 3.6M, which was measured by a motion-capture system [1–4]. One research discussed human motion prediction in real-time by using three-dimensional (3D) body-joint information, and the estimation of the body position was realized after 0.5 s, for a jump motion [5]. Some studies tried to estimate the applied force while subjects manipulated an object, based on a neural network (NN) model [6–8]. In these studies, they focused on estimating the present or future state of a person, from their motion. In our research, in contrast, we estimate not the information of the person but that of the object that they manipulate, which makes our work quite different from these previous studies.

Whenever a rough and quick measure of the weight of an object is needed, our system can be used to evaluate it from the human motion data captured using a smartphone. This may be useful, for example, to quickly estimate the excess weight of baggage before checking-in at the airport. This system can also be used to evaluate many illusions related to weight perception. It is known that humans misjudge the mass of an object from its information such as size, shape, temperature, and so on [9]. If such perceptual illusions are reflected in human-body movements, we can quantitatively evaluate them by using the proposed system.

In our work, as a first step toward body-motion–based object-mass estimation, we conducted an experimental study to examine the feasibility of such an estimation. The subject was one of the authors, and the object lifted was always the same. The manner of lifting and the object shape were fixed. Under these conditions, we conducted regression learning for the object mass and 25 body joints, using a five-layered NN. From the experimental results from a single person who provided the training data, we confirmed that the object mass could be estimated with error less than approximately 0.8 kg, for objects with mass in the range of 2 to 12 kg.

2 Method

Figure 2 shows the schematic illustration of our proposed system. We measured 3D positions of 25 body joints while lifting an object. From these points, we calculated the 3D positions of the center of gravity (COG) of the whole body. From these 26 points, we created an NN model that output the estimated mass of the object. After off-line learning, we estimated the mass of the object by using the parameters achieved during the learning process. The following subsections show the details of our system.

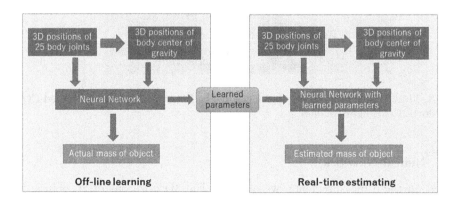

Fig. 2. Schematic illustration of the system

2.1   Measurement of Human Skeleton Data

To measure the body motion, we used Kinect V2, which is a depth camera that can be used to estimate human skeleton data. The system measured 3D positions of 25 body joints at 30 fps. Figure 3 shows the joints that were detected by Kinect V2. Based on our assumption that the position of the COG of whole body was an important factor for estimating the mass of the object, we calculated the 3D positions of the COG from the 3D positions of these 25 points. It was known that the 3D positions of the COG could be calculated from the 3D positions of each joint and the assumed masses of each body segment [10]. For each body segment, we used the same parameters used in [10].

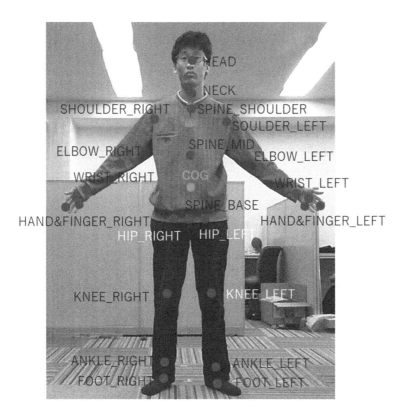

Fig. 3. The 25 body joints (blue dots) measured by Kinect V2 and the calculated COG (red dot). (Color figure online)

2.2   Neural Network

Based on these measurements, we obtained the 3D positions of 26 points: 25 joints and the calculated COG, for every frame. However, these data included the position and orientation of the whole body, which were unrelated to the mass of the object. Therefore, we normalized the data according to the following procedure. First, we rotated the orientation of the body by multiplying the rotational matrix with the data so that the body faced the front of Kinect's camera. Then, we converted the position of the whole body to 3D velocity data by subtracting the current position data from that of a previous frame, to reduce the position dependency.

After the preprocessing phase, we input the converted 3D velocity data to the NN. In this paper, in the first step of the research, we use whole body information as input. We believe that lifting a heavy object requires whole body action. Consequently, the use of whole body joints for learning is natural to achieve accurate estimation. Of course, some body parts may not affect the estimation of the object mass. Detailed discussions are provided in the discussion section.

In order to utilize the sequential patterns of body motions, we combined one second (30 frames) data of 26 body points, from the start of lifting the object, as a one learning data set, as shown in Fig. 4. Thus, one input dataset was composed of 26 points (25 joints + COG) 3 dimensions (x, y, z) 30 frames = 2340 data.

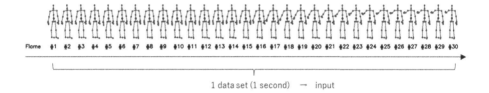

Fig. 4. Input dataset

Figure 5 shows the NN model used in our system. The NN has an all-combined five-layered model and a rectified linear unit as the activation function. The model structure was determined experimentally with reference to the previous research. We used the mass of the object for the correct data, which was compared with the outputs. In our model, for the error function, we used the root mean squared (RMS) error, which is given by

$$RMS : E(\mathbf{w}) = \sqrt{\frac{1}{N}\sum_{n=1}^{N}(y_n - d_n)^2} \tag{1}$$

where $\mathbf{w}$ is the weight vector, whose value is determined from the learning process, y_n is the estimated mass, d_n is the actual mass, and N is the batch size, which is the number of data used to update one set of parameters. For example, when the batch size is 10, 10 datasets and the related correct outputs y_n are set for the NN. With this setup, the error function $E(\mathbf{w})$ was calculated, to update the weight vector $\mathbf{w}$ to improve the model. The learning proceeded by repeating this process. As a result, the NN outputs estimated the weight as a continuous value.

It is known that differences in the data distributions for each minibatch make the learning process unstable. This is because it depends greatly on the initial value. To solve this problem, we used batch normalization [11], which normalized the input distribution at each layer so that the average became 0 and the variance became 1. When a minibatch B contained m data

$$B = \{x_1, \cdots, x_m\} \tag{2}$$

the output of batch normalization $Y = \{y_1, \cdots, y_m\}$ was given by

$$\mu_B = \frac{1}{m} \sum_{i=1}^{m} m x_i \tag{3}$$

$$\sigma_B^2 = \frac{1}{m} \sum_{i=1}^{m} (x_i - \mu_B)^2 \tag{4}$$

$$\hat{x}_i = \frac{x_i - \mu}{\sqrt{\sigma_B^2 + \epsilon}} \tag{5}$$

$$y_i = \gamma \hat{x}_i + \beta \tag{6}$$

where γ, β are the learned parameters and ϵ is the parameter for stabilization whose value is empirically set to be 10^{-5}.

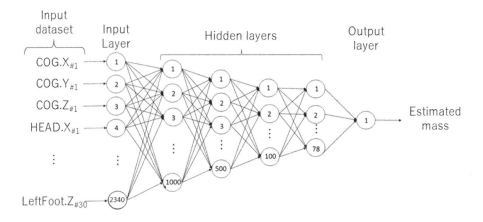

Fig. 5. Neural network structure for estimating mass of object

3   Experiment

3.1   Neural Network

In this paper, we show the relation between human motion and the weight of the lifted object, using data from one person, to confirm our concept. One male subject in his twenties, who is 175 cm tall and slender, participated in motion capturing. We asked the subject to lift objects of various weights and measured the motions using Kinect V2 at 30 fps. In this paper, the shapes of the objects to be lifted and the manner of lifting were fixed. We used a carry bag, shown in Fig. 6, as the object to be lifted, and changed its mass by placing weights inside it. For the total mass (carry bag + weights), 11 patterns were prepared in increments of 1 kg from 2.13 kg to 12.13 kg. We asked the subject to stand upright and to hold the handle of the bag with his right hand. Sound signals were used to inform the timing of lifting the bag. The subject repeated this trial 50 times for each mass. He was allowed to take a break during the measurement to reduce the effects of fatigue. The lift up process finished in one second in all trials. These one second motion data were used as one dataset for learning.

Fig. 6. Carry bag used as the object to be lifted

3.2   Evaluation

We evaluated our learning results as follows. We asked the same subject to perform the same measurement, but with different masses from the learning data, and used them as validation data. Since our NN model was a regression model, the system could estimate intermediate values between the discrete learned weight values. These data were not used for learning; they were used for evaluation only. The validation data were measured 10 times from 2.63 kg to 9.63 kg in 1 kg increments for each of the eight types of masses. The results were compared with the actual masses for both the training and validation datasets.

4   Result

Figure 7 shows the trend of the RMS error during learning. The orange curve is the error between the training and correct data, and the blue one is that between the validation and correct data. The horizontal axis shows the epoch, which is the number of cycles required for learning. As the epoch increases, both errors decrease and converge to certain values. For the validation data, the RMS error converges to approximately 0.82 kg. This result is sufficiently accurate, when compared to the results from human senses. From this, we confirmed that it was possible to estimate the approximate mass of objects from human motion, without using weighing scales.

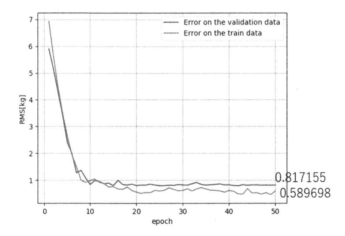

Fig. 7. RMS error for validation and training data (Color figure online)

Figure 8 shows the estimation results for the validation data after learning. The horizontal axis shows the true mass and the vertical axis shows the estimated mass. The blue dots are the average values of the estimated masses and the green bars show the standard deviations. The orange line shows the correct line. It is observed that the standard deviations are between approximately 0.5 and 1.0 kg. As described above, the weights of these validation data were not used in the learning phase. Our system could correctly estimate unknown weights based on the learning of body motions with discrete weights.

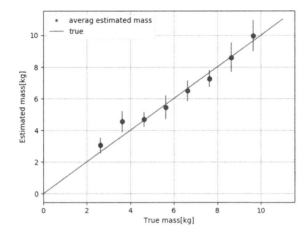

Fig. 8. Estimation results for the validation data (Color figure online)

5   Discussion

In this paper, the learning data were measured from one subject only. There may be individual differences in the manner of lifting objects, for different persons, and it is assumed that muscle strength influences the motion. If we input motions of other subjects in this model, or if we make an NN model from the motion data of multiple people, the results would be different. There are two possible ways to make a model: (1) a personalized model and (2) a universal model for everyone. From the viewpoint of accuracy, of course, making a personalized model is better than the universal model; however, it is practically difficult to acquire data and train a model, in a personalized manner. It may be possible to construct the universal model by considering the individual differences by using physical information for each individual, such as height, shoulder width, etc., as input data. The type of model to be used depends greatly on the type of application that is to be supported. In this paper, we showed that a personalized learning model could be constructed with accuracy of 0.8 kg.

For simplicity, in our work, we fixed the shape of the object and the manner of lifting it. In actual situations, however, the manner of lifting changes depending on the shape of the object; for example, whether it has a handle or not. Adaptation to other lifting methods remains a future work. It is conceivable to classify lifting methods into several types and construct a network model for each lifting method.

In this paper, we used 3D positions of whole body joints for learning, as we believed that the lifting action utilized whole body parts. However, the validity of using whole body parts is not clear at the moment. By limiting the number of joints for learning, we can know the important body parts to estimate the weight of a lifting object. We might also reduce the depth information so that we can learn with a typical 2D camera.

In this research, we used the special depth sensor Kinect V2 to estimate the body joints for learning. Using the special sensor may be a problem while dealing with ordinary situations; however, recent studies have developed a method to estimate the skeleton information from images from a monocular camera [12,13]. Moreover, depth sensors are increasingly being mounted on smartphones, such as the ones used for face authentication in iPhoneX. We expect that, in the future, we will be able to measure body motions with a smartphone and estimate the mass of a lifted object.

In our experimental result, the standard deviation was approximately 0.69 kg. In order to achieve more accurate results for practical use, multiple trials can be performed and the estimation results can be averaged. In this case, the averaged value will converge to the true weight, as the estimated values in Fig. 8 fit on the theoretical line. This strategy is similar to the way people try to estimate the weight of an object. If one wants to know whether an object is heavier or lighter than a certain mass, for example, to avoid overfilling baggage at the airport, the model can be constructed targeting that particular mass.

We believe that our method can also be used to evaluate many types of haptic weight illusions. It is known that a person cannot accurately determine the mass of an object from additional information such as the size, shape, and temperature of the object [9]. For example, in the size–weight illusion, when there are two objects of the same mass, the smaller one feels heavier. Such an illusion of weight perception would be reflected in the body motion when lifting it. The mass estimation by machine learning shown in this research is also useful for verifying if such an illusion is reflected in the body motion. This system can be applied to the quantitative evaluation of such illusions.

6   Conclusion

In this paper, we proposed a system that estimated the mass of an object from the human motion of lifting it. We assumed that the weight information was reflected in the human lifting motion and that an NN model could be used to estimate the mass of the object. We made an NN model for one subject to confirm whether our approach was possible or not. Our experimental results showed that the mass could be estimated with an accuracy of 0.82 kg in the weight range of 2.13 kg to 12.13 kg.

Acknowledgments. This research was supported by JST PRESTO 17939983. We would like to thank Editage (www.editage.jp) for English language editing.

References

1. Ionescu, C., Papava, D., Olaru, V., Sminchisescu, C.: Human3.6M: large scale datasets and predictive methods for 3D human sensing in natural environments. IEEE Trans. Pattern Anal. Mach. Intell. **36**(7), 1325–1339 (2014). https://doi.org/10.1109/TPAMI.2013.248

2. Martinez, J., Black, M.J., Romero, J.: On human motion prediction using recurrent neural networks. In: 2017 IEEE Conference on Computer Vision and Pattern Recognition, pp. 4674–4683 (2017). https://doi.org/10.1109/CVPR.2017.497

3. Jain, A., Zamir, A.R., Savarese, S., Saxena, A.: Structural-RNN: deep learning on spatio-temporal graphs. In: Proceedings of the IEEE Conference on Computer Vision and Pattern Recognition, pp. 5308–5317 (2016). https://doi.org/10.1109/CVPR.2016.573

4. Fragkiadaki, K., Levine, S., Felsen, P., Malik, J.: Recurrent network models for human dynamics. In: Proceedings of the IEEE International Conference on Computer Vision, pp. 4346–4354 (2015). https://doi.org/10.1109/ICCV.2015.494

5. Horiuchi, Y., Makino, Y., Shinoda, H.: Computational foresight: forecasting human body motion in real-time for reducing delays in interactive system. In: Proceedings of the 2017 ACM International Conference on Interactive Surfaces and Spaces, pp. 312–317 (2017). https://doi.org/10.1145/3132272.3135076

6. Fermüller, C., Wang, F., Yang, Y., Zampogiannis, K., Zhang, Y., Barranco, F., Pfeiffer, M.: Prediction of manipulation actions. Int. J. Comput. Vis. **126**(2–4), 358–374 (2018). https://doi.org/10.1007/s11263-017-0992-z

7. Pham, T.-H., Kyriazis, N., Argyros, A.A., Kheddar, A.: Hand-object contact force estimation from markerless visual tracking. IEEE Trans. Pattern Anal. Mach. Intell. (2017). https://doi.org/10.1109/TPAMI.2017.2759736

8. Hwang, W., Lim, S.-C.: Inferring interaction force from visual information without using physical force sensors. Sensors **17**(11), 2455 (2017). https://doi.org/10.3390/s17112455

9. Lederman, S.J., Jones, L.A.: Tactile and haptic illusions. IEEE Trans. Haptics **4**(4), 273–294 (2011). https://doi.org/10.1109/TOH.2011.2

10. Park, S.-B., Kim, S.-Y., Hyeong, J.-H., Chung, K.-R.: A study on the development of image analysis instrument and estimation of mass, volume and center of gravity using CT image in Korean. J. Mech. Sci. Technol. **28**(3), 971–977 (2014). https://doi.org/10.1007/s12206-013-1168-6

11. Ioffe, S., Szegedy, C.: Batch normalization: accelerating deep network training by reducing internal covariate shift. In: Proceedings of the 32nd International Conference on Machine Learning (2015)

12. Cao, Z., Simon, T., Wei, S.-E., Sheikh, Y.: Realtime multi-person 2D pose estimation using part affinity fields. In: 2017 IEEE Conference on Computer Vision and Pattern Recognition, pp. 1302–1310 (2017). https://doi.org/10.1109/CVPR.2017.143

13. Mehta, D., Sridhar, S., Sotnychenko, O., Rhodin, H., Shafiei, M., Seidel, H.-P., Xu, W., Casas, D., Theobalt, C.: VNect: real-time 3D human pose estimation with a single RGB camera. ACM Trans. Graph. **36**, 4 (2017). https://doi.org/10.1145/3072959.3073596

Electromagnetic Actuator
for Tactile Communication

Basil Duvernoy[1](✉), Ildar Farkhatdinov[2], Sven Topp[3],
and Vincent Hayward[4,5] ⓘ

[1] Sorbonne Université, Institut des Systèmes Intelligents et de Robotique,
75005 Paris, France
duvernoy@isir.upmc.fr
[2] School of Electronic Engineering and Computer Science,
Queen Mary University of London, London E1 4FZ, UK
[3] School of Psychology, The University of Sydney, Sydney, NSW 2006, Australia
[4] Institute of Philosophy, School of Advanced Study,
University of London, London, UK
[5] Actronika SAS, Paris, France

Abstract. Fingerspelling is a tactile code that enables linguistic communication with people who are Deafblind. We describe and undertake initial testing of a crucial component of a device that is designed to perform tactile fingerspelling with the speed and the clarity approaching that of a human signer. The component in question is a tactile actuator, which is based on a conventional electromagnetic motor, but which is carefully configured to meet the requirements of communication by tactile spelling. The actuator is intended to be easy to manufacture, reliable, inexpensive, to be made in many variants and to be safe to use.

Keywords: Fingerspelling · Tactile displays · Actuators

1 Introduction

The practical realisation of tactile displays has long been a challenge. One factor which is frequently cited is the lack of availability of actuators that are sufficiently small, fast, strong, reliable, cost effective and have other desirable application-specific properties. In the past fifty years many tactile display designs have been described but are not surveyed here because numerous review articles are readily available and continue to be published at a steady pace. A result of the lack of adequate actuators is that today, with the exception of refreshable Braille displays, most commercially or pre-commercially available (i.e. evaluation kits) devices are single or few actuator systems. Multiple actuator tactile displays typically remain laboratory prototypes. From this perspective the current situation is not much different from that in 1927, see [2, Figs. 3 and 4].

ⓒ Springer International Publishing AG, part of Springer Nature 2018
D. Prattichizzo et al. (Eds.): EuroHaptics 2018, LNCS 10894, pp. 14–24, 2018.
https://doi.org/10.1007/978-3-319-93399-3_2

1.1 Why the Development of Purpose-Specific Tactile Actuators Is Needed

These observations justify the consideration of tactile displays, like R. H. Gault did almost a century ago, from the view point of narrowly defined use-cases. In this article, we focus on one such single use-case: The stimulation that is necessary to bring about linguistic communication by touch. One mode of tactile communication that enjoys widespread practice, besides Braille text reading, is the family of signing and spelling languages that is utilised by the Deafblind community. This community comprises hundreds of thousands of individuals in Europe (349,000 individuals in the UK alone with an estimated population density of 1:250 [5]). The primary form of communication within the Deafblind domain is reliant of the sense of touch but may also include auditory or visual codes (dependent on visual and auditory acuity). For reasons that range from aetiology to life opportunities, approximately a quarter of this community communicates linguistically by placing tactile symbols into the palm of the hand. The development of a technology capable of conveying the relevant tactile codes rapidly and clearly would nevertheless be worthwhile, provided of course, that the technology would be economically viable.

1.2 Brief Introduction to Tactile Spelling

Due to isolation of individuals with Deafblindness, methods of tactile communication have evolved separately within countries and historically across continents and sub-continents. The category of interest here is that of the tactile *finger-spelling* codes (as opposed to *hands-on-signing*) that are used in the British Commonwealth, Italy, Germany and several other countries. These codes are signed by touching the sensitive inside region of the hand and represent a letter,

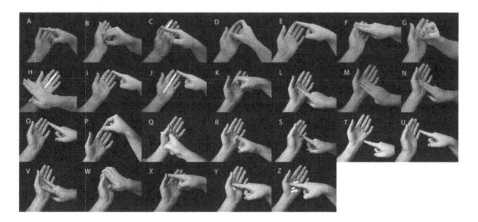

Fig. 1. Alphabet coding of British the "Deafblind Manual" and the Australian "Deafblind Tactile Fingerspelling".

word, concept or even an entire phrase. A significant downside of tactile finger-spelling is the ergonomic discomfort and bio-mechanical stress to which tactile signers are subjected with prolonged signing leading to Repetitive Stress Injuries (RSI) in the fingers, wrist and shoulders. At its core, fingerspelling is based on brief finger tapping actions and swift swiping movements on the palm to sign letters and numbers. Figure 1 illustrates the basis of the UK and Australian system. Some code extensions also use secondary interactions such as finger tap closely followed by a finger 'flick'.

One should not assume, however, that fingerspelling, like Braille code, can only encode letters and numbers. The reality is that its expressiveness is akin to that of auditory and visual codes. This fact is particularly true of Deafblind Tactile Fingerspelling, a system developed in Australia and which at the time of writing is the primary focus of our attention [3,6]. There is prosody, emphasis, and other forms of modulation that are like those of speech and that operate at the lexical, grammatical, semantic, and emotional levels, in addition to the use of non-lexical short-hand symbols, abbreviations, smileys, geometric figures, directional cues, nicknames among others. Useful tactile communication technologies should account for, reproduce, and represent these natural forms of modulation.

An observation which is highly relevant to design of actuators specifically tailored for tactile communication through fingerspelling is the fact that professional tactile interpreters can sign continuously at a rate of up to five symbols per second. To estimate the speed requirement of a tactile display capable of reproducing natural signing, an informal test was performed with the help of a volunteering professional interpreter. The interpreter was asked to sign the pangramic sentence "The quick brown fox jumps over the lazy dog". A total of nine seconds was required to convey thirty-five letters. A breakdown of this sentence by symbol type indicates that six were signed by sliding, fifteen were signed with a single tap, fourteen by place-and-hold, and one by a pinch. Rough estimates suggest that symbols requiring swiping can take up to 300 ms in duration while the much shorter tapping motions are executed under 30 ms. While this test was conducted at the maximum speed of the interpreter it should be noted that this pace cannot be comfortably sustained for more than a few minutes.

Before we review the requirements for an actuator suitably designed for tactile fingerspelling, the complete device is now briefly described. This device will be more fully described and evaluated in future publications.

1.3   Brief Overall Device Description

The design philosophy follows from the need to provide a device capable of supporting prolonged use while not impeding the freedom of movement of the person using it. It is evident that in actual practice, the hand of a user may be called upon at a moment's notice to tasks other than receiving tactile code. These basic, pragmatic requirements disqualify approaches based on "tactile gloves" which are impractical to don and doff, and which cause discomfort and sweating after a few minutes of use. Moreover, tactile gloves fail at providing clean channel separation during stimulus generation — a requirement that is essential for intelligibility. Human hands are sensitive to vibrations of very low amplitude, viz. of one micrometer or less. Attaching actuators to textiles in continuous contact with the skin cause mechanical signals to propagate away from the locus of stimulation, irremediably blurring the signals being transmitted.

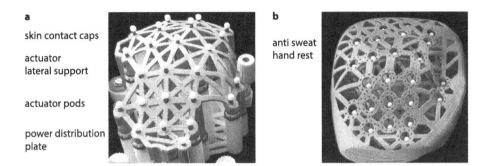

a

skin contact caps

actuator
lateral support

actuator pods

power distribution
plate

b

anti sweat
hand rest

Fig. 2. Whole-hand tactile display. **a**. Array of twenty four actuators housed in individual pods. **b**. View of the device with the hand rest shell positioned above the array without direct contact.

We developed instead a hand interface that comprises two components. There is an array of twenty-four actuators (this number is to be justified in future publications), see Fig. 2s, which are distributed in three dimensions to maximise their mutual distances ensuring a minimum of mechanical and magnetic interference between them. The individual actuators are held inside pods and are precisely positioned laterally. The moving parts of the actuators, termed 'plungers', drive vertical rods that terminate with customisable, skin-contacting caps. The rods transmit movement through loose tolerance guidance, thus operating with little friction and without special guiding elements.

The actuator array is covered by a hand-supporting shell that serves a triple purpose. It mechanically isolates the hand from the actuator array with the result that tactile stimulation takes place only when and where actuators are activated. When not used, the skin contacting caps are recessed and parasitic vibrations are not transmitted to the hand at undesired loci of the volar region of the hand. In other words, only the activated actuators stimulate the skin at a specific locations, and the signals do not leak elsewhere. The second purpose of the shell is to support the hand against gravity, a key requirement for prolonged use. The third purpose is to provide for a removable interface that can be cleaned and can be customised.

1.4   Summary of Requirements

We can now specify more accurately the desired properties of suitable actuators. Ten requirements are weighted equally and must be met without exception, namely,

1. to be small enough to accommodate twenty to thirty actuators in a space delimited by a human hand above a table;
2. to be capable of delivering impacts on the hand similar in nature to those made by human fingers. The energy dissipated by such impacts may be estimated at 0.2 mJ. This figure can be worked out from acceleration data from human fingers [1];
3. to achieve repeating these impacts at a rate of at least four per second distributed over the device. Here, the performance of the transducer shouldn't be specified with respect to the perceptual performance of the receiver, but rather with respect to the motor performance of signers. Most experienced Tactile Interpreters can finger tap three times per second on average [4];
4. to assume a recessed position when not in use to avoid unwanted parasitic stimulation, even when not activated;
5. to provide vibro-tactile stimulation in the range 100–500 Hz such that frictional noise can be simulated with the aim of producing good apparent motion, a commonly accepted range of frequencies [7];
6. to be safe to use and to interact with, even in the case of malfunction;
7. to be easy to be manufactured and replicated given basic technical skills, and operate at nominal performance even with low tolerance manufacturing;
8. to have a moderate cost and to rely on widely available materials and components;
9. to be easily maintainable, interchangeable, and if possible washable;
10. and to be reliable, maintainable, and support millions of cycles before failure.

2   Motor Design and Realisation

To achieve the stated objectives, it became apparent early in the design process that the guiding mechanism on which the moving parts relied would be the weak point of any design. From this observation, it was concluded that vertical displacement would be a primary constraint owing to its simplicity. Vertical displacement can be achieved with no other mechanism than a plunger moving in a vertical bore. The second, early decision concerned the type of primary actuation. Unless shown otherwise, the electrodynamic motor which vastly dominates the transducer industry, was the only available option. Any of other known modes of realisation of actuation failed to meet one or several of the constraints outlined in Sect. 1.4. Design iterations, using well-known principles of realisation of electrodynamic motors [8], rapidly converged to a design based on an axial organisation of the magnets. The presently realised motor is represented in Fig. 3a.

The motor comprises only two subassemblies. The first is a thin-walled mandrel on which a coil is wound. The mandrel includes thicker walls at either end to increase its structural strength. The second is a moving subassembly comprises two axially polarised ring magnets secured around a non-ferromagnetic rod. It is made of a carbon fibre composite but this is not essential. The moving subassembly acts like a plunger which is inserted in the bore of the coil

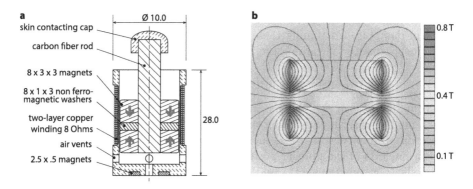

Fig. 3. Actuator Design. **a.** Grey arrows indicate the magnet polarities. **b.** Dimensional optimisation of the magnetic circuit.

subassembly, remaining there under the action of gravity, and is free-moving. The present design produces a nomimal force of approximately 0.15 N, meaning that for a plunger mass of about 3 g, it is capable of an acceleration five times that of gravity.

Recal that the central design goal was to provide for two modes of stimulation. The first mode is an impulsive mode aimed at reproducing the impact of a finger and the second is aimed at providing for vibro-tactile stimulation in an intermittent fashion.

2.1 Impact Mode

An impact was achieved by simply pulsing current in the coil. The plunger shot up from which two scenarios can arise. If there is a hand in range of the motor — the pods and the hand rest shell were strategically designed to locate the skin within 3.0–4.0 mm of the cap in its rest position —, then a collision occurred. The sensation of impact was very similar to that generated by a tapping finger. If for any reason no hand was present to determine a collision, then the plunger continued to rise. However, see Fig. 3b, the magnetic field interfering with the coil soon reversed and so did the electrodynamic force, causing the plunger to be pushed back into the bore. If for any reason current should ceased, a hard stop prevented the plunger from exiting, at the cost of an unpleasant knocking noise. During normal operation, current timing and intensity could be judiciously selected to ensure silent operation of the motor.

It is important to recall that vibration-free operation was an essential requirement for intelligibility which required precise timing of current reversal to stop the plunger before striking the bottom of the bore. Precise timing could not be achieved without a complex closed-loop operation. A solution was to provide for passive braking when approaching the end of the downward movement by tiny magnets inserted at the bottom of the bore that interfered with the main magnets to create a repelling force of the form $1/a^2$, where, a is the magnet-to-magnet distance. A secondary braking mechanism was a viscous force caused by the flow of air through small vents that were calibrated to provide a desired amount of damping. Combining these elements makes it possible to determine the nonlinear equation governing the motor,

$$m\ddot{z}(t) + b\dot{z}(t) + k(z)z(t) + mg = a(z(t), i(t)),$$

where m is the mass of the plunger, $z(t)$ is the vertical position of the plunger, $k(z)$ is a nonlinear spring modelling the action of the braking magnets, g is the acceleration of gravity, and $a(z, i)$ models the variation of the electrodynamics force as a function of the plunger position, $z(t)$, and of the current, $i(t)$, flowing in the coils. The functions $k(z)$ and $a(z, i)$ were not empirically determined, owing to the final design of the actuator not being frozen. An interesting "slingshot" effect involved the reversal of the current during an initial pulse followed by switching to a positive pulse in a second phase.

2.2   Vibro-Tactile Mode

While in this mode of operation, the motor was biased to cause the plunger to lift upward and push gently against the skin. Remaining in this position, the motor could be used as a wide-bandwidth electrodynamic transducer. In our present design the lifting and gentle push on the skin was achieved for only 10% of the nominal current capacity, allowing plenty of headroom for oscillatory stimulation. In this mode, we may model the actuator as a linear system working around a biased operating point,

$$m\ddot{z}(t) + b\dot{z}(t) = c_b(i(t)) + f(d, t),$$

where, c_b represents the motor's Bl product at the point of operation, where $f(d, t)$ is the dynamic model of the mechanical load given by a finger, and where d stands for the surface deflection of the finger. Estimates for $f(d, t)$ can be found in [9].

3   Fabrication

Various dimensions and materials were optimised using CAD tools. In particular it was found that the magnet geometry indicated in Fig. 3 provided good performance with conventional, commercially available neodymium magnets. With some precautions, a 3D-printing process using fused deposition gave satisfactory manufacturing of the mandrel. The coil winding was initially undertaken manually. A desk-top winding machine was designed in-house to speedup the winding process and achieve tight and regular wire packing. It was found that an 8 Ω, two-layer coil gave a good compromise, similar to coils incorporated in audio loudspeakers. The magnets were bonded to stock carbon fibre rods cut at length. Not accounting for labor, an overall costing of the components for small scale production came to a total of 13 € (9 € for the mandrel and 4 € for the plunger). Large cost savings could certainly be obtained through bulk procurements.

4   Evaluation

4.1   Time Domain, Large Signal Response

This test was intended to verify that our actuator could effect rapid taps at speeds and intensities outlined in the requirements. The actuator was commanded with brief 20 ms, 3.3 V pulses at 90 ms intervals and its movements were monitored using a miniature accelerometer (ADXL 335, Analog Device, PC-board-less custom commissioning, mass 50 mg). The response is in Fig. 4, showing that the motor was clearly capable of repeating ten taps per second. Figure 4b shows that acceleration (smoothed by a second-order lowpass Butterworth filter) tracked the input command with some disturbances due to the frictional noise of the magnet sliding inside the bore. Figure 4a shows the numerically integrated raw acceleration signal that estimated, after de-trending, the plunger velocity and position. Decreasing velocities were when the plunger was falling back inside the bore under the action of gravity and increasing velocities is when it was propelled upward. It can be observed that the plunger velocity reached 0.4 m/s when the vertical displacement was 4 mm, leading to an inelastic impact energy of 0.24 mJ.

4.2   Frequency Domain, Small Signal Response

We analysed the frequency response of the actuator by interposing the miniature accelerometer between the rod and the cap in contact with the finger of a volunteer, as in Fig. 5a. The motor was biased at 20% of its current capacity and a small oscillatory voltage was superposed to the bias. The actuator was driven

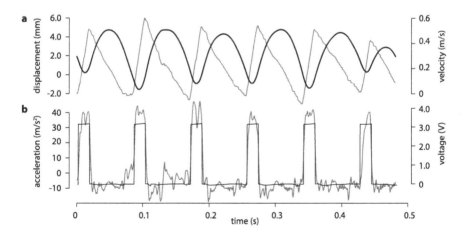

Fig. 4. Large signal, time domain performance. **a.** Estimated velocity (thin gray line) and position (black line) as a function time. **b,** Voltage input (thin gray line) and resulting acceleration (smoothed) starting at the value of negative acceleration of gravity.

with sinusoidal signals at frequencies ranging from 20 Hz to 1000 Hz (by steps of 10 Hz from 20 to 500 Hz and of 50 Hz between 500 and 1000 Hz). The measured acceleration and input voltage recordings for each frequency were used to produce the frequency response shown in Fig. 5b using the Fast Fourier Transform function of Matlab. The plot demonstrates that for the range of frequencies 20–200 Hz the actuator can be modelled by a mass. The slight ~3 dB drop around 250 Hz may be attributed to the viscous damping properties of the finger [9], while the rise in signal magnitude in the high frequencies can be explained by the increasing contribution of frictional noise in this range. This effect can be observed in Fig. 5c showing the noise-sensitive acceleration signal in the time domain.

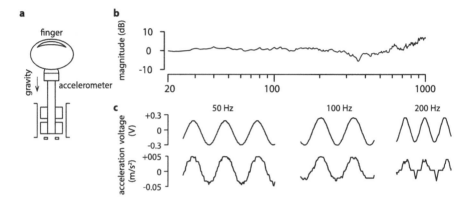

Fig. 5. Small signal performance. **a**. Measurement condition. **b**. Bode plot of the acceleration response. **c**. Time domain response at different frequencies.

5   Discussion/Conclusion

We set out to design and produce an actuator suited to the purpose of generating the sensations required for the reproduction of tactile codes used in Deafblind Tactile Communication. Whilst we have no doubts that further iterations of design will be required, our initial investigations and characterisation of the motor provided promising results.

Its small overall size gives it the capacity to be utilised in a high-resolution displays. An array of twenty actuators spread over the sensitive area of the volar part of the hand is feasible for the greatest majority of hand sizes and shapes. In some cases, the capacity to create even denser groupings of actuators is a practical proposition.

The pricing of materials, of the manufacturing costs, and of the complexity of production have all been kept to a minimum. Materials are easily sourced from the market and the possibility for cost reduction by a factor ten is quite achievable. Manufacturing costs and complexity are low with construction requiring little expertise other than care. The modular design means that, in the event of failure, actuators be rapidly reproduced and replaced, or stocked as spares.

On a mechanical level, the plunger component of the design can easily be seen meeting our requirement of being recessed when not in use. The impact capabilities could be classified as equivalent to, greater or less than those exerted by a human interpreter. Initial evaluations made by the third co-author, a Deafblind researcher, suggests that forces being exerted are in some cases too high for prolonged usage.

While it is noted that professional interpreters can sign at a speed of four symbols per second and we aimed to reproduce this performance. Our volunteering interpreter suggested that such speeds are impractical to maintain over extended periods of time. An estimates of two symbols per second is a more realistic base line. The proposed actuator design easily produced ten taps per second demonstrating a fair amount of performance headroom for more rapid contacts. Whether these higher speeds would be intelligible will require further investigation.

Our operating frequency range and quiet operation also meet initial requirements but may need some further refinement. Activation of the motor below 400 Hz frequencies appears to generate little or no noise. However, a noisy response was observed when the driving signals exceeded 400 Hz. Possibilities for this inconvenience may be that the skin contacting cap decoupled from the skin or that the higher frequency excited a nonlinear clattering regime. Further investigations will be required to clarify and resolve this issue before rigorous human trials can be undertaken.

Acknowledgements. The research reported herein is a component of a larger project which was, and is generously supported by three consecutive Google Faculty Awards to V.H. and S.T ("Tactile Communicator for Use by The Deafblind; Software Layers for Deafblind Tactile Communication; Hand-to-Hand Remote Deafblind Tactile Communication"). B.D. was awarded a post-graduate fellowship by the project SMART of the Faculté des Sciences de Sorbonne Université.

References

1. Christou, E.A., Shinohara, M., Enoka, R.M.: Fluctuations in acceleration during voluntary contractions lead to greater impairment of movement accuracy in old adults. J. Appl. Physiol. **95**(1), 373–384 (2003)
2. Gault, R.H.: "Hearing" through the sense organs of touch and vibration. J. Franklin Inst. **204**, 329–358 (1927)
3. Johnston, T., Schembri, A.: Australian Sign Language: An Introduction to Sign Language Linguistics. Cambridge University Press, Auslan (2007)
4. Peters, M., Durding, B.M.: Handedness measured by finger tapping: a continuous variable. Can. J. Exp. Psychol./Revue canadienne de psychologie experimentale **32**(4), 257–261 (1978)
5. Robertson, J., Emerson, E.: Estimating the number of people with co-occurring vision and hearing impairments in the uk. Technical Report 2010:1, CeDR, Lancaster University, UK (2010)

6. Topp, S.: Deafblind haptic speech, a vibrotactile device proposal. Master's thesis, School of Computer Science and Engineering, University of New South Wales, Australia (2013)
7. Verrillo, R.T.: Psychophysics of vibrotactile stimulation. J. Acoust. Soc. Am. **77**(1), 225–232 (1985)
8. Wang, J., Jewell, G.W., Howe, D.: Analysis and design of tubular linear permanent magnet machines. IEEE Trans. Magn. **35**(3), 1986–2000 (1999)
9. Wiertlewski, M., Hayward, V.: Mechanical behavior of the fingertip in the range of frequencies and displacements relevant to touch. J. Biomech. **45**(11), 1869–1874 (2012)

Vibrotactile Signal Generation from Texture Images or Attributes Using Generative Adversarial Network

Yusuke Ujitoko[1] and Yuki Ban[2](✉)

[1] Hitachi, Ltd., Yokohama, Japan
yusuke.ujitoko.uz@hitachi.com
[2] The University of Tokyo, Tokyo, Chiba, Japan
ban@edu.k.u-tokyo.ac.jp

Abstract. Providing vibrotactile feedback that corresponds to the state of the virtual texture surfaces allows users to sense haptic properties of them. However, hand-tuning such vibrotactile stimuli for every state of the texture takes much time. Therefore, we propose a new approach to create models that realize the automatic vibrotactile generation from texture images or attributes. In this paper, we make the first attempt to generate the vibrotactile stimuli leveraging the power of deep generative adversarial training. Specifically, we use conditional generative adversarial networks (GANs) to achieve generation of vibration during moving a pen on the surface. The preliminary user study showed that users could not discriminate generated signals and genuine ones and users felt realism for generated signals. Thus our model could provide the appropriate vibration according to the texture images or the attributes of them. Our approach is applicable to any case where the users touch the various surfaces in a predefined way.

Keywords: Vibrotactile signals · Generative Adversarial Network

1 Introduction

The vibrotactile sense enables humans to perceive texture surface properties through tool-surface interaction. Unfortunately, the richness of the vibrotactile responses from virtual texture surfaces is missing from current tool-surface interactions on a touchscreen. The tool-surface interactions are composed of simple gestures such as tapping or flickering, so vibrotactile designer should find the appropriate vibrotactile sig-nals for each gesture. However, it is difficult to find ones. Though there are vibrotactile datasets which is made public, it is rare to find the appropriate vibrotactile signals from them. It is because such datasets contains at most 100 kinds of textures, as compared to countless kind of texture in the real world.

Instead of looking into datasets, vibrotactile modeling has been studied for a long time to provide such responses. However, there is no model that interactively generates vibrotactile responses based on the state of the tool and the state of the surfaces. Such model should learn the complex mapping between large input and output space; Inputs

© Springer International Publishing AG, part of Springer Nature 2018
D. Prattichizzo et al. (Eds.): EuroHaptics 2018, LNCS 10894, pp. 25–36, 2018.
https://doi.org/10.1007/978-3-319-93399-3_3

are state of the tool (ex. tool's velocity) and the state of the texture surface (ex. texture's attributes), on the other hand, outputs are vibrotactile signals. Considering a limitation of a representational power that a trained single model can have, it is difficult to train the model that get both states of the tool and state of the texture surface as input. In other words, there is a trade-off between the model's interactivity for the tool's state and the one for the texture surface's state.

Emerging, recent data-driven approach for haptic modeling mainly focus on the interactivity of the tool's state. Prior studies mapped the normal force and the velocity magnitude of the tool with vibrational patterns [1, 2]. These vibrational patterns were encoded in the autoregressive model. Their model succeeded in mapping the tool's state and the vibration patterns. They are suitable for interactions where there is much variability with tool's velocity and applied force. However, the single model generating vibrational signals only supported single kind of texture that is used during training. Thus, when you try to generate vibrations of another kind of texture, you need to replace the model with another one.

This paper, on the other hand, focuses on the interactivity for the texture's state instead of the tool's state. Current touchscreen interactions are composed of simple gestures such as tapping or flickering, which is completed in a short time. With such gestures, the tool's velocity or applied force is approximately constant. On the other hand, such gestures are generally used for various texture surfaces. Thus, we pose the modeling task of generating appropriate vibrotactile signals that correspond to the visual information or attributes of texture. Such capabilities realize generating haptic signals for even unseen textures automatically or manipulating vibrotactile signals by changing attribute values. As an application of this model, we assume a vibrotactile designing toolkit for tool-surface interactions where designers can (1) set attributes of texture or (2) prepare texture images to generate the appropriate signals for gestures. The model that accomplishes it is required to have the capability to capture rich distribution.

Recently, generative methods that produce novel samples from high-dimensional data distributions, such as images, are finding widespread use. Specifically, Generative Adversarial Networks (GANs) [3] have shown promising results in synthesizing real-world images. Prior research demonstrated that GANs could effectively generate images conditioned on labels [4], texts [5], and so on. In spite of these promising results, there are few studies that used GANs to model time-series data distribution. Indeed, the generation of vibration by GANs has not been realized for now. In this study, we make full use of GANs for indirectly generating vibrotactile signals via time-frequency domain representation, which can be calculated as the image. We train the model so that it can generate vibrotactile signals conditioned on texture images or texture attributes.

The contribution of this study is three-fold. First, to our best knowledge, we introduce the problem of vibrotactile generation and are the first to use GANs to solve it. Second, we succeed in indirectly generate time-series data via time-frequency representation using GANs. Third, our trained single model meets the demand for interactiveness for the state of textures by providing the appropriate vibration that corresponds to the texture images or texture attributes.

2   Related Work

Modern data-driven texture modeling mapped the tool's state and the vibrational response of contact in autoregressive coefficients [1] or in neural network [2]. However, their single model could generate vibrotactile signals only for single texture. When generating vibrations of another kind of texture, the model was needed to be replaced with another one. Therefore, in this paper, we train the single model that generates appropriate haptic signals that correspond to the visual information or attributes of texture. The model that accomplishes it is required to have the capability to capture rich distribution.

Generative methods that produce novel samples from high-dimensional data distributions, such as images, are finding widespread use, for example in image-to-image translation [6], image super-resolution [7], and so on. In this study, we use GANs framework to generate sharp time-frequency samples for vibrotactile feedback. GANs were introduced in the seminal work of Goodfellow et al. [3], and are composed of two models: generator and discriminator. They are alternatively trained to compete with each other. Given a distribution, the generator is trained to generate samples from noise vector z so that the generated samples resemble this true distribution. On the other hand, the discriminator is trained to distinguish whether the samples are genuine. After training, the generator can generate samples from noise vector z, which are indistinguishable from genuine samples by the discriminator.

Utilizing the GANs' capability to capture rich data distributions, there are several methods to manipulate the output samples of GANs. As one of the representative method, conditional sample generation has been studied. AC-GAN [8] is a promising variant of conditional GANs in which generator conditions the generated samples on its class label c and the discriminator performs an auxiliary task of classifying the generated and the genuine samples into the respective class labels. In this setting, every generated sample is associated with a class label c and a noise z, which are used by the generator to generate images $G(c, z)$.

By using conditional GANs, cross-modal generation has been studied. Text to image generation was implemented by [5]. In their studies, plausible images for birds and flowers were generated from their text descriptions. Cross-modal audio-visual generation was studied in [9]. Though they tried to generate spectrogram convertible to sound, they generated the rough spectrogram, which was not convertible to good sound. The reason for the poor generation is that the network architecture and optimization technique was not sophisticated. Inspired by their work, we construct the cross-modal visuo-vibrotactile generating model. We use the improved network architecture and optimization technique, and thus, our model is able to generate the spectrogram that is convertible to the vibrotactile signals.

3   Vibrotactile Signal Generation

3.1   Concept of Overall Model

By utilizing GANs' capability to capture rich data distributions, we would like to make the single generative model that has following features: automatic generation of vibrotactile signals either (1) from given texture images or (2) from given texture attributes. Though prior research focuses on the interactive generation based on tool's state, this paper proves the concept above for predefined tool's state under constrained touch interactions. Among various touch interactions, we focus on the task of moving a pen on the texture surface.

The overall diagram of our model is shown in Fig. 1. It consists of two parts: an encoder network, and a generator network. They are trained separately. The encoder is trained as an image classifier and it encodes texture images into a label vector c. The generator is trained with discriminator in GANs training framework and generates spectrogram that is a representation of vibration in a time-frequency domain. We describe the training details for each network in the following sections. The overall model enables end-to-end generation from visual images or label attributes of texture to the vibrotactile wave.

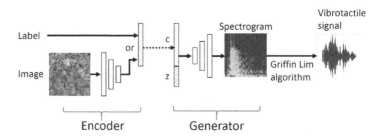

Fig. 1. Overall diagram of our model.

We describe the data flow step by step based on Fig. 1. The input into the model is either a class label that represents the tactile attributes of the texture or a texture image. When the image is input, the label vector c is extracted from the texture image through encoder network. The label vector c is a categorical variable that shows the attributes of the texture. Next, the label vector c is passed into the generator network. The generator concatenates the label c and the random noise z and transforms them into the spectrogram. The generated spectrogram is converted into the acceleration wave format by Griffin-Lim algorithm [10]. Then the wave format data is output to the user. With this overall model, users can input either label information or texture images to obtain vibration. That is why we do not adopt the network like pix2pix [6], which only supports input as images and converts images directory into signals.

Acceleration signals are used as vibrotactile stimulus in our model. In order to train the whole network, we use dataset [11], which contains acceleration signals and captured images during movement task. The pairs of signals and images are annotated with 108 classes.

3.2   Encoder

We trained the image encoder that encoded texture images into the label vector c. We adopted the deep residual network (ResNet-50) [12] architecture. We fine-tuned all the layers of the ResNet-50 that had been pre-trained with ImageNet [13]. We used Adam optimizer with a mini-batch size of 64. The learning rate started from 1e-3 and was decreased by a factor of 0.1 when the training error plateaued.

The size of provided images by [11] is 320×480. We fed them into the encoder network. For training phase of encoder network, we followed ordinary data augmentation settings. We scaled an image with factors in [1, 1.3], randomly cropped 128×128 size of it, flipped it horizontally and vertically, rotated it by a random angle. The recent data augmentation technique of random erasing and mixup were also used.

As a result of training, the trained encoder achieved a classification accuracy of more than 95% on the testing set. After the network was trained, its last layer was removed, and the feature vector of the second to the last layer having dimension of label vector was used as the image encoding in our generator network.

3.3   Generator

Network Architecture and Training Settings.   Generator was trained with discriminator in GANs framework. During training, the discriminator learned to discriminate between genuine and generated samples, while the generator learned to fool the discriminator. Generator output samples $x = G(z, c)$ conditioned on both random noise vector z and a label vector c from dataset. Discriminator had two outputs: $D(x)$ the probability of the sample x being genuine, and $P(x) = c$, the predicted label vector of x. After training, the discriminator was removed and the generator was only used in our model. Inspired by [14], we employed architecture and loss function, which was based on SRResNet [7], DRAGAN [15], and AC-GAN [8]. The architecture of generator and discriminator are shown in Fig. 2.

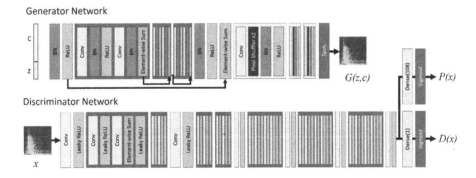

Fig. 2.   Network architecture of generator and discriminator.

Acceleration signals orthogonal to the surface during movement task were used as vibrotactile stimulus and we aim at generating the signals by generator. For now, there are few studies generating time series data using GANs. It is because GANs are poor at generating time-series data though they are good at generating 2D images. Therefore, we chose amplitude spectrogram as a representation of the acceleration signals and trained GANs to generate spectrogram as if that was 2D image. The same dataset used for training encoder contained acceleration signals during movement task. Each signal had 4 s long and the sampling rate was 10 kHz. We computed the spectrogram from wave format using 512-point Short-Time Fourier Transform (STFT) with a 512 hamming window and a 128 hop size. Then, the linear amplitude of the spectrogram was converted to the logarithmic scale. We cropped the spectrogram and resized it into 128×128 size. As a result, the spectrogram contained the information of time-frequency domain up to 256 Hz for 1.625 s long. The values in the spectrogram were normalized into the range from 0 to 1.

We selected 9 textures out of 108 textures for GANs' training because it is stable to train conditional GANs with fewer number of conditional label dimensions. Thus, the dimension of categorical label c was 9. On the other hand, the dimension of noise z was 50. The selected 9 textures were representative of 9 groups of LMT haptic texture database [11] (Fig. 3). We used Adam optimizer with a mini-batch size of 64. The learning rate was fixed at 2e-4.

Fig. 3. Selected textures for GANs training.

Training Results of Generator. The spectrogram in test dataset and the one generated by generator are shown in Fig. 4. The comparison between them shows the trained generator could generate the spectrograms that appear indistinguishable from test ones.

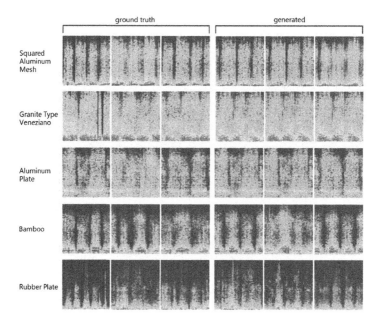

Fig. 4. The spectrogram for each class label in test dataset and the one generated by generator.

We describe the qualitative evaluation by user study in Sect. 4. On the other hand, it is generally difficult to quantitatively evaluate the GANs. The ordinary evaluation metric of GANs, namely the "inception score" cannot to be applied to our case because the "inception score" is only applied to standard dataset such as CIFAR-10. Instead, we observe that t-SNE is a good tool to examine the distribution of generated images. A two dimensional t-SNE visualization is shown in Fig. 5. It is shown that the generated and test samples made group for each class label.

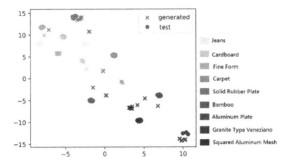

Fig. 5. t-SNE visualization of test dataset and the one generated by generator.

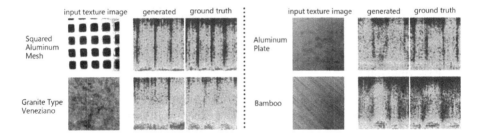

Fig. 6. E2E generation from texture images into spectrogram.

3.4 End-to End (E2E) Network

E2E cross modal generation of signals from texture images are realized by combining encoder and generator. The encoder was trained with 9 classes instead of 108 classes in accordance with input dimension of conditional generator. Figure 7 shows the generated spectrogram from the texture image and genuine one for each test image in the dataset. The comparison between them shows the E2E network could generate the spectrograms that seem indistinguishable from test one. We describe the qualitative evaluation by user study in Sect. 4 (Fig. 6).

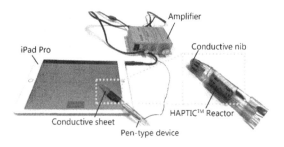

Fig. 7. Setting of the experimental system.

4   User Study

User studies were conducted to investigate that whether our method could generate perceptually realistic vibrotactile stimuli. Two studies were conducted to evaluate Generator (Generator Ex.) and E2E network (E2E Ex.). Ten participants whose ages ranged from 22 to 25 (eight males and two females) participated in these studies. All of them were right handed. They were screened to determine that they were not depressed, terribly tired because the perception would be affected by physical or emotional states. Each of them participated in those two studies on another day. The data acquisition was approved by the University of Tokyo Ethics committee (approbation number: KE17-63) and written informed consent was obtained from all participants.

4.1   Experimental System

In user studies, participants' task was to move a pen-type device on a surface of a tablet device while receiving vibrotactile feedback. Our experimental system was constituted of the tablet device (Apple Inc., iPad Pro 9.7 inch), an amplifier (Lepai Inc., LP-2020A +), and a pen-type device with a vibrator (Fig. 8). The pen-type device, which we hand-crafted, is specifically described in the next paragraph.

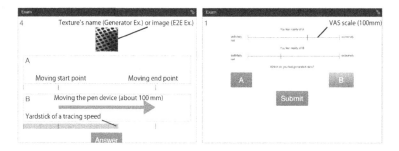

Fig. 8. Experimental windows.

The pen-type device was about 20 g weight and about 140 mm long. The diameter of the grip part of the pen was about 10 mm. The pen tip wore conductive material that is ordinary used for the stylus. Since the shaft of the pen used in these studies was made of plastic and does not conduct to the grip part, we winded a conductive sheet on the grip to react with a capacitance type touch screen. Inside the pen-type device, the vibrator (ALPS Inc., HAPTIC™ Reactor) was embedded at the position of 2 cm distance from the tip of the pen where participants gripped. The vibrator was small (35.0 mm $\times$ 5.0 mm $\times$ 7.5 mm) and light (about 5 g) enough not to prevent participants from moving the pen.

When participants touched and moved the pen on the surface, the vibration signal was output from earphone jack of the tablet, and amplified by the amplifier, and vibrator embedded on the pen presented the vibration to the participants' fingers.

4.2   Task Design

These studies used a within-participant design. Participants moved the pen-type device along the two different predefined path on screen in succession, while receiving either test or generated vibrational feedback. After that, participants tried to distinguish which stimulus was generated one. They also evaluated the realism of stimuli. In Generator Ex., generated signals were generated by feeding a label vector that represented each class into the generator. In E2E Ex., generated signals were generated by feeding a test image that represented each class into the encoder network. Corresponding class label texts or texture images were displayed on the touch screen. Participants' task was the same in Generator Ex. and E2E Ex. except that what they saw on screen was class label texts or texture images.

The procedure of one trial in participant's task is described in this paragraph. Participants moved the pen on a virtual texture surface from left to right for about 100 mm distance at fixed speed with their dominant hands. To control the movement speed and distance, the touch screen visualized a bar that indicated where and how much speed to move. According to the bar elongation, participants moved the pen approximately 100 mm distance in 1.6 s. Participants were told to hold the pen at the position where a vibrator was embedded. After completing movement on two surfaces, they answered which stimulus was felt generated one by tapping one of the two answer buttons. Besides, they answered the degree of realism for each stimulus by visual analogue scale (VAS) ratings [16] (Fig. 9 Right). Participants rated the realism that they felt on an analogue scale in this testing method. They answered the question "How much realism did you feel?" by rating realism on a 100 mm line on the touch screen anchored by "definitely not" on the left and "felt realism extremely" on the right. They used the pen-type device to check on this line. The displayed order of test and generated stimuli in one trial was shuffled.

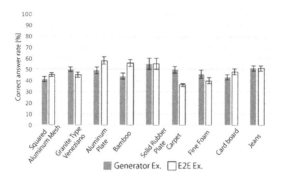

Fig. 9. Percentage of identifying which stimuli were generated one out of two.

Vibration signals that belonged to nine classes of textures that are modeled in Sect. 3 (Fig. 4) were prepared for this study. Test signals are randomly extracted from test dataset corresponds to each class, and generated signals are generated for each trial. Participants performed the trial ten times for each class. Therefore, each participant performed 180 trials in total for both Generator Ex. and in E2E Ex. E2E Ex. was conducted after Generator Ex. and these studies were held on separate days in order to prevent any satiation effects. To prevent sequential effects, the presentation order of these factors was randomly assigned and counter-balanced across participants.

4.3 Result

Figure 10 shows the percentage of correctly identifying which stimulus was generated. We call this value as "Correct answer rate". If this value is close to 50%, it means that participants failed to distinguish test data from generated data. Thus, it is confirmed that our method could generate the vibrational stimuli that were close to the genuine stimuli. The average and the standard error (SE) of "Correct answer rate" were $47.7 \pm 1.49\%$ for Generator Ex., and $48.2 \pm 2.49\%$ for E2E Ex. To investigate whether these rates were out of 50%, we applied the Chi-Square goodness of fit test. It revealed that the rate of Carpet and Fine Foam condition in E2E Ex. were significantly lower than 50% (Carpet: $p < 0.01$, Fine Foam: $p < 0.05$).

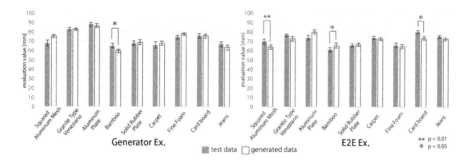

Fig. 10. The score of realism participants felt.

On the other hand, Fig. 10 shows the results of how much realism participants felt for each class. The score of the realism of test data was 72.9 ± 1.49 and that of generated data was 73.1 ± 2.93 in Generator Ex. In E2E Ex., the score of the realism of test data was 71.4 ± 2.04 and that of generated data was 70.3 ± 1.81. We used a Student's paired t-test to each texture condition, and revealed that there were significant differences between the average score of test and generated data for Bamboo in Generator Ex. ($p = 0.025$), and Squared Aluminum Mesh, Bamboo, Card board in E2E Ex. ($p = 0.026, 0.025, 0.025$). There was no significant difference between the average score of test and generated data in total.

4.4 Discussion

"Correct answer rate" of most texture conditions were almost 50%, thus participants could not distinguish test data from generated data. In the post questionnaire, all participants answered that they did not find the difference between the test stimulus and the generated stimulus. Therefore, it can be said that our system has the potential to generate the high realistic vibrotactile signals from given texture attributes or given texture images. "Correct answer rate" of Carpet and Fine Foam class in E2E Ex. were significantly lower than 50% so that participants tended to misunderstand the generated stimulus as an genuine stimulus for these two classes. On the contrary, there were no significant differences in the realism that participants felt between test and generated data in Carpet and Fine Foam classes. There was no correlation between the realism evaluation value and the discrimination rate of generated data.

Most scores about realism were over 60 and there was no significant difference between the scores of generated and test data in total. These results suggest that the generated vibrotactile stimuli had certain realism equivalent to the genuine stimuli. Focusing on the data for each class, the scores about realism were different between Generator Ex. and E2E Ex. This difference seems to be derived from the impression gap between texture attributes and images. Four out of ten participants answered in the post questionnaire that the impression of test image and label name were different, especially for Bamboo. Also, some participants said that it is difficult to imagine the texture surface from label name displayed in Generator Ex. These answers suggested that we should re-design the attribute axes, which we used class labels as they are in this study. For example, if we use some onomatopoeia as attribute axes, users can intuitively set and manipulate attributes and usability would be improved.

Users rated generated data significantly higher than test data for Squared Aluminum Mesh in E2E Ex. Five participants answered that they felt periodic vibrotactile stimuli like moving on the mesh as the generated stimuli, so it can be considered that the trained model has enhanced the characteristic attribute like a mesh too much.

5 Conclusion

In this study, we introduced the problem of vibrotactile generation based on various texture images or attributes during predefined tool-surface interaction, and solved it by adversarial training. The user study showed that users could not discriminate generated signals and genuine ones. Our approach is applicable to any case where the users touch the various surfaces in a predefined way. Thus, our study contributes to the broadening the options of vibrotactile signal preparation in such cases.

References

1. Culbertson, H., Unwin, J., Kuchenbecker, K.J.: Modeling and rendering realistic textures from unconstrained tool-surface interactions. IEEE Trans. Haptics **7**(3), 381–393 (2014)
2. Shin, S., Osgouei, R.H., Kim, K.D., Choi, S.: Data-driven modeling of isotropic haptic textures using frequency-decomposed neural networks. In: IEEE World Haptics Conference, WHC 2015, pp. 131–138 (2015)
3. Goodfellow, I., Pouget-Abadie, J., Mirza, M., et al.: Generative Adversarial Nets. Adv. Neural. Inf. Process. Syst. **27**, 2672–2680 (2014)
4. Mirza, M., Osindero, S.: Conditional Generative Adversarial Nets. arXiv preprint arXiv: 1411.1784 (2014)
5. Reed, S., Akata, Z., Yan, X., et al.: Generative adversarial text to image synthesis. In: ICML, pp. 1060–1069 (2016)
6. Isola, P., Zhu, J.-Y., Zhou, T., Efros, A.A.: Image-to-Image Translation with Conditional Adversarial Networks. In: CVPR (2017)
7. Ledig, C., Theis, L., Huszar, F., et al.: Photo-Realistic Single Image Super-Resolution Using a Generative Adversarial Network. arXiv preprint arXiv:1609.04802 (2016)
8. Odena, A., Olah, C., Shlens, J.: Conditional Image Synthesis With Auxiliary Classifier GANs. arXiv preprint arXiv:1610.09585 (2016)
9. Chen, L., Srivastava, S., Duan, Z., Xu, C.: Deep Cross-Modal Audio-Visual Generation. arXiv preprint arXiv:1704.08292 (2017)
10. Griffin, D.: Signal estimation from modified short-time Fourier transform. IEEE Trans. Acoust. Speech Sig. Process. **32**(2), 236–243 (1984)
11. Strese, M., Schuwerk, C.: Multimodal feature-based surface material classification. IEEE Trans. Haptics **10**(2), 226–239 (2017)
12. He, K., Zhang, X., Ren, S., Sun, J.: Deep residual learning for image recognition. In: CVPR, pp. 770–778 (2016)
13. Russakovsky, O., Deng, J., Su, H., et al.: ImageNet large scale visual recognition challenge. Int. J. Comput. Vis. **115**(3), 211–252 (2015)
14. Jin, Y., Zhang, J., Li, M., et al.: Towards the Automatic Anime Characters Creation with Generative Adversarial Networks. arXiv preprint arXiv:1708.05509 (2017)
15. Kodali, N., Abernethy, J., Hays, J., Kira, Z.: On Convergence and Stability of GANs. arXiv preprint arXiv:1705.07215 (2017)
16. Lee, K., Hicks, G., Nino-Murcia, G.: Validity and reliability of a scale to assess fatigue. Psychiatry Res. **36**, 291–298 (1991)

Haptic Material: A Holistic Approach for Haptic Texture Mapping

Antoine Costes[1,2(✉)], Fabien Danieau[1], Ferran Argelaguet[2], Anatole Lécuyer[2], and Philippe Guillotel[1]

[1] Technicolor R&I, Rennes, France
antoine.costes@technicolor.com
[2] Univ. Rennes, Inria, CNRS, IRISA, Rennes, France

Abstract. In this paper, we propose a new format for haptic texture mapping which is not dependent on the haptic rendering setup hardware. Our "haptic material" format encodes ten elementary haptic features in dedicated maps, similarly to "materials" used in computer graphics. These ten different features enable the expression of compliance, surface geometry and friction attributes through vibratory, cutaneous and kinesthetic cues, as well as thermal rendering. The diversity of haptic data allows various hardware to share this single format, each of them selecting which features to render depending on its capabilities.

Keywords: Texture · Compliance · Roughness · Friction
Temperature · Haptic material

1 Introduction

3D scanning techniques have flourished in the last decade, giving the possibility of digitizing real-life objects in a photo-realistic way. How could and should such virtual objects be enhanced with haptic properties in a touch-realistic way? Which features are to be considered, and how to store them in a standard format?

As for today, there is no obvious, generalized way to provide haptic properties to a virtual object, and most haptic rendering setups rely on custom and specific data formats which are not interoperable. This lack of standard representation impedes the whole computer haptics pipeline, from acquisition to rendering. A common, standardized way of storing haptic data would help to unify the approaches, to simplify the processes, to facilitate setups compatibility, and to spread haptic databases.

We propose the notion of "haptic material" as a reference to the similar notion of "materials" in computer graphics. In computer graphics, materials are handy packages with all the data required for the visual rendering of a virtual object. As an analogy, the haptic material should provide all the necessary elements for haptic rendering. Our format takes in account ten different spatially distributed haptic features, which we extracted from previous literature in order to cover the possible combinations of four haptic percepts and four rendering cues.

© Springer International Publishing AG, part of Springer Nature 2018
D. Prattichizzo et al. (Eds.): EuroHaptics 2018, LNCS 10894, pp. 37–45, 2018.
https://doi.org/10.1007/978-3-319-93399-3_4

The ten haptic features are stored in haptic maps, which provide an intuitive way to visualize them and facilitate many tasks related to haptic design.

2   Ten Relevant Features for Haptic Surfaces

Decades of research on touch perception showed that pressure forces, vibrations, friction forces and temperature are perceived in a complementary way, resulting in four distinct percepts (for review see [28] and [35]): **compliance** refers to the perception of deformation modalities; **surface geometry** refers to shape, reliefs and asperities; **friction** refers to sliding-related sensation; **warmth** refers to perceived temperature differences.

These perceptual dimensions, or percepts, arise from the reception of different types of cues by various body receptors: **cutaneous cues**, relating to contact area and skin deformation, are mainly sensed by SA-I, SA-II and FA-I in the region of contact; **vibratory cues**, relating to rapid deformation, propagate through the limbs and are mainly sensed by FA-II receptors in deep tissues and joints; **kinesthetic cues**, relating to limb movements and efforts, are mainly sensed by proprioceptors located in muscles and joints; **thermal cues**, relating to the heat flux transmitted by contact, are sensed by thermoreceptors in the region of contact.

Despite a tempting correspondence, these four types of cues do not match directly the four perceptual dimensions of texture perception. Indeed, finger pad deformations, contact vibrations and constrained motion are not specific to a given property, but can rather arise from compliance, geometry or friction attributes. Table 1 summarizes the perceptual metrics from the literature for the various combinations of percepts and cues.

Table 1. Representative quantities for the ten haptic percept/cue combinations.

Percepts → Cue Types ↓	Compliance	Geometry	Friction	Warmth
Kinesthetic	Rate-hardness [7]	Local surface orientation [14]	Kinetic friction [32]	/
Cutaneous	Contact area spread rate [6]	Local indentation [4]	Static friction [26]	/
Vibratory	Dynamic stiffness [40]	Stroke spectral response [17]	Stick-slip [19]	/
Thermal	/	/	/	Thermal profile [27]

Yet, very little is known about the relative importance of each cues for a given percept. For instance, in the case of compliance, the relative importance of vibratory cues is unknown. The systematic study of cues relative importance for compliance, surface geometry and friction perception is needed to determine an optimal combination of stimuli for a given haptic experience to be realistic.

Table 2. Typical rendering devices used to render each of the ten percept/cue combinations.

	Compliance	Geometry	Friction	Warmth
Kinesthetic	Normal force feedback [7]	Parallel platform [14]	Variable friction display [30]	/
Cutaneous	CASR display [6]	Micro-pin array [4]	Tangential force feedback [22]	/
Vibratory	Vibrator (tapping transients) [40]	Vibrator (stroking response) [17]	Vibrator (stroking transients) [19]	/
Thermal	/	/	/	Peltier module [9]

It should be kept in mind that the proposed conceptual distinction between cues is not tight and comprises some overlap. The clearest case is certainly the one of surface geometry. The well-documented "duplex theory" states that vibratory cues are necessary to perceive reliefs below 0.1 mm, and that coarser asperities are correctly perceived with static contact only, however vibratory cues contribute to coarse roughness perception through dynamic contact [5]. Also, it can be argued that the cutaneous and kinesthetic perceptions are hardly separable, as both local indentation and surface orientation integrate finger pad deformation with trajectory to form a spatially distributed percept. Nevertheless, the display of haptic shape at different scale involve different stimuli [11], and it seems reasonable to consider three different orders of magnitude relatively to the size of a finger. Insofar the finger is clearly affected in three different ways, namely vibrations, indentation and compression.

Finally, the vibrations conveying either roughness or friction information are hardly separable in practice, whether for acquisition or rendering, as they both arise from the rubbing of the surface. One can hypothesize that they match different spectral or temporal patterns: for instance the friction information being mainly characterized by abrupt changes and transient dynamics while the roughness information would be expressed by stable patterns for a given speed and force. However this hypothesis remains hard to evaluate experimentally.

3   Holistic Haptic Texture Mapping

Texture mapping is a method, commonly used in computer graphics, to render high frequency geometric details at low cost by wrapping on a 3D surface the pixels from textures [1]. If texture mapping has been extensively used for haptic rendering, it has been mainly focused on small-scale geometry (see [24] for a review). Although a few authors considered other haptic features, each of them involved a custom format for haptic data that is not directly compatible with the other setups [13, 20, 34].

We propose to associate an image with ten dedicated haptic maps based on the ten complementary haptic features identified in the previous section. By extending texture mapping to a variety of features, our holistic image format benefits from its intuitive visualization and rapid editing possibilities. The ten haptic maps can be elaborated either from real-world measurements and/or perceptual models, but can also be sketched manually.

In our illustrative example, a wooden texture image (see Fig. 1a), taken from a high quality scan-based texture package [41], is augmented with ten haptic maps. For sake of simplicity our haptic maps are all defined either as regular grayscale or RGB images. In addition, we will assume that vibratory features are defined in the form of regression models [33, 40], defined in specific files stored together with the haptic image. Therefore, the vibratory maps store only the references to vibration models, similarly to [34].

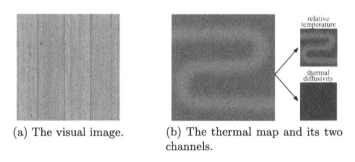

(a) The visual image.   (b) The thermal map and its two channels.

Fig. 1. Example of a visual image and thermal map revealing a hidden piping system. (Color figure online)

Figure 2 presents an example of the ten haptics maps. The normal map (Fig. 2b) stores the orientation of the surface for any point on the image. The height map (Fig. 2e) contains the vertical coordinates of the surface with respect to the 3D mesh. Both are defined as it commonly is in computer graphics, and were provided within the texture package. In the absence of measurement from the real material, all other maps were visually sketched from the texture visuals. The rate-hardness, CASR, static friction and kinectic friction maps (respectively Fig. 2a, d, c, and f) store eponymous values in 8-bit maps. Finally, the dynamic stiffness, stroke spectral response and stick-slip maps provide references to their respective models stored in separate files.

The thermal map (Fig. 1b) is a 24-bit RGB image. The R and G channels are respectively used to store the local values for relative temperature and the thermal diffusivity (B channel is not used). The local temperature values are defined relatively to ambient temperature (which is assigned to the whole virtual

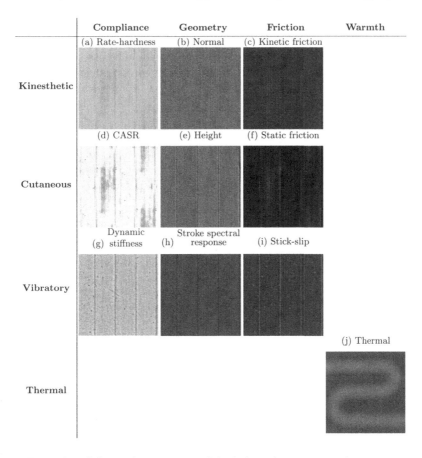

Fig. 2. Examples of the ten haptic maps of the holistic haptic image format, organized along perceptual dimensions and physical cues.

object, like mass). As detailed on (Fig. 1b), the color shades arise from a uniform dark green value expressing the uniform low thermal diffusivity of wood, and uneven local temperatures due to an potentially invisible heat source.

3.1   Format Specification Table

Our haptic format benefits from technical maturity of texture mapping: when using haptic materials, user can seamlessly make use of tiling or unwrapping.

Texture mapping techniques also extensively addressed the trade-off problem between resolution and performance, leading to various tricks like anti-aliasing and mipmapping. When applying this approach to haptics however, the question remains delicate as the different haptic maps address different physical quantities, matching different perceptual thresholds that might not have been directly address in previous literature. As an example, it is not trivial to decide which range and resolution should be required for a static friction coefficient.

Therefore, we propose a general-case specification table to define the format, range and resolution for haptic maps content. In specific contexts requiring other ranges or enhanced precision, custom specifications could be used to interpret the maps in the appropriate way. Table 3 summarizes the units, range and resolutions for each metric.

Table 3. General specification table for the features stored in the haptic maps. Vibratory maps are not considered as they store only references.

Haptic feature	Format	Range	Resolution
Rate-hardness	8-bit	0-10000 N.s^{-1}/m.s^{-1}	40 N.s^{-1}/m.s^{-1}
Contact area spread rate	8-bit	0-25.6 N/cm^2	0.1 N/cm^2
Local surface orientation	3x8-bit	2 x 0-180°	0.002°
Local indentation	8-bit	± 5mm	0.04 mm
Kinetic friction	8-bit	±5	0.04
Static friction	8-bit	±5	0.04
Relative temperature	8-bit	±25.4°	0.2°
Temperature slope	8-bit	0-5.0°/s	0.02°/s

4 Conclusion and Future Work

In this paper, we presented a new format for haptic texturing taking into account ten different haptic features, which are complementary both from a technical and a perceptual point of view. This format provides a generic description of haptic materials without prior knowledge on display hardware. The possibility to edit haptic properties directly on volumetric objects through a haptic interface opens the way to fast-prototyping *haptic design*, providing means of quick experimental iterations to sensory designers in the production of multi-sensory experiences. Besides, this format especially suited for the constitution of haptic databases, which are meant to be shared between haptic researchers using various devices.

Yet, the optimal complementarity between the ten features remains to be ensured by the systematic study of pyschophysical thresholds and relative importance of each cues, which represents a consequent body for future research. An unified rendering software solution remains also a challenging following. Finally, the topic of haptic material acquisition is still an open research question, as both real-world measurements and synthesis models have strengths and limitations.

References

1. Heckbert, P.: Survey of texture mapping. IEEE CG Appl. **6**(11), 56–57 (1986)
2. Armstrong-Helouvry, B., Dupont, P., De Wit, C.C.: Survey of models, analysis tools and compensation methods for the control of machines with friction. Automatica **30**(7), 1083–1138 (1994)

3. Kontarinis, D.A., Son, J.S., Peine, W., Howe, R.D.: A tactile shape sensing and display system for teleoperated manipulation. In: IEEE International Conference on Robotics and Automation, vol. 1, pp. 641–646 (1995)
4. Shimojo, M., Shinohara, M., Fukui, Y.: Human shape recognition performance for 3D tactile display. IEEE Trans. Syst. Man Cybern. Part A Syst. Hum. **29**(6), 637–64 (1999)
5. Hollins, M., Risner, S.R.: Evidence for the duplex theory of tactile texture perception. Attention Percept. Psychophy. **62**, 695–705 (2000)
6. Bicchi, A., Scilingo, E.P., De Rossi, D.: Haptic discrimination of softness in teleoperation: the role of the contact area spread rate. IEEE Trans. Robot. Autom. **16**, 496–504 (2000)
7. Lawrence, D.A., Pao, L.Y., Dougherty, A.M., Salada, M.A., Pavlou, Y.: Rate-hardness: a new performance metric for haptic interfaces. IEEE Trans. Robot. Autom. **16**, 357–371 (2000)
8. Okamura, A.M., Cutkosky, M.R., Dennerlein, J.T.: Reality-based models for vibration feedback in virtual environments. IEEE/ASME Trans. Mechatron. **6**(3), 245–252 (2001)
9. Jones, L. A., Berris, M.: Material discrimination and thermal perception. In: 11th Symposium on Haptic Interfaces for Virtual Environment and Teleoperator Systems, pp. 171–178 (2003)
10. Hwang, J.D., Williams, M.D., Niemeyer, G.: Toward event-based haptics: rendering contact using open-loop force pulses. In: Haptic Interfaces for Virtual Environment and Teleoperator Systems, p. 24 (2004)
11. Hayward, V.: Display of haptic shape at different scales. In: Proceedings of Eurohaptics, pp. 20–27 (2004)
12. Kammermeier, P., Kron, A., Hoogen, J., Schmidt, G.: Display of holistic haptic sensations by combined tactile and kinesthetic feedback. Presence: Teleoper. Virtual Environ. **13**(1), 1–15 (2004)
13. Kim, L., Sukhatme, G.S., Desbrun, M.: A haptic-rendering technique based on hybrid surface representation. IEEE Comput. Graph. Appl. **24**(2), 66–75 (2004)
14. Dostmohamed, H., Hayward, V.: Trajectory of contact region on the fingerpad gives the illusion of haptic shape. Exp. Brain Res. **164**(3), 387–394 (2005)
15. Yang, G.H., Kyung, K.U., Jeong, Y.J., Kwon, D.S.: Novel haptic mouse system for holistic haptic display and potential of vibrotactile stimulation. In: IEEE/RSJ International Conference on Intelligent Robots and Systems, pp. 1980–1985 (2005)
16. Kikuuwe, R., Takesue, N., Sano, A., Mochiyama, H., Fujimoto, H.: Fixed-step friction simulation: from classical Coulomb model to modern continuous models. In: IEEE/RSJ International Conference on Intelligent Robots and Systems, pp. 1009–1016 (2005)
17. Kuchenbecker, K.J., Fiene, J., Niemeyer, G.: Improving contact realism through event-based haptic feedback. IEEE Trans. Vis. Comput. Graph. **12**(2), 219–230 (2006)
18. Tiest, W.M.B., Kappers, A.M.L.: Haptic and visual perception of roughness. Acta Psychol. **124**(2), 177–189 (2007)
19. Konyo, M., Yamada, H., Okamoto, S., Tadokoro, S.: Alternative display of friction represented by tactile stimulation without tangential force. In: Haptics: Perception, Devices and Scenarios, pp. 619–629 (2008)
20. Wakita, W., Murakami, K., Ido, S.: A texturebased haptic model design with 3D brush. In: 18th International Conference on Artificial Reality and Telexistence, pp. 51–56 (2008)

21. Friedman, R.M., Hester, K.D., Green, B.G., LaMotte, R.H.: Magnitude estimation of softness. Exp. Brain Res. **191**(2), 133–142 (2008)
22. Drif, A., Le Mercier, B., Kheddar, A.: Design of a multilevel haptic display. In: Bicchi, A., Buss, M., Ernst, M.O., Peer, A. (eds.) The Sense of Touch and Its Rendering, vol. 45, pp. 207–224. Springer, Heidelberg (2008). https://doi.org/10.1007/978-3-540-79035-8_10
23. Bergmann Tiest, W.M., Kappers, A.M.L.: Cues for haptic perception of compliance. IEEE Trans. Haptics **2**(4), 189–199 (2009)
24. Theoktisto Colmenares, V. A., Fairn Gonzlez, M., and Navazo lvaro, I.: A hybrid rugosity mesostructure (HRM) for rendering fine haptic detail (2009)
25. Wijntjes, M.W., Sato, A., Hayward, V., Kappers, A.M.: Local surface orientation dominates haptic curvature discrimination. IEEE Trans. Haptics **2**(2), 94–102 (2009)
26. Provancher, W.R., Sylvester, N.D.: Fingerpad skin stretch increases the perception of virtual friction. IEEE Trans. Haptics **2**(4), 212–223 (2009)
27. Tiest, W.M.B., Kappers, A.M.: Tactile perception of thermal diffusivity. Attention Percept. Psychophy. **71**(3), 481–489 (2009)
28. Tiest, W.M.B.: Tactual perception of material properties. Vis. Res. **50**(24), 2775–2782 (2010)
29. McMahan, W., Romano, J.M., Rahuman, A.M.A., Kuchenbecker, K.J.: High frequency acceleration feedback significantly increases the realism of haptically rendered textured surfaces. In: IEEE Haptics Symposium, pp. 141–148 (2010)
30. Bau, O., Poupyrev, I., Israr, A., Harrison, C.: TeslaTouch: electrovibration for touch surfaces. In: UIST, pp. 283–292 (2010)
31. Kim, S.C., Kyung, K.U., Kwon, D.S.: Haptic annotation for an interactive image. In: 5th International Conference on Ubiquitous Information Management and Communication, p. 51 (2011)
32. Mullenbach, J., Johnson, D., Colgate, J.E., Peshkin, M.A.: ActivePaD surface haptic device. In: IEEE Haptics Symposium, pp. 407–414 (2012)
33. Culbertson, H., Romano, J.M., Castillo, P., Mintz, M., Kuchenbecker, K.J.: Refined methods for creating realistic haptic virtual textures from tool-mediated contact acceleration data. In: IEEE Haptics Symposium, pp. 385–391 (2012)
34. Kamuro, S., Takeuchi, Y., Minamizawa, K., Tachi, S.: Haptic editor. In: SIGGRAPH Asia Emerging Technologies, p. 14 (2012)
35. Okamoto, S., Nagano, H., Yamada, Y.: Psychophysical dimensions of tactile perception of textures. IEEE Trans. Haptics **6**(1), 81–93 (2012)
36. Moscatelli, A., Bianchi, M., Serio, A., Al Atassi, O., Fani, S., Terekhov, A., Hayward, V., Ernst, M., Bicchi, A.: A change in the fingertip contact area induces an illusory displacement of the finger. In: Auvray, M., Duriez, C. (eds.) EUROHAPTICS 2014. LNCS, vol. 8619, pp. 72–79. Springer, Heidelberg (2014). https://doi.org/10.1007/978-3-662-44196-1_10
37. van Beek, F.E., Heck, D.J., Nijmeijer, H., Tiest, W.M.B., Kappers, A.M.: The effect of damping on the perception of hardness. In: World Haptics Conference, pp. 82–87 (2015)
38. Higashi, K., Okamoto, S., Nagano, H., Yamada, Y.: Effects of mechanical parameters on hardness experienced by damped natural vibration stimulation. In: Systems, Man, and Cybernetics, pp. 1539–1544 (2015)
39. Benko, H., Holz, C., Sinclair, M., Ofek, E.: Normaltouch and texturetouch: high-fidelity 3d haptic shape rendering on handheld virtual reality controllers. In: Proceedings of the 29th Annual Symposium on User Interface Software and Technology, pp. 717–728 (2016)

40. Higashi, K., Okamoto, S., Yamada, Y., Nagano, H., Konyo, M.: Hardness perception by tapping: effect of dynamic stiffness of objects. In: World Haptics Conference, pp. 37–41 (2017)
41. Mura Vision. https://www.muravision.com

Estimation of the Pressing Force
from Finger Image by Using Neural Network

Yoshinori Inoue[1(✉)], Yasutoshi Makino[1,2], and Hiroyuki Shinoda[1]

[1] University of Tokyo, 5-1-5 Kashiwanoha, Kashiwa, Chiba 277-0882, Japan
y.inoue@hapis.k.u-tokyo.ac.jp
[2] JST PRESTO, Kashiwa, Japan

Abstract. In this paper, we propose a method that estimates contact force to hard surface from a single visual image of a finger by using a neural network. In general, it is hard to estimate applied force to hard object only from visual images as the object surface hardly moves. In this paper, we focus on the human side. When persons push an object, posture of hand reflects how hard he/she pushes the surface. Observation of human body condition will tell the haptic information. We used the Convolutional Neural Network to make the system learn the relationship between the applied force and the finger posture. We created a neural network model individually. The evaluation result shows that a root mean square error from the actual force is approximately 0.5 N for the best case, which is 2.5% to the dynamic range (0–20 N) of applied force.

Keywords: Force sensing · Convolutional neural network · Augmented reality

1 Introduction

Thanks to the improvement of recent technologies, it is promising that VR and AR will become more important. At present, mainstream of VR and AR uses Head-Mounted Displays (HMDs), however, the other types of methods such as mid-air imaging technology also will be popular. One possible development in AR is to use projection mapping technique as a tool for superimposing additional images onto real objects.

There are some previous systems that achieved interaction with a projected images. For example, for Xperia Touch by SONY, it is possible to directly interact with the projected images through hands by measuring the motion of the fingertip and it is possible to input anywhere on the projected area. Hasegawa et al. [1]. proposed "Tactile Projector" system which allowed users to interact with projected images with tactile feedback by using ultrasound airborne tactile display. As is shown in these previous cases, we can say that users can interact with projected image in both input and output.

In these studies, they mainly judged whether the finger is touching to the projected image or not. In order to improve the quality of these types of experiences, it is desirable to measure how strongly a user pushes a projected surface. This types of improvement had been seen in the case of smartphones. The operability of recent smartphones have been improved because they can estimate such pressing force by installing a new force sensor. The interaction with projected image must be improved as the same manner.

© Springer International Publishing AG, part of Springer Nature 2018
D. Prattichizzo et al. (Eds.): EuroHaptics 2018, LNCS 10894, pp. 46–57, 2018.
https://doi.org/10.1007/978-3-319-93399-3_5

Here we assume one application, as an example, that project images of instruments such as piano keyboard and a user interacts with it as shown in Fig. 1(a). For example in the realistic piano case, players put his/her fingers on keys even when they do not play the sound. Thus the projected piano system must detect not only contact/non-contact condition but also its force. The purpose of this research is to estimate the pressing force in such projection-based interaction system by using a simple camera. The projection-based interactive system can detect the pressing force of each finger to enrich the experience.

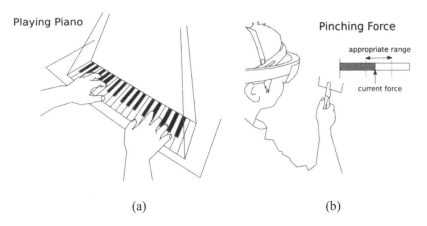

Fig. 1. Schematic images of our system. (a) The projection-based interactive system. (b) The system instructs appropriate force range by estimating the pinching force.

This system can be also used for HMD-based AR system as shown in Fig. 1(b). When a user utilizes a tool such as a plier, the camera on the HMD measures the condition of the finger, estimates the applied force, and indicates the appropriate force to handle the object.

In this paper, as a first step to achieve the vision-based force sensing scheme, we show how the system accurately estimates applied force by using finger images. We use Convolutional Neural Network (CNN) to learn the relationship between the applied force, which is measured with a load cell, and image of finger as shown in Fig. 2. There are some previous studies that uses the color change of a fingernail to predict pressing force and direction [2–4]. In that case, it is hard to use it with projection mapping as the projected image interferes with the measurement of the color of the fingernail. We use the posture of the finger to predict pressing force.

Our experimental result shows that the root mean square (RMS) error of estimated value is 0.5 N for the best case provided the learning model parameters are tuned for individual user.

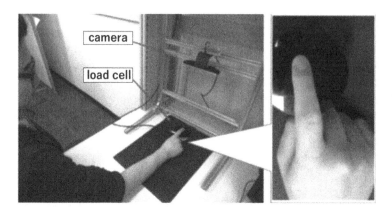

Fig. 2. Left: Measurement setup. It consists of the camera and the load cell. Right: A subject pushes the load cell with his/her index finger.

2   Related Works

2.1   Push Force Estimation by Fingernail Color

In the current paper, the pressing force is estimated from the image of entire hand. There have been some previous studies that estimate applied force to fingertip by measuring the change of the color of a fingernail. In those studies, the average error was approximately 1 N [5–7]. They mainly used a set of visible LED and photodiode to detect the color change. In the study [5] the authors used an image of the tip of fingernail by using a special camera device. The resulting error was 0.5 to 1 N.

In these studies, they attached a sensor onto a fingernail. Although the device seemed sufficiently small, it sometimes makes users hard to handle object naturally. The proposed system in this study differs from the previously proposed color-change based method in that the force can be estimated without attaching a sensor to a finger. Even when the color change is recorded remotely with camera, the color change seems difficult to use with the projected images as they interfere with the color detection. By contrast, the force information in the proposed method is estimated not only from the color change of a fingernail but also the posture of whole finger to try to make the estimation accuracy robust against the lighting condition.

2.2   Estimate Force from Images

There have been some studies that predicted manipulation force through images [8–10]. In these studies, they tried to estimate applied force for each finger when a user hold some particular objects such as a cup and a bottle. Their research assumed the case when a user grabs some object. Our research differs in that we do not grasp the object and estimate the applied force by pressing down on any surfaces.

In the previous studies [2–4], they estimated the force through hand images in the range of relatively small force up to 5 N, as they focused on handling cups and objects. In that case users do not hold such targets so strongly. By contrast, we assume the application that grasp a pliers as shown in Fig. 1, it is necessary to be able to estimate larger force. Our experiment allow users to add approximately 20 N for estimation.

2.3 Detecting Contact by Camera

In the previous study [11], Echtler et al. proposed a method to detect contact/non-contact condition by using IR camera. They used IR light source which is guided to the thin transparent glass plate. Due to the total internal reflection, the light diffuses only when the finger touches the glass plate. The camera can see the contact/non-contact condition by measuring the diffused light from the contact position. This might be used to estimate contact force since the intensity of diffused light would be affected by how strong a finger pushes the object. One restriction, in this case, is the target surface. The system detects the contact condition only on the designated glass plate. Our system focuses on to detect contact force on arbitrary hard surface.

OmniTouch system [12] detects the contact condition by using a depth image sensor put on a user's shoulder. The concept of OmniTouch is to use body surface as a new input surface. Since they assumed to detect contact condition on human skin, the surface deforms and its displacement can be measured with depth sensor. In the current study, we assume the contact with hard surface. Measuring contact condition by depth image sensor cannot be applied to those hard surface.

2.4 Deep Learning

The multilayered neural network has excellent results in ILSVRS (Image Net Large Scale Visual Recognition Challenge) held in September 2012 [13]. It shows high performance in the field of image processing, and in recent years it has been applied to face recognition, object identification and many other fields. Before the deep neural network emerged, most of image recognition methods extract necessary features from an input and perform machine learning on them and thus it was impossible to extract features that human beings cannot recognize or information unknowingly acquired. However, in the multilayer deep neural network, used in these days, important features are automatically extracted in the calculation process without specifying the feature quantity. In this research, we believe that by using a neural network, we can acquire more feature quantity appearing in hand including fingernail color change.

3 Proposed System

3.1 Data Measurement

Figure 2 shows the equipment to capture hand image and to measure applied force. The equipment consists of a camera that captures images and a load cell (FS 10, Unipulse

Corp.) that measures the pressing force. The camera is installed above the load cell to sufficiently record the state of the finger when pressed. Images are captured at 30 fps by the RGB camera, and at the same time, the pressing force is measured by the load cell. The accuracy of the load cell, shown in its datasheet, is that the error to the full-scaled value range is less than 0.02%.

The relative position of the camera and the load cell is fixed by using aluminum and acrylic frames. The pushing surface and its surroundings are covered with black paper to reduce light reflection, which can be noise for images for learning process. We cut out unnecessary parts of the captured images that do not show the hand from the original image. Only the part of the hand is used as the learning data since we assumed that the non-hand part was meaningless for estimating the applied force. The border line to be cut was fixed and visualized for the subjects at the time of measurement. Subjects were instructed to put their hands within the range. The cut image is shown in the right in Fig. 2. This preparation helps to reduce computational time for learning.

3.2   Pushing Trial

For learning dataset, we measured the finger images under the following conditions. Five male subjects (ages from 23–26) pushed the load cell surface under the same lighting conditions.

- Subjects are instructed to put their index finger on the load cell surface and keep their wrist always on the desk.
- Only the index finger is allowed to stretch to press the load cell as shown in Fig. 2. They are not allowed to move their arm intentionally to prevent applying their own weight to the load cell.
- Measurement duration is 90 s. Subjects freely apply forces by moving index finger whose force range is from 0 N to 20 N. The applied force value is displayed on a PC screen so that they can control the force range.
- No intentional shear force shall be applied.

3.3   Dataset Creation

Based on the measured data, we create a dataset for learning. The captured color image is converted to grayscale for shortening the calculation time and related force value is tagged as shown in Fig. 3 for teacher data. We obtained 2,700 (30 fps × 90 s) datasets from the measurement process for each subject. As we discussed later, we create the machine learning model for all 5 subjects and individual ones. We used 70% of 2,700 data as training process to determine weight parameters in a neural network. The remaining 30% of the data were used for evaluating the learned parameters.

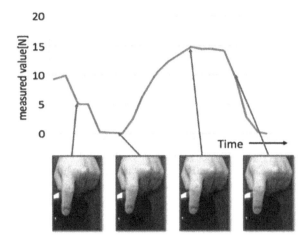

Fig. 3. Schematic image of dataset creation. Although only 4 images are shown for ease of viewing, the related force value was tagged to all the data which is taken at 30 fps.

3.4 Machine Learning

We used the CNN as shown in Fig. 4. Learning is performed by using the created dataset. The input is the brightness value of each pixel of the single grayscale image of the finger as shown in Fig. 3 and the output is the estimated value of the pressing force. Therefore, the number of units of the input layer is the number of pixels of the image data. The number of units of the output layer is 1. We changed the convolution size step by step from 32 filters 6x6 to 96 filters 4x4. The pooling layers are inserted between the convolutional layers.

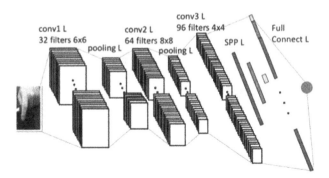

Fig. 4. Convolutional neural network model used in experiments.

We used the backpropagation method and Root Mean Square (RMS) error as the error function and parameters are updated to minimize RMS error of test data. The Rectified Linear Unit (ReLU) function is used as the activation function in the network, and RMSpropGraves [14] (rate = 0.0001, alpha = 0.95, momentum = 0.9, eps = 0.0001) is used as the optimization method. In addition, Spatial Pyramid Pooling (SPP) layer is used between CONV 3, which is the last layer of the convolutional layers, and the full-connect layer as is used in [15]. We used Chainer as a framework for constructing a neural network. These network structures are determined empirically to achieve higher performance of estimation.

4   Evaluation

The transition of the loss function for learning of five subjects individually is shown in Fig. 5. The horizontal axis is the epoch number, which represents iteration of learning process, and the vertical axis is the RMS error of the estimated force from the single finger image. We made learners for each subject and it shows 5 different curves for Fig. 5. As we described in the previous section, 70% of the dataset is used for learning to update the model parameters, and the transition of RMS error, shown in Fig. 5, is evaluated with the rest 30% of data.

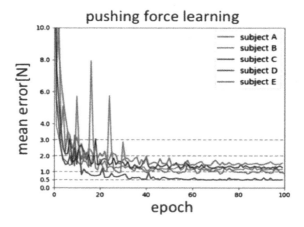

Fig. 5. Transition of error function during learning for individual model.

The result shows that the RMS error of subject C is the smallest among five subjects, which converges to approximately 0.5 N. This RMS error corresponds to 2.5% of the dynamic range from 0 N to 20 N. Subject E has the largest RMS error, which converges to approximately 1.5 N. This value corresponds to 7.5% of the 20 N range.

Figure 6 shows the same result to the model made from the all 5 subjects. Its error converges to approximately 1.6 N. The result is not as good as the best case in individual model.

Table 1 summarizes the learning results of five subjects and all 5 subjects dataset. The final error means the RMS error of the last epoch. The rate shows the RMS error rate to the full dynamic range: 20 N. The elapsed time is the time required for learning with Windows PC (CPU: Intel Core-i7-6700 @3.4 GHz, GPU: GeForce GTX 1080, and Memory: 16 GB). In order to accomplish 100 epoch of individual learning with 2,700 data, it needs approximately 10 min. By contrast, it needs 43 min for 5 subjects data at once.

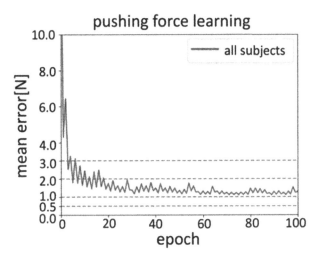

Fig. 6. Transition of error function during learning for all 5 subjects model.

Table 1. Comparison of the performance of learning systems

Tester	Final error (N)	Rate (%)	Elapsed time (s)
Subject A	0.9754	4.7	590 (5.9 s/epoch)
Subject B	1.1621	5.8	598 (6.0 s/epoch)
Subject C	0.5120	2.5	595 (6.0 s/epoch)
Subject D	1.2698	6.3	597 (6.0 s/epoch)
Subject E	1.5444	7.7	599 (6.0 s/epoch)
All subjects	1.5982	8.0	2564 (25.6 s/epoch)

Figure 7 plots the evaluation results with 200 test dataset, which are not used for making each model. The horizontal axis is the measured force by the load cell, and the vertical axis is the estimated force by the CNN. When the estimated force by learning is equal to the measured value, they form the straight line of $y = x$. As is shown in the Fig. 7, the estimated values seems to fit on the theoretical line for all the cases.

Figure 8 shows the absolute value of the error of the learning result, which means how much force estimated by learning is different from the true value. The horizontal axis shows the measured force by the load cell, and the vertical axis is the value of RMS error. There seem no significant differences depending on the applied force (Fig. 6).

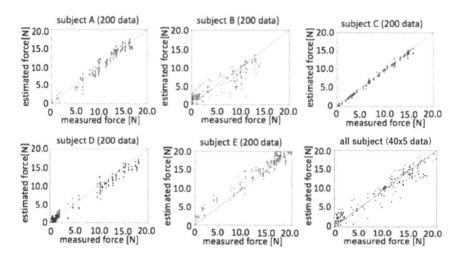

Fig. 7. Validation of learning results for each subject and all 5 subjects

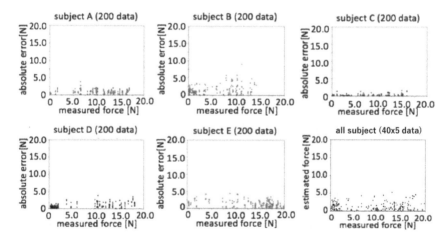

Fig. 8. The absolute value of the error of the learning result for each subject and all 5 subjects.

Figure 9 shows the comparison between the individual model and the general model made from all 5 subjects. We used the same parameters of all 5 model which is shown in Fig. 7 and separate the result so that it can be compared easily. It is clear that the variance becomes larger for the all 5 subjects model. This means the current model cannot generalize the individual characteristics of pushing the surface. However, the average of each standard deviation is 0.9934 N, which would be acceptable depending on the applications.

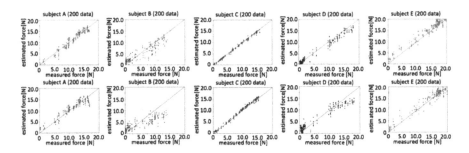

Fig. 9. Comparison of learning results. Five graphs in the top row shows the same one in Fig. 7 and the bottom row shows the validation with the same dataset of 5 subjects by using the model made from all 5 subjects.

5   Discussions

5.1   Generalization

As is shown in the results, the individual model showed better performance than the generalized model made from all 5 subjects. This is because there might be an individual difference in the image representing the pressing force. The finger posture they pushed the load cell and the change in color of fingernail and surrounding skin seemed different from person to person.

There are two ways to manage this problem. One is to make individual model all the time as we showed in this paper. When the system is supposed to be used in some particular area such as in factory or logistics warehouse with HMD as we illustrated in Fig. 1(b), it is possible to prepare individual model since the users are limited. As we shown in Table 1, the computational time for one subject is approximately 10 min for 90 s pushing action and it is relatively short time.

The other way is to use sequential information for learning. The current system only uses a single image of the finger. The sequential image of the finger may contain the typical force information. Learning from those data, there might be general features in pressing motion rather than static image. Making use of sequential images for improving generalization of the system is one of our future works.

In the current study, the number of subjects: 5, is thought to be too small to generalize the pushing action. Using more sample dataset can improve the learner to realize universal prediction model.

5.2   Effect of Dataset Variation

According to Fig. 7, when the measured force is in the range of 5 N to 15 N, it is found that the estimated value of the subject B is judged to be smaller than the actual value. On the contrary, the estimated value of subject E is estimated to be relatively large.

The reason for this is thought to be the variation in training dataset. In the experiment, the subjects were asked to apply force freely to the force sensor between 0 to 20 N. From that viewpoint, subject B pushed the load cell weaker and subject E pushed it stronger in average. In these cases, the learners tended to judge the applied forces to be weaker/ stronger than actual forces, respectively.

Considering the variation in subject C, there seems no bias in variation of dataset and the system succeeded in guessing closely to the true value.

These data suggest that the influence of learning accuracy depending on the frequency of pushing data. We suppose that learning accuracy can be improved by measuring data with the similar frequency with respect to a given force.

5.3   Robustness

In this paper, we restricted to obtain hand image at a fixed position and angle under the same lighting condition. In order to achieve higher robustness against many external conditions, we have to record many types of conditions of hand such as different lighting, angle of the camera, left hand, and so on. Appropriate data augmentation for neural network might be helpful to solve this issue.

6   Conclusions

In this study, we tried to estimate pressing force through a single frame of hand image by using the CNN. To capture a finger image and related pressing force for learning and evaluation of the estimator, we measured them with a camera and a load cell.

A learning model was constructed in which a single image was input to a CNN. Our evaluation experiment showed that Root Mean Square (RMS) error of estimated force was 0.5 N for the best performance condition with its dynamic range of 0–20 N. On the other hand, the worst case showed that the RMS error was 1.5 N in average. These RMS errors correspond to 2 and 8% of the range of 20 N, respectively.

In the current study, we made individual CNN model to achieve the higher accuracy of estimation. We cannot realize a generalized learning model in this study. However, the current system only needs 10 min for calculating the CNN parameters with 90 s data measurement. This would be practical to make individual estimator if the use case matches. To generalize the model, we suppose to utilize the sequential information of the finger for learning.

As mentioned in the introduction, this research aims to use it for HMD such as Google Glass and Holo-Lens, but at this stage, the accuracy depends on the position and angle of the camera. It is necessary to construct robustness which is not influenced by the condition of the camera and lighting condition.

Acknowledgments. This work is supported by JST PRESTO 17939983.

References

1. Kazuma, Y., Keisuke, H., Hiroyuki, S.: Measuring visio-tactile threshold for visio-tactile projector. In: Proceedings of SICE Annual Conference 2012, pp. 1996–2000 (2012)
2. Stephen, M., Harry, A.: Measurement of finger posture and three-axis fingertip touch force using fingernail sensors. IEEE Trans. Robot. Autom. **20**, 26–35 (2004)
3. Thomas, G., John, H., Stephen, M.: 3-D fingertip touch force prediction using fingernail imaging with automated calibration. IEEE Trans. Rob. **31**, 1116–1129 (2015)
4. Thomas, G., Lucas, L., Yu, S., John, H., Stephen, M.: 3D force prediction using fingernail imaging with automated calibration. In: 2010 IEEE Haptics Symposium, pp. 113–120 (2010)
5. Cornelia, F., Fang, W., Yezhou, Y., Konstantinos, Z., Yi, Z., Francisco, B., Michael, P.: Prediction of Manipulation Actions. arXiv.org. https://arxiv.org/abs/1610.00759. Accessed 20 Jan 2018
6. Tu-Hoa, P., Nikolaos, K., Antonis, A., Abderrahmane, K.: Hand-object contact force estimation from markerless visual tracking. IEEE Trans. Patt. Anal. Mach. Intell. **PP**, 1 (2017)
7. Wonjun, H., Soo-Chul, L.: Inferring Interaction Force from Visual Information without Using Physical Force Sensors. Sensors, Basel (2017)
8. Florian, E., Andreas, D., Marcus, T., Gudrun, K.: Inverted FTIR: easy multitouch sensing for flatscreens. In: ITS 2009 Proceedings of the ACM International Conference on Interactive Tabletops and Surfaces, pp. 29–32 (2009)
9. Chris, H., Hrvoje, B., Andrew, W.: OmniTouch: wearable multitouch interaction everywhere. In: UIST 2011 Proceedings of the 24th Annual ACM Symposium on User Interface Software and Technology, pp. 441–450 (2011)
10. Alex, K., Ilya, S., Geoffrey, H.: ImageNet classification with deep convolutional neural networks. In: NIPS 2012 Proceedings of the 25th International Conference on Neural Information Processing Systems, vol. 1, pp. 1097–1105 (2012)
11. Alex, G.: Generating Sequences With Recurrent Neural Network. arXiv.org. https://arxiv.org/abs/1308.0850. Accessed 20 Jan 2018
12. Shaoqing, R., Kaiming, H., Ross, G., Jian, S.: Faster R-CNN: Towards Real-Time Object Detection with Region Proposal Networks. arXiv.org. https://arxiv.org/abs/1506.01497. Accessed 20 Jan 2018

Multi-point Pressure Sensation Display Using Pneumatic Actuators

Takaaki Taniguchi[✉], Sho Sakurai, Takuya Nojima, and Koichi Hirota

The University of Electro Communications, 1-5-1 Chofugaoka, Chofu, Tokyo, Japan
takaaki16@vogue.is.uec.ac.jp

Abstract. In this research, we developed the device that makes it possible to present a haptic sense in a wide range of a hand with high-density. This device is composed of a plurality of modules with built-in pin arrays and pneumatically drives the pins in the module compress the skin and present the haptic sense. There is 2 type of devices, one's density of pins evenly distributed on the whole hand (device1), and the other's density of pins are arranged with high-density of fingertips based on a 2-point threshold (device2). The total number of pins was 128 for both devices. The Controller of the device was composed of electro-pneumatic regulators, a control circuit, and a PC. Force presented by each actuator was computed based on the simulation of contact between the virtual hand and object. In order to evaluate the performance of these devices, 3-dimensional shape recognition experiment of virtual objects was conducted. Measurement results of correct answer rate and response time were 65.6% and 46.1 s in device1. The results of device2 were 70.3% and 40.2 s. From these results, it was suggested that the arrangement of the presentation stimuli based on the 2-point discrimination threshold is effective for the tactile recognition.

Keywords: Virtual reality · Haptic device · Pneumatic

1 Introduction

Virtual Reality (VR) is a technology creates a similar environment as a function does not exist in reality by giving various stimuli to various kinds of human senses. In the recent year, anyone can easily construct a VR environment because of the improvement of computer performance and the advancement of 3D technology. Many VR technologies related to visual and auditory sensation are present in our surroundings, they are familiar with our lives. Other than visual and auditory sensation, many types of research on VR technology regarding haptic sense have been progressing, and haptic devices using various methods have been developed. In addition, technologies for measuring shapes and motions of a human body in a real environment by using various sensors, and reflecting those data in the VR environment are progressing. However, most of these haptic devices limited in the range of stimulation or inadequate stimulation density. Therefore, we developed the device that performs high-density tactile stimulation throughout the hand.

© Springer International Publishing AG, part of Springer Nature 2018
D. Prattichizzo et al. (Eds.): EuroHaptics 2018, LNCS 10894, pp. 58–67, 2018.
https://doi.org/10.1007/978-3-319-93399-3_6

2 Related Work

In elements that are emphasized as tactile interaction in the current VR environment, there is object information such as weight and shape of a virtual object. Usually, people often use hands to acquire these objects information in reality. Therefore, many types of wearable haptic devices for hand have been developed for a long time.

Phantom Premium [1] and Force Dimension [2] are grounded type haptic devices, which can express very accurate and wide range forces. However, these devices have a weak point that user cannot perform tactile recognition by freely moving their hands.

In above respect, wearable haptic devices have a relatively high degree of freedom of hand at the time of interaction. CyberGrasp [3] is the device attaches a wire passing mechanism to the back of the hand and presents a force sense to the fingertip by pulling a wire. The Rutgers Master II [4] adopts a specification that presents reaction force from the actuator against the flexion of the finger. These devices are classified as exoskeleton type. Although it is wearable, it becomes heavier because of the structure using multiple actuators. Therefore, in recent years, many devices have been developed that are smaller, lighter, and do not impair the wearer's movements as compared with the exoskeleton type, even in wearable devices by limiting the range of stimulation only to the fingertip. Prattichizzo et al. [5] proposed the wearable haptic device that can directly apply a force vector to the fingertip. Choi et al. [6] developed the device called Wolverine, specialized for presenting a grasping sensation of a rigid body. Minamizawa et al. [7] created a device that deforms the fingertip and presents the sense of virtual objects weight. A lot of pin array type devices have been developed as tactile presentation devices to fingertip. [8, 9] High stimulation density is an advantage of the pin array type haptic device. These devices are suitable for expressing the force like manipulating the object by pinching it with the fingertip, however for the operation and the tactile recognition by using a wide range of the hand is not enough because they limit the presentation range to the fingertip. In tactile recognition, it has been reported that the extent of the area of contact affects the accuracy of recognition. [10] Although this study was conducted using real objects, it also shows that it is necessary to cover a wider area of the hand even in tactile recognition in the VR environment.

Although there are not many haptic devices covering the whole hand, Some devices using vibration presentation are developed. Vibration can be realized by a relatively small actuator, and some are commercialized. [11] The research of Tanabe et al. [12] can be cited as a full-scale study. In this research, they developed the glove type device with 52 vibro-actuators placed throughout the hand. Also, they conducted an experiment of 3-dimensional shape recognition by using their device. In this experiment, 4 type of virtual objects were used. The correct answer rate was about 70% and the response time was about 20 s in the recognition using only their device. However, according to Klatzky et al. [10], the correct answer rate in recognition of 36 familiar objects in reality is 95% and the response time is 6.12 s. Comparing these results, we can see the large gap between the virtual object recognition and the real one.

Regarding above gap, we focused on the density of the stimulation. As the indicator of the tactile resolution of the hand, 2-point discrimination threshold has been used since long. According to Weinstein [13], 2-point threshold is narrowest at the fingertip of

2 mm and is also about 10 mm in the palm, so it is necessary to increase the stimulation density to cover these. In addition, Antfolk et al. [14] carried out a tactile recognition experiment against limb amputees by using artificial hand, and showed that feedback by pressure is more effective for touch recognition than feedback by vibration.

Considering the above, in this research, we proposed a method of attaching multiple modules with built-in pin arrays throughout the hand in order to improve the stimulation density while keeping the stimulus in the whole hand. Although it becomes possible to present a high-density stimulation by the pin array to the whole hand, the problems of enlarging the apparatus and increasing the weight also exist. To solve these problems, we adopted the pneumatic drive of the module. Driving by pneumatic pressure makes it possible to separate the device and control unit, so it is possible to reduce the size and weight of the device. In addition, we create the device with pins equally placed throughout the hand and the device with pins based on the 2-point threshold and examined the difference in tactile recognition by pin arrangement.

3   Device and System

In our study, two prototype devices of pressure sensation display were developed. Both of them have 128 pneumatic actuators that affect force on the skin. The pneumatic actuator is a kind of air cylinder where force is presented by a pin that works as a piston. Two devices are different regarding the distribution of actuators. In the first device, the actuators are arranged in a homogeneous manner, or without considering the difference in the tactile resolution among hand (called Device 1). In the second device, the actuators were arranged so that their density becomes approximately proportional to the 2-point threshold on each part of the hand (called Device 2).

3.1   Device 1

The device is composed of actuator modules and supporting materials. Actuator module is a block of actuators. In this device, four types of modules as in Fig. 1(a) were used depending on the shape of the surface on which the module is placed. Modules were arranged on the palm and fingers as in Fig. 1(b) to cover the entire area. Modules for the ball of fingers had a curved shape to so that they will fit the finger surface although the individual difference in the finger size was not considered. Variation of the dimension of the module depending on the fingers is shown in Table 1. Modules were created using the 3D printer (Replicator 2X, MakerBot) and holes in modules were finished by the milling machine. The diameter of all pins was 3 mm, hence each pin generate a force of 3.5 N when the air pressure of 0.5 MPa, which is the maximum pressure used in the following experiment, was supplied. Top of the module was covered with air permeable cloth to let out the air leaking from the gap between the cylinder and the pin.

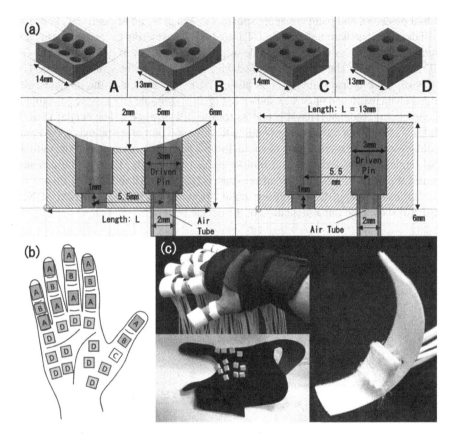

Fig. 1. Device 1 (a) Shape of modules, (b) Arrangement of each module, (c) Implementation

Table 1. Length of module: L and the number of pins

Phalanx	Thumb	Index	Middle	Ring	Small	Pin number
Distal	18	13	15	13	11	6
Middle	–	15	15	15	13	4
Proximal	18	15	15	15	13	6 (4:only thumb)

Modules on fingers and palm were supported by Velcro tape strips and a hand supporter. Figure 1(c) shows the implementation of the device. The device was connected to the air control unit by urethane tubes.

3.2   Device 2

As described above, the density of actuators of this device was designed based on the knowledge on the 2-point discrimination threshold. According to Weinstein [13], 2-point discrimination threshold on fingertip (distal phalanx), side of finger (middle and proximal phalanx), and palm are approximately 2, 4, and 8 mm respectively, hence the ratio of density of actuators should be 1/4:1/16:1/64. Considering the area of these parts, the number of actuators on fingertip, side of finger, and palm was determined as 14, 8, and 22, respectively. The structure of the device is basically same with the device 1. In this device, three types of modules as in Fig. 2(a) were used, and the modules were arranged on the palm and fingers as shown in Fig. 2(b). Module E comprise 14 actuators for fingertip, and module F has 4 actuators for the side of fingers. The height: H of the module G is 6 mm, but only 5 corresponding to the center part of the palm is set to 8 mm. The dimension of the modules is shown in Table 2 and 3. The diameter of the cylinder of this module E was reduced to 2 mm to realize the density. Each of the actuators generates the force of 1.5 N when air pressure is 0.5 MPa. All modules of this device were fabricated using CNC milling cutter (kitmill QT100, ORIGINALMIND). Figure 2(c) shows the implementation of the device.

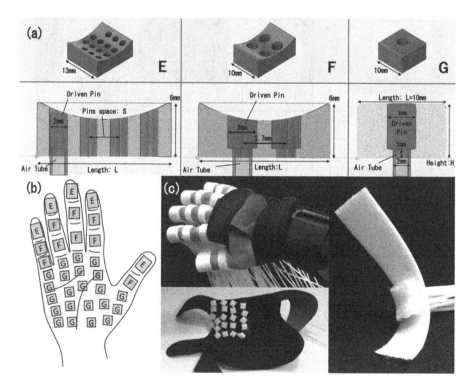

Fig. 2. Device 2 (a) Shape of modules, (b) Arrangement of modules, (c) Implementation

Table 2. Pins space: S(mm) (Device2_Distal)

	Thumb	Index	Middle	Ring	Small
S	4.06	3.46	3.46	3.46	3.06

Table 3. Length of module: L(mm) and pins number

Phalanx	Thumb	Index	Middle	Ring	Small	Pins number
Distal	18	15	15	15	13	14
Middle	–	15	15	15	15	4
Proximal	18	15	15	15	15	4

3.3 Device Drive System

Block diagram of the system is shown in Fig. 3. The Controller of the device was composed of electro-pneumatic regulators, the control circuit, and the PC. An air compressor was used as the air source. The pressure of the air was reduced by the electro-pneumatic regulators and transmitted to the actuators. The output pressure of the regulator was commanded by the PC (called controller PC) through the control circuit (Fig. 3).

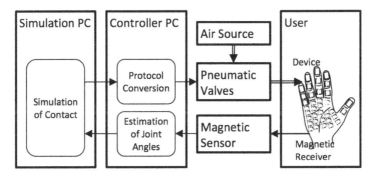

Fig. 3. Device drive system

Force presented by each actuator was computed based on the simulation of contact between the virtual hand and object. The simulation was performed using the deformable hand model previously developed by our group [15]. The contact force was computed on each surface node of the hand model, and the output force of each actuator was computed by summing up the forces on nodes that are close to the actuator. More precisely, Voronoi-diagram regarding actuator positions on a plain that approximate the surface of the palm (x-z plane of the hand model) was computed, and nodes inside each cell were mapped to the corresponding actuator. The mapping for device 1 and 2 are shown in Fig. 4.

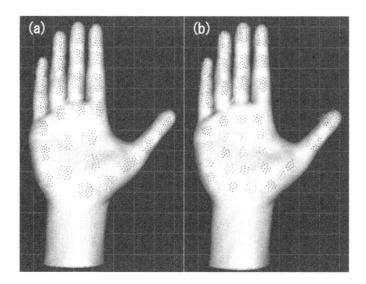

Fig. 4. Mapping of nodes (a) Device 1, (b) Device 2

The motion of the hand was measured by a magnetic sensor (Liberty 240, Polhemus), hand posture was estimated in the controller PC (shared with the controller of the device), and information of position/orientation of the hand and angles of skeleton joints were transmitted to the simulation PC through Ethernet. The resulting force data from the simulation were sent back to the controller PC and presented by the device to the user.

4   Experiment

A preliminary experiment on evaluation of the device was carried out. The task of the evaluation was the recognition of 3D object shape. This experiment was intended to test our hypotheses as follows: (a) the performance using our device is higher compared with other researchers using smaller number of actuators, and (b) the performance using Device 2 is higher than using Device 1. These hypotheses are based on our assumption that the difficulty of shape recognition by haptic device is partly because of the resolution of tactile feedback.

4.1   Method

The procedure of the experiment is composed of practice and evaluation stages. The practice stage was intended for the subjects to get used to the task. Subjects were instructed to put their hand on the virtual object so as not to cause deep penetration into the object. In this stage, the virtual hand and object are visually presented on the display, and subjects could see them to visually confirm the relationship between the hand and the object. The shape of objects used in this stage is shown in Fig. 5(a–d). At the end of the stage, the subjects took a quiz on the identification of shapes from the above four objects without vision.

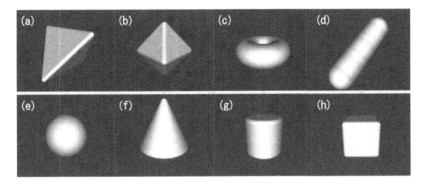

Fig. 5. Virtual objects for experiment (scale: 0.004 m^3) (a) Tetra, (b) Octa, (c) Torus, (d) Stick, (e) Shape, (f) Cone, (g) Cylinder, (h) Cube

After a break for 5 to 10 min, the evaluation stage was started. In this stage, subjects performed the task of identifying the shape of objects without visual information using device 1 and 2. The shapes of the virtual objects are shown in Fig. 5(e–f).

The scale of each object is 0.004 m^3. In one set of tasks, each subject performed the task twice on each of shapes. The order of the task in a set was determined by the Latin square rating method to mitigate the effect of order. Each subject performed two sets of tasks using different haptic device respectively; the order of the device was changed depending on the subject and the evaluation using two different devices were scheduled on different days to eliminate the order effect. Correct answer of the task was not informed to avoid learning in the evaluation stage. The participants consisted of 6 male and 2 female, aged 20–23.

4.2 Result

The result of the experiment is shown in Fig. 6. Ration of correct response for device 1 and 2 was 65.6% and 70.3% respectively (Fig. 6 left). According to the 2-way analysis of variance that deals with the difference of subjects and devices as two factors, no significant main effects and interaction by those factors were found. The completion time using device 1 and 2 was 46.1 and 40.2 s respectively (Fig. 6 right). These results include the time when the subjects answer was wrong. The 2-way analysis of variance with factors of the difference between the subjects and the devices was performed, and main effect by the difference of the device was proved to be significant. Difference was found in the difference in response time by the device ($p = 3.47*-10^3 < 0.05$).

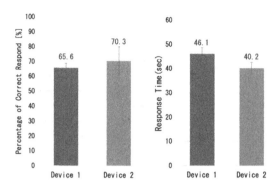

Fig. 6. Percentage of correct respond and response time

4.3 Discussion

Regarding the ration of correct answer, device 2 has a result exceeding 70%. There is a possibility that clear difference may appear by increasing the number of subjects and trials in future.

As stated in Sect. 2, Tanabe et al carried out an experiment on the recognition of 3D shape using vibro-tactile grove device and reported that correct answer ration was 75.8% [11], which is higher than that of our result. However, it should be noted that there is the difference in the condition of experiment. In the Tanabe's experiment, the same objects shapes were used in both practice and evaluation stages, which is allows users to tell the shapes apart just from the features specific to the experimental shapes. In contrast, in our experiment, different shapes were used for the two stages. Under this condition, more generic ability of shape recognition is required for the subject.

The results of the experiment suggest that the device 2 (designed based on 2-point threshold) is advantageous compared with the device 1(homogeneous design) in that completion time is reduced while the correct answer ration kept unchanged.

5   Conclusion

In this paper, we developed a multi-point pressure haptic device that drives pins in multiple modules attached to the hand by air pressure. We tested 3–dimensional shape identification of virtual objects in absence of visual feedback using devices we developed. Due to high-density and wide range pressure sense stimulation by the device, it was possible to obtain a high correct answer rate even when using objects different from the practice stage. In addition, in the case of using a device whose pin arrangement based on 2-point threshold, improvement of correct answer rate and response time was observed. Although the experimental results showed the effectiveness of improvement of stimulation density and arrangement based on 2-point threshold, it was far from actual touch recognition. We aimed to present a high-density tactile stimulus to the whole hand, but the number of pins is 128 points, and in order to reproduce haptic sense like a real hand, a higher density stimulation seems to be necessary.

In addition, although our device is lighter than the exoskeleton type, the burden on the user is a subject to be improved before. There is also a problem that the air tubes impede the movement of the hand, therefore it is necessary to improve these problem in the future.

References

1. 3D Systems. https://ja.3dsystems.com/haptics-devices/3d-systems-phantom-premium. Accessed 30 Jan 2018
2. Force Dimension. http://www.forcedimension.com. Accessed 29 Jan 2018
3. CyberGloveSystems. http://www.cyberglovesystems.com/cybergrasp. Accessed 24 Jan 2018
4. Bouzit, M., Burdea, G., Popescu, G., Boian, R.: The rutgers master II-new design force-feedback glove. IEEE/ASME Trans. Mechatron. **7**(2), 256–263 (2002)
5. Prattichizzo, D., Pacchierotti, C., Malvezzi, M.: Towards wearability in fingertip haptics: a 3-DoF wearable device for cutaneous force feedback. IEEE Trans. Haptics **6**(4), 506–516 (2013)
6. Choi, I., Hawkes, E.W., Christensen, D.L., Ploch, C.J., Follmer, S.: Wolverine: a wearable haptic interface for grasping in virtual reality. In: Proceedings IEEE/RSJ International Conference on Intelligent Robots and Systems (IROS), pp. 986–993 (2016)
7. Minamizawa, K., Kajimoto, H., Kawakami, N., Tachi, S.: A wearable haptic display to present the gravity sensation. In: Second Joint EuroHaptics Conference and Symposium on Haptic Interface for Virtual Environment and Teleoperator Systems (WHC 2007), 22–24 March 2007
8. Kim, S.-C., Kim, C.-H., Yang, G.-H., Yang, T.-H., Han, B.-K., Kang, S.-C., Kwon, D.-S.: Small and lightweight tactile display (SaLT) and its application. In: Proceedings WorldHaptics, pp. 69–74 (2009)
9. Sarakoglou, I., Tsagarakis, N., Caldwell, D.G.: A portable fingertip tactile feedback array – transmission system reliability and modelling. In: Eurohaptics Conference, 2005 and Symposium on Haptic Interfaces for Virtual Environment and Teleoperator Systems, World Haptics 2005, First Joint, pp. 547–548 (2005)
10. Klatzky, R.L., Loomis, J.M., Lederman, S.J., Wake, H., Fujita, N.: Haptic identification of objects and their depictions. Percept. Psychophysics **54**(2), 170–178 (1993)
11. CyberGloveSystems. http://www.cyberglovesystems.com/cybertouch/. Accessed 11 April 2018
12. Tanabe, K., Kakei, S., Kajimoto, H.: The whole hand haptic glove using numerous linear resonant actuators. In: IEEE World Haptics Conference 2015, 22–26 June 2015, Northwestern University, Eanston, Illinoi (2015)
13. Weinstein, S.: Intensive and extensive aspects of tactile sensitivity as a function of body part, sex, and laterally. In: The Skin Sense, pp. 195–222 (1968)
14. Antfolk, C., Controzzi, M.D.M., Lundborg, C., Rosén, B., Sebelius, F., Cipriani, C.: Artificial redirection of sensation from prosthetic fingers to the phantom hand map on transradial amputees: vibrotactile versus mechanotactile sensory feedback. IEEE Trans. Neural Syst. Rehabil. Eng. **21**(1), 112–120 (2013)
15. Hirota, K., Tagawa, K.: Interaction with virtual object using deformable hand. In: Proceedings VR2016, pp. 49–56 (2016)

A Simple Minimum Cable-Tension Algorithm for a 2-DOF Planar Cable-Driven Robot Driven by 4 Cables

Gabriel Baud-Bovy[1,2(✉)] and Kamil Cetin[1]

[1] Robotics Brain Cognitive Science Department,
Italian Institute of Technology, Genova, Italy
{gabriel.baud-bovy,kamil.cetin}@iit.it
[2] Faculty of Psychology, Vita-Salute San Raffaele University and Unit
of Experimental Psychology, IRCCS San Raffaele Scientific Institute,
Milan, Italy

Abstract. In this study, we propose an optimum non-iterative algorithm for the minimum cable tension solution of two degree-of-freedom cable-driven robots. The problem is specifically defined for a cable-driven robot with one end-effector connected to four motors by four cables. A two-cable algorithm and a three-cable algorithm are presented with examples, then the optimal two-cable and three-cable solutions are proven for the absolute value norm and Euclidean norm.

Keywords: Cable-driven robot · Cable tension · Projection method
Optimal solution

1 Introduction

A cable-driven robot consists of a moving point-mass end-effector/platform, fixed points with actuated motors/pulleys, and cables connecting the end-effector to the fixed points. Thanks to the advantages of lightweight cables, cable-driven robots have little inertia, high velocity/accelerations, a large workspace and high load capability. These advantages make them suitable to be used in force feedback haptic applications (e.g. [1–3]). However, the cable-driven robots have some disadvantages such as the fact that cables can only pull the end-effector but not push it. In addition, it is necessary to achieve positive tension in all the cables to avoid slacking, which might prevent proper winding around the pulleys.

According to the number of cables m and the number of degrees-of-freedom (DOF) n, cable-driven robots can be classified into two groups: (i) under-constrained if $m \leq n$ and (ii) fully- or over constrained if $m > n$. As pointed out in the literature [1, 2], in order to be able to produce an end-effector force in any direction while maintaining positive tension in all cables, the number of cables must be at least $n + 1$ or there must be an external force such as gravity or a spring if the cable-driven robots are under-constrained. When $m > n + 1$, cable-driven robots are redundantly actuated and there is an infinite number of feasible solutions with positive cable tensions.

© Springer International Publishing AG, part of Springer Nature 2018
D. Prattichizzo et al. (Eds.): EuroHaptics 2018, LNCS 10894, pp. 68–81, 2018.
https://doi.org/10.1007/978-3-319-93399-3_7

Many methods have been proposed in the literature (see reviews in [1–4]) to deal with the minimization of positive cable tension and the determination of the feasible wrench workspace. These minimization methods can be classified as numerical and analytical. The numerical methods are based on iterative calculations and mostly give approximate solutions. They include a convex optimization method using Dykstra's alternating projection algorithm to solve minimum L_2-norm cable tensions of cable-driven robots [6]. They also include linear programming formulations for optimal tension distribution [7] as well as a quadratic programming formulation, which can yield good solutions even when the optimal solution is outside the feasible workspace [11]. In [9, 10], the authors used the Karush-Kuhn-Tucker algorithm to iteratively solve the redundancy resolution of cable-driven robots. Tang et al. [12] developed a geometrical-based convex analysis method with less iterative calculation and complexity to calculate the workspace of fully-constrained cable-driven robots and to optimize cable tension distribution. While numerical methods based on the iterative computation of the optimal solution are quite general and can be applied to a wide variety of cable-driven systems, they are also usually very computationally intensive and normally not suited for real-time control because of time constraints.

In contrast to numerical methods, analytical methods produce closed-form solutions. While they are usually less general, they are preferable for real-time implementations due to lesser complexity and time demands. In [5], Fang et al. presented an analytically-based method for optimum cable tension distribution of a 6-DOF cable-driven robot with seven cables. However, this method can only be applied to cable-driven robots having $n + 1$ actuators. Pott [8] focused on computational speed, real-time capability, maximum redundancy, and continuity of force distribution. He improved a closed-form method but the minimization of cable tension has weak solutions due to the medium feasible cable force. In [13], Mikelsons et al. focused on the continuous solution of the cable tensions and developed an algorithm without iterative steps for the real-time control of cable-driven robots. Since this algorithm needs to calculate the QR decomposition of the structure matrix for each vertex of the polytope, the approach is still computationally intensive and time inefficient. In order to avoid discrete cases and complex calculation of the cable tension distribution, Gosselin and Gernier [14] proposed a non-iterative algorithm to minimize the L_2- and L_p-norm of the relative force vector. However, this method can only be applied to cable-driven robots having $m = n + 1$ cables because the n degree of formulation of cable tensions is symbolically written in terms of one extra cable and a unique solution is calculated for that cable tension, and then the remaining cable tensions are straightforwardly determined. In [15, 16], for computationally efficient tension distribution of the cable-driven robots having only two actuated redundancies, the authors extended the barycenter algorithm of [13] by using the centroid of a two-dimensional polytope as the desired cable tension distribution. However, this method is computationally costly to find the feasible continuous cable tensions. In [17], Williams et al. proposed a non-iterative method to maintain positive cable tension for a 4-cable planar device by utilizing the method of Shen et al. in [18].

In this study, we present a simple algorithm to compute the minimum cable tension solutions for a 2-DOF planar robot driven by four cables ($n = 2$ and $m = 4$). We provide geometrical proofs of the validity of the algorithm. We consider both the absolute value (L_1) and the Euclidian (L_2) norms. Our algorithm is simpler than other non-iterative algorithms [13, 14, 16] and provides some geometrical insight about the solution.

2 Problem Definition

Let us consider a cable-driven robot with one end-effector connected to four motors by four cables. Each cable has a fixed entry point with the other extremity attached to a central end-effector. All entry points A_i are on the same plane. The end-effector position x corresponds to the point where the cables are connected together. We define the workspace as the area where it might be possible to move x by controlling the cable lengths. Typically, the four entry points are arranged to form a rectangle.

Let u_i be the cable directions (unit vectors) corresponding to some end-effector position x inside the workspace.

$$u_i = \frac{A_i - x}{A_i - x} \tag{1}$$

We want to find a set $\{t_i, i = 1, \ldots, 4\}$ of cable tensions such that

$$f = t_1 u_1 + t_2 u_2 + t_3 u_3 + t_4 u_4 \tag{2}$$

with the constraint that cable tensions are positive or null $t_i \geq 0$ and the L_2 (or Euclidian) norm is minimum.

$$\|T\|_2 = \sqrt{t_1^2 + t_2^2 + t_3^2 + t_4^2} \to \min \tag{3}$$

Since the square function is monotonic, the minimum for this norm is the same as that of the squares of the cable tensions.

Another possible optimal solution might correspond to the minimum of the absolute value (L_1 or Manhattan) norm.

$$\|T\|_1 = |t_1| + |t_2| + |t_3| + |t_4| \to \min \tag{4}$$

In the following sections, we first present the two-cable algorithm and the three-cable algorithm, then consider the optimal cable tension solutions for the Euclidian norm and then for the absolute value norm. A priori, the optimal solution might involve any number of cables.

3 The Two-Cable Solution

Two cables are necessary and sufficient to produce an arbitrary force in the entire workspace. To show this, one can pick the two cables $T_{12} = [t_1, t_2]$ that bracket the force direction and project the force on them.

Let u_1 and u_2 be the direction of the two cables that bracket the force:

$$\varphi_1 = \tan^{-1}\frac{u_{1y}}{u_{1x}} < \varphi = \tan^{-1}\frac{f_y}{f_x} \leq \varphi_2 = \tan^{-1}\frac{u_{2y}}{u_{2x}} \tag{5}$$

By construction, the force is

$$f = t_1 u_1 + t_2 u_2 = \underbrace{[u_1 \quad u_2]}_{U}\begin{bmatrix} t_1 \\ t_2 \end{bmatrix} = UT_{12} \tag{6}$$

The solution for the cable tension is

$$T_{12} = \begin{bmatrix} t_1 \\ t_2 \end{bmatrix} = U^{-1}f \tag{7}$$

Geometrically, the matrix U^{-1} projects the force f on the cable directions u_1 and u_2 as seen in Fig. 1. The fact that the two cables bracket the force insures that t_1 and t_2 are always positive. For the same reason, U is always invertible (the two cable directions bracketing f are never collinear).

Remark 1. When the force is aligned with a cable direction (u_2), the two-cable algorithm yields a one-cable solution. This is easy to show geometrically since the oblique projections of f on u_1 and u_2 are 0 and $|f|$, respectively when f is aligned with u_2.

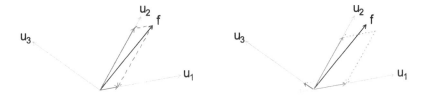

Fig. 1. Example of two- and three-cable solutions in a planar workspace. Angles between the force f and the cable directions u_1, u_2 and u_3 correspond to -40, 10 and $95°$, respectively. *Left*: For the two-cable solution, the cable tensions are $t_1 = 0.227$, $t_2 = 0.839$. The L_1 and L_2-norms are $|T|_1 = 1.066$ and $|T|_2 = 0.755$ respectively. *Right*: For the three-cable solution, the cable tensions are $t_1 = 0.403$, $t_2 = 0.714$, $t_3 = 0.135$, and the norms are $\|T\|_1 = 1.252$ and $\|T\|_2 = 0.691$, respectively. In this example, the three-cable algorithm is better than the two-cable algorithm. The decrease of the cable tension t_2 in the three-cable algorithm relative to the two-cable algorithm is enough to compensate for the increase in cable tension t_1 and t_3.

Further on, we demonstrate that the two-cable algorithm is always optimal for the absolute value (L_1) norm. However, as illustrated in Fig. 1, the two-cable algorithm does not always provide a solution that minimizes the Euclidian (L_2) norm.

4   The Euclidian Norm and the Three-Cable Solution

In this section, we describe an algorithm to compute the optimal solution for the L_2-norm. Depending on the position of the end-effector in the workspace and on the direction of the force, this solution might involve up to three cables. The problem is (i) to know how many cables are involved in the optimal L_2-norm solution, (ii) which cables are involved and, (iii) to compute the tensions for all cables involved.

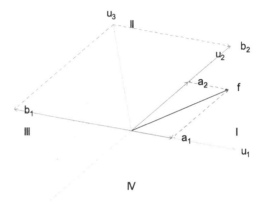

Fig. 2. Geometric interpretation of the components of vector A and vector B. Sectors I, II, III and IV define the cable directions u_i where u_1 and u_2 are the force directions that bracket the force and u_3 is the direction of the third that belongs to the optimal solution.

The complete algorithm is described below. For the moment, let us assume that we know that the optimal solution involves the three cables u_1, u_2 and u_3. The question is how to compute the corresponding tension.

By assumption, the external force is a linear combination of the three cable forces:

$$f = \begin{bmatrix} u_1 & u_2 \end{bmatrix} \begin{bmatrix} t_1 \\ t_2 \end{bmatrix} + t_3 u_3 = U T_{12} + t_3 u_3 \tag{8}$$

Cable tensions t_1 and t_2 can be expressed as a function of cable tension t_3:

$$T_{12} = U^{-1}(f - t_3 u_3) = U^{-1}f - t_3 U^{-1}u_3 = A - t_3 B \tag{9}$$

where U^{-1} is the inverse of the 2×2 matrix U. Written in components we have an expression for t_1 and t_2 as a function of t_3

$$\begin{bmatrix} t_1 \\ t_2 \end{bmatrix} = \begin{bmatrix} a_1 \\ a_2 \end{bmatrix} - t_3 \begin{bmatrix} b_1 \\ b_2 \end{bmatrix} \tag{10}$$

As shown in Fig. 2, geometrically, vector A is the projection of force f on cable direction u_1 and u_2. Vector B is the projection of u_3 on u_1 and u_2.

If u_1 and u_2 are the cable directions that bracket f, then a_1 and a_2 correspond to the two-cable algorithm and must be positive. b_1 and b_2 are the projection of u_3 on u_1 and u_2. If u_3 is in sector II, b_1 is negative and b_2 is positive. The opposite is true if u_3 is in sector IV. b_1 and b_2 are negative if u_4 is in sector IV. Note that u_3 cannot be in sector I because we have assumed that u_1 and u_2 bracket the force.

In order to minimize the total cable tension for the Euclidian (L_2) norm, we can write the function for the three-cable algorithm as

$$\|T\|_2 = t_1^2 + t_2^2 + t_3^2 \rightarrow \min \tag{11}$$

This implies that

$$0 = \frac{\delta}{\delta t_3}\left(t_1^2 + t_2^2 + t_3^2\right) = 2t_1 \frac{\delta t_1}{\delta t_3} + 2t_2 \frac{\delta t_2}{\delta t_3} + 2t_3 \tag{12}$$

Substituting Eq. (10) with the partial derivatives into Eq. (12), can be solved for t_3 as follows:

$$t_3 = \frac{a_1 b_1 + a_2 b_2}{1 + b_1^2 + b_2^2} \tag{13}$$

t_1 and t_2 can now be computed using Eq. (10). Because we have assumed that the optimal solution involved these three cables, t_1, t_2 and t_3 must be positive.

The complete algorithm addresses the remaining issues, i.e. how to select the cables involved in the optimal solution in addition to how to compute the tension for these cables.

Minimum Cable Tension Algorithm

1. Select the two cable directions u_1 and u_2 that bracket force f. Compute the inverse of $U = [u_1 \quad u_2]$ and $A = U^{-1}f$. Note that A corresponds to the two-cable solution.
2. Compute $B = U^{-1}u_i$ and t_i (i =3 or 4) according to equation (13) separately for the two possible three-cable solutions $\{u_1, u_2$ and $u_3\}$ and $\{u_1, u_2$ and $u_4\}$
3. Check the sign of t_i for the two possible three-cable solutions.
   a. If the two values of t_i are negative, the two-cable solution A is optimal.
   b. If one of the two t_i has a positive sign, compute $T_{12} = A - t_i B$ for this value of t_i and return the corresponding three-cable solution $\{t_1, t_2,$ and $t_i\}$.

Remark 2. Geometrical intuition might suggest that a cable must make an angle of less than 90° with the external force as a necessary condition to be part of the optimal solution. The example of Fig. 1 shows, however, that this is not the case. A small contribution along cable direction u_3 can improve the L_2-norm solution even though this cable makes an angle larger than 90° with respect to the external force. The above algorithm resolves the problem of determining when the three cable solution is valid by looking at the sign of the third cable in the two possible three-cable solutions.

Remark 3. As presented above, using the position of the end-effector and the direction of the force, minimum cable tension algorithm makes simple calculations with square-invertible matrix to solve how many and which cables with minimum tensions. In addition, our algorithm does not need to calculate all the intersection points of the feasible tension distribution polytopes like other non-iterative methods [13, 14, 16]. In terms of computational simplicity or efficiency, our algorithm is very fast and convenient for real-time implementations.

5 Proofs

In this section, we provide simple proofs, based on geometric reasoning, to establish the correctness of this algorithm. We also demonstrate that the two-cable solution is always optimal for the absolute value (L_1) norm.

We start by considering the optimal solution for a three-cable device.

Theorem 1. *The two-cable algorithm gives the optimal solution for a cable-driven system with only three cables. This is true for the L_1 and L_2 norms.*

Proof. Let u_1 and u_2 be the cable directions that bracket force f. We want to show that u_3 cannot contribute to the solution. In a system with three cables, the angle between u_3 and u_1 or u_2 is always less than π for any position inside the workspace.

We know that the optimal three-cable solution corresponds to $t_1 = a_1 - t_3b_1$ and $t_2 = a_2 - t_3b_2$. Let us select u_1 and u_2 as the cable directions that bracket force f. In this case, it is easy to see that a_1 and a_2, the parallel projections of f on u_1 and u_2, must be positive. Similarly, b_1 and b_2, the parallel projections of u_3 on u_1 and u_2, must be negative.

The L_1 and L_2 norms for the two-cable solution are $|a_1| + |a_2|$ and $a_1^2 + a_2^2$ respectively, since a_1 and a_2 correspond to the two-cable solution. Since b_1 and b_2 are negative and t_3 must be positive, it is easy to see that any positive value of t_3 will also increase t_1 and t_2 with respect to the two-cable solution for both norms. Therefore, the optimal solution corresponds to the two-cable solution.

Note that this demonstration does not hold for a four-cable device because there might be a case where b_1 and b_2 have a different sign with four cables (this is the case in Fig. 2 where the projection of u_3 on u_1 is negative and the projection of u_3 on u_2 is positive).

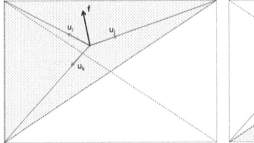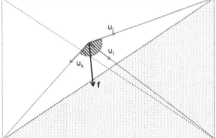

Fig. 3. Representation of the end-effector inside and outside of the triangular workspace (grey area) in the left and right panels respectively.

Lemma 1. *If $\{u_i, u_j, u_k\}$ is an optimal three-cable solution for a four-cable system, the end-effector must be outside the triangular workspace defined by the corresponding attachment points.*

Proof. The lemma is proven by showing that the end-effector cannot be inside the workspace. Let us assume that the end-effector is inside the triangular workspace defined by attachment points of the optimal three-cable solution (see Fig. 3, left panel). Since the fourth cable does not contribute to the optimal solution by assumption, the three-cable solution should be optimal for this reduced three-cable system. However, this is not possible because Theorem 1 states that all optimal solutions for a three-cable system are two-cable solutions. Therefore, the end-effector must be outside the workspace as shown in Fig. 3 (right panel).

Lemma 2. *If* $\{u_i, u_j, u_k\}$ *is an optimal three-cable solution for a four-cable system, then the direction of the force is bracketed by the cable directions of this reduced system.*

Proof. From Lemma 1, we know that the end-effector position must be outside the triangular workspace defined by the attachment points of the three-cable optimal solution. In this configuration, the external force is necessarily bracketed by two of the cables of this system (see gray filled area in Fig. 3, right panel).

Theorem 2. *For a four-cable system, the optimal solution always involves the two cables direction bracketing the force.*

Proof. To prove this theorem, we consider separately all possible cases. (1) If optimal solution involves only two-cables, then the force is necessarily bracketed by those two cables that are part of the solution because the cables can only pull. (2) The one-cable solution is a special case of the two-cable solution. (3) If the solution involves three cables, Lemma 1 tells us that the end-effector must be outside the corresponding workspace and Lemma 2 tells us that the force direction must be bracketed by two of the three cables involved in the corresponding reduced system. (4) If a four-cable solution existed (but see below), it would necessarily involve the two cables bracketing the force.

This theorem is key to justifying the initial choice of cable directions u_1 and u_2 in the above algorithm (see point 1).

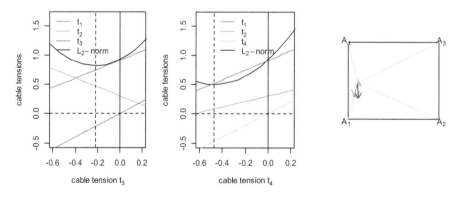

Fig. 4. Example of a configuration where the minimum L2-norm three-cable solution (*vertical dotted line*) is not valid because the tension for the third cable is negative. The first two cables correspond to the cables bracketing the force. The third cable (t_3 in the *left panel* and t_4 in the middle panel) corresponds to the cables attached to A_3 and A_4 respectively. The best valid solution is obtained by setting this cable tension to zero (*vertical solid line*), which corresponds to the two-cable solution plotted in the *right panel*.

Theorem 3. *This theorem states the other assumptions on which the algorithm relies:*
　　A1. *A negative* t_3 *value obtained from Eq. (13) implies that the optimal solution involves two cables.*
　　A2. *A positive* t_3 *obtained from Eq. (13) implies* t_1 *and* t_2 *must be positive.*
　　A3. *The three-cable solution is unique.*
　　A4. *For a four-cable system, the optimal solution cannot involve all cables.*

Assumption 1 is used in point 3.a. Assumption 2 is used in point 3.b in the sense that the algorithm only checks the value of t_3 to identify a valid three-cable solution. Assumption 3 is used in the sense that the algorithm does not check for the validity of the second three-cable solution if the first one is valid.

Proof. By definition, we know that the value of t_3 obtained by Eq. (13) minimizes the L_2 norm. By the formula $t_i = a_i - t_3 b_i$, the changes in t_1 and t_2 are linearly related to the change in t_3. Since the L_2-norm is convex, we need to change t_3 (and t_1 and t_2) as little as possible.

To prove A1, it is enough to note that the smallest adjustment of a negative t_3 needed to make it compatible with a non-null constraint corresponds to $t_3 = 0$, which also corresponds to the two-cable solution since $T_{12} = A$ when $t_i = 0$ ($i = 3$ or 4, see Fig. 4).

A2 is proven *by absurdum*. We start by assuming that t_3 is positive and t_1 negative and show that this leads to a contradiction. To keep the L_2-norm as small as possible, t_1 and t_3 should change as little as possible. This means setting t_3 so that $t_1 = a_1 - t_3 b_1 = 0$. However, setting $t_1 = 0$ would mean that the optimal solution did not involve one of the two cables that bracket the force. Since this is not possible (Theorem 2), t_1 (or t_2) cannot be negative if t_3 is positive.

A3 is a consequence of the convexity of the L_2-norm.

To prove A4, assume that an optimal four-cable solution exists, with u_1 and u_2 bracketing the force. We can consider the contribution of the two other cables u_3 and u_4 and replace this four cable system by a three cable system where the third cable u_{34} is placed so that its contribution is aligned with the sum of the two contributions $t_{34} u_{34} = t_3 u_3 + t_4 u_4$. The L_2 and L_1 norms for this three-cable system are better than the corresponding norms for the optimal four-cable solution since $t_{34}^2 < t_3^2 + t_4^2$ or $|t_{34}| < |t_3| + |t_4|$. However, from Theorem 1 we know that the optimal solution for a three-cable system involves only the two cables bracketing u_1 and u_2, therefore this three-cable solution cannot not be optimal. This implies that our assumption that a four-cable solution exists is not true.

Theorem 4. *The two-cable solution is optimal for the L_1 norm.*

Proof. From Eq. (10) and the L_1 norm, we have

$$\|T\|_1 = |t_1| + |t_2| + |t_3| = |a_1 - t_3 b_1| + |a_2 - t_3 b_2| + |t_3| \tag{14}$$

where $[a_1 \; a_2] = U^{-1} f$ and $[b_1 \; b_2] = U^{-1} u_3$ are the projection of f and u_3 on u_1 and u_2 respectively. The cable tensions t_1 and t_2 must be positive since u_1 and u_2 are the two cable directions that bracket the force and are part of any optimal solution (see Theorem 2). Moreover, t_3 must also be positive to be part of the optimal solution. Therefore, we can remove the absolute value and rewrite the objective function as

$$\|T\|_1 = a_1 - t_3 b_1 + a_2 - t_3 b_2 + t_3 = (a_1 + a_2) - t_3(b_1 + b_2 - 1) \tag{15}$$

with the constraint $t_3 \geq 0$.

$a_1 + a_2$ is the L_1 norm for the two-cable algorithm since a_1 and a_2 are the projections of f on u_1 and u_2. The L_1-norm for the three-cable solution will be smaller only if $b_1 + b_2 - 1$ is positive since t_3 cannot be negative. To prove that the two-cable algorithm gives an optimal solution, we therefore need to prove that the three-cable solution is impossible; that is, $b_1 + b_2 - 1$ is always negative or $b_1 + b_2 < 1$.

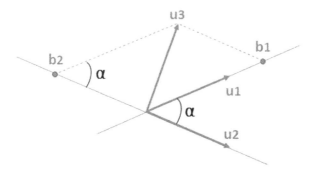

Fig. 5. Projection of u_3 on u_1 and u_2.

First, b_1 and b_2 cannot both be positive since u_3 must be outside the sector defined by u_1 and u_2, which brackets the force. If both b_1 and b_2 are negative, the demonstration is finished since $b_1 + b_2 < 1$ because $b_1 < 0$ and $b_2 < 0$. Thus, we need to consider only the case where b_1 and b_2 have a different sign.

To that end, we consider the parallelogram formed by the projection of u_3 on u_1 and u_2 as shown in Fig. 5. The length of the diagonal corresponding to u_3 is 1

$$|u_3| = \sqrt{b_1^2 + b_2^2 - 2b_1 b_2 \cos \alpha} = 1 \tag{16}$$

Thus, we have

$$1 = b_1^2 + b_2^2 - 2b_1 b_2 \cos \alpha \tag{17}$$

We want to demonstrate

$$b_1 + b_2 < 1 \tag{18}$$

or

$$(b_1 + b_2)^2 = b_1^2 + b_2^2 + 2b_1 b_2 < 1 \tag{19}$$

Substituting (17) into (19), we need to verify that

$$b_1^2 + b_2^2 + 2b_1 b_2 < b_1^2 + b_2^2 - 2b_1 b_2 \cos \alpha \tag{20}$$

Since $b_1 b_2$ is always negative, the division will change the sign of the inequality (20) and we can rewrite it as

$$1 > -\cos\alpha \tag{21}$$

which is always true for $\pi \geq \alpha > 0$.

Extensive simulations showed that this algorithm works. We think that we have also proven that it is correct. It would be nice to have a geometric criterion that indicated when there is a two- or three-cable solution for the L_2-norm rather than relying on the sign of t_3 but the algorithm is also quite computationally efficient. It only requires inverting a 2×2 matrix and a few additional operations and tests.

6 Conclusion

The main contribution of this study is the description of an efficient algorithm to minimize the cable tensions of a four-cable system with two DOFs. We have also shown that (i) the optimal solution always involves the two cables bracketing the force, (ii) the two-cable solution is always optimal for a three-cable system, (iii) the two-cable solution is always optimal for the L_1 norm. For a four-cable system, we described the algorithm to compute cable tensions that minimize the L_2 norm, and also identified conditions for the three-cable solution.

The reason why the L_1 norm solutions involve only two cables is that the increase in tension of the third is greater than the decrease in tension of the cable(s) bracketing the external force. Compared to the solutions for the L_1 norm, the solutions for the L_2 norm tend to avoid having a relatively large cable tension. In other words, the L_2 norm will distribute the force in a way that equalizes the tension across cables more so than the L_1 norm.

The difference between the L_2-norm for the two- and three-cable solutions is generally relatively small. One might wonder from a practical point of view whether it is worth it to consider the optimal three-cable solution for the L_2 norm. One reason might be that three maximal tension-limited cables are able to produce markedly larger end-effector forces in some configurations than two cables.

We readily acknowledge the limits of our algorithm. In particular, we did not consider the fact that cable tensions must generally be somewhat above zero to avoid slacking when the end-effector moves. This problem could be handled by assuming a minimum tension $t_{\min}$ on all cables and calculating the net force $f_{\min}$ resulting from the minimum cable tensions. Then our algorithm could be applied to the difference $f - f_{\min}$ with the desired force f to find the optimal cable tensions t_i that correspond to this difference. These cable tensions could then be added to $t_{\min}$ to produce the desired force.

When we compared our algorithm against other non-iterative algorithms [13, 14, 16], from geometric point of view it provides the minimum and faster solution with a few simple mathematical calculations. In the future, we intend to implement the proposed algorithm in a planar cable-driven force-feedback device with four motors under development for haptic applications in an educational context.

Acknowledgment. The authors gratefully acknowledge the financial support of the weDRAW project funded by the European Union's Horizon 2020 Research and Innovation Program under Grant Agreement No. 732391.

References

1. Pott, A., Bruckmann, T. (eds.): Cable-Driven Parallel Robots. MMS, vol. 32. Springer, Cham (2015). https://doi.org/10.1007/978-3-319-09489-2
2. Gosselin, C., Cardou, P., Bruckmann, T., Pott, A. (eds.): Cable-Driven Parallel Robots. MMS, vol. 53. Springer, Cham (2018). https://doi.org/10.1007/978-3-319-61431-1
3. Gosselin, C.: Cable-driven parallel mechanisms: state of the art and perspectives. Mech. Eng. Rev. **1**(1), DSM0004 (2014)
4. Tang, X.: An overview of the development for cable-driven parallel manipulator. J. Adv. Mech. Eng. **6**, 823028 (2014)
5. Fang, S., Franitza, D., Torlo, M., Bekes, F., Hiller, M.: Motion control of a tendon-based parallel manipulator using optimal tension distribution. IEEE/ASME Trans. Mechatron. **9**(3), 561–568 (2004)
6. Hassan, M., Khajepour, A.: Minimization of bounded cable tensions in cable-based parallel manipulators. In: International Design Engineering Technical Conferences and Computers and Information in Engineering Conference, vol. 8, Las Vegas, USA, pp. 991–999 (2007)
7. Borgstrom, P.H., Jordan, B.L., Sukhatme, G.S., Batalin, M.A., Kaiser, W.J.: Rapid computation of optimally safe tension distributions for parallel cable-driven robots. IEEE Trans. Rob. **25**(6), 1271–1281 (2009)
8. Pott, A.: An improved force distribution algorithm for over-constrained cable-driven parallel robots. In: Thomas, F., Pérez Gracia, A. (eds.) Computational Kinematics. MMS, vol. 15, pp. 139–146. Springer, Dordrecht (2014). https://doi.org/10.1007/978-94-007-7214-4_16
9. Bedoustani, Y.B., Taghirad, H.D.: Iterative-analytic redundancy resolution scheme for a cable-driven redundant parallel manipulator. In: International Conference on Advanced Intelligent Mechatronics, Montreal, USA, pp. 219–224 (2010)
10. Taghirad, H.D., Bedoustani, Y.B.: An analytic-iterative redundancy resolution scheme for cable-driven redundant parallel manipulators. IEEE Trans. Rob. **27**(6), 1137–1143 (2011)
11. Côté, A.F., Cardou, P., Gosselin, C.: A tension distribution algorithm for cable-driven parallel robots operating beyond their wrench-feasible workspace. In: International Conference on Control, Automation and Systems, Gyeongju, South Korea, pp. 68–73 (2016)
12. Tang, X., Wang, W., Tang, L.: A geometrical workspace calculation method for cable-driven parallel manipulators on minimum tension condition. Adv. Rob. **30**(16), 1061–1071 (2016)
13. Mikelsons, L., Bruckmann, T., Hiller, M., Schramm, D.: A real-time capable force calculation algorithm for redundant tendon-based parallel manipulators. In: International Conference on Robotics and Automation, Pasadena, CA, pp. 3869–3874 (2008)
14. Gosselin, C., Grenier, M.: On the determination of the force distribution in over constrained cable-driven parallel mechanisms. Meccanica **46**(1), 3–15 (2011)
15. Lamaury, J., Gouttefarde, M.: A tension distribution method with improved computational efficiency. Mech. Mach. Sci. **12**, 71–85 (2013)

16. Gouttefarde, M., Lamaury, J., Reichert, C., Bruckmann, T.: A versatile tension distribution algorithm for n-DOF parallel robots driven by n + 2 cables. IEEE Trans. Rob. **31**(6), 1444–1457 (2015)
17. Williams II, R.L, Vadia, J.: Planar translational cable-direct-driven robots: hardware implementation. In: International Design Engineering Technical Conferences and Computers and Information in Engineering Conference, vol. 2, pp. 1135–1142 (2003)
18. Shen, Y., Osumi, H., Arai, T.: Manipulability measures for multi-wire driven parallel mechanisms. In: IEEE International Conference on Industrial Technology, Guangzhou, pp. 550–554 (1994)

Autonomous Reconfigurable Dynamic Investigation Test-rig on hAptics (ARDITA)

Maria Laura D'Angelo and Ferdinando Cannella[✉]

Istituto Italiano di Tecnologia, 16163 Genova, Italy
{marialaura.dangelo,ferdinando.cannella}@iit.it

Abstract. Autonomous Reconfigurable Dynamic Investigation Test-rig on hAptics (ARDITA). It is detailed in its kinematics and methodology. We tested 40 people in order to demonstrate the accuracy of this new device. The ARDITA measurement system was tested on the index fingertip. The results were analyzed from several points of view: fingertip size, area, age of the subjects, and sex. Age (20–40 years old) did not affect the performances, while the length and the sex shown some difference. It was possible to determine the threshold of the tactile sensitivity of subject in healthy: 27 correct answers out 40. The accuracy was better than current screening methods used during the physical inspection for peripheral neuropathy.

1 Introduction

Therefore, it is not surprising that the investigation of fingertip sensing and mechanical properties has gained increasing attention not only in the field of human behavior modeling, but also in humanoid robotics, where there is the need for compliant robotic fingers endowed with tactile sensors/devices. Due to the concentration of different types of mechanoreceptors within the fingers and fingerpads [1, 2] many different forms of tactile feedback have been investigated as alternatives to kinesthetic devices for conveying similar force information. Additionally, in terms of the area covered by the senses, the transduction of tactile signals is distributed over a considerably wider surface than in a single localized sensory organ, such as, eyes and ears. Secondly, tactile sensing has a complex nature and to find suitable technological analogies in science or engineering it is not an easy task [3, 4]. The nature of tactile sensing through the skin is not simply the transduction of one physical property into an electronic signal. This is mainly because the sense of touch assumes many forms [5, 6]. These "forms" include the detection of temperature, texture, shape, force, friction, pain and other related physical properties. The relation between these different aspects of the tactile features is not clearly understood. Third, unlike the visual and auditory senses, the touch signal is not a well-defined quantity and the researchers of this field are still dealing with the basics of collecting the most relevant data [7–9]. Last not least, more recent study have focused on the sexes differences (between male and female) to resolve the spatial structure of surfaces pressed upon the skin [10]. Peters et al. tested 50 women and 50 men on a tactile grating orientation task and measured the surface area of the participants' index

© Springer International Publishing AG, part of Springer Nature 2018
D. Prattichizzo et al. (Eds.): EuroHaptics 2018, LNCS 10894, pp. 82–93, 2018.
https://doi.org/10.1007/978-3-319-93399-3_8

fingertips. They found as the tactile perception improves with decreasing finger size, and that this correlation fully explains the better perception of women, who on average have smaller fingers than men [10]. Consequently, the same research of human tactile acuity and perception was related to the fingertip surface area of children [11]. Several children were tested and was found that, as in adults, children with larger fingertips (at a given age) had significantly poorer acuity, yet paradoxically acuity did not worsen significantly with age [11].

In this work, a new approach to assess the peripheral neuropathies is presented, exploiting the former test rig DITA that was used to begin to improve the current screening during the medical inspections [9, 12]. The principle is to give an repeatable stimulus to the patient and to record its response. That permits to the doctors to have an objective evaluation and data comparable with the future investigations. Then the ARDITA (Autonomous Reconfigurable Dynamic Investigation Test-rig on hAptics) was developed to generate a well determined stimulus for the fingertip and reconfigurable in order to change the input.

2 Material

2.1 Kinematics

ARDITA consists of 28 stepper linear actuators. The actuator resolution is 0.010 mm/step and the maximum displacement is 15 mm, with steps of about 100 µm. The maximum static and dynamic force of each actuator are 2.8 N and 11.1 N, respectively. Each stepper linear actuator (driven by a 12 V source), through a complex system of 28 aluminum levers (one per each motor), moves one lamina that is able to create (together with other laminae) different tactile stimuli (sinusoidal shape). To reproduce the tactile stimulus, like the one generated by the passage over passive gratings, an array of thin laminae (28 mm total width) is built. Since laminae are produced in brass and steel (see Fig. 2) and placed alternated, they can slide up and down each other, one next to the other without friction problems, as shown in Fig. 3(a). During each experimental test, the participant's fingertip was positioned on the tactile stimulus which is set to "zero position" (all the laminae are at the zero level of indentation), as shown in Fig. 3(b). Then, during the stepper motors actuation, the tactile stimulus is created and the fingertip follows the shape as show in Fig. 3(c). Moreover, the stepper linear actuators, levers and laminae are assembled and mounted on two actuated sliders by Igus (Milan, Italy) that could translate the tactile stimuli during the experimental tests to activate the proprioceptive human system. The maximum stroke of the actuated slider is 500 mm and it is actuated by a stepper linear actuator NEMA 17 (by Nanotec), driven by a 24 VDC. In these first experimental tests, the participant's proprioceptive system is not considered because I want that each subject was focusing exclusively on the perception of the tactile stimulus without introducing the proprioceptive system. Future experimental tests could introduce the proprioceptive system during the exploration of the tactile stimulus. All the electronics, the actuated stepper motors, the levers and the laminae have been enclosed within a steel case. A metallic support was build and fixed on the top of ARDITA case, to support the right arm of the subject and to improve the subject's comfort during the experimental test. The whole ARDITA device is controlled by a fully programmable algorithm that is able, trial by trial, to change the sequence of the tactile stimuli and to better investigate the tactile performance of each subject.

2.2   Tactile Stimuli

ARDITA Based on the previous detailed description of ARDITA, the main components of this device are 28 stepper linear actuators, 28 brass and steel laminae and 28 levers. Five different tactile stimuli have been chosen, represented and then combined between each other to perform the whole experimental test (Fig. 1). It is important to highlight as each tactile stimulus is different from the others solely based on its wavelength [mm] and not on the temporal frequency [Hz] or amplitude [mm]. In other words, although per each stimulus the wavelength changes, the amplitude and the temporal frequency are always equal to 1 mm (10 steps - 1 step = 0.1016 mm) and 2 Hz, respectively. In this way, since the duration of the tactile stimulus is always 3 s, those one with higher spatial frequency (shorter wavelength equal to 5 mm and 7 mm) will be repeated multiple times within the same time interval than stimuli with a low spatial frequency (11 mm and 13 mm), as shown in Fig. 4.

(a)

(b)

Fig. 1. The ARDITA device, from top to bottom: (a) ARDITA without steel case (b) ARDITA with steel case, during experimental test.

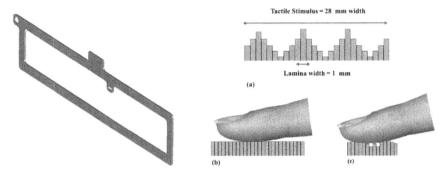

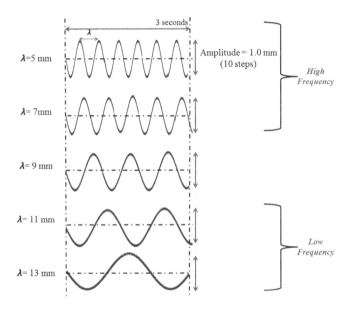

Fig. 2. Lamina

Fig. 3. From left to right: (a) ARDITA tactile stimulus created by actuated laminae array. (b) fingertip positions on the tactile stimulus at zero position, (c) fingertip during an experimental test.

Fig. 4. Sinusoidal tactile stimuli representation with their wavelength [mm] and amplitude [mm or steps]. Respective

From the first to the fifth the tactile stimuli wavelength are 5 mm, 7 mm, 9 mm, 11 mm and 13 mm. Based on the aforementioned selected five tactile stimuli, they were randomly combined in order to have 8 different trials (from 01 to 08), as shown in the Table 1.

Table 1. Experimental Test: Trial Combinations

ID Trial	1st Stimulus	2nd Stimulus
Trial 01	5 mm	9 mm
Trial 02	9 mm	13 mm
Trial 03	7 mm	9 mm
Trial 04	9 mm	11 mm
Trial 05	11 mm	9 mm
Trial 06	9 mm	7 mm
Trial 07	13 mm	9 mm
Trial 08	9 mm	5 mm

Each trial (from 01 to 08) was repeated 5 times during the same experimental test, so the best tactile performance (in terms of correct answers) could be equal to 40. Moreover, in order to check how the participant's answers were given randomly, the trial 09 has been introduced and repeated, within the same experimental test, 10 times. This trial consists of the tactile "reference stimulus" with 9 mm of wavelength, both before and after the interval of 0.5 s. In this way, as already said, a complete experimental test includes 50 (40 + 10) trials.

In order to verify the real amplitude of the laminae and their temporal frequency [Hz] during the stepper motor actuation, per each tactile stimulus (5 mm, 7 mm, 9 mm, 11 mm and 13 mm), I acquired for 10 s the signal of 10 laminae using an optoNCDT 1302-20 laser by MicroEpsilon (Ortenburg, Germany), with a resolution of 10 μm.

Per each stimulus and per each lamina selected the amplitude average values and the standard deviation between several laminae of the same tactile stimulus are reported in Table 2.

Table 2. Amplitude value [Mm] for different laminae and tactile stimulus. Average and standard deviation value.

Tactitile stimulus wavelength [mm]					
ID trial	5	7	9	11	13
1 lamina	0.86	0.97	1.02	0.97	1.02
3 lamina	0.71	1.10	1.04	1.01	1.04
7 lamina	0.75	0.15	0.94	0.94	0.89
10 lamina	0.96	1.02	1.00	0.99	1.07
13 lamina	0.65	0.86	0.81	0.88	0.91
16 lamina	0.83	1.02	0.94	0.91	0.89
19 lamina	0.92	1.09	1.04	0.99	1.05
22 lamina	0.91	1.23	1.25	1.00	1.23
25 lamina	1.00	0.70	0.66	1.11	1.17
27 lamina	1.22	1.15	1.23	1.23	1.27
AVERAGE [mm]	0.88	1.03	0.99	1.00	1.05
STD [mm]	0.08	0.08	0.09	0.05	0.07

3   Methods

Forty healthy right-handed volunteers (21 female and 19 male), aged between 25 to 60 years, were invited to participate in this study. The tactile sensitivity was tested on the index finger of their right hand, using the ARDITA device. The fingertip was free of calluses and, each participant gave her/his informed consent to the experiments. Then, a demographic survey was completed, including age and gender. At the beginning of each experimental test, the participant's fingerpad was correctly positioned on the array of laminae and then, it was asked the subject to wait for the entire duration of the experiment. In order to guarantee the same initial conditions, at the beginning of each experimental test, the following procedure was established:

- all the tactile sensitivity tests were carried out on early morning at the same time to prevent the daily stress on the finger pulp and skin;
- to each subject was given informed consent to participate in the experiment: they read and then, signed it;
- every subject was conveniently and comfortably located next to the ARDITA device, as shown in Fig. 5;

Fig. 5.   Participant positioning during the tactile experimental tests.

- in order to improve subject's attention on the tactile sensation, they wore a face mask and earphones.
- the index finger of the right hand was positioned on its specific point on the laminae array;
- the exploration of the tactile stimuli started.

Moreover, at the end of each experimental test, the participant's fingertip was measured. To each subject, was asked to press the distal phalanx of the index finger on the ink pad. Then, using an electronic caliper, the fingerprint dimensions in length [mm] and width [mm] were measured and, consequently, the fingertip surface area [mm^2] was obtained.

Per each subject, one experimental test was performed. Each experimental test consist of fifty trials and, the duration of the whole experimental test was about 16 min.

Five sinusoidal tactile stimuli, created by the 28 actuated stepper motors and levers, were chosen for the experimental test. Each trial consist of two tactile stimuli that are subjected consecutively to the participant's fingertip: one is always the "reference stimulus", the other one is chosen randomly. The reference stimulus's wavelength is 9 mm, while the other stimuli's wavelength are 5 mm, 7 mm, 11 mm and 13 mm. The duration of the each stimulus is 3 s and, between the first and the second stimulus there is an interval of 0.5 s. So, the whole duration of the single trial is 10 s, counting also the subject's answer. I always tested the participant's fingertip in the morning, when the fingertip skin was not affected by any mechanical stress due to the daily duties. At the end of each trial, the participant has been subjected to the following question: "Which of the two tactile stimuli, the first or the second, have you perceived with greater spatial frequency?". The answer could be: "First stimulus" or "Second stimulus". Finally, the number of correct answers (tactile performances) were collected and analyzed. Moreover, the tactile performances are related statistically to the subject's age, sex and fingertip length.

4 Results and Discussion

Overall result was that the subjects (people in healthy) responses were analyzed and the minimum number of correct answers means was 27 out of 40 tests. That was established as threshold. Testing the patients (people affected by peripheral neuropathies; in our case the Carpal Tunnel Syndrome), all their correct answers were less than 27. Another result was the investigation between the answers and the other parameters: gender, finger length and age. First of all a consideration about the finger geometry properties was shown: the subject's index geometry in terms of fingertip length [mm] and contact area [mm^2] was evaluated. As shown in Fig. 6 the trend is clearly enough: there is a good linear correlation (with R = 0.87) between the fingertip length and the subject's index finger contact area [mm^2]. Then an important result, obtained during the statistical analysis, confirms the sex difference in tactile sensitivity performances (p-value $\leq$ 0.001), as shown in Fig. 7. In other words, considering only the subject's performances and the sex, the mean performances difference between male and female is statistically significant (p-value $\leq$ 0.001). Moreover the results in terms of age and tactile sensitivity performances were evaluated. The population was divided in two different groups: from 25 to 40 years old and from 40 to 60 years old. Statistically, the means of tactile performances of the two groups were compared. Once verified the normal distribution and evaluated the sample variances, the T-test was performed (p-value = 0.9903). In this case, since the p-value is greater than 0.05 the hypothesis H0 was accepted and, the difference in terms of tactile performance between the two age groups results not statistically significant, as shown in Fig. 8.

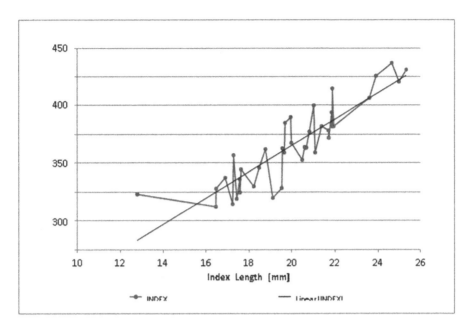

Fig. 6. Correlation between the index finger length [mm] vs the finger area [mm²]. The regression line is added.

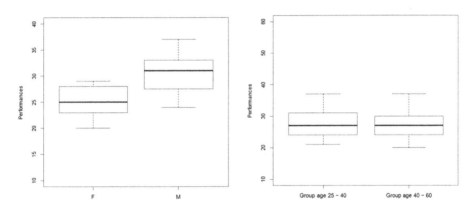

Fig. 7. Tactile performances by sex. Higher performances correspond to better tactile sensitivity.

Fig. 8. Tactile performances by age: no statistically significant difference in terms of tactile performances.

At this point, according with the first result obtained, men outperform women because men have longer index fingers. As expected, men's fingers were significantly bigger than women's (unpaired, $t = -3.40$, p-value $= 0.001567$). So, to investigate whether this accounted for the better tactile sensitivity of the men, a sex-by-fingertip length ANCOVA on the tactile performances data was performed. A data-set was created: the sex variable is a factor with two levels (male and female), while the other two variables (tactile performances and fingertip length) are numeric in their type. The ANCOVA analysis was performed on two different models: the first one considered the tactile performances as the dependent variable with sex as factor and fingertip's length as the covariate. The summary of these results shows a significant effect of fingertip length and sex (p = 0.0003 and p = 0.0033), but no significant interaction (p = 0.611). These results suggest that the slope of the regression between fingertip length and tactile performances is similar between males and females. Moreover, a second model should be fit without the interaction to test for a significant differences in the slope. This second model shows that sex has a significant effects of the dependent variable which in this case can be interpreted as a significant difference in "intercepts" between the regression lines of males and females. Now, the model 1 and the model 2 with anova command were compared in order to asses if the interaction significantly affects the fit of the model. The anova command clearly shows that removing the interaction (fingertip length and sex) does not significantly affect the fit of the model (F = 0.263, p = 0.611). So, at this point, it is possible to say that the fingertip length has a significant and positive effect on the tactile performances and the effect is similar for males and females. Thus, when finger size (length) was considered, the apparent sex effect on tactile sensitivity vanished. At this point, the fit linear regression between the tactile sensitivity performances and the fingertip's length dimensions, not only across the entire participant sample (Pearson's R = 0.5, p ≤ 0.001) (see Fig. 9) but also within both the male (R = 0.432, p = 0.044) and female (R = 0.43, p = 0.049) (see Fig. 10) groups, are reported. These results strongly support that tactile sensitivity is determined not by sex per se but by finger length dimension.

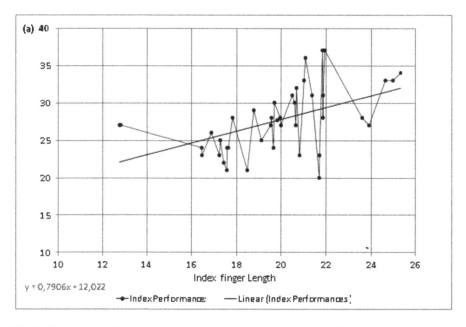

Fig. 9. Scatter-plot of performances (correct answers of the subjects/patients, vertical axis) vs Index distal phalanx length with regression line.

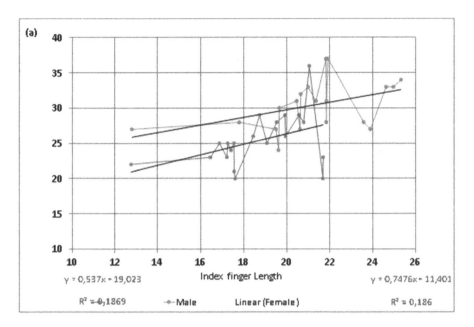

Fig. 10. Scatter-plot of performances (correct answers of the subjects/patients, vertical axis) vs Index distal phalanx length in female (pink) and male (blue) groups. The regression lines are added (Color figure online)

5   Conclusions

In this study, the whole knowledge of the mechanisms involved in the touch (neurophysiology and psychophysics) were well-considered and deeply studied to obtain interesting results related to the human tactile sensitivity. In particular, following the DITA results, an innovative and autonomous device called ARDITA was designed, developed and built. Forty healthy subjects experienced five different tactile stimuli, combined between each other and their tactile sensitivity ware evaluated related to the subject's age, sex and fingertip's length.

Among all the interesting results, two can be selected as the main ones:

- the threshold of the tactile sensitivity equal to 27;
- the participant's tactile performances are strongly influenced by the fingertip length and not by the sex or the age.

These results demonstrate the ARDITA is aligned with the previous works and then it is useful to investigate the tactile sensitivity: for instance it can be used for detecting the Carpal Tunnel Syndrome neuropathy in the patients.

As future work, the proprioception will be introduced in this study exploiting the linear actuators of ARDITA. So its influence on the tactile sensitivity will be investigated. Moreover this device will be used to investigate the peripheral neuropathies diseases in order to have more accurate screening than current devices [29].

References

1. Birznieks, I., Jenmalm, P., Goodwin, A., Johansson, R.: Encoding of direction of fingertip forces by human tactile afferents. J. Neurosci. Official J. Soc. Neurosci. **21**(20), 8222–8237 (2001)
2. Brown, J.D., Ibrahim, M., Chase, E.D.Z., Pacchierotti, C., Kuchenbecker, K.J.: Data-driven comparison of four cutaneous displays for pinching palpation in robotic surgery. In: 2016 IEEE Haptics Symposium (HAPTICS), pp. 147–154 (2016)
3. Cadoret, G., Smith, A.M.: Friction, not texture, dictates grip forces used during object manipulation. J. Neurophysiol. **75**(5), 1963–1969 (1996)
4. D'Angelo, M. L., Cannella, F., Liberini, P.: Self-training influence in peripheral neuropathy diagnosis (2015)
5. Dargahi, J., Payandeh, S.: Surface texture measurement by combining signals from two sensing elements of a piezoelectric tactile sensor, vol. 3376, pp. 122–128 (1998)
6. Dario, P.: Tactile sensing-technology and applications, sensors and actuators. A-Physical **26**, 251–261 (1991)
7. Drewing, K., Fritschi, M., Zopf, R., Ernst, M.O., Buss, M.: First evaluation of a novel tactile display exerting shear force via lateral displacement. ACM Trans. Appl. Percept. **2**(2), 118–131 (2005)
8. Dros, J., Wewerinke, A., Bindels, P.J., van Weert, H.C.: Accuracy of monofilament testing to diagnose peripheral neuropathy: a systematic review. Ann. Family Med. **7**(6), 555–558 (2009)
9. Fearing, R.S., Moy, G., Tan, E.: Some basic issues in teletaction. In: Proceedings of IEEE International Conference on Robotics and Automation, 1997, vol. 4, pp. 3093–3099 (1997)
10. Gleeson, B.T., Horschel, S.K., Provancher, W.R.: Perception of direction for applied tangential skin displacement: effects of speed, displacement, and repetition. IEEE Trans. Haptics **3**(3), 177–188 (2010)
11. Hayward, V., Astley, O.R., Cruz-Hernandez, M., Grant, D., de-la Torre, G.R., Haptic, M.: Interfaces and devices. Sens. Rev. **24**(1), 16–29 (2004)
12. Johansson, R.S., Vallbo, A.B.: Tactile sensibility in the human hand: relative and absolute densities of four types of mechanoreceptive units in glabrous skin. J. Physiol. **286**(1), 283–300 (1979)
13. Johnson, K.O.: The roles and functions of cutaneous mechanoreceptors. Curr. Opin. Neurobiol. **11**(4), 455–461 (2001)
14. Kenshalo, D.R.: The Skin Senses Proceedings. Thomas, Print, Springfield, Ill (1968)
15. Krueger, L.E.: David katz's der aufbau der tastwelt (the world of touch): a synopsis. Percept. Psychophys. **7**(6), 337–341 (1970)
16. McMahan, W., Gewirtz, J., Standish, D., Martin, P., Kunkel, J.A., Lilavois, M., Wedmid, A., Lee, D.I., Kuchenbecker, K.J.: Tool contact acceleration feedback for telerobotic surgery. IEEE Trans. Haptics **4**(3), 210–220 (2011)
17. Pacchierotti, C., Prattichizzo, D., Kuchenbecker, K.J.: Cutaneous feedback of fingertip deformation and vibration for palpation in robotic surgery. IEEE Trans. Biomed. Eng. **63**(2), 278–287 (2016)
18. Peine, W.J., Howe, R.D.: Do humans sense finger deformation or distributed pressure to detect lumps in soft tissue. In: Proceedings of ASME Dynamic Systems and Control Division, DSC, vol. 64, pp. 273–278 (1998)
19. Perez, A.G., Lobo, D., Chinello, F., Cirio, G., Malvezzi, M., Martín, J.S., Prattichizzo, D., Otaduy, M.A.: Soft finger tactile rendering for wearable haptics. In: 2015 IEEE World Haptics Conference (WHC), pp. 327–332 (2015)

20. Peters, R.M., Goldreich, D.: Tactile spatial acuity in childhood: effects of age and fingertip size. PLOS ONE **8**(12), e84650 (2013)
21. Peters, R.M., Hackeman, E., Goldreich, D.: Diminutive digits discern delicate details: Fingertip size and the sex difference in tactile spatial acuity. J. Neurosci. **29**(50), 15756–15761 (2009)
22. Prattichizzo, D., Pacchierotti, C., Rosati, G.: Cutaneous force feedback as a sensory subtraction technique in haptics. IEEE Trans. Haptics **5**(4), 289–300 (2012)
23. Provancher, W.R., Sylvester, N.D.: Fingerpad skin stretch increases the perception of virtual friction. IEEE Trans. Haptics **2**(4), 212–223 (2009)
24. Quek, Z.F., Schorr, S.B., Nisky, I., Okamura, A.M., Provancher, W.R.: Augmentation of stiffness perception with a 1-degree-of-freedom skin stretch device. IEEE Trans. Hum. Mach. Syst. **44**(6), 731–742 (2014)
25. Schoonmaker, R., Cao, C.G.L.: Vibrotactile force feedback system for minimally invasive surgical procedures. In: 2006 IEEE International Conference on Systems, Man and Cybernetics, vol. 3, pp. 2464–2469 (2006)
26. Schorr, S.B., Quek, Z.F., Romano, R.Y., Nisky, I., Provancher, W.R., Okamura, A.M.: Sensory substitution via cutaneous skin stretch feedback. In: 2013 IEEE International Conference on Robotics and Automation, pp. 2341–2346 (2013)
27. Watson, J.C., Dyck, J.P.B.: Peripheral neuropathy: a practical approach to diagnosis and symptom management, vol. 90(7), pp. 940–951 (2015)
28. Weber, E., Ross Der Tastsinn, H., Murray, D., Mollon, J.: The Sense of Touch. Publication for Experimental Psychology Society by Academic, London (1978)
29. Willison, H., Winer, J.B.: Clinical evaluation and investigation of neuropathy. J. Neurol. Neurosurg. Psychiatry **74**(Suppl. 2), ii3–ii8 (2003)

Modelling the Air-Gap Field Strength of Electric Machines to Improve Performance of Haptic Mechanisms

William S. Harwin$^{(\boxtimes)}$

University of Reading, Reading, UK
w.s.harwin@reading.ac.uk
http://www.reading.ac.uk/~shshawin

Abstract. The air-gap of electro-magnetic (EM) actuators determines key operating parameters such as their ability to generate force. In haptic devices these parameters are not optimised for the conditions typically seen in operation and include the heat produced in the air-gap, the volume of the air-gap, and the intensity and direction of the magnetic field. The relationship between these parameters is complex thus design decisions are difficult to make. This paper considers the role of the radial magnetic field in cylindrical electric motors, a type often used in haptic devices. Two models are derived and compared with experimental measurements. The first model is a closed form solution, the second is a classic Poisson solution to Ampere's equation. These models are shown to be valid for making more general design decisions in relation to haptic actuators, and in particular allow an evaluation of the trade off between the volume of the air-gap, the resulting radial magnetic field and hence heat generated and the resulting forces.

Keywords: Electrical machines · Electro-magnetic actuators
DC motors · Radial magnetic field · Diametrically polarised
Cylindrical magnet

1 Introduction

An overlooked aspect of haptic interface research is the demands required of the actuators to deliver the needed forces to the individual. There are few bespoke commercial actuators designed for haptic applications. One exception is the Apple Taptic engine designed to provide haptic feed back in the Apple Watch, iPhone, iPad and MacBook laptops etc. In most other cases haptic interface designers use off the shelf motors and actuators that are often intended for different operating conditions such as gear based transmissions where the actuator should operate at high speeds and low torque in a single direction. In most haptic applications, the preference would be for an actuator that can deliver high force with minimal delay at more modest speeds.

© Springer International Publishing AG, part of Springer Nature 2018
D. Prattichizzo et al. (Eds.): EuroHaptics 2018, LNCS 10894, pp. 94–105, 2018.
https://doi.org/10.1007/978-3-319-93399-3_9

As well as delivering forces with minimal delay, actuators for haptic devices need to transfer kinetic energy into and out of the individual. If we consider an interaction such as simulating the taps of a small (virtual) hammer, we can consider the bounce as nearly an ideal elastic collision. To achieve this in a haptic context requires the movement of the persons hand and arm to be arrested and then accelerated in the opposite direction. This represents a transfer of kinetic energy out of, and back into the person's hand and arm. Managing this energy transferring is the responsibility of the haptic actuators, coupled to any motor amplifiers and the power supply. The energy absorbed by the device must either appear primarily as heat loss in the mechanism or actuator, or potentially be transferred back to the power source for storage. Several authors have tried to divert this energy into programmable or auxiliary damping. For example Weir et al. used both passive damping and controlled damping implemented in analogue electronics [12], Harwin et al. used magnetic particle brakes [4] whereas Gosline and Hayward [3] and Mohand-Ousaid et al. [6] used eddy current braking. Although the haptic fidelity and stability are improved, this is at the expense of complexity. It may be possible to reduce this complexity by careful consideration of energy management in a bespoke haptic actuator as it is the actuator that takes the primary burden for delivering the force and managing this energy flow into and out of the person.

Novel actuators may eventually provide useful solutions, and in particular actuators using graphene or low temperature superconductors would have many desirable characteristics for electro-magnetic actuators. High conductivity implies less heat loss through i^2R heating, and the thermal properties of graphene would make the management of any of this undesirable heat much easier. However more research will be needed to address difficulties with the fabrication and assembly of graphene components before this material can be applied in the production of efficient commercial actuators for haptic applications. Similarly, although superconducting materials would allow high currents and high magnetic fields to be produced to deliver the necessary forces in a haptic actuator, current materials have a significant overhead in terms of thermal management that would need to be addressed.

Adapting off-the-shelf actuators to haptic devices usually mandates a high efficiency transmission to deliver meaningful forces onto the person [10, 11]. The most common approach is to use a backdrivable transmission principal that assumes that there is a loss-less relation between the motor torques and the endpoint forces [2]. In most 'backdrive' mechanisms the motor spends time operating 'stalled' when the motors do not move, yet need to provide a significant torque. Limitations of off-the-shelf components to operate in these conditions result in haptic devices with an inability to portray hard contact without a 'spongy' feel. Although accuracy and delays in sensing, and the dynamics of the motor and drive electronics all contribute to these problems, this paper focuses on the motor air-gap and the potential for managing energy (including heat) in that space.

A calculation derived in [5] (Eq. 2) shows the importance of energy management in the air-gap of an electromagnetic actuator intended for haptic interfaces. In an ideal electrical machine with an air-gap volume V it can be shown [5] that the generated force F is given by

$$F = \frac{1}{\rho^{\frac{1}{2}}} B \sqrt{P_{\text{loss}}} \sqrt{V} \qquad (1)$$

where B is the magnetic field, and ρ is the resistivity of the armature wire and P_{loss} is the power lost as heat (i.e. $i^2 R$ heating).

Thus to maximise the available force requires management of these four variables. This paper will not consider ρ, a material property of the armature conductor, nor P_{loss}, a necessary consequence of generating high forces, rather it will focus on the inter relationship between air-gap volume V and available magnetic field B.

Equation 1 can also be written in terms of the power loss i.e. $P_{\text{loss}} = \frac{F^2 \rho}{B^2 V}$. It is then evident that a reduction in this power can be achieved by increasing the magnetic field and the air-gap volume. However these two variables are coupled so for any given magnetic material is there a benefit to increasing the volume of the air-gap given that there will inevitably be a reduction of the magnetic field across the air-gap? But if air-gap volume can be increased there may be a secondary benefit in terms of the design of mechanisms to allow efficient extraction of heat from the armature and hence allow for higher actuator forces [5].

The paper will only consider actuators with two pole cylindrical magnets that are diametrically polarised as these are most common in the small DC electric motors used in devices such as the Sensible/3D systems Phantom range, the Novint Falcon, Entact robotics W5D etc.

2   Theory

Modelling the magnetic field in a motor air-gap is non-trivial usually requiring a piece-wise solution to the Maxwell equations such as the method of finite element analysis. However simply models are possible and may be of value in gaining a better understanding of the conditions that must be optimised to improve the performance of electro-magnetic actuators for use in haptics. A close form solution to Ampere's non time varying equation $\nabla \times \boldsymbol{H} = \boldsymbol{J}$ is explored in Sect. 2.1. This equation can be used to get a first approximation of the trade-off between air-gap volume and magnetic field. Section 2.2 overviews a common method used to simplify Ampere's and Gauss's equations for 2 dimensional analysis. The relationship of these results to experimental measurements is given in Sects. 3 and 4. Discussions and conclusions follow.

2.1   A Two Dimensional Closed Form Estimation of the Magnetic Field in a Diametrically Polarised Cylindrical Magnet

A simplified two dimensional version of a static magnetic field for a two pole cylindrical magnet polarised along a radius can be found in closed form. This type of magnet is commonly used in cylindrical motors for haptic applications. As typical of this type of solution we can exploit symmetries in the solution, in particular the field will be symmetric with respect to the $x - z$ plane shown in Fig. 1. Although the material properties of the cylindrical magnet as characterised by first order reversal curves or second quadrant B-H hysteresis curves could be considered, these do not adapt easily to more general modelling. The approach used in this paper is to characterise the magnetic material properties by a notional surface current representing the underlying causes of the field. In Fig. 1 this surface current will flow into the paper $(-z)$ for the region $-\pi/2 < \phi < \pi/2$ and reverse to be out of the paper for the region $\pi/2 < \phi < 3\pi/2$. This surface current results in the classic concept of a north and a south pole. The location of the peak radial magnetic field occurs along two magnetic poles lines (north pole line - NPL and south pole line - SPL as indicated in Fig. 1). An instantaneous reversal of current at these two pole lines is initially assumed although this is later relaxed to avoid a singularity in the solution.

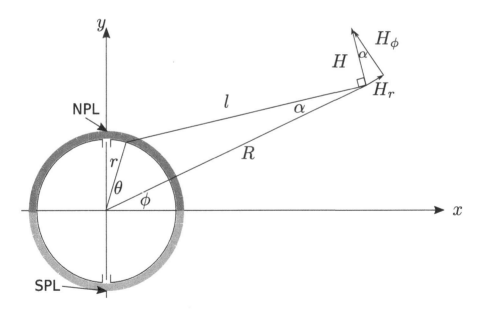

Fig. 1. Calculation of the magnetic field of a diametrically magnetised cylindrical magnet. A north pole line (NPL) and a south pole line (SPL) can be considered as the intersection between the magnet and the $y - z$ plane

With these assumptions we can calculate the radial field at a distance R from the centre of the magnet by considering the current contributions from all the surface currents by integrating θ through a full circle noting the current reversals as the angle $\phi + \theta$ crosses the y-axis.

Radial Field. The static magnetic field strength H due to a straight line current $I\,d\theta$ flowing down the length of the cylinder and situated a distance l from $r\,d\theta$ can be approximated from Ampere's equation as

$$H 2\pi l = I$$

This field must ensure that the cross product is maintained so that the direction of H must be perpendicular to both the line current in the z direction, and the vector pointing along the measurement l. By considering the radial component of H as $H_r = H \sin\alpha$ we can then identify the field due to each current element and integrate this equation to compute the field due to the cylindrical magnet.

From Fig. 1 it is possible to show that the radial magnetic field will be

$$H_r = \int_{-\pi/2-\phi}^{\pi/2-\phi} \frac{I}{2\pi} \frac{\sin\alpha}{l} d\theta + \int_{\pi/2-\phi}^{3\pi/2-\phi} \frac{-I}{2\pi} \frac{\sin\alpha}{l} d\theta \tag{2}$$

Using the geometrical relationships $r\sin\theta = l\sin\alpha$ and $l^2 = (R - r\cos\theta)^2 + (r\sin\theta)^2$, and using the negative sign on the current to reverse the limits of the second term in Eq. 1 these two integrals can be solved as

$$H_r = \frac{I}{\pi} \int_{-\pi/2-\phi}^{\pi/2-\phi} \frac{r\sin(\theta)}{(R - r\cos\theta)^2 + (r\sin\theta)^2} d\theta$$

On integration this becomes

$$H_r = \frac{I}{2\pi R} \ln\left(R^2 + r^2 - 2\,r\,R\cos\theta\right)\Big|_{-\pi/2-\phi}^{\pi/2-\phi}$$

or

$$B_r = \frac{\mu I}{2\pi R} \ln\left(\frac{R^2 + r^2 + 2\,R\,r\sin(\phi)}{R^2 + r^2 - 2\,R\,r\sin(\phi)}\right) \tag{3}$$

A similar process can be used to compute the tangential field, but it is not necessary to derive this as it does not contribute to the ability of a cylindrical motor to produce torque.

Adjustment for Modelling the Field at the Pole Lines. The calculation of the magnetic field at the two pole lines poses a problem when instantaneous current reversal at the pole lines is assumed. If the radial field at the surface of the magnet is needed along this line the solution is infinite because the sin terms in Eq. 3 take on the values ± 1 and the equation reduces to

$$B_r' = \frac{\mu I}{2\pi R} \left(\ln(R + r)^2 - \ln(R - r)^2\right)$$

where B'_r is the radial field along the pole line. Thus there is a singularity when trying to calculate the field along the pole lines at the surface of the cylinder when a division by zero occurs. The obvious solution is to allow a space along the pole line where the surface current is assumed to be zero. This is readily done by changing the integration limits of Eq. 2 thus

$$H_r = \frac{I}{\pi} \int_{-\pi/2-\phi+\Delta}^{\pi/2-\phi-\Delta} \frac{r \sin(\theta)}{R^2 + r^2 - 2rR\cos\theta} d\theta + \frac{I}{\pi} \int_{-\pi/2-\phi-\Delta}^{\pi/2-\phi+\Delta} \text{ditto } d\theta$$

hence

$$B_r \frac{2\pi R}{\mu I} = \ln \frac{R^2 + r^2 - 2Rr\sin(\phi + \Delta)}{R^2 + r^2 + 2Rr\sin(\phi - \Delta)} + \ln \frac{R^2 + r^2 - 2Rr\sin(\phi - \Delta)}{R^2 + r^2 + 2Rr\sin(\phi + \Delta)} \quad (4)$$

where 2Δ now represents the angle at the two pole lines where there is no surface current.

2.2 Air-Gap Field Estimation Using 2D Numerical Solutions to Maxwell Equations

The theoretical formula described in Sect. 2.1 does not account for the role of the casing in motor design, that helps to intensify the field in the air gap.

An alternative way to estimate this magnetic field is to consider 2D solutions to the Maxwell equations. The following method is well described in standard text books such as [8,9].

The approach used here is to assume that A_z (magnetic vector potential) and J_z (current density) are scalar and represent the z value of their 3D equivalents. Assume $\boldsymbol{H}$, $\boldsymbol{B}$, the magnetic field strength, and magnetic flux density are 2D vector fields in the x-y plane. It is then possible to reconfigure the static version of Ampere's equation ($\nabla \times \boldsymbol{H} = \boldsymbol{J}$) as $\nabla \cdot C\boldsymbol{H} = J_z$ where C is the matrix

$$C = \begin{bmatrix} 0 & 1 \\ -1 & 0 \end{bmatrix}$$

C serves a similar function to the 3D curl operation $\nabla\times$.

Likewise the gauge equation $\boldsymbol{B} = \nabla \times \boldsymbol{A}$ that ensures flux conservation $\nabla \cdot \boldsymbol{B} = 0$ can be rewritten for two dimensional solutions as $\boldsymbol{B} = C\nabla A_z$. Finally the relationship $\boldsymbol{B} = \mu\boldsymbol{H}$ where μ is a property of the material will be used throughout, including an assumption that it will apply to the hard magnetic material of the motor core magnet. Instead the magnetising strength of this material will be modelled as a surface current J_z that reverses at the half way line between the two pole lines (NPL/SPL).

These assumptions allow the solution to be written as a Poisson problem

$$-\nabla \cdot (\frac{1}{\mu}\nabla A_z) = J_z$$

By adding boundary conditions, this class of problem can be solved with tools such as the Matlab PDE (partial differential equation) toolbox.

Numerical Simulation of the Air-Gap of a Cylindrical Motor. Figure 2 shows a solution as a quarter representation of the field in the air-gap of a cylindrical motor. Dimensions are approximately those of the Maxon RE25 motor, that is an air-gap width of 2 mm and a magnet radius of 8.5 mm. This figure shows the field as a scaled direction vector. The estimated radial field strength results of this simulation are plotted along with experimental measurements in Fig. 5.

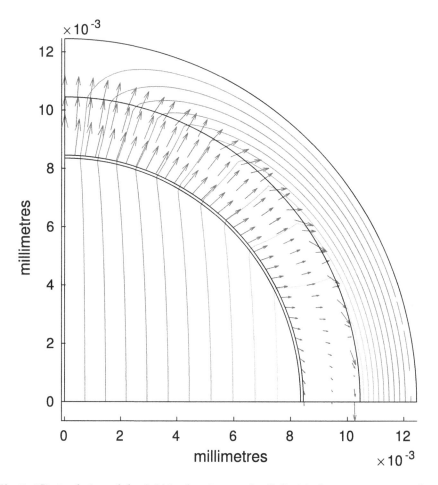

Fig. 2. 2D simulation of the field in the air-gap of a Cylindrical magnet motor such as the Maxon RE25 using Matlab PDE toolbox. Arrows show the direction and magnitude of the magnetic field in the air-gap

3 Experimental Measurement of the Radial Field of a Cylindrical Magnet

The radial field was measured on two cylindrical magnet configurations to assess the validity of the proposed models. The first configuration was a cylindrical magnet with a diameter of 23 mm that was sufficiently removed from magnetic material to assume a free space condition. The second was the air-gap of a partially disassembled Maxon RE25 motor. The field was measured using a GMET H001 Gauss meter (CERMAG Ltd.) with a 1–3000 Gauss range and a 1 Gauss resolution using a transverse (thin) probe.

All experiments were done using an indexing head at 9° increments - this was for convenience since this particular indexing head had a 40:1 gear ratio.

4 Results

4.1 Field of a Cylindrical Magnet

Figure 3 shows the measured radial field of the isolated cylindrical magnet. Also shown in the graph are the theoretical result as predicted by Eq. 3. The figure clearly shows that the model works well away from the surface of the magnet and away from the pole lines. The model does not predict the field well along the two pole lines. This is as expected by consideration of Eq. 3.

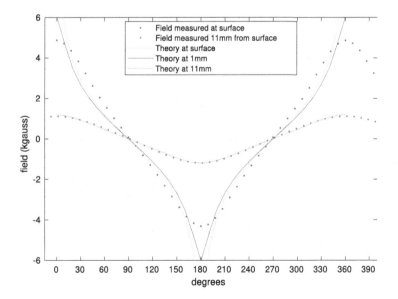

Fig. 3. Theoretical radial field vs experimental results for a free standing 23 mm diameter cylindrical magnet. The current density is assumed to be 6.6×10^4 A rad^{-1}

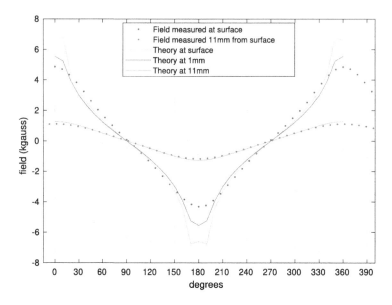

Fig. 4. Theoretical radial field vs experimental results for a free standing 23 mm diameter cylindrical magnet. Theory assumes a region of about $15°$ at each pole where magnetising current density is assumed to be zero. Elsewhere the current density is assumed to be 3.6×10^4 A rad^{-1}

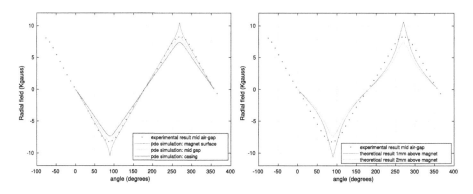

Fig. 5. Measured and computed radial magnetic field in the air-gap of a Maxon RE25 motor (magnet diameter 8.5 mm air-gap 2 mm). Experimental results are common to both graphs as described in Sect. 3. Left graph shows the prediction from a numerical solution to the simplified Ampere equations. Right graph shows the prediction made using Eq. 3 of a free standing cylindrical magnet

Figure 4 shows that the revised model as described by Eq. 4 is a better fit to the experimental data. This supports the premise that the surface current density may not change instantaneously along the pole line. This may be a consequence of the magnetisation procedure or a material limitation. Like the simpler model, the prediction of field away from magnet surface and away from the pole line is good.

Figure 5 shows the radial field as measured at the mid radius in the air-gap of a Maxon RE25 motor. The comparison between the measured results and the numerical solution to the simplified Ampere equation can be seen in the left hand graph, and the right hand graph overlays a computed value of the radial magnetic field as given in Eq. 3. Table 1 uses the results of the 2D simulation described in Sect. 2 solved with the Matlab PDE toolbox to estimate the mid air-gap field of a cylindrical magnet with enclosure and shows the trade-off between air-gap volume and field strength.

Table 1. Numerical estimates (via Matlab PDE toolbox) of the mean and maximum magnetic field in the mid air-gap of a theoretical motor with a 2-pole cylindrical magnet with a 20 mm diameter. The 2 mm air-gap results are directly comparable with the results shown in Fig. 5 (left)

Air-gap mm	Max field kGauss	Mean field kGauss
2	8.213	4.236
4	4.099	2.171
6	2.648	1.435
8	1.910	1.056

5 Discussion

Both the partial differential equation based numerical model and the closed form model of a cylindrical magnet field are viable for modelling the field in the air-gap of a cylindrical motor and hence evaluating the potential for better motor efficiency for a haptic application. It is evident that the numerical solution based on a 2D solution to Ampere's equation provides better accuracy, particularly at the pole lines, and can include the effects of the casing in enhancing the field, however the closed form with adjustment for the pole line singularity may be acceptable and is much simpler to calculate.

Using these methods the loss in field strength as the diametrical air-gap radius is increased is shown to be roughly in proportion (Table 1), so increasing the air-gap volume is countered (as expected) by the loss in magnetic field strength. This suggests that management of heat in an actuator designed specifically for haptic applications will need to consider more than just an increase in the air-gap volume to improve efficiency, and more consideration will be needed to ensure that heat is conducted away from the air-gap. However it would seem feasible to increase the air-gap volume and accept a lower magnetic field strength given the potential that may allow for better heat management.

Future work will now need to consider thermal modelling (e.g. [1,7]) in addition to field modelling to optimise electrical machines for haptic applications. As has been shown, the modelling of this field just over the pole lines is difficult so the calculations could use an offset, possibly by 15 to 30° where the surface current is assumed to be zero so as to get best use out of the magnetic field models.

6   Conclusion

The two models of the radial magnetic field of a cylindrical magnet presented in this paper have been validated against experimental results for both an exposed cylindrical magnet, and the air-gap of a typical motor used in haptic applications. In both cases there is good agreement between the models and the measured radial magnetic field. The derivation of a robust and believable framework for the field in the air-gap of a cylindrical motor will allow better evaluation of the inter-relationships between the volume of an actuator air-gap and the resulting field and hence ability to produce continuous and controllable forces via the motor. In turn this may enable better design decisions about the managing the heat generated by the armature and hence the ability of the actuator to produce a sustained force. The understanding the relationships between the ability of the actuator to generate high sustained forces and the air-gap volume will require careful evaluation for haptics applications as the i^2R heat generated by the armature is a necessary condition for force generation in an electro-magnetic haptic actuator. Increasing the air-gap volume may provide a rational approach to improving the extraction of this heat without compromising the actuator performance.

Acknowledgements. With thanks to Peter Tolson and Mike Charij for assisting with the experiments and to Maxon motors for providing old stock motors.

References

1. Buckley, P., et al.: Effects of thermal protection methods on haptic perception. In: 2011 IEEE World Haptics Conference (WHC), pp. 143–148. IEEE (2011). https:// doi.org/10.1109/WHC.2011.5945476
2. Carignan, C.R., Cleary, K.R.: Closed-loop force control for haptic simulation of virtual environments. In: haptics-e.org 1.2 (2000). http://www.haptics-e.org/Vol_01/index.html
3. Gosline, A.H.C., Hayward, V.: Dual-channel haptic synthesis of viscoelastic tissue properties using programmable eddy current brakes. Int. J. Robot. Res. **28**(10), 1387–1399 (2009)
4. Harwin, W.S., et al.: Design and clinical potential of programmable mechanical impedance. Robotica **5**, 523–530 (1998). ISSN 0263–5747. https://doi.org/10.1017/S026357479800068X

5. Jarman, R., Janko, B., Harwin, W.S.: Current overstressing small DC motors to evaluate performance limits of electrome chanical actuators for haptic applications. In: 2015 IEEE World Haptics Conference, pp. 171–176 (2015). https://doi.org/10.1109/WHC.2015.7177709
6. Mohand-Ousaid, A., et al.: Haptic interface transparency achieved through viscous coupling. Int. J. Robot. Res. **31**(3), 319–329 (2012)
7. Rios, M., et al.: Thermal performance modeling of foil wound concentrated coils in electric machines. In: 2016 IEEE Energy Conversion Congress and Exposition (ECCE), pp. 1–8 (2016). https://doi.org/10.1109/ECCE.2016.7855512
8. Salon, S.J.: Finite Element Analysis of Electrical Machines. Springer, New York (1995). ISBN 978-0-7923-9594-2. http://books.google.co.uk/
9. Strang, G.: Computational Science and Engineering. Wellesley-Cambridge Press (2007)
10. Townsend, W.T., Salisbury, J.K.: The efficiency limit of belt and cable drives. J. Mech. Transmissions Autom. Des. **110**(3), 303–307 (1988)
11. Townsend, W.T.: The effect of transmission design on force-controlled manipulator performance. Cable efficiency discussed in chapter x 67–77. Ph.D. thesis. MSME: MIT (1988). https://dspace.mit.edu/bitstream/handle/1721.1/6835/AITR-1054.pdf
12. Weir, D.W., Colgate, J.E., Peshkin, M.A.: Measuring and increasing Z-width with active electrical damping. In: Symposium on Haptic Interfaces for Virtual Environment and Teleoperator Systems, haptics 2008. IEEE, pp. 169–175 (2008)

Assessment of Perceived Intensity and Thermal Comfort Associated with Area of Warm Stimulation to the Waist

Katsunari Sato[(✉)] and Manami Usui

Nara Women's University, Nara, Japan
`Katsu-sato@cc.nara-wu.ac.jp`

Abstract. A wearable thermal stimulation device can easily provide a thermally comfortable environment that suits personal preferences using lower electric power than air conditioning devices. This study investigates the influence of an area of warm stimulation on the waist to efficiently design a device that can provide higher thermal comfort to users. A device that could apply warmth on the waist by using four thermal units that utilize the Peltier element was developed. The experiment performed to determine spatial perception showed that the participants could not recognize a difference in the spatial pattern of stimulation using the developed device correctly. Furthermore, the results of experiments that evaluated the perceived intensity and the comfort indicated that a larger area of warm stimulation increased not only the perceived intensity but also the thermal comfort, whereas the intensity of the stimulation had less effect on the thermal comfort than the perceived intensity. Therefore, it is better to increase the area rather than the intensity of warm stimulation to improve the comfort provided by the thermal device.

Keywords: Warm stimulation · Thermal comfort · Spatial summation

1 Introduction

An appropriate thermal environment is important for people to live comfortably [1]. The main way to induce such a thermal environment is by air conditioning; however, it is known that local thermal stimulation of the body is also effective [1, 2]. Devices that induce local thermal stimulation can solve the challenges of individual preferences for thermal comfort and the high cost of electric power of air conditioning.

This study investigates a more optimal design of such a thermal stimulation device. Previous studies on human thermal sensation have revealed that the sense of thermal stimulation is affected by its intensity, time, area, and other factors [3]. These parameters may affect not only the thermal sensation, but also the thermal comfort, because thermal comfort appears to be induced from thermal sensation [1, 2]. While previous studies and conventional devices focused predominantly on the temperature (intensity of stimulation) and stimulation position of the body [1, 2], this study focuses on the effect of the area of warm stimulation on the waist. The waist is generally used as the location for

© Springer International Publishing AG, part of Springer Nature 2018
D. Prattichizzo et al. (Eds.): EuroHaptics 2018, LNCS 10894, pp. 106–113, 2018.
https://doi.org/10.1007/978-3-319-93399-3_10

provision of warm stimulation, and a number of devices that warm the waist are commercially available. Furthermore, the area of thermal stimulation is important in the design of the size and shape of the thermal stimulation device.

It is known that the area of thermal stimulation affects thermal sensation as a spatial summation [4–6]. The large area of stimulation decreases and increases the thermal thresholds and the perceived intensity of stimulation, respectively. If the area of stimulation also affects the thermal comfort, this finding may be useful for realizing a device that provides greater comfort more efficiently.

Section 2 details the examination of the influence of the area of warm stimulation on thermal comfort, and introduces the warm device used in the experiments. The experiment described in Sect. 3 examines the spatial perception ability for warm stimulation of the waist. Then, the results of the thermal comfort comparison of different stimulation areas are presented in Sect. 4.

2   Warm Stimulation Device for the Waist

Figures 1 and 2 show the warm stimulation device for the waist. The device consists of four thermal units and a fabric belt to affix the units to the waist (Fig. 1a). One thermal unit consists of a Peltier element (40×40 mm, TEC1-12706, Vktech Inc.), thermistor (103JT-025, SEMITEC Inc.), heat sink, and fan (Fig. 1b). The Peltier element is connected to the driver circuit that uses the motor driver IC to control the surface temperature of the Peltier element by passing electric current. The AC adaptors (12 V, 0.5 A) are connected to each controller. This thermal unit maintains the surface temperature of the Peltier element at the target temperature using the proportional control method based on the temperature measured by the thermistor. The control is carried out using an Arduino Nano and a laptop PC (Windows 10 Professional) with Processing software. Proportional control is applied to the thermal units, and the surface temperature of the Peltier element reaches the target one within one second when the difference between the target and current temperature is approximately 5 °C.

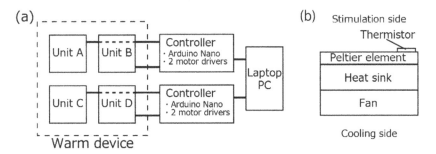

Fig. 1.   (a) Configuration of the warm stimulation device for the waist. (b) Configuration of thermal units

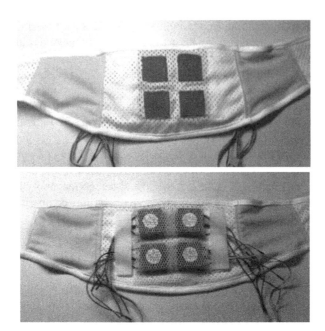

Fig. 2. Warm stimulation device for the waist with four thermal units. Above: surface for stimulation (Peltier element); below: surface for cooling of thermal unit (fan).

Figure 2 shows the constructed warm display for the waist device used in this experiment. The total weight of the waist device is approximately 250 gf. There is a gap of 20 mm between the thermal units. Since the spatial resolution of the temperature stimulation on the waist is more than 20 mm [7], the user of this warm device cannot detect the position of the warm stimulation correctly. The surfaces of the Peltier elements are covered by a conductive cloth (MedTex P-130, Technical Textiles, Inc.) that has high electrical and thermal conductivity to improve the feel of the touch. The surfaces of the fans are covered by mesh cloth with good breathability.

3   Experiment 1: Spatial Warm Perception on the Waist

3.1   Participants and Environment

Five students (all women, aged 21–22 years) of Nara Women's University participated in this experiment. The average skin temperature of their waists was approximately 34 °C. The experiment was conducted with the consent of participants under the approval of the ethics review committee of Nara Women's University.

The temperature and humidity of the room in which the experiments were conducted were approximately 25 °C and 50% RH, respectively.

3.2   Procedure and Conditions

The participants sat on chairs wearing the developed devices on their waists; the temperature of each thermal unit of the device was controlled at randomly selected stimulation conditions prior to being worn. After 30 s had elapsed, the participants selected the perceived spatial pattern from the five patterns shown in Fig. 3. Then, the participants removed the devices and rested for 10 min before the next stimulation condition was applied. The participants sat in their chairs throughout the experiment.

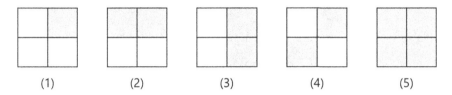

Fig. 3. Spatial patterns of warm stimulation. The colored cell represent the positions of warm stimulation, the temperatures of which are set at 37 °C or 40 °C. The temperature of the blank cells is set at 34 °C. There are three different spatial patterns for the stimulation using two Peltier elements. (Color figure online)

There were tem stimulation conditions with different temperatures and spatial patterns. The temperature of the thermal units with no warm stimulation was 34 °C because this was the average skin temperature of the participants and it is within the insensitive temperature zone. The surface temperature of the thermal units during thermal stimulation was maintained at 37 °C or 40 °C as a painless stimulation intensity. There were five spatial patterns for the warm stimulation: one stimulation area, two stimulation areas with three different patterns, and four stimulation areas (Fig. 3).

3.3   Results and Discussion

Figure 4 shows the response rate of each stimulation pattern. The correct answer ratios are small under all conditions: the average correct answer ratio is 32.7% (the chance level is 20%). At the stimulation temperature 37 °C, the participants recognized the spatial pattern of pattern 3 relatively accurately (60%). At the stimulation temperature 40 °C, the participants recognized the spatial patterns of patterns 3 and 5 relatively accurately (53.3% and 66.7%, respectively).

37℃		Response				
		1	2	3	4	5
Pattern	1	46.7	13.3	26.7	13.3	0.0
	2	46.7	13.3	6.7	26.7	6.7
	3	33.3	6.7	60.0	0.0	0.0
	4	46.7	13.3	20.0	13.3	6.7
	5	20.0	40.0	20.0	6.7	13.3

40℃		Response				
		1	2	3	4	5
Pattern	1	20.0	6.7	53.3	13.3	6.7
	2	0.0	20.0	20.0	26.7	33.3
	3	6.7	6.7	53.3	20.0	13.3
	4	6.7	20.0	40.0	20.0	13.3
	5	0.0	13.3	13.3	6.7	66.7

Fig. 4. Percentage of response for the spatial patterns of warm stimulation shown in Fig. 2. Colored cells represent the percentage of participants recognized the correct pattern. (Color figure online)

These results indicate that it is difficult for the participants to recognize the spatial pattern on their waist when using the developed device. The relatively high accuracy for pattern 3 at both 37 °C and 40 °C indicates that the participants could recognize the spatial difference of the stimulation in the case of the stimulation spreading in the spine direction without sandwiching the midline. Furthermore, the participants could recognize when the intensity of the stimulation was strong (pattern 4 under the 40 °C condition). We consider that the perception might change from warmth to pain owing to heat because a previous study showed that the spatial perception for warm stimulation increased when the stimulation was strong [8].

4 Experiment 2: Perceived Intensity and Thermal Comfort of Warm Stimulation on the Waist

4.1 Participants and Environment

The participants and experimental environment for this experiment were the same as in Experiment 1.

4.2 Procedure and Conditions

The participants sat on chairs wearing developed devices on their waists; the temperature of each thermal unit of the device was pre-controlled at randomly selected stimulation conditions. Then, participants answered two questions every minute, regarding the perceived intensity and feeling of comfort on their waists. The participants' responses were gathered using a seven-level Likert scale (7 is the most intense or comfortable, and 1 is the weakest or highest level of discomfort), and the results were analyzed on an ordinal scale. The participants answered based on a comparison with the neutral state, i.e., without the device, (where 1 and 4 represent neutral intensity and comfort, respectively). The stimulation time was 10 min, and the participants removed the devices after the stimulation. The interval between different stimulation conditions was 10 min. The participants sitting on their chairs throughout the experiment.

There were seven stimulation conditions with different temperatures and areas. The surface temperature of all thermal units was 34 °C (condition corresponding to "None"), and during the provision of thermal stimulation, the units were maintained at 37 °C or 40 °C. There were three spatial patterns for warm stimulation: one (Small), two (Middle), and four (Large) areas of thermal units ((1), (2), and (5), respectively, as shown in Fig. 3). Based on the results of Experiment 1, side-by-side units were selected for the stimulation of the two-area condition.

4.3 Results and Discussion

The graphs in Fig. 5 show the averaged time change in perceived intensity and comfort on the waist. The red and orange lines represent the stimulation temperatures of 37 °C and 40 °C, respectively. The straight, dashed, and dotted lines represent the four (L), two (M), and one (S) areas, respectively.

It appears that the averaged perceived intensity increases with increasing temperature and time elapsed. The effect of time indicates that temporal summation might occur. The participants also perceived a warm sensation under "None" stimulation condition. We consider that the device prevented the natural heat loss from the skin and the skin temperature was increased under the "None" condition. The averaged comfort sensation also appears to show the same tendency as that of the perceived intensity: the maximum value appears for 40 °C for case L, and minimum for 37 °C for case S. However, the difference in comfort between the conditions is smaller than that of perceived intensity.

The three-way tests for area, temperature, and time were conducted using the results, with the exception of the result of the no stimulation condition. The ANOVA result for perceived intensity shows a significant difference in the main effect of area ($F(2, 329)$ $= 42.49$, $p < 0.01$) and marginal difference in the main effect of temperature ($F(1, 329)$ $= 5.83$, $p = 0.073$). The result for thermal comfort shows a marginal difference in the main effect of area ($F(2, 329) = 3.14$, $p = 0.098$). There is no significant or marginal difference in the other main effects.

The results show that spatial summation occurred in the perceived intensity: the participants perceived a stronger intensity when the stimulation area was wider, and they could not recognize the differences in area, as shown in Experiment 1. Furthermore, it indicated that the larger area of the warm stimulation increased the thermal comfort, whereas the intensity of the stimulation had less effect on the thermal comfort than the perceived intensity. When comparing the results of each condition, the conditions of "40 °C S" and "40 °C M" show a stronger perceived intensity than that of "37 °C L", although they were less comfortable than the "37 °C L" case. Therefore, it is better to

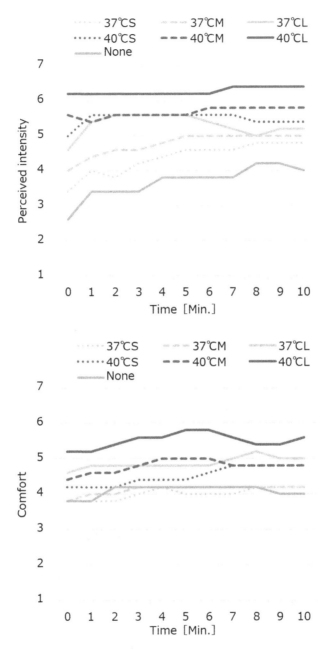

Fig. 5. Changes in perceived intensity (above) and comfort (below) on the waist with time. The horizontal and vertical axes represent the elapsed time from the beginning of the stimulation and averaged response of all participants, respectively. The color and type of line represent the conditions of temperature and area, respectively. (Color figure online)

increase the area rather than the intensity of warm stimulation to improve the thermal comfort provided by a device. This conclusion contributes to the design of the size of wearable thermal stimulation devices to provide thermal comfort.

5   Conclusion

This study investigated the influence of the area of warm stimulation on thermal comfort on the waist. The results indicated that when the perceived intensity and thermal comfort increased with increasing area of warm stimulation. However, the intensity of the stimulation had less effect on the thermal comfort than on the perceived intensity.

In the future, we aim to examine if a similar phenomenon of thermal comfort occurs in the case of warmer or colder stimulation and for different body parts to design another device that can provide thermal comfort by local stimulation.

Acknowledgement. This study was supported by JST ACCEL Grant Number JPMJAC1404 (Embodied Media Project) and JSPS KAKENHI Grant Number JP 17H01956.

References

1. Arens, E., Zhang, H.: The skin's role in human thermoregulation and comfort. In: Pan, N., Gibson, P. (eds.) Thermal and Moisture Transport in Fibrous Materials, pp. 560–602. Woodhead Publishing Ltd. (2006)
2. Nakamura, M., Yoda, T., Crawshaw, L., Yasuhara, S., Saito, Y., Kasuga, M., Nagashima, K., Kanosue, K.: Regional differences in temperature sensation and thermal comfort in humans. J. Appl. Physiol. **105**, 1897–1906 (2008)
3. Jones, L.A., Ho, H.-N.: Warm or cool, large or small? The challenge of thermal displays. IEEE Trans. Haptics **1**(1), 53–70 (2008)
4. Hardy, J.D., Oppel, T.W.: Studies in temperature sensation. III. The sensitivity of the body to heat and the spatial summation of the end organ responses. J. Clin. Invest. **16**, 533–540 (1937)
5. Stevens, J.C., Marks, L.E.: Spatial summation and the dynamics of warmth sensation. Percept. Psychophys. **9**, 391–398 (1971)
6. Kenshalo, D.R., Decker, T., Hamilton, A.: Comparisons of spatial summation on the forehead, forearm, and back produced by radiant and conducted heat. J. Comp. Physiol. Psychol. **63**, 510–515 (1967)
7. Cain, W.S.: Spatial discrimination of cutaneous warmth. Am. J. Psychology **86**, 169–181 (1973)
8. Simmel, M.L., Shapiro, A.: The localization of non-tactile thermal sensations. Psychophysiology **5**, 415–425 (1969)

Vibrotactile Feedback to Combine with Swing Presentation for Virtual Reality Applications

Hirotaka Shionoiri[✉], Rei Sakuragi, Ryo Kodama, and Hiroyuki Kajimoto

The University of Electro-Communications, 1-5-1 Chofugaoka, Chofu, Tokyo 182-8585, Japan
{shionoiri,sakuragi,kodama,kajimoto}@kaji-lab.jp

Abstract. We have developed a virtual reality (VR) system that uses an automobile as its motion platform. To improve the user's experience of this VR system, we mounted transducers on the system to present vibration in accordance with the swing of the motion platform. In this paper, we report the parameters of a vibration waveform that is suitable for the vibrotactile feedback that is to be combined with the front-to-back swing. First, vibration parameters (including these of rubber, wood, and aluminum) that are suitable for combination with the swing were created by adjustments performed by expert users based on a previous study. Next, a user study was conducted to validate the created parameters. As a result of the user study, the vibration waveforms of rubber and aluminum were found to be well matched with videos showing collisions with the same material, whereas when the participants watched a video of collision with wood, both the rubber and wood vibrations were evaluated as being natural.

Keywords: Virtual reality · Vibrotactile · Cross-Modal

1 Introduction

Amusement facilities can provide virtual reality (VR) content using a motion platform. Because commercial motion platforms are expensive and require a large-scale footprint, it is difficult to use this type of platform at home. To address this issue, we have developed a VR system that uses an automobile as a motion platform [1] (Fig. 1). Automobiles are industrial products that are already commonly present in daily life, and this VR system thus makes it possible to enjoy VR content while using a motion platform at home. However, because this VR system presents body motion via control of the accelerator and brake of the automobile, the system is limited by the fact that the presentable swing frequency is restricted to lower frequencies when compared with that of commercial motion platforms. This limitation causes a problem in that high-quality feedback cannot be provided for VR contents requiring feedback with a wider range of frequency components, such as a collision. To solve this problem, we have devised a method to expand the range of presentable frequency components by adding transducers to the VR system and presenting the vibrations at the same time as the swing presentation.

© Springer International Publishing AG, part of Springer Nature 2018
D. Prattichizzo et al. (Eds.): EuroHaptics 2018, LNCS 10894, pp. 114–124, 2018.
https://doi.org/10.1007/978-3-319-93399-3_11

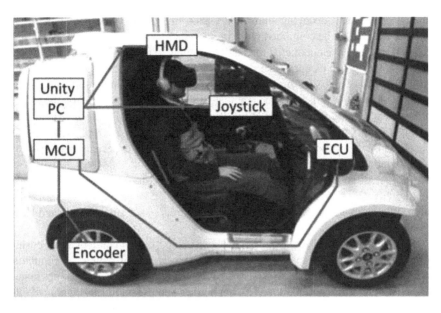

Fig. 1. Overall view and system configuration of VR system using an automobile as its motion platform (from [1]).

In this work, we have investigated vibration waveform parameters that are suitable for combination with the swing when watching VR content. We studied collisions with three different materials: rubber tires, wooden cubes, and aluminum cubes, which was inspired by Okamura's previous work that proposed a method to present the material feeling of a tapped object using a decaying sinusoidal waveform and a desktop haptic device [2, 3]. Because these situations are quite different (where one is the swing plus vibration and the other is force plus vibration), vibration parameters that were suitable for combination with the swing were created via adjustments performed by expert users based on the previously proposed parameters, and a user study was then conducted to verify the validity of the created parameters. The contributions of this paper is to make it possible to express material feeling in VR contents using automobiles as MPs.

2 Related Work

Okamura proposed parameters that could be used in a haptic device to present the material feelings of virtual objects that were based on actual measured waveforms [2, 3]. The parameters were proposed for rubber, wood and aluminum, and the measurements were performed by actually tapping these material cubes with the haptic device. As a result of these measurements, she reported that the vibration waveforms produced by tapping these materials can be represented by a decaying sinusoidal waveform with three specific parameters: amplitude, frequency, and decay rate. She also reported that the frequency remained constant, regardless of moderate differences in tapping speed. Based on these findings, we selected a decaying sinusoidal waveform with the same frequency as the vibration waveform to be combined with the swing.

Several studies have conducted the tactile stimulus to the whole of the user's body. The Emoti-Chair is one example that improves music and video experiences by presentation of vibrations and shaking [4]. Music experiences were improved by driving a number of voice coil motors and linear actuators that had been mounted on the chair in accordance with music being played. While the input signals in this case were essentially based on the sound, we do not use the same strategy of recording and replaying the sound signals, because the purpose of this work is to improve the VR experience using a tactile stimulus, which has a much lower frequency than sound.

Several studies have attempted to improve the entertainment experience by presenting vibrations to the user's body [5], finger [6, 7], forearm [8], and foot [9]. In addition, it is known that the presentation of vibrations is not strongly affected by the user's clothing [10].

Steinemann [11] suggested low-cost feedback using a combination of an air cushion with pull mechanisms to improve the immersive experience of racing car simulators. Haptic Turk is another example of an inexpensive motion platform that combines manual swing and acceleration presentation [12], but neither of these platforms combined other signals with vibration. Ryu [13] proposed that vibrotactile feedback is an effective means for presentation of information in a car following experiments using various signal frequencies. Vibrotactile presentations via the driver's seat [14] or backrest [15] have been used to present directional or spatial information.

A motion platform with vibration presentation has also been developed [16]. However, to the best of the authors' knowledge, no studies to date have evaluated the effects of a combination of vibration and body swing.

3 Hardware Configuration

To ensure that the experiment was conducted safely, we did not use actual cars; instead, we developed a device that imitates a car and conducted experiments using this device.

Figure 2 shows an overview of the experimental device. We used a hand trolley (DSK-101, Nansin Inc. Tokyo, Japan) as a base vehicle to perform a front-to-back swing. We set a wooden plate (lumber core, 155[W] × 46[D] × 2[H] cm) on top of the trolley to act as the floor of the car. We then installed a gaming chair (playseat, Playseat Company) on the wooden plate to act as the driver's seat, along with a handle and a pedal, which are accessories of the Playseat. We installed a linear actuator (F 1420-200, Yamaha) to provide the for front-to-back motion, which is controlled using a personal computer via a serial communication link.

To present vibrations, we mounted vibrotactile transducers at the main contact points between the human user's body and the device. The selected installation locations were the steering wheel, the accelerator pedal, the seat surface, and the backrest, but we used only the transducers at the steering wheel and the seat surface in this work. One transducer (Vp 408, Acuve Laboratory, Inc.) was fixed to the upper part of the steering wheel.

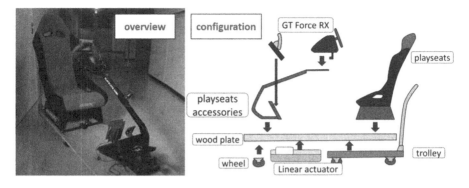

Fig. 2. Overview of the experimental device and the device configuration.

On the seat, part of the urethane cushion used for the seating surface was cut out and a transducer (Vt 708, Acuve Laboratory, Inc.) was embedded into the seat (Fig. 3).

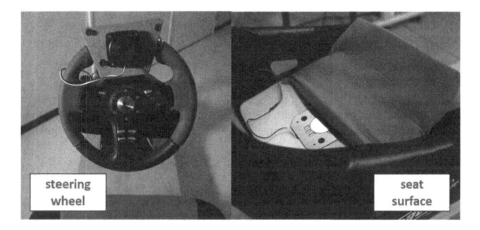

Fig. 3. Transducer mounting locations.

The signal input to the transducer was performed using a microcontroller (mbed NXP LPC 1768, ARM). An acceleration sensor (ADXL 345, Analog Devices) was connected to the microcontroller and the vibration was output when it detected the swing presentation. The swing that was used in this work was generated using a method in which the linear actuator moves forward by 20 cm and then stops. Strong acceleration can be presented at the moment of stopping, because of the characteristics of the linear actuator. The vibration output was prepared at the time when forward acceleration was detected and the vibration was output at the time when the direction of acceleration switched to backwards (Fig. 4).

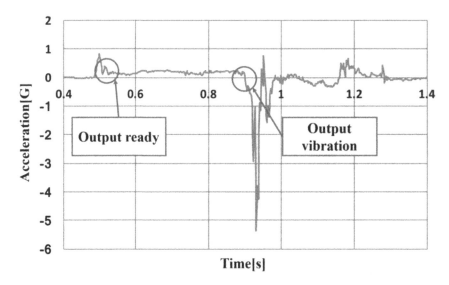

Fig. 4. Example of swing presentation with the timing of the vibration output.

4 Building of Vibrotactile Wave for Combination with Swing

Based on the parameters that were proposed by Okamura [2, 3], the vibration parameters that are suitable for combination with the swing were determined. The vibration feedback model is a decaying sinusoidal waveform that can be expressed using the following equation.

$$V(t) = Ae^{-Bt} \sin(2\pi ft) \qquad (1)$$

Here, V is the command value of the voltage that is input from the microcontroller to the transducer. The maximum value of V was set at 0.5, and the minimum value was set at −0.5. A is a term that expresses the initial amplitude and dependent on the speed in contact. In our experimental environment, because the linear actuator is the position controller and it was difficult to change its velocity, we fixed the actuator speed and the initial vibration amplitude was fixed for each material. B expresses the rate of decay of the decaying sinusoidal waveform, while fω expresses the frequency of this waveform. The vibration amplitudes produced by the transducers in the steering wheel and the seat were measured in advance and the vibration intensity presented by each transducer was adjusted to ensure that the two intensities were equal. The vibration parameters were determined to match the video and the swing through adjustments performed by expert users. The swing was performed by a linear actuator. This swing was generated by advancing forward about 20 cm and stopping. While performing these adjustment, we used a head-mounted display (HMD; Oculus Rift, Oculus) to show the video, in which the user collides with the object, and presented the swing and the vibration simultaneously (Fig. 5).

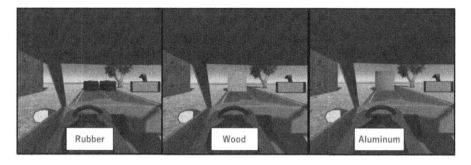

Fig. 5. Screenshots of the experimental VR system.

Table 1 shows the vibration parameters that were perceived to be natural when combined with the swing. There were several findings during the adjustment process. When we presented the vibration and swing simultaneously, we found that the sensation presented differed clearly from that which was presented by vibration alone. In particular, when the vibration decayed immediately, it could hardly be perceived by the user. This is probably because the perception of the vibration presentation was masked by the strong acceleration that was presented by the swing. The sensation was also perceived to be more natural when the vibration continued during the swing. Based on these observations, the decay factors were greatly reduced from the original, values to present the vibration for longer periods.

Table 1. Vibration parameters as determined by expert users for combination with the swing.

Material	A	B (s^{-1})	f (Hz)
Rubber	0.325	6.5	30
Wood	0.021	6.0	100
Aluminum	0.295	4.0	300

Furthermore, presentation of the vibration and swing at the same time, gave the sense that the two stimuli were fused. In particular, when the amplitude A was varied, the shock or heaviness of the swing was also felt to change, and when the decay factor B was changed, the reverberation of the object with which the system had collided was also felt to change. Based on these observations, we designed the parameters of the materials to be felt by the user as follows: rubber presented a heavy shock without resonance, wood presented a light shock with a small resonance, and aluminum presented a heavy shock with a large resonance.

5 Experiment

Experiments were conducted to verify the effectiveness of the vibration waveform parameters that were determined by the expert users.

5.1 Procedure

Ten people (one female, nine males, ranging from 21 to 24 years old) participated in the experiments. Each participant boarded the experimental device and used the HMD to watch first-person view videos in which the car collided with the target objects. At the moment of collision in the video, the swing and the vibration were presented to the participant simultaneously. For each trial, participants were asked to answer a questionnaire about their experiences. The experimental conditions included three conditions for the material of the object (rubber, wood, aluminum) with which the car collided in the video and three vibration conditions (rubber, wood, aluminum) that we prepared, giving nine combinations in total. The swing, the vibration waveforms and the videos were the same as those that were used in the previous section.

To prevent the participants being surprised by the stimuli, they all experienced the swing, the three vibrations, and the three videos once before the main trials began. Sound cues were masked using white noise from earphones, with earmuffs above these earphones. Each participant conducted one trial per condition, giving a total of nine trials, in random order. Table 2 shows the questionnaire that was presented to the participants. All answers were made on the Likert scale of 1 to 7 (Fig. 6).

Table 2. Questions used in the experiment.

Question 1	How heavy did you imagine the collided object to be?
Question 2	How strongly did you feel the reverberation of the object with which you collided?
Question 3	How natural did the experience feel?

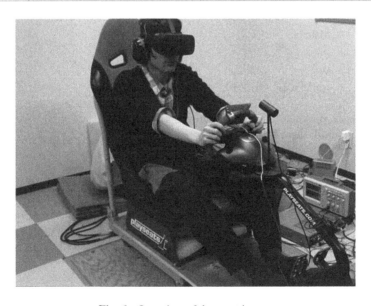

Fig. 6. Overview of the experiment.

5.2 Results

The results for the evaluations of the weight, the reverberation, and the naturalness of the experience are shown in Figs. 7, 8, and 9, respectively. "Object" in each figure represents the material of the object that was presented visually, while the material in each graph shows the material that was presented using vibrotactile sensation. Significant differences observed using the Steel-Dwass test are indicated by *.

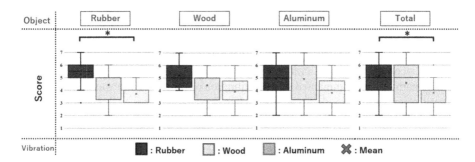

Fig. 7. Evaluations of perceived heaviness.

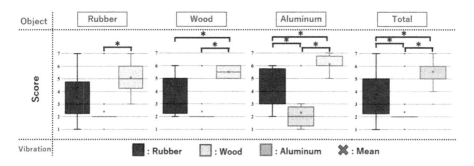

Fig. 8. Evaluations of perceived reverberation.

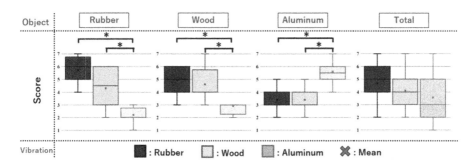

Fig. 9. Evaluations of perceived naturalness.

6   Discussion

From the results for naturalness for rubber and aluminum, we found that a natural experience can be realized when combining the material shown in the video with the same material's vibration, which means that our designed rubber and aluminum vibrations were well matched with the participants' subjective impressions. For the video of collision with the wood, however, the vibrations of wood and rubber produced similar results. We believe that this similarity was caused by individual differences in the impression of the wood from the video. Some participants commented that it was difficult to estimate the weight of the wood cube from the video when the collision occurred, and this uncertainty may have led to the above results. In fact, participants who imagined heavy wood from the video preferred the vibration of the rubber.

Many participants commented that the vibration of the aluminum was characteristic of the material, which might have resulted in low naturalness evaluation when the vibration of aluminum was presented with the visual scenes of the other two materials.

For the vibration waveform of the rubber, there was a comment that the naturalness of the collision was high overall because the impacts were felt strongly. This comment corresponds with the fact that the vibration waveform of the rubber was highly evaluated overall. In the comments after the experiment, one participant mentioned that the weight of the impact varied according to the strength of the vibration, while four participants stated that it varied according to the frequency, and four participants stated that they judged based on the overall impression. Among these participants, two people stated that the feeling of collision with the object was particularly strong in the case of the vibration of the rubber.

With regard to the reverberation of the object that was received from the collision, it can be seen that the score for the vibration of the wood was always extremely low. The comments after the experiment indicated that the vibration of the wood had too weak an amplitude and it was then difficult to perceive the differences based on the stimulus of the swing alone. This is considered to be a natural consequence because the amplitude of the wood vibration was set to be small. Three of the participants judged the reverberations from the frequency, while two judged based on the length of the vibration, and three judged based on both parameters.

Some of the participants commented that the impressions of the weight and the reverberations changed with the material in the video, but the scores for the weight and the reverberations showed similar trends, regardless of the video shown, and this included the scores of the persons who made these comments.

7   Conclusion

We have designed a vibration parameter that is suitable for expression of the feeling of specific materials of objects with which the user collided in a VR system that presents a combination of front-to-back swing and vibration. Videos in which the user's vehicle collided with rubber tires, wood cubes, and aluminum cubes were prepared; suitable vibration presentation parameters were then created for each video by expert users, who adjusted the initial parameters. We performed a user study to verify the validity of the parameters that were created. In the user study, the participants saw videos of collisions with rubber tires, wood cubes, and aluminum cubes, and were presented with the swing and vibration at the moment of collision. The results indicated that the vibration waveforms of rubber and aluminum were well matched with the videos of the collisions with rubber and aluminum, respectively. For the video of the wood, however, because of individual differences in the estimated impact from the videos by individual users, the waveforms of wood and rubber produces similar results.

References

1. Kodama, R., Koge, M., Taguchi, S., Kajimoto, H.: COMS-VR: mobile virtual reality entertainment system using electric car and head-mounted display. In: Proceedings of the IEEE Symposium on 3D User Interfaces, pp. 130–133. IEEE, Los Angeles (2017)
2. Okamura, A.M., Cutkosky, M.R., Dennerlein, J.T.: Reality-based models for vibration feedback in virtual environments. IEEE/ASME Trans. Mechatron. 6(3), 245–252 (2001)
3. Okamura, A.M., Hage, M., Dennerlein, J.T., Cutkosky, M.R.: Improving reality-based models for vibration feedback. In: Proceedings of the ASME Dynamic System and Control Division (2000)
4. Branje, C., Karam, M., Fels, D., Russo, F.: Enhancing entertainment through a multimodal chair interface. In: IEEE Toronto International Conference Science and Technology for Humanity, pp. 636–641, IEEE, Toronto (2009)
5. Yamazaki, Y., Mitake, H., Hasegawa, S.: Tension-based wearable vibroacoustic device for music appreciation. In: Bello, F., Kajimoto, H., Visell, Y. (eds.) EuroHaptics 2016. LNCS, vol. 9775, pp. 273–283. Springer, Cham (2016). https://doi.org/10.1007/978-3-319-42324-1_27
6. Hachisu, T., Kajimoto, H.: HACHIStack: dual-layer photo touch sensing for haptic and auditory tapping interaction. In: Proceedings of the SIGCHI Conference on Human Factors in Computing Systems, pp. 1411–1420, ACM, Paris (2013)
7. Tanabe, K., Takahashi, A., Hoshino, K., Ogawa, D., Hachisu, T., Kajimoto, H.: HapTONE: haptic instrument for enriched musical play (II)—system detail. In: Hasegawa, S., Konyo, M., Kyung, K.-U., Nojima, T., Kajimoto, H. (eds.) AsiaHaptics 2016. LNEE, vol. 432, pp. 461–465. Springer, Singapore (2018). https://doi.org/10.1007/978-981-10-4157-0_77
8. Sakata, S., Nagano, H., Konyo, M., Tadokoro, S.: Multipoint vibrotactile stimuli based on vibration propagation enhance collision sensation. In: Bello, F., Kajimoto, H., Visell, Y. (eds.) EuroHaptics 2016. LNCS, vol. 9775, pp. 65–74. Springer, Cham (2016). https://doi.org/10.1007/978-3-319-42324-1_7
9. Farkhatdinov, I., Ouarti, N., Hayward, V.: Vibrotactile inputs to the feet can modulate vection. In: Proceedings of IEEE World Haptics Conference, pp. 677–681. IEEE, Daejeon (2013)
10. Duthoit, V., Sieffermann, J.-M., Enrègle, E., Blumenthal, D.: Perceived intensity of vibrotactile stimuli: do your clothes really matter? In: Bello, F., Kajimoto, H., Visell, Y. (eds.) EuroHaptics 2016. LNCS, vol. 9774, pp. 412–418. Springer, Cham (2016). https://doi.org/10.1007/978-3-319-42321-0_38
11. Steinemann, A., Tschudi, S., Kunz, A.: Full body haptic display for low-cost racing car driving simulators. In: Proceedings of IEEE Virtual Reality, pp. 245–246. IEEE, Singapore (2011)
12. Cheng, L., Luhne, P., Lopes, P., Sterz, C., Baudisch, P.: Haptic Turk: a motion platform based on people. In: Proceedings of the SIGCHI Conference on Human Factors in Computing Systems, pp. 3463–3472, ACM, Toronto (2014)

13. Ryu, J., Chun, J., Park, G., Choi, S., Han, S.H.: Vibrotactile feedback for information delivery in the vehicle. IEEE Trans. Haptics **3**(2), 138–149 (2010)
14. Hogema, J.H., De Vries, S.C., Van Erp, J.B.F., Kiefer, R.J.: A tactile seat for direction coding in car driving: field evaluation. IEEE Trans. Haptics **2**(4), 181–188 (2009)
15. Morrell, J., Wasilewski, K.: Design and evaluation of a vibrotactile seat to improve spatial awareness while driving. In: Proceedings of IEEE Haptics Symposium, pp. 281–288. IEEE, Boston (2010)
16. Bellmann, T., Heindl, J., Hellerer, M., Kuchar, R., Sharma, K., Hirzinger, G.: The DLR robot motion simulator part I: design and setup. In: Proceedings of IEEE International Conference on Robotics and Automation, pp. 4694–4701. IEEE, Shanghai (2010)

The Rice Haptic Rocker: Comparing Longitudinal and Lateral Upper-Limb Skin Stretch Perception

Janelle P. Clark$^{(\boxtimes)}$, Sung Y. Kim, and Marcia K. O'Malley

Rice University, Houston, TX 77005, USA
janelle.clark@rice.edu

Abstract. Skin stretch, when mapped to joint position, provides haptic feedback using a mechanism similar to our sense of proprioception . Rocker-type skin stretch devices typically actuate in the lateral direction of the arm, though during limb movement stretch about joint angles is in the longitudinal direction. In this paper, human perceptual performance in a target-hitting task is compared for two orientations of the Rice Haptic Rocker. The longitudinal direction is expected to be more intuitive due to the biological similarities, creating a more effective form of haptic feedback. The rockers are placed on the upper arm, and convey the position of a cursor among five vertically aligned targets. The longitudinal orientation results in smaller errors compared to the lateral case. Additionally, the outer targets were reached with less error than the inner targets for the longitudinal rocker. This result suggests longitudinal stretch is more easily discerned than laterally oriented stretch.

1 Introduction

Skin stretch devices of various forms have been successfully studied for several applications, by stretching the skin to varying of degrees and directions to convey information to the user. The motivation behind all haptic devices is to provide easily understood information through the sense of touch. For skin stretch in particular, it remains an open question if the orientation of the stretch impacts perception. In this work, the Rice Haptic Rocker is used to compare the user's perception in its current configuration, stretching skin laterally from side to side, or a longitudinal configuration, stretching skin along the length of the arm.

Haptic devices are becoming an increasingly important form of communication, utilizing the sense of touch to offload visual, auditory, or situational information. For example, customizable vibration patterns can be used for phone notifications, or a user can be informed through the controller of a gaming system of some danger to the avatar. In the research community, the applications of haptic interfaces are more extensive, in both actuation mode and application, to create easily perceived and understood information, for instance allowing users to increase skill performance in surgery [19] or receive directional guidance [21]. In addition to vibratory modes mentioned above [9], haptic modes such as squeeze

© Springer International Publishing AG, part of Springer Nature 2018
D. Prattichizzo et al. (Eds.): EuroHaptics 2018, LNCS 10894, pp. 125–134, 2018.
https://doi.org/10.1007/978-3-319-93399-3_12

[6], pneumatic [2], and normal forces [3] have also been studied, along with the skin stretch mechanisms which are the focus of this work.

Skin stretch devices have been developed to provide user feedback, and can be separated into those actuating on the fingertip, wrist, and arm. For finger-tip devices, the applications vary between virtual mass and forces [18, 20], friction rendering [22], and directional cues [13, 14]. Among them, longitudinal, lateral, and combination devices are present, as well as devices using both directions with success. The workspace of these devices is significantly smaller than those on the wrist and arm, attributable to the density of mechanoreceptors in the fingertips. For this work, fingertip devices are useful to review, however the results presented here are expected to only apply to more gross movements on the wrist and arm.

Wrist mounted skin stretch devices also actuate in lateral [8] and combined lateral and longitudinal systems [16, 24], with similar application to the fingertip designs, guidance and force feedback. The mechanisms vary in design, in [24], several motors rotate a silicone ball on either side of the wrist. A bracelet of four rocker-shaped actuators in [8] create a variety of possible cooperative or antagonistic pairs. There are two pads in [16] which can move both in the longitudinal direction and rotate about the base of a lever, creating a lateral effect. However in this experiment, where the device was intended for force feedback, users reported wanting to move their arm in the direction of the stretch cue. This type of user response has made skin stretch successful in guidance and positional error applications listed above, as well as for devices on the arm utilized for prosthetic control. .

The remaining skin stretch devices discussed here are designed to actuate on the upper arm. For those presented, the feedback is mapped to positional information, either absolute angular position or positional error. The device in [23] has a unique design, with two small contacts rotating about an axis between them, creating a twisting stretch on the arm to indicate angular position errors. The portable device in [7] has a small protrusion mounted to a plate allowing to move both laterally and longitudinally to convey directional cues. Rather than a compact device, the system in [1] has cables for each prosthetic finger run from the prosthesis to a terminating button adhered to the forearm. The longitudinal stretch from the cables serve to indicate the hand aperture. The Rice Haptic Rocker has a rocker design similar to those in the wrist design presented in [8], which at Rice was preceded by [5]. It was first introduced in combination with the Pisa/IIT SoftHand to complete object discrimination tasks for a grasping spheres with a prosthetic hand [4]. One rocker is mounted laterally to convey the relative aperture of the hand. These devices are similar in the method they use to communicate with the user, however the actuation scheme varies considerably.

When selecting a type of haptic feedback for a given task, the concept of modality matching has been beneficial by suggesting the haptic mode should reflect the type of information it is used to convey [15, 17]. Research in the biological mechanisms behind proprioception in humans suggest that, in addition to muscle spindles, joint position information is in part realized through the repeatable patterns of skin stretch about the joints [11,12]. Then skin stretch is particularly suitable for positional information, and demonstrated through the body of work previously referenced.

We hypothesize, in consideration of the biological mechanisms, stretch in the longitudinal direction is more intuitive to a user than lateral stretch. In this work, the perceptual accuracy of a target task is assessed using the Rice Haptic Rocker in its initial lateral configuration compared to a revised longitudinal one. Results of this work serve to compare the relative effectiveness of two stretch directions for haptic feedback on the upper arm.

2   Device Description

The Rice Haptic Rocker is a haptic device consisting of a rocker shaped geometry with a high friction interface with the skin. Its rotation by a servo creates a tangential force, stretching the skin as the servo is actuated. It has been proposed and utilized already in the lateral orientation, as described in [4], where the axis of rotation is parallel to the length of the arm and the skin is stretched from side to side. In this work, it is compared to the longitudinal direction, where the skin is stretched along the length of the arm and the axis of rotation is perpendicular to it, see Fig. 1.

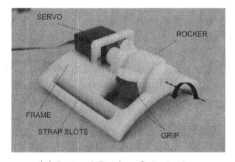
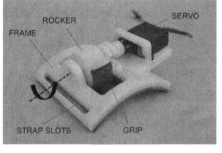

(a) Lateral Rocker Orientation   (b) Longitudinal Rocker Orientation

Fig. 1. The rocker is mounted in two orientations in order to compare user perception between the previously studied lateral orientation to the proposed longitudinal orientation.

The frame and rocker are made of a hard ABS-like plastic and 3-D printed by a Connex Objet 260 printer. The contact surface of the rocker is a half inch diameter silicone rubber, different than the rectangular neoprene foam used in [4], in order to increase comfort. The frame holds a servo (Hitec HS-5070 MH), which actuates the rocker, with two socket head screws and nuts (M1.6 × 0.35 mm). The assembly of the frame, rocker, and servo are placed on the upper arm with the rocker toward the outside of the arm.

3   Methods

Participants were asked to complete a virtual navigational task to determine the effects of different skin stretch orientations on sensory perception. The navigation was facilitated by skin stretch feedback in lateral or longitudinal directions. We hypothesize that stretch in the longitudinal direction would garner a lower error value than stretch in the lateral direction.

3.1   Experimental Participants

The experiment included twenty-three able-bodied subjects (age 21.5 ± 2.1 years, 4 female, one left handed). The participants did not claim any physical or cognitive impairment that could interfere with their ability to follow the instructions of the study, nor any pathology that could affect tactile sensation of the upper arm. The methods and procedures described in this paper were carried out in accordance with the recommendations of the Institutional Review Board of Rice University with written informed consent obtained from all users.

3.2   Experimental Set-Up

The rocker was placed and secured on the upper arm of the subject with a frame, held with a Velcro strap. The tightness of the device was dependent on the comfort of the subject, but sufficient to facilitate skin stretch with the rocker with no slipping. During the assessment, the participant was seated at a workbench in front of a monitor and keyboard, see Fig. 2. Once seated, the participants were asked to place their arm on the table in a relaxed position, with the rocker assembly secured on their right arm. The arm and rocker were visually occluded by a black curtain to cause participants to rely only on the haptic sensations of the rocker. Headphones with pink noise prevented possible auditory cues from the servo actuation.

Participants moved the cursor to the desired position using the 8 and 2 keys, and indicating a complete trial by pressing the enter key when they believed the target had been reached. The assessment environment was implemented with MATLAB, Simulink and QUARC visualization software, and sampled at 1000 Hz. Five targets positioned in a vertical line were displayed on the monitor, all equally spaced at 48, 24, 0, −24, −48 units, as shown in Fig. 3. In each trial, one of the four non-center targets would brighten, indicating the desired target the participant should navigate toward. Starting from the center target, the cursor moved a uniform distance with each key press within each trial. Across trials the increment at which the cursor moved varied randomly between 1, 2, 3, 4, or 6 units per key press, to prevent the participants from counting key presses rather than relying solely on the stretch. The rocker position on the arm is proportional to the cursor position on the screen. The visibility of the cursor was dependent on the experimental block, as described in Sect. 3.3. Each target and increment combination was shown an equal number of times in each experimental block with a randomized order.

Fig. 2. The participant is seated at the bench facing the monitor, their right arm rests on the workbench with the rocker secured to the upper arm. Headphones provide pink noise to eliminate audio cues.

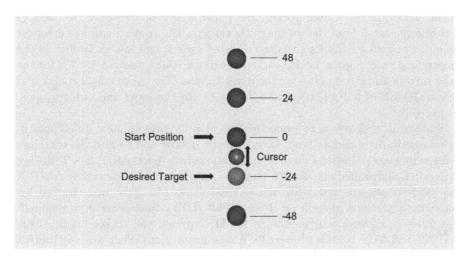

Fig. 3. The visualization for the perceptual task, the desired target blinks and the cursor is controlled using the keyboard.

3.3   Experimental Protocol

This navigation task was completed for the two rocker orientations, lateral and longitudinal, and each subject completed the task with both orientations in a single one-hour session. Trial times were determined by the subjects with no time limitations. To prevent possible training bias and effects of fatigue, half of the participants completed the task with the laterally oriented rocker first and the other half completed the longitudinally oriented rocker first.

The task comprised of three blocks: two training blocks and one assessment block. The blocks differed in the visibility of the cursor, which was included during training to create an association between the target positions on the screen and the stretch from the Rocker, and removed during the assessment to test their ability to reach the targets by relying solely on the rocker feedback. In the first training block, comprised of 20 trials, the cursor was present at all times during the trial. In the second training block, comprised of 60 trials, the cursor was not present until the participant confirmed they believed the target had been reached, when the cursor would display the final position. In the assessment block, comprised of 20 trials, the cursor was not visible at any point throughout the entire block. In all three blocks, an equal number of each increment and target were represented within each block.

4   Results

The differences in perception of the two rocker designs were quantified by the root mean squared error (RMSE) of the cursor position with respect to the desired target in the assessment phase, see Fig. 4. As well as comparing the overall performance of each rocker, the performance of the inner two targets were differentiated from that of the outer targets. The results show less error for the outer targets for the longitudinal oriented rocker, and less variability in the longitudinal case. For the lateral rocker, the mean RMSE was $9.3 \pm 4.7\%$ for the inner targets and $9.6 \pm 4.0\%$ for the outer targets. The longitudinal rocker had a mean RMSE of $9.2 \pm 2.0\%$ and $7.2 \pm 3.2\%$ for the inner and outer targets, respectively.

Statistical analyses were performed to identify performance differences in rocker orientations and between targets in the middle and toward the extremes of the workspace, as well as possible interactions between them. A 2×2 [Rocker (Lateral; Longitudinal) $\times$ Target (Inner; Outer)] repeated-measures ANOVA was used to assess the RMSE across conditions. The data was checked for sphericity deviations, though no Huynh-Feldt (HF) adjustments were required. The analysis showed a difference in RMSE between the rocker orientations, $F(1, 22) = 5.40$, $p = .03$, $\eta^2 = 0.20$. A significant main effect was not present between the inner and outer targets, however the interaction approached significance, $F(1, 22) = 3.41$, $p = .08$, $\eta^2 = 0.13$, causing the interaction to be investigated. The longitudinal rocker orientation did result in a significant difference between the inner and outer targets, $t(22) = 2.55$, $p = .018$, $d = 0.76$, though none was present in the lateral case.

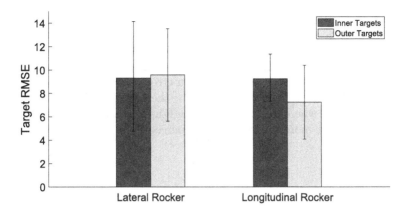

Fig. 4. The mean RMSE across all users for each experimental condition, error bars represent the RMSE standard deviation. The rocker orientation has a significant effect ($p = .03$), where the lateral rocker has higher errors than the longitudinal rocker. In the longitudinal case, outer targets are easier to discern than the inner targets ($p = .018$).

5   Discussion

In this work, impact of stretch direction in user perception for a target task is tested with the Rice Haptic Rocker. Lateral, or side to side, movement was compared to the more biologically accurate longitudinal, or up and down, stretch. Feedback provided with the longitudinal orientation of the rocker resulted significantly less positional errors compared to lateral cue orientation. This agrees with the initial hypothesis, that the presence of longitudinal stretch as a source of proprioceptive information makes the orientation more intuitive for the user compared to the lateral direction, though with a small effect size.

Other factors may also contribute to this result. By inspection, we observe more possible skin movement in the lateral direction compared to stretch along the length of the arm. Other factors could be related to the biology of the skin, in the mechanoreceptors or muscle and fat composition, requiring further research. Though the longitudinal direction has been shown to result in more accurate perception, because of the prominence of this mode in the human's existing proprioceptive system, the information may become confounded during dynamic tasks due to natural skin stretch existing in the arm. The haptic devices should be designed to be as inert as possible to external stimuli in the environment, and certainly during navigational and prosthetic applications the device will be used while the user is moving their arm. The impact of dynamic tasks and possibility of confounding the stretch cue should be investigated. In addition, the impact of the arm choice could be evaluated. One left-handed subject was included in this experiment, however the importance of arm dominance in feedback remains open.

The decrease in target error for the outer targets compared to the inner ones for the longitudinal rocker suggest some sort of nonlinear behavior. The torsional device used in [8] utilized an s-curve mapping in the device position to create larger increments near the neutral position and smaller ones toward the extrema in order to address this tendency. A similar s-curve mapping does not impact the target accuracy in [10], however this was using the lateral orientation of the rocker, which did not show a difference in errors between the targets in the presented work. This also could be related to the increased skin movement in the lateral direction, where insufficient skin tightness is achieved at the extrema of the lateral case for more sensitive change perceptions.

6   Conclusion

Skin stretch has been implemented in a variety of forms for haptic feedback to human users. In this experiment two stretch directions were compared using the Rice Haptic Rocker, in lateral and longitudinal directions on the upper arm. The longitudinal rocker produced smaller errors in a target task compared to the lateral orientation. For the longitudinal rocker, the outer targets had a smaller error compared to the inner targets, whereas the lateral rocker did not have a difference in the target location. These results could be due to at least two possible sources. One relates to the possible intuitiveness of the longitudinal direction from the use of skin stretch in joint motion for proprioceptive information. The second is the observed smaller amount of skin movement possible in the longitudinal direction, allowing smaller changes to be discerned in pre-stretched skin, perhaps not extensive enough in the lateral case. These results can assist in haptic device choice and design for applications relating to proprioceptive, navigation, compliance, and force feedback.

References

1. Akhtar, A., Nguyen, M., Wan, L., Boyce, B., Slade, P., Bretl, T.: Passive Mechanical Skin Stretch for Multiple Degree-of-Freedom Proprioception in a Hand Prosthesis. In: Auvray, M., Duriez, C. (eds.) EUROHAPTICS 2014. LNCS, vol. 8619, pp. 120–128. Springer, Heidelberg (2014). https://doi.org/10.1007/978-3-662-44196-1_16
2. Antfolk, C., Björkman, A., Frank, S.O., Sebelius, F., Lundborg, G., Rosen, B.: Sensory feedback from a prosthetic hand based on air-mediated pressure from the hand to the forearm skin. J. Rehabil. Med. **44**(8), 702–707 (2012)
3. Antfolk, C., D'Alonzo, M., Controzzi, M., Lundborg, G., Rosén, B., Sebelius, F., Cipriani, C.: Artificial redirection of sensation from prosthetic fingers to the phantom hand map on transradial amputees: vibrotactile versus mechanotactile sensory feedback. IEEE Trans. Neural Syst. Rehabil. Eng. **21**(1), 112–120 (2013)
4. Battaglia, E., Clark, J.P., Bianchi, M., Catalano, M.G., Bicchi, A., O'Malley, M.K.: The rice haptic rocker: skin stretch haptic feedback with the pisa/iit softhand. In: Proceedings of the IEEE World Haptics Conference (2017)
5. Blank, A., Brookshier, C.A., O'Malley, M.: Skin stretch feedback of gripper aperture for prosthetic hands in a grasp and lift task (work in progress). In: Proceedings of the IEEE World Haptics Conference (2015)

6. Casini, S., Morvidoni, M., Bianchi, M., Catalano, M., Grioli, G., Bicchi, A.: Design and realization of the cuff-clenching upper-limb force feedback wearable device for distributed mechano-tactile stimulation of normal and tangential skin forces. In: IEEE/RSJ International Conference on Intelligent Robots and Systems. pp. 1186–1193. IEEE (2015)

7. Caswell, N.A., Yardley, R.T., Montandon, M.N., Provancher, W.R.: Design of a forearm-mounted directional skin stretch device. In: Proceedings of the IEEE Haptics Symposium. pp. 365–370 (2012)

8. Chinello, F., Pacchierotti, C., Tsagarakis, N.G., Prattichizzo, D.: Design of a wearable skin stretch cutaneous device for the upper limb. In: Proceedings of the IEEE Haptics Symposium. pp. 14–20 (2016)

9. Cipriani, C.: DAlonzo, M., Carrozza, M.C.: A miniature vibrotactile sensory substitution device for multifingered hand prosthetics. IEEE Trans. Biomed. Eng. **59**(2), 400–408 (2012)

10. Clark, J.P., Kim, S.Y., O'Malley, M.K.: The rice haptic rocker: Altering the perception of skin stretch through mapping and geometric design. In: the Proceedings of IEEE Eurohaptics Conference (2018)

11. Collins, D.F., Refshauge, K.M., Todd, G., Gandevia, S.C.: Cutaneous receptors contribute to kinesthesia at the index finger, elbow, and knee. J. Neurophysiol. **94**(3), 1699–1706 (2005)

12. Edin, B.B., Johansson, N.: Skin strain patterns provide kinaesthetic information to the human central nervous system. The Journal of physiology **487**(1), 243–251 (1995)

13. Gleeson, B.T., Horschel, S.K., Provancher, W.R.: Communication of direction through lateral skin stretch at the fingertip. In: World Haptics 2009 - Third Joint EuroHaptics conference and Symposium on Haptic Interfaces for Virtual Environment and Teleoperator Systems. pp. 172–177 (2009)

14. Guinan, A.L., Hornbaker, N.C., Montandon, M.N., Doxon, A.J., Provancher, W.R.: Back-to-back skin stretch feedback for communicating five degree-of-freedom direction cues. In: Proceedings of the IEEE World Haptics Conference. pp. 13–18 (2013)

15. Kim, K., Colgate, J.E., Santos-Munné, J.J., Makhlin, A., Peshkin, M.A.: On the design of miniature haptic devices for upper extremity prosthetics. IEEE/ASME Trans. Mechatron. **15**(1), 27–39 (2010)

16. Kuniyasu, Y., Sato, M., Fukushima, S., Kajimoto, H.: Transmission of forearm motion by tangential deformation of the skin. In: Proceedings of the 3rd Augmented Human International Conference. pp. 16:1–16:4. ACM (2012)

17. Meek, S.G., Jacobsen, S.C., Goulding, P.P.: Extended physiologic taction: design and evaluation of a proportional force feedback system. Journal of Rehabilitation Research & Development **26**(3), 53–62 (1989)

18. Minamizawa, K., Fukamachi, S., Kajimoto, H., Kawakami, N., Tachi, S.: Gravity grabber: Wearable haptic display to present virtual mass sensation. In: ACM SIGGRAPH Emerging Technologies. ACM (2007)

19. Okamura, A.: Methods for haptic feedback in teleoperated robotassisted surgery. Industrial Robot: the international journal of robotics research and application **31**(6), 499–508 (2004)

20. Schorr, S.B., Quek, Z.F., Romano, R.Y., Nisky, I., Provancher, W.R., Okamura, A.M.: Sensory substitution via cutaneous skin stretch feedback. In: 2013 IEEE International Conference on Robotics and Automation. pp. 2341–2346 (2013)

21. Stanley, A.A., Kuchenbecker, K.J.: Evaluation of tactile feedback methods for wrist rotation guidance. IEEE Trans. Haptics **5**(3), 240–251 (2012)

22. Sylvester, N.D., Provancher, W.R.: Effects of longitudinal skin stretch on the perception of friction. In: Second Joint EuroHaptics Conference and Symposium on Haptic Interfaces for Virtual Environment and Teleoperator Systems (WHC'07). pp. 373–378 (2007)

23. Wheeler, J., Bark, K., Savall, J., Cutkosky, M.: Investigation of rotational skin stretch for proprioceptive feedback with application to myoelectric systems. IEEE Trans. Neural Syst. Rehabil. Eng. **18**(1), 58–66 (2010)

24. Yem, V., Otsuki, M., Kuzuoka, H.: Development of wearable outer-covering haptic display using ball effector for hand motion guidance. In: Kajimoto, H., Ando, H., Kyung, K.U. (eds.) Haptic Interaction: Perception, Devices and Applications, pp. 85–89. Springer Japan (2015)

Buttock Skin Stretch: Inducing Shear Force Perception and Acceleration Illusion on Self-motion Perception

Arata Horie[(✉)], Hikaru Nagano, Masashi Konyo, and Satoshi Tadokoro

Graduate School of Information Sciences, Tohoku University,
6-6-01 Aramaki Aza Aoba, Aoba-ku, Sendai-shi, Miyagi 980-8579, Japan
`horie.arata@rm.is.tohoku.ac.jp`

Abstract. This study presents a new concept of buttock skin stretch to induce the perception of shear force while sitting. Skin stretch is a potential approach to deliver kinesthetic information by cutaneous stimuli with a compact and portable device. We first introduce the buttock skin stretch approach for a virtual motion platform to enhance the experience of self-motion acceleration. We developed a single degree-of-freedom skin stretch device to deform the buttock skin in the lateral direction of the frontal plane. To deal with the shape difference of buttocks, the initial position of the sliding contactors was calibrated with the buttock pressure distribution on the seat. We investigated the relationship between the contactor displacement and the perceived shear force on each lateral side. The estimated magnitudes of the perceived force showed a monotonically increasing trend corresponding to the skin stretch displacement on each side. The observed similarity between the left and right sides suggests the good reproducibility of the proposed method. We also investigated the bias effect of the buttock skin stretch to the perceived acceleration of self-motion, which was induced by the vection illusion presented with an optical flow. The results of the magnitude estimation suggest that skin displacement of 9 mm biased the perceived acceleration more than that of 3 mm displacement. These findings suggest that the shear force induced by the buttock skin stretch can enhance the perception of self-motion.

Keywords: Skin stretch device · Force perception
Self-motion perception · Buttock skin

1 Introduction

Skin stretch is a potential approach to deliver kinesthetic information by cutaneous stimuli. It is known that tangential displacement on the surface of the skin induces the perception of force including directions. Different types of the skin stretch devices have been proposed for the fingerpad [1–4], palm [5], and the upper limb [6,7] in the past. For instance, Gleeson et al. proposed a skin stretch

© Springer International Publishing AG, part of Springer Nature 2018
D. Prattichizzo et al. (Eds.): EuroHaptics 2018, LNCS 10894, pp. 135–147, 2018.
https://doi.org/10.1007/978-3-319-93399-3_13

display with a 2-DoF shear contactor to produce tangential skin displacement on the fingertip held by a thimble [1]. Minamizawa et al. proposed a wearable device with two motors and a belt able to deform the fingertip [2]. Wheeler et al. investigated a rotational skin stretch on the upper limb for navigating position and movement of the arm [6]. In general, the skin stretch approach has limitations in accurately controlling the amount of force compared to the physical force feedback devices, because the shear deformation depends on skin thickness, stiffness, and other frictional properties. On the other hand, the skin stretch has a great advantage of realizing a compact and portable mechanism since large actuators are not necessary for producing lateral skin deformations. In this study, we first introduce a skin stretch device for buttocks to induce kinesthetic illusions on a seated body. There are many studies or commercial products to provide vibrotactile feedback for the seated body, but no study has applied skin stretch on buttocks to the best of our knowledge. A possible issue to be addressed for the buttock skin stretch device is in controlling the skin stretch by adjusting the contact location by taking into account the individual differences in body shape and clothing. We also need to investigate the relationship between the applied displacement and the perceived force, which might vary from person to person.

Furthermore, this study tries to enhance the perception of self-motion as a potential application of buttock skin stretch. The goal is to develop a virtual motion platform to ride or drive on a seat equipped with the skin stretch device, which is expected to enhance the experiences of motion acceleration by incorporating with visual information via a large screen or head-mounted display. The main advantage of a buttock skin stretch approach for the motion platform is a compact device, as described above. If it is small enough, we can mount it on an existing seat and facilities like a cushion.

Enhancing the self-motion perception has been studied by many researchers. The first approach was to use a motion platform that stimulates somatosensory and vestibular sensations by providing actual tilts or movement to the human body. The second approach used was inducing sensory illusion by exciting human sensations such as visual cue [8], auditory cue [9], and galvanic vestibular stimulation [10]. Notably, Amemiya et al. also reported that vibrotactile apparent motion on the torso could modulate the perceived velocity of the self-motion [11]. The buttock skin stretch approach proposed in the present study could have the similar effect on the self-motion. However, the perception enhanced by the skin stretch is expected to be the acceleration, not the velocity, because the skin stretch induces force perception, which could be proportional to the acceleration if we assume a motion equation.

This study reports the initial results conducted to investigate the feasibility of buttock skin stretch. Particularly, the present study reports the following three topics: (1) Development of a single-DoF skin stretch device to deform the buttock skin in the lateral direction of the frontal plane, (2) Investigation of the relationship between the contactor displacement and the perceived shear force on either side, and (3) Investigation of the bias effect of the buttock skin stretch on the perceived acceleration of the self-motion. The proposed device controls

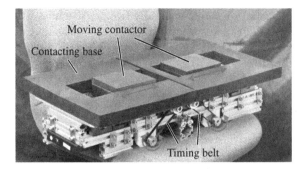

Fig. 1. Buttock skin stretch display placing on a chair

the skin stretch by sliding contactors at the center of each buttock, which is stationarily fixed by a surrounding soft seat. The basic idea is the same as that of a conventional skin stretch device for the fingerpad [1]. However, we propose a calibration method to adjust the personal shape differences by locating the initial contactor positions at the peak of pressure distribution loaded by the buttock in a sitting posture. The perceived force is evaluated by the magnitude estimation to confirm a monotonous increasing tendency corresponding to the skin stretch displacement. For the last topic, we investigate the bias effect of the vection illusion presented using an optical-flow of dots to induce the perception of the self-motion, which is a commonly used method to assess the perceived self-motion for audio [12] and vibrotactile stimuli [11]. In Conclusion, we also show a sample application of the prototype device.

2   Buttock Skin-Stretch Device

2.1   Device Design

We developed a tactile device to present buttock skin stretches. Figure 1 shows a photograph of the developed device. Users activate the device by sitting at the top of it. Two contactors are placed on the left and right of the device to make contact with each buttock. The outer circumference of the buttock is on the contacting base, and the two contactors move to the left and right. The contactors are bonded to the belt conveyor inside the device. The belt conveyors are each controlled by two motors (Maxon RE25, Maxon Motor), two motor drivers (ESCON 50/5, Maxon Motor), and two encoders (RE30E, Nidec Copal Corp.).

There are two important issues with regard to the buttock skin stretch device. The first is to control the position of the contactor according to the shape of the user's buttocks. The second is that the contactors and the buttocks must not slide. Therefore, in this study, we decided to control the amount of deformation by setting the pressure center occurring in the vicinity of the sciatic bone while seated as the initial position of the contactor.

The pressure distribution shows generally two peaks while sitting on the seat, as shown in Fig. 2(a). This pressure distribution was measured using a pressure sensor sheet (BIG-MAT2000P3BS, Nitta Corp, size: 440×480 mm, resolution: 10×10 mm) as shown in Fig. 2(b).

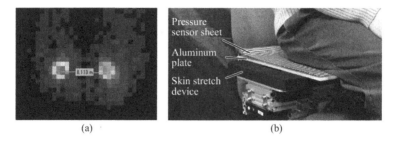

(a)   (b)

Fig. 2. (a) One example of measured pressure distribution is shown. Red-colored area is high pressured. The distance between the left and right peak pressure positions can be estimated. (b) Pressure is measured by the pressure sensor sheet on the aluminum plate. (Color figure online)

In order to prevent sliding between the contactor and the buttocks, we adopted a rubber sponge (hard chloroprene rubber) as the material of the contactor and contacting base. The displacement range of the contactor was also set to a range that does not slip empirically (maximum 9 mm). However, unlike the conventional skin stretch device, the contactors make contact with the buttocks through clothing. For this reason, the sliding of clothes and skin cannot be excluded. However, in a sitting position, because the weight of the upper body is added, sufficient pressing force can be obtained so that sliding rarely occurs within the set range.

2.2   Control of Contactor Displacement

The position of the contactor is controlled by feeding back the value of the encoder. The position resolution by the encoder is 0.3 mm. The sampling frequency of measuring encoder value and controlling command to the microcontroller is 100 Hz with a single-board microcontroller (Arduino UNO).

The accuracy of position control by this system was confirmed by preliminary experiment.

In the state where the participant is placed, the command value and the measured value by the encoder are compared. A participant whose weight is 69 kg was placed on the device. The input commands were given in 10 s to command 3 mm which is the minimum displacement used in the experiment and 9 mm which is the maximum displacement.

The results of the experiment are shown in Figs. 3(a) and (b). The accuracy of position were enough for presenting the place we need. There is a delay in the input command value and the output displacement. This is due to the suppression of the control gain for safety.

3   Experiment 1: Relationship Between Buttock Skin Stretch and Perceived Shear Force

In the first experiment, we investigated the relationships between the perceived shear force and the lateral displacement of contactor through magnitude estimation. All experimental procedures, including the recruitment of participants, were approved by the Ethics Committee of the Graduate School of Information Sciences at Tohoku University, which was also applied to the second experiment.

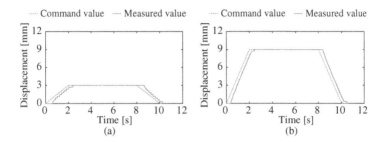

Fig. 3. Two examples of response of contactor displacement. (a) The stimulus with the maximum displacement of 3 mm. (b) The stimulus with the maximum displacement of 9 mm.

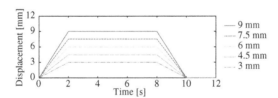

Fig. 4. Five types of stimuli of the first experiment

3.1   Participants

Ten participants (aged 18–25 years, right-handed) took part in the study. All subjects had no motor or sensory limitations by self-report. They were not aware of the purpose of the experiments.

3.2   Stimuli

Figure 4 shows the five types of stimuli used in the first experiment. They have different maximum displacements ($d = 3, 4.5, 6, 7.5$, and 9 mm.) For each stimulus, the displacement monotonically increased during first 2 s of reaching the maximum value, retained the maximum value for 6 s, and then monotonically decreased during the first 2 s to reach zero. These values were selected through pre-tests in which the authors perceived shear displacements but did not perceive slippage between the buttocks and contactors.

3.3   Procedure

Before performing the experiments, we made the center positions of the two contactors to the peak positions of pressure at buttocks. The participants sat on the pressure sensor (BIG-MAT2000P3BS, Nitta Corp, size: 440×480 mm, resolution: 10×10 mm) which were located on the skin stretch device with an aluminum plate interlaid as shown in Fig. 2(b). From the measured pressure distribution, we calculated the center positions at left and right buttocks respectively as shown in Fig. 2(a). The left and right contactors were moved so that the center positions coincide with the peak positions of pressure distribution. After this adjustment, we removed the pressure sensor and the aluminum plate.

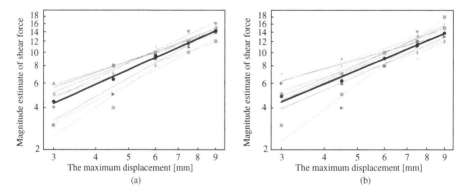

Fig. 5. Magnitude estimates of shear force. Solid black line shows geometric mean and the other colored lines show individual data. (a) Left direction. (b) Right direction. (Color figure online)

In the experiments, the participants sat directly on the skin stretch device. While the experiments, the participants heard pink noise through headphones for sound insulation. For each trial, the modulus of which the maximum displacement of 6 mm was presented at first, and a test stimuli was presented after 2 s interval. The displacement direction of a test stimulus was same to the direction of the modulus. After providing two stimuli, the participants answered the magnitude estimate of maximum tangential force of a test stimulus compared to the modulus whose magnitude was set to 10. The scale of answered magnitude estimate is not limited. The five types of test stimuli ($d = 3, 4.5, 6, 7.5$, and 9 mm) are used once on each side; for each participant, 10 trials were totally performed.

3.4   Results

Figure 5 show the relationships between the estimated magnitude of the shear force and the maximum buttock skin displacement to the left and right directions, respectively. For each participant, the data were fitted to the power function defined as $f = kd^b$, where d is the maximum displacement, f is estimated magnitude of shear force, and k and b are proportionality constants.

Thin lines are the lines fitted to each participant's data. All the participants tended to perceive larger shear force with larger skin displacement, although individual differences can be observed. In addition, for each participant, the Spearman correlation coefficient between the maximum displacement and perceived shear force was measured. For all the participants, high correlation coefficients ($\rho > 0.9$, $p < 0.05$) were found, which support the theory that larger skin displacement leads to larger perceived shear force. Moreover, the solid black thick lines are the lines fitted to the geometric means of the estimated magnitudes of shear force. The power exponents b are 1.08 (left direction) and 1.03 (right direction), which mean that the perceived shear force monotonically (almost linearly) increases with the amount of maximum skin displacement.

The experimental results suggest that buttock skin stretch induced the perception of shear force. Although there are individual differences in the perceived shear force, the trend observed for all participants is that the increase in maximum skin displacement monotonically increased the perceived shear force. Moreover, the similar trend in relationships in the right and left directions was observed, which suggests that the developed skin stretch system functions stably for both the right and left directions.

The experimental results suggested that the increment of maximum skin displacement almost linearly increased perceived shear force. Moreover, the similar tendency in the relationships was observed in right and left directions, which suggested that the operation of the developed skin stretch system is stable in both the right and left directions.

4   Experiment 2: Evaluation of Bias on Perceived Self-motion Acceleration Induced by Skin Stretch

We investigated the possibility of bias in acceleration sensation by buttock skin stretch as a pilot study, and not as an accurate control of the feeling of acceleration. We conducted the second experiment to determine whether buttock skin stretch creates a bias in favor of the illusion of self-motion acceleration by visual stimulus (vection).

4.1   Participants

The participants were the same 10 participants in the first experiment. They were also unaware of the purpose of the experiments.

4.2   Stimuli

One modulus stimulus and 30 test stimuli were used to estimate the magnitude of the perceived acceleration in the experiment.

The modulus stimulus is the visual stimulus, which is an optical flow of laterally-moving images containing 50 white particles on a black background in each frame. In each trial, the acceleration of lateral movement has the following profile: linearly increasing (2 s), lasting (6 s), linearly decreasing (2 s), and the same shape of profile in opposite direction of the first (10 s). The initial velocity is zero; thus, the velocity finally returns to zero. The maximum acceleration of the modulus is $0.12 \, \mathrm{m/s^2}$.

The test stimulus is the combination of visual and haptic stimuli. Visual stimuli are five types of optical flow with maximum acceleration ($a = 0.06, 0.09, 0.12, 0.15$, and $0.18 \, \mathrm{m/s^2}$). The acceleration profile of the five test stimuli is same as the profile of the modulus mentioned above. This value was empirically chosen in order to deliver the perception of self-motion. The haptic stimuli are five types of buttock skin stretches with different maximum displacement ($d = 3, 4.5, 6, 7.5$, and $9 \, \mathrm{mm}$), as shown in Fig. 6; these are similar to the acceleration profile of optical flow image. To avoid slippage between contactors and buttocks during movement, the maximum displacement were adopted. Totally, 30 test stimuli (five visual conditions $\times$ six haptic conditions containing $d = 0$). The direction of buttock skin displacement was opposite to that of the acceleration of optical flow. The two contactors constantly followed the same displacement profile.

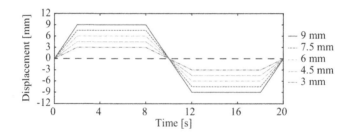

Fig. 6. Five types of stimuli of the second experiment

4.3   Procedure

The initial positions of contactors were adjusted according to the shape of the participant's buttocks before performing the experiment. We set the center positions of the two contactors as the peak positions of the pressure measured at the buttocks.

Figure 7 shows the experimental conditions. The participants sat on the buttock skin stretch device, placed their chin on the chin rest, and put on the

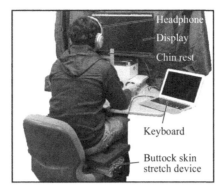

Fig. 7. Experimental condition

headphones. The participants focused on the display in front of them and used the keyboard to start the stimuli and answer questionnaires.

In each trial, the modulus stimulus was presented for 20 s followed by a test stimulus for 20 s. The time interval between the two stimuli was 2 s. After receiving two stimuli, the participants answered questions on the subjective magnitude of the maximum acceleration toward the moving direction of the test stimulus. They were instructed that the magnitude of the modulus is 10. Thus, if a participant answers 10, he/she is shifted to the forced choice task to answer whether the intensity of the acceleration sensation induced by the test stimulus is larger or smaller than the modulus stimulus; however, the results of this questionnaire were not used in this paper.

Each participant undertook 60 trials (30 test stimuli × left and right directions) with 1-min breaks after every five trials.

4.4   Results

Figure 8 shows the relationship between the maximum acceleration of optical flow and the geometric mean of the estimated magnitudes of self-motion acceleration.

The perceived acceleration tended to increase according to the increasing acceleration of the visual stimulus in all 12 conditions (six stimuli ($d = 0, 3, 4.5, 6, 7.5,$ and 9 mm) × left and right directions). This tendency suggests that the participants perceived the illusion of self-motion acceleration even though buttock skin stretch was added to the visual stimulus.

When the acceleration of the visual stimulus is small, the variation of estimated magnitudes between the conditions tends to be large; when the acceleration of the visual stimulus is large, the variation tends to be small.

We predicted that acceleration will always be estimated greater by adding tactile stimulus to the visual stimulus, but it can be seen that there are conditions that tend to estimates lower by presenting a tactile stimulus. In addition, for 3 mm contactor displacement, the acceleration was estimated to be lower compared to the other conditions, whereas the tendency that the 9 mm is estimated

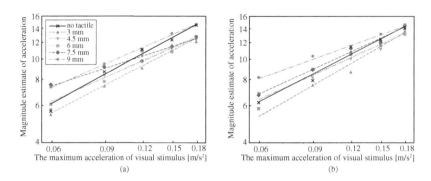

Fig. 8. Magnitude estimates of acceleration. (a) Left direction. (b) Right direction.

to be high can be seen. Thus, it is considered that participants felt different acceleration induced by haptic stimuli, which affected self-motion sensation. We analyzed statistically whether the perceived acceleration changes depended on tactile presentation and amount of deformation.

To investigate the bias effect of buttock skin stretch on the illusion of self-motion acceleration by visual stimulus (vection), we calculated the individual subjective equivalent acceleration, which is the visual stimulus acceleration the same as the modulus visual stimulus ($= 10$).

Figure 9 shows the relationships between the maximum displacement of buttock skin stretch and the subjective equivalent self-motion acceleration without extreme outliers. The Shapiro-Wilk test showed that all the conditions had a normal distribution. One-way ANOVA with repeated measures showed that subjective acceleration differed significantly among the different tactile conditions for both left and right movements ($p = 0.023, p = 0.022$). The Tukey-Kramer test showed that there was no significant difference between the zero tactile condition and the other tactile conditions. However, there was a signifi-

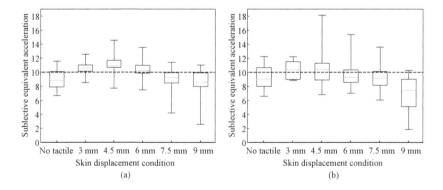

Fig. 9. Subjective equivalent acceleration. (a) Left direction. (b) Right direction.

cant difference between the conditions of different maximum displacement (3 and 9 mm) ($p = 0.035$ (left) and $p = 0.041$ (right)). The difference in the maximum displacement of buttock skin stretch modulated the perception of self-motion.

The results suggest that the buttock skin stretch affected the illusion of self-motion acceleration. Increasing the maximum buttock skin displacement increased the perceived acceleration.

5   Discussion

The first experiments investigated the relationship between the contactor displacement and the perceived shear force on users' buttocks. The results showed that the perceived shear force almost linearly increased corresponding to the skin stretch displacement, where the fitted model's power exponents were almost 1 in either direction. The similar linearity is reported in the related studies on the fingerpad skin stretch. Pare et al. found the linear relationship in the magnitude estimation of the tangential force applied to the fingerpad [13], and Gleeson et al. reported the linearity between the tangential skin displacement and the perceived tangential force [1]. Although there is a difference between the actual skin stretch and the displacement of the device contactors, our buttock skin stretch device could induce the perceived force in the same manner of the conventional studies.

Also, we confirmed the similar tendency in the magnitude estimation of the perceived force in either direction, where the fitted model's power exponents were 1.08 (left direction) and 1.03 (right direction). These results show the proposed buttock skin stretch device has the good reproducibility of the induced forces. It suggests that the proposed calibration method of the initial contact points worked well.

The second experiments investigated the bias effect of the buttock skin stretch to the self-motion acceleration induced by the vection illusion. The results showed that lateral displacement on buttock skin of 9 mm biased the perceived acceleration more than that of 3 mm. The results suggest the induced shear force by the buttock skin stretch could enhance the perceived acceleration of self-motion. As a limitation of the second experiment, there is a possibility that the intensity of the stimuli might bias the participants' answer. However, we also confirmed a tendency that the small skin stretch has a negative effect on the bias. Amemiya et al. also reported the similar tendency in the bias on the self-motion velocity induced by vibrotactile apparent motion [11]. We need a further investigation towards the details.

To improve the control method of the induced acceleration of self-motion, it is more reasonable to assume that the presented force is proportional to the acceleration in terms of physics. We expect that the relationship investigated in the first experiment can be applied to control the targeted perceived force.

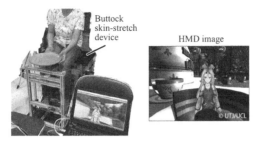

Fig. 10. Application example: virtual riding system of amusement teacup

6   Conclusion

We developed a novel haptic device that provides lateral skin stretches at the user's left and right buttocks, respectively. We conducted two experiments to investigate whether buttock skin stretch would induce the perception of shear force and self-motion. The first experiment evaluated the perceived shear force caused by buttock skin deformation using a magnitude estimation method. The results showed that the displacement of buttock skin stretch increased the perceived shear force. In the second experiment, we investigated whether the representation of buttock skin displacement affected the self-motion perception caused by the visual stimulus of optical flow. The representation of buttock skin stretch did not significantly enhance the self-motion sensation caused by the modulus (no skin stretch). However, we found that the difference in the maximum displacement of buttock skin stretch modulated the perceived acceleration of self-motion. Hence, it is confirmed that buttock skin stretch induced the perception of shear force and affected self-motion perception.

The developed skin stretch device can be extended to a two-dimensional buttock skin stretch device on a transverse plane. A longitudinal skin stretch mechanism will realize longitudinal translational and rotational motions by the same and opposite directional right and left stretches, respectively. The integration of lateral and longitudinal skin stretch devices is expected in future implementation.

The buttock skin stretch device can be a substitute for a motion platform, and is easily used by simply placing it on a chair. We have already tried to apply the skin stretch device to the compact and portable virtual reality system that represents the sensation of riding a teacup in an amusement park (Fig. 10). Skin displacement changes according to the rotational movement of a teacup that a user controls actively or is controlled passively by an avatar, which provides an immersive and interactive haptic experience. Consequently, the buttock skin stretch has a high potential for several applications such as consumer amusement systems and convenient flight or driving simulators.

Acknowledgment. This work was in part supported by ImPACT Program "Tough Robotics Challenge." We would like to thank Akito Nomura, Ayaki Nishimura, and Ren Sugimoto for their assistance in building the buttock skin stretch device.

References

1. Gleeson, B.T., Horschel, S.K., Provancher, W.R.: Design of a fingertip-mounted tactile display with tangential skin displacement feedback. IEEE Trans. Haptics **3**(4), 297–301 (2010)
2. Minamizawa, K., Fukamachi, S., Kajimoto, H., Kawakami, N., Tachi, S.: Gravity grabber: wearable haptic display to present virtual mass sensation. In: ACM SIGGRAPH 2007 Emerging Technologies. ACM (2007). Article no. 8
3. Prattichizzo, D., Chinello, F., Pacchierotti, C., Malvezzi, M.: Towards wearability in fingertip haptics: a 3-DoF wearable device for cutaneous force feedback. IEEE Trans. Haptics **6**(4), 506–516 (2013)
4. Schorr, S.B., Quek, Z.F., Nisky, I., Provancher, W.R., Okamura, A.M.: Tactor-induced skin stretch as a sensory substitution method in teleoperated palpation. IEEE Trans. Hum. Mach. Syst. **45**(6), 714–726 (2015)
5. Guinan, A.L., Montandon, M.N., Doxon, A.J., Provancher, W.R.: Discrimination thresholds for communicating rotational inertia and torque using differential skin stretch feedback in virtual environments. In: 2014 IEEE Haptics Symposium (HAPTICS), pp. 277–282, February 2014
6. Wheeler, J., Bark, K., Savall, J., Cutkosky, M.: Investigation of rotational skin stretch for proprioceptive feedback with application to myoelectric systems. IEEE Trans. Neural Syst. Rehabil. Eng. **18**(1), 58–66 (2010)
7. Chinello, F., Pacchierotti, C., Bimbo, J., Tsagarakis, N.G., Prattichizzo, D.: Design and evaluation of a wearable skin stretch device for haptic guidance. IEEE Rob. Autom. Lett. **3**(1), 524–531 (2018)
8. Berthoz, A., Pavard, B., Young, L.: Perception of linear horizontal self-motion induced by peripheral vision (linearvection) basic characteristics and visual-vestibular interactions. Exp. Brain Res. **23**(5), 471–489 (1975)
9. Valjamae, A., Larsson, P., Vastfjall, D., Kleiner, M.: Travelling without moving: auditory scene cues for translational self-motion. Georgia Institute of Technology (2005)
10. Maeda, T., Ando, H., Sugimoto, M.: Virtual acceleration with galvanic vestibular stimulation in a virtual reality environment. In: 2005 Proceedings of the Virtual Reality, VR 2005, pp. 289–290. IEEE (2005)
11. Amemiya, T., Hirota, K., Ikei, Y.: Tactile apparent motion on the torso modulates perceived forward self-motion velocity. IEEE Trans. Haptics **9**(4), 474–482 (2016)
12. Riecke, B.E., Väljamäe, A., Schulte-Pelkum, J.: Moving sounds enhance the visually-induced self-motion illusion (circular vection) in virtual reality. ACM Trans. Appl. Percept. (TAP) **6**(2), 7 (2009)
13. Paré, M., Carnahan, H., Smith, A.M.: Magnitude estimation of tangential force applied to the fingerpad. Exp. Brain Res. **142**(3), 342–348 (2002)

A Soft Vibrotactile Actuator with Knitted PVC Gel Fabric

Won-Hyeong Park[1], Yongjae Yoo[2], Gobong Choi[1], Seungmoon Choi[2], and Sang-Youn Kim[1(✉)]

[1] Interaction Laboratory, Advanced Research Technology Center,
KOREATECH, 330-708 Cheonan, ChungNam, Korea
sykim@koreatech.ac.kr
[2] Haptic and Virtual Reality Laboratory, Department of Computer Science and Engineering,
POSTECH, 790-784 Pohang, Gyeongbuk, Korea

Abstract. This paper proposes a soft vibrotactile actuator providing users with more functions in less space and improved usability in wearable and/or shape-changing devices. Previously, we have developed a soft vibrotactile actuator based on non-petroleum-based, eco-friendly, and electroactive plasticized poly-vinyl-chloride (PVC) gel formed as wave shape. One of the key differences between the electroactive PVC gel and the traditional electroactive polymers is that PVC gel does not need any stretchable electrodes. Although wave-shaped actuator improves the performance, it is possible that the ridges in PVC gel based actuators will be flayed from the body. In this paper, we introduce a new soft vibrotactile actuator using knitted PVC gel fabric. We measure the displacement of the actuator to quantitatively investigate the performance of the proposed actuator, and furthermore we performed a perceptual evaluation to compare the vibration strength of the proposed actuator and a rigid commercialized actuator. The results show that the proposed actuator can create vibration amplitude strong enough to stimulate human skin.

Keywords: Soft actuator · Tactile · Flexible · Bendable · Vibration · Haptic · VR

1 Introduction

Beyond the rigid frame based electronic mobile devices, recently many users focus on a consumer electronics with flexible frame which has the several advantages of the flexible devices, such as lightweight, flexibility, mobility, thin thickness, and etc. By users' demand, many flexible devices consisting of a flexible battery, a flexible display, a flexible speaker, a flexible electronic circuit, and a flexible touch screen [1–5] are actively being developed. To fabricate flexible haptic actuator, a wide variety of intelligent materials, which can respond to external stimuli such as pH, temperature, light, magnetic field, and electric field, have been intensively studied [6–8]. Among the several smart materials, many researchers have focused on electroactive polymers (EAPs), which are divided into two categories of ionic and non-ionic EAPs, for flexible haptic

© Springer International Publishing AG, part of Springer Nature 2018
D. Prattichizzo et al. (Eds.): EuroHaptics 2018, LNCS 10894, pp. 148–156, 2018.
https://doi.org/10.1007/978-3-319-93399-3_14

actuators. In the case of the ionic EAP represented by ionic polymer-metal composites (IPMC), its shape can be deformed by moving positive ions toward a cathode under electric field. Normally the ionic EAP consists of an ion exchange membrane sandwiched between two electrodes, and it exhibits a large bending displacement in the presence of a low applied voltage (under 5 V). Although the ionic EAP shows large deformation under low voltage, the polyelectrolyte is vulnerable to solvent evaporation and is inevitably accompanied by an electrolysis reaction. So, it is not easy to be embedded into consumer electronic devices. Another weak point is that the force generated from the ionic EAPs is too weak to stimulate human's skin.

In contrast of ionic polymers, non-ionic EAPs have simple configuration, fast response, and high operation efficiency. Furthermore, they are operated in air condition, and their vibrational force is strong enough to stimulate human's skin. For these reasons, the non-ionic EAPs are drawing attention as a material for haptic actuators despite of their high-voltage requirement. Generally, the non-ionic EAP based haptic actuators are composed of two compliant electrodes and a non-ionic EAP membrane. The non-ionic EAP membrane is sandwiched between the two electrodes. When a voltage is applied to the electrodes, the generating electrostatic pressure compresses the dielectric layer in thickness direction and thus the non-ionic EAP expands in planar direction. Furthermore, the non-ionic EAP quickly returns to its original shape as soon as the applied voltage is disappeared. According to this phenomenon, they can make vibrations under AC voltage inputs. However, to increase haptic performance of the non-ionic EAP based actuator, we have to consider a pre-strain procedure [9]. Also, non-ionic EAP has to consider flexible and electrically conductive electrodes to be operated. To solve the problems of the conventional non-ionic EAP, a poly-vinyl chloride gel (PVC gel) has been receiving a great deal of attention as a raw material for a thin film-type soft vibrotactile actuator [10]. When a voltage input is applied to the PVC gel, the PVC gel deforms toward an anode by the movement of the dipoles and PVC chains. Due to this behavior, the PVC gel based vibrotactile actuator does not need not only the compliant electrodes but also the pre-stretching process. A vibrotactile actuator should generate force strong enough to stimulate human skin and should be actuated in a wide frequency range. The PVC gel is sandwiched between two parallel electrodes. To improve the haptic performance of a small and thin vibrotactile actuator, previously we combined more than two phenomena mechanically in the actuators. The first phenomenon is the electric-field-induced deformation of the PVC gel and another effect is electrostatic force in the proposed actuator [10].

Generally, the elastic restoring force is proportional to the displacement. For maximizing the displacement in a small and thin actuator, wave-shaped PVC gel, which has valleys and ridges, was designed [10]. Even though we can improve the haptic performance of the PVC gel based actuator, the wave-shaped actuator brought a new problem. There is a possibility that the ridges in PVC gel based actuators will be flayed from the body. In order to overcome the limitation, we propose a new vibrotactile actuator using a knitted PVC gel fabric. To investigate whether the proposed knitted PVC gel fabric can be used for a soft vibrotactile actuator or not, we carried out experiments. Furthermore, we perform a perceptual evaluation to compare the vibration strength of the proposed actuator and a rigid commercialized actuator. According to these experiments, we show that the proposed actuator can be used for flexible devices.

2   Design and Fabrication of a Knitted PVC Gel Fabric Based Soft Vibrotactile Actuator

Acetyl tributyl citrate (ATBC, Sigma-Aldrich), which is known as an eco-friendly green plasticizer [11], polyvinyl chloride (PVC, Sigma-Aldrich, Mw = ~282,000) powders, and tetrahydrofuran (THF, Sigma-Aldrich, 99.9%) as a solvent were prepared to fabricate a PVC gel. Figure 1 shows the fabrication process of the PVC gel. The ATBC and the PVC powders were inserted into the exceed THF, and they were stirred during 4 h in an air condition for completely dissolving them into the THF. The well-mixed PVC-ATBC solution was poured into a flat Teflon dish, and the solution was evaporated in a fume hood during 48 h for completely evaporating the THF solvent. After the evaporation, we detached the PVC gel from the Teflon dish, and then cut the PVC gel in rectangular whose size is 25 mm (height) × 2 mm (width) × 2 mm (thickness). Finally, knitted PVC gel fabric could be obtained after weaving the long and slender PVC gel strips.

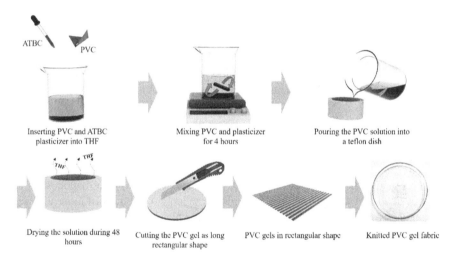

Fig. 1. Fabrication process of the proposed knitted PVC gel fabric.

Figure 2 shows the overall structure of the knitted PVC gel fabric based soft vibrotactile actuator. The proposed actuator is composed of an upper layer, a rectangular double-sided adhesive tape, a knitted PVC gel fabric, and a lower layer (Fig. 2(a)). The upper layer is composed of an actuation membrane, four flexible bridges, a flexible frame, and an input terminal (Fig. 2(b)). We applied a gold electrode on the lower side of the actuation membrane for the upper layer (and on the upper side of the actuation membrane for the lower layer). Figure 2(c) shows the fabricated soft vibrotactile actuator. The size of the actuation membrane is 23 mm (width) × 23 mm (height) × 1 mm

(thickness), and the total size of the actuator except input terminal is 36 mm (width) ×
36 mm (height) × 1 mm (thickness). The cross-sectional view of the proposed actuator
is shown in Fig. 2(d). As we mentioned before, knitted PVC gel fabric was sandwiched
between two electrodes (in the upper and lower layers). In this structure, the upper layer
and the lower layer are used for a cathode and an anode, respectively.

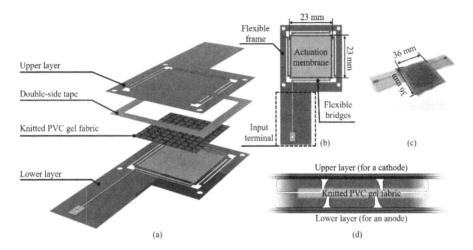

Fig. 2. Overall structure of the proposed soft vibrotactile actuator based on knitted PVC gel
fabric. (a) The perspective view of the proposed actuator. (b) Composition of the upper and lower
layers. (c) Fabricated knitted PVC gel fabric based soft vibrotactile actuator. (d) Cross-sectional
illustration of the proposed actuator. (Color figure online)

Under voltage input, the PVC gel deforms toward an anode by moving the dipoles
with PVC chains [12]. We called it electric-field-induced deformation. Figure 2(d)
shows the cross-sectional view of the proposed actuator where two long and slender
PVC gels are twisted. We applied the anode to the electrode in the lower layer (colored
in red) and the applied the cathode to the electrode in the upper layer (colored in black).
When a voltage input is applied to the actuator, twisted two PVC gel deformed toward
the anode by the electric-field-induced deformation of the PVC gel. According to this
electric-field-induced deformation, the thickness of the actuator becomes thinner. As we
can see in Fig. 2(d), there are two parallel electrodes in the actuator. Due to the parallel
electrodes, electrostatic force is created between the upper layer and the lower layer.
The electrostatic force makes the actuation part move downward. Because two
phenomena are merged in the proposed actuator, we can improve its performance. As
soon as we remove the voltage input, the twisted PVC gel quickly returns to its initial
shape by the elastic restoring force. Therefore, under AC voltage input, the actuator
vibrates.

3   Vibrotactile Performance of the Proposed Actuator

Displacement behavior was measured for investigating the characteristics of the proposed soft actuator. We constructed an experimental environment consisting of a function generator (Agilent 33220A), a high voltage amplifier (trek 20/20), a proposed soft vibrotactile actuator based on knitted PVC gel fabric, a laser scanning vibrometer (PSV-500), a data management system (Vibrometer Front-End), and a PC. An AC voltage input is created by the function generator and then is conveyed to the high voltage amplifier to be amplified 1000 times. The AC voltage input is also transmitted to the data management system. The amplified input signal is applied to the proposed actuator, and the transmitted input voltage signal to the data management system is displayed on a PC. In vibrating, the laser scanning vibrometer measures the displacement of the actuator. The measured displacement signal was transmitted to the data management system, and the signal was displayed on the PC. Therefore, we can simultaneously observe and compare two signals (input voltage and the measured displacement).

In this experiment, a square wave input of frequency 1 Hz was applied to our flexible actuator. Note that the actuation layer moves down and then back to the initial state because of the contraction force produced by the electrostatic effect between the negative and positive electrodes. The displacement of the actuation layer increases monotonically with the amplitude of electric potential. Figure 3(a) shows that the measured displacement was increased from 0.242 μm (200 V) to 21.63 μm (1500 V) for the input with frequency 1 Hz. We also measured the maximum displacements of the proposed actuator from 1 Hz to 300 Hz interval with 10 Hz (Fig. 3(b)). This test was done in five times in constant temperature of 25 °C, and relative humidity of 50% and then the values reported were an average of the five tests. The input voltage was fixed at 1500 V. The error bar means the standard deviation of the displacement.

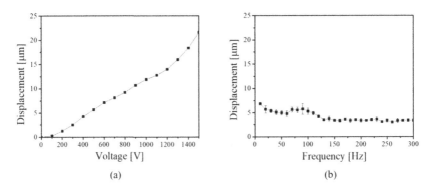

Fig. 3. Displacement of the proposed knitted PVC gel fabric based soft vibrotactile actuator. (a) and (b) are displacement behaviors according to input voltage sweep and frequency sweep, respectively.

The proposed actuator has a great advantage of flexibility, but its vibrating part is inevitably light. The light apparent mass at contact would cause an adverse effect on the skin stimulation. Hence, the perceptual strength of vibration that users feel with our flexible actuator can be lower than other heavier actuators if the vibration strength of a soft actuator is same as that of a rigid actuator. In addition, the contact area of our soft actuator on the skin varies during stimulation due to the flexibility, whereas solid contactors maintain the same contact area. So, in this section, we conducted an experiment to find the point of subjective equality (PSE).

Thirteen university students (11 males and 2 females; 21–31 years old with an average of 24.5) participated in this experiment. No participants reported a sensory disorder. They were paid 10,000 KRW (about 10 USD) after the experiment. Two actuators were used in this experiment. One was our flexible actuator with a custom power amplifier for standard stimuli. The other one was a mechanical mini-shaker (Brüel and Kjær, model 4810; dynamic mass of 20 g, including a 22 mm × 22 mm plastic contactor) with an amplifier (Brüel and Kjær, model 2709) for generating comparison stimuli. All stimuli were controlled by a computer via a 16-bit data acquisition board (National Instrument, USB-6251). An earmuff (3M, Optime 98) was used to prevent the effects of external auditory noises. Each participant placed his/her index finger on the flexible actuator and another index finger on the mini-shaker to perceive stimuli. The stimulus locations were counterbalanced between participants. They were instructed not to move their index fingers to the best of their ability to maintain the same contact condition during each staircase series of trials (the left panel of Fig. 4).

The 1-up, 1-down interleaved adaptive staircase procedure [13] was used to measure the PSE of comparison stimuli to the standard stimulus (see the right panel of Fig. 4). The vibrotactile stimuli used in the experiment had one of four frequencies (70, 100, 200, and 300 Hz). For each frequency, the standard stimulus was presented by our actuator with the amplitude of 1.5 kV_{p-p} in a sinusoidal waveform. Comparison stimuli were provided by the mini-shaker at the same frequency, but with varying amplitudes. The initial amplitude of comparison stimuli was randomly chosen between 0.5 and 0.6 g (measured with an accelerometer (Kistler, 8794A500) attached on the mini-shaker) for downward staircases and between 0.03 to 0.05 g for upward staircases. Each stimulus was 1 s long, and inter-stimulus interval (ISI) was 0.2 s.

On each trial, a participant perceived two vibrations and reported to the experimenter which one was stronger. The experimenter entered the participant's response to the computer, after which the next trial began. If the participant answered that the comparison stimulus was perceived stronger, its amplitude decreased by a certain step size in the next trial. In the case of weaker comparison stimuli, the amplitude of the next comparison stimulus increased by the same step size.

The initial step size was 4 dB, and it was halved after every response reversal for each staircase (4, 2, 1, 0.5, and 0.25 dB). Each of upward and downward staircases was terminated after five respective response reversals were observed. The PSE was taken as the average of the last three reversal points of both upward and downward staircases.

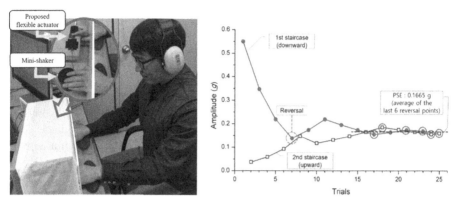

Fig. 4. Experimental setup (left) and an illustration of interleaved staircase procedure (right).

Two cases in the within-trial presentation order of two stimuli (the standard stimulus first or the comparison first) and another two cases in the initial direction of staircases (downward first or upward first) were tested with each participant, resulting in four PSE estimates for each frequency. The PSE for a frequency was calculated by the average of the four. Thus, the main experiment consisted of a total of 16 staircases per participant. Prior to the main experiment, participants went through a training session with four randomly selected staircases. The presentation order was randomized. A 2-min break was given to participants after finishing every four staircases. After the experiment, participants described the sensations that they perceived from the vibrations produced by each actuator. The experiment was done within an hour for a participant.

The contact forces of the participants measured before the main experiment are ranged from 0.07 to 0.43 N with a mean of 0.25 N. All participants reported that they could perceive clear stimuli generated by both actuators. The mean PSEs measured in the experiment are shown as a box plot in Fig. 5. The mean PSEs were 0.098 g for 70 Hz, 0.094 g for 100 Hz, 0.095 g for 200 Hz, and 0.152 g for 300 Hz. This means that our flexible actuator perceived as strong as the vibrations of amplitude 0.1–0.15 g generated by the shaker that had the dynamic mass of 20 g. They cannot be said as strong, but they are sufficient for clear perception (about 10 dB SL for all the frequencies, calculated from [14]). Therefore, our flexible actuator could become good use cases where the flexibility is required but excessive contact force is not applied. For example, smart-watches, smart clothes, and haptic VR suits can be nice application areas of our flexible actuator.

Participants reported that our flexible actuator tended to impart light and shivering sensation, that is quite different from typical vibrotactile sensations they have been felt. It seems that the lightweight of actuating part causes the phenomenon, and it is an interesting topic to be investigated. Also, widening the designing space of vibrotactile stimuli by utilizing both traditional actuators and flexible actuator would be a plausible approach in HCI and VR applications.

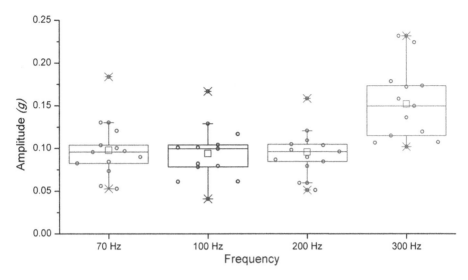

Fig. 5. Box plot of the 13 participants' PSEs. Squares: means, boxes: 25 to 75 percentile points, centerlines in the boxes: medians, X marks: 1 and 99 percentile points.

4 Conclusion

According to the advance of hardware technology, we can easily imagine a life with flexible devices that can be easily bent or rolled. To fabricate a soft and flexible actuator, in this paper, we made a long and slender PVC gels and then weaved the gels into knitted PVC gel fabric. Based on the PVC gel fabric, we developed a tiny and thin soft actuator that can selectively stimulate human mechanoreceptors. Due to the electric-field-induced deformation of the PVC gel and the electrostatic attraction force, proposed actuator could create vibration signal with large frequency bandwidth. The experiments clearly show that the proposed actuator creates enough output force to stimulate human skin across a large frequency bandwidth and to convey a variety of vibrotactile sensations to users.

Acknowledgements. This research was supported by Institute for Information & communications Technology Promotion (IITP) grant funded by the Korea government (MSIP) (No. 2017-0-00179, HD Haptic Technology for Hyper Reality Contents). This work was also supported by the Industrial Strategic technology development program (10077643, development of shape-adaptive electro-adhesive gripper for grasping arbitrary shaped objects) funded by the Ministry of Trade, industry & Energy (MOTIE, Korea).

References

1. Yoon, J., Kwon, H., Lee, M., Yu, Y., Cheong, N., Min, S., Choi, J., Im, H., Lee, K., Jo, J., Kim, H., Choi, H., Lee, Y., Yoo, C., Kuk, S., Cho, M., Kwon, S., Park, W., Yoon, S., Kang, I., Yeo, S.: 65.1: Invited Paper: World 1st Large Size 18-inch Flexible OLED Display and the Key Technologies. SID Symposium Digest of Technical Papers, vol. 46(1) (2015)

2. Kim, J.-S., Ko, D., Yoo, D.-J., Jung, D.S., Yavuz, C.T., Kim, N.-I., Choi, I.-S., Song, J.Y., Choi, J.W.: A half millimeter thick coplanar flexible battery with wireless recharging capability. Nano Lett. **15**(4), 2350–2357 (2015)

3. Yao, X., Jia, T., Xie, C., Fu, J., He, Y.: Facial fabrication of paper-based flexible electronics with flash foam stamp lithography. Microsyst. Technol. **20**(10), 4419–4426 (2016)

4. Xu, S.C., Man, B.Y., Jiang, S.Z., Chen, C.S., Yang, C., Liu, M., Gao, X.G., Sun, Z.C., Zhang, C.: Flexible and transparent graphene-based loudspeakers. Appl. Phys. Lett. **102**(15), 151902 (2013)

5. Wang, J., Liang, M., Fang, Y., Qui, T., Zhang, J., Zhi, L.: Rod-coating: towards large-area fabrication of uniform reduced graphene oxide films for flexible touch screens. Adv. Mater. **24**(21), 2874–2878 (2012)

6. Cheng, B., Li, Z., Li, Q., Ju, J., Kang, W., Naebe, M.: Development of smart poly(vinylidene fluoride)-graft-poly(acrylic acid) tree-like nanofiber membrane for pH-responsive oil/water separation. J. Membr. Sci. **534**, 1–8 (2017)

7. Wang, H. S., Cho, J., Song, D. S., Jang, J. H., Jho, J. Y., Park, J. H.: High-performance electroactive polymer actuators based on ultra thick ionic polymer–metal composites with nanodispersed metal electrodes. ACS Appl. Mater. Interfaces. (2017)

8. Pastorczak, M., Okrasa, L., Yoon, J.A., Kowalewski, T., Matyjaszewski, K.: Kinetics of the temperature-induced volume phase transition in poly(2-(2-methoxyethoxy)ethyl methacrylate) hydrogels of various topologies. Polymer **110**, 25–35 (2017)

9. Rosset, S., Shea, H.R.: Small, fast, and tough: shrinking down integrated elastomer transducers. Appl. Phys. Rev. **3**(3) (2016)

10. Park, W.-H., Bae, J.W., Shin, E.-J., Kim, S.-Y.: Development of a flexible and bendable vibrotactile actuator based on wave-shaped poly(vinyl chloride)/acetyl tributyl citrate gels for wearable electronic devices. Smart Mater. Struct. **25**(11), 115020 (2016)

11. Zhang, X., Li, Y., Hankett, J.M., Chen, Z.: The molecular interfacial structure and plasticizer migration behavior of green' plasticized poly(vinyl chloride). Phys. Chem. Chem. Phys. **17**, 4472–4482 (2015)

12. Shin, E.-J., Bae, J.W., Jeong, J., Choi, D.-S., Lee, J.E., Nam, B.U., Lin, L., Kim, S.-Y.: High-performance PVC gel for adaptive micro-lenses with variable focal length. Sci. Rep. **7** (2017)

13. Leek, M.R.: Adaptive procedures in psychophysical research. Attention Percept. Psychophysics **63**(8), 1279–1292 (2001)

14. Ryu, J., Jung, J., Park, G., Choi, S.: Psychophysical model for vibrotactile rendering in mobile devices. Presence Teleoperators Virtual Environ. **19**(4), 364–387 (2010)

A Tangible Surface for Digital Sculpting in Virtual Environments

Edouard Callens[1], Fabien Danieau[2(✉)], Antoine Costes[2,3],
and Philippe Guillotel[2]

[1] INSA Lyon, Villeurbanne, France
[2] Technicolor, Cesson-Sévigné, France
fabien.danieau@technicolor.com
[3] IRISA/Inria, Rennes, France

Abstract. With the growth of virtual reality setups, digital sculpting tools become more and more immersive. It is now possible to create a piece of art within a virtual environment, directly with the controllers. However, these devices do not allow to touch the virtual material as a sculptor would do. To tackle this issue we investigate in this paper the use of a tangible surface that could be used in virtual reality setups. We designed a low-cost prototype composed of two layers of sensors in order to measure a wide range of pressure. We also propose two mapping techniques to fit our device to a virtual 3D mesh to be sculpted. Participants of an informal test were asked to reproduce a pattern on three meshes: a plane, a sphere and a teapot. They succeeded in this task, showing the potential of our approach.

Keywords: Tangible interface · Haptic sculpting
Virtual environment

1 Introduction

With the recent technological developments in Virtual Reality (VR), users can now naturally interact with 3D content: they are fully immersed in virtual environments where they can walk around and manipulate 3D objects. Relying on this technology, first tools are already available to enable content creation. Using controllers, a user can paint or sculpt virtual objects. Although this approach is more intuitive than using a keyboard and a mouse, it is still far away from the direct hand manipulation and it lacks touch feedback [9].

In line with this observation, research has been conducted for decades to improve the creation of 3D models of objects and characters. The manipulation of complex data like those is addressed by the research field of Tangible Interfaces [12], enabling users to naturally manipulate physical objects mapped to virtual ones. Numerous materials have been experimented to manipulate 3D models through physical devices, from curved rubber tape [2] to fabric [7]. Nevertheless there are still challenges to tackle to design a device allowing to sculpt

© Springer International Publishing AG, part of Springer Nature 2018
D. Prattichizzo et al. (Eds.): EuroHaptics 2018, LNCS 10894, pp. 157–168, 2018.
https://doi.org/10.1007/978-3-319-93399-3_15

any 3D model in a large scale virtual environment. First the hardware should be light enough to be held and displaced around a 3D model. Second the mapping of the device onto a 3D model must be explicit enough and fit any shape.

In this context, we propose a new device that users can touch and press to sculpt a 3D mesh with their bare fingers. The device is a surface composed of foam and two layers of pressure sensitive materials: a custom fabric-based pressure matrix relying on Velostat and a matrix of FSRs (Force Sensitive Resistor). The top layer handles light pressure and localization, while the bottom layer handles medium and strong pressure. This device is connected to a 3D modeling environment, where it is represented by a proxy. Two mapping methods between this proxy and the 3D mesh to be modified were designed to fit the two shapes.

2   Related Work

This research work focuses on tangible interfaces for virtual sculpting, where an input device represents a 3D object. The concept of virtual clay has been extensively studied by Ishii et al. with their Illuminating Clay and SandScape [5]. The users alter the topography of a clay or sand landscape model with their hands. Meanwhile the changing geometry is captured in real-time by a ceiling-mounted laser scanner or IR (infra-red) light sensing technology. This technology is well adapted for the manipulation of landscape-like shapes but hardly adaptable to a random 3D object. Besides, it is not possible to manipulate an existing object. In a similar way, Tabrizian et al. use a malleable surface to enable the creation of virtual landscape [14]. In addition to the modeling, the user can select a tool to add grass, water or routes. The final model can be directly viewed within a head mounted display. More flexible systems based on a deformable membrane allowing to change the shape of a 3D object were proposed [3,15]. The mapping of the physical to the virtual surface is direct: bumps are created according to the pressure distribution on the surface. The SOFTii prototype, based on conductive foam, is also a flexible interface although it has not been applied to sculpting [10].

Other materials have been embedded in tangible interfaces. Hook et al. designed a reconfigurable tactile surface based on ferromagnetic technology [4]. This approach is still a proof-of-concept but the authors showed that it might be applicable for virtual sculpting. Foam is also a suitable material for a sculpting device [8]. The user removes part of an actual foam which is tracked and digitally represented. While intuitive, this system does not allow to undo an operation or to work on existing 3D models.

In their review on tangible user interfaces, Shaer and Hornecker pointed out the issue of mapping a physical device to digital information [12]. The direct mapping where the device fully represents the digital information is the more intuitive for the user. But when they cannot be mapped (in the case of abstract digital information for instance), indirect mapping or metaphor has to be used. In the context of virtual sculpting, indirect mapping is necessary when the physical object cannot perfectly match any 3D model. The work of Sheng et al. evokes the idea of a proxy representing the physical device in the virtual world [13]. It helps users to understand how they can interact within this world and how this proxy can be mapped to a virtual object. The authors proposed a global non-linear mapping and three local relative mappings. Although they detailed the advantages and limitations of each mapping they did not evaluated them.

3   Tangible Surface for 3D Sculpting

The overview of our system is depicted in Fig. 1. First, a multi-layered and multi-cells device has been designed, based on pressure sensors. The pressure measurements, forwarded to a computer, are pre-processed and filtered by a Processing code providing a pressure and position estimation to the virtual environment (VE) running under Unity3D[1]. In this VE, a proxy represents the physical device. The user may adjust the mapping of the proxy to a target mesh, and press the physical device to deform this mesh.

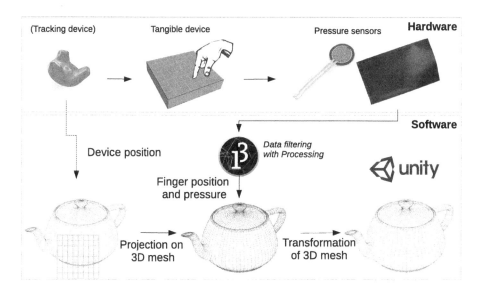

Fig. 1. Workflow overview. The tangible interface is made of foam and pressure sensors (FSRs and Velostat). A proxy maps the physical device to the virtual object surface.

This prototype was designed in such a way that it could be attached to an existing VR controller. Thus, it relies on low cost technology that is light, robust and easily powered. In this work we were interested in the tangible surface itself and therefore we did not consider the tracking part.

---

[1] https://unity3d.com.

3.1 Hardware

Our approach is inspired from the multi-cells architecture [11,16], where several pressure sensors are arranged in a 2D array in order to estimate the pressure location. To provide a wide range of pressure values, a 2-layers matrix architecture has been used (see Fig. 2). The top layer handles light pressures and touch localization, while the bottom layer handles middle and intense pressures with lower localization accuracy.

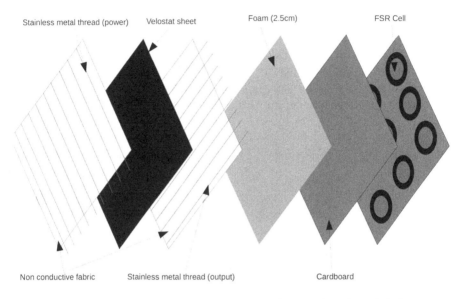

Stainless metal thread (power)   Velostat sheet   Foam (2.5cm)   FSR Cell

Non conductive fabric   Stainless metal thread (output)   Cardboard

Fig. 2. The multi-layers architecture. The top layer (Velostat) deals with light pressure and touch localization, while the second layer (FSR) handles stronger pressures.

Both layers have been designed as a matrix configuration. To get a high accuracy for the position value, a line per line scanning method has been preferred to independent wiring, arranged in a two-dimensional grid. Each cell can thus be addressed by sharing a common electrode per column and sharing the other one per line with a single voltage divider. Connecting alternatively each column to V_{in} and measuring the voltage V on each line allows to scan the whole matrix.

Top Layer: Light Pressure Sensing and Localization. The upper layer is a custom pressure sensor made of Velostat fabric, in-between two grids of stainless steel perpendicular lines. The Velostat sheet is a piezo-resistive material made of carbonized polymer that have its resistance changing depending on the applied pressure. Layered between the two electrodes grids, it acts like a variable resistor.

The resistance value is captured by a micro-controller using a simple voltage divider. The Velostat, variable resistor R_{var}, is connected between an input voltage V_{in} and a resistor R connected to the ground. The voltage V between the R poles is measured thanks to an analog digital converter (ADC) integrated into the micro-controller. The ADC gives a digital value proportional to the measured voltage in the range $[0\text{–}V_{in}]$. V follows the voltage divider equation defined as:

$$V = V_{in}\frac{R}{R + R_{var}} \tag{1}$$

As described, the Velostat is stacked between two grids of conductors (see Fig. 2). The columns of steel thread on the top grid power each cell, while the lines of conductor on the bottom grid provide the voltage value. The conductive wire has been sewed on a regular cotton fabric in narrow lines. This leads to a resolution suitable for position tracking, as well as it provides a nicer tactile sensation than other materials like foam. The sewing was made to get the conductive Velostat in contact with the thread, while being isolated from the user's fingers. Additional detachable clips were also sewed with the conductive thread on the fabric for an easy connection with the other parts of the system, as shown in Fig. 3.

Fig. 3. From left to right: overview of the Velostat layer, close up of Velostat sheet and fabric underneath, close up of the detachable clips.

Because of the number of pins (9 columns + 9 lines = 18 pins), a multiplexer is used to simplify the sensing process. It is based on Adafruits ADS1015 breakouts, more specifically, a 12-bit 4 channels ADC multiplexer communicating in I2C to the micro-controller, including its own ADC converter. Up to four boards with different I2C addresses can be used together, providing 16 analog channels, which is enough for the size of the matrix. On the top grid, a regular 16 channels multiplexer is used to power each line independently, while the others are set to high impedance.

Figure 4 shows a measurement of the Velostat resistance over time. A pressure was linearly (as much as possible) applied with one finger.

Bottom Layer: Intense Pressure Sensing. The bottom layer embeds a 3×3 *Interlink 402 FSRs* matrix of round pressure sensors (see Fig. 5). The 3×3 matrix between a layer of foam and a rigid material surface allows to get a uniform distribution of the pressure, even if FSRs detect local pressures. The foam also provides a passive haptic feedback. The same idea, as for the top layer of line scanning, is used to scan the 3×3 matrix using the microcontroller pins to power the columns and reading the 10-bits ADC values. Figure 4 shows the resistance of one FSR sensor over time. The resistance range is two orders of magnitude higher than the Velostat one, but it reaches faster a minimum resistance. Hence, this layer is more suitable for high pressure sensing.

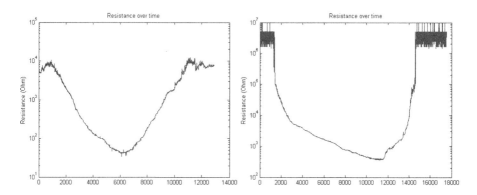

Fig. 4. Resistance over time for the Velostat (left) and for one FSR unit (right).

Micro-controller. The micro-controller board used is a Teensy 3.1, based on the Cortex-M4 chip. The Arduino IDE code is supported through the Tennsy-duino add-on. This leads to a full device capable of sensing a wide range of pressure on a 2D array (Fig. 5). By optimizing ADCs conversion time and I2C communications, the full scan of all the matrices cells takes 90 ms, leading to a 11 Hz refreshing rate which is enough for finger interactions [6].

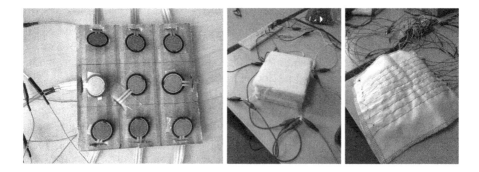

Fig. 5. Left: the 3×3 FSR matrix on a rigid surface. Middle: the bottom layer and foam. Right: the final device on which the user interacts.

3.2   Software

Driver and Filtering. With I2C boards and matrices cells addresses set up, a dedicated program scans the lines of the two matrices, reads and arranges the data. The ADS1015 ADC output data are converted to 10-bit resolution values providing a 3.3 V range. Then the values are packed into OSC messages, transmitted to the PC over USB using the SLIP[2] encapsulated serial communication protocol.

After the SLIP encapsulated serial message is decoded, the raw pressure values are directly filtered in Processing with a 1€ filter [1]. It is an adaptive low-pass filter specifically designed for interactive systems. Easily configurable, two parameters control static jitter and lag. It provides satisfactory results with minor tweaks and is reliable with fast and slow movements on the device (this filter adapts its cut-off frequency depending on the speed of the input). The next step maps the data value from a 10-bit integer to a floating-point number in the range [0–1].

The finger position is computed using the top layer data (with the Velostat). The barycenter of the cells closed to the touch point (selected as the highest pressure value on the matrix) is computed as the final finger position. Finally, the global pressure is computed as an average between the top layer pressure (Velostat) and the bottom layer pressure (FSR matrix). Only cells above a certain threshold are taken into account.

Virtual Environment and Proxy. The virtual environment has been prototyped with Unity3D. The device is manipulated through a proxy that takes the form of a semi-transparent square plane (Fig. 6). The key challenge here is to map this planar proxy to any target mesh to be sculpted (parametrization problem). Besides the mapping has to be explicit enough for the users to know what they are manipulating.

The mapping consists in two steps. First, there is an alignment between the proxy and the expected virtual object location. The current prototype is not yet tracked in space, the user has to manually place the proxy on the target mesh. To do so, the user selects a vertex on the target mesh with the mouse, then the center of the proxy is matched to the vertex position. The proxy is also rotated so that the normal of its central vertex is aligned to the normal of the target vertex as shown in Fig. 6.

The second step is the geometrical morphing of the proxy to the virtual object mesh. Two solutions have been implemented. The first technique consists in a **projection** of the proxy onto the targeted mesh. Each vertex of the proxy iteratively casts a ray along its normal in direction of the target mesh. If the ray hits a part of the target mesh, the vertex moves along the ray towards the target mesh as seen Fig. 7.

The second technique adds an extra **wrapping** step. The goal is to wrap the proxy around the object, for a better accuracy in small parts of a target mesh

---

[2] Serial Line Interface Protocol, see https://github.com/CNMAT/OSC.

Fig. 6. Left: Proxy aligned to a side of a teapot mesh. Right: Proxy aligned to the top of the teapot.

Fig. 7. Projection mapping. The proxy is mapped onto the surface of the teapot. Each iteration moves the vertices in the direction of the target mesh normal vectors. (a) Initial position, (b) Halfway through the process, (c) Completely mapped proxy.

(like the teapot handle for instance). Each vertex of the device is scanned from the central vertex to the edges in a circular manner. For each, a ray along its normal is cast, and its normal is aligned to the normal of the hit point. Then, the vertex is moved following previous method, along the normal. All vertices not scanned yet change their normal according to the current one. This way, through the different iterations, the proxy will progressively bend around the targeted mesh as depicted in Fig. 8.

Fig. 8. Wrapping mapping. The proxy is mapped onto the surface of the teapot. Each iteration moves the vertices in the direction of the target mesh normal vectors. (a) Initial position, (b) Halfway through the process, (c) Completely mapped proxy.

Once the proxy matched to the target mesh, the user sculpts the virtual object with simple stroke and press gestures on the device, altering the mesh in the area delimited by the mapped proxy. The effect on the mesh is determined by a radius parameter and a deformation speed parameter. Each vertex is moved along the average normal direction computed in the radius around the hit point, with a weighting factor related to the distance to the hit point.

4   Results

A pilot test has been conducted to investigate the usability of our prototype, and the influence of the mapping on a sculpting task. In this study, only the top layer with the Velostat was used, as it provides localization and enough pressure information to perform a simple sculpting task. Six participants, including one female, have taken part into the test.

A simple 3D scene has been created in which the user can deform one object (a plane, a sphere or a teapot). The proxy representing the device is also displayed (such as in Fig. 6). Three mapping techniques were implemented: the two techniques, "projection" and "wrapping", presented above, and a control technique, "no mapping". This latest technique does not change the shape of the proxy. It remains a plane and a ray is also cast to hit a vertex of the target mesh.

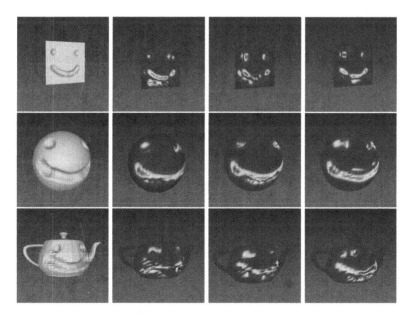

Fig. 9. Results from one participant. From left to right: reference mesh, no mapping condition, wrapping technique and projection technique. Colors go from blue (no difference to the reference) to red (maximum difference, normalized with bounding box). (Color figure online)

Three deformed objects were created with a professional digital sculpting tool (Sculptris[3]). They served as a reference that the participants had to reproduce (Fig. 9 - Left column). The pattern to sculpt was a smiley face on the round or flat part of the objects. This particular shape was chosen to see if the participants could use the whole area of the physical device and trace lines on a curved object.

Once the task completed, we first performed a visual analysis of the meshes deformed by the participants. The Hausdorff distance to the reference was computed with Meshlab and the meshes were colorized accordingly (see Fig. 9). All participants succeeded to complete the task: the features of the pattern, eye and smile, are present on the output meshes. Yet, from this visual analysis, we cannot conclude that one method outperformed another.

We also observed that on the sphere and the teapot, resulting patterns seem to be more centered or compact than on the references. This is probably because the proxy had to be moved or rescaled to perform the task on these objects. By default the proxy was too small to cover the area needed to reproduce accurately the whole pattern. Then, a strategy often adopted by participants was to draw the entire pattern after having moved the proxy.

Finally, we looked at the average time spent by the participants on each object. No significant difference was observed, letting us believe that the mapping techniques seems to not decrease the user's performance.

5   Discussion

This first test provided interesting insights that will be taken into consideration to improve our setup. Overall, we observed that the participants succeeded to reproduce the pattern created with a digital sculpting software. At first, the participants directly tried to reproduce the reference shape. Then they erased these attempts, first because of a misplacement of the eyes, then because of a misplacement of the smile. Eventually the participants made something they liked and went to the next object. This observation illustrates well the mapping issue between our flat device and a random object. Interestingly we noticed two strategies to draw the curved line representing the smile. Half of the participants were using a continuous movement pressure on the device, drawing the line in one single gesture. The others were tracing the line by applying multiple touches on the device, forming a series of little holes on the resulted mesh eventually forming a smile.

From the interviews, it seems that working with a mapping technique allows the participant to subjectively feel more efficient with the device. Participants reported that the interaction was perceived as more comfortable and better understood. Further studies are however needed to establish the efficiency difference between the two mapping techniques. To differentiate these techniques, a larger set of objects has to be used, including objects with concavity. Obviously more participants are required to properly evaluate the device, but their

---

[3] http://pixologic.com/sculptris.

expertise should be carefully identified. Professional 3D artists using tablets are familiar with 3D interaction through planar devices.

A visual guide could be displayed both on the physical device and the proxy in order to help the user. Such a guide could be a grid printed on the device that would be deformed on the proxy. Also the top layer, sensible to light touch, could be used to indicate the user's finger location and the deformation would be only triggered when the bottom layer is activated (stronger pressure).

The use of this two-layer configuration should be also investigated. In this work we made sure that the top layer is enough to perform a sculpting task. The bottom layer would easily extend the pressure amplitude. But other interactions could be designed. Fine details could be edited with the top layer (as a knife would cut clay) while rough details may be handled by the bottom layer (as if a finger presses clay).

In our current implementation the device is a planar surface, but it could easily be shaped differently such as a sphere or a half-sphere with the same sensors and materials. A specific shape could be more adapted to a target model. For instance a sphere would be suitable for face modeling while a plane to landscape modeling. More investigation are to be conducted to determine the limits of the mapping and in which case the shape of the device must be changed.

Finally, the device is currently suitable for interaction with one finger. It can be extended to multiple fingers. For example, blob detection could detect multiple finger inputs on the device. With this feature more interaction techniques could also be supported such as twisting, bending or stretching a 3D mesh.

6   Conclusions and Perspectives

In this paper, we introduced a low-cost tactile surface device designed to sculpt 3D meshes. It is composed of two layers of sensors to spatially capture both light touch and strong pressure. We also proposed two methods to map the planar device to an arbitrary 3D mesh. Finally we identified in an informal user test the strengths and weaknesses of the device. In this test participants succeeded in sculpting a pattern on various virtual objects.

This work is a first step toward an intuitive mesh manipulation within virtual environments, and highlights many aspects to be studied. Our fabric-based approach allows for a variety of device shapes, which raises several questions: should the device be flat or curved? Could it handles other gestures, like squeeze or pinch? In a next step, the device will be tracked in space. Added to standard VR controllers like the Oculus touch or the Vive controller, it could be usable inside Unity3D in a straightforward way. Such a setup would be relevant for the already existing sculpting or painting tools.

References

1. Casiez, G., Roussel, N., Vogel, D.: 1€ filter: a simple speed-based low-pass filter for noisy input in interactive systems. In: Proceedings of the SIGCHI Conference on Human Factors in Computing Systems, pp. 2527–2530. ACM (2012)

2. Grossman, T., Balakrishnan, R., Singh, K.: An interface for creating and manipulating curves using a high degree-of-freedom curve input device. In: Proceedings of the SIGCHI Conference on Human Factors in Computing Systems, pp. 185–192. ACM (2003)

3. Han, J., Gu, J., Lee, G.: Trampoline: a double-sided elastic touch device for creating reliefs. In: Proceedings of the 27th Annual ACM Symposium on User Interface Software and Technology, UIST 2014, pp. 383–388. ACM (2014)

4. Hook, J., Taylor, S., Butler, A., Villar, N., Izadi, S.: A reconfigurable ferromagnetic input device. In: Proceedings of the 22nd Annual ACM Symposium on User Interface Software and Technology, pp. 51–54. ACM (2009)

5. Ishii, H., Ratti, C., Piper, B., Wang, Y., Biderman, A., Ben-Joseph, E.: Bringing clay and sand into digital design continuous tangible user interfaces. BT Technol. J. **22**(4), 287–299 (2004)

6. Jones, L.A.: Kinesthetic sensing. In: Human and Machine Haptics (2000)

7. Leal, A., Bowman, D., Schaefer, L., Quek, F., Stiles, C.K.: 3D sketching using interactive fabric for tangible and bimanual input. In: Proceedings of Graphics Interface 2011, pp. 49–56. Canadian Human-Computer Communications Society (2011)

8. Marner, M.R., Thomas, B.H.: Augmented foam sculpting for capturing 3D models. In: 2010 IEEE Symposium on 3D User Interfaces (3DUI), pp. 63–70. IEEE (2010)

9. Massie, T.: A tangible goal for 3D modeling. IEEE Comput. Graph. Appl. **18**(3), 62–65 (1998)

10. Nguyen, V., Kumar, P., Yoon, S.H., Verma, A., Ramani, K.: SOFTii: soft tangible interface for continuous control of virtual objects with pressure-based input. In: Proceedings of the Ninth International Conference on Tangible, Embedded, and Embodied Interaction, pp. 539–544. ACM (2015)

11. Saenz-Cogollo, J.F., Pau, M., Fraboni, B., Bonfiglio, A.: Pressure mapping mat for tele-home care applications. Sensors **16**(3), 365 (2016)

12. Shaer, O., Hornecker, E.: Tangible user interfaces: past, present, and future directions. Found. Trends Hum. Comput. Interact. **3**(1–2), 1–137 (2010)

13. Sheng, J., Balakrishnan, R., Singh, K.: An interface for virtual 3D sculpting via physical proxy. GRAPHITE **6**, 213–220 (2006)

14. Tabrizian, P., Petrasova, A., Harmon, B., Petras, V., Mitasova, H., Meentemeyer, R.: Immersive tangible geospatial modeling. In: Proceedings of the 24th ACM SIGSPATIAL International Conference on Advances in Geographic Information Systems, p. 88. ACM (2016)

15. Watanabe, Y., Cassinelli, A., Komuro, T., Ishikawa, M.: The deformable workspace: a membrane between real and virtual space. In: 2008 3rd IEEE International Workshop on Horizontal Interactive Human Computer Systems, TABLETOP 2008, pp. 145–152. IEEE (2008)

16. Zhou, B., Lukowicz, P.: Textile pressure force mapping. In: Schneegass, S., Amft, O. (eds.) Smart Textiles, pp. 31–47. Springer, Cham (2017). https://doi.org/10.1007/978-3-319-50124-6_3

A Tactile Feedback Glove for Reproducing Realistic Surface Roughness and Continual Lateral Stroking Perception

Ping-Hua Lin and Shana Smith[✉]

Department of Mechanical Engineering, National Taiwan University,
Taipei 10617, Taiwan
ssmith@ntu.edu.tw

Abstract. Haptic feedback has been widely applied to many virtual reality (VR) applications and electronic products to offer more information and sensation to users. This research aims to recreate lateral stroking stimuli in a virtual environment using a wearable tactile feedback glove. Tactile perception controlling factors for laterally stroking on physical surfaces with different roughnesses were recorded. A neural network was trained to find the driving voltages for the actuators. Piezoelectric actuators were used to create realistic tactile sensations. Two experiments were conducted. One was the roughness discrimination experiment, which was used to test if the participants can match the simulated roughness with physical templates. The other experiment was the continual lateral stroking experiment, which was used to find a representation method which can give users the most realistic continual stroking sensations. User tests showed that the developed tactile feedback system can reproduce realistic surface roughness sensations.

Keywords: Tactile feedback · Wearable haptic feedback glove
Surface roughness · Lateral stroking · Virtual reality · Neural network

1 Introduction

Over the past decade, virtual reality (VR) has been widely applied to education, job training, medical surgery, entertainment, and military. Other than visual and audio feedback, recently, haptic feedback has drawn a lot of attention for enhancing the realism and immersiveness of the virtual environments.

Haptic feedback can be classified into kinesthetic force feedback and tactile feedback. Kinesthetic feedback is related to human limb position and movement in space [1], and the corresponding mechanoreceptors are in muscles, tendons, and joints. On the other hand, tactile feedback is activated by skin deformation, pressure, and thermo-differences, and its mechanoreceptors are found across the body surface, beneath both hairy and hairless (glabrous) skin.

Although much interest has been placed on the field of kinesthetic force feedback, few design guidelines have been specified regarding creating realistic simulated tactile sensations. In addition, wearable and portable tactile feedback devices have become the

© Springer International Publishing AG, part of Springer Nature 2018
D. Prattichizzo et al. (Eds.): EuroHaptics 2018, LNCS 10894, pp. 169–179, 2018.
https://doi.org/10.1007/978-3-319-93399-3_16

main stream of technology [2]. Thus, light-weight and small volume actuators, such as DC motors, micro speakers, voice coil motors, and piezoelectric actuators, are often used to deliver tactile sensations.

For example, DC motors can provide vertical stress and shear stress to human's fingertips [3–5]. Hashimoto et al. [6] used a speaker to create pushing force and suction force to users' palms. Wu et al. [7] used micro speakers to create complex waveform and provide realistic simulated key click haptic feedback to users. Different actuators can also be integrated to create multiple tactile sensations. For example, Nishimura et al. [8] used a voice coil actuator and two DC motors to render vertical force and tangential force to user's finger.

Compared to other actuators, piezoelectric actuators have the advantages of wide frequency response, fast response time, light weight, and small size. Therefore, some researchers used piezoelectric actuators to create complex vibration waveforms to simulate object surface texture information [9, 10].

However, human's discrimination of object surface texture is not only determined by the physical texture information, but also by the movement patterns of users' hands. Lederman and Klatzky [11] categorized human's typical movement patterns for exploratory procedures into six categories, among which lateral motion is considered as the only exploratory procedure which can perceive object texture information. Moreover, surface roughness is one of the texture information which can be perceived using only vibrotactile stimuli [12].

Surface roughness perception involves relative motions between hands and objects. Although some researchers created vibrotactile travelling waves using different actuators, they only provided simulated dynamic motions on a device [13, 14]. There is very few research concerning creating simulated travelling waves on human hands to create dynamic continual lateral stroking sensations.

Raisamo et al. [15] put three C-2 linear vibrotactile voice coil actuators on participants' arms and used 3 motion presentation methods, saltation, modulation, and hybrid, to test cognition-related scale of continuity and emotion-related scales of pleasantness and arousal. Saltation provides three separate pulses on three actuators. Modulation makes use of dynamic transition of amplitude between the actuators. Hybrid combines separate pulses of saltation to modulation. Raisamo et al. found that the modulation method was rated significantly more continuous and pleasant, compared to saltation and hybrid methods.

Instead of delivering meaningless arousal alarm to users, realistic tactile feedback should not only consider object surface texture characteristics, but also the motion of human hands [16, 17]. In this research, a vibrotactile feedback glove, which can deliver simulated surface roughness and continual lateral stroking perceptions to users in a VR environment, was developed. Unlike mechanoreceptors on arms, the mechanoreceptors on each finger are independent. Therefore, when creating realistic continual lateral stroking movement, users' hand motion directions and speeds needed to be considered.

The organization of this paper is organized as follows. Section 2 gives an overview concerning the hardware and software of the system. Section 3 addresses the surface texture data processing method. Section 4 introduces the user interface. Section 5 mentioned the user tests and test results. Finally, Sect. 6 offers conclusions.

2   System Overview

The system was composed of a tracking interface, a VR interface, and a haptic interface, as shown in Fig. 1. Leap motion was used to track hand position when users interacted with virtual objects. Unity 3D was used as a central hub for detecting collisions and giving commands to the haptic interface. The commands were sent to the MCUs through PC's serial COM port. Then, the digital signals were converted into analog voltage signals and amplified, using a vibration table programmed inside the MCUs. Piezoelectric actuators would receive amplified voltage signals and be activated to create vibrotactile feedback to users.

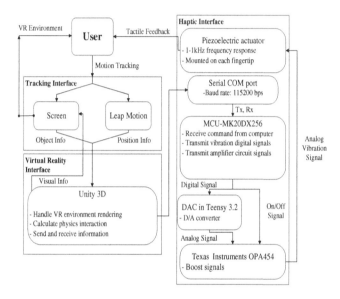

Fig. 1. System flowchart of the haptic feedback system

The wearable tactile feedback glove was composed of three parts, actuator holders, glove body, and piezoelectric actuators, as shown in Fig. 2. The actuator holders were used to mount piezoelectric actuators onto the fingertips. Users' fingertips would be in contact with the end part of the piezoelectric actuators. The piezoelectric actuators worked like a cantilever beam to transmit vibration to users' fingertips. Therefore, users would receive tactile sensations on their fingertips when actuators vibrated. In this research, piezoelectric actuators (V_{pp} = 96 V, length = 38 mm, width = 12 mm) from Unictron Technologies Corp. were used.

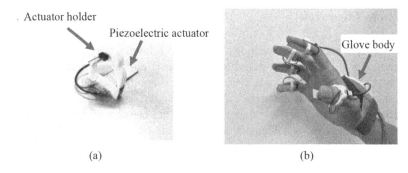

(a)   (b)

Fig. 2. Tactile feedback glove

Figure 3 shows the VR interface developed using Unity3D. Each button was related to a different surface roughness or different lateral stroking presentation method. When a virtual button was clicked, it would activate the MCU to send corresponding driving voltages to vibrate the piezoelectric actuators on the glove. The motions and gestures of the virtual hands were corresponding to the physical hands. Through the VR interface, users would be able to interact with virtual scenes.

Fig. 3. VR interface

3   Texture Data Processing System

The texture data processing system covers texture data recording, texture data training, and texture data reproducing steps.

3.1   Texture Data Recording

Roughness perception can be described as a function of groove width, ridge width, hand moving speed, and fingertip contact force [18–20]. Therefore, other than the roughness characteristic of a surface texture, in this study, hand moving speed and fingertip contact force were considered.

Therefore, while recording surface texture data, tactile perception controlling factors, such like lateral movement speed (v_x), lateral acceleration (a_x), normal contact force (f_n), and vibrotactile acceleration (a_z) should all be recorded. The hand lateral movement speed (v_x) was obtained by the integral of the lateral acceleration (a_x).

Prior research showed that groove width had a stronger impact on roughness perception than ridge width [21]. In this study, three templates with different groove widths, 2 mm, 3 mm, and 4 mm, were tested. The ridge widths of the three templates were all set to 1 mm. The indentation depth and the length of the templates were 2 mm and 120 mm, respectively.

Two different compressive forces, heavy (above 2 N) and light (equal or below 2 N), were used for testing. Each condition was repeated for 20 times to acquire more accurate information concerning lateral stroking perception.

3.2 Texture Data Training

In this study, a back propagation neural network (NN) model was trained to find the relationship between ($a_x, v_x, \Delta f_n$) and (a_z). Discrete Fourier transformation was used to convert the time domain information into frequency domain. The input data included lateral acceleration (a_x), lateral velocity (v_x), and normal compressive force (Δf_n), and the output data included the z-axis acceleration (a_z). The first 70% of the input and output data was used for training process, computing and updating the gradient weightings, the next 15% of the data was used for validation, and the last 15% of the data was for testing.

The initial input weights, input bias weights, output weights, and output bias weights were randomly set between [−10, 10]. The log sigmoid function f_1 was used as the active function in the hidden layer. The hyperbolic tangent sigmoid function was used as the active function in the output layer.

The learning rate of the training process was set to 90%. The back propagation process, steepest descent approximations, and over-fitting controls were used to train the neural network model. The training process stopped when 20000 epochs or less than 10^{-9} of the total error were reached.

3.3 Texture Reproducing

The output acceleration $a_{z,NN}$ were linearly mapped to the digital unit in the MCU to find the driving voltages for the tactile feedback glove. Using the 12-bit DAC in Teensy 3.2 USB board, the predicted acceleration ($a_{z,NN}$) can be divided into 4096 units. The minimum and the maximum $a_{z,NN}$ were mapped to the digital unit of 0 and 4095. Then, a look-up vibration table was built and programmed into MCU MK20DX256 through Teensyduino to find the driving voltages.

The piezoelectric actuator on each finger of the tactile glove was controlled by a Teensy 3.2 USB board (MK20DA256) with a pre-defined ID. Each byte delivered by Unity 3D was separated into two parts. The first 3 bits were used to identify the finger ID in a binary form, and the next 5 bits were used to determine the corresponding driving voltages from the vibration table to activate the actuator.

4   User Interface

In Fig. 3, virtual buttons 1 to 3 represent light stroking for templates 1 to 3, and virtual buttons 4 to 6 represent heavy stroking of templates 1 to 3, respectively. Participants put on the tactile feedback glove and activated virtual buttons 1 to 6, randomly. Since lateral movement speed was a factor affecting roughness perception, users needed to follow the moving speed of the track bar on top of the graphical user interface from left to right.

The average stroking time on the physical templates was 3.3 s for all five fingers, and 2.1 s for each finger. Therefore, the time difference between each finger was roughly 0.3 s. In order to observe how the vibration representations affected the continual lateral stroking perception, four different representation methods were designed to simulate continual stroking sensations: heavy press (H), saltation (S), modulation (M), and trapezoid (T), as shown in Fig. 4.

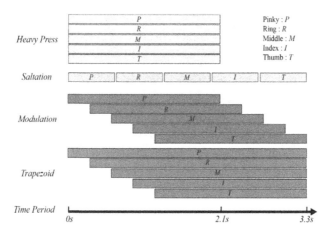

Fig. 4. Representation methods for virtual continual lateral stroking

Heavy press representation method was design to deliver the roughness stimuli to five fingers simultaneously. Time period of this method was 2.1 s. Saltation method provides stimulus to each finger individually and sequentially. The total stroking time period was 3.3 s. Prior research showed that the time for the sensory organs to receive stimulus from the environment and activate the nerve impulse was about 30 ms [22]. Therefore, the interval between each finger for the saltation method was set to be 30 ms to ensure the finger receptors would be activated sequentially. The time period for each finger was 0.64 s.

Modulation method provided stimulus to each finger for 2.1 s, but the actuating time was 0.3 s difference between the fingers. The total stroking time period was 3.3 s. Therefore, some overlapping existed among the fingers. Trapezoid method was designed to provide stimulus to each finger with 0.3 s difference from the adjacent fingers, but all fingers stopped vibrating at the same time. The total stroking time period was 3.3 s.

The four representation methods were applied to display the three virtual template roughness. In this test, all representation methods used heavy compressive forces, which were over 2 N. Three series of simulated lateral stroking sensations were created: series 1 (H1, S1, M1, T1), series 2 (H2, S2, M2, T2), and series 3 (H3, S3, M3, T3), which were corresponding to heavy press (H), saltation (S), modulation (M), and trapezoid (T) representations for virtual templates 1 to 3.

5   Tactile Sensation Experiment

The main purpose of this research was to provide users realistic continual lateral stroking tactile sensations in virtual environments. Two experiments were conducted. One was roughness discrimination experiment and the other one was continual lateral stroking experiment. Forty participants, 20 females and 20 males, took the experiments (mean age 22.7 years, SD = 2.17).

5.1   Roughness Discrimination Experiment

The purpose of the roughness discrimination experiment was to test if the participants can match the simulated roughness with the physical templates. Before conducting the virtual roughness discriminability experiment, a physical roughness discrimination test, using the three templates, was conducted to see if the participants can discriminate different physical roughness.

The physical roughness discrimination test was a repeated measure within-subject two-way design experiment. Six conditions were randomly tested (3 roughness × 2 normal compressive forces). Subjects were asked to conduct lateral stroking from left to right to perceive the roughness of the physical templates, as shown in Fig. 5(a). After each stroking, participants were asked to rate the roughness from +1 (smooth) to +7 (coarse).

(a)   (b)

Fig. 5. Roughness discrimination experiment. (a) physical roughness discrimination test (b) virtual roughness discrimination test.

The virtual roughness discrimination test was also a repeated measure within-subject two-way design experiment. Six conditions (3 roughness × 2 normal compress forces corresponding to buttons 1 to buttons 6 in Fig. 3) were randomly tested. Subjects were asked to wear the tactile glove and follow the speed of the track bar to move their hands from left to right, as shown in Fig. 5(b). Subjects perceived the roughness through the vibrotactile glove. After each stroking, participants were asked to rate the simulated roughness from +1 (smooth) to +7 (coarse).

Results. *Physical Roughness Discrimination Test.* Two-way ANOVA was used to analyze the effects of the design attributes on roughness ratings. The results showed that compressive   normal   forces   significantly   affected   roughness   perception ($F_{1,40} = 127.335, p = .000$), so did the groove widths ($F_{1.72,40} = 717.492, p = .000$).

The main effect of the two variables showed that heavy force (higher than 2 N) gave participants more coarser feeling than light force (lower than 2 N). Groove widths also played an important role on roughness perception. Template 3 with 4 mm groove width was rated coarser than template 2 with 3 mm groove width. Template 2 was rated coarser than template 1.

Virtual Roughness Discrimination Test. Two-way ANOVA was used to analyze the roughness perception of the virtual roughness. Groove widths and normal compressive forces   significantly   affected   the   roughness   perception ($F_{2,40} = 1771.195, p = .000; F_{1,40} = 73.649, p = .000$).

Virtual roughness with template 1-heavy (M = 1.950, SD = 0.749) was perceived coarser than template 1-light (M = 1.250, SD = 0.439, p = .000). Virtual roughness with template 2-heavy (M = 4.750, SD = 0.776) was perceived coarser than template 2-light (M = 3.525, SD = 0.716, p = .000). Virtual roughness with template 3-heavy (M = 6.950, SD = 0.221) was perceived coarser than 3-light (M = 5.800, SD = 0.758, p = .000). According to the results of the virtual roughness discriminability test, both groove widths and normal compressive forces were strongly relative to participant's roughness perception.

Comparison of the Virtual Buttons and the Real Templates. Correlation analysis was used to show the relationships between the roughness ratings for the physical templates and the virtual roughness. The Pearson's correlation coefficient, *r*, was 0.97. The result rejected the null hypothesis that the physical templates and virtual templates was non-correlated ($p = .001 < .05$), which means that the developed tactile glove could be regarded as a faithful texture reproducing device.

5.2 Continual Lateral Stroking Experiment

The purpose of the continual lateral stroking experiment was to test which representation method could give users the most realistic continual stroking sensations. The virtual continual lateral stroking experiment included twelve buttons with three series: series 1 (H1, S1, M1, T1), series 2 (H2, S2, M2, T2), and series 3 (H3, S3, M3, T3). The virtual continual lateral stroking experiment was also a repeated measure within-subject one-way design (representation method) for three times (three templates).

Participants first laterally stroked physical template 1 with heavy compressive force. Then, they put on the vibrotactile glove and randomly activated any button in series 1 and followed the motion and speed of the track bar to move their hands from left to right to experience the simulated tactile representations. After each stroking, participants were asked to rate the realism of the simulated roughness from +1 (unrealistic) to +7 (realistic). The same procedure was repeated for templates 2 and 3.

Results. *Result of Realistic Rating for Template 1 (2 mm).* The results showed that the representation method was a dominant factor in realistic perception ratings for template 1 ($F_{2.21,40} = 194.442, p = .000$). According to the results of the post hoc pairwise comparison, modulation representation method ($M = 6.73, SD = 0.68$) was perceived more realistic than heavy press ($M = 1.20, SD = 0.65, p = .000$), saltation ($M = 2.50, SD = 1.20, p = .000$), and trapezoid ($M = 5.13, SD = 1.38, p = .000$).

Result of Realistic Rating for Template 2 (3 mm). The results showed that the representation method was a dominant factor in realistic perception ratings for template 2 ($F_{2.58,40} = 161.291, p = .000$). According to the results of the post hoc pairwise comparison, modulation representation method ($M = 6.30, SD = 1.11, p = .000$) was perceived more realistic than heavy press ($M = 1.23, SD = 0.58, p = .000$) and saltation ($M = 2.60, SD = 1.37, p = .000$). However, the ratings for modulation and trapezoid ($M = 5.78, SD = 1.23, p = .408$) were not significantly different.

Result of Realistic Rating for Template 3 (4 mm). The results showed that the representation method was a dominant factor in realistic perception ratings for template 3 ($F_{2.23,40} = 240.527, p = .000$). According to the result of the post hoc pairwise comparison, modulation representation method ($M = 6.28, SD = 0.14$) was perceived more realistic than heavy press ($M = 1.23, SD = 0.08, p = .000$), and saltation ($M = 2.35, SD = 0.22, p = .000$). However, the ratings for modulation and trapezoid ($M = 6.15, SD = 0.13, p = 1.000$) were not significantly different.

6   Conclusions

This research developed an intuitive and realistic tactile feedback system, which can be applied to increase the sense of realism in VR applications. The system includes a tactile feedback glove, a hand position tracking device, and a VR environment. A texture recording device and a neural network model were created to realistically reproduce surface texture information.

Two experiments were conducted to evaluate the stimuli rendered by the system. First, the roughness discriminability experiment was conducted to observe participants' tactual perception on virtual roughness. The roughness ratings showed that the virtual roughness was highly correlated to the physical roughness ($r^2 > 0.9$).

Then, the continual lateral stroking experiment was conducted to find a method which can deliver the most realistic continual stroking sensation. The results showed that the modulation representation method had the highest rating. Nevertheless, for template 1 (2 mm groove width), modulation representation method was distinguishable from trapezoid method ($p = .000$). However, with template 2 (3 mm groove width) and template 3 (4 mm groove width), modulation method was not perceived significantly different from trapezoid method. The reasons that cause modulation representation method not distinguishable from trapezoid method for larger groove widths need to be further investigated in the future research.

Acknowledgement. This research was supported by the Ministry of Science and Technology of Taiwan under Contract MOST 106-2221-E-002-120.

References

1. Smith, J.L., Crawford, M., Proske, U., Taylor, J.L., Gandevia, S.C.: Signals of motor command bias joint position sense in the presence of feedback from proprioceptors. J. Appl. Physiol. **106**(3), 950–958 (2009)
2. Santís, M., Jaramillo, D., Pérez, V.Z.: Vibrotactile system for the replication of textures. VII Latin American Congress on Biomedical Engineering CLAIB 2016, Bucaramanga, Santander, Colombia, 26th–28th October 2016. IP, vol. 60, pp. 512–515. Springer, Singapore (2017). https://doi.org/10.1007/978-981-10-4086-3_129
3. Zappi, V., Gaudina, M., Brogni, A., Caldwell, D.: Virtual sequencing with a tactile feedback device. In: Nordahl, R., Serafin, S., Fontana, F., Brewster, S. (eds.) HAID 2010. LNCS, vol. 6306, pp. 149–159. Springer, Heidelberg (2010). https://doi.org/10.1007/978-3-642-15841-4_16
4. Aoki, T., Mitake, H., Keoki, D., Hasegawa, S., Sato, M.: Wearable haptic device to present contact sensation based on cutaneous sensation using thin wire. In: Proceedings of the International Conference on Advances in Computer Entertainment Technology, pp. 115–122. ACM (2009)
5. Minamizawa, K., Fukamachi, S., Kajimoto, H., Kawakami, N., Tachi, S.: Gravity grabber: wearable haptic display to present virtual mass sensation. In: ACM SIGGRAPH 2007 Emerging Technologies, p. 8. ACM (2007)
6. Hashimoto, Y., Nakata, S., Kajimoto, H.: Novel tactile display for emotional tactile experience. In: Proceedings of the International Conference on Advances in Computer Entertainment Technology, pp. 124–131. ACM (2009)
7. Wu, C.-M., Hsu, C.-W., Lee, T.-K., Smith, S.: A virtual reality keyboard with realistic haptic feedback in a fully immersive virtual environment. Virtual Reality **21**(1), 19–29 (2017)
8. Nishimura, N., Leonardis, D., Solazzi, M., Frisoli, A., Kajimoto, H.: Wearable encounter-type haptic device with 2-DoF motion and vibration for presentation of friction. In: Haptics Symposium (HAPTICS), pp. 303–306. IEEE (2014)
9. Kyung, K.-U., Son, S.-W., Kwon, D.-S., Kim, M.-S.: Design of an integrated tactile display system. In: 2004 IEEE International Conference on Robotics and Automation, vol. 1, pp. 776–781. IEEE (2004)
10. Smith, S., Smith, G., Lee, J.L.: The effects of realistic tactile haptic feedback on user surface texture perception. J. VibroEng. **17**(2), 1004–1016 (2015)
11. Lederman, S.J., Klatzky, R.L.: Hand movements: a window into haptic object recognition. Cogn. Psychol. **19**(3), 342–368 (1987)
12. Klatzky, R.L., Lederman, S.J.: Tactile roughness perception with a rigid link interposed between skin and surface. Percept. Psychophys. **61**(4), 591–607 (1999)
13. Kim, S.-Y., Kim, J.-O., Kim, K.Y.: Traveling vibrotactile wave-a new vibrotactile rendering method for mobile devices. IEEE Trans. Consum. Electr. **55**(3), 1032–1038 (2009)

14. Kim, S.-Y., Kim, J.C.: Vibrotactile rendering for a traveling vibrotactile wave based on a haptic processor. IEEE Trans. Haptics **5**(1), 14–20 (2012)
15. Raisamo, J., Raisamo, R., Surakka, V.: Comparison of saltation, amplitude modulation, and a hybrid method of vibrotactile stimulation. IEEE Trans. Haptics **6**(4), 517–521 (2013)
16. Asano, S., Okamoto, S., Yamada, Y.: Vibrotactile stimulation to increase and decrease texture roughness. IEEE Trans. Hum. Mach. Syst. **45**(3), 393–398 (2015)
17. Iizuka, S., Nagano, H., Konyo, M., Tadokoro, S.: Whole hand interaction with multi-finger movement-based vibrotactile stimulation. In: Hasegawa, S., Konyo, M., Kyung, K.-U., Nojima, T., Kajimoto, H. (eds.) AsiaHaptics 2016. LNEE, vol. 432, pp. 157–161. Springer, Singapore (2018). https://doi.org/10.1007/978-981-10-4157-0_27
18. Cascio, C.J., Sathian, K.: Temporal cues contribute to tactile perception of roughness. J. Neurosci. **21**(14), 5289–5296 (2001)
19. Lederman, S.J.: Tactile roughness of grooved surfaces: the touching process and effects of macro-and microsurface structure. Percept. Psychophys. **16**(2), 385–395 (1974)
20. Taylor, M., Lederman, S.J.: Tactile roughness of grooved surfaces: a model and the effect of friction. Atten. Percept. Psychophys. **17**(1), 23–36 (1975)
21. Lederman, S.J., Taylor, M.M.: Fingertip force, surface geometry, and the perception of roughness by active touch. Atten. Percept. Psychophys. **12**(5), 401–408 (1972)
22. Koeppen, B.M., Stanton, B.A.: Berne & Levy Physiology. Elsevier Health Sciences, Philadelphia (2009)

3D Printed Haptics: Creating Pneumatic Haptic Display Based on 3D Printed Airbags

Yuan-Ling Feng$^{(\boxtimes)}$, Roshan Lalintha Peiris, Charith Lasantha Fernando, and Kouta Minamizawa

Keio University Graduate School of Media Design,
Yokohama-city, Kanagawa 223-8526, Japan
xxfylxx@kmd.keio.ac.jp

Abstract. In this paper, we provide a rapid fabrication method to create customizable pneumatic haptic displays using 3D printing technology. Based on the 3d printed miniature airbag which is built form a simple modeling process, various shapes of the haptic display can be made. Not only altering the shape of a single airbag to make a one-dimensional haptic display, but also combining multi airbags as spacial distributed to construct a multi DoF haptic display is possible. The 3D printed airbag is scalable, light to wear and waterproof. Each airbag is inflated by a full-range speaker which mounted on a closed air chamber where the air is transferred back and forth through a tiny nozzle to the airbag. So both low-frequency pressure and high-frequency vibration could be presented. Our technical evaluation identified that the airbag is capable of presenting a wide range of mechanical vibration from 2 Hz to 800 Hz. In addition, a user study was done to investigate the capability of rendering multi degree-of-freedom tactile sensation. The average accuracy of distinguishing directional information is over 80%.

1 Introduction

The 3D printing technology provides a rapid prototype process for getting a pre-assembled object. It is used to print goods for daily use, art works, even interactive objects. With the advances in the variety of raw materials, faster printing speed and lower cost of 3d printers, we can illustrate a future view of creating any personalized products, even a haptic display, via a household 3D printer. Recent wearable haptic displays are actuated with an electro-mechanical structure, such as a small mobile moving belt [8] or a platform [6] which contacts with the skin through a DC motor for providing pressure and torque, or with a voice coil actuator to realize a faster dynamic response [17]. Such devices are generally bulky and are limited by their rigid structure, that they are hard to be reshaped for personalized requirements. Other wearable haptic displays created with a pneumatic structure are constructed by a grounded inflation system and inflatable airbags. In such systems, airbags utilized to provide the haptic feedback

© Springer International Publishing AG, part of Springer Nature 2018
D. Prattichizzo et al. (Eds.): EuroHaptics 2018, LNCS 10894, pp. 180–192, 2018.
https://doi.org/10.1007/978-3-319-93399-3_17

are much lighter and more customizable. However, such researches usually use more complex fabrication methods and use traditional air pumps which can not render the precision texture with high speed inflation and deflation.

In this work, we present a rapid fabrication method of creating a haptic display based on 3D printed miniature airbags, and renders haptic feedbacks through a voice coil based inflation system. Main contributions are: (1) Presenting a novel 3d modeling process easy to be handled for building various and customized haptic airbags (2) An inflation system that can render both the high frequency vibration and low frequency pressure based on full-range speakers. (3) A user evaluation that has confirmed the ability of rendering multi degree of freedom directional vibration when the haptic display consists of multi-airbags.

2   Related Work

2.1   3D Printed Pneumatics

With the advancement of 3D printing technologies, some researchers start to work on 3d printed pneumatic objects. Blossom by Richard Clarkson[1] prints a flower which blends two materials with varying physical properties transitioning from flexible to rigid and forcing air into the cavities of the flower causing it to bloom. Further research has investigated combining electro-mechanical components to realize interactions. [16] presents a method for rapid prototyping interactive robot skins using flexible 3D printed material and analog air pressure sensors. This work senses air pressure in chambers passively to prototype particular manipulation affordances on robot skins. Another example from Vázquez et al. [18] also used printing pneumatic objects with air pressure sensor in their interior to provide haptic feedback or render computational states. This research used the 3D printer creating pneumatic controls whose haptic feedbacks can be manipulated programmatically through the pneumatic actuation. In particular, by manipulating the internal air pressure of various pneumatic elements, they can create mechanisms that require different levels of actuation force and can also change their shape. They discuss a series of example 3D printed pneumatic controls which include conventional controls, such as buttons, knobs, and sliders, then extend to domains such as toys and deformable interfaces. Majority of these researches look at pneumatic input devices with several levels of activation forces for inputting with the haptic feedback. However, our work focus on providing an output haptic display with wide bandwidth for simulating texture or force direction.

2.2   Pneumatic Haptic Displays

Actuating air can generate a suction or inflation pressure that is used for deforming the human skin to stimulate haptic feedbacks. The suction pressure contacts with the skin directly [7], but the inflation pressure is usually provided via a

---

[1] https://www.richardclarkson.com/blossom.

closed and inflatable air chamber. [10] uses silicon to fabricate miniature air chamber arrays which are attached on fingertips for the compliant tactile sensation. [11,21] indicate different approaches on creating a pneumatic shape changing interface which is able to provide haptic feedbacks. Also, some researchers use big airbags which are low-definition but provide powerful pressures to make the haptic display able to provide a user directional information. For example, the Sarotis Project[2] uses silicon to fabricate a set of airbags which are worn on the arms, legs, neck, and waist to provide spatial information of a room through pressures. Another example from Kon et al. [4] is a waist-type Hanger Reflex navigation system based on spacial distributed airbags. As well as WRAP [12], a wristband type pneumatically actuated haptic guidance consists of four airbags. Except the directional information, some works try to simulate richer feedbacks, such as KOR-FX gaming vest[3], a vest type pneumatic haptic display made for enhancing game experience that can simulate the strike feeling. To provide the directional information and richer tactile feedbacks, we explored a method which is briefly described in [2] for creating and actuating the haptic display consists of 3D miniature airbags. [2] explained a previous prototype of this paper and focused on the underwater application.

In addition to wearable displays, grounded haptic display too have been created based on the pneumatically actuation systems. For example, Russomanno et al. [14] mounted pneumatic bubbles on the touchscreen to augment the haptic feedback.

2.3   Tactile Rendering

Tactile feedbacks are rendered via generating vibrations or pressures on the skin. Some previous works use the mechanical vibration to alter friction of the display surface [1], or based on the electrovibration system to display the texture and the shape of virtual objects [15,20]. Another way to render tactile feedbacks is to record vibrations as waveforms when the skin touches objects, then output the waveform from an actuator. The vibration is recorded by an accelerometer [5,13] or a microphone [9], and provides a reliable sensation. The actuator used for outputting is usually the voice coil vibrator like Vp2[4]. As a kind of voice coil actuators, the speaker is used for generating vibrations to the skin directly. In previous researches like Kaneko et al. [3] use the same speaker with this work but make a tactile display which attaches aluminum plates to speakers.

Most of conventional researches of vibratory texture display are only able to provide one-dimensional vibrations. To deform the skin for displaying multi-dimension tactile feedbacks, multi motors or additional mechanical structures is required [15,19].

In 3D Printed Haptics, speakers are used as a part of the actuation system for inflating the airbag. It can present a nimble and wide bandwidth vibration

---

[2] http://www.interactivearchitecture.org/sarotis-the-new-sense.html.

[3] http://www.korfx.com.

[4] http://www.acouve.co.jp/product/pd_vp2.html.

or pressure to simulating abundant textures. Furthermore, we explore providing one-dimension vibrations and multi-dimension vibrations that can be presented via changing the design of the airbag.

3   Implementation

3.1   System Overview

As shown in Fig. 1, the system consists of three main components. (1) The actuator that consists of a single airbag or multi airbags (2) A speaker based actuation mechanism to produce the air pressure waves to actuate the airbags (3) A personal computer (PC) for generating the necessary low and high frequency audio waveforms to drive the speaker based actuation mechanism. For the purpose of this prototype we utilize the Max MSP software to generate the audio wave forms.

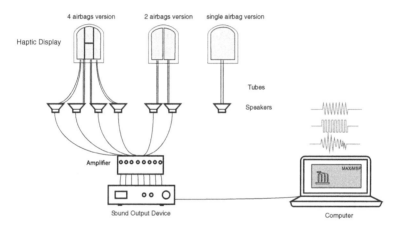

Fig. 1. System overview

3.2   Airbag Design

The main component of the pneumatic haptic display is the 3D printed airbag. In this work, we use the Autodesk Fusion360[5] software for modeling the airbag and the Stratasys Objet260 Connex3[6] multi-material printer which is a kind of the PolyJet printer for 3d printing. The Objet260 Connex3 3D printer offers printing with a wide variety of material and with varying softness levels. For this work, we used two kinds of materials used: the hard white material named RGD and the soft transparent material named Tango+.

---

[5] https://www.autodesk.com/products/fusion-360/overview.
[6] http://www.stratasys.com/3d-printers/objet260-connex3.

The structure of the basic pattern airbag is separately shown in Fig. 2. Only the surface where the human skin will attach needs to be deformable, so there is one surface made out of soft materials. The other surfaces should be made out of hard materials for concentrating air pressures on the soft layer. Furthermore, the hole which connects with an air tube should be opened on a solid surface to avoid the air leak. Thus, as indicated in the Fig. 2, the airbag is printed as two individual components. One is a multi-material main body consisting of three layers: a soft layer which contacts with the skin on the top, a hard layer which connects with the tube at the bottom, and a mix-material (70% RGD + 30% Tango+) transition layer in between for combining the soft layer and the hard layer tighter. Except the soft layer is a surface, the hard layer and mix layer are frames. There are two guidelines for design the hard layer and the soft layer. One is that the hard layer (Fig. 2A) should be 0.7 mm greater than the outer diameter of the tube to avoid weakened structures near the hole. Next the thickness of the soft layer (Fig. 2A) is recommended between 0.1 mm and 1.0 mm. The soft layer thickness under 0.1 mm could easily rupture during repeated actuation use and thickness over 1.0 mm would require more powerful actuation system. The other is a hard cover that needs to be assembled using Epoxy resin adhesive after printing. We adopted this mechanism of printing the airbag as two separate components to avoid building up of support materials inside the vacant area when printing hollow objects.

A typically modelled standard airbag is shown in Fig. 2A. The modeling process is simply and can be generalized to other CAD softwares. It is summarized as three steps: (1) Draw the shape of the airbag in the 2d sketch plane. (2) Extrude each 3d components from the sketch plane. (3) Arrange the position

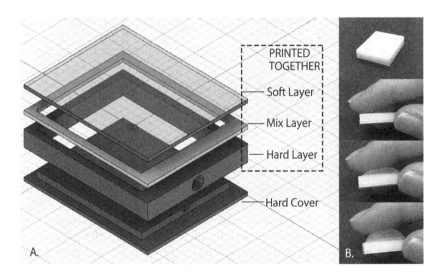

Fig. 2. Exploded design view of the structure of the airbag's basic pattern (b) The soft material inflated to various levels by pressuring the air bag.

of each component according to the basic structure of the airbag as shown in Fig. 2A. Except the cover component, other components that construct the main body of the object should joined in order.

3.3   Actuation System

As shown in the system overview, airbags are inflated and deflated by the speaker's movements which are actuated by audio signals from PC. The actuation system is consists of a PC, an audio interface, an amplifier board set, and a speaker set, shown in Fig. 3. Each air bag is attached to a single speaker. Each speaker is attached to an independent audio channel on an eight channel amplifier board which was used as an interface to convert the pre-amplified signal to the speakers from a multi-channel USB audio interface (Roland - OCTA-CAPTURE[7]). The speakers (AURASOUND NSW2-326-8A[8]) were mounted on the closed air chamber where the air is transferred through a tiny nozzle where the audio signal is converted to a the air pressure. When the speaker is actuated by an audio wave generated on the PC. The speaker generates the air pressure due to the continuous and rapid movement of the cone. This movement pushes and pulls the air in and out of the chamber, to inflate and deflate the airbag. On the PC side, Max MSP was used to generate the required audio signals for push/pull movements of the speaker cone. By creating different audio patterns, we were able to render low frequency pressure and high frequency vibration.

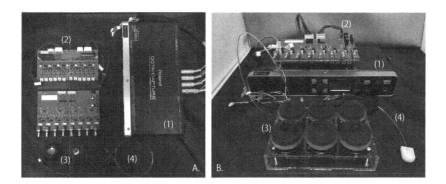

Fig. 3. Hardware of the actuation system. (1) The audio interface. (2) Audio cables. (3) The amplifier. (4) The speaker set. (5) The air tube.

The audio signal is controlled by MAX/MSP in the PC side, and the sound resource of it could be sinusoids or captured/rendered texture based audio waveforms.

---

[7] https://www.roland.com/jp/products/octa-capture/features/.
[8] http://www.ari-web.com/aurasound/NSW2-326-8A/index.html.

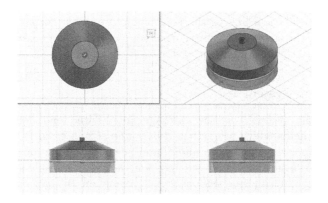

Fig. 4. 3D model of the speaker cover

4   Evaluation

4.1   Frequency Measurements

The objective of this evaluation is to measure the frequency response characteristics of a standard miniature airbag. The airbag used for evaluation is one of the
basic pattern (Fig. 2(b)) whose specification is $20\,\mathrm{mm} \times 20\,\mathrm{mm} \times 0.5\,\mathrm{mm}(length \times width \times surfacethickness)$. Its bottom was fixed on a horizontal table plane, and
we used an accelerometer on its inflatable surface. The accelerometer, ADXL345[9]
(max sampling rate: 3200 Hz) is attached to measure the vibration horizontal

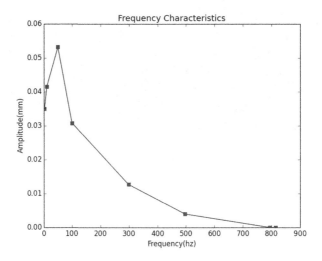

Fig. 5. Frequency characteristics of the airbag surface.

---

[9] http://akizukidenshi.com/catalog/g/gM-06724/.

frequency and without any external force. We used a NUCLEO-F767ZI[10] at a 2000 Hz sampling rate to capture the data. The displacement was obtained through double the double integral of the sensed acceleration value.

Ten sinewaves with the frequency of 2 Hz, 10 Hz, 50 Hz, 100 Hz, 300 Hz, 500 Hz, 800 Hz, and 850 Hz were presented as input signals for this evaluation. The volume of the amplifier was set to a quarter of the max volume. The result processed by Fast Fourier Transform are shown in Fig. 5.

4.2 User Test for Multi-dimension Vibration Rendering

The purpose of this evaluation is for evaluating the accuracy of rendering the multi-dimension vibration patterns on a user's fingertip. Both the 2-DoF and 3-DoF tactile feedback have been evaluated. As shown in Fig. 6, the experimental design is as follows:

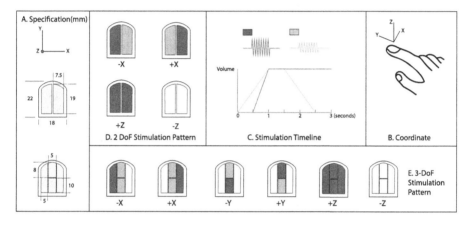

Fig. 6. Experiment design of multi-dimension vibration rendering. (A. The specification of airbags what used for the experiment. B. The coordinate of fingertips. C. The stimulation given to participants each term. D. Four stimulation patterns for the 2-DoF experiment. E. Six stimulation patterns for the 3-DoF experiment.)

Coordinates are defined as B when referenced to the participants' fingertip, where the positive x-axis is towards the right of the fingertips, the positive y-axis is forwards with the fingertips, and the positive z-axis is towards the direction where vertical to the fingerpad.

Haptic displays employed in the experiment are characterized in A. One consists of two airbags to present the 2-DoF tactile sensation in the x and z axises. The other consists of four airbags to present the 3-DoF tactile sensation.

---

[10] https://os.mbed.com/platforms/ST-Nucleo-F767ZI/.

Signals for stimulation are two sinusoidal vibration with the frequency at
30 Hz. One of them whose amplitude is half of the other is sent to the airbag
earlier, according to the timeline which is shown in C.

Patterns of stimulation which represent to each directional information are
shown in D and E. There are four patterns for the 2-DoF experiment and six
patterns for the 3-DoF experiment. The colors filled up airbags are matched
with stimulation signals. White means non-forces rendered.

We provided each pattern of stimulation randomly at 5 times for each participant
for both 2-DoF and 3-Dof patterns. 10 participants (4 males and 6 females, ages
between 24 and 28) took part in the experiment. The experimental tool for this
test was programmed in MAX/MSP. The tool plays a stimulation randomly after
its start button being pressed, and writes the pattern of the stimulation into a txt
file. When a stimulation is finished, the participants will be reminded to select
a pattern according to their intuitions. During the experiment, participants are
required to wear on a headphone where the white noise is playing to avoid the
disruption. Figure 7 shows the scene of a participant doing the test.

The results of the experiment are processed as the confusion matrix shown in
the Fig. 8. The accuracy of negative z-axis which is removed from forms is 100%,
which means the vibration is absolutely sensible. As observed, all the accuracies
are over 76% and the max accuracy is up to 96%. The overall accuracy of the
3-DoF experiment is higher than the 2-DoF experiment, even the airbags used
for it are smaller. This could be due to the design of the 2-DoF which has a
larger contact surface with the finger-tip than the 3-DoF design. According to
the feedbacks from participants, there are two participants have mentioned that
they had clearly sensed the directions at the beginning, but they had gradually

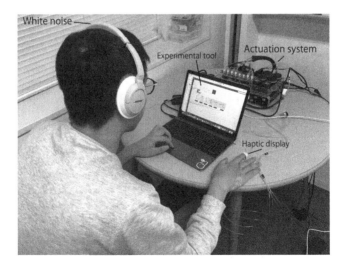

Fig. 7. Experimental setup of the user evaluation

become confused with the test going on. We identify that this reason of tiredness too may have contributed to the lower accuracies of the 2-DoF design.

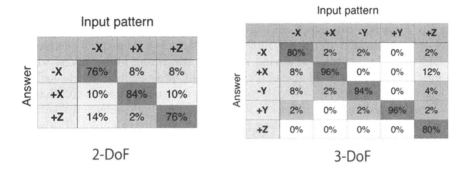

Fig. 8. Results of the experiment

5   Customized Haptic Display Designs

With the 3D printing technology, the pneumatic display based on the airbag is easy to be designed for personalized sizes and various shapes, which was not easy to be realized before. The modeling method provided in this research allows users to redesign and revise the haptic display easily. All you need to do is just

Fig. 9. Various designs of the haptic display (A. Wearable haptic displays for fingers and ungrounded haptic displays consisting of an array of air chambers. B. Tangible objects embedded with airbags. C. Wearing the haptic displays)

revises the sketch drew in the first modeling step, then the shape of the airbag will be changed correspondingly by Fusion 360.

Based on the basic pattern which is explained on the previous section, we created several types of haptic displays which could be used in different applications. The first type is a wearable display such as Fig. 9C which is made for the fingertip. Fingertip patterns consist of a single airbag to present one-dimension force, or multi airbags to present multi-dimension force. Among all the haptic displays made by us, the one having max DoF consists of four airbags, which can present 3-DoF force. The second type is built into tangible objects such as the heart shown in Fig. 9B, where the objects are designed as meaningful shapes. Also arraying multi airbags in Fusion 360 to merge as a multi-cells active surface like Fig. 9A is possible. The displays presented above are examples of original haptic displays which are completely modeled from scratch. However, another way to create the haptic display is embedding the airbag into the existing 3D models. For example, as shown in Fig. 9B, adding a heart shape airbag into a bunny to let a static object become a dynamic haptic display. The haptic feedback could simulate bunny's heartbeats or fish's breath and make the toy vivid. Even the feedback of the fish toy can be felt clearly underwater, as we explored in [2]. In addition to embedding haptic displays, if an airbag is added to some joints of a 3D model, it could actuate movements of parts of the model. For example, the dolphin's (Fig. 9B) tail joint is embedded with an airbag, so that the tail will wave during actuating.

6   Discussion and Limitations

In this paper, we presented a comprehensive way of producing miniature haptic airbags using 3D printing. Through our evaluations we identified that the basic pattern of the airbag is capable of producing haptic frequencies up to 800 Hz. In addition, we explored the capabilities of providing multi-dimensional vibration patterns with different designs of fingertip haptic airbags. However, we identify few limitations of this work.

As a starting point, these evaluation was limited to the 0.5 mm thickness of the surface material and a few selected patterns for providing multi-dimensional vibration patterns. With our future works we plan to expand these parameters to further understand the capabilities of this system.

The current hardware system of the actuation system is bulky and relatively heavy for mobile applications. However, the hardware used are for general purposes and can be further miniaturized for specific application purposes.

7   Conclusion

3D Printed Haptics proposed a rapid fabrication method for creating pneumatic haptic displays based on the 3D printed airbags, and evaluated the performance of the haptic display to render the tactile feedback. The haptic display printed by the 3d printer do not have internal electro-mechanical elements, so it is washable and can be used under water. Even in some tough environments like factory, it can works without misgivings. Because the low-cost display is separable with the actuation system, it could be regarded as disposable. The fabrication process via 3D printing technology we proposed uses readily available softwares and simple processes that are friendly for beginners and could enjoy all of the advantages of the 3D printing. In addition, as the 3D printer becomes faster and more portable, anyone could get their own haptic display anytime anywhere if they want.

As the future work, we are able to fix the defect discovered in the experiment to improve our haptic display, such as adjusting the softness or height of fingertip-pattern haptic display to attach fingerpad more compliantly. Furthermore, attaching airbag into the joints of 3D models will create movements which perhaps can be used for making soft robotic toys. Also, the new way to use the actuation system could be found, like generating vibrations while altering the displacement of the speaker-corn.

Acknowledgement. This work was supported by JST ACCEL Embodied Media project (JPMJAC1404), Japan.

References

1. Chubb, E.C., Colgate, J.E., Peshkin, M.A.: ShiverPaD: a glass haptic surface that produces shear force on a bare finger. IEEE Trans. Haptics **3**(3), 189–198 (2010)
2. Feng, Y.L., Fernando, C.L., et al.: Submerged haptics. In: ACM SIGGRAPH E-Tech (2017)
3. Kaneko, S., Kajimoto, H.: Development of a one-dimensional lateral tactile display for the sensation of texture using a speaker array. In: Hasegawa, S., Konyo, M., Kyung, K.-U., Nojima, T., Kajimoto, H. (eds.) AsiaHaptics 2016. LNEE, vol. 432, pp. 143–149. Springer, Singapore (2018). https://doi.org/10.1007/978-981-10-4157-0_25
4. Kon, Y., Nakamura, T., Kajimoto, H.: Interpretation of navigation information modulates the effect of the waist-type hanger reflex on walking. In: 2017 IEEE Symposium on 3D User Interfaces (3DUI), pp. 107–115. IEEE (2017)
5. Kuchenbecker, K.J., Gewirtz, J., McMahan, W., Standish, D., Martin, P., Bohren, J., Mendoza, P.J., Lee, D.I.: VerroTouch: high-frequency acceleration feedback for telerobotic surgery. In: Kappers, A.M.L., van Erp, J.B.F., Bergmann Tiest, W.M., van der Helm, F.C.T. (eds.) EuroHaptics 2010. LNCS, vol. 6191, pp. 189–196. Springer, Heidelberg (2010). https://doi.org/10.1007/978-3-642-14064-8_28
6. Leonardis, D., Solazzi, M., Bortone, I., Frisoli, A.: A 3-RSR haptic wearable device for rendering fingertip contact forces. IEEE Trans. Haptics **10**, 305–316 (2017)
7. Makino, Y., Asamura, N., Shinoda, H.: A cutaneous feeling display using suction pressure. In: SICE 2003 Annual Conference, vol. 3, pp. 2931–2934. IEEE (2003)
8. Minamizawa, K., Fukamachi, S., et al.: Gravity grabber: wearable haptic display to present virtual mass sensation. In: SIGGRAPH Emerging Technologies, p. 8. ACM (2007)
9. Minamizawa, K., Kakehi, Y., Nakatani, M., Mihara, S., Tachi, S.: TECHTILE toolkit: a prototyping tool for design and education of haptic media. In: Virtual Reality International Conference, p. 26. ACM (2012)

10. Moy, G., Wagner, C., Fearing, R.S.: A compliant tactile display for teletaction. In: ICRA, vol. 4, pp. 3409–3415. IEEE (2000)
11. Ou, J., Skouras, M., et al.: aeroMorph-heat-sealing inflatable shape-change materials for interaction design. In: UIST, pp. 121–132. ACM (2016)
12. Raitor, M., Walker, J.M., Okamura, A.M., Culbertson, H.: WRAP: wearable, restricted-aperture pneumatics for haptic guidance. In: ICRA, pp. 427–432. IEEE (2017)
13. Romano, J.M., Kuchenbecker, K.J.: Creating realistic virtual textures from contact acceleration data. IEEE Trans. Haptics **5**(2), 109–119 (2012)
14. Russomanno, A., Xu, Z., O'Modhrain, S., Gillespie, B.: A pneu shape display: physical buttons with programmable touch response. In: World Haptics Conference (WHC), pp. 641–646. IEEE (2017)
15. Saga, S., Raskar, R.: Simultaneous geometry and texture display based on lateral force for touchscreen. In: 2013 World Haptics Conference (WHC), pp. 437–442. IEEE (2013)
16. Slyper, R., Hodgins, J.: Prototyping robot appearance, movement, and interactions using flexible 3D printing and air pressure sensors. In: RO-MAN, pp. 6–11. IEEE (2012)
17. Solazzi, M., Frisoli, A., Bergamasco, M.: Design of a novel finger haptic interface for contact and orientation display. In: 2010 IEEE Haptics Symposium, pp. 129–132. IEEE (2010)
18. Vázquez, M., Brockmeyer, E., Desai, R., Harrison, C., Hudson, S.E.: 3D printing pneumatic device controls with variable activation force capabilities. In: Proceedings of the 33rd Annual ACM Conference on Human Factors in Computing Systems, pp. 1295–1304. ACM (2015)
19. Wang, Q., Hayward, V.: Biomechanically optimized distributed tactile transducer based on lateral skin deformation. Int. J. Rob. Res. **29**(4), 323–335 (2010)
20. Yamamoto, A., Ishii, T., Higuchi, T.: Electrostatic tactile display for presenting surface roughness sensation. In: International Conference on Industrial Technology, vol. 2, pp. 680–684. IEEE (2003)
21. Yao, L., Niiyama, R., Ou, J., Follmer, S., Della Silva, C., Ishii, H.: Pneui: pneumatically actuated soft composite materials for shape changing interfaces. In: Proceedings of the 26th Annual ACM Symposium on User Interface Software and Technology, pp. 13–22. ACM (2013)

HaptI/O: Physical I/O Node
over the Internet

Satoshi Matsuzono$^{(\boxtimes)}$, Haruki Nakamura, Daiya Kato, Roshan Peiris,
and Kouta Minamizawa

Keio University Graduate School of Media Design,
4-1-1 Hiyoshi Kohoku-ku, Yokohama, Kanagawa 223-8526, Japan
{s.matsuzono,h.nakamura,i.mas.trunk,roshan,Kouta}@kmd.keio.ac.jp
http://embodiedmedia.org/

Abstract. Along with the development of information technology and
tactile technology, it has become possible to share human haptic experiences via the Internet. In this research, we propose HaptI/O a technology that allows easy sharing and communication of haptic experiences.
HaptI/O devices are physical network nodes that can perform as gateways to both input or output the haptic information from a source such as
the human body or a tangible object. HaptI/O proposed in this research
focuses on the (1) ease of sharing haptic information with a focus on
usability (2) share Haptic information among multiple users (3) usage of
the HaptI/O as a mobile device. As a result of user testing of the implemented HaptI/O, it was confirmed that user's information perception in
remote communication was improved.

Keywords: Haptics · Internet · Haptic transmission · I/O device

1 Introduction

Since the Internet service became popular since the 1990's, information technology has made tremoundous strides to this day. In recent years, the spread of
smartphones and tablets has enabled sharing an individual's experiences with
others by using social networks (SNS). Currently, the information shared through
SNS mainly focuses on sharing text and images (and videos), limiting the ability
to convey multimodal experiences and the feeling of presence.

Recently, the advancement of the haptic technology has enabled us to record
and playback haptic experiences [7,8]. Especially in the fields of virtual reality (VR) and entertainment, in addition to reproducing the experiences mainly
based on audio-visual awareness, the addition of "haptic feedback" which can
actually obtain "touch feeling (haptic sensation)" has presents a physical experience with increased presence and reality. Furthermore, with the next generation
high-speed Internet network infrastructure (such as 5G), the transmission, collection and analysis technologies of large-capacity data has been developed. As
such, the future 5G Internet is targeting to allow the mainstream Haptic Internet

© Springer International Publishing AG, part of Springer Nature 2018
D. Prattichizzo et al. (Eds.): EuroHaptics 2018, LNCS 10894, pp. 193–203, 2018.
https://doi.org/10.1007/978-3-319-93399-3_18

applications to enable and share real time haptic experiences with remote users at an anytime, anywhere basis [1–3].

Therefore, we propose HaptI/O which makes it possible to communicate and share haptic experiences easily. HaptI/O devices are physical network nodes that can perform as gateways to both input or output the haptic information from haptic sources such as the human body or tangible objects. The HaptI/O Cloud connects multiple HaptI/O devices and manages the transmission of haptic information from one to multiple nodes as well as one to a single node mutual connection. This system can be activated with a single button, and can be easily combined with other audio/video communication mediums (for example Skype) enabling us to share our experiences with the sense of touch.

2   Previous Haptic Transmission Technologies

Progress of haptic technology has become inexpensive, high performance, compact as compared with the past, and it is possible to reproduce by recording various feelings that people obtain through the body experiences with a sensor and reproducing them with actuators.

From about 20 years ago to 2005, transmitted haptic sensations by physical movement. inTouch [4] shares the rotation of a stick with a person far away and realizes interpersonal communication between remote areas. RobotPhone [5] can communicate via a robot by synchronizing the shape and motion of multiple robots placed at remote locations. Unlike the electronic avatar displayed on the display, it is also possible to actually touch the person to convey the force or move the object to perform the work. Haptic Video [6] can record physical skills by recording expert's work and dynamically playing it with a force sense presentation device.

Following these developments, it became possible to reproduce fine haptic sensation by vibration tactile sense etc. TECHTILE toolkit [7] makes it possible to record and reproduce acoustic signals as a tactile sensation on a contact microphone and to share feel. Unlike a conventional vibration tactile sense using a conventional vibration motor etc., application of it to the field of reproduction of tactile is expected as real time property and vibration resolution are increased. StereoHaptics [8] makes it possible to impart a feeling of movement to the vibrotactile sense by attaching an actuator that generates vibration to the palm of the hand, and it is possible to present the feeling of attack in the video game and the movement of objects in the video content. Haptoclone [9] is a system that interacts by three-dimensional "cloning" of tactile information and visual information, and the two who are away from each other can touch each other with bare hands and naked eyes. Kissenger [10] is an device that provides a physical interface for transmitting a kiss between two remotely connected people. It can sense and transmit the amount of force produced by the active user, and recreate it on the passive side. Their work greatly promotes intimacy between people in long distance relationships.

Furthermore, recent developments have enabled digitizing and transmitting haptic information over the Internet. Tactile transmission over the Internet presents challenges [11] such as haptic input and output devices, delay, synchronization with voice and video. With the establishment of recent high speed network infrastructures, it is now possible to connect tactile information to the Internet and share haptic experiences with others. HapticAid [12] can share sensation of fingertip with skin vibration sensor and mobile platform. Twech [13] can record moving pictures containing tactile sensation by using a tactile recording/playback device attached to iPodTouch, it is possible to upload it as it is on the SNS and share the feeling of touch. TELESAR V [14] makes it possible to create a phenomenon that the user's body possessed in a robot in a remote place and is expected to be applied to various applications between remote areas. In the communication protocol, UDP multicast transmits tactile information and joint motion data. It is realized by lowering the resolution of video to reduce information synchronization and transmission delay. inFORM [15] is a Dynamic Shape Display that can render 3D content physically, so users can interact with digital information in a tangible way. Remote participants in a video conference can be displayed physically, allowing for a strong sense of presence and the ability to interact physically at a distance. Huggy Pajama [16] is a pajama that reproduces a wearable embrace with a hugging interface device connected via the Internet. They propose a system aimed at promoting physical exchanges in remote communication of parents and children by tying each other over the Internet. Zhang [17] created a system that vibrates the vest and knows where they are being touched when touching the user's body wearing the vibrating vest reflected in the video on the display. It combines with video and maintains high compatibility with conventional audio video remote conference system.

3 Design and Implementation

3.1 Design Requirement

If haptic information such as video and audio can be conveyed over the Internet, it is thought that it will be possible to convey the presence feeling and be able to come in contact with people among remote areas through the video phone. Also it would enable sharing texture and the touch feelings of the materials remote communication scenarios. As discussed in the previous section, many of the research presents many challenges yet to be addressed for sharing of haptic sensations via the internet.

In order to address these points, the design goals of the HaptI/O proposed in this research is to (1) enable easy sharing of haptic information with a focus on usability (2) enable sharing Haptic information to multiple users from a single source (3) needs to be mobile. In order to satisfy the requirement of (1), HaptI/O is designed to start its service with a single button. In addition, HaptI/O operation can also be performed with a smartphone or tablet, with a simple user interface. The user can connect the sensor node and the actuator node between the devices using a Web browser and selectively transmit the haptic information to another person. In order to satisfy the requirement of (2), HaptI/O is implemented using IP multicast communication protocol [18]. In the IP multicast protocol, since the source sender needs to transmit the packet only once, the network can be used efficiently. Multiple HaptI/Os are designed to have their own IP addresses and are controlled on the network, thereby constructing a network capable of performing haptic transmission by one-to-one mutual communication or multicast from one node to multiple nodes. In order to satisfy the requirement (3), it is necessary to use cheap and compact electronic components in this implementation and to mount it in a size that fits in the palm of a human being. As a reason for not implementing on smartphones and tablets as a base, this research presents haptic information in addition to video and audio, so it is necessary to be a compact device independent of them. Also, the current smartphone does not include enough sensors and actuators to input and output the tactile sense.

3.2   Hardware Design

We developed HaptI/O as a physical network node that can perform as a gateway to input or output the haptic information. Hardware concept of HaptI/O is small and simple. As shown in Fig. 1, the device includes a sensor (PREIMO, EM246U100B1), an actuator (Alps ElectronicsHaptic Reactor tough type), a communication module (Intel Edison), a battery (Lithium ion battery, 3.7 V, 900 mAh), an audio interface (BUFFALOBSHSAU01BK) and an amplifier (TECHTILE Amplier [7]) in one module. A sensor that can output with emphasizing the low frequency band was used as the sensor. The selected actuator is a voice coil type actuator (Haptic Reactor tough type) which can respond quickly and generate various tactile sensations depending on frequencies. The compact communication module used (Intel Edison) contains RAM: 1 GB and 802.11n Wireless LAN-The Haptic sensor is attached to the HaptI/O module via the audio interface. The sensed tactile information is converted from analog data to digital data at the audio interface. Next, the captured haptic information is transmitted to the HaptI/O cloud via the communication module. On the receiver's end, the haptic information received through the communication

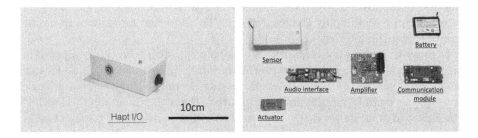

Fig. 1. The HaptI/O prototype hardware design and it opened to reveal its contents: a sensor, an actuator, communication module, a battery, an audio interface and an amplifier.

module is processed through the audio interface (converted into analog information), and the amplifier and output on to the actuator. The module size which is 45 90 35 mm fits comfortably in the palm of a human hand. Another main advantage of this device is that the user of this device can simultaneously be a receiver and/or a transmitter of haptic information.

3.3   Network System Implementation

HaptI/O uses an IP multicast protocol in order to communicate between the sensor node and the actuator node using the Internet. IP multicast protocol is a communication method to realize one-to-many and many-to-many real-time communication over IP networks. Figure 2 shows the implemented network configuration diagram. The user can get haptic information by selecting the actuator node and sensor node that you want to connect from the Web browser. For this prototype of HaptI/O, the communication network is built in the local network environment where the IP addresses for each nodes are allocated from the DHCP [19] server to distinguish each HaptI/O device. The management of network communication was constructed using Nodejs [20].

When HaptI/O starts up, the IP address of HaptI/O is registered on the server. Next, as the communication from the Web browser to the server, the IP addresses of HaptI/O functioning as the sensor node (selected from the browser), the IP address of HaptI/O functioning as the actuator node, and the data of the multicast group are transmitted to the server. We used the JSON [21] format as the data format. This transmitted data is processed by the server, and identifies the sensor node and the actuator node of HaptI/O to be connected, and determines the multicast group.

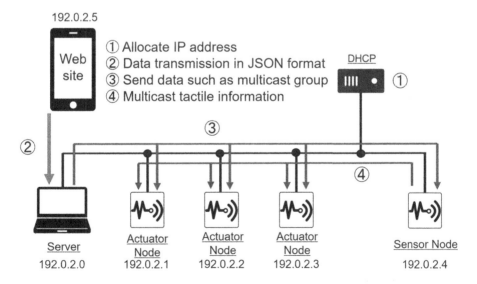

Fig. 2. Network system configuration diagram. (Color figure online)

Next, in the communication from the server to HaptI/O, the data of the identified HaptI/O mode and multicast group processed by the server is transmitted in JSON format. Packets such as 192.0.2.4: Sender, Group: 234.192.0.2, Color: Green, 192.0.2.3: Receiver, Group: 234.192.0.2, Color: Green are received for each HaptI/O. Each HaptI/O refers to the Sender/receiver mode and multicast group associated with its own IP address, HaptI/O of the sensor node transmits the haptic information to the multicast group by sending the data in User Datagram Protocol (UDP). HaptI/O of the actuator node can receive data of haptic information transmitted from the sensor node by accessing the multicast group IP address. Haptic multicast was realized with the network routing.

3.4   User Interface

For ease of operation, the system was designed to operate from a web interface in order to connect HaptI/O on the network (Fig. 3). The UI of the website was constructed using HTML, Javascript, CSS. When the server is launched, the Web browser is automatically released on the same subnet. If the user selects a haptic multicast communication with HaptI/O, they would be prompted to select the multicast group, the HaptI/O mode, and the button item for determining the setting. Since IP multicast protocol is used as a method to realize multicast, multicast group was identified by three colors red, green and blue.

HaptI/O uses distinctive colours such as red, green and blue to easily present the user's group information (red if the group address is 234.192.0.2, green, if 234.198.51.100, blue, if the group address is 234.203.0.113). When the HaptI/O to which the IP address is allocated is registered on the server, the IP

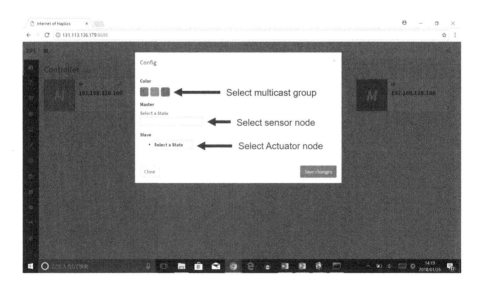

Fig. 3. User interface for configuring HaptI/O. (Color figure online)

address of the registered Hapt I/O is entered on the Web browser. The mode of HaptI/O is selected by selecting the IP address allocated to each node from the sender/receiver selection bar. Upon selection of these 3 items of the multicast group HaptI/O mode and pressing the enter button, the packet is sent to the server. Figure 4 shows how the Implemented HaptI/O works.

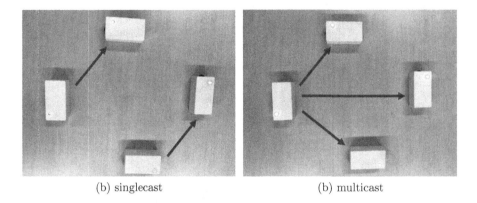

(b) singlecast   (b) multicast

Fig. 4. Operating state of HaptI/O implemented

4   Technical Evaluation

4.1   Experiment

In this experiment, we verify whether user's information perception in remote communication is improved by presenting tactile information in addition to audio/visual information using the HaptI/O. We prepared two separate rooms to recreate the actual remote communication. For room-to-room communication, used the Skype software that allows audio/visual communication. Communication between HaptI/Os was done on the same subnet. We used the RT-AC 85 router with the maximum data transfer rate of 800 Mbps. The texture of the material used four types of rasp with different roughness (Roughness standard th [22]: 240, 320, 400, 600). In the beginning, two types of different roughness rasp are randomly presented to a user in another room and asked which one is rough by visual inspection only. Likewise, all other combinations (240 and 320, 240 and 400, 240 and 600, 320 and 400, 320 and 600, 400 and 600) are randomly presented and answered. Next, a user in another room has HaptI/O of Actuator Node, and two types of different roughness rasp are traced with HaptI/O of Sensor Node over the camera and asked which one is rough. At this time, the user is asked to make the same movement as the tracing action of the opponent. Likewise, all combinations are randomly presented and answered. We compared the response rates in the case of adding only audiovisual information and tactile information with each combination. We recruited 12 participants, between 22 and 27 years old from a nearby organization. Figure 5 shows the experiment.

Fig. 5. Experimental situation: transmission of tactile information to participants through Skype

4.2   Results and Discussion

The results of this experiment are shown in Fig. 6. In this figure, the response rate is shown on the vertical axis and the combination of two kinds of materials on the horizontal axis. From the results in Fig. 6, it was confirmed that recognition of information is improved by presenting haptic information in addition to audiovisual information. Significant differences were observed in the combination of 240 and 600, which differ greatly in roughness. From this result, it was confirmed that HaptI/O can sense and present coarse and smooth differences. However, with the combination of 400 and 600, the response rate was better for the condition without haptic presentation. It is considered that it is difficult to sense tactile information because high frequency components increase as Roughness th increases.

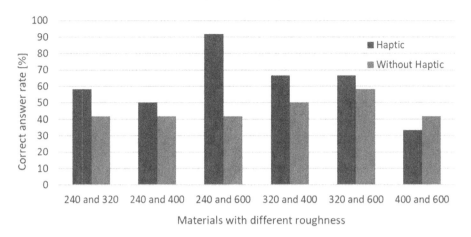

Fig. 6. Evaluation results of materials with different roughness.

5   Conclusion

We propose the HaptI/O which makes it possible to make haptic communication easy and easy. HaptI/O devices are physical network nodes that can perform as gateways to both input or output the haptic information on human body or tangible objects. This system can multicast haptic sensation from one Sensor-Node to multiple Actuator-Node. As a result of verification experiments on whether user recognition of information in remote communication is improved using HaptI/O, it was confirmed that information awareness is improved by presenting tactile information in addition to audiovisual information. Therefore this system can be easily combined with other audio/video communication mediums enabling us to share our experiences with the sense of touch.

In the current version, this HaptI/O can transmit only tactile information. Therefore in the future, we plan to develop devices that will be able to transmit temperature and pressure, so that we can more realistically share information with the sense of touch. In addition, we will formulate communication protocols and data formats for haptic transmission.

Acknowledgment. This work was supported by JST ACCEL Embodied Media project (JPMJAC1404), Japan.

References

1. Fettweis, G., Alamouti, S.: 5G: personal mobile Internet beyond what cellular did to telephony. IEEE Commun. Mag. **52**, 140–145 (2014)
2. Aijaz, A., Dohler, M., Aghvami, A.H., Friderikos, V., Frodigh, M.: Realizing the tactile internet: haptic communications over next generation 5G cellular networks. IEEE Wirel. Commun. **24**(2), 82–89 (2017)

3. Simsek, M., Aijaz, A., Dohler, M., Sachs, J., Fettweis, G.: 5G-enabled tactile internet. IEEE J. Sel. Areas Commun. **34**(3), 460–473 (2016)
4. Brave, S., Dahley, A.: inTouch: a medium for haptic interpersonal communication. In: CHI97 Extended Abstracts on Human Factors in Computing Systems. ACM (1997)
5. Sekiguchi, D., Inami, M., Tachi, S.: RobotPHONE: RUI for interpersonal communication. In: CHI01 Extended Abstracts on Human Factors in Computing Systems. ACM (2001)
6. Saga, S., et al.: Haptic video. In: ACM SIGGRAPH 2005 Emerging Technologies. ACM (2005)
7. Minamizawa, K., Kakehi, Y., Nakatani, M., Mihara, S., Tachi, S.: TECHTILE toolkit: a prototyping tool for designing haptic media. In: ACM SIGGRAPH 2012 Emerging Technologies, p. 22. ACM, August 2012
8. Israr, A., Zhao, S., Mcintosh, K., Schwemler, Z., Fritz, A., Mars, J., Koniaris, B.: Stereohaptics: a haptic interaction toolkit for tangible virtual experiences. In: ACM SIGGRAPH 2016 Studio, p. 13. ACM, July 2016
9. Makino, Y., Furuyama, Y., Inoue, S., Shinoda, H.: HaptoClone (Haptic-Optical Clone) for mutual tele-environment by real-time 3D image transfer with midair force Feedback. In: Proceedings of the 2016 CHI Conference on Human Factors in Computing Systems, pp. 1980–1990. ACM, May 2016
10. Samani, H.A., Parsani, R., Rodriguez, L.T., Saadatian, E., Dissanayake, K.H., Cheok, A.D.: Kissenger: design of a kiss transmission device. In: Proceedings of the Designing Interactive Systems Conference, pp. 48–57. ACM, June 2012
11. Fettweis, G.P.: The tactile internet: applications and challenges. IEEE Veh. Technol. Mag. **9**(1), 64–70 (2014)
12. Maeda, T., Tsuchiya, K., Peiris, R., Tanaka, Y., Minamizawa, K.: HapticAid: haptic experiences system using mobile platform. In: Proceedings of the Tenth International Conference on Tangible, Embedded, and Embodied Interaction, pp. 397–402. ACM, March 2017
13. Hanamitsu, N., Nakamura, H., Nakatani, M., Minamizawa, K.: Twech: a mobile platform to search and share visuo-tactile experiences. In: SIGGRAPH Asia 2015 Mobile Graphics and Interactive Applications, p. 10. ACM, November 2015
14. Fernando, C.L., Furukawa, M., Kurogi, T., Kamuro, S., Sato, K., Minamizawa, K., Tachi, S.: Design of TELESAR V for transferring bodily consciousness in telexistence. In: 2012 IEEE/RSJ International Conference on Intelligent Robots and Systems (IROS), pp. 5112–5118. IEEE (2012)
15. Follmer, S., Leithinger, D., Olwal, A., Hogge, A., Ishii, H.: inFORM: dynamic physical affordances and constraints through shape and object actuation. In: Uist, vol. 13, pp. 417–426, October 2013
16. Teh, J.K.S., Cheok, A.D., Peiris, R.L., Choi, Y., Thuong, V., Lai, S.: Huggy Pajama: a mobile parent and child hugging communication system. In: Proceedings of the 7th International Conference on Interaction Design and Children, pp. 250–257. ACM, June 2008
17. Zhang, L., Saboune, J., El Saddik, A.: Development of a haptic video chat system. Multimedia Tools Appl. **74**(15), 5489–5512 (2015)

18. Rosenberg, J., Kaufman, M., Hiie, M., Audet, F.: An architectural framework for browser based real-time communications. IETF Request for Comments Draft (2011)
19. Droms, R.: Automated configuration of TCP/IP with DHCP. IEEE Internet Comput. **3**(4), 45–53 (1999)
20. Nodejs Homepage. https://nodejs.org/en/
21. JOSN Homepage. https://www.json.org/index.html
22. JIS R 6010, Coated Abrasive Sizes (1991)

Synergy-Based Multi-fingers Forces Reconstruction and Discrimination from Forearm EMG

Luis Pelaez Murciego, Michele Barsotti[✉], and Antonio Frisoli

PERCRO Laboratory, TeCIP Institute, Scuola Superiore Sant'Anna of Pisa, Pisa, Italy
michele.barsotti@santannapisa.it

Abstract. In this paper we propose a novel synergy-based myocontrol scheme for finger force estimation and classification which is able to simultaneously control 4 fingers with a training phase based only on individual-finger data. The proposed method has been tested using the online-available NinaPro database and validated in a preliminary experiment conducted with the use of a hand-exoskeleton. Results show how the presented approach outperforms considerably the linear regression method which is considered standard approach in myoelectric control. The low error rate obtained (smaller than 10% of the targeted force) and the effectiveness in decreasing the number of false activation open the possibilities for future uses in fields such as haptics and neuro-rehabilitation.

1 Introduction

Myoelectric control can decode human motor intent from non-invasive electromyographic signals (EMG) into control signals. The rapid growing of multifunction hand-prosthesis and robotic-exoskeletons open the challenge for dexterous myocontrol schemes to be exploited in the neuro- rehabilitation field [1,2]. Patter recognition techniques have been widely studied during the last four decades, achieving more than 90% of accuracy when recognizing hand gestures [3,4]. More recently, Rasool et al. proposed a synergy-based classifier able to discriminate up to 12 multi-degree-of-freedom (DoF) tasks involving wrist and hand movements [5]. Additionally, [6] successfully proposed the use of task-related synergy classifier for recognizing more than 10 hand gestures. However, the lack of simultaneity between DoFs and the high cost of the errors (i.e. an error in classification will compromise the entire gesture and may lead to a frustrating and unsafe situation for the user) have kept pattern recognition approaches restricted to laboratories. As a result, proportional and simultaneous control paradigm (i.e. regression methods) has been gaining more attention over the last years [7,8], establishing itself as promising tool to reduce the gap between research and commercial applications [9]. In fact, using regression methods might allow to recognize movements that are not included in the training dataset. In

© Springer International Publishing AG, part of Springer Nature 2018
D. Prattichizzo et al. (Eds.): EuroHaptics 2018, LNCS 10894, pp. 204–213, 2018.
https://doi.org/10.1007/978-3-319-93399-3_19

this way, it could be possible to dramatically reduce the time needed to train the system and thus, avoid muscle fatigue before start the exercises. This aspect is particular relevant in clinical scenarios where saving time in the setup phase it is translated into more time focused on rehabilitation tasks.

It is particular interesting the DoF-wise strategy presented in [10], which allows to cosntrol different DoFs simultaneously by extracting the synergies for each DoF independently using a semi-supervised version of the non-negative matrix factorization (NMF) algorithm. This method has been successfully used to control two DoFs of the wrist movements, but documented a substantial error increment when a third DoF was included. The approach assumes that, when crosstalk between the surface EMG channels is small, two synergies are sufficient to represent the positive and negative force patterns respectively for each DoF. The case of dexterous finger control is particularly challenging due to the high number of muscles involved and the small space of forearm they share. Despite the levels of crosstalk may be important, the mentioned approach has been proven to be suitable for reconstructing the force of 3 fingers simultaneously (thumb, index and middle finger) [11].

We aimed at training a model using only data from individual fingers to estimate the force during both single and multiple-fingers tasks. For the case of study, four fingers are considered: index (I), middle (M), ring (R) and little (L). The thumb has been intentionally excluded due to the needed of measure intrinsic muscle activity for a correct estimation. In this paper a modified version of the DoF-wise algorithm is introduced, which includes also an investigation on how the number of synergies extracted for each DoF affects the accuracy of the reconstructed force. Since unintended finger activations are a recurrent issue in myoelectric finger control [11], is proposed a novel synergy-based control scheme which allows to exploit the synergies properties also for finger discrimination. The inclusion of the classification stage provides the benefits of the pattern recognition method without resign to the advantages of a natural and simultaneous proportional control granted by the regression model. The implemented algorithm has been validated using the public available dataset NinaPro [12] and then preliminary tested on a custom-made setup which incorporates the use of a hand-exoskeleton.

2   Materials and Methods

In this Section both datasets are described: the NinaPro database, used for testing the proposed approach; and the custom setup with the hand-exoskeleton, used for preliminary validation of the results.

2.1   NinaPro Database

In the second version of the NinaPro database [12] is also introduced the data-force at fingertips in addition to the most common hand gestures. Only the set of exercises corresponding to the fingers forces patterns has been used in this work. Muscle activity was measured from 40 able-body subjects during the performing of 6 different tasks: 4 single finger flexion (I, M, R and L) and 2 multiple finger flexion (I-L and M-R). Each task consisted in 6 repetitions of 5 s each in a trapezoidal shape with 3 s resting time between repetitions. Eight bipolar electrodes were placed around the forearm equally spaced in a ring disposition and four were muscle targeted for extensors, flexors, biceps and triceps respectively. Since biceps and triceps muscles are not involved in finger force generation, only the first ten channels were considered. Additionally, six subjects were removed from the list after visual inspection of the raw data (e.g. critically low signal-to-noise ratio, multiple finger activation for single finger tasks, etc.). EMG signals were sampled at a rate of 2 KHz and cleaned from 50 Hz power-line interference using built-in notch filter. The forces at fingertips were measured using Force Linear Sensors (FLS) at a sample rate of 100 Hz.

2.2   Experimental Setup with the Hand Exoskeleton

EMG data were recorded using 16 monopolar self-adhesive Ag-AgCl electrodes placed equally spaced around the forearm in two bracelets at a distance of 1/3 and 2/3 of the forearm length respectively from the elbow (see Fig. 1). The signals were acquired by a commercial bio-signal amplifier (g-tec, g.USBamp, Austria) at a sample rate of 1200 Hz. Each channel was band-pass filtered 5–500 Hz and cleaned from 50 Hz power-line interference through built-in filters. A hand exoskeleton equipped with 5 linear force sensors was used to measure the finger forces at middle phalanges at a sample rate of 120 Hz (see [13] for an extensive description of the hand-exoskeleton). The subject sat in a comfortable position in front of an LCD screen while wearing the hand-exoskelton on their right (dominant) hand. A visual feedback of the finger forces was provided to the subject through a graphical interface illustrated in Fig. 1. The visual cues included 5 empty bars representing each finger (only 4 were used during the experiment). The bars were filled from the middle to the bottom, proportionally to the force exerted when flexing the fingers. The middle of the bar corresponded to resting position. The gestures set included four 1-finger tasks (I, M, R and L), four 2-fingers tasks (I-M, M-R, R-L and I-L), two 3-finger tasks (I-M-R and M-R-I) and one 4-fingers task. Each task contained three repetitions of the same gesture, which consisted in following a trapezoidal force pattern with 2 s rising/falling slope and 3 s at constant force of 7 Newton (i.e. half of the averaged maximum finger forces [14]). A resting time of 3 s between repetitions and 30 s between tasks was introduced to avoid fatigue.

2.3   Performance Analysis

As mentioned above, the training data set only contains information of single finger tasks. In the case of NinaPro dataset, single finger data have been split into 50% for training and 50% for test. In the case of the self-acquired database, data was divided in one repetition for training and two repetitions for test. The root-mean-square error (RMSE) between the reconstructed and the measured force was used as a performance index and is defined as

$$RMSE(F, C) = \sqrt{\frac{\sum_i (f_i - c_i)^2}{n}} \tag{1}$$

where F and C are the sensor measurements and the reconstructed force respectively and f_i and c_i are their i-th samples. A 1-way ANOVA test was conducted for assessing significant differences in the RMSE of the reconstruction using different number of synergies (ranging from 0 to 9, as shown in Fig. 3(a)). The effect of the introduction of the FSD classification stage has been evaluated with another 1-way ANOVA. In case of significant main effect Bonferroni corrected multiple comparisons were conducted. Normality of data distributions have been assessed through the Lilliefors test.

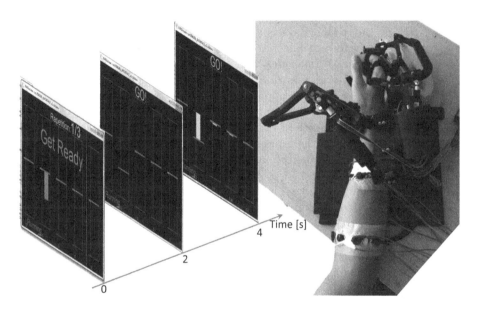

Fig. 1. Left: Graphical user interface. Each bar represents a finger, cues of targeted fingers (pink bar) are shown to the subject for 2 s before start. The subject is asked to follow the horizontal red lines, while the yellow bars indicates the force measured by the sensors. Right: Subject wearing the hand exoskeleton before the experiment. (Color figure online)

3   Procedure

All the numerical procedures presented in the subsequent sections have been used for both datasets.

3.1   Data Processing

The EMG signals were band-pass filtered in the 20–450 Hz band using a 4 order Butterworth filter. The modified version of the Bayesian envelope estimator [15] presented in [16] has been used as feature extracted from EMG signals in a moving window of 300 ms with a 50% overlap. The parameters that define the time evolution equation of the Bayesian estimator have been manually tuned using training data.

3.2   Synergy-Based Force Estimation

The synergy estimation approach (see "Synergy-based force estimation" block on Fig. 2) is based on the semi-supervised NMF algorithm proposed by Jiang et al. [10]. The muscle synergy model can be defined as

$$X_i(t) = W_i * H_i(t) \tag{2}$$

where $X_i(t)$ is the EMG Bayesian envelopes matrix of size $[Channels \times Samples]$ when only the ith finger is active, Wi represents its synergy matrix $[Channels \times Number\,of\,Synergies]$ and $H_i(t)$ corresponds to the muscle activation $[Number\,of\,Synergies \times Samples]$ of the same finger. Training data was used to solve (2) in a DOF-wise approach (i.e. one finger at a time). Therefore, the final synergy matrix W is calculated by concatenating all synergy matrix resulting of solving i instances of (2). The scale factors β were used to set the activation signals levels to the same range of exerted forces. There were calculated by using a multilinear regression between the signals $H(t)$ and the targeted force measured by the sensors.

During the offline test, finger activation signals $H(t)$ were estimated as the product between the pseudo-inverse synergy matrix W and the Bayesian filtered EMG signal $X(t)$ corresponding to any given task, such as

$$H(t) = W^+ * X(t) \tag{3}$$

The reconstructed force of the ith finger $C_i(t)$ was then obtained by multiplying the estimated activation signals with the scale factors β as following

$$C_i(t) = \beta_{i1} * H_{i1}(t) + ... + \beta_{ij} * H_{ij}(t) \tag{4}$$

where j identifies the number of synergies. An analysis of performance results using different number of synergies is presented in Sect. 4.1.

3.3   Finger Synergy Discrimination

As shown in the work of Rasool et al. [5,6], it can be expected that the Bayesian signal obtained from a given task $X(t)$ will be best reconstructed ($\hat{X}(t)$) by using the set of synergies corresponding to the DoF active during that particular task such that

$$\hat{X}_i(t) = W_i * H_i(t) \tag{5}$$

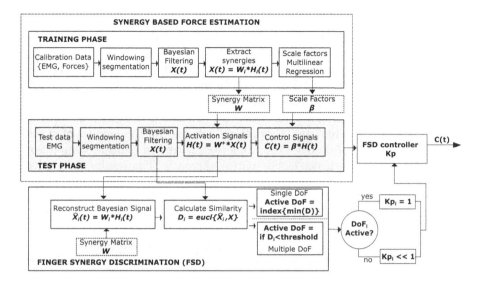

Fig. 2. Block diagram of the proposed control scheme. Synergies extracted using single DoF data are used during the FSD block to modify the value of the proportional controller Kp.

where W_i and $H_i(t)$ are the synergies and activation signals of the ith DoF respectively and $\hat{X}_i(t)$ is the reconstructed Bayesian signal obtained for that pair of parameters. When only single-finger tasks are considered, the problem of finding the active finger can be solved by running i instances of (5) using the pair $\{W_i, H_i(t)\}$ corresponding to each finger and comparing the results $\hat{X}_i(t)$ with the original signal $X(t)$ by means of a similarity measurement (e.g. euclidean distance). The index of the minimum distance is expected to correspond to the intended finger. With the information of the active fingers, removing the unintended fingers activations became a trivial problem. In this proposal, a simple proportional controller Kp is used to attenuate all the untargeted finger control signals estimated during the synergy-based control stage. In case of multiple-finger tasks were considered, a decision threshold was used to determine which are the targeted fingers. The value of the threshold is empirically calculated for each finger using training data. An illustration of the algorithm can be seen in Fig. 2.

4 Results

4.1 Results with the NinaPro Database

Synergy Investigation. Figure 3(a) shows the RMSE errors between the measured force and the control output averaged across 34 subjects for different number of synergies (k). Performance index is calculated separately for single-finger task, multiple-fingers tasks and all the tasks combined. The results are compared with the standard linear regression (LR) method to provide context to the reader. As expected, since the model was trained only using single finger gestures, the error is noticeable higher during multiple-fingers tasks execution. This effect is mainly due to the fact that during multiple-fingers tasks, muscle activity corresponding to one finger may be obscured by stronger muscles related to any of the other fingers involved in the task. The ANOVA tests conducted on the three sets of tasks reported a significant influence of the number of synergies variation. Figure 3(a) shows the Bonferroni corrected multiple comparison between the LR and synergy-based control approach. The results shows that increasing the number of synergies to more than four ($k \geq 4$) provides a significant improvement in the reconstruction accuracy with respect to the standard approach (LR). As shown previously in the literature, for an accurate estimation is expected to require at least the same number of synergies as the total number of DoFs involved. It is also noticeable that using more than four synergies had no significant effect in the reconstruction accuracy improvement. According to the results, the number of synergies extracted for each finger in this work has been set to four.

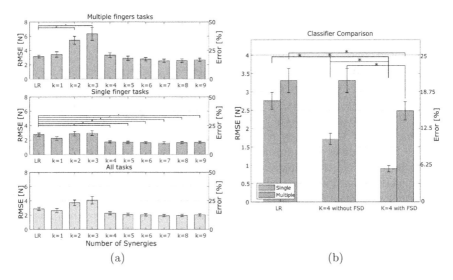

(a)   (b)

Fig. 3. Performance results in terms of RMSE [N] and percentage error of the averaged maximum force. Asterisks mark Bonferroni corrected significant differences. (a) Error results obtained using different number of synergies for the three sets of tasks. (b) Comparison between the LR approach and the modified DoF-wise proposed with and without the Finger Synergy Discrimination (FSD) block.

FSD Performance. Figure 3(b) illustrates the RMSE reconstruction error averaged across 34 subjects for the three methods described above: standard linear regression (LR), DoF-wise approach with $k = 4$ and DoF-wise approach when adding the FSD control stage described in Sect. 3.3. It can be seen how the synergistic method without FSD outperforms the Linear Regression when only single fingers are considered. With the introduction of the FSD stage there is a significant improvement in both single and multiple fingers force reconstruction.

4.2   Results with the Hand-Exoskeleton Setup

Preliminary results obtained in the pilot experiment described in Sect. 2.2 are reported in Fig. 4. In particular, RMSE performance is reported in Fig. 4(a) and a representative graph of the finger forces estimation for a single-finger task is shown in Fig. 4(b). Even though only one subject performed the pilot experiment, the results acquired are in line with those obtained using the NinaPro database (see Sect. 4.1). In fact, considering that the maximum force requested for the exercises was 7 Newtons, the averaged error percentage obtained with the FSD inclusion is close to 6%.

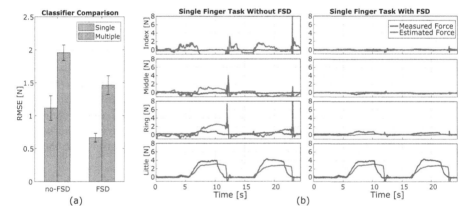

Fig. 4. Performance obtained with the Hand-Exos setup. (a) the averaged RMSE error bars show the results of including the FSD control stage for 4 single-finger and 6 multiple-finger tasks. A representative graph of the finger forces estimation can be seen in (b). The effect of introducing the FSD is clearly perceptible in the right image.

5   Discussion and Future Work

We validated a novel synergy-based control scheme to estimate finger forces using a model trained only with data from single-finger exercises. In this work is presented an extended model of the DoF-wise approach introduced in [10] in which we investigated how the number of synergies extracted for each DoF can affect the force reconstruction performance. We found that there is a significant improvement with respect to the standard linear regression approach when using at least the same number of synergies as the number of DoFs (i.e. 4 in this case) involved in the problem. It has been observed that increasing the number to more than 6 does not provide any significant improvement. The classification stage introduced allows to potentially recognize which are the active fingers during the gesture performance and used this information to remove false activations generated by untargeted fingers. The combination of both stages has been proven to provide a more accurate estimation of the force exerted in comparison to the same scheme without the FSD block. Significant differences between the performance obtained with single and multiple-fingers tasks (6% Vs 15% error respectively) have been also documented. This discrepancy may be explained by two main reasons. First, in order to keep a short training session which increases the usability of future myocontrol-based applications, the model was trained using only on single finger exercises. The second reason it can be physiologically explained by the covariation of forces [17,18] and it would be associated to the non-linear synergistic combination occurred when generating multi-finger forces. The inability of the synergies to accurately separate the neural information when more than one finger is involved is still a challenge to be solved. The proposed method has the potential of satisfactorily merging regression and classification paradigms. As shown in Fig. 4(b), the classification approach can dramatically reduce false activations and hence augmenting the usability of possible clinical applications. On the other hand, the regression methods, thank to their capability of generalization, may allow to shortening the time needed for training the system. A regular training session can be complete in less than 5 min when 4 fingers are involved in the tasks. Moreover, we noticed that, in the case of the self acquired data, increasing the ratio training:test data to 2:1 did not observably improve the accuracy of the results. Future work will include the online validation of the proposed scheme to control the hand-exoskeleton carrying the experiments with healthy and stroke patients.

Acknowledgments. This work has been partially funded by: the EU Horizon2020 project nr. 644839 ICT-23-2014 CENTAURO; the national PRIN-2015 ModuLimb (Prot. 2015HFWRYY), the RONDA project (Regione Toscana, Italy FAS Salute 2014 program).

References

1. Vujaklija I., Amsuess S., Roche A.D., Farina D., Aszmann, O.C.: Clinical evaluation of a socket-ready naturally controlled multichannel upper limb prosthetic system. In: González-Vargas, J., Ibáñez, J., Contreras-Vidal, J., van der Kooij, H., Pons, J. (eds.) Wearable Robotics: Challenges and Trends. Biosystems & Biorobotics, vol. 16, pp. 3–7. Springer, Cham (2017). https://doi.org/10.1007/978-3-319-46532-6_1
2. Leonardis, D., Barsotti, M., Loconsole, C., Solazzi, M., Troncossi, M., Mazzotti, C., Castelli, V.P., Procopio, C., Lamola, G., Chisari, C., et al.: An emg-controlled robotic hand exoskeleton for bilateral rehabilitation. IEEE Trans. Haptics **8**(2), 140–151 (2015)

3. Khushaba, R.N., Al-Ani, A., Al-Jumaily, A.: Orthogonal fuzzy neighborhood discriminant analysis for multifunction myoelectric hand control. IEEE Trans. Biomed. Eng. **57**(6), 1410–1419 (2010)
4. Celadon, N., Došen, S., Binder, I., Ariano, P., Farina, D.: Proportional estimation of finger movements from high-density surface electromyography. J. NeuroEng. Rehabil. **13**(1), 73 (2016)
5. Rasool, G., Iqbal, K., Bouaynaya, N., White, G.: Real-time task discrimination for myoelectric control employing task-specific muscle synergies. IEEE Trans. Neural Syst. Rehabil. Eng. **24**(1), 98–108 (2016)
6. Zhang, S., Zhang, X., Cao, S., Gao, X., Chen, X., Zhou, P.: Myoelectric pattern recognition based on muscle synergies for simultaneous control of dexterous finger movements. IEEE Trans. Hum. Mach Syst. **47**(4), 576–582 (2017)
7. Jiang, N., Dosen, S., Muller, K.R., Farina, D.: Myoelectric control of artificial limbs: is there a need to change focus? [In the Spotlight]. IEEE Signal Process. Mag. **29**(5), 150–152 (2012)
8. Rehbaum, H., Jiang, N., Farina, D.: Real time simultaneous and proportional control of multiple degree of freedom: initial results of amputee tests. In: 34th Annual International Conference of the IEEE Engineering in Medicine and Biology Society, pp. 1346–1349 (2012)
9. Roche, A.D., Rehbaum, H., Farina, D., Aszmann, O.C.: Prosthetic myoelectric control strategies: a clinical perspective. Curr. Surg. Rep. **2**(3), 44 (2014)
10. Jiang, N., Englehart, K.B., Parker, P.A.: Extracting simultaneous and proportional neural control information for multiple-dof prostheses from the surface electromyographic signal. IEEE Trans. Biomed. Eng. **56**(4), 1070–1080 (2009)
11. Kim, P., Kim, K.S., Kim, S.: Modified nonnegative matrix factorization using the hadamard product to estimate real-time continuous finger-motion intentions. IEEE Trans. Hum. Mach. Syst. **47**(6), 1089–1099 (2017)
12. Gijsberts, A., Atzori, M., Castellini, C., Müller, H., Caputo, B.: Movement error rate for evaluation of machine learning methods for semg-based hand movement classification. IEEE Trans. Neural Syst. Rehabil. Eng. **22**(4), 735–744 (2014)
13. Sarac, M., Solazzi, M., Sotgiu, E., Bergamasco, M., Frisoli, A.: Design and kinematic optimization of a novel underactuated robotic hand exoskeleton. Meccanica **52**(3), 749–761 (2017)
14. Koiva, R., Hilsenbeck, B., Castellini, C.: FFLS: an accurate linear device for measuring synergistic finger contractions. In: 2012 Annual International Conference of the IEEE Engineering in Medicine and Biology Society (EMBC), pp. 531–534. IEEE (2012)
15. Sanger, T.D.: Bayesian filtering of myoelectric signals. J. Neurophysiol. **97**(2), 1839–1845 (2007)
16. Hofmann, D., Jiang, N., Vujaklija, I.: Bayesian filtering of surface EMG for accurate simultaneous and proportional prosthetic control. IEEE Trans. Neural Syst. Rehabil. Eng. **24**(12), 1333–1341 (2016)
17. Tomiak, T., Abramovych, T.I., Gorkovenko, A.V., Vereshchaka, I.V., Mishchenko, V.S., Dornowski, M., Kostyukov, A.I.: The movement-and load-dependent differences in the emg patterns of the human arm muscles during two-joint movements (a preliminary study). Fronti. Physiol. **7**, 218 (2016)
18. Santello, M., Bianchi, M., Gabiccini, M., Ricciardi, E., Salvietti, G., Prattichizzo, D., Ernst, M., Moscatelli, A., Jörntell, H., Kappers, A.M., et al.: Hand synergies: integration of robotics and neuroscience for understanding the control of biological and artificial hands. Phys. Life Rev. **17**, 1–23 (2016)

Basic Design on Blocking
Part of Skin-Propagated Vibration
for Artificial Hand

Yuki Kito[1(✉)], Yoshihiro Tanaka[1], Noritaka Kawashima[2],
and Masahiro Yoshikawa[3]

[1] Nagoya Institute of Technology, Nagoya, Japan
y.kito.737@nitech.jp, tanaka.yoshihiro@nitech.ac.jp
[2] Research Institute of National Rehabilitation
Center for Persons with Disabilities, Tokorozawa, Japan
kws456123@gmail.com
[3] Osaka Institute of Technology, Osaka, Japan
masahiro.yoshikawa@oit.ac.jp

Abstract. We aim at developing a prosthetic hand having vibration-based sensors and actuators that provide feedback to enhance body recognition. Detection of skin-propagated vibration on the prosthetic hand is reasonable because of a small number of sensors thanks to a large receptive field by the propagation and a high-temporal response. However, limiting the receptive field of each sensor is required for each finger, in order to reduce the vibration originating from an undesired area. For this issue, the present study proposes the addition of a blocking part on the skeleton of the prosthetic hand. A rigid rod covered with silicone was assembled, as a simple model of the hand, and a skin vibration sensor with a PVDF film and the blocking part were set. Results on materials and dimensions show that making a part of the rod thicker with a certain thickness and width is effective for reducing the vibration.

Keywords: Skin-propagated vibration · Blocking part
Tactile sensor · Prosthetic hand

1 Introduction

1.1 Background

Tactile sense is strongly involved in body recognition, as indicated by the Rubber Hand Illusion [1,2]. Applications on body recognition have attracted extensive attention from robotics researchers on teleoperation, human-augmented extra arms, and prosthetic hands. For example, Arata et al. demonstrated that the effect of the Rubber Hand Illusion can be enhanced with master slave robots for accurate manipulation [3]. Parietti et al. developed Supernumerary Robotic Limbs, which is a wearable robot designed to assist a human worker by using

© Springer International Publishing AG, part of Springer Nature 2018
D. Prattichizzo et al. (Eds.): EuroHaptics 2018, LNCS 10894, pp. 214–225, 2018.
https://doi.org/10.1007/978-3-319-93399-3_20

additional arms and legs attached to the worker's body [4]. There is an issue with these devices however; how the worker expands their body recognition into the additional arms and legs. Ehrsson et al. showed that upper limb amputees felt a rubber hand like theirs when the stump and the index finger of the rubber hand were simultaneously tapped [5]. Enhancement of body recognition has the potential to increase the operability of robot hands, to help rehabilitation, to reduce phantom pain, and to enable tactile recognition of objects.

We aim at developing a passive prosthetic hand having vibration-based sensors and actuators that provide feedback. Generally, embedding tactile sensors to prosthetic or robot hands has been tried in order to enable their accurate manipulation, as can be seen from the sensory-motor control of humans. For example, Godfrey et al. showed that force feedback reduces grasping force during manipulation using a myoelectric prosthesis [6]. Implementing force sensors is effective for manipulation with a prosthetic hand, as well as contributing to the body recognition of the prosthetic hand. However, the implementation of force sensors still has many issues such as the need for a large number of them, high sensitivity, measurement of 3-axis force, and a systematic method of feedback for multi sensor outputs.

In this study, we focused on skin-propagated vibration in order to obtain the body recognition of artificial hands such as prosthetic hands. Shao et al. demonstrated that skin vibration is propagated to a remote area from a contact area by attaching many acceleration sensors on humans' hands when they touch objects with their fingertips [7]. Natsume et al. demonstrated that skin-propagated vibration has a good relation with subjective roughness rating while rubbing surfaces [8]. Thus, the use of the skin-propagated vibration can contribute to the contact detection with a wide receptive field as well as texture recognition.

We think that the contact detection based on skin-propagated vibrations is useful to generate body recognition because of the small number of sensors required, thanks to their large receptive field and high-temporal response to stimulation. Although accurate spatial information derived from contact is difficult to achieve without a large number of sensors, the sight sense might help to obtain the spatial information together with touch. To achieve this, it is required to place sensors for detecting the skin-propagated vibration on each finger of the prosthetic hand since vibrotactile feedback is required for each finger in order to imitate humans. However, when sensors are placed on each finger, they respond to contact stimulation on, not only the corresponding finger, but also the neighboring fingers, since the elicited vibration is propagated throughout the rubber surface.

1.2 PVDF Sensor

A polyvinylidene fluoride (PVDF) film which is polymer piezo material, has been used for tactile sensors. For instance, Sokhanvar et al. showed that endoscopic graspers with a PVDF sensor can be employed for softness sensing in minimally invasive surgery [9]. Takamuku et al. showed that a PVDF sensor and strain gauges are useful for haptic discrimination of material properties by a robotic hand [10]. On these sensors, PVDF films were set on the contact area in order

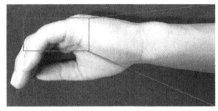
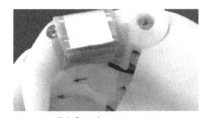

(a) State covering a rubber hand   (b) Inside structure

Fig. 1. Structure of the prosthetic hand with the PVDF sensor

to detect the force or vibration, directly. Here, we focused on using the PVDF film to detect the skin-propagated vibration.

We attempted to apply a PVDF film onto a prosthetic hand, considering a wearable tactile sensor with a PVDF film used by Natsume et al. [8]. In the previous study, the PVDF film was wrapped on the finger pad between the distal interphalangeal (DIP) and the proximal interphalangeal (PIP) joints and detected skin-propagated vibration from the fingertip contacting with an object. The PVDF film generates a charge proportional to the tension stress. Therefore, the sensor output is relative to the acceleration. Thus, the previous sensor responds only to the vibration elicited on the finger, rather than responding to the movement of the finger as a whole. Acceleration sensors respond to both the vibration and the movement of the finger. In addition, the response of the above PVDF sensors shows small influence from the orientation of the contact area, due to wrapping the sensor around the finger pad. The PVDF film features also advantages in the assembly. The PVDF sensor is thin, flexible, and easy to place.

In a similar way to the above sensor, a PVDF film was wrapped on the area between PIP and metacarpophalangeal (MCP) joints on the skeleton of the index finger of the prosthetic hand with a rubber medium and a hand-shaped rubber covering the skeleton. Figure 1 shows the state of the rubber hand and the inside structure that houses the sensor. The sensor can detect the propagated vibration in a similar way to the human fingers. However, there is still the problem on applying PVDF sensors into multi prosthetic fingers, as mentioned above. Blocking the undesired propagation of the vibration across the fingers is required.

1.3   Block of Propagated Vibration

Thus, this paper presents a basic research to enable the design of the receptive field of PVDF sensors on a prosthetic hand. We propose a simple method to block artificial skin-propagated vibration by placing mechanical elements partially on the skeleton of the prosthetic hand. As a basic design, we assembled a simple model based on the structure of the artificial finger having the sensor. The simple model is a rigid rod covered with a silicone rubber. A PVDF sensor, which has the same structure as the one shown in Fig. 1, was used on the

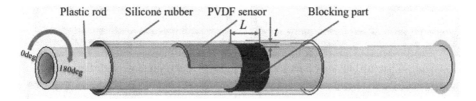

Fig. 2. Simple model based on the structure of the finger

model. As a blocking part, we prepared soft mediums between the rod and the rubber, and the partially thick rod. Effects of the materials and dimensions of the proposed blocking part were investigated with the simple model.

2   Method to Control a Receptive Field of the Vibration Sensor

Figure 2 shows the structure of the model with the PVDF sensor and the blocking part. The model was composed of a rigid plastic rod covered with a silicone rubber. The rod and the silicone rubber correspond to the skeleton and the rubber skin of the prosthetic hand, respectively. The PVDF film was attached on the middle area of the rod with a rubber medium. The length of the rod was 150 mm, and the inner and outer diameters were 10 and 14 mm, respectively. The silicone rubber was 80 mm in length, and the inner and outer diameters were 16 and 18 mm, respectively. The PVDF sensor with the rubber medium was 20 mm in width, and the thickness was 0.9 mm. A blocking part was set on the area close to the sensor.

We propose a method to place the blocking part on the rod. Two kinds of blocking parts were investigated. One is a soft medium, which is sandwiched partially between the rod and the rubber. In the other type, the thickness of a part of the rod was increased. Since the blocking part might work as a boundary, reducing the propagated vibration, the PVDF sensor has a high response to the stimulation given to the side with the sensor, but it has a low response to the stimulation given to the side without the sensor.

3   Experiment 1: Material

First, we investigated the effect of the material on the proposed blocking part.

3.1   Models

All models are presented in Fig. 3 (without the silicone rubber). Four different materials were prepared for soft mediums employed as the blocking part: urethane sponge, high density urethane sponge, gel, and nitrile rubber. Dimensions

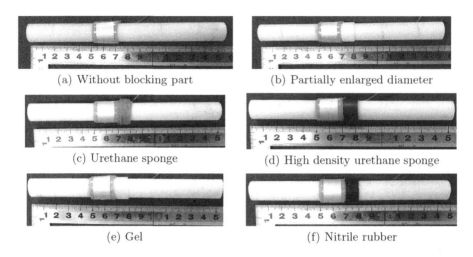

(a) Without blocking part   (b) Partially enlarged diameter

(c) Urethane sponge   (d) High density urethane sponge

(e) Gel   (f) Nitrile rubber

Fig. 3. Model with each blocking part or without blocking part

of all materials were $L = 10$ mm in width (axial direction) and $t = 1$ mm in thickness as shown in Figs. 2 and 3. All materials were attached to the same position on the rod with an adhesive tape. A model with partially enlarged diameter (partially-thick part) was prepared with the same material as the rod and the same dimensions ($L = 10$ mm, $t = 1$ mm) as the soft mediums. In addition to the test models, a model without any blocking part was prepared for comparison.

3.2   Method

Stimulator. A stimulator, which generates sinusoidal vibration to the model, was assembled for this study. Figure 4 shows its structure. It was composed of a vibrator (TL-002-14R Haptuator Redesign, Tactile Labs) for vibration stimulation, an acceleration sensor (2302B, SHOWA SOKKI) for measuring the amplitude of the vibration, and a load cell (LMA-A, KYOWA) for measuring the contact force. They were embedded in a rigid plastic case as shown in Fig. 4. A hemisphere contactor was placed at the extremity of the stimulator. The vibrator was connected to an amplifier and a function generator. An experimenter could control the intensity and frequency of the stimulation, as well as the contact force, by watching the vibration and contact force measured by the embedded sensors displayed on a monitor.

Procedure. The experimental setup is shown in Fig. 5. All models were covered with the silicone rubber, and the end of the rod with a blocking part was clamped in a vice, to mimic the finger of a prosthetic hand. The stimulator contact points were at 30, 40, 50, 60 (the position of the PVDF), 70 (the position of the blocking part), 80 and 90 mm from the other end of the rod, at a constant angle of $90°$ (the center of the PVDF sensor in circumferential direction as shown in Fig. 2).

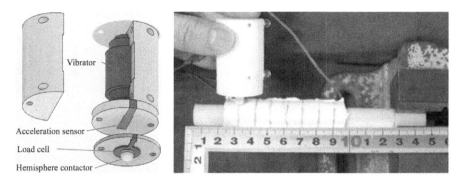

Fig. 4. Structure of stimulator   **Fig. 5.** Experimental state

In addition, contact angles of 0, 45, 90, 135 and 180° at a constant distance of 30 mm were investigated. The contact force was set at 0.5 N, and the vibration was set at 100 Hz in the frequency and 10 μm in the amplitude (peak-to-peak). The exerted contact force was 0.5 ± 0.1 N, and the amplitude of the vibration was 10 ± 3 μm throughout the trials. The rod was subjected to vibration during 10 s for each position, and the sensor output was collected during the stimulation at a sampling frequency of 10 kHz and filtered by a high pass with a cut off frequency of 10 Hz. The sensor output was extracted in the duration of 5 s when the input vibration was stable and the root mean square (RMS) of the extracted sensor output was calculated for the evaluation of the intensity of the sensor output for each trial. Then, means of the intensity and its standard deviation were calculated from 5 measurements per position.

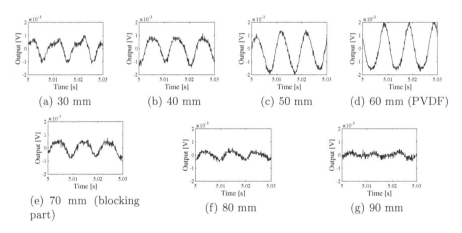

Fig. 6. Examples of sensor outputs to the propagated vibration from different positions (case of the model with partially-thick rod)

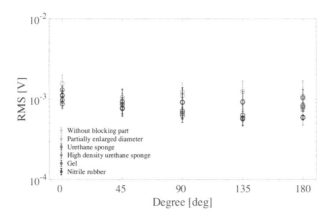

Fig. 7. Results of stimulation at different circumferential angles at 30 mm on each model with different materials

3.3   Results and Discussion

Examples of the sensor outputs on the model with partially enlarged diameter are shown in Fig. 6. The results show that the sensor output was large to the stimulation at the closer positions of the sensor and decreased after 70 mm thanks to the blocking part.

The experimental results on different circumferential angles at 30 mm and on different axial distances at 90° are shown in Figs. 7 and 8, respectively. Regarding the circumferential angle, it seems that there is no large difference between the models. Since the sensor is attached within 0–180°, the sensor output might not have been affected among the circumferential angles. For the axial detection, it was found that the sensor output appeared symmetrically around the sensor in the model without the blocking part. This occurs because the structure around the sensor is the same. When the vibration was close to the position of the sensor, the sensor output was large because the vibration was directly applied. On the other models, in Figs. 8(b)–(f), the intensity of the sensor outputs was lower on the stimulation at 80 and 90 mm as compared with that on the stimulation at 30 and 40 mm. It can be seen that the intensity of the sensor outputs largely decreased to the stimulation over the location of the blocking part. These results indicate that all blocking parts reduced the skin-propagated vibration.

Figure 9 shows the intensity of the sensor output for the stimulation at 90 mm for comparison of the blocking effects among models. There is no large difference between the models with the blocking parts. This result indicates that materials do not strongly affect the blocking effect. Considering the geometry of the models, which were composed of the rod, the rubber, the sensor and the blocking part, it is supposed that a strong factor is the distance between the sensor and the rubber. The thickness is the same among models with the blocking part, and the diameter of the blocking part was the same as the inner diameter of the silicone rubber. Therefore, some tension might have been given to the rubber at the

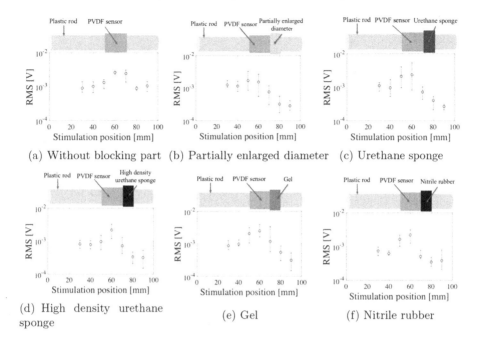

(a) Without blocking part   (b) Partially enlarged diameter   (c) Urethane sponge

(d) High density urethane sponge

(e) Gel

(f) Nitrile rubber

Fig. 8. Results on the stimulation of each model with different materials to different axial positions at 90°

position of the blocking part, whereas the intensity of the tension was slightly different among materials due to the different stiffness. In addition, Fig. 10 shows the intensity of the sensor output for the stimulation at 30 mm. There are small differences between models. This result might derive from the different reflection of the waves generated by the blocking part due to the different materials.

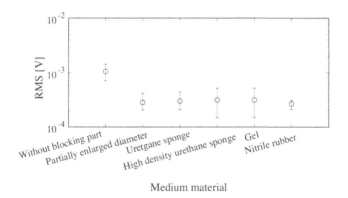

Medium material

Fig. 9. Results on the stimulation of different materials at 90 mm on 90°

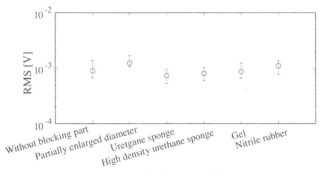

Fig. 10. Results on the stimulation of different materials at 30 mm on 90°

Next, we conducted experiments with partially-thick models having different thicknesses and width.

4   Experiment 2: Thickness and Width

In experiment 2 we studied the influence of the dimensions of the blocking part on the vibration-blocking effect. Thus, focusing on the model with the partially-thick part only (corresponding to Fig. 8(b)), the thickness and width of the thick part were investigated.

4.1   Models

Partially-thick rods with different thicknesses ($t = 0$, 0.2, 0.4, 0.6, 0.8, 1.0, and 1.2 mm) were prepared, and the width of all models was set as $L = 10$ mm. Moreover, partially-thick rods with different widths ($L = 0$, 2, 4, 6, 8, 10, and 12 mm) were prepared with a constant thickness of $t = 1.0$ mm.

4.2   Method

The same stimulator was used as in Experiment 1.

First, to evaluate the blocking effect and the reflection of the waves generated by the blocking part, the vibration contact point was set at 30 and 90 mm on 90° for the partially-thick rods with different thicknesses. Then, the vibration contact point was set at 90 mm on 90° for the partially-thick rods with different widths.

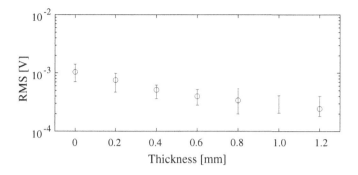

Fig. 11. Results on the stimulation to models with different thicknesses at 90 mm on 90°

4.3   Results and Discussion

The intensity of the sensor output on the stimulation of the models with different thicknesses at 90 mm is shown in Fig. 11. The result shows that the sensor output is inversely related to the thickness. This indicates that the blocking effect was enhanced with the increase in thickness. A possible reason is that the tension given to the rubber increases due to the partially-thick part. When the tension is large, it might be more difficult for the corresponding area of the rubber hand to elicit the vibration. Thus, the sensor output decreased. The results on thickness supports our assumption.

The intensity of the sensor output on the stimulation of models with different thicknesses at 30 mm is shown in Fig. 12. The result shows that when the thickness is thicker than 1 mm, the intensity of the sensor output is slightly increased. This might be caused by the reflection of the waves generated by the blocking part. Considering the reflection wave, there is a possibility that the frequency characteristic of the sensor output was changed by the reflection of the waves as well as material. Here, a preliminary experiment showed that the frequency characteristic of the PVDF sensor with the blocking part had a moderate peak.

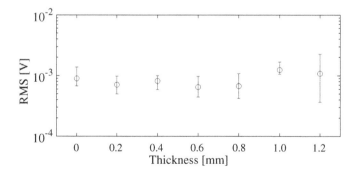

Fig. 12. Results on the stimulation of models with different thicknesses at 30 mm on 90°

Although the influence of the reflection waves might not be large, frequency response is relevant to associate it with the human's frequency response for the vibrotactile feedback. In future work, phenomenon of the blocking effect and frequency response will be investigated in more detail.

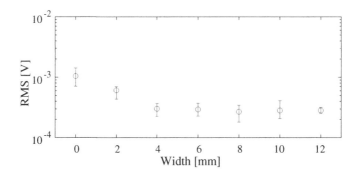

Fig. 13. Results on the stimulation of models with different widths at 90 mm on 90°

The intensity of the sensor output on models with different widths is shown in Fig. 13. The result shows that the sensor output decreased as the width increased, however when the width is thicker than 4 mm, there is no difference in the sensor output. When the width is small, the vibration does not decreases enough since the area where the tension is induced is small. When the model has a relatively wide blocking part, the tension is induced to a sufficiently large area to diminish the propagated vibration. Thus, the effect was not changed under the width more than 4 mm.

These results showed that the method of blocking vibration by making a part of the rod thicker at a certain thickness and width is useful for designing the receptive field of vibration on the prosthetic hand. This method is advantageous in the aspect of the simple structure and fabrication. It does not require any additional materials or assembling process, and it is easy to fabricate.

5   Conclusion

We proposed a basic structure that enables the design of a receptive area of a PVDF sensor for detecting skin-propagated vibration on an artificial hand. We assembled a rigid rod covered with silicone based on the structure of the prosthetic finger having the PVDF sensor. We proposed a method to put the blocking part on the skeleton of the artificial hand to diminish the propagation of vibration from an undesired area. The results showed that the effect of the materials of the blocking part was small, however the effect of thickness and width were important. Finally, we concluded that, making a part of the rod thicker with a certain thickness and width is effective for diminishing the vibration. This is useful for designing the prosthetic hand because it does not require any additional materials or assembling process, and it is easy to fabricate.

The next step will be to apply this design to a prosthetic hand equipped with one sensor on each finger and evaluate the influence of the frequency characteristics.

Acknowledgment. This work was supported in part by JSPS KAKENHI Grant number JP17H01252.

References

1. Matthew, B., Jonathan, C.: Rubber hands 'feel' touch that eyes see. Nature **391**, 756 (1998)
2. Armel, K.C., Ramachandran, V.S.: Projecting sensations to external objects: evidence from skin conductance response. Proc. Roy. Soc. Lond. Ser. B Biol. Sci. **270**(1523), 1449–1506 (2003)
3. Arata, J., Hattori, M., Ichikawa, S., Sakaguchi, M.: Robotically enhanced rubber hand illusion. IEEE Trans. Haptics **7**(4), 526–532 (2014)
4. Parietti, F., Asada, H.H.: Dynamic analysis and state estimation for wearable robotic limbs subject to human-induced disturbances. In: 2013 IEEE International Conference on Robotics and Automation, vol. 7, no. 4, pp. 3880–3887 (2013)
5. Ehrsson, H.H., Rosén, B., Stockselius, A., Ragnö, C., Kőhler, P., Lundborg, G.: Upper limb amputees can be induced to experience a rubber hand as their own. Brain **131**(12), 3443–3452 (2008)
6. Godfrey, S.B., Bianchi, M., Bicchi, A., Santello, M.: Influence of force feedback on grasp force modulation in prosthetic applications: a preliminary study. In: 38th Annual International Conference of the IEEE Engineering in Medicine and Biology Society (EMBC), pp. 5439–5442 (2016)
7. Shao, Y., Hayward, V., Visell, Y.: Spatial patterns of cutaneous vibration during whole-hand haptic interactions. Proc. Natl. Acad. Sci. USA. **113**(15), 4188–4193 (2016)
8. Natsume, M., Tanaka, Y., Sano, A.: Skin-propagated vibration for roughness and textures. In: World Automation Congress (WAC). IEEE (2016)
9. Sokhanvar, S., Packirisamy, M., Dargahi, J.: A multifunctional PVDF-based tactile sensor for minimally invasive surgery, vol. 16, no. 4. IOP Publishing Ltd. (2007)
10. Takamuku, S., Gomez, G., Hosoda, K., Pfeifer, R.: Haptic discrimination of material properties by a robotic hand. In: IEEE 6th International Conference on Development and Learning (2007)

Estimating the Direction of Force Applied to the Grasped Object Using the Surface EMG

Yuki Ban[(✉)] [iD]

The University of Tokyo, Chiba, Japan
ban@edu.k.u-tokyo.ac.jp

Abstract. In the passive haptic system and other VR fields, there is a great demand for measuring the direction and magnitude of various forces applied to a grasped object. To acquire this force, there are mainly two kinds of methods; one is directly measuring it by the sensor attached or embedded to the object surface or the glove type device, and the other is estimating it by measuring the change of the surface electromyography (sEMG) of the forearm. The former is used a lot but has problems that it is difficult to stick the sensor due to the object's surface, and sensors prevent fingers and objects from touching directly. The latter approach has a potential to release us from above problems. However, most of their works focused on estimating a certain direction of force, like a grip force, thus, there is no research to estimate multidirectional loading forces.

To solve these problems, we propose a solution for estimating direction and magnitude of the force applied to the grasped object using sEMG of the forearm with the convolutional neural network (CNN), as the gesture recognition field uses. By constructing training system that can measure sEMG signals and the force applied to the grasped object, we trained a model, and this model realized over 95% accurate directional estimation and the estimation of force magnitude with less than 7% NRMSE.

Keywords: Grasp Force direction estimation · EMG · Machine learning

1 Introduction

Lots of research have been done to present the haptic sensation in a virtual environment (VE). There are currently two main methods to present the haptic sensation while touching a virtual object. The first method is realized by dynamically moving real objects so that it matches the location of virtual objects' shapes. This method, which is called "active haptics" is realized by utilizing robotic arms or transformable surfaces [1]. The second method is realized by placing static, physical props around users in the real environment in advance to match their virtual counterparts. This method is called "passive haptics" [2]. The technique of the passive haptics has a potential to present realistic haptic sensation without costly actuators. Moreover, several studies have established the method to display various feeling of contact by manipulating the visualized position of a virtual object, using physical props at a fixed position in the real world. For example, Azmandian et al. have provided passive haptic feedback in VE by warping the

© Springer International Publishing AG, part of Springer Nature 2018
D. Prattichizzo et al. (Eds.): EuroHaptics 2018, LNCS 10894, pp. 226–238, 2018.
https://doi.org/10.1007/978-3-319-93399-3_21

virtual space to match the location of a physical prop in a person's surrounding [3]. With this system, a single physical prop can provide passive haptics for multiple virtual objects. We also have been trying to modify the shape perception for virtual object and a wall by distorting the movement of the virtual hand [4, 5]. In these studies, sensing the position of actual hand and props are indispensable.

These passive haptic techniques can be extended to the presentation of stiffness sensation during grasping virtual objects. This extension can be realized by sensing the grasping force, instead of position. In other words, by measuring the force applied to a real object and reflecting it in the deformation of the virtual object, it is possible to manipulate the perception of stiffness [6, 7]. Although these techniques have a potential to display the various stiffness, it is difficult to accurately measure the force magnitude and direction applied to the real object, and thus the method of measurement is now under research.

To measure the force applied to the grasped object, there are mainly two kinds of methods; one is directly measuring it by the sensor attached or embedded to the object surface or the glove type device, and the other is estimating it by measuring the change of the surface electromyography (sEMG) of the forearm when we grasp an object. The merit of the former method is that you can accurately measure the grasping force if you can attach a sensor. However, it is necessary to attach and embed sensors to all objects to be measured, and when attaching a sensor to the fingertip, there is a problem that the way to move the fingers is constrained because it cannot touch the object directly. The latter method, using sEMG, is mainly utilized in many motion support systems, such as HAL [8], as well as in rehabilitation, nursing care support, etc. A muscle is composed of many motor units and the "discharge" or "firing" of each motor unit generates a "motor unit action potential" (MUAP), which is the sum of the contributions of the individual fibers that comprise each motor unit. sEMG records a muscle's electrical activity from the surface of the skin, meaning that it reflects the generation and propagation of MUAPs. Therefore, sEMG signals can help us to estimate user's movement and force generation.

Thus, sEMG signals are considered to be useful in the VR system that needs to use the force to grasp objects. However, such force estimation has been applied only to situations where the direction of force applied is limited, such as the grip force direction and the elbow flexion direction. One of the major reasons of this is that discrimination of the multidirectional force was difficult with a linear discriminator such as Support Vector Machine (SVM) due to the fact that the myoelectric information is highly noisy.

On the other hand, rapid progress of deep learning research in recent years has greatly improved the discrimination accuracy of images and sounds, and it is becoming possible to solve the problem thought to be impossible by conventional machine learning methods. Regarding EMG, for example, it has been confirmed that by inputting sEMG of the forearm to the convolutional neural network (CNN), the gesture identification accuracy can be greatly improved compared to previous studies that did not use deep learning method [9]. Based on these points, we considered that it would be possible to easily estimate various forces applied to an object during twisting and bending, if the applicant can learn the correspondence between the forearm sEMG signals and the direction and magnitude of the force applied to the grasped object using these approaches.

In this paper, we focus on the change of the forearm sEMG when a force is applied to a grasped object, and aim to realize a method for estimating the direction and magnitude of various forces during grasping operations such as pulling, bending and twisting of an object (Fig. 1). If this method can be realized, it is possible to easily realize a visuo-haptic display that modifies the stiffness perception for the virtual object by manipulating the deformation of vitual objects based on the measured force applied to actual objects. In this paper, as a first step to realize "a method to estimate the direction and magnitude of various forces applied to grasped objects" for constructing such a visuo-haptic display, we constructed a system that can simultaneously measure the force with various directions applied to a grasping object and the forearm sEMG signals.

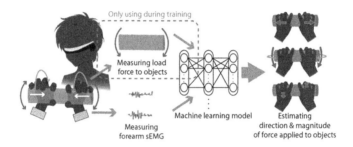

Fig. 1. Estimating the direction and magnitude of forces applied to the object using sEMG.

2 Previous Works

2.1 Measuring the Force Applied to a Grasped Object

The methods for measuring force on a grasped object can be roughly divided into methods of attaching or embed pressure sensors on a grasped object, and methods of attaching sensors to the fingers by using a glove-type device. The former is easy to operate because it only needs to paste the sensor on the object. However, if the object's shape is difficult to attach a sensor to, such as a sphere, it is necessary to embed the sensor directly inside the object [10]. Although an accurate force vector distribution measurement can be achieved with this method, the effort of embedding the sensor directly into the object is too high to apply it to lots of objects.

The approach of attaching a sensor to a finger by using a glove-type device is becoming more feasible with the ongoing development of sensor technology, which is making these devices easier to manufacture and configure for each user. For instance, Sagisaka et al. developed highly flexible, small-scale sensor for tactile sensing gloves [11]. However, this device could only measure the grip force, so we cannot measure the load force when a user twists, pulls or pushes an object. Additionally, because the glove lies between the finger and the object to be grasped, it alters the original contact and friction sensations. For these reasons, we sought a method to avoid attaching sensors to objects or gloves.

2.2   Estimating the Grasping Force and Gestures Using sEMG Signals

The relation between sEMG signals and exerted force has been largely studied. Focusing on the arm forces, models were developed to estimate the exerted force during specific movements [12, 13]. All researchers show that a relationship between sEMG signal and exerted force exists and that is non-linear. Researchers also found that this relationship is not simple because lots of factors influence the sEMG signal and make it difficult to develop a general model. Although some researchers have tried to estimate the hand grip force and the weight of the handled object using the neural network, their methods could not realize highly accurate estimation [14, 15]. Most of their works focused on a certain direction of force, like a grip force, thus, there is no research to estimate multi-directional loading force on objects as we are seeking.

On the contrary, in the field of gesture recognition using sEMG, several types of research reported that they realized highly accurate estimation than the existing method using the deep learning method [9, 16]. For instance, Park and Lee reported that a better classification accuracy for CNN compared to SVM. Thus, we focus on these approaches to estimate the direction and magnitude of force applied to the grasped objects.

3   Estimating the Force Magnitude Applied to a Grasped Object

3.1   Concept of Overall System

The related research using sEMG signals, described above, mainly focuses on estimating the grip force (normal direction force). The estimation of load force (tangential direction force), such as pulling or twisting, has received little attention. However, considering the possibility of distinguishing between various gestures using sEMG signals, it should be possible to estimate the direction and magnitude of the force applied to a grasped object. Therefore, in this research, we aim to implement a method for estimating force direction and magnitude for actions such as pulling, bending, and twisting of a grasped object based on changes in the sEMG signals of the forearm.

In this section, we describe the configuration of our proposed learning system that can simultaneously measure the force applied to a grasping object and the forearm sEMG signals, and the data flow of training the model.

3.2   System Configuration

There are three possible conditions that affect this training: user's difference, the difference in shape of held object, the difference in grasping posture. Among them, in this paper, we focus on the effect of the user's difference on the training result as the first step, and create and verify the system with the other two conditions fixed. Our system consists of two parts. One is the part of measuring various force applied to an object, and the other is the part measuring the forearm sEMG. The former part is only used for training phase, and the latter part is used for training and estimation phase (Fig. 2). For the former part, we used a cylindrical acrylic object as the grasped object. This cylindrical object is 300 mm length and 50 mm diameter, and this object is fixed at the height of 120 mm from the desk. The reason for the cylindrical shape setting of the grasping object is that it is easy to grasp because it has few corner faces and force can be easily applied in the rotational direction around the axis, such as in the twisting motion. A strain gauge is used to acquire the magnitude of the force applied to an object. Strain gauges are affixed to the surface of the object, and the applied force is determined by acquiring the degree of deformation when a force is applied to the object. The gauges are affixed in six locations in order to enable the measurement of pulling, pushing, bending, and twisting (Fig. 3). Since the changes in the resistances of the strain gauges due to deformation are very small, the voltage changes are amplified by 100 times in the instrumentation amplifier (INA128) after each strain gauge passes the Wheatstone bridge.

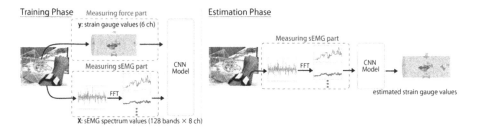

Fig. 2. Data flow of training and estimation phases.

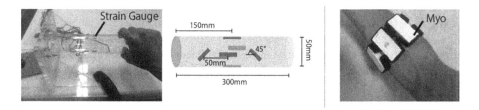

Fig. 3. Devices for two parts. Left: strain gauges attached on a grasped object. Center: the position of strain gauges. Right: how to wear Myo in this study.

For the measuring sEMG part, we used the Myo sensor, manufactured by Thalmic Lab [17]. This sensor has an 8-channel sEMG sensor, 3-axis acceleration sensors, and 3-axis gyro sensors (Fig. 3).

Advance Preparation and Signal Preprocessing. For the measuring force part, we determined the relationship between the magnitude of the applied force and the deformation amount of the object measured with strain gauges. We hanged multiple kinds of weight (1 kg, 3 kg, 5 kg) to the acrylic cylinder and measured the strain gauge values under each weight condition (Fig. 4). Through this measurement, it is confirmed that the strain gauge value increases linearly according to the weight, in the range up to 5 kg, and these measurement results were used in the user study described below.

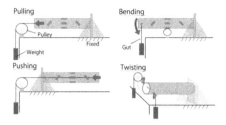

Fig. 4. Measuring the corresponding of strain gauge values and force magnitudes

For the measuring sEMG part, Myo's 8-channel sEMG sensor obtains a digital value between −128 and 127 as the myoelectric potential of the forearm at a sampling rate of 200 Hz. This data is multiplied by a Hamming window every 128 frames. For the numerical values obtained in this manner, a moving average of five frames was calculated for each channel and used as input data for estimation.

Network Architecture and Training Settings. The numerical values from the FFT analysis on the data obtained from the Myo 8-channel myoelectric potential sensor contain different values for individual sensors. In order to estimate the direction of the force applied to a grasped object, these values are fed into the CNN. The reason why we convolute the value of FFT analyzed data is that there is some relation between adjacent channels, and the frequency spectrum makes a characteristic form depending on the direction of force applied to the object. As Fig. 5 shows, the architecture of the CNN was structured as follows:

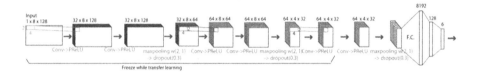

Fig. 5. Architecture of the convolutional neural network used on the sEMG signal.

The input data corresponds to time windows of 128 frames, meaning its size is 128 bands × 8 channels after preprocessing. These windows are consistent with typical practices in the field (i.e., analyzing time windows in order to allow control in real time) [18]. The first block of the network is comprised of the following four pieces. The first and second pieces are convolutional layers with 32 filters of size 4 × 2. The third piece is a non-linear activation function (rectified linear unit). The fourth piece is a subsampling layer that performs average pooling with filters of size 2 × 1.

The second and third blocks of the network are comprised of the following four pieces. The first and second pieces are convolutional layers with 64 filters of size 4 × 2. The third piece is a non-linear activation function (rectified linear unit). The fourth piece is a subsampling layer that performs average pooling with filters of size 2 × 1.

The fourth block of the network is comprised of the following three pieces. The first piece is a fully-connected layer of size 8192. The second piece is a fully-connected layer of size 128. The third piece is a fully connected layer of size 6.

Several different weight initializations were tested. In the end, the weights of the convolutional layers were initialized with random values in ranges determined by percentages of the data ranges in order to achieve reasonable training time and stability. We applied a dropout function after each pooling with a rate of 0.3, which we determined based on the results of test trials. The loss function used was mean squared error.

Hyper-parameters were identified via random search and manual hyper-parameter tuning [19] was performed on a validation set comprised of one participant randomly selected from two datasets. After several tests, we decided to use Adam optimizer with a mini-batch size of 128. The learning rate was fixed at 2e−4.

Calibration. To improve the estimation accuracy, it is assumed that constructing the model with only a single user's data is better. However, for that purpose, each user has to gather data before using the system and the system needs to train a model. These efforts lack convenience. Therefore, it is ideal that highly accurate estimation can be performed with a learning model constructed from multi-person's data that does not include herself/himself. However, it is expected that the maximum potential muscular force and magnitude of the force applied to the grasped object differ greatly between individuals, so highly accurate estimation cannot be expected with this method. Thus, in this case, calibration is required to make the model suitable for individual users. In this paper, we use a method of transfer learning for each subject as a calibration method.

Transfer learning is one of the common learning methods used in the field of machine learning. In the field of machine learning, transfer learning is defined as "the process of using knowledge gained through one or more different tasks and applying it in order to efficiently find effective hypotheses for new tasks" [20]. For a CNN, when using features in a too low level layer, we cannot take full advantage of the highly discriminative structure of the convolutional layers. Conversely, when using features in a too high level layer, there is a possibility of overfitting the training dataset during learning, which will negatively impact the performance of the model.

Although the potential muscular force varies for each user, the frequency spectrum still has common features, meaning transfer learning can be used in this case. Recently, Côté-Allard et al. reported that they succeeded in improving gesture recognition accuracy with sEMG by using transfer learning [21]. Following these previous knowledge, we re-trained the network up to the last convolutional layer (Fig. 5).

4   User Study

To evaluate the accuracy of our method, we conducted a user study. This study followed standard ethical practices, and it underwent the ethical review by the Ethics Review Committee in our research institution. 15 participants whose ages ranged from 22 to 25 (13 males and 2 females) participated in the experiment. All of them were right-handed, and every one had daily exercise habits less than 2 h per week. Also, no one had any experience using Myo. The device was attached to the dominant arm, and its logo mark came inside the elbow like Fig. 3. A participant sat a seat and grasped a cylindrical object's right edge with her/his right hand.

4.1   Task Design

In this experiment, eight different types of grasping forces on a cylindrical object were used for identification of gesture as follows: pulling, pushing, bending (up, down, front, and back for a total of four directions), twisting (with the right hand toward the back or front for a total of two directions) (Fig. 6). Participants were told to keep the posture of the right hand so that their finger's third joints were on top (Fig. 3, Left). They were told to apply force ten times in each direction to get the training and validation data. Each applying force trial took 10 s, and participants were told to increase applying power gradually for first 5 s to the target magnitude, then to keep their power for next 5 s. The time count was displayed with the sound and the vision on a monitor (Fig. 7). On a monitor, there was a bar which showed the force magnitude calculated by the calibrated value of a strain gauge. The system displayed the target magnitude of the force that a participant should apply to an object, and s/he was told to control applying force to reach this target magnitude by watching this bar's length.

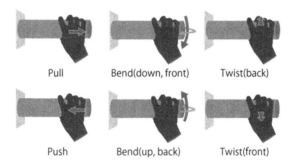

Pull	Bend(down, front)	Twist(back)
Push	Bend(up, back)	Twist(front)

Fig. 6. Force direction of training dataset. (left side of the object is fixed)

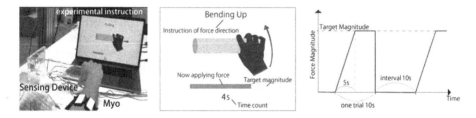

Fig. 7. Left: The setup of the experiment, Center: Experimental instruction. Right: Instructed time line of the force magnitude in one trail.

This target magnitude was equal to the value when 5 kg weight was hanged to the cylindrical object. Between each trial, they had a break for 10 s. The trial order of the force direction was randomly assigned and counterbalanced across participants to eliminate any order effect. Therefore, each participant performed 96 trials (=8 (force directions) × 12). After that, each participant performed 32 trials (=8 (force directions) × 4) to create the dataset for the transfer learning that we called "TL data."

4.2   Training and Accuracy Evaluation

To remove noise, we excluded sEMG values which were smaller than the sensor's value when hanging a 1 kg weight to the cylindrical object in each force direction task. Three types of models were trained in this experiment; Model α was trained with only one participant's data and we used 10-fold cross validation on the data set in order to have a simple and reliable measure of the accuracy; Model β was trained with multi participants' data. This model was trained with participants' data other than a participant to be tested. Thus, we produced 15 models constructed from the data of 14 people excluding test participant's data; Model γ was trained by calibrating Model β with each participant's TL data, and we used 10-fold cross validation on the dataset as Model α.

Learning was carried out with batch size of 128 and 200 epochs for Model α and Model β, and with batch size of 128 and 30 epochs for model γ. For the continuous detection of the strain gauge's output value, the main metric was the Normalized Root Mean Square Error (NRMSE) of the estimated strain gauge's output value to the real value. The variation tests were done with each direction of force.

In addition to this evaluation, we verified whether the type of force direction was correctly recognized. To prove this, we performed following processing; First, absolute values of six strain gauges were calculated, and the upper two were selected. After that, we checked whether these two sensor's values were positive or negative. When this combination of values was the same between the test and generated data, we could recognize the direction of force correctly. For example, in bending down situation, the absolute values of strain gauge should be the largest at the top side sensor (sensor 1) and the bottom side sensor (sensor 2) (Fig. 8). At this time, since the top side is elongated and the bottom side is shrinking, the value of the sensor 1 should be negative and the value of the sensor 2 should be positive. Whether or not this combination matched

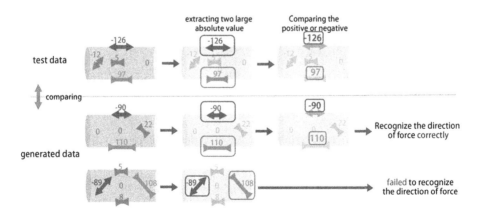

Fig. 8.   How to determine whether identification of force direction was correct.

between test and generated data was verified for input of each force direction. The ratio of the time in which the force direction was correctly recognized at the total input time in each direction was taken as the accuracy of the force direction estimation.

4.3 Result

As the experimental result, we show two types of data, one is the accuracy of the force direction estimation calculated with the method described above (named Direction accuracy), and the other is the accuracy of the force direction and magnitude estimation with NRMSE (named Magnitude accuracy).

Figure 9 Left shows the Direction accuracy. The average and its standard error of the accuracy of the force direction estimation for each condition of the training model were: Model α (Individual): $95.1 \pm 1.50\%$; Model β (All): $86.6 \pm 4.02\%$; Model γ (Transfer): $93.5 \pm 2.44\%$. We used repeated measures ANOVA with Bonferroni-Holm correction. This test revealed a significant effect of the type of the training model ($F(2, 336) = 14.34$, $p < .01$), with the Bonferroni-Holm correction showing a significant difference between the estimation accuracy percentage in all conditions ($p < .01$).

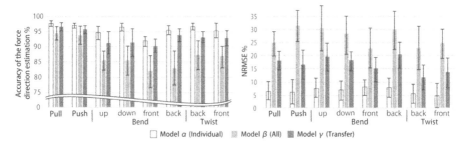

Fig. 9. Result of estimation accuracy (Left: Direction accuracy, Right: Magnitude accuracy)

On the other hand, Fig. 9 Right shows Magnitude accuracy. The percentages of NRMSE of the predicted strain gauge's output value to the real value over all directions of force were: Model α (Individual): 6.71 ± 2.41; Model β (All): 26.9 ± 8.24; Model γ (Transfer): 15.2 ± 4.13. We used repeated measures ANOVA with Bonferroni-Holm correction. This test revealed a significant effect of the diameter of a grasped object ($F(2, 336) = 80.43$, $p < .01$), with the Bonferroni-Holm correction showing a significant difference between the classification accuracy percentage in all conditions ($p < .01$).

4.4 Discussion

Because there are individual differences in the muscle load required to demonstrate the magnitude of a certain force, sEMG when exerting the same magnitude of force also makes a difference between individuals. Therefore, it is convincing that the accuracy of the case of the Model α trained and evaluated within the individual is the highest, and the accuracy of the case of the Model β evaluated by the model not trained with its own data is the lowest. On the other hand, the accuracy of the Model γ which was applied transfer learning by each subject data based on the Model β is superior to that of the Model β both in Direction accuracy and Magnitude accuracy, so it suggests that the usefulness of transfer learning in this case.

For Direction accuracy, the accuracy of bending situation was lower than that of pulling/pushing or twisting situations especially with Model β. The reason of this is considered that although participants were told to grasp the object with fixed posture, the relationship of position between a hand and a grasped object was subtly different between participants, so if the direction of force applied to the object was equal, the force applied to the arm was changed. From the result that Direction accuracy was over 95% using the model trained with only one participant's data, our method is useful for estimating the force direction applied to the grasped object, and has highly potential to be used to the visuo-haptic system that displays stiffness with passive haptics. Moreover, the result that Direction accuracy using the transfer learning was over 90% suggested that we can adapt a model to individuals with less time consuming simple calibration, if we have a model trained with multi users' data.

On the contrary, Magnitude accuracy using Model γ seems to be not high enough to use for VR system, although its accuracy improved from that with Model β. It can be considered that individual differences concerning magnitude of the force is too large to absorb the difference by using transfer learning. However, Magnitude accuracy using Model αwas high enough so that we can use the model trained with individual data not only to estimate the direction of force but also the magnitude of force. Besides, regarding model γ using the transfer learning, even though it is impossible to estimate accurate intensity, since estimation of direction can be performed with a high degree of accuracy, it is considered to be useful for rough estimation of magnitude, like determination strong or weak, with the directional estimation.

5   Conclusion

We have presented a solution for estimating direction and magnitude of force applied to the grasped object using sEMG of the forearm. By constructing training system that can measure sEMG signals and the force applied to the grasped object, we realized highly accurate estimation by learning the relation between grasping force in multiple directions and sEMG at that time, and applied the method of transfer learning to improve accuracy. The accuracy of estimating magnitude of force using the transfer learning was not satisfactory, however, this method gained high accuracy of over 90% for force direction estimation.

As the next step, we should investigate the influence of the grasped object's shape and the hand posture on the accuracy of estimation. It can be possible that the transfer learning helps us to enhance the accuracy of it, even when these parameters change. Since our proposed system makes it easy to acquire various force input to an object, it is expected to play an active part in various scenes.

References

1. Tachi, S., Maeda, T., Hirata, R., Hoshino, H.A.: Construction method of virtual haptic space. In: Proceedings of the 4th International Conference on Artificial Reality and Tele-Existence, pp. 131–138 (1994)
2. Hinckley, K., Pausch, R., Goble, J.C., Kassell, N.F.: Passive real-world interface props for neurosurgical visualization. In: Proceedings of the SIGCHI Conference on Human Factors in Computing Systems, vol. 452 (1994)
3. Azmandian, M., Hancock, M., Benko, H., Ofek, E., Wilson, A.D.: Haptic retargeting: dynamic repurposing of passive haptics for enhanced virtual reality experiences. In: Proceedings of the SIGCHI Conference on Human Factors in Computing Systems, pp. 1968–1979 (2016)
4. Ban, Y., Kajinami, T., Narumi, T., Tanikawa, T., Hirose, M.: Modifying an identified angle of edged shapes using pseudo-haptic effects. In: Isokoski, P., Springare, J. (eds.) EuroHaptics 2012. LNCS, vol. 7282, pp. 25–36. Springer, Heidelberg (2012). https://doi.org/10.1007/978-3-642-31401-8_3
5. Matsumoto, K., Ban, Y., et al.: Unlimited corridor: redirected walking techniques using visuo haptic interaction. In: ACM SIGGRAPH 2016 Emerging Technologies, p. 20 (2016)
6. Ban, Y., Narumi, T., et al.: Controlling perceived stiffness of pinched objects using visual feedback of hand deformation. In: Haptics Symposium (HAPTICS), pp. 557–562 (2014)
7. Kimura, T., Nojima, T.: Pseudo-haptic feedback on softness induced by grasping motion. In: Isokoski, P., Springare, J. (eds.) EuroHaptics 2012. LNCS, vol. 7283, pp. 202–205. Springer, Heidelberg (2012). https://doi.org/10.1007/978-3-642-31404-9_36
8. Kawamoto, H., Sankai, Y.: Power assist system HAL-3 for gait disorder person. In: Miesenberger, K., Klaus, J., Zagler, W. (eds.) ICCHP 2002. LNCS, vol. 2398, pp. 196–203. Springer, Heidelberg (2002). https://doi.org/10.1007/3-540-45491-8_43
9. Park, K.H., Lee, S.W.: Movement intention decoding based on deep learning for multiuser myoelectric interfaces. In: 2016 4th International Winter Conference Brain-Computer Interface (BCI), pp. 1–2 (2016)
10. Nitta, K., Sato, T., Koike, H., Nojima, T.: Photoelastic Ball: a touch detectable ball using photoelasticity. In: the 5th Augmented Human International Conference, vol. 16, pp. 1–8 (2014)
11. Sagisaka, T., Ohmura, Y., Nagakubo, A., Ozaki, K., Kuniyoshi, Y.: Development and applications of high-density tactile sensing glove. In: Isokoski, P., Springare, J. (eds.) EuroHaptics 2012. LNCS, vol. 7282, pp. 445–456. Springer, Heidelberg (2012). https://doi.org/10.1007/978-3-642-31401-8_40
12. Misener, D.L., Morin, E.L.: An EMG to force model for the human elbow derived from surface EMG parameters. In: IEEE 17th Annual Conference Engineering in Medicine and Biology Society, vol. 2, pp. 1205–1206 (1995)
13. Doheny, E.P., Lowery, M.M., FitzPatrick, D.P., O'Malley, M.J.: Effect of elbow joint angle on force-EMG relationships in human elbow flexor and extensor muscles. J. Electromyogr. Kinesiol. **18**(5), 760–770 (2008)
14. Jazlan, A., Sidek, S.N.: Development of a myoelectric interface for indirect hand grip force and wrist angle measurement/analysis. Int. J. Biomechatronics Biomed. Robot. **3**(1), 42–53 (2014)
15. Oboe, R., Tonin, A., Yu, K., et al.: Weight estimation system using surface EMG armband. In: 2017 IEEE International Conference Industrial Technology (ICIT), pp. 688–693 (2017)

16. Atzori, M., Cognolato, M., Müller, H.: Deep learning with convolutional neural networks applied to electromyography data: a resource for the classification of movements for prosthetic hands. Front. Neurorobot. **10**, 9 (2016)
17. Myo, Thalmic Labs Inc. (2013). https://www.myo.com/
18. Englehart, K., Hudgins, B., et al.: Classification of the myoelectric signal using time-frequency based representations. Med. Eng. Phys. **21**(6), 431–438 (1999)
19. LeCun, Y., Bengio, Y.: Deep learning. Nature **521**(7553), 436–444 (2015)
20. Silver, D., et al.: NIPS Workshop on "Inductive Transfer: 10 Years Later. Whistler (2005)
21. Côté-Allard, U., et al.: Transfer Learning for sEMG Hand Gestures Recognition Using Convolutional Neural Networks, Systems, Man, and Cybernetics (SMC) (2017). https://doi.org/10.1109/smc.2017.8122854

Substitution of Hand-Object Pressure Cues with the Sole of the Foot for Haptic Presentation Using a Tactile Pin Array

Keigo Hiki[1], Tetsuhiro Okano[1], Sho Sakurai[1], Takuya Nojima[1],
Michiteru Kitazaki[2], Yasushi Ikei[3], and Koichi Hirota[1(✉)]

[1] University of Electro-Communications, Tokyo, Japan
hirota@vogue.is.uec.ac.jp
[2] Toyohashi University of Technology, Toyohashi, Aichi, Japan
[3] Tokyo Metropolitan University, Tokyo, Japan

Abstract. This paper discusses a preliminary study on haptic recognition by presenting pressure to the sole of the foot as an alternative to the hand. Various methods to present haptic sensation have been proposed. However, a method that sufficiently mimics the haptic sensation of the entire hand has not been established. The authors investigate an approach of presenting haptic stimuli acting on the hand to another body part as an alternative. This approach will alleviate the difficulty of wearing a device on the hand. However, it raises the question if we will be able to integrate the somatic sensation of the hand with force/tactile sensations that are presented to a different body part. In our study, a system that presents pressure sensations to the sole of the foot was constructed, and experiments to evaluate weight, stiffness, and two-dimensional shape recognition using the system were conducted. Regarding weight and stiffness, the experiments showed that recognition similar to that of the hand is possible. Regarding shape recognition, similar recognition was possible in cases where the pressure was presented to the hand and to the foot.

Keywords: Alternative presentation · Pressure sensation

1 Introduction

The human hand is used for interaction with objects and with the environment. There have been many studies that introduce interaction using the hand to a virtual environment. Given that haptic feedback is essentially important for the interaction, a haptic device that feeds back touch and force sensations to the user has been investigated. However, a technology to present haptic sensation that is similar to that of real interaction has not been established. Some devices are successful in presenting haptic sensation of restricted interaction, such as manipulating a pen-like tool or pinching an object with two fingers. In cases where the user interacts freely with the object, however, higher degrees of freedom are required for the device; distribution of force on the surface of the hand that will be caused in the interaction must be presented. It is difficult to implement such a device because of the following features of the hand. The hand has a complex shape, deforms drastically, and is covered by soft tissue. Moreover, the resolution of tactile sensation of

© Springer International Publishing AG, part of Springer Nature 2018
D. Prattichizzo et al. (Eds.): EuroHaptics 2018, LNCS 10894, pp. 239–251, 2018.
https://doi.org/10.1007/978-3-319-93399-3_22

the hand is relatively high among skin surfaces. Devices with high degrees of freedom tend to become heavy and bulky and often interfere with the motion of the hand and fingers. This difficulty seems hard to overcome immediately with current technology.

To circumvent this difficulty, we are investigating a method that presents haptic sensations to a skin surface other than the hand. In the proposed method, the user touches the virtual object using the hand while the sensation of touch is felt on another part of the body. This method frees the hand from the burden of wearing haptic devices. For the method to work, the person must be capable of integrating somatic sensations of the hand with haptic sensations in the other part of the body. Alternative presentations of haptic sensation have been investigated in previous studies of prosthetic hands. However, the degree of freedom of the presentation is somewhat limited because of the sensors that are worn on the prosthetic hand. Our proposed investigation is focused on the foot sole as the target area for the substituted presentation. The tactile resolution of the sole is relatively high among skin surfaces although lower than that of the hand. In many virtual reality (VR) systems designed for use in a seated state, the user's feet are free from tasks and hence can be used as alternative areas for haptic presentation.

The goal of our research is to investigate the feasibility of the alternative presentation approach in VR and telepresence applications. An important function of the hand in such applications is haptic recognition of objects and environment. Hence, our study began by investigating the fundamental characteristic of recognition base on the approach. This paper reports our preliminary experiments on the recognition of weight, stiffness, and two-dimensional shapes.

2   Related Research

2.1   Presentation of Haptic Sensation to Hands and Fingers

Many studies have been conducted on devices for haptic presentation in the virtual environment. Most of them were intended for presentation on hands and fingers. For example, CyberGrasp could present an extending force to the fingers [1]. The SPIDAR-MF method was capable of presenting a force vector to each of the five fingertips [2]. Generally, the design of such devices becomes increasingly difficult as the degree of freedom increases.

Presentation of vibration is relatively easy to achieve by attaching vibrators on the hand. CyberTouch is a device with six vibrators for fingers and palm [1]. Ooka et al. investigated presenting the feeling of contact and slip by controlling the vibration stimulus of 4 points presented to the index finger [3]. Tanabe et al. implemented and evaluated a haptic glove that was equipped with 52 liner resonant actuators on fingers and palm [4]. Although more freedom is achieved by using compact vibrators, increasing the number of vibration devices also causes restrictions on the movement of the hand and causes a burden due to excessive weight. In addition, according to the empirical impression, vibrations lack reality in the sensation of contact.

Methods of presenting force sensation by deforming the skin have also been proposed. Deformation of the skin of the fingertip can be realized with a relatively small mechanism, and it is suitable for expressing a sensation of force accompanying operations like manipulation. Minamizawa et al. are developing a device with two degrees of freedom to deform the skin with a belt [5]. Leonardis et al. are developing 3-degree-of-freedom devices that move contact points by a link structure [6]. Yem et al. have developed a one-degree-of-freedom device focusing on shear deformation [7]. However, it is considered difficult to extend such a mechanism to other areas of the hand to increase the degree of freedom.

Technology to present tactile sensation using convergent ultrasonic waves has been investigated [8]. This method is excellent in that no equipment attached to the user is required. A restriction of the method is that the ultrasonic waves must not be shielded by other objects. Further investigation will be necessary to apply a method to the hand that is allowed to take arbitrary pauses, such as grasping.

Despite considerable research, a suitable and successful technology that enables presentation of haptic stimulation to the hands and fingers has not been developed. For this reason, our research is interested in alternative presentation.

2.2   Presentation of Haptic Sensation to Feet

Presentation of force and tactile sensations to the foot sole has been investigated both in the context of VR and of navigation. Most studies conducted in the realm of VR aim to simulate the sensation of walking. Iwata et al. developed devices that simulate ground contact and apply pressure on the sole of the foot [9]. Sakai et al. proposed a method to reproduce vibrations transmitted to the foot during walking by recording the vibration during walking and presenting this to the toenail [10]. Kato et al. developed a device that presents the sense of friction generated during walking in the virtual environment [11].

Most studies related to navigation focused on the transmission of symbolic messages to the walking users. Some of them deal with vibrotactile devices that present spatial patterns using multiple vibrators. Velázquez et al. developed and evaluated a device with 16 (4×4) vibrating motors [12]. It is reported that the recognition ratios of dynamic patterns (sequential activation of lines) and static shapes ranged from 64–83% and 31–32%, respectively. Meier et al. also investigated recognition of message using vibration patterns [13]. They reported that the ratio of discriminating four directional messages was 96% while walking and 78% while jogging. Some other research investigated presentation of the message by temporal patterns of vibration [14, 15]. The interest of our research is different from previous studies in that our research will not deal with the sensation of walking or symbolic messages.

2.3   Alternative Presentation of Force/Tactile Sensation

In a broader sense, an alternative presentation includes cases in which sensory information is presented using multiple modalities on various regions of the body. The former case includes many studies that deal with visual to tactile transformation [16, 17]. The latter case includes studies on the prosthetic hand with sensory feedback where information of touch on the artificial hand is presented on other skin regions [18, 19]. Generally, the degree of freedom of tactile feedback in those systems was relatively small and, depending on the implementation, only symbolic information of contact was transmitted. The latter approach has been investigated also in the field of computer-human interaction. Khurelbaatar et al. [20] proposed a system that performs visual to tactile conversion; the location of a finger on the display was measured by a touch panel, and the image pattern around the touch area was presented to another finger by an electro-tactile device. To the best of our knowledge, no prior research has been conducted that deals with an alternative presentation of force on the hand to the foot sole.

2.4   Characteristics of Haptic Perception and Recognition

A two-point discrimination threshold is commonly used as a representative index of tactile spatial resolution. It is known that the two-point discrimination threshold of the hand is 2–10 mm and that of the soles is 10–20 mm [21]. This knowledge gives useful information for the design of haptic devices.

Klatzky et al. proposed a taxonomy on the modalities of haptic recognition in which eight exploratory procedures (EPs) were defined [22]. Four of those are closely related to the perceptions of mechanical stimuli: lifting an object to recognize the weight (or unsupported holding), pushing an object to recognize the stiffness (or pressure), wrapping by hand or tracing the contour for shape recognition (or enclosure and contour following, respectively). The items of evaluation in the following experiments (i.e. weight, stiffness, and shape) were determined based on this taxonomy corresponding to the above four modalities.

3   Alternative Presentation of Pressure to the Sole of the Foot

A system that presents the pressure sensation acting on the sole of the foot instead of the hand was developed. This system involves the simulation of contact force with respect to hand movement and presentation of pressure on the sole of the foot.

3.1   Contact Force Simulation 1: Calculation Using a Hand Model

In experiments on the characteristics of weight and stiffness recognition, contact force simulation was performed using a deformable hand model [23]. The position and orientation of the hands and fingers were measured using a magnetic sensor (Liberty 240, Polhemus), and the state of the hand model (virtual hand) was updated based on the data. The contact force between the virtual hand and the virtual object was calculated by deformation analysis of the virtual hand using the finite element method (FEM).

As is described in Sect. 3.3, the pressure presentation is realized by a pin array device. Given that the contact force is calculated for each node of the hand model, it is necessary to calculate the output force of each pin based on the forces exerted on the nodes. In the proposed implementation, nodes and pins are mapped as follows: First, the hand model was deformed so that the palm was flat and the fingers were aligned. In this state, the two-dimensional positions of the nodes were calculated and superimposed on the pin positions of the pin array. In this two-dimensional plane, each node is associated with the nearest pin. The nodes located at the back of the hand were excluded. This calculation was made using the sign of the inner product of the plane normal and the surface normal at the node. The resulting correspondence between the nodes and pins is shown in Fig. 1(a–d), in which the nodes associated with the respective pins are indicated by different colors. The update rate of the simulation calculation is approximately 100 Hz although it fluctuates depending on the increase/decrease of the contact area (the number of nodes).

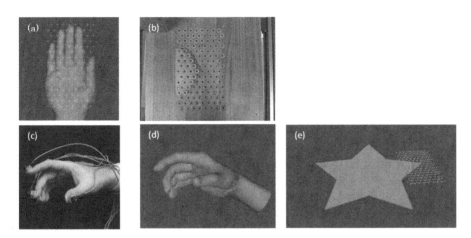

Fig. 1. Contact simulation and computation of pressure

3.2   Haptic Simulation 2: Presentation of Pressure Patterns

For experiments performed to assess the characteristics of recognition of two-dimensional shapes, a contact force applied to an object was approximated by a two-dimensional force pattern without using the hand model. A virtual pin array was defined to represent the contact point of each pin in the interaction. The position and orientation of the virtual pin array were updated by the motion of the hand or the pressure device, depending on the experimental condition, as obtained by the magnetic sensor (Fastrak, Polhemus). The intensity of force at each virtual pin corresponds to the pattern (see Fig. 1(e)). In the following Experiment 2, the subject was asked to place his/her hand similarly to Fig. 1(a). The force pattern was defined as a 2-dimensional image of 256 gradations of monochrome 512×512 pixels and the gradation was associated with the force. The update rate of stimulation, including the tracking by the magnetic sensor, was 60 Hz.

3.3   Pressure Sense Presentation

A device composed of an array of air cylinders was used to generate a pressure sensation stimulus. The air cylinder has a structure in which a metal pin is inserted into a plastic pipe, and the diameter of the pin was 3 mm. Air cylinders were arranged in an equilateral triangular lattice and cover an area of 70 mm × 130 mm with 128 cylinders at intervals of 10 mm. An air compressor was used as the pressure source, and the pressure acting on the air cylinder was controlled by the electro-pneumatic regulator (VY1B, SMC). The pressures of all the air cylinders can be controlled independently. The output force of each pin was 3.5 N when the operating air pressure was 0.5 MPa. Analog voltages that command output pressure to electro-pneumatic regulators were generated by micro-computers (H8/3664F, RENESAS) and DA converters (LTC1660CN, Linear Technology). By sending the command value from the PC to the microcomputer by serial communication, the generating force of the pin is changed. The update frequency of the analog voltage was approximately 50 Hz.

In experiments using the device for the foot, the gap between the skin surface and the pin was decreased by adjusting the heights of the air cylinders in the arch. In contrast, when the device is used for hands, a ball caster is attached to the device so that it can move with the hand within a horizontal plane. The lattice spacing of the device was determined based on the sole two-point discrimination threshold [21], and the density is thought to be insufficient for presentation to the hand. This issue will be discussed in Sect. 5.2.

4 Experiment 1: Recognition of Weight and Stiffness

The intensity of the force applied while lifting an object with the hand provides an estimation of the weight of the object. Also, the relationship between the force and displacement when pushing the surface of the object can help recognize the stiffness of the object. In this experiment, the recognition accuracy of the weight and stiffness in the case of alternative presentation to the soles was evaluated. Regarding the recognition of stiffness, it is known that the change in the contact area of the skin surface is also used as a clue to recognize stiffness [24]. In the present experiment, the contact area changes due to the deformation of the virtual hand, but the object does not deform. Contact with deformable objects will be studied in future research.

4.1 Experimental Method

The weight and stiffness recognition characteristics by alternative presentation were evaluated by the adjustment method. In the task of weight recognition, the standard stimulus was presented by a real sphere hung on a string (Fig. 2(a)); the subject received a stimulation by lifting it on the palm. The value of the standard stimulus (mass of the real sphere) was changed in 0.5, 1.0, and 1.5 kg. The comparison stimulus was presented by a physics-based simulation of the virtual sphere. The adjustable range of the comparison stimulus was 0.1–2 kg (in 0.01 kg increments). The diameter of the real and virtual sphere was 100 mm.

In the task of stiffness recognition, the standard stimulus was presented by a device that was composed of a spring and a hemispherical surface (Fig. 2(b)); when a force is exerted on the spherical surface by hand, the spring shrinks, and a displacement proportional to the force is generated. The motion of the spherical surface was restricted so that displacement occurs only in the vertical direction. The value of the standard stimulus was changed in 0.15, 0.30, and 0.50 N/mm. The comparative stimulus was computed by simulating the repulsive force of the spring model (virtual spring). The variable range of the comparison stimulus was 0.01–0.70 N/mm (in increments of 0.01 N/mm). The diameter of the real and virtual hemispherical surface was 100 mm.

After experiencing the standard stimulus, the subject adjusted the comparative stimulus to be equal to the standard stimulus. The subject was allowed to repeat the process of feeling real stimulus and adjusting the comparison stimulus freely. To alleviate the order effect, the order of the standard stimulus presented for each subject was changed. The subjects were 12 (10 males, 2 females) aged 22–26; all right-handed with a foot size range of 21.5–28.5 cm. Before starting the experiment, subjects experienced the task for about 10 min to become acclimated.

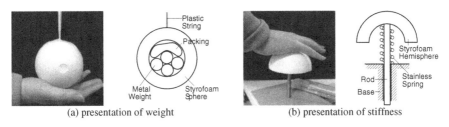

(a) presentation of weight   (b) presentation of stiffness

Fig. 2. Presentation of standard stimuli

4.2   Results and Discussion

The values of the comparison stimulus set by the subject under each standard stimulation condition were plotted in Fig. 3. Cross marks represent average values at each standard stimulus. Table 1 shows the average value, standard deviation (SD), just noticeable difference (JND), and Weber ratio of weight recognition or sensitivity (JND/Stimulus) of stiffness recognition.

According to the results, the weight estimated by the subject was close to that of the real object. This result demonstrates that the weight acting on the hand can be recognized by alternative presentation to the sole of the foot. A relatively large error was observed with the 0.5 kg sphere. This is probably due to a problem with the device that the compensation of the output force for the pin weight was not performed. The influence of this problem is expected to be more noticeable under the condition that the standard stimulus is small.

The result also suggests that stiffness of the spring was recognized with an error of 20% on average with respect to the standard stimulus. As the stiffness of the standard stimulus increases (harder), the resulting value of the comparative stimulus deviates to lower (softer), and the variation tends to increase, however the sensitivity of recognition (JND/stimulus intensity) was almost constant irrespective of the stimulus value. This result demonstrates that it is possible to recognize stiffness by alternative presentation to the sole of the foot.

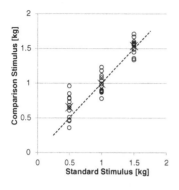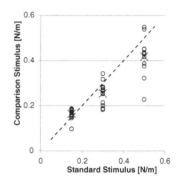

Fig. 3. Recognition of weight (left) and stiffness (right)

Table 1. Indices obtained from recognition of weight (left) and stiffness (right)

Stimulus [kg]	0.5	1.0	1.5	Stimulus [N/m]	0.15	0.30	0.50
Average	0.65	0.99	1.54	Average	0.165	0.255	0.418
SD	0.172	0.132	0.107	SD	0.024	0.048	0.083
JND	0.116	0.089	0.072	JND	0.016	0.032	0.056
Weber Ratio [-]	0.232	0.089	0.048	Sensitivity [-]	0.108	0.108	0.112

5   Experiment 2: Recognition of Two-Dimensional Shapes

The shape of an object is recognized by touching by hand. In this experiment, the characteristics of recognition under alternative presentation of pressure to the soles of the foot were evaluated.

5.1   Experiment Method

According to the motion of the hand on the table, the force computed by the method described in Sect. 3.2 was presented to the foot or hand of the subject. The performance (recognition ratio and completion time) was measured under two conditions where the pressure was fed back to the foot and to the hand. In the case of the hand, the device was attached to a ball caster, put on the table, and the subject moved the device with the hand (Fig. 4 (left)). In case of the foot, the device was placed on the floor, and the subject put his/her foot on it (Fig. 4 (right)). By placing the hand on the carriage with the ball casters, the subject could move the hand with less friction. In the experiment, also the effect of the area of pressure presentation was investigated. The task was performed under two conditions where pressure presentation was given in the whole area of the hand and when it was restricted to a narrow range of the fingertip. In the latter condition, only the pin in the region of the distal bones of the index and middle fingers was driven. In summary, the experiment was carried out under four conditions: the whole area of hand (PA), the fingertip area of the hand (PF), the whole area of sole (SA), the toe area of sole (SF).

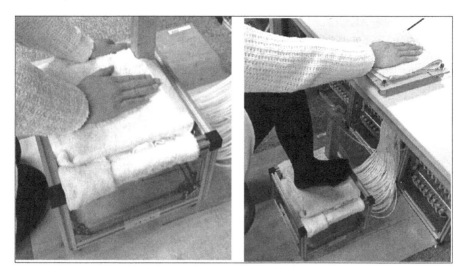

Fig. 4. Experimental setup (left: for hand, right: for foot)

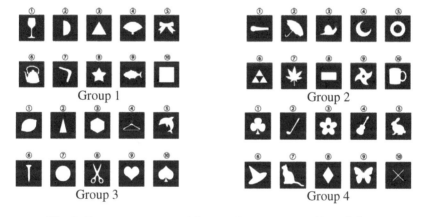

Fig. 5. Pressure patterns used for experiment on recognition of shape

The shapes, or pressure patterns, presented in the experiment are shown in Fig. 5. Force proportional to the pixel intensity was output by the device. In the experiment, the proportional coefficient was determined so that a force of 1.4 N was output when the luminance was 255 (white part of the image). In the virtual environment, the shape of the figure was mapped to the area of 460 mm × 460 mm. The shapes were divided into four groups, and each group was used to perform five recognition tasks, where different shapes are presented from the group. The grouping was performed randomly without considering the feature of the shape. The experiment did not intend to investigate the effect of the feature of the shape on the performance. The subject performed the task without any visual cues and selected the result from the images of the group, and provides the answers in numbers. The shapes not presented in the group were included to reduce the potential impact of chance. Also, in order to reduce the order effect, the combination of groups of presentation shapes and conditions was changed for each subject. Ten subjects (8 males, 2 females) aged 22 to 26, participated in the experiment, all were right-handed. Before starting the experiment, subjects experienced the task for about 10 min to become acclimated.

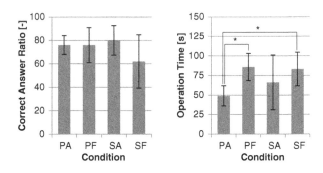

Fig. 6. Recognition ratio (left) and completion time (right)

5.2   Results and Discussion

Results of correct answer ratio and completion time are shown in Fig. 6. The correct answer ratio was over 75% under conditions other than SF. Although the SF condition is lower than other conditions, it is higher than the chance level. A two-way analysis of variance with two factors of the portion of feedback (P/S) and the area of presentation (A/F) were performed, and it was found that neither of the factors had any significant impact on the results (P/S: $F_{1,36} = 0.93$, $p = 0.34$, A/F: $F_{1,36} = 3.02$, $p = 0.09$, interaction: $F_{1,36} = 3.02$, $p = 0.09$). A two-way analysis of variance with factors P/S and A/F was also performed with respect to the completion time and it was proved that the effect of A/F was significant ($F_{1,36} = 12.8$, $p = 0.001$) while the effect of P/S and the interaction between P/S and A/F were not significant ($F_{1,36} = 0.94$, $p = 0.33$, and $F_{1,36} = 1.77$, $p = 0.19$, respectively). Post hoc analysis using Tukey method was performed, and significant differences were found between PA-PF and PA-SF condition pairs ($p < 0.05$).

Based on the results of this experiment, no significant difference was observed between the hand (P) and the foot (S) conditions. Hence, it can be assumed that the alternative presentation to the foot provided the same effect as presentation to the hand. This result demonstrates that the alternative presentation method is successful for recognizing two-dimensional shapes. In addition, the practice time allowed for each subject before the experiment was as short as 10 min, which suggests that alternative presentation was relatively naturally accepted by the subjects. However, the result is a comparison with the case where the pressure was presented by the device to the hand, and the result of alternative presentation does not indicate recognition equivalent to that by the real hand. To verify the possibility of alternatively presenting comparable to the real hand, a more sophisticated haptic device is required.

Average recognition ratio in the SA condition was 80%. This recognition ratio is relatively high compared with the result of a previous study by Velázquez [12], in which the recognition ratio of static shape was 31–32%. A possible reason for the difference includes the difference in the density of stimuli and condition of recognition (active exploration in our case). Also it is conceivable that presentation of pressure rather than vibration matches the presentation of contact as suggested in [19].

6 Conclusion

This study reported the results of our experiments conducted to assess the fundamental recognition characteristics when pressure is applied to the foot. A system was constructed to apply pressure to the foot instead of the hand. Experiments were conducted to assess the impact of using the alternative method on the recognition of weight, stiffness, and two-dimensional shape. Regarding weight and stiffness, the experiments demonstrated that recognition similar to hand recognition is possible by using the foot as an alternative. Regarding shape recognition, the experiments showed that similar recognition was possible in cases where the pressure was presented to the hand and to the foot.

The experiment described here could be refined in some points. In the experiment of recognition of stiffness, deformation of the object was not simulated. As discussed above, the change in contact area on the skin due to deformation of the object can be a clue to stiffness as well. In order to verify this effect, it is necessary to simulate interaction with a deformable virtual object. In the experiment of shape recognition, only two-dimensional shapes were used. In real environments the recognition of three-dimensional shapes is more common. Additionally, experiments with real hands show that recognition performance is better in the case of three-dimensional shapes than two-dimensional shapes [25]. These issues will be examined in our future research.

Acknowledgements. This research was funded by Grant-in-Aid for Scientific Research (16K12474) and Ministry of Internal Affairs and Communications SCOPE (141203019). This research was implemented with the approval of the Ethics Committee of the University of Electro-Communications (No. 16037, 16039).

References

1. CyberGlove Systems. http://www.cyberglovesystems.com/
2. Liu, L., Miyake, S., Akahane, K., Sato, M.: Development of string-based multi-finger haptic interface SPIDAR-MF. In: Proceedings of ICAT 2013, pp. 67–71 (2013)
3. Ooka, T., Fujita, K.: Virtual object manipulation system with Substitutive display of tangential force and slip by control of vibrotactile phantom sensation. In: Proceedings of Haptics Symposium 2010, pp. 215–218 (2010)
4. Tanabe, K., Takei, S., Kajimoto, H.: The whole hand haptic glove using numerous linear resonant actuators. In: Proceedings of IEEE World Haptics 2015 (2015)

5. Minamizawa, K., Kajimoto, H., Kawakami, N., Tachi, S.: A wearable haptic display to present the gravity sensation - preliminary observations and device design. In: Proceeding of World Haptics 2007, pp. 133–138 (2007)
6. Leonardis, D., Solazzi, M., Bortone1, I., Frisoli, A.: A wearable fingertip haptic device with 3 DoF asymmetric 3-RSR kinematics. In: Proceedings of WHC2015, pp. 388–393 (2015)
7. Yem, V., Shibahara, M., Sato, K., Kajimoto, H.: Expression of 2DOF fingertip traction with 1DOF lateral skin stretch. In: Hasegawa, S., Konyo, M., Kyung, K.-U., Nojima, T., Kajimoto, H. (eds.) AsiaHaptics 2016. LNEE, vol. 432, pp. 21–25. Springer, Singapore (2018). https://doi.org/10.1007/978-981-10-4157-0_4
8. Yoshino, K., Shinoda, H.: Contactless touch interface supporting blind touch interaction by aerial tactile stimulation. In: Proceedings of IEEE Haptics 2014, pp. 347–350 (2014)
9. Iwata, H., Yano, H., Nakaizumi, F.: Gait master: a versatile locomotion interface for uneven virtual terrain. In: Proceedings of IEEE VR 2001, pp. 131–137 (2001)
10. Sakai, K., Hachisu, T., Hashimoto, Y.: Sole tactile display using tactile illusion by vibration on toenail. In: Hasegawa, S., Konyo, M., Kyung, K.-U., Nojima, T., Kajimoto, H. (eds.) AsiaHaptics 2016. LNEE, vol. 432, pp. 95–97. Springer, Singapore (2018). https://doi.org/10.1007/978-981-10-4157-0_16
11. Kato, G., Kuroda, Y., Kiyokawa, K., Takemura, H.: HapStep: a novel method to sense footsteps while remaining seated using longitudinal friction on the sole of the foot. In: Hasegawa, S., Konyo, M., Kyung, K.-U., Nojima, T., Kajimoto, H. (eds.) AsiaHaptics 2016. LNEE, vol. 432, pp. 105–111. Springer, Singapore (2018). https://doi.org/10.1007/978-981-10-4157-0_18
12. Velázquez, R., Bazán, O., Magaña, M.: A shoe-integrated tactile display for directional navigation. In: Proceedings of IROS 2017, pp. 1235–1240 (2017)
13. Meier, A., Matthies, D.J.C., Urban, B., Wettach, R.: Exploring vibrotactile feedback on the body and foot for the purpose of pedestrian navigation. In: Proceedings of WOAR 2015, Article 11 (2015)
14. Visell, Y., Law, A., Cooperstock, J.R.: Touch is everywhere: floor surfaces as ambient haptic interfaces. IEEE Trans. Haptics 2(3), 148–159 (2009)
15. Menelas, B.-A.J., Otis, M.J.-D.: Design of a serious game for learning vibrotactile messages. In: Proceedings of HAVE 2012, pp. 124–129 (2012)
16. Linvill, J.G., Bliss, J.C.: A direct translation reading aid for the blind. Proc. IEEE 54(1), 40–51 (1966)
17. Kajimoto, H., Kanno, Y., Tachi, S.: Forehead electro-tactile display for vision substitution. In: Proceedings of EuroHaptics 2006, pp. 75–79 (2006)
18. Antfolk, C., Björkman, A., Frank, S.-O., Sebelius, F., Lundborg, G., Rosen, B.: Sensory feedback from a prosthetic hand based on air-mediated pressure from the hand to the forearm skin. J. Rehabil. Med. 44(8), 702–707 (2012)
19. Antfolk, C., D'Alonzo, M., Controzzi, M., Lundborg, G., Rosén, B., Sebelius, F., Cipriani, C.: Artificial redirection of sensation from prosthetic fingers to the phantom hand map on transradial amputees: vibrotactile versus mechanotactile sensory feedback. IEEE Trans. Neural Syst. Rehabil. Eng. 21(1), 112–120 (2013)
20. Khurelbaatar, S., Nakai, Y., Okazaki, R., Yem, V., Kajimoto, H.: Tactile presentation to the back of a smartphone with simultaneous screen operation. In: Proceedings of CHI 2016, pp. 3717–3721 (2016)
21. Weinstein, S.: Intensive and extensive aspects of tactile sensitivity as a function of body part, sex and laterality. In: Proceedings of the First International Symposium on the Skin Senses, pp. 223–261 (1968)

22. Klatzky, R.L., Loomis, J.M., Lederman, S.J., Wake, H., Fujita, N.: Haptic identification of objects and their depictions. Percept. Psychophys. **54**(2), 170–178 (1993)
23. Hirota, K., Tagawa, K.: Interaction with virtual object using deformable hand. In: Proceedings of VR 2016, pp. 49–56 (2016)
24. Yazdian, S., Doxon, A.J., Johnson, D.E., Tan, H.Z., Provancher, W.R.: Compliance display using a tilting-plate tactile feedback device. In: Proceedings of Haptics 2014, pp. 13–18 (2014)
25. Lederman, S.J., Klatzky, R.L.: Haptic identification of common objects: effects of constraining the manual exploration process. Percept. Psychophys. **66**(4), 618–628 (2003)

Motor Shaft Vibrations
May Have a Negative Effect on Ability
to Implement a Stiff Haptic Wall

Louis Swaidani[1]([✉]), Luke Steele[2], and William Harwin[1]

[1] Department of Biological Sciences, University of Reading, Reading, UK
louis.swaidani@pgr.reading.ac.uk
[2] Generic Robotics, Building L014, University of Reading,
London Road Campus, Reading RG1 5AQ, UK
L.Steele@genericrobotics.com

Abstract. A one degree of freedom experimental test bed is used to investigate the effects of elastic vibration in haptic devices. Strong angular vibration occurs at the motor rotor due to elastic deformation in the shaft. These vibrations occur due to large discontinuities in the virtual environment such as stiff contact which is common in haptics. Also looked at was the effect of these vibrations on stability and control. It was found that the vibrations may negatively affect the stability of the haptic device by introducing large measurement errors to the controller. The experiments investigated using different types of damping in controller feedback. Adding damping to the system whilst these elastic vibrations are present can successfully damp the system, but also tend to increase the magnitude of vibrations sometimes resulting in greater instability. Finally, a second non co-located encoder was used to try to eliminate measurement error from the system due to vibration. It was found that by simply placing the encoder closer to the link where the angle is being measured, error due to rotational flex in the shaft is eliminated. This yielded the greatest improvement in controller performance, nearly eliminating the presence of the vibrations and their effects.

Keywords: Stiffness · Elastic · Torsional deflection · Vibration
Limit cycle · Gyro · Damping · Non-collocated control
Haptic device control · Modelling

1 Introduction

Haptic interfaces provide a tactile and proprioceptive mode of interaction with a virtual environment. One of the persistent challenges with haptics is producing consistently realistic contact with objects in the virtual environment whilst eliminating instability and unwanted vibration.

There has been much research on the stability of haptic devices with regards to the controller. Time delay, quantisation error and interaction with the human

© Springer International Publishing AG, part of Springer Nature 2018
D. Prattichizzo et al. (Eds.): EuroHaptics 2018, LNCS 10894, pp. 252–263, 2018.
https://doi.org/10.1007/978-3-319-93399-3_23

operator have all been cited as causes of instability or causes of non-passive behaviour [1–6]. There is less in the literature looking at the effects of stiffness and elastic deformation of the haptic device itself potentially resulting in vibrations. These vibrations can affect the kinematics of the device by introducing measurement error into the control system or by storing energy elastically and releasing it later. This can ultimately impact on stability of the system. In addition to this, vibration is important to the user's haptic perception of the virtual environment.

Elastic vibration can occur in systems where inertial bodies are connected by stiff components. In haptic devices this is usually in the transmission, such as a shaft or cable drive rather than the links themselves. Whilst elastic deflection of the linkages are known to contribute to error in end effector position and poor trajectory tracking in robotics [7] in addition to adding vibrations, the case of flexible joints and transmissions is of more relevance to the majority of haptic applications.

Haptic interfaces, like the W5D from Entact Robotics, have the links of the device directly mounted on the motor shaft whereas devices like the PHANToM are driven by steel cable drives. The elastic strains resulting from normal operating conditions have a significant effect on kinematics and control of the device as well as setting up elastic vibration. Angular vibrations can the occur both in the motor rotor or the links of the device. Cable drives are noticeably elastic in nature and thus haptic or tele-robotic systems designed in this way exhibit significant error in end effector position. Shaft driven transmissions do not suffer significant error in end effector position due to having relatively high stiffness but the small deflections that do occur can lead to instability in the haptic controller producing strong vibrations that can be seen and felt by the user.

One of the difficulties with haptics is implementing stiff contact with virtual objects whilst avoiding unstable behaviour [8]. It is possible that vibration in the haptic device plays some role in this instability. Stiff contact introduces a sudden change in torque to the haptic device. Similar shock-loading usually leads to harmonic vibrations in non-rigid systems, this may be responsible for some of the vibrations found in haptic devices.

The purpose of this paper is to investigate the cause of these vibrations, and evaluate their effects on the stability of a haptic device. Furthermore, it intends to develop solutions to minimise the adverse effects of these vibrations by investigating different types of sensor for damping and the advantages of non-collocated sensors and actuators.

2   Methods

2.1   Haptic Interface Design

The experimental testbed used was a one degree of freedom (1-DOF) device consisting of a single motor attached to a lever arm which the user would normally operate holding at the tip shown in Fig. 1. This is similar to a 'paddle' style haptic device [9] and, due to its simplicity, is good for looking in detail at vibrations in

Fig. 1. The experimental test bed which is a 1-DOF haptic interface. The user holds the tip of the beam and moves it till reaching the haptic wall where the motor is turned on.

the device and subtle changes in sensors or the controller. The construction of the device is robust to eliminate the effects of vibrations or play anywhere apart from the unconstrained motion of the motor (Maxon RE40 148877) and end effector. The beam used was also designed to have a high enough stiffness to eliminate any vibration in the beam. The beam was 200 mm long with a cross section of 10 mm by 20 mm giving it a second moment of inertia of 1.66×10^{-3} mm^4. The aluminium beam is mounted directly to the motor shaft and the motor shaft itself is doubly supported with ball bearings; as shown in Fig. 1. Figure 2 shows a free body diagram of the moving components in the device. Assuming the shaft as a rigid body (ignoring stiffness) the motor rotor, shaft and beam can be modelled as a single body. However, considering stiffness, the device can be considered as two inertial masses connected by a stiff shaft as shown in Fig. 3. In this system, the inertial bodies may rotate separately with the first (the motor) as θ_1 and the second (the beam) as θ_2. The rotational movements of the two are constrained only by the stiffness and damping terms related to the shaft. The stiffness of the 6 mm diameter shaft was calculated as 143.59 Nm/rad.

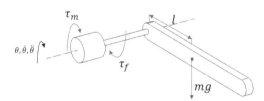

Fig. 2. Free body diagram of the moving components of the haptic device. Depicted are the motor rotor, motor shaft and the solid beam which constitutes the end effector. τ_m is the motor torque and τ_f is the torque applied at the other end of the motor shaft.

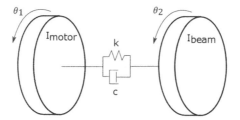

Fig. 3. Simplified model of the haptic device as a two mass system connected by a stiff shaft (represented here with a spring and dashpot). Where I_{motor} and I_{beam} are the respective inertial masses of the motor rotor and the beam, k is the angular stiffness of the motor shaft and c is an angular damping term.

2.2   Sensors and Placement

Encoders are commonly used, in haptics and other control applications, for accurate measurement of the position of the motor. They are usually mounted on the motor itself; an arrangement provides a precise measurement of the position of the motor but in a system that is sufficiently non-rigid may lose accuracy if trying to measure end effector position. The haptic device was fitted with two identical encoders for these experiments, one at normal mounting location at the rear of the motor (Encoder 1) and one at the distal end of the shaft (Encoder 2).

Both of the encoders used were identical 20000 count/rev quadrature encoders (Quantum Devices LP12-20000-A-C-D-C-A). An additional gyro sensor was fitted on the beam about halfway along the length. The gyro sensor used was Analog Device's ADXRS613. The range of which is ± 150 deg /s with a sensitivity of 12.5 mV/ deg /s and a bandwidth of 3000 Hz.

Adding damping to the haptic device requires a measurement of angular velocity. This is usually done by taking the derivative of the position measurement. Since this is a sampled system this is a discrete derivative and requires a small amount of low-pass filtering. The resulting velocity estimate therefore has a minimum delay of half the sample time but with the filtering is about 3.5 ms when running the control loop at 1000 Hz. The resolution of the encoder for angular velocity is 0.314 rad/s. The rate measurement from the gyro did not have additional filtering and while its effective resolution depends on the noise in the analogue signal it was a factor of ten better than that of the encoder at about 0.0382 rad/s.

2.3   Experiments

A set of experiments were conducted with different gains set for the stiffness and damping of the haptic device. For each experiment the end effector was placed carefully at the surface of the virtual wall (0 rad) and not held by a human user. The controller was set with a high wall stiffness (high proportional gain k) which will initiate a limit cycle which will grow and settle at a marginally stable state.

In this way the end effector is seen to bounce on the surface of the virtual wall and exhibit other vibrations.

The experiments were repeated under different conditions, namely which sensor was used to measure the angular position and velocity of the haptic device and feedback to the motor as well as their placement in the case of the encoders. The two encoders used, one located on the back of the motor as is commonly seen in control applications and one located at the other end of the motor shaft closest to the beam, are hereon referred to as encoder 1 and 2 respectively and their measurements as q_1 and q_2. The entire system was controlled using Matlab and Simulink with the real-time toolbox operating via a Simulink Real-time target PC fitted with a Quanser Q8 data card. The values for controller gains were chosen to produce a usable stiffness for a 'haptic wall' and so that the limit cycles of the device would settle to a marginally stable state and within reasonable time so that they can be compared.

Table 1. List of the sensors and signals used in each experiment for control of the haptic device.

Experiment	Angle (q)		Angular velocity ($\dot{q}$)		Control gains	
	Encoder 1	Encoder 2	Difference filter	Gyro rate	k_p	k_d
1	x	-	-	-	800	-
2	x	-	x	-	800	1
3	x	-	-	x	800	1
4	-	x	-	-	800	-
5	-	x	x	-	800	1
6	-	x	-	x	800	1

3   Results

Figure 4 shows the a portion of the data from Experiment 1 where the end effector of the haptic device was left to rest on the virtual wall (at 0 rad) but due to the high stiffness gain k and no damping (except the inherent damping of the hardware due to friction) resulted in a continuous and predictable limit cycle. This snapshot of the data is one sample of one of these limit cycles or 'bounces' on the virtual wall. The figure shows four graphs from produced from the data over the same time window, the first two of which show the states of the system as recorded by the sensors. Encoders 1 and 2 measured angular position in quadrature mode at 20000 counts/rev. Plot (a) compares position from encoder 1 and encoder 2 in Experiment 1, which used the ordinary motor encoder (encoder 1) for position control which is the most common mounting position. Although the signal from encoder 2 was not used for control purposes in experiment 1 it shows the actual position of the beam and end effector. The second plot (b) shows the velocity signals from the gyro and the

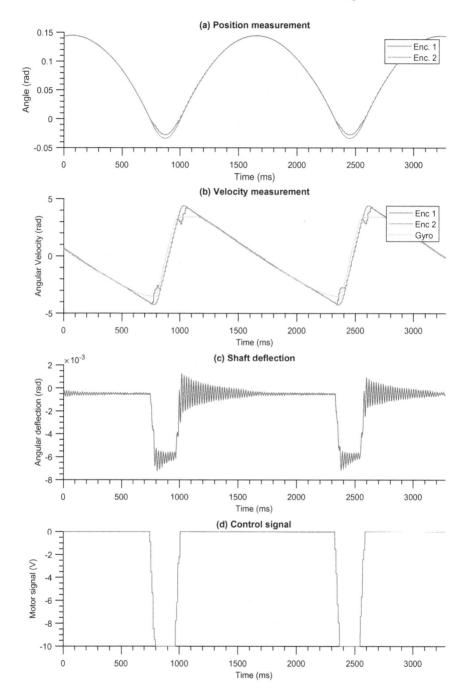

Fig. 4. Four different plots of data from experiment 1 (see Table 1): (a) plots encoder angle measurement against time (b) velocity against time from encoder differentiation and gyro sensor (c) angular deformation of the motor shaft due to torsion (d) control signal u sent to the motor corresponds to angular deformation

differentiated encoder position measured by encoders 1 and 2. Plot (c) shows the
deflection in the rotor shaft by taking the difference in angle measured between
the two encoders. Below this plot (d) shows the feedback to the motor from the
controller. The effect of adding different methods of damping and only the motor
encoder for position was tested in experiments 1, 2 and 3. The angular position
measurement from these tests can be seen in Fig. 5 which compares the position
and velocity signals of these experiments. The rest of the results displayed in
Figs. 6, 7 and 8 show selected comparisons of the measured shaft deflections
under different control conditions and the control signal to the motor during
interaction with the haptic wall. Figure 6 compares the elastic vibrations using
encoder 1 with and without damping as performed in experiments 1 and 2.
Figure 7 shows the resulting reduction in vibration from switching from encoder
1 to encoder 2 without adding damping which corresponds with experiments 1
and 4. Figure 8 compares the damping achieved using the gyro rate measurement
versus differentiated encoder signal whilst using only the beam encoder (experiments 5 and 6). In each figure the upper plot (a) shows the angular deflection of
the shaft whilst the end effector is resting on the whilst below (b) is the control
signal u to the motor.

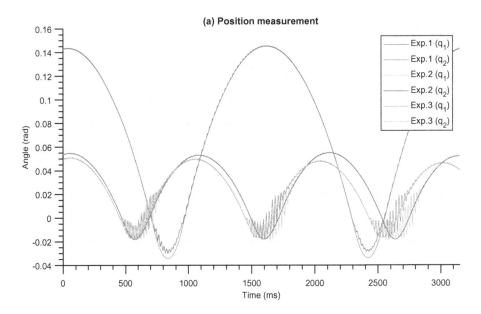

Fig. 5. Shows the angle measured for experiments 1, 2 and 3 (see Table 1) with both
encoders against time. Motor encoder is q_1 and beam encoder is q_2. Large vibrations
can be seen in the motor encoder which is the motor rotor vibrating due to shock
loading of the motor shaft.

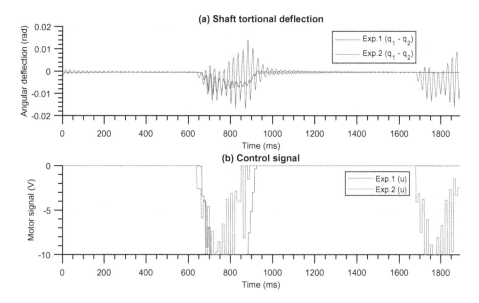

Fig. 6. The effect on vibrations and the control signal to the haptic device when adding damping and measuring position and velocity with the motor encoder. Upper plot (a) shows the angular deflection in the motor shaft. The lower plot (b) shows the control signal u to the motor driver produced by the controller.

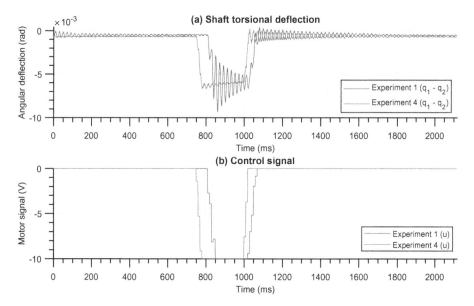

Fig. 7. Comparison of angular deformation and control signal whilst using encoders 1 and 2 for measuring angle and no damping (experiments 1 and 4). Upper plot (a) shows the torsional deflection in the motor shaft found by subtracting the difference in encoder position. Lower plot (b) shows the signal to the motor of the haptic device.

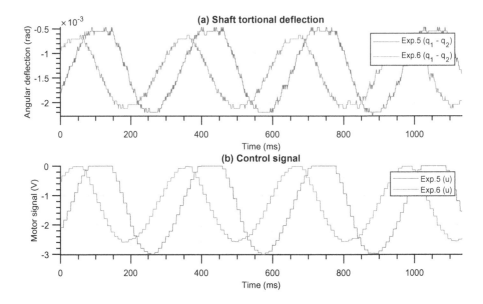

Fig. 8. Comparison of angular deformation and control signal using encoder and gyro damping with angular measurements taken from the beam encoder (experiments 5 and 6). (a) The torsional deflection in the motor shaft found by subtracting the difference in encoder position. (b) The signal to the motor driving the haptic device.

4 Discussion

The results from Experiment 1 suggests that the two mass model of the test bed device can be applied to this scenario. As the encoder reading crosses zero and the controller recognises the beam as having entered the haptic wall, the motor is turned on. This, due to the high wall stiffness, results in shock loading and a large vibration in the haptic device. These vibrations are audible but can also be felt if the user holds the end effector. Figure 4 also shows that the same transient vibrations occur when the position measurement crosses zero in the opposite direction thus leaving the haptic wall and turning the motor off. This is due to the motor shaft being suddenly released from torsion. Finally, it can be seen that regardless of the scenario these transient vibrations occur at the same natural frequency as it is independent of the control parameters.

This behaviour supports the model of the haptic device as a shaft with rotation masses exhibiting harmonic vibration. The shock loading and unloading of the motor shaft due to the unilateral constraint at the haptic wall initiate the vibrations at the natural frequency of the system. The ratio of amplitude of angular vibration of the two bodies in the two mass system is given by Eq. 1.

$$\frac{\hat{\theta}_1}{\hat{\theta}_2} = \frac{I_2}{I_1} \tag{1}$$

where:
I_n = Inertia of mass n
$\hat{\theta}_n$ = amplitude of vibration in mass n.

The difference in inertia of the motor rotor and the beam is sufficiently large that the amplitude in the beam is 0.86% of what is seen in the motor. Thus in this particular scenario it is reasonable to simplify the model of torsional vibration from a shaft with two rotating masses to a shaft with one rotating mass and one fixed end. The base natural frequency of the system should be given by the Eq. 2.

$$\omega_{nf} = \sqrt{\frac{k_t}{I_m}} \tag{2}$$

where:
k_t = the torsional stiffness
I_m = the motor inertia.

Modelling the vibrations of the device using the simplified case of a shaft with one fixed end and a single rotating mass at the other gives a natural frequency equal to 503 Hz. The data from the experiments show that the vibrations do indeed occur at approximately 500 Hz. Crucially these vibrations are within the range that will not be filtered out by a 1 kHz control loop and will therefore introduce oscillation in the control signal u that is fed back to the motor. To ensure that the observed vibrations were not subject to aliasing as the sample rate is just high enough to observe 500 kHz vibration, the measurement data seen here was sampled at 10 kHz, 10 times the control loop sampling rate. This did not reveal any higher frequency vibration but simply confirmed the observations.

Care was taken to ensure these vibrations were not as a result of play in the joints or loose mounting of the beam. These would also present as discontinuities in the angular motion rather than continuous elastic vibration. Looking at Fig. 7, the only discontinuity we see is when crossing the boundary at the haptic wall and after this we see simple harmonic motion which decays with time.

Adding damping to the system when using the motor encoder did not improve the suppression of the vibrations. Figure 6 shows the difference in vibrations and controller feedback that resulted from implementing damping with an encoder based velocity estimate. Whilst it did reduce the amplitude of limit cycles of the device it did not damp them sufficiently for the beam to come to rest on the haptic wall. Additionally, the amplitude of the vibrations in the motor increased. This is also seen in the lower plot (b) where the motor vibrations are so large that they introduce fluctuations in the control signal u. Figure 5 shows the position measurement for experiments 1 and 2 where we can see from the beam encoder that during each bounce or limit cycle the beam encoder reading only crosses zero once in each direction. However, the motor encoder measurement, particularly when damping is added, crosses zero multiple times. The measurement error caused by the vibrations can cause unstable behaviour by causing the controller to think the end effector has left the haptic wall whilst it is still in it and vice versa. Therefore, it seems that the stiffness of the motor shaft is a factor in whether the end effector of the haptic device can to come to rest near or at a stiff virtual wall.

The gyro damping was seen to be more effective whilst using the motor encoder and only marginally better whilst using the beam encoder. Figure 5 shows the gyro damps the limit cycles of the haptic device more effectively but does not remove the vibration present in the motor at all. When switching to the motor encoder, the vibrations are nearly completely removed and the encoder damping performs far more comparably to the gyro. Figure 8 show this where the amplitude of angular deflection in the shaft is similar in both cases. Since the gyro is more effective at reducing the limit cycle amplitude due to smaller delay and better effective resolution it can be said to be more effective at least when operating below saturation.

5   Conclusion

The results show that modelling haptic devices as rigid bodies may not be appropriate in most cases. Even in such a robust haptic device as seen in this experiment, the effect of torsional deflection of the motor shaft result in perceptible disturbances due to vibration which are even audible at high gains. More analysis of haptic devices is needed where key components that exhibit elastic behaviour are modelled as stiff bodies. In this example the vibrations occurred in the motor shaft but in other examples such as a Phantom haptic device, the cable drives are likely to exhibit these kinds of vibrations. In cases such as these, it may be possible to improve stability and reduce unwanted vibration simply by better placement of encoders.

The angular velocity measurement from the gyro sensor resulted in more effective damping at lower velocities relative to the differentiated encoder signal. This performance is only achieved if the bandwidth of the gyro is high enough (>1000 Hz) to accurately measure vibrations at the natural frequency of the system. The gyro rate has several advantages such as higher effective resolution, no delay and does not require filtering. The encoder has limited resolution for measuring angular velocity which is hampered by the high sampling rate, it always incurs a delay from discrete differentiation and is relatively noisy due to the quantisation error and requires filtering adding further control delay. At higher velocities the encoder signal is less noisy and the gyro will begin to saturate and at this point the encoder velocity estimate is preferable.

An alternative approach to haptic device control is to include better models of the elastic properties of the mechanism and use these to provide a better estimate of end point position. Of course these models would need to adapt to the passive properties of the human.

References

1. Hannaford, B., Ryu, J.H.: Time-domain passivity control of haptic interfaces. IEEE Trans. Robot. Autom. **18**(1), 1–10 (2002)
2. Colgate, J., Schenkel, G.: Passivity of a class of sampled-data systems: application to haptic interfaces. In: Proceedings of 1994 American Control Conference, ACC 1994, vol. 3, pp. 3236–3240. IEEE (1994). http://ieeexplore.ieee.org/document/735172/
3. Wyatt, J.L., Chua, L.O., Gannett, J.W., Goknar, I.C., Green, D.N.: Energy concepts in the state-space theory of nonlinear n-Ports: part 11 losslessness. IEEE Trans. Circ. Syst. **29**(7), 417–430 (1982)
4. Tanaka, H., Ohnishi, K., Nishi, H., Kawai, T., Morikawa, Y., Ozawa, S., Furukawa, T.: Implementation of bilateral control system based on acceleration control using FPGA for multi DOF haptic endoscopic surgery robot. IEEE Trans. Ind. Electron. **56**(3), 618–627 (2009). https://doi.org/10.1109/TIE.2008.2005710
5. Adams, R.J., Moreyra, M.R., Hannaford, B.: Stability and performance of haptic displays: theory and experiments. In: Proceedings ASME International Mechanical Engineering Congress and Exhibition, pp. 227–234 (1998)
6. Ryu, J.H., Kim, Y.S., Hannaford, B.: Sampled-and continuous-time passivity and stability of virtual environments. IEEE Trans. Robot. **20**(4), 772–776 (2004)
7. Ryu, J.H., Kwon, D.S., Hannaford, B.: Control of a flexible manipulator with non-collocated feedback: time-domain passivity approach. IEEE Trans. Robot. **20**(4), 776–780 (2004)
8. Colgate, J., Grafing, P., Stanley, M., Schenkel, G.: Implementation of stiff virtual walls in force-reflecting interfaces. In: Proceedings of IEEE Virtual Reality Annual International Symposium, pp. 202–208 (1993)
9. Okamura, A.M., Richard, C., Cutkosky, M.R.: Feeling is believing: using a force-feedback joystick to teach dynamic systems. J. Eng. Educ. **91**(3), 345–349 (2002). https://doi.org/10.1002/j.2168-9830.2002.tb00713.x

Virtual Reality: Impact of Vibro-Kinetic Technology on Immersion and Psychophysiological State in Passive Seated Vehicular Movement

Alexandre Gardé[1]([✉]), Pierre-Majorique Léger[1]([✉]), Sylvain Sénécal[1]([✉]),
Marc Fredette[1]([✉]), Shang-Lin Chen[1]([✉]), Élise Labonté-Lemoyne[1]([✉]),
and Jean-François Ménard[2]([✉])

[1] HEC Montréal, Montréal, Canada
{alexandre.garde,pml,sylvain.senecal,marc.fredette,
shang-lin.chen,elise.labonte-lemoyne}@hec.ca
[2] D-BOX Technologies Inc., Longueuil, Canada
jfmenard@d-box.com

Abstract. In this paper, we investigate the effect of a vibro-kinetic seat, i.e., a seat using movement and vibration synchronized with a given media, on psychophysiological states and head movements of users immersed in virtual reality. The aim of this study is to explore the extent to which a vibro-kinetic seat can contribute to create a more immersive virtual reality experience than with a classic seat, including fewer cybersickness discomfort symptoms. We test our hypothesis with a between-subject design where we assigned 45 participants to a specific condition: Vibro-kinetic condition (with the seat moving according to the virtual reality experience) or non-vibro-kinetic condition (where the seat was motionless). Users' physiological states were captured using electrodermal activity and heart rate variability. Users' head movements were captured using automatic video detection. The results suggest that the vibro-kinetic condition leads to more immersion and a better psycho-physiological state to livirtual learning environmentve a more optimal virtual reality experience without cybersickness symptoms. Also, based on the head movement detection, the vibro-kinetic seat seems to contribute to increasing head movements for a large number of users, an indication of the increased presence feeling in virtual reality. Moreover, users in the vibro-kinetic condition live an enhanced experience and are more immersed in the VR experience.

Keywords: Vibro-kinetic · Virtual reality · Cybersickness · Motion sickness
Psychophysiological · Movement · Immersion · Parasympathetic
Haptic feedback · Oculus Rift · ECG · HRV · HF · EDA · SCR

1 Introduction

This paper investigates the effect of vibro-kinetic (VK) technology on a user's psycho-physiological states in a virtual reality (VR) context, specifically in the context of a head mounted device (HMD). We investigate the impact of a VK seat, i.e., a seat using movement and vibration synchronized with a given media, on the immersive VR

© Springer International Publishing AG, part of Springer Nature 2018
D. Prattichizzo et al. (Eds.): EuroHaptics 2018, LNCS 10894, pp. 264–275, 2018.
https://doi.org/10.1007/978-3-319-93399-3_24

experience of the user. We explore the extent to which VK can augment the experience emotionally and physiologically, while helping to reduce negative side effects such as cybersickness.

For the study, a commercial vibro-kinetic seat was used. This technology is proprietary, thus technical information about the seat is not available. However, this technology is patented, we thus included one of the patent reference in the paper [10], which provide some additional information. VK technologies are relatively new technologies that can manage a specific type of media channel called motion code. This code is used to produce motion and vibration synchronized with a given media. Indeed, VK technology can be defined as artifacts providing whole-body motion and vibration feedback (frequency response between 0 and 100 Hz) adjusted with the media scenes. The aim of this artifact is to actively produce feedback to reinforce the audiovisual input from the media. It can induce a physical feedback such as the feeling of driving on a bumpy road or the feeling of a strong impact during a car crash. In this study, the seat used generates multiple vibrations and trembling motions according to what the user sees in the virtual world. In the case of a rollercoaster stimuli, if the user goes up, the VK seat induces the feeling of a wagon that is going up the slope, trembling in contact with the rails.

VR, also called virtual environment (VE), is a three-dimensional computer-generated simulation [22]. VR technology aims at creating a digital world inspired by human imagination or recreated from reality that can be immersive, interactive, and multisensory [9].

Immersion can be defined as the experience of being surrounded by a completely different reality, of being transported to an elaborately simulated place [6, 13, 20, 24]. Other authors also affirm that immersion is about sensory fidelity, i.e., sensory cues similar to those experienced in the real world [5].

According to Witmer and Singer [38], when immersion is optimal, users experience a high feeling of presence. Presence is defined as the natural recognition of an environment [24] and the conscious feeling on the part of the viewer of being in a virtual world, caused by unconscious spatial perception processes [31]. If the VR experience does not induce a sense of presence, the experience is also likely to be less emotionally strong [30]. Few researchers studied immersion and gender, but some suggest that there is a possible difference between women and men when it comes to feelings of presence [2].

Cybersickness is also an important factor in the VR user experience. Cybersickness is a well-known issue in VR and VE experiences [18]. Cybersickness, also called VR sickness, occurs only in VE contexts [33]. To our knowledge, VK technology has not been tested to measure its impact on cybersickness [26]. This form of motion sickness generally results in felling symptoms such as nausea, headache, or simply by a feeling of general discomfort [1]. Research suggests that cybersickness could be linked with feelings of presence. In fact, there is an inverse relation between cybersickness and sense of presence [7, 38]. According to Bles et al. [4] and their work on motion sickness and rearrangement theory [28], cybersickness; and more generally all types of motion sickness, find their origin in the conflict about subjective vertical (SV), i.e., the internal representation of gravity [4]. Rearrangement theory is the main motions sickness theory in the research and is widely accepted. Basically, it states that motion sickness is due to a mismatch between signals transmitted by the eyes, the vestibular system and the nonvestibular proprioceptors to the brain [27]. Bles et al. [4] simplify this main theory with their so-called SV-conflict theory. SV-conflict theory demonstrated that most of motion sickness experimental data can be explained by the conflict regarding the subjective vertical. It's defined as "all situations which provoke motion sickness are characterized by a condition in which the sensed vertical as determined on the basis of integrated information from the eyes, the vestibular system and the nonvestibular proprioceptors is at variance with the subjective vertical as predicted on the basis of previous experience [4, pp. 481–482]."

H1: Building on this literature, previous studies have shown that the VK experience can significantly enhance the emotional experience and generate greater arousal [26]. In line with Slater and Wilbur [35], we hypothesize that the VK condition (when the seat is moving according to the VR stimuli) enhances the immersion (H1). Immersion is positively correlated with the increase in emotion intensity [37] which can be seen through electrodermal activity (EDA) data. EDA refers to the change in the electrical properties of the skin in response to sweat secretion by the eccrine sweat glands [11] influenced by the activity of the sympathetic nervous system (SNS). The physiological basis of EDA is an involuntary reaction that occurs in the skin and subcutaneous tissue in response to changes in emotions. Thus, we expect a significative difference in terms of EDA between VR experienced with or without a VK seat.

H2: Moreover, research suggests that a person who moves his head during VR would feel a stronger sense of presence during his immersion [34]. VR is a 360° world, inviting users to look all around, above and below them. If the users feel really present in the VE, they will look everywhere and not only right in front of them like in a cinema context. We hypothesize that the VK condition should lead to more significant head movement during the experience, a proxy of their sense of presence (H2). Based on SV-conflict theory, head movement should be particularly significant on the x and z-axis, y-axis being not concerned by SV.

H3: We argue that a VK seat can contribute to a psychophysiological state that is likely to help to maintain users in an optimal immersive experience. Subjects shouldn't have to make continuous autoregulation efforts to reach or stay in this homeostatic state and be relaxed. To monitor this state, we watched the influence of the autonomic nervous system (ANS) on the heart rate variability (HRV). The parasympathetic nervous system (PNS), one of the two parts of the ANS, induces a relaxation response in the body which decreases blood pressure, slows respiratory activity and heart rate to help one reach a homeostatic state [3]. When someone is taking control of his diaphragmatic breathing to calm down, he/she tries to regulate himself consciously. This conscious autoregulation increases heart rate variability and lowers heart rate [8]. Strong correlation between the high frequencies (HF) and respiration have been shown in the literature [17, 36]. HF reflects respiration [17] and positively impacts the PNS [21]. We hypothesis that the VK condition should lead to a more optimal state that requires less conscious autoregulation (H3).

2 Method

2.1 Sample and Design

We conducted a between-subject experiment in which 45 participants were either assigned to a VK condition with the seat moving according to the VR experience, or a non-VK condition where the seat was motionless like a classic seat. This experiment was approved by the IRB of our institution.

Participants' gender and susceptibility to motion sickness were taken into consideration when assigned to conditions. Our objective was to ensure that conditions were well balanced according to these two variables since motion sickness is an important issue when it comes to VR [18]. To recruit subjects with a large range of motion sickness susceptibility, we use the Motion Sickness Susceptibility Questionnaire (MSSQ) [16]. In this questionnaire, respondents have to rate their past experience in different types of vehicles (boat, aircraft, cars, swings in playgrounds, etc.). The final score is between 0, with no experience of motion sickness at all; to 54, when the maximum score in all kind of vehicle (average = 10.54; SD = 9.39). Furthermore, to reduce potential biases related to recent VR experiences, participants must have had no VR usage in the last 30 days and should be able to use VR head-mounted device without glasses.

The final sample was composed of 24 males and 22 females with an average age of 24-year-old (4.9 standard deviations). Twenty-four (24) participants (12 females) were assigned to the VK condition and 22 (10 females) to the non-VK condition. In addition, no significant difference was found in the MSSQ scores of the two groups (p-value > 0.05). Each participant received a $30 compensation for their participation.

2.2 Procedure and Stimuli

For the experiment, participants were seated during a 10-min VR stimulus in which they experience a passive vehicular movement with a VR headset (Fig. 1).

Fig. 1. Experimental montage

A D-Box (Longueuil, Canada) VK seat specifically designed for VR was used. It was only activated for participants in VK condition. Its movements were designed by specialized movement artists in order to enhance the VR stimulus (See patent for additional information [10]). For both conditions, we used an Oculus Rift Cv1 (Menlo Park, CA) headset.

A pretest was conducted (n = 7) to ensure that participants clearly understood the instructions and to address technical issues.

We designed a stimulus which was composed of three short Passive Seated Vehicular Movement VR experiences where users did not have to and could not interact with the Virtual Environment (VE). They only have to sit, look around and enjoy the stimuli. These VR experiences were seen consecutively to make a global 10 min experience. The aim of this was to build a stimulus that was more and more susceptible to induce motion sickness. Seven pretests were done to validate the final stimuli. The stimuli presented to the participants were composed with (1) two laps as a co-pilot in a race car, (2) a roller coaster ride, and (3) a cartoon snow ride. All participants experienced the stimuli in this order. During the stimuli, participants saw the scene from the point of view of a passenger in car or wagon, depending on the moment of the stimuli.

We placed the participants with the physiological sensors in the D-box seat. We performed a baseline measurement of 1 min and 30 s for stabilizing the physiological equipment before the experiment. Participants were given instructions to take off the Oculus Rift if they felt uncomfortable due to cybersickness symptoms, at which point we would stop the experiment. We also specified that stopping the experiment would not impact their compensation, and that it was all part of the experience. Following the instructions, we helped them to correctly put the Oculus Rift on their head and we launched the stimuli. Fifteen participants interrupted the experience before the end of the stimuli (no difference between VK and non-VK conditions, p-value = 0.596). On average, participants saw 90.0% of the VR stimuli (no difference between conditions, p-value = 0.503).

2.3   Instruments and Measures

To track head movements, we used Facereader (Wageningen, Netherlands), an automatic video analysis software. This software has a robust head orientation tracking system [23] and can give the position of the head in degree between $-45°$ and $+45°$ (0 on each axis when the face is perfectly right). This angle is measured simultaneously around the 3 axes: x, y and z. In other words, when subjects say "no" with their heads, we see data points changing on the x-axis. When they say "yes" with their heads, we see data points changing on the y-axis. And when they are tilting their heads like clockwise, we see data points changing on the z-axis.

In order to measure the psychophysiological state, we use electrodermal activity (EDA) and electrocardiography (ECG). More specifically, we focus on skin conductance response (SCR), which corresponds to the physical change of electrical conductivity of the skin, to measure the activity of the Sympathetic nervous system (SNS) and the HF of the HRV to measure the activity of the Parasympathetic nervous system (PNS). SNS and PNS are both parts of the autonomic nervous system (ANS) and have different influences on the body. The activation of the SNS prepares an individual's body for action. In response to stress, it orchestrates a "fight or flight" response, which leads to some phenomenon like a dilation of the bronchi, an acceleration of cardiac and respiratory activity, an increase in blood pressure, etc. [3]. The activation of the PNS, or vagal system, corresponds to a relaxation response. When activated, functions of the organism will generally slowdown. Heart rate gets slower as well as the respiratory activity [3]. HF are generated by the heart and can be seen between 0.15 and 0.4 Hz [14, 19].

HF is presenting as a self-regulation index [32] and is considered a proxy of regulatory strength i.e., the ability to exert self-control and to override or alter one's dominant response tendencies [15]. Thus, in our experimental design, an HF increase is linked to the participants attempting to self-regulate by focusing on their breathing and taking deeper breaths to avoid any sickness feeling. SCR and HRV were captured using Biopac wireless sensors (Goleta, USA). Noldus Observer XT (Wageningen, Netherlands) was used to synchronize the presentation of the experimental stimuli with the DBox Cinemotion player (Longueuil, Canada). Biopac Acknowledge (Goleta, USA) was used to analyze EDA and ECG data.

2.4   Analysis

Concerning head movement, a logistic regression was performed to model the effect of z-axis head movement on the probability of stopping the experiment before its end, as the response variable is binary (quit or not). The number of observations N = 15. Moreover, for men older than 23 years old (15 males out of 24) a Wilcoxon Sum Rank test was performed to compare the head movement on z-axis between participants in VK and non-VK condition, given the between-subject design of the experiment and the small number of participants in each group (N = 8 in VK condition, N = 7 in non-VK condition).

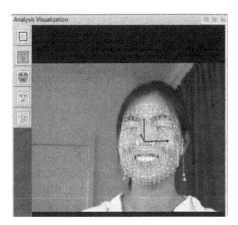

Fig. 2. Head tracking axis (in order: x, y, z) [25]

To compare psychophysiological states of participants in VK and non-VK conditions, we use the means of physiological measurements between the two groups. Heteroskedastic Student tests with unequal variances were performed. In our experimental design, we asked participants to get off the HMD if they were feeling any discomfort. For this reason, we analyzed two times periods: the last minute of the participant's experience and the whole experience.

3   Results

H1: Fig. 2 shows the augmentation in SCR apparition rate during the whole experience normalized with the baseline. Results show that VK condition lead to more activation compare to the group in non-VK condition (p-value = 0.0029). Subject's group in VK condition know 44.7% more SCR, with a 95% confidence interval ranging from 30.5% to 59.0%. Residue analysis reveals damaged signal and outlier data. Four participants (3 in VK condition) had to be removed from this ANOVA analysis. Better immersions being linked to higher SCR, this results support vigorously H1: VK seat pushes the immersion further.

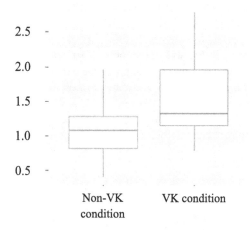

Fig. 3. Augmentation in the SCR rate during the experiment

H2: When users are more immersed in VR, they tend to move their head more on the z-axis to stay perfectly aligned with the visual. Then, we hypothesize that participants in VK condition should have more head movement around the z-axis. Results of head movements give us interesting patterns for male older than 23 years old (15 men on 24 of our sample) on this axis. We found that VK condition induces more head movement on the z-axis for this kind of users (p-value = 0.054). Moreover, in our sample, head movements around z are linked to a lower probability to stop the VR experience before the end of the stimuli (p-value = 0.073). These results support partially our H2 which says that VK condition should enhance the movement of the head in a more natural way that translates a better feeling of presence of participants (Fig. 4).

H3: Here, we hypothesis that VK seat contributes to better psychophysiological states for an optimal VR experience that is defined by a less conscious autoregulation and so less activation of the parasympathetic nervous system (PNS). Our results support this hypothesis. We compare participants of the two conditions in term of HF ratio from their HRV. This ratio is normalized using the HF average for the last minute of the stimuli experienced by the user divided by the HF average of the rest of the experience. A significant difference was found between the HF of the VK group and the non-VK

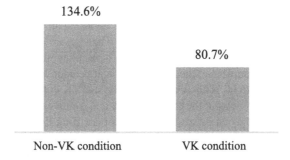

Fig. 4. HF ratio in non-VK and VK condition during last minute

group (p-value = 0.040). HF increased by 134,6% in the non-VK condition compared to only 80,7% in the VK condition in the last minute of the VR experience (Fig. 3). This result supports our H3 and clearly demonstrates that VK seat helps users to have a better autoregulation.

4   Discussion and Conclusion

This study investigated the influence of vibro-kinetic (VK) technology on immersion in the context of a passive seated vehicular shifting in virtual reality (VR). We conducted a between-subject experiment in which we used a 10 min stimulus to immerse 45 subjects. Results of the analysis of psychophysiological data and head tracking support that VK contributes to induce a more immersive VR experience for the users. Our results contribute to the literature by filling a gap on the effect of VK seats in a passive VR experiment.

VR is all about bringing the users into another world. The users must feel physically there, in this recreated world, as if it were real. If the users aren't totally immersed, if they don't feel present in the virtual world, then their experience will be less emotionally strong [30]. We find that the seat that we used in this experiment, i.e., a seat moving in accordance with the VR scene, enhanced the emotions that the user was experiencing, pushing further his/her immersion in the virtual environment (VE).

Analysis of head movements reinforces findings about immersion. In our experimental design, no specific instructions were given to participants with regards to head movement in the virtual scene. A large part of male participants (62.5%) naturally aligned their heads on the z-axis. This axis is the one where results are the most meaningful when it comes to cybersickness [29]. According to the subjective vertical (SV)-conflict theory [4], cybersickness is due to a conflict regarding the SV i.e., the internal representation of gravity. This theory states that motion sickness is due to a mismatch between SV, determined by previous experiences; and the sensed vertical, predicted on the basis of information sent from the eyes, the vestibular system and the nonvestibular proprioceptors. If we interpret this theory with a 3D point of view, it could suggest that conflict appears with changes on the x-axis and the z-axis (the y-axis being the only one that didn't change the aspect of SV). Our head movement results support Bles et al. work

[4]. Based on the SV-conflict theory, in the case of vehicular movement in VR, when participants align their head around the z-axis, it could mean that the user feels like moving with the virtual car. In real life conditions, when we are in a vehicle, it is natural to see people leaning during a turn or a curve. This is the phenomenon that we observed for 62.5% of our male sample. So, the VK condition appears to help users move as they would in real life conditions. Thus we can say that the VK condition leads to a more natural movement of the head in the context of vehicular movement in VR.

Moreover, results show an interesting pattern concerning ECG analysis for cybersickness literature. It is pertinent to investigate the effect of VK technology on the brain considering that motion sickness symptoms are psychophysiological. The brain's nervous system includes two parts that work simultaneously: the autonomic nervous system (ANS) and the parasympathetic nervous system (PNS). We observed the reaction of the PNS using high frequencies (HF) of the heart, HF being an index of PNS [19, 39]. PNS governs the resting and rehabilitation of the body. When activated, the brain aims to return to its homeostatic state contrary to the stress response that is induced by ANS, also called "fight or flight" reaction [3]. During our analysis, we focused on the whole experience and on the last minute of each participant. The last minute is important in our experimental design because the participants were free to stop the experience when they started to feel any discomfort due to cybersickness. The last minute tells us what the psychophysiological state of the participant was just before ending the VR immersion. We find an augmentation of HF during the last minute for subjects with a still seat (non-VK condition). HF is a synonym of PNS activation and is a proxy of respiration [17, 21, 36]. It means that, when subjects are seated on a normal chair, they need to regulate themselves using deep breaths in order to calm their body and decrease discomfort. Based on this, VK technology could help VR users to autoregulate and stay in a relaxed state leading to fewer symptoms of cybersickness. This study provides encouraging results for future research in this area.

To better understand how VK technology impacts cybersickness, future studies should use longer stimuli It is well known in the literature that the probability of cybersickness highly increases over time [12]. Furthermore, our study was conducted with a passive VR stimuli. Interactive VR stimuli should be tested as well to determine if our results can be extended to other types of VR experiments.

In summary, results show that VK contributes to the VR experience by pushing the immersion further, inducing a better psychophysiological state that is more optimal for VR experience and by fostering more natural head movements for a large number of users, leading to a higher sense of presence in the VR. This study also illustrates that VK technology is an opportunity for the VR industry to reduce cybersickness, a major issue when it comes to VR experiences.

Acknowledgments. We thank all the study participants and we are thankful for the financial support of the Natural Sciences and Engineering Research Council of Canada.

References

1. Abrams, C., Earl, W.K., Baker, C.H., Buckner, D.N.: Studies of the effects of sea motion on human performance. Office of Naval Research, Technical report, pp. 791–796 (1971)
2. Annetta, L., Klesath, M., John, M.: Taking science online: evaluating presence and immersion through a laboratory experience in a virtual learning environment for entomology students. J. Coll. Sci. Teach. **39**(1), 27–34 (2009)
3. Bear, M.F., Connors, B.W.: Neurosciences (4e édition): A la découverte du cerveau (2016)
4. Bles, W., Bos, J.E., De Graaf, B., Groen, E., Wertheim, A.H.: Motion sickness: only one provocative conflict? Brain Res. Bull. **47**, 481–487 (1998). https://doi.org/10.1016/S0361-9230(98)00115-4
5. Bowman, D.A., Mcmahana, R.P., Tech, V.: Virtual reality: how much immersion is enough? (Cover story). Comput. (Long Beach Calif.) **40**, 36–43 (2007). https://doi.org/10.1109/MC.2007.257
6. Brown, E., Cairns, P.: A grounded investigation of game immersion. In: CHI EA 2004 CHI 2004 Extended Abstracts on Human Factors in Computing Systems, p. 1297 (2004). https://doi.org/10.1145/985921.986048
7. Busscher, B., de Vliegher, D., Ling, Y., Brinkman, W.P.: Physiological measures and self-report to evaluate neutral virtual reality worlds. J. Cyber. Ther. Rehabil. **4**, 15–25 (2011)
8. Cottin, F., Médigue, C., Papelier, Y.: Effect of heavy exercise on spectral baroreflex sensitivity, heart rate, and blood pressure variability in well-trained humans. Am. J. Physiol. Hear. Circ. Physiol. **295**, H1150–H1155 (2008). https://doi.org/10.1152/ajpheart.00003.2008
9. Cruz-Neira, C.: Virtual reality overview. In: SIGGRAPH, p. 1 (1993)
10. D-Box Technologies Inc.: Media Recognition and Synchronisation to a Motion Signal (2016). https://patents.justia.com/patent/9640046
11. Dawson, M.E., Schell, A.M., Filion, D.L.: The electrodermal system. In: Foundations of Psychophysiology, pp. 200–223 (2000)
12. Drexler, J.M.: Identification of system design features that affect sickness in virtual environments (2006)
13. Ermi, L., Mäyrä, F.: Fundamental components of the gameplay experience: analysing immersion. In: Changing Views Worlds Play, pp. 15–27 (2005). https://doi.org/10.1080/10641260490479818
14. Gacek, A., Pedryez, W.: ECG Signal Processing Classification and Interpretation. Springer, London (2015). https://doi.org/10.1007/978-0-85729-868-3
15. Geisler, F.C.M., Vennewald, N., Kubiak, T., Weber, H.: The impact of heart rate variability on subjective well-being is mediated by emotion regulation. Pers. Individ. Differ. **49**, 723–728 (2010). https://doi.org/10.1016/j.paid.2010.06.015
16. Golding, J.F.: Predicting individual differences in motion sickness susceptibility by questionnaire. Pers. Individ. Differ. **41**, 237–248 (2006). https://doi.org/10.1016/j.paid.2006.01.012
17. Goldstein, D.S., Bentho, O., Park, M.-Y., Sharabi, Y.: Low-frequency power of heart rate variability is not a measure of cardiac sympathetic tone but may be a measure of modulation of cardiac autonomic outflows by baroreflexes. Exp. Physiol. **96**, 1255–1261 (2011). https://doi.org/10.1113/expphysiol.2010.056259
18. Gownder, J.P., McQuivey, J.L., Johnson, C.: The Coming Wave Of Virtual Reality (2016)
19. Hufnagel, C., Chambres, P., Auxiette, C.: Les systèmes de monitoring du bien-être: application à l' anxiété dans les troubles du spectre autistique. le Bull Sci l'arapi **34**, 50–55 (2014)

20. Jennett, C., Cox, A.L., Cairns, P., Dhoparee, S., Epps, A., Tijs, T., Walton, A.: Measuring and defining the experience of immersion in games. Int. J. Hum. Comput. Stud. **66**, 641–661 (2008). https://doi.org/10.1016/j.ijhcs.2008.04.004

21. De Jonckheere, J., Rommel, D., Nandrino, J., Jeanne, M., Logier, R.: Heart rate variability analysis as an index of emotion regulation processes: interest of the Analgesia Nociception Index (ANI). In: Proceedings of Annual International Conference of the IEEE Engineering in Medicine and Biology Society EMBS, pp. 3432–3435 (2012). https://doi.org/10.1109/embc.2012.6346703

22. Kolasinski, E.: Prediction of simulator sickness in a virtual environment (1996)

23. Van Kuilenburg, H., Den Uyl, M.J., Israël, M.L., Ivan, P.: Advances in face and gesture analysis. In: Proceedings of Measuring Behavior, pp. 371–372 (2008)

24. McMahan, A.: Immersion, engagement, and presence. Video Game Theor. Read Immers. **67**, 86 (2003)

25. Noldus: FaceReader 6: Reference Manual (2011)

26. Pauna, H., Léger, P.-M., Sénécal, S., Fredette, M., Courtemanche, F., Chen, S.-L., Labonté-Lemoyne, É., Ménard, J.-F.: The psychophysiological effect of a vibro-kinetic movie experience: the case of the D-BOX movie seat. In: Davis, Fred D., Riedl, R., vom Brocke, J., Léger, P.-M., Randolph, Adriane B. (eds.) Information Systems and Neuroscience. LNISO, vol. 25, pp. 1–7. Springer, Cham (2018). https://doi.org/10.1007/978-3-319-67431-5_1

27. Reason, J.T.: Motion sickness adaptation: a neural mismatch model. J. R. Soc. Med. **71**, 819–829 (1978). https://doi.org/10.1177/014107687807101109

28. Reason, J.T., Brand, J.J.: Motion Sickness. Academic Press, Oxford (1975)

29. Rebenitsch, L.R.: Cybersickness Prioritization and Modeling. Michigan State University (2015)

30. Riva, G., Mantovani, F., Capideville, C.S., Preziosa, A., Morganti, F., Villani, D., Gaggioli, A., Botella, C., Alcañiz, M.: Affective interactions using virtual reality: the link between presence and emotions. CyberPsychol. Behav. **10**, 45–56 (2007). https://doi.org/10.1089/cpb.2006.9993

31. Schubert, T.W.: A new conception of spatial presence: once again, with feeling. Commun. Theor. **19**, 161–187 (2009). https://doi.org/10.1111/j.1468-2885.2009.01340.x

32. Segerstrom, S.C., Nes, L.S.: Heart rate variability reflects effort, strength, and fatigue. Psychol. Sci. **18**, 275–281 (2007). https://doi.org/10.1111/j.1467-9280.2007.01888.x

33. Simon, D., Keith, N., Eugene, N.: A systematic review of Cybersickness. Br. J. Health. Psychol. **19**, 149–180 (2014). https://doi.org/10.1145/2677758.2677780

34. Slater, M., Steed, A., McCarthy, J., Maringelli, F.: The influence of body movement on subjective presence in virtual environments. Hum. Factors **40**, 469–477 (1998). https://doi.org/10.1518/001872098779591368

35. Slater, M., Wilbur, S.: A Framework for Immersive Virtual Environments (FIVE): speculations on the role of presence in virtual environments. Presence Teleoperators Virtual Environ. **6**, 603–616 (1997). https://doi.org/10.1007/s10750-008-9541-7

36. Vaderrama, M., Navarro, V., Le van Quyen, M.: Heart Rate Variability as measurement of heart-brain interaction.pdf. Epilespie et coeur **22**, 194–200 (2010). https://doi.org/10.1684/epi.2010.0323

37. Visch, V.T., Tan, E.S., Molenaar, D.: The emotional and cognitive effect of immersion in film viewing. Cogn. Emot. **24**, 1439–1445 (2010). https://doi.org/10.1080/02699930903498186

38. Witmer, B.G., Singer, M.J.: Measuring presence in virtual environments: a presence questionnaire. Presence Teleoperators Virtual Environ. **7**, 225–240 (1998). https://doi.org/10.1162/105474698565686
39. Wu, W., Lee, J.: Improvement of HRV methodology for positive/negative emotion assessment. In: Proceedings of 5th International ICST Conference on Collaborative Computing: Networking, Applications and Worksharing (2009). https://doi.org/10.4108/icst.collaboratecom2009.8296

Lateral Modulation of Midair Ultrasound Focus for Intensified Vibrotactile Stimuli

Ryoko Takahashi[1(✉)], Keisuke Hasegawa[2], and Hiroyuki Shinoda[2]

[1] Graduate School of Information Science and Technology,
The University of Tokyo, Tokyo, Japan
takahashi@hapis.k.u-tokyo.ac.jp
[2] Graduate School of Frontier Sciences, The University of Tokyo, Chiba, Japan
Keisuke_Hasegawa@ipc.i.u-tokyo.ac.jp, Hiroyuki_Shinoda@k.u-tokyo.ac.jp

Abstract. In this paper, we propose a new modulation method of midair ultrasound focus named Lateral Modulation (LM), which provides significantly stronger vibrotactile stimuli on the skin surface compared to that provided by conventional Amplitude Modulation (AM) in the realm of midair ultrasound haptics. We experimentally validated the effectiveness of the LM method by showing that it significantly lowered the vibrotactile detection threshold compared with the AM method, for a wide range of modulation frequencies. The method was found to be valid both on the glabrous and hairy skins, and is expected to be applied to whole-body midair haptics. We demonstrate that the LM method relies on the characteristics of human perception of moving stimuli on the skin surface.

Keywords: Midair haptics · Haptic display · Human perception

1 Introduction

Airborne Ultrasound Tactile Display (AUTD) [1,2] can present tactile stimulus on a human body surface without direct contact. AUTD creates an ultrasound focus at an arbitrary position in the workspace by controlling the phase shift and amplitude of the output emission of the ultrasound transducers. The focus presents tactile stimuli by applying acoustic radiation pressure, which pushes the skin surface inside the focal region. This display can superimpose tactile feedback onto 3D human-computer interfaces such as AR and VR systems. As examples of such aerial vibrotactile systems, an aerial touch panel with haptic feedback called HaptoMime [3] and a mutual real-time telepresence system called HaptoClone [4], which allows two users over a distance to simultaneously share a virtually identical three-dimensional workspace that includes visual and tactile information, have been developed so far, in addition to many other related technologies [5,6].

The standard method of presenting vibrotactile sensation with a current AUTD is temporally modulating the amplitude of the acoustic radiation pressure

© Springer International Publishing AG, part of Springer Nature 2018
D. Prattichizzo et al. (Eds.): EuroHaptics 2018, LNCS 10894, pp. 276–288, 2018.
https://doi.org/10.1007/978-3-319-93399-3_25

with a waveform so that it has vibration components of about 100 to 200 Hz. With this method, the presentation position is limited to the glabrous part of the skin (often a palm), which is the most sensitive region available for tactile stimulation for most cases.

This is because the maximum pressure that the device can generate is firmly limited by its specification, and consequently, it is highly difficult to present relatively low frequency vibration components lower than several tens of hertz as distinctly perceivable passive tactile stimuli. Although it is true that users can perceive those lower-frequency-modulated focus by actively and carefully moving their hands, in those cases, it is only possible to let the users feel smooth protrusion when they pay sufficient attention to it. The most straightforward solution for improving the focal intensity is to increase the presentation pressure by employing a larger number of AUTDs [7]. Nevertheless, it is not always desirable to emit such a strong ultrasound from the viewpoint of safety. In addition, for some applications, it may be difficult to assume a hardware configuration that occupies a large space. If we achieve clear tactile presentation to areas other than hairless skin, we can make full use of the intrinsic advantage of midair ultrasound haptics that stimulus can be presented at an arbitrary timing on any position on the body. For instance, new applications such as presentation of a trigger evoking the user's attention, presentation of midair trajectory, or instruction of specific body actions, can be realized for an unspecified number of users in a purely haptic manner.

In fact, haptic technology targeting the whole body is still under development, however, it is a field with great expectations in terms of practical application. The fundamental assumption among current whole-body haptic displays is that the users wear specific devices in touch with their bodies [8,9]. Those "wearable" methods are indeed promising for many potential applications. However, those devices have some inevitable inconveniences such as constrained body movement of the user and bulky device size due to the wiring and actuators. As for AUTDs, it can reliably apply force on the exposed body surface such as hands, arms, and face. It should be noted that successful stimulation of the skin under clothes is still difficult with the method proposed in this paper.

The conventional amplitude modulation (AM) method temporally modulates the ultrasound pressure, which means that the average output acoustic power is lower than the maximum non-modulated power. At the same time, a non-modulated spatially-fixed ultrasound focus, which yields temporally constant radiation pressure, cannot be felt as a vivid passive tactile sensation as described above even when the focal acoustic power is much greater than that of perceivable AM focuses.

The main idea of this research is that the temporally non-modulated focus yields vibrotactile sensation on multiple points on the skin when the focus is horizontally moving in a continuous manner, while employing the maximum possible output of the device. In other words, it is not the focal amplitude but the horizontal focal location that is modulated in the proposed method. We define this spatial modulation technique as Lateral Modulation (LM). Current AUTD systems can locate ultrasound focus with a spatial resolution in the submillimeter range and a temporal refresh rate of 1,000 Hz, resulting in smooth focal movements on the skin. In addition, some researches have suggested the existence of somatosensory areas that are selectively activated by spatially moving stimuli [10], though its mechanism is still not completely understood. Therefore, with the LM method, it is expected that the resulting vibrotactile stimuli can be stronger owing to the fully utilized acoustic power and enlarged vibrated skin region, compared with conventional spatially fixed AM focus.

In this paper, we have experimentally clarified that the LM method is able to present subjectively stronger vibrotactile sensation to both the palm and the dorsal side on the lower arm, compared with the conventional AM method. In addition, we have also confirmed that this lowering of the detection threshold of vibrotactile stimuli with the LM method is observed among a wide range of modulation frequencies in the range of 50 to 200 Hz.

2   Principle

2.1   Tactile Stimulation by Ultrasound Focus

AUTD is a device containing ultrasound transducers arranged in a lattice pattern. The phase and amplitude of the output waveform of each transducer can be individually controlled. AUTD concentrates the acoustic power in a narrow area with a controlled set of output phase and amplitude. The maximum possible energy concentration is achieved when the acoustic pressure from all the transducers converge to one point. This is realized by setting the phase shifts of the transducers in such a way that they are proportional to the distance between the desired focal position and each transducer. Although it is possible to generate spacing patterns with multi focus instead of a single focus [11,12], we focus on presenting a single focal point in this paper, because it is the strongest possible acoustic field.

It is known that when an object blocks intense acoustic propagation, a quasistatic pressure proportional to the acoustic power is generated on its surface. This phenomenon is called acoustic radiation pressure [13], which is the fundamental physical principle of aerial ultrasound tactile presentation. Although the instantaneous ultrasound pressure varies with time, the time average value of the radiation pressure is proportional to the acoustic power on a macroscopic time scale. As a result, theoretically, the squared ultrasound waveform envelope is detected and perceived as vibrotactile stimuli [7].

Theoretically, the sound pressure distribution around the ultrasound focus created by transducers arranged in a lattice is given as a two-dimensional squared sinc function. Here, the focus refers to the region between two central zero-cross lines. The size of the perceivable focus can be narrowed down to about the wavelength depending on the distance from the emitting surface [2]. The AUTD used in this paper has transducers resonating at 40 kHz, and therefore it presents a spot of about 8.5 mm in size, which is equal to the wavelength. The acoustic power outside the focus is much lower, which contributes little to the perceivable vibrotactile stimuli.

Note that the ultrasound focus only generates pressure normal to the skin surface. Regardless of the modulation mode, no shear force is thought to be generated on the skin surface. Thus, the focal movement described in the following section does not include any tangential force such as friction. It includes only the spatiotemporal changes of the normal force on the skin.

2.2 Vibrotactile Presentation Method: Amplitude Modulation vs Lateral Modulation

Conventional Method: Amplitude Modulation. From the earliest research stages of ultrasound midair haptics [1], it has been a common strategy to increase the subjective stimulus intensity by temporally modulating the ultrasound pressure. This method involves temporally varying the amplitude of the waveform while keeping the focal position fixed. In this paper, we define this method as "Amplitude Modulation," and hereinafter call it "AM." Note that what the AUTD directly controls is the exerted acoustic radiation pressure on a rigid target, and not its displacement. In presenting vibrotactile stimulation with sinusoidal AM, it is known that the identification threshold is the lowest for a modulation frequency of around 200 Hz when targeting the palm [7]. It is thought that this is because the vibrotactile detection threshold of the Pacini corpuscles has a minimum value around 200 Hz, and is superior in sensitivity to the other receptors. However, to the best of our knowledge, there are no examples of similar sensitivity curves for ultrasound stimulation in hairy parts without Pacini corpuscles. Nevertheless, it is empirically known that AM ultrasound focuses are difficult to perceive by hairy skin, especially when the modulation frequency surpasses 200 Hz. As stated above, theoretically, a squared envelope of the waveform corresponds to the vibrotactile sensation. Nevertheless, we simply created the focal waveform so that the envelope of the (non-squared) waveform was sinusoidal. This is because of the simplicity in implementation, and we considered that this incongruity has little effect on the perceived stimuli.

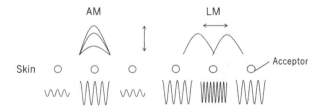

Fig. 1. Two vibrotactile presentation methods. The waveforms represent the strength and cycle of pressure given to the acceptors. The left figure shows conventional Amplitude Modulation, and the right figure shows Lateral Modulation.

Proposed Method: Lateral Modulation. In this paper, we propose a new method of modulation. This method involves keeping the amplitude of the waveform constant while temporally changing the horizontal position of the focus in a periodic manner. We define this method as "Lateral Modulation," and hereinafter call it "LM." We switched the focal position at a refresh rate of 1,000 Hz. Figure 1 shows the concept of the two methods.

Here, we compare the time average of the acoustic power applied to the entire skin in AM and LM. Let ω_c be the carrier angular frequency of the ultrasound wave, $\omega_m(<\omega_c)$ be the AM angular frequency, and $p_{AM}(t)$ and $p_{LM}(t)$ be the instantaneous acoustic pressure at the focal point in AM and LM, respectively, with t denoting the time. In our setup, ω_c is $2\pi \times 40$ kHz. With a modulation index of 100%, the instantaneous acoustic pressure at the focal point is given as:

$$p_{AM}(t) = p_0 \sin(\omega_c t) \sin(\omega_m t), \ p_{LM}(t) = p_0 \sin(\omega_c t), \tag{1}$$

where p_0 is the maximum amplitude. We have the time-averaged acoustic powers P_{AM} and P_{LM} radiated from the phased array as:

$$P_{AM} = \frac{a}{T} \int_0^T (p_{AM}(t))^2 \, dt, \ P_{LM} = \frac{a}{T} \int_0^T (p_{LM}(t))^2 \, dt, \tag{2}$$

where $T = \frac{2\pi}{\omega_m}$, and a is a constant, concluding that $P_{LM} = 2P_{AM}$. Since the radiation pressure is proportional to the acoustic power [13], when the maximum output of the device is constant, LM can apply twice the acoustic power to the entire skin as that of AM in time average.

Next, we consider the fluctuation of pressure on a specific fixed spatial point on the skin. In this paper, we define LM as the horizontal sinusoidal movement of a focus with a fixed amplitude. Here, the LM frequency is defined as the frequency of the focal movement. The excitation waveform at a fixed point on the skin depends on the shape of the focus and the distance from the LM center. For instance, if the focus has an edgy power distribution, the resulting excitation waveform will correspondingly contain steep parts. Note that the excitation waveform is not always a sine wave with a single frequency. For example, at the center point of the LM, the skin surface is excited by a waveform having a frequency component double that of the LM frequency, because the focus crosses twice in one cycle. The existence of these harmonics and the vibration on multiple adjacent receptors with spatially dependent phase delays is what differentiates LM from AM.

3   Experiment

We constructed an experiment workspace with 4 AUTDs mounted on the ceiling of an aluminum frame (Fig. 7). The ultrasound emitted from the AUTDs propagate downwards. All experiments were performed with this workspace.

3.1   Experiment 1: Measurement of Acoustic Radiation Pressure

The first experiment was the waveform measurement of acoustic radiation pressure generated by the LM method with an electric condenser microphone (ECM) from Kingstate (KECG2738PBJ-A). The waveform was captured by an oscilloscope (PicoScope 4262). All the waveforms shown in this section were processed by the software low-pass filter of the PicoScope with the cut-off frequency set to 2,000 Hz so that it corresponds to the waveform of the acoustic radiation pressure. We verified how the LM vibrotactile stimuli varied spatially.

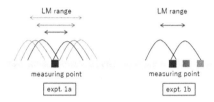

Fig. 2. Conceptual diagram of experiments 1a and 1b. In experiment 1a, the measurement position was fixed and the spatial amplitude was changed. In 1b, we fixed the spatial amplitude and changed the measurement position.

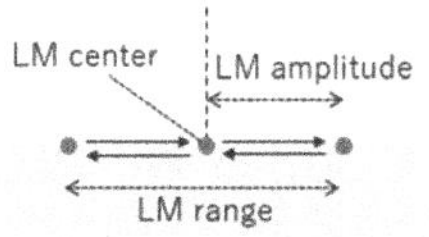

Fig. 3. Definition of LM terms. The circle in the figure indicates the focus position.

Procedures. In this experiment, the LM frequency was set to 25 Hz, resulting in a period of 40 ms. Figure 2 shows the schematic descriptions of the two experiments, 1a and 1b. In both the experiments, the distance from the emission plane of the AUTD to the ECM was 230 mm.

(Experiment 1a): We fixed the ECM at the center of the workspace, which corresponded to the center of the generated LM focus. We measured the ECM outputs for sinusoidal LM amplitudes of 2, 4.5, and 7 mm. Here, we define LM amplitude as the halved horizontal swinging length of the LM focus (Fig. 3).

(Experiment 1b): Next, we fixed the LM amplitude to 7 mm and measured the radiation pressure waveforms while shifting the horizontal position of the ECM with respect to the LM center by 0 to 9 mm in steps of 1 mm.

Results. Figure 4 shows the ECM output waveform at the LM center. The blue, red, and green lines are the outputs for the LM amplitudes 2, 4.5, and 7 mm, respectively. In all the lines, two peaks are observed within one LM cycle (40 ms). These results agree with the theoretical speculation that the doubled frequency component is observed at the LM center. The variation of the ECM output is seen to increase with increase in the LM amplitude. Note that the focal size in the experiment was approximately 10 mm.

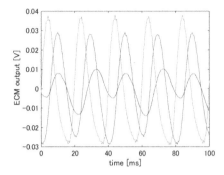

Fig. 4. Output voltages of the ECM installed at the LM center. The LM frequency was 25 Hz, and the blue, red, and green lines are for the LM vibration amplitudes of 2, 4.5, and 7 mm, respectively. Harmonics were observed in all the lines, and the ECM output amplitude became larger for larger lateral vibration amplitude. (Color figure online)

Figure 5 shows the ECM output waveforms for experiment 1b, when the measurement positions were set to 1, 3, 5, and 7 mm away from the LM center, with the LM amplitude fixed to 7 mm. Figure 5 shows that the interval between the two peaks varies depending on the measurement position. This is understood by calculating the timing when the focal center traverses the measurement point.

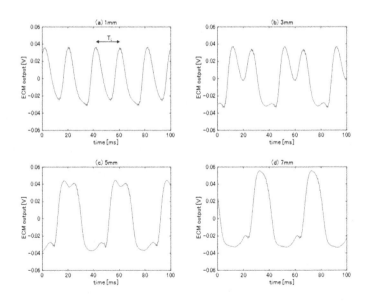

Fig. 5. Output voltages of the ECM for 25 Hz LM with a lateral vibration amplitude of 7 mm in experiment 1b. Figures a, b, c, and d are for the distances 1, 3, 5, and 7 mm between the ECM and the LM center, respectively.

The position of the focal center in the LM direction can be represented as $A\sin(\omega_{LM}t)$, where A is the LM amplitude, t is the time, and ω_{LM} is the LM angular frequency. The peaking time t of the radiation pressure at the measurement point x_0 is obtained by solving $x_0 = A\sin(\omega_{LM}t)$. For $x_0 > A$, the focal center does not cross during the LM cycle, where a single peak is expected in the LM cycle. However, small secondary peaks were seen in the graph of 7 mm. This is because of the secondary peak in the squared sinc function adjacent to the focal region.

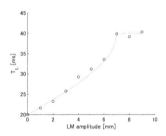

Fig. 6. Theoretical curve of T_L and the measured values.

We define the longer interval between the two peaks as T_L. Figure 6 shows the theoretical curve of T_L and the actually measured values along the measurement positions. The theoretical curve is consistent with the measured values of T_L, which indicates that current AUTDs could generate LM focus in a theoretically predictable way.

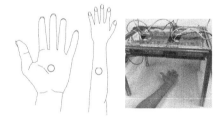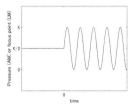

Fig. 7. Left figure shows the focus point in experiment 2, center figure shows the focus point in experiments 3 and 4, and right picture shows a view of the experiment.

Fig. 8. Modulation of ultrasound pressure amplitude or focal position over time. The unmodulated acoustic radiation pressure is presented at the center of the workspace and the modulation starts with the sound of the signal (time = 0). X is the amplitude of each modulation.

3.2   Experiment 2: Vibration Detection Threshold on Hairless Part

We experimentally obtained the vibration detection threshold of AM and LM stimuli on the palm with respect to several modulation frequencies and LM amplitudes.

Procedures. Figure 7 shows a view of the experiment. We had five male and one female subjects, whose age ranged from 22 to 32. The subjects placed left hand on the center of the workspace, with the palm facing upward (Fig. 7). During the experiment, the subjects wore headphones playing white noise to nullify auditory clues. In every trial, the subjects heard the cue sound as the stimuli was presented. Then, they answered whether they felt the vibrotactile sensation after the signal sound. We varied the stimulus intensity and obtained the detection threshold for each condition by using the method of limits. For each condition, the trial was done once. The distance from the emission plane of the AUTD to the palm was 270 mm.

Figure 8 shows the modulation waveform of the ultrasound amplitude in AM stimulation. Because negative radiation pressure cannot be produced, proper offset pressure was required. However, the DC offset caused static pressure and mass flow, called acoustic streaming. In order to get rid of these factors, which were irrelevant to the experiments, we presented a focus modulated with this DC offset for seconds prior to each time the AM focus was displayed. This DC offset was set to the 50% value in the waveform. A similar procedure was also done for LM stimuli: every trial started with presenting a still focus that lasted for seconds followed by an LM modulated focus. The intensity of stimuli in both

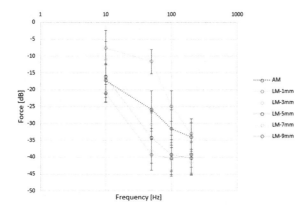

Fig. 9. Comparison of the average thresholds for AM and LM on hairless skin. 0 dB corresponds to the upper limit of the output ultrasound pressure of the device. Error bars indicates standard deviations. The cases in which vibration was not felt even at the maximum output were eliminated. 10 Hz AM stimuli could not be felt by one subject, and 1 mm and 10 Hz LM stimuli could not be felt by two subjects. "LM-X mm" indicates the LM that has X mm LM amplitude.

AM and LM is defined as the maximum instantaneous output pressure from the AUTD. The maximum amplitude was varied with 51 levels. For both AM and LM stimuli, we set the modulation frequency to 10, 50, 100, and 200 Hz. The LM amplitude was set to 1, 3, 5, 7, and 9 mm.

Result. Figure 9 shows the result. Here, 0 dB corresponds to the upper limit of the output ultrasound pressure of the device. 10 Hz AM stimuli could not be felt by one subject, and (1 mm, 10 Hz) LM stimuli could not be felt by two subjects. The overall tendency in LM stimuli is that the increase in the LM amplitude lowers the detecting threshold. It can be observed that the LM stimuli with more than 5 mm amplitude was felt stronger than the AM stimuli. (1 mm, 50 Hz), (3 mm, 100 Hz), (5 mm, 50, 100, or 200 Hz), (7 mm, 50, 100, or 200 Hz), or (9 mm, 50 Hz) LM stimuli were significantly different from the AM stimuli in the paired t-test ($p < 0.05$). This tendency is reasonably understood with the results in experiment 1.

3.3   Experiment 3: Vibration Detection Threshold on Hairy Part

Procedures. Experiment 3 was performed in the same fashion as that of experiment 2, except that the stimulation position was changed to the center of the forearm hairy part (Fig. 7). We presented both AM and LM stimuli. For LM stimuli, the LM amplitude was fixed to 7 mm. The modulation frequency was set to 10, 50, 100, and 200 Hz. The distance from the emission plane of the AUTD and the palm was 230 mm to 250 mm.

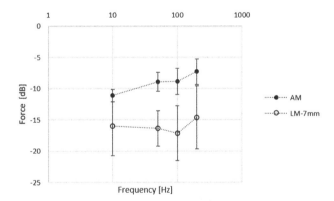

Fig. 10. Comparison of the average thresholds for AM and LM on hairy skin. 0 dB corresponds to the upper limit of the output ultrasound pressure of the device. Error bars indicate standard deviations. The cases in which vibration was not felt even at the maximum output were eliminated. 100 Hz AM stimuli could not be felt by one subject, and 200 Hz AM stimuli could not be felt by two subjects.

Result. Figure 10 shows the result. The result that the LM threshold takes lower values among all modulation frequencies is consistent with the result of the previous experiment. The difference is that thresholds are flatter among the modulation frequencies. This is due to the absence of Pacini corpuscles, which exhibit extreme sensitivity around a specific stimulation frequency. Since the AM threshold does not decrease as the modulation frequency increases, we conclude that the threshold decrease in LM stimuli is not because of the harmonics that LM contains. It is also worth noting that a drop in detection threshold of at most 10 dB was observed. The difference between AM and LM stimuli was significant in the paired t-test ($p < 0.05$), when the LM frequency was 50, 100, or 200 Hz.

3.4   Experiment 4: Subjective Evaluation of Two Vibrotactile

In this experiment, the subjects evaluated the difference between AM and LM stimuli by subjective impressions of the stimuli. We presented AM vibrotactile and 7 mm LM vibrotactile at the maximum intensity on the middle of the hairy part of their forearm. For both the conditions, the modulation frequency was set to 50 Hz. After two stimuli, the subjects answered which stimulus was stronger. They were also asked to express how each of the vibration felt like. As a result, 100% of the subjects answered that LM was a stronger stimulus ($n = 5$). For both the stimuli, some subjects answered that they felt as if wind was blowing on their arm. This was presumably because of the wind caused by acoustic streaming. It should be clearly noted that what the subjects felt was not only the wind since the vibrotactile stimuli was surely felt as demonstrated in the above experiments.

4   Discussion

While an AM focus is thought to activate both shallow and deep receptors (Meissner and Pacini corpuscle), LM modulation can be considered to stimulate mainly shallow receptors. We expect this because the sum of the applied pressure in the region of LM range is constant, and the size of the receptive fields in these two receptors are different. Since deep receptors receive sums of stimuli on wider areas, they are unable to perceive the small spatial changes of the stimuli point. If selective stimulation of different mechanoreceptors is achieved with our method, it may be possible to present a variety of realistic tactile textures [14,15].

As stated above, the harmonics entailed by the LM focus was not the essential aspect of enhancement of vibrotactile stimuli. In addition, although the LM focus contains twice the acoustic power as that of the AM focus as stated above, the lowering of detection threshold cannot be explained merely by this effect. As referred to in the introduction, some researches refer to the activation of somatosensory areas by spatially moving the stimuli on the skin surface [10]. More detailed investigation about the perceptive effect of those spatial stimuli will lead to a more efficient way of subjectively intensifying the presented vibrotactile stimuli.

5 Conclusion

We proposed the lateral modulation (LM) method to present midair ultrasound vibrotactile stimuli. We verified the effectiveness of the LM method in terms of enhancing the subjective strength of the presented vibrotactile stimuli on the glabrous and hairy skin regions, compared with the conventional AM methods. We demonstrated that this effect was valid for modulations of 50 to 200 Hz with an LM amplitude of 5 mm and more. We also found that this effect cannot be explained by the harmonics caused by the LM focus, concluding that it is due to the characteristics of human perception of spatially modulated stimuli. Our achievement will be utilized in realizing full-body haptic systems that are free from mechanical constraints as stated in the introduction. In future, we will investigate the underlying mechanism that causes the LM enhancement, as well as construct a practical system based on this method.

References

1. Iwamoto, T., Tatezono, M., Shinoda, H.: Non-contact method for producing tactile sensation using airborne ultrasound. In: Proceedings of Eurohaptics 2008, pp. 504–513 (2008)
2. Hoshi, T., Takahashi, M., Iwamoto, T., Shinoda, H.: Noncontact tactile display based on radiation pressure of airborne ultrasound. IEEE Trans. Haptics **3**(3), 155–165 (2010)
3. Monnai, Y., Hasegawa, K., Fujiwara, M., Yoshino, K., Inoue, S., Shinoda, H.: HaptoMime: mid-airhaptic interaction with a floating virtual screen. In: Proceedings of 27th Annual ACM Symposium on User Interface Software Technology, pp. 663–667 (2014)
4. Makino, Y., Furuyama, Y., Inoue, S., Shinoda, H.: HaptoClone (Haptic-Optical Clone) for mutual tele-environment by real-time 3D image transfer with Midair force feedback. In: Proceedings of 2016 CHI Conference on Human Factors Computing System, pp. 1980–1990 (2016)
5. Korres, G., Eid, M.: Haptogram: ultrasonic point-cloud tactile stimulation. IEEE Access **4**, 7758–7769 (2016)
6. Carter, T., Seah, S.A., Long, B., Drinkwater, B., Subramanian, S.: Ultrahaptics: multi-point mid-air haptic feedback for touch surfaces. In: Proceedings of the 26th Annual ACM Symposium on User Interface Software and Technology, UIST 2013, pp. 505–514. ACM, New York (2013)
7. Hasegawa, K., Shinoda, H.: Aerial vibrotactile display based on multiunit ultrasound phased array. IEEE Trans. Haptics. https://doi.org/10.1109/TOH.2018.2799220
8. Teslasuit. http://teslasuit.io/
9. NullSpace VR. http://nullspacevr.com/
10. Bodegard, A., Geyer, S., Naito, E., Zilles, K., Roland, P.E.: Somatosensory areas in man activated by moving stimuli: cytoarchitectonic mapping and PET. NeuroReport **11**, 187–191 (2000)
11. Long, B., Seah, S.A., Carter, T., Subramanian, S.: Rendering volumetric haptic shapes in mid-air using ultrasound. ACM Trans. Graph. **33**(6) (2014). Article No. 181

12. Inoue, S., Makino, Y., Shinoda, H.: Active touch perception produced by airborne ultrasonic haptic hologram. In: 2015 IEEE World Haptics Conference (WHC), Evanston, IL, pp. 362–367 (2015)
13. Awatani, J.: Studies on acoustic radiation pressure. I. (General Considerations). J. Acoust. Soc. Am. **27**, 278–281 (1955)
14. Asamura, N., Yokoyama, N., Shinoda, H.: Selectively stimulating skin receptors for tactile display. IEEE Comput. Graph. Appl. **18**(6), 32–37 (1998)
15. Konyo, M., Tadokoro, S., Yoshida, A., Saiwaki, N.: A tactile synthesis method using multiple frequency vibrations for representing virtual touch. In: 2005 IEEE/RSJ International Conference on Intelligent Robots and Systems (IROS 2005), pp. 3965–3971 (2005)

Improving Perception Accuracy
with Multi-sensory Haptic Cue Delivery

Nathan Dunkelberger[1]([✉]), Joshua Bradley[1], Jennifer L. Sullivan[1], Ali Israr[2],
Frances Lau[2], Keith Klumb[2], Freddy Abnousi[2], and Marcia K. O'Malley[1]

[1] Mechatronics and Haptic Interfaces Laboratory,
Department of Mechanical Engineering, Rice University,
Houston, TX 77005, USA
nbd2@rice.edu
[2] Facebook, Incorporated, Menlo Park, CA 94025, USA
http://mahilab.rice.edu/

Abstract. This paper presents a novel, wearable, and multi-sensory haptic feedback system intended to support the transmission of large sets of haptic cues that are accurately perceived by the human user. Previous devices have focused on the optimization of haptic cue transmission using a single modality and have typically employed arrays of haptic tactile actuators to maximize information throughput to a user. However, when large cue sets are to be transmitted, perceptual interference between transmitted cues can decrease the efficacy of single-sensory systems. Therefore, we present MISSIVE (Multi-sensory Interface of Stretch, Squeeze, and Integrated Vibration Elements), a wearable system that conveys multi-sensory haptic cues to the user's upper arm, allowing for increased perceptual accuracy compared to a single-sensory vibrotactile array of a comparable size, conveying the same number of cues. Our multi-sensory haptic cues are comprised of concurrently rendered, yet perceptually distinct elements: radial squeeze, lateral skin stretch, and localized cutaneous vibration. Our experiments demonstrate that our approach can increase perceptual accuracy compared to a single-sensory vibrotactile system of comparable size and that users prefer MISSIVE.

1 Introduction

Wearable haptic feedback devices are appealing for their ability to convey rich and varied tactile information to a human user in a compact form-factor. A range of applications for haptic cueing have been explored, from navigational assistance to sensory substitution feedback for individuals with vision, hearing, or proprioception impairments. Haptic cueing using wearable tactile actuators has been effectively used for encoding speech [8,10,15,17,18,26,28,29], providing movement guidance [14,19], and performing audio- [11] and video- to-tactile translation [12]. Tactile feedback can also be an effective form of communication in contexts where individuals are already visually or aurally saturated [23].

© Springer International Publishing AG, part of Springer Nature 2018
D. Prattichizzo et al. (Eds.): EuroHaptics 2018, LNCS 10894, pp. 289–301, 2018.
https://doi.org/10.1007/978-3-319-93399-3_26

A variety of mechanisms have been designed to render haptic feedback, the majority of which utilize cutaneous sensory channels such as skin stretch, pressure, or vibration. These modalities of haptic feedback are favorable for wearable devices because they can be actuated with low voltage servos or motors, and require only a small on-board battery and microcontroller to operate. Skin stretch devices leverage a no-slip contact between an end effector and skin so that when the end effector is displaced, a mild skin shear sensation is produced. They can be rocker-based [3,5,13], linear [1], or rotational [4,27]. These mechanisms have been used primarily for directional guidance to indicate desired forearm rotations and translations, as well as for sensory feedback [5]. Pressure-inducing devices often consist of a motorized or pneumatically-actuated band that tightens around the arm. These devices have been successfully used for emotional indicators in digital communication [20] and to provide directional information [19]. The third category of wearable haptic feedback, vibration, is the most widely reported in the literature. Vibration feedback is most commonly implemented with vibrotactors due to their small form factor and ability to be driven at varying frequencies and amplitudes. By arranging multiple vibrotactors in a specific spatial configuration, an extensive number of actuation patterns can be rendered. Vibration has been used to convey a wide variety of meaningful metrics, including: grasping force [19], deviation from a postural set point [6,9], object slip [25], real-time quality of task performance [16], or navigational cues [21].

It is clear that there are not only many ways to implement haptic feedback, but also many pertinent applications for which it would be beneficial. What is not clear, however, is what methods should be used in which contexts in order to maximize the efficacy of the feedback. Ideal haptic feedback delivers the desired information quickly through tactile cues that users can perceive and distinguish accurately. When the information is simple and can be encoded within a few haptic cues (forward, back, right, left navigation cues, for example), the methods described previously are suitable. To communicate more complex information, a higher information transfer rate is required. Although information transfer rates can be increased simply by presenting low-information cues at a faster rate, studies have shown that it is more effective to present information-rich cues at a slower rate [2,22]. In other words, the key to increasing information transfer through the haptic channel is not to increase the presentation *rate* of cues, but rather to increase the information *content* of each cue [22].

In order to increase the information content of a haptic cue, more actuators are needed. However, integrating a substantial number of actuators into a wearable device is difficult because the inter-actuator spacing must be large enough to maintain high localization accuracy and minimize perceptual interference. As a result, these devices are sizable and can quickly become impractical for many wearable applications.

A number of the haptic devices reported in the literature encounter these challenges because they are uni-modal, that is, they only utilize a single actuator type. Given the diversity of mechanoreceptors in the skin, it is probable that wearable haptic devices that stimulate a range of mechanoreceptors may be able to overcome the limitations of single-modality wearable haptic feedback devices that have been prevalent in the literature. We hypothesize that a multi-sensory device, which can render a more diverse range of stimulations, will allow for the creation of a large set of perceptually-distinct cues while still maintaining a small, wearable form-factor. Multi-sensory devices are advantageous because they integrate actuators that operate at different frequencies, thereby allowing multiple stimuli to be rendered at once. Studies have indeed shown that more reliable perception of a physical attribute is possible when multiple tactile stimuli are combined [7]. The integration of multiple haptic modalities into a single system can also help reduce the inter-actuator spacing and perceptual interference between cues.

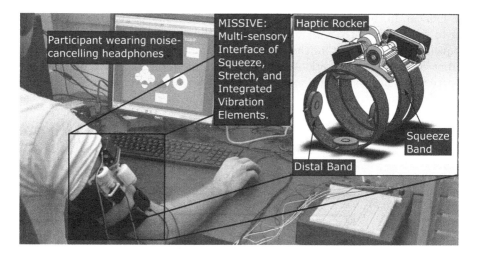

Fig. 1. The participant wears the MISSIVE on their upper arm. The bands are spaced three inches center-to-center. The Proximal Band comprises the lateral skin stretch and radial squeeze devices, and the Distal Band houses an array of four vibrotactors spaced 90° apart around the arm.

In this paper, we introduce MISSIVE (Multi-sensory Interface of Stretch, Squeeze, and Vibration Elements), a novel, multi-sensory, wearable haptic actuator that delivers concurrent tactile cues through combinations of vibration, radial squeeze, and lateral skin stretch. We present the design of this novel haptic device, as well as an assessment of the perceptual accuracy of our multi-sensory system compared with that of an analogous single-sensory device. Our study results show that MISSIVE outperformed the single-sensory system with respect to both presentation identification accuracy as well as user preference.

2   MISSIVE: Multi-sensory Haptic Device

MISSIVE is a compact device capable of delivering a variety of tactile cues to the upper arm of the user. It integrates three types of haptic actuators—a vibrotactor band, radial squeeze band, and haptic rocker—to produce concurrent sensations of vibration, radial squeeze, and lateral skin stretch, as shown in Fig. 1. To make the wearable actuator more compact, the squeeze band and the haptic rocker are mounted on the same frame, worn approximately 3 in. above (on the proximal side of) the vibrotactor band. We will refer to the two bands by their position on the arm (i.e. the Proximal Band and the Distal Band).

2.1 Distal Band

The Distal Band consists of four vibrotactors (C2 Tactors, Engineering Acoustics Inc., USA) positioned on the top, right, bottom, and left sides of the user's upper arm. The tactors are 1.2 in. in diameter and are actuated by a voice coil mechanism. In this study, they are driven at a frequency of 265 Hz, corresponding to the maximum vibration amplitude of the vibrotactors. In addition, this frequency value falls within the region of maximum sensitivity for the Pacinian corpuscle, the skin's vibration-sensing mechanoreceptor. This design allows for a large set of haptic cues to be defined using combinations of tactor location(s) and vibration patterns.

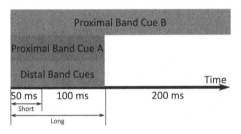

Fig. 2. Relative timing of the three haptic cues within a single presentation. The total duration of the haptic presentation is 350 ms. All three cues begin at the same time but have different durations. The Proximal Band Cue B actuates for 350 ms, the Proximal Band Cue A actuates for 150 ms, and a single Distal Band vibrotactor actuates for either 50 ms (short cue) or 150 ms (long cue).

2.2 Radial Squeeze Band

The design of the radial squeeze band is based on a similar device developed in the MAHI Lab, the Rice Squeeze Band [24]. It consists of a strap that is connected to a servomotor on one end and wraps around the user's arm. When the servomotor is actuated, it tightens the band and squeezes the user's arm. The servomotor (HS-485HB, Hitec RCD USA, Inc.) has a maximum torque output of 588 mNm.

2.3   Haptic Rocker

The lateral skin stretch actuator is the Rice Haptic Rocker, which was designed by Clark and described in [3]. The device comprises a servomotor connected to a rubber-coated, semi-circular end-effector that is pressed against the user's arm. When the servomotor is actuated, it induces a mild skin-shear sensation by rotating the end-effector and stretching the skin. The servomotor (HS-5070MH, Hitec RCD USA, Inc.) has a maximum torque of 375 mNm.

3   Methods

3.1   Participants

Eight able-bodied participants (four male, six right-handed, 18–24 years old) took part in the experiment. The participants did not suffer from any physical or cognitive impairment that could interfere with their ability to follow the instructions of the study, nor any pathology that could affect tactile sensation or muscular activity of the forearm. They had little to no prior experience with haptic devices. The methods and procedures described in this paper were carried out in accordance with the recommendations of the Institutional Review Board of Rice University with written informed consent obtained from all participants.

Table 1. Corresponding cues between MISSIVE and single-sensory devices (see Fig. 1)

	ACTUATORS		CUES
	MISSIVE	Single-sensory System	Description
Distal Band	4 vibrotactors	4 vibrotactors	Short/long pulse
Proximal Band Cue A	Haptic Rocker	1 vibrotactor (top)	On/off (150 ms)
Proximal Band Cue B	Radial Squeeze Band	1 vibrotactor (bottom)	On/off (350 ms)

3.2   Haptic Presentation Set

We developed a set of 32 haptic presentations to use in this identification experiment. Each presentation contained three components: a vibration cue, a lateral skin stretch cue, and a radial squeeze cue, which were all actuated concurrently. The vibration cues were rendered by activating a single tactor (top, right, bottom, or left) for a short (50 ms) or long (150 ms) pulse, resulting in eight unique cues. The radial squeeze and lateral skin stretch cues were rendered as binary, on/off cues. The radial squeeze cue was rendered by tightening the radial squeeze band for 175 ms and then releasing for 175 ms, resulting in a total cue duration of 350 ms. The lateral skin stretch cue was rendered by rotating the haptic rocker 30° and then returning it back to its center position, resulting in a total cue duration of 150 ms. Pilot testing was used to determine these cue actuation patterns to be easily perceptible and of similar intensity. A visualization of the relative timing of the three cues is shown in Fig. 2.

3.3   Single-Sensory Format

To compare the distinguishability of multi-sensory versus single-sensory presentations, we designed an analogous vibration-only device by replacing each of the Proximal Band actuators with vibrotactors. The haptic rocker was replaced by a vibrotactor in the Proximal Band positioned on the top side of the user's arm, and the radial squeeze band was replaced by a vibrotactor in the Proximal Band positioned on the bottom side of the user's arm. The Proximal Band cues on the single-sensory system were rendered in the same way (i.e. on/off) and for the same amount of time as the corresponding cues on the multi-sensory system. For simplicity, we will use "Cue A" to refer to the haptic rocker or top vibrotactor cue and "Cue B" to refer to the radial squeeze band or bottom vibrotactor cue. Thus, on both devices, Proximal Band Cue A is a 150 ms on/off cue, and Proximal Band Cue B is a 350 ms on/off cue. A summary of the cues and actuators in each system is presented in Table 1.

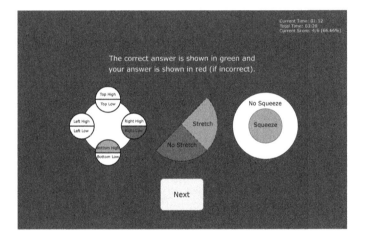

Fig. 3. Testing Graphical User Interface - After the user clicks "next", three haptic presentations are played one after the other with an inter-cue interval of 400 ms. The user responds by clicking on the images corresponding with the cue that they felt on their arm (in the single-sensory condition, participants are taught to interpret the lateral skin stretch and radial squeeze buttons as Cue A and Cue B respectively). After they submit their response, the correct answer is displayed in green, and the haptic cue is played again on their arm. (Color figure online)

3.4   Procedure

A repeated-measures, cross-over design was used in which half of the participants performed training and testing with MISSIVE first followed by the single-sensory system. The other half started with the single-sensory system, followed by MISSIVE.

Training. Participants interacted with the haptic devices through the graphical user interface (GUI) shown in Fig. 3. Participants were given ten minutes of self-guided training immediately before testing for each system. The self-guided training consisted of two interfaces which could be navigated between freely. The first interface allowed participants to explore the haptic cues by selecting an activation pattern for each component and clicking the mouse to feel it rendered on their arm. The second interface allowed users to simulate the testing protocol by clicking the mouse to feel three presentations. After responding which presentation was the second one, they were shown the correct answer and the presentation was replayed.

Testing. During the testing phase, the haptic presentations were rendered with either MISSIVE or with the single-sensory device, and participants were asked to identify them through the computer interface. Each of the 32 presentations was presented five times, in random order, for a total of 160 trials. Participants advanced through the 160 trials at their own pace, and no time constraint was imposed. However, in order to mimic a more realistic application of haptic cue identification, cues were masked during testing using an AXB presentation format. On each trial, participants were presented with three haptic presentations, 400 ms apart, and were asked to identify the second (target) cue.

Table 2. MISSIVE and single-sensory system average accuracy scores and p-values for statistical comparisons

	Overall score	Distal Band Cue	Proximal Band Cue A	Proximal Band Cue B
Multi-sensory	41.4%	62.5%	69.4%	87.3%
Single-sensory	30.5%	42.8%	73.6%	81.3%
p	<.01	<.01	.07	.26

A masked paradigm allows for variable response rates because it separates the time taken for the mental identification process from the physical act of clicking on the chosen response. After the testing, users were asked if they had any preference for either haptic device on a three point scale (i.e. preference for the single-sensory device, no preference, or preference for MISSIVE).

3.5   Data Analysis

An overall presentation accuracy score for each participant on each system was calculated as the percent of *presentations* correctly identified during testing. Accuracy scores for each cue component were also calculated. Paired, within-subjects t-tests were run on the accuracy scores to evaluate whether single- or multi-sensory cues were more easily identifiable. Confusion matrices were generated to visualize overall perceptual performance by aggregating the presentation and response data across all participants for each system.

4 Results

4.1 Perception Accuracy

In the multi-sensory condition, there was an overall mean presentation accuracy of 41.4%, which was greater than the overall mean presentation accuracy of 30.5% in the single-sensory condition ($t(7) = 3.6, p < .01$). For the Distal Band, accuracy in the multi-sensory condition was 62.5%, higher than the 42.8% in the single-sensory condition ($t(7) = 5, p < .01$). The accuracy of Proximal Band Cue A in the multi-sensory condition (69.4%) was not significantly lower than in the single-sensory condition (73.6%) ($t(7) = 2.2, p = .07$). Finally, the accuracy of Proximal Band Cue B in the multi-sensory condition (87.7%) was not significantly higher than the accuracy in the single-sensory condition (81.3%) ($t(7) = 1.2, p = .26$). Five of the users preferred MISSIVE to the single-sensory system, two had no marked preference, and one preferred the single-sensory system. These results are summarized in Table 2 and in Fig. 4.

4.2 Confusion Matrices

Confusion matrices for both systems are presented in Figs. 5 and 6, where rows are the perceived cues and columns are the actual presented cues. The 32-by-32 matrix is divided into a 4-by-4 matrix of sub-matrices with heavy lines corresponding to different levels of activation of Proximal Band Cue A, and B (on/off). Cells are filled in with a percentage according to the proportion of times the participants responded a certain way when presented with a given cue. The main diagonal of the confusion matrix illustrates the correct answers (i.e. the perceived presentation matches the actual presentation).

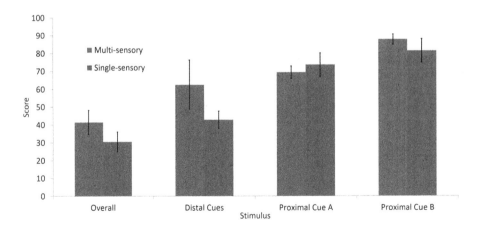

Fig. 4. The mean percent correct for both systems is compared ($N = 8$). The overall scores are significantly different ($p < .01$), and the Distal Band vibrotactor accuracies are significantly different ($p < .01$). Error bars denote the 95% confidence interval.

5   Discussion

The objective of this study was to compare users' ability to discern haptic cues when they were presented with MISSIVE and with a comparable single-sensory device. Data were analyzed both in terms of overall presentation accuracy and

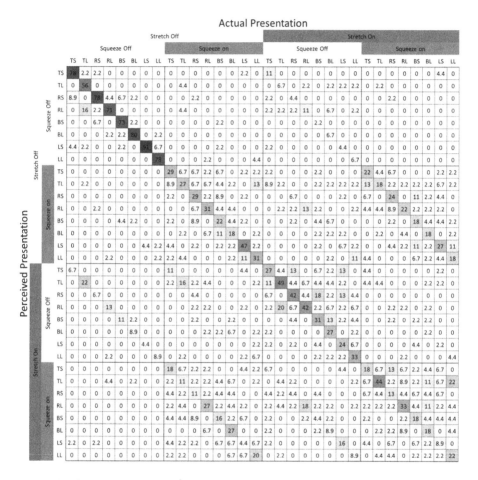

Fig. 5. Confusion matrix for the multi-sensory system ($N = 8$): The 32-by-32 matrix is divided into a 4-by-4 matrix of sub-matrices with heavy lines corresponding to different levels of activation of Proximal Band Cue A, and B (on/off). Vibrotactors are labeled by their location: T/L/B/R and pulse duration: S/L. Cells are filled in with a percentage according to the proportion of times the participants responded a certain way when presented with a given cue. The main diagonal of the confusion matrix illustrates the correct answers (i.e. the perceived presentation matches the actual presentation). With the multi-sensory system, more confusion consistently occurs mistaking which actuators (i.e. lateral skin stretch, radial squeeze, or both) are active. The vibrotactor accuracy is strong (errors are inconsistently distributed) even in off-diagonal sub-matrices, indicating that even when the participants mistook one actuator for another, they could still accurately identify the vibrotactor.

cue accuracy. Distal Band cue perceptual accuracy for MISSIVE exceeded that of the single-sensory case—even though they are identical in design—highlighting an advantage of the multi-sensory approach. The Distal Band vibration cues were masked by Proximal Band vibration cues in the single-sensory system, while in MISSIVE the vibration cues were masked by lower frequency radial squeeze and lateral skin stretch cues in the Proximal Band. This distinction is likely the

Actual Presentation — Columns are grouped as: cols 1–8 = Proximal Band Cue A OFF / Cue B OFF; cols 9–16 = Cue A OFF / Cue B ON; cols 17–24 = Cue A ON / Cue B OFF; cols 25–32 = Cue A ON / Cue B ON. Rows (Perceived Presentation) follow the same four groupings. Vibrotactors labeled by location T/L/B/R and pulse duration S/L.

Perceived	TS	TL	RS	RL	BS	BL	LS	LL	TS	TL	RS	RL	BS	BL	LS	LL	TS	TL	RS	RL	BS	BL	LS	LL	TS	TL	RS	RL	BS	BL	LS	LL
A OFF/B OFF TS	71	8.9	0	0	2.2	0	2.2	0	0	0	0	0	0	0	0	0	2.2	0	0	0	2.2	2.2	2.2	0	0	0	2.2	0	0	0	0	0
TL	6.7	47	0	0	0	2.2	0	0	2.2	6.7	0	0	0	0	0	4.4	27	27	4.4	2.2	8.9	0	13	2.2	2.2	0	0	0	0	2.2	0	0
RS	2.2	0	71	6.7	8.9	2.2	0	0	0	0	0	0	0	0	0	0	0	0	2.2	0	4.4	0	0	0	0	0	0	0	2.2	0	0	0
RL	0	4.4	2.2	71	0	2.2	0	0	2.2	0	2.2	4.4	0	0	0	0	2.2	6.7	11	11	0	4.4	0	0	0	0	0	0	0	0	0	0
BS	0	0	0	0	67	18	2.2	0	0	0	0	0	0	0	0	0	0	0	0	0	0	0	0	0	0	0	0	0	0	0	0	0
BL	0	0	0	0	0	42	0	0	2.2	0	4.4	0	18	8.9	6.7	2.2	0	0	0	0	0	0	0	0	0	0	0	2.2	0	0	0	0
LS	0	0	0	0	2.2	0	73	16	0	0	0	0	0	0	0	0	0	0	0	0	0	0	0	0	0	0	0	0	0	0	0	0
LL	0	0	0	0	0	2.2	0	58	0	0	0	0	0	0	0	4.4	0	2.2	0	0	0	2.2	13	16	0	0	0	0	0	0	0	0
A OFF/B ON TS	2.2	0	2.2	0	0	0	0	0	8.9	6.7	0	2.2	0	0	4.4	0	0	0	2.2	0	4.4	0	2.2	0	6.7	4.4	0	0	0	4.4	2.2	0
TL	0	2.2	0	0	0	0	0	0	8.9	11	0	4.4	2.2	0	2.2	2.2	4.4	0	4.4	0	4.4	2.2	2.2	0	11	4.4	4.4	2.2	6.7	2.2	2.2	0
RS	0	0	0	0	0	0	0	0	4.4	0	6.7	4.4	4.4	4.4	0	0	0	0	0	0	0	0	0	0	0	0	0	2.2	4.4	0	0	0
RL	0	2.2	0	0	0	0	0	0	8.9	11	24	36	2.2	0	4.4	0	2.2	0	4.4	16	0	0	0	0	6.7	6.7	8.9	18	6.7	2.2	2.2	4.4
BS	0	0	0	0	2.2	2.2	0	0	2.2	2.2	2.2	4.4	8.9	6.7	2.2	4.4	0	0	0	0	0	0	0	0	0	0	0	0	0	2.2	0	0
BL	0	0	0	2.2	0	6.7	0	0	8.9	0	20	2.2	38	51	18	11	2.2	0	0	0	0	0	0	0	2.2	2.2	2.2	2.2	2.2	2.2	2.2	2.2
LS	0	0	0	0	0	0	4.4	0	0	0	0	0	0	0	0	0	4.4	0	0	0	2.2	2.2	0	0	0	0	0	0	0	0	0	0
LL	0	0	2.2	0	0	0	0	2.2	0	4.4	0	0	0	2.2	11	27	0	0	0	0	0	2.2	2.2	2.2	0	2.2	2.2	2.2	2.2	2.2	8.9	16
A ON/B OFF TS	0	4.4	0	0	0	0	0	0	2.2	0	0	0	0	0	0	0	16	13	13	0	11	4.4	13	2.2	0	2.2	0	0	2.2	2.2	0	0
TL	0	8.9	0	0	2.2	0	0	0	2.2	4.4	0	0	0	0	0	0	22	24	16	13	13	11	11	8.9	6.7	6.7	2.2	2.2	6.7	2.2	4.4	0
RS	0	0	8.9	4.4	2.2	2.2	0	0	0	0	0	0	2.2	0	0	0	0	8.9	0	0	0	2.2	0	0	2.2	0	0	0	0	2.2	0	0
RL	2.2	2.2	0	2.2	0	2.2	0	0	2.2	0	8.9	11	0	0	0	0	0	0	6.7	27	2.2	6.7	0	0	0	2.2	4.4	6.7	2.2	2.2	0	0
BS	0	0	0	0	2.2	0	0	0	0	2.2	0	2.2	0	0	0	0	2.2	2.2	0	8.9	4.4	0	4.4	2.2	4.4	0	0	0	0	0	0	0
BL	2.2	0	0	0	4.4	0	0	0	0	2.2	4.4	0	6.7	2.2	0	0	2.2	4.4	0	6.7	6.7	4.4	0	0	4.4	11	2.2	2.2	6.7	8.9	4.4	2.2
LS	0	2.2	0	0	0	0	6.7	8.9	0	0	0	0	0	0	0	2.2	0	2.2	0	2.2	2.2	0	2.2	0	0	0	0	0	0	2.2	0	4.4
LL	0	0	0	0	0	0	0	0	2.2	0	0	0	0	0	13	8.9	0	0	0	0	4.4	0	8.9	40	0	0	0	0	2.2	6.7	2.2	
A ON/B ON TS	0	4.4	0	0	0	0	0	0	6.7	4.4	4.4	0	2.2	2.2	0	4.4	2.2	0	2.2	2.2	16	11	8.9	8.9	11	4.4	11	8.9	11	6.7	4.4	
TL	0	2.2	0	0	0	0	0	0	8.9	6.7	0	0	0	2.2	0	0	2.2	4.4	6.7	0	0	2.2	2.2	0	20	16	18	2.2	20	8.9	27	4.4
RS	2.2	0	2.2	2.2	0	0	0	0	2.2	8.9	4.4	2.2	0	0	2.2	0	0	4.4	4.4	2.2	4.4	0	0	4.4	4.4	4.4	2.2	4.4	0	2.2	0	2.2
RL	0	0	0	0	0	0	0	0	2.2	6.7	2.2	8.9	0	0	0	0	0	0	4.4	0	0	0	2.2	4.4	16	20	0	8.9	0	6.7		
BS	0	0	0	0	2.2	0	0	0	4.4	4.4	0	2.2	2.2	2.2	2.2	4.4	0	0	0	2.2	6.7	0	2.2	2.2	2.2	2.2	6.7	8.9	8.9	0		
BL	0	0	0	0	0	0	0	0	4.4	2.2	2.2	6.7	2.2	6.7	2.2	2.2	0	0	0	4.4	2.2	0	8.9	4.4	2.2	6.7	8.9	6.7	0	8.9		
LS	0	0	0	0	0	0	0	0	2.2	0	4.4	0	0	0	8.9	8.9	0	0	2.2	0	2.2	4.4	2.2	0	2.2	0	2.2	0	0	8.9		
LL	0	0	0	0	0	0	2.2	0	2.2	2.2	2.2	0	0	0	2.2	11	0	0	2.2	0	2.2	4.4	0	2.2	2.2	0	4.4	2.2	0	2.2	11	22

Fig. 6. Confusion matrix for the single-sensory system ($N = 8$): The 32-by-32 matrix is divided into a 4-by-4 matrix of sub-matrices with heavy lines corresponding to different levels of activation of Proximal Band Cue A, and B (on/off). Vibrotactors are labeled by their location: T/L/B/R and pulse duration: S/L. Cells are filled in with a percentage according to the proportion of times the participant responded a certain way when presented with a given cue. The main diagonal of the confusion matrix illustrates the correct answers (i.e. the perceived presentation matches the actual presentation). With the single-sensory system, vibrotactor accuracy deteriorates significantly ($t(7) = 5.0, p = .002$).

explanation for the superior performance of vibration cue identification in the multi-sensory condition.

Proximal Band Cue A and B perceptual accuracies were not significantly different between the single- and multi-sensory systems. The accuracy observed in these cues was higher than the accuracy recorded for the distal band, likely because the Proximal Band cues were longer and were therefore more easily identified. However, because these cues were so prominent, they tended to mask the distal band cues.

The confusion matrices show more specifically where errors occurred. Off-diagonal elements in the same sub-matrices as the main diagonal denote Distal Band errors. Elements in off-diagonal sub-matrices denote incorrect Proximal Band responses (i.e. not correctly identifying radial squeeze or lateral skin stretch). Within those off-diagonal sub-matrices, the cells follow the same pattern, where the diagonal corresponds to correct Distal Band responses, and off-diagonal elements denote Distal Band errors.

The results indicate that the identification mistakes made with the MIS-SIVE were far more consistent than on the single-sensory device. Specifically, when stretch and squeeze were both active, users had trouble perceiving the stretch cue. However, with the unimodal system, confusion consistently occurred in identifying which of the vibrotactors was active in the Distal Band, along with errors in mistaking the Proximal Band cues. This suggests that the vibrotactors in the Proximal Band hindered the participants' ability to accurately perceive the vibrotactors in the Distal Band. The regularity of the type of errors observed with the MISSIVE device point to potential opportunities for design improvements that could increase perceptual accuracy.

6   Conclusion

In this work, we present a novel, multi-sensory approach to increase perceptual accuracy of concurrently rendered cues. We combined multiple modalities of haptic cues (vibration, lateral skin stretch, and radial squeeze) that are perceptually distinct and can be recognized when presented concurrently. Experimental results showed that participants were better able to identify concurrent multi-sensory haptic cues compared to a concurrent single-sensory haptic cues. In addition, qualitative feedback from the participants revealed a preference for MISSIVE over the single-sensory system.

Acknowledgements. This work was supported by Facebook, Inc.

References

1. Akhtar, A., Nguyen, M., Wan, L., Boyce, B., Slade, P., Bretl, T.: Passive mechanical skin stretch for multiple degree-of-freedom proprioception in a hand prosthesis. In: Auvray, M., Duriez, C. (eds.) EUROHAPTICS 2014. LNCS, vol. 8619, pp. 120–128. Springer, Heidelberg (2014). https://doi.org/10.1007/978-3-662-44196-1_16
2. Alluisi, E.A., Muller Jr., P.F., Fitts, P.M.: An information analysis of verbal and motor responses in a forced-paced serial task. J. Exp. Psychol. 53(3), 153 (1957)
3. Battaglia, E., Clark, J.P., Bianchi, M., Catalano, M.G., Bicchi, A., O'Malley, M.K.: The rice haptic rocker: skin stretch haptic feedback with the Pisa/IIT softhand. In: IEEE World Haptics Conference, pp. 7–12. IEEE (2017)
4. Casini, S., Morvidoni, M., Bianchi, M., Catalano, M., Grioli, G., Bicchi, A.: Design and realization of the cuff - clenching upper-limb force feedback wearable device for distributed mechano-tactile stimulation of normal and tangential skin forces. In: IEEE/RSJ International Conference on Intelligent Robots and Systems, pp. 1186–1193 (2015)
5. Chinello, F., Pacchierotti, C., Tsagarakis, N.G., Prattichizzo, D.: Design of a wearable skin stretch cutaneous device for the upper limb. In: Haptics Symposium, pp. 14–20. IEEE (2016)
6. Christiansen, R., Contreras-Vidal, J.L., Gillespie, R.B., Shewokis, P.A., O'Malley, M.K.: Vibrotactile feedback of pose error enhances myoelectric control of a prosthetic hand. In: 2013 World Haptics Conference, pp. 531–536 (2013)
7. Ernst, M.O.: A bayesian view on multimodal cue integration. In: Human Body Perception from the Inside Out, vol. 131, pp. 105–131 (2006)
8. Gault, R.H.: Progress in experiments on tactual interpretation of oral speech. J. Abnormal Psychol. Soc. Psychol. 19(2), 155 (1924)
9. Gopalai, A.A., Senanayake, S.A.A.: A wearable real-time intelligent posture corrective system using vibrotactile feedback. IEEE/ASME Trans. Mechatron. 16(5), 827–834 (2011)
10. Israr, A., Meckl, P.H., Tan, H.Z.: A two Dof controller for a multi-finger tactual display using a loop-shaping technique. In: Proceedings of the ASME International Mechanical Engineering Congress and Exposition (IMECE 2004), pp. 1083–1089 (2004)
11. Karam, M., Russo, F.A., Fels, D.I.: Designing the model human cochlea: an ambient crossmodal audio-tactile display. IEEE Trans. Haptics 2(3), 160–169 (2009)
12. Kim, M., Lee, S., Choi, S.: Saliency-driven real-time video-to-tactile translation. IEEE Trans. Haptics 7(3), 394–404 (2014)
13. Liang, X., Makatura, C.R., Schubert, M., Solomon, B.H., Walker, J.M., Blank, A.A., O'Malley, M.K.: [D86] skin-stretch proprioceptive feedback for a robotic gripper. In: 2014 IEEE Haptics Symposium, p. 1 (2014)
14. Norman, S.L., Doxon, A.J., Gleeson, B.T., Provancher, W.R.: Planar hand motion guidance using fingertip skin-stretch feedback. IEEE Trans. Haptics 7(2), 121–130 (2014)
15. Novich, S.D., Eagleman, D.M.: Using space and time to encode vibrotactile information: toward an estimate of the skin's achievable throughput. Exp. Brain Res. 233(10), 2777–2788 (2015)
16. Pandey, S., Byrne, M.D., Jantscher, W.H., O'Malley, M.K., Agarwal, P.: Toward training surgeons with motion-based feedback: initial validation of smoothness as a measure of motor learning. In: Proceedings of the Human Factors and Ergonomics Society Annual Meeting, vol. 61, no. 1, pp. 1531–1535 (2017)

17. Reed, C.M., Delhorne, L.A.: Current results of a field study of adult users of tactile aids. In: Seminars in Hearing, vol. 16, pp. 305–315. Thieme Medical Publishers, Inc. (1995)
18. Reed, C.M., Durlach, N.I., Braida, L.D.: Research on tactile communication of speech: a review. ASHA Monographs **20**, 1 (1982)
19. Stanley, A.A., Kuchenbecker, K.J.: Evaluation of tactile feedback methods for wrist rotation guidance. IEEE Trans. Haptics **5**(3), 240–251 (2012)
20. Suhonen, K., Müller, S., Rantala, J., Väänänen-Vainio-Mattila, K., Raisamo, R., Lantz, V.: Haptically augmented remote speech communication: a study of user practices and experiences. In: Proceedings of the 7th Nordic Conference on Human-Computer Interaction: Making Sense Through Design, pp. 361–369. ACM (2012)
21. Tan, H., Gray, R., Young, J.J., Taylor, R.: A haptic back display for attentional and directional cueing (2003)
22. Tan, H.Z., Reed, C.M., Durlach, N.I.: Optimum information transfer rates for communication through haptic and other sensory modalities. IEEE Trans. Haptics **3**(2), 98–108 (2010)
23. Tang, A., McLachlan, P., Lowe, K., Saka, C.R., MacLean, K.: Perceiving ordinal data haptically under workload. In: Proceedings of the 7th International Conference on Multimodal interfaces, pp. 317–324. ACM (2005)
24. Treadway, E., Gillespie, B., Bolger, D., Blank, A., O'Malley, M.K., Davis, A.: The role of auxiliary and referred haptic feedback in myoelectric control. In: World Haptics Conference, WHC, pp. 13–18. Northwestern University, IEEE (2015)
25. Walker, J.M., Blank, A.A., Shewokis, P.A., O'Malley, M.K.: Tactile feedback of object slip facilitates virtual object manipulation. IEEE Trans. Haptics **8**(4), 454–466 (2015)
26. Weisenberger, J.M., Broadstone, S.M., Kozma-Spytek, L.: Relative performance of single-channel and multichannel tactile aids for speech perception. J. Rehabil. Res. Dev. **28**(2), 45 (1991)
27. Wheeler, J., Bark, K., Savall, J., Cutkosky, M.: Investigation of rotational skin stretch for proprioceptive feedback with application to myoelectric systems. IEEE Trans. Neural Syst. Rehabil. Eng. **18**(1), 58–66 (2010)
28. Wong, E.Y., Israr, A., O'Malley, M.K.: Discrimination of consonant articulation location by tactile stimulation of the forearm. In: 2010 IEEE Haptics Symposium, pp. 47–54 (2010)
29. Yuan, H., Reed, C.M., Durlach, N.I.: Tactual display of consonant voicing as a supplement to lipreading. J. Acoust. Soc. Am. **118**(2), 1003–1015 (2005)

Travelling Ultrasonic Wave Enhances Keyclick Sensation

David Gueorguiev[1,3](✉), Anis Kaci[2], Michel Amberg[2], Frédéric Giraud[2], and Betty Lemaire-Semail[2]

[1] Inria Lille Nord Europe, 59650 Villeneuve d'Asq, France
[2] Univ. Lille, Centrale Lille, Arts et Métiers Paris Tech, HEI, EA 2697 - L2EP, 59000 Lille, France
anis.kaci@etudiant.univ-lille1.fr, Michel.Amberg@univ-lille1.fr, frederic.giraud@polytech-lille.fr
[3] Max-Planck Institute for Intelligent Systems, 70569 Stuttgart, Germany
dgueorguiev@is.mpg.de

Abstract. A realistic keyclick sensation is a serious challenge for haptic feedback since vibrotactile rendering faces the limitation of the absence of contact force as experienced on physical buttons. It has been shown that creating a keyclick sensation is possible with stepwise ultrasonic friction modulation. However, the intensity of the sensation is limited by the impedance of the fingertip and by the absence of a lateral force component external to the finger. In our study, we compare this technique to rendering with an ultrasonic travelling wave, which exerts a lateral force on the fingertip. For both techniques, participants were asked to report the detection (or not) of a keyclick during a forced choice one interval procedure. In experiment 1, participants could press the surface as many time as they wanted for a given trial. In experiment 2, they were constrained to press only once. The results show a lower perceptual threshold for travelling waves. Moreover, participants pressed less times per trial and exerted smaller normal force on the surface. The subjective quality of the sensation was found similar for both techniques. In general, haptic feedback based on travelling ultrasonic waves is promising for applications without lateral motion of the finger.

Keywords: Haptic display · Tactile perception
Ultrasonic vibration · Travelling wave · Keyclick · Button click

1 Introduction

Haptic interaction is essential to our capacity to use portable interactive screens without physical keyboard [1]. In the last decades, tactile displays have greatly improved with the development of naive on-screen physics that are intuitive to the user [20] and rapid progress in the ability to deliver force-based tactile feedback [11,15]. However, it is still difficult to type a large text on the keyboard of a tablet. The difficulty of this task partly comes from the ergonomics of the

© Springer International Publishing AG, part of Springer Nature 2018
D. Prattichizzo et al. (Eds.): EuroHaptics 2018, LNCS 10894, pp. 302–312, 2018.
https://doi.org/10.1007/978-3-319-93399-3_27

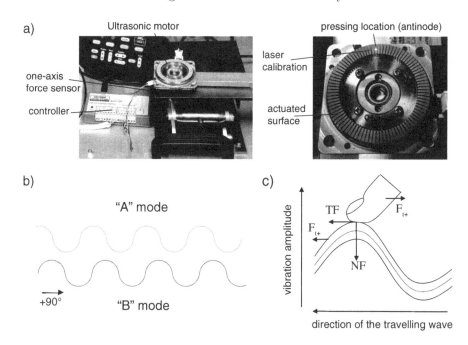

Fig. 1. (a) The apparatus used for the generation of the keyclick. The actuation was performed on an ultrasonic motor. (b) The ultrasonic travelling wave was generated by the superposition of two stationary waves, which are shifted by either $-90°, 0°$ or $+90°$. (c) The travelling wave generates an additional tangential force F_{t+} on the fingertip compared to the stationary ultrasonic vibration.

screen but also from the lack of tactile feedback that current tactile displays provide to us while typing. At best, they deliver timely vibrations that replace the contact mechanics occurring during the push of a classical keyboard button. The absent or impaired sensation compared to an old-fashioned physical keyboard is an important shortcoming of the current smartphones and tablets and one of the major challenges ahead of the realistic rendering of haptic feedback. In addition to the poor user experience, unnatural feedback also impairs the user's typing performance on the device. Several vibration-based technologies for creating a button-click have been suggested. 250 Hz vibration with up and down ramps have proven effective to improve finger-based text entry [7]. It was also suggested that a higher fidelity of the vibrotactile signal hence a more pleasant click sensation could be achieved by using piezo actuators instead of conventional vibrating motors [8]. A recent study showed that, in addition to the improved performance, the feeling of an haptic click can be recreated by using three repeated cycles of a 250 Hz sinusoidal signal generated by piezo actuators [2,10].

However, vibrotactile feedback is inherently different to the force feedback generated by the keys of physical keyboards, which apply contact forces to the fingertip [18]. It has been suggested that a button click sensation can be achieved by modulating the friction between a finger and an ultrasonically vibrating surface at the moment of contact in order to recreate the rapid change in force induced by the buckling of a mechanical push button [14]. Indeed, the human perception of transient frictional cues is particularly accurate at the onset of the tactile interaction with a surface and [5] and event-base feedback is known to create a more realistic haptic sensation [9] compared to position-based feedback. Therefore, frictional modulations driven by the user's behavior are very salient for the sense of touch and small differences in their timing or sharpness can have a large perceptual impact [4].

2   Earlier Work

A recent study has built on these principles to show that a realistic keyclick sensation can be generated by an event-based stepwise modulation of the ultrasonic vibration [12]. Two types of stimulation were tried: a step of falling friction and a step of rising friction occurring at a predefined normal force level. Users detected more easily the falling friction than the rising friction and reported to feel it as a convincing keyclick sensation. The proposed method relies on sudden changes in the impedance of the finger [13], which are provoked by the influence of the ultrasonic lubrication [16,19] on the compression of the fingerpad. Lateral motion of the finger is generally necessary to the occurrence of friction modulation by ultrasonic lubrication. In its absence, the subtle mechanics generating the keyclick sensation require a high amplitude of ultrasonic vibration to be perceivable and the threshold for perceiving the clickbutton is several times higher than the threshold for perceiving frictional steps during dynamic tactile exploration [6]. The quality of the sensation was also found to be strongly influenced by the natural impedance of the fingertip with an impaired sensation for extreme impedances.

It is also possible to enhance the modulation of friction hence the tactile sensation generated by ultrasonic actuation on the fingertip through the implementation of an ultrasonic travelling wave instead of a stationary wave. When vibrating, the particles of a surface on which a travelling wave is propagating undergo an elliptic motion. For specific operating conditions, they can help to propel the finger if they move in the same direction as the finger pulp when they come in contact with it. This effect additionally decreases the equivalent friction coefficient compared with a pure stationary wave [3]. Conversely, a travelling wave decreases the friction reduction when the direction is reversed.

Progressive ultrasonic waves can be wisely used to generate a keyclick sensation during pressing on an actuated surface. Our method consists in a stepwise switching on of a travelling ultrasonic wave at a predefined normal force threshold and a reversal of its direction when a second predefined normal force threshold is reached. This method exploits the frictional force exerted by the ultrasonic travelling wave to deliver a click sensation to the user during the pressing of the surface. This study aims to compare both methods for generating a keyclick sensation in terms of psychophysical threshold, quality of the sensation and pressing behavior of the participants. In a first experiment, we let participants free to explore the sensation by not restricting the number of pressings by trial in order to see if they would choose different exploratory strategies for the two methods. In a second experiment, we increased the comparability between the methods by estimating the perceptual threshold when participants were constrained to press only once by trial on the surface.

3 Materials and Methods

3.1 Participants

Data were collected from 20 healthy volunteers aged between 22 and 62 (5 females). 10 participated in experiment 1 and 10 additional participants were recruited for experiment 2. Participants were wearing noise-cancelling headphones in order to prevent potential interference from auditory cues. All participants gave written informed consent. The investigation conformed to the principles of the Declaration of Helsinki and experiments were performed in accordance with relevant guidelines and regulations.

3.2 Experimental Set-Up

For this experiment, the stator of a USR60 ultrasonic motor (Shinsei Corporation, Japan) was used (Fig. 1a). It is constituted by a bronze disk on which a ring of 16 piezoelectric actuators is glued. Half of these actuators are arranged so that they can excite the 9th bending mode denoted by cos hereafter, which is characterized by a resonance frequency of 40 kHz, and a wavelength $\lambda = 21$ mm. The other actuators are arranged with a spatial shift of $\lambda/4$ on the ring, thus exciting a doublet of the cos mode, which is denoted sin. The excitation of modes cos and sin in quadrature, i.e. with a temporal phase shift of $\pi/2$ (Fig. 1b) produces a travelling wave (Fig. 1c). Changing the sign of the phase shift will invert the direction of the wave; cancelling the phase shift produces a stationary wave. A laser doppler vibrometer (OFV 505, Polytec, Germany) was used to localize the antinodes of the stationary wave, and was marked as a target for the pressing. The normal force during pressing on the actuated surface was measured by a one-axis force sensor, located below the pressing area, with a resolution of 0.01N. The acquisition of the force values was performed by a in-house acquisition board at a 42 Hz sampling rate. In addition, the laser vibrometer was used to compute the values in μm corresponding to the arbitrary units (from 1 to 15) controlling the intensity of the ultrasonic vibration (Fig. 2a).

The keyclick rendering when using a stationary wave was performed as in [12] by a step increase of the amplitude of vibration when a predefined threshold of the normal force was reached (Fig. 2b). For the travelling wave method, two normal force thresholds f_{th1} and f_{th2} were predefined (Fig. 2c). At f_{th1}, the travelling wave was switched on by a step increase in the amplitude of vibration. Above the normal force threshold f_{th2}, which was set 0.33N higher than f_{th1}, the direction of the travelling wave was reversed in order to enhance the tactile feedback on the fingertip.

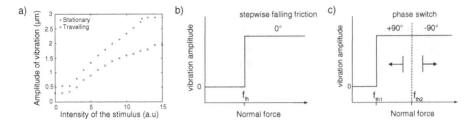

Fig. 2. (a) The correspondance between the arbitrary intensity values and the amplitude of ultrasonic vibration. (b) The keyclick actuated by the stationary wave was generated by a stepwise switch on of the ultrasonic vibration at a predefined threshold value of the normal force (c) For the travelling wave, the stepwise increase in amplitude at f_{th1} is followed by a second normal force threshold f_{th2} at which the direction of the ultrasonic wave is reversed.

3.3   Experimental Procedure

In both experiments, participants were asked to press on the actuated surface with their index finger. The target location was chosen on a vibration *antinode* and labelled with a color marker in order to ensure that participants experienced consistent ultrasonic vibration across trials. The estimation of the psychophysical threshold was performed with a one-up one-down staircase procedure, which targeted the intensity at which a keyclick sensation was felt 50% of the time, a procedure also referred as Bekesy tracking method [17]. At each trial, after pressing on the actuated surface, the participants had to report if they felt a keyclick sensation or not. We chose a non-forced choice procedure despite its proneness for criterion bias for two reasons: 1/ we wanted the participants to focus on the keyclick sensation rather than on the perception of the variation of the finger-surface friction. 2/ for a given participant, the psychophysical estimation for the progressive and stationary wave are likely to be identically influenced by its criterion bias. Thus, the influence of the criterion on the comparison is lower than if the aim of the study was to estimate the absolute psychophysical threshold. Before each block, participants were allowed to familiarize themselves with the haptic feedback by testing several clicks at maximum intensity.

To avoid potential biases due to prediction of the next stimulation intensity by participants, three staircases with different force thresholds were interlaced (0.11, 0.44 and 0.77N). For each trial, the probability to be presented with a trial from a given staircase was 1/3 (Fig. 3a). The experiment ended when 5 turnovers or 30 trials were achieved for all three staircases. For each staircase, the perceptual threshold was then computed as the mean of the last 3 turnovers. One participant in experiment 2 made less than three turnovers in one of the conditions and we had to discard its data. The experiment was performed two times: one with the stationary wave method and another time with the progressive wave method. The order of the two conditions was pseudo-randomized across participants to avoid learning curve effects.

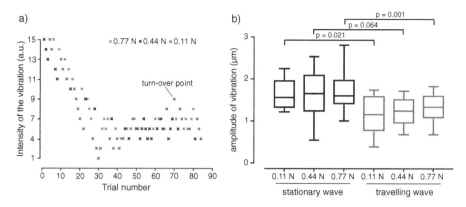

Fig. 3. (a) Typical example of three interlaced psychophysical staircases, which target the 50% perceptual threshold by a one-up one-down paradigm. At each trial, the implemented staircase is chosen at random with a probability of 1/3. (b) In experiment 1 (multiple clicks), the 50% perceptual threshold was computed for both actuation techniques. The error bars, the whisker boxes and the horizontal bars show respectively the min. and max. values, their interquartile range and the median value.

4 Results

4.1 Multiple Clicks

For all tested actuation criteria (0.11N, 0.44N and 0.77N), we computed the 50% detection thresholds for both methods to generate a keyclick sensation (Fig. 3b). For the stationary ultrasonic vibration, the median value of the individual thresholds for 0.11N, 0.44N and 0.77N were respectively 1.56 μm (IQR = 1.98 − 1.30), 1.65 μm (IQR = 2.11 − 1.21) and 1.60 μm (IQR = 2.00 − 1.39). For the travelling ultrasonic vibration, the median values of the individual thresholds for 0.11N, 0.44N and 0.77N were respectively 1.16 μm (IQR = 1.61 − 0.76), 1.24 μm (IQR = 1.54 − 0.94) and 1.34 μm (IQR = 1.62 − 1.06). The results showed a significantly lower threshold for the rendering technique based on travelling ultrasonic vibration (Friedman test: $\chi^2 = 16.09$, p = 0.0066). A further post-hoc analysis with Wilcoxon matched-pairs signed rank test showed that the difference between the two techniques was statistically significant for the 0.11N and 0.77N thresholds (respectively n = 10, W = −44, p = 0.0215 and n = 10, W = −49, p = 0.001) while a trend was observed for the 0.44N threshold (n = 10, W = −37, p = 0.064). Overall, rendering with travelling ultrasonic vibration decreased the detection threshold by around 25–30% compared to actuation with a stationary ultrasonic wave.

In the first experiment, participants were allowed to press as many times as they wanted on the actuated surface for a given trial. For each participant, the average number of presses across the experiment did not differ significantly between the two actuation methods and the three possible force thresholds (nonparametric Friedman test: $\chi^2 = 7.77$, p = 0.1693) (Fig. 4a). However, large numbers of consecutive surface presses (clicks) were mostly found close to the psychophysical threshold. Thus, we computed the average number of clicks across participants for each trial number and we compared both techniques for the first 52 trials (Fig. 4b), which was the number of trials available for all participants. The results showed a significantly higher average number of clicks for the actuation by a stationary wave (Wilcoxon matched-pairs signed rank statistical: $N = 52$, $W = 712$, $p = 0.0006$). Similarly, we computed the peak force during pressing for the first 52 trials and compared it for both techniques (Fig. 4c). The peak force during pressing was found significantly higher for the actuation with a stationary wave (Wilcoxon matched-pairs signed rank statistical: $N = 52$, $W = 1022$, $p < 0.0001$). Overall, these results show that, in the case of the stationary wave, the participants tended to press more times and harder when the actuation intensity was close to their psychophysical threshold.

4.2   One Click

In the second experiment, participants were instructed to press only once per trial on the actuated surface. For the stationary ultrasonic vibration, the median value of the individual thresholds for 0.11N, 0.44N and 0.77N were found to be respectively 1.86 μm (IQR $= 2.85 - 1.04$), 1.88 μm (IQR $= 2.73 - 1.26$) and 2.27 μm (IQR $= 2.85 - 1.75$). For the progressive ultrasonic vibration, the medians of the individual thresholds for 0.11N, 0.44N and 0.77N were respectively 1.49 μm (IQR $= 1.75 - 0.51$), 1.54 μm (IQR $= 1.73 - 0.37$) and 1.63 μm (IQR $= 1.82 - 0.62$) (Fig. 4d). The results showed a significantly lower threshold for the rendering technique based on travelling ultrasonic vibration (Friedman test: $\chi^2 = 25.14$, $p = 0.0001$). A further post-hoc analysis with Wilcoxon matched-pairs signed rank test showed that differences were statistically significant for all threshold conditions. (respectively $n = 10$, $W = -42$, $p = 0.011$; $n = 10$, $W = -39$, $p = 0.019$ and $n = 10$, $W = -45$, $p = 0.004$ for 0.11N, 0.44N and 0.77N). Thus, rendering with travelling ultrasonic vibration when only one click was allowed decreased the median detection threshold compared to stationary vibration by similar percentage to the one observed when multiple clicks were possible.

We further compared the psychophysical thresholds of the second experiment to those observed in the first one (Fig. 5a) and although they showed a slight increase, the difference was not significant (Mann-Whitney test: $U = 300.5$, $p = 0.096$ for the stationary actuation and $U = 373$, $p = 0.614$ for the actuation by a travelling wave). Thus, pressing numerous times did not significantly influence the keyclick perception threshold of the users.

As in experiment 1, we measured the peak normal force that the participant exerted and we averaged its value across all participants for each trial number of the staircase. In the second experiment, 47 trials were available for all participants and we compared the peak forces between the two actuation techniques (Fig. 5b). The results showed a significantly higher average peak force during pressing for the actuation by a stationary wave (Wilcoxon matched-pairs signed rank statistical test: $N = 43$, $W = 946$, $p < 0.0001$). In this experiment, even the

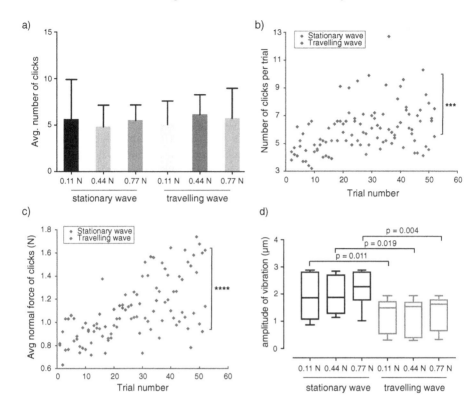

Fig. 4. (a) The average number of key presses (clicks) per condition for all six conditions. The boxplots and error bars show respectively the median values and the interquartile ranges. (b) Scatter plot of the average number of clicks for a given trial number. (c) Scatter plot of the average peak normal force during clicking for a given trial number. (d) In experiment 2 (one click), the 50% perceptual threshold was computed for both actuation techniques. The error bars, the whisker boxes and the horizontal bars respectively show the min. and max. values, their interquartile range and the median value.

early trials with a high amplitude of vibration showed a large difference between both techniques.

In both experiments, we asked participants which technique rendered the more realistic keyclick sensation. Seven out of ten participants preferred actuation with the travelling wave in experiment 1 and five out of ten in experiment 2, suggesting that the travelling wave generates a quality of the keyclick sensation similar to the stationary actuation.

5   Discussion

Our study shows that the actuation of an ultrasonic keyclick by a travelling wave decreases the amount of vibration amplitude which is necessary to render the click. We also found that the users are less prone to use excessive normal force or click multiple times compared to rendering with a stationary wave. Interestingly, pressing one or multiple times did not significantly influence the psychophysical threshold. This suggests that for a given set of parameters, the keyclick induces a consistent sensation and that the temptation for repeated pressing is mainly done to confirm the sensation of the first click. The difference between both techniques in the pressing normal force was larger when participants were constrained to one click. This suggests that participants felt that they are maximizing their perception of the stationary ultrasonic keyclick by pressing harder hence inducing a larger compression of their fingertip. Although the reflex to push harder when the stimulus becomes subtle was still present, it was less pronounced for the travelling wave, probably because they felt that this type of stimulation mostly induces a lateral force on the fingertip.

We explain these results by the capacity of the travelling wave to produce more tangential force contrast than a stationary wave, whose feedback intensity depends on the lateral component of the fingerpad's compression. This larger contrast stems of the wave's constant pushing force F_{t+} that exists independently of lateral motion of the finger. The strong lateral force component of the actuation by a travelling wave raises the question of the perceived quality of the keyclick sensation since the force exerted by a physical keyboard is purely normal. To that end, we compared the subjective perception of keyclick rendering generated by the travelling wave to the one generated by the stationary wave by asking participants to report their preferred rendering. The reports did not show an overwhelming preference for one of the techniques confirming that the travelling wave method generates a genuine keyclick sensation on the fingertip.

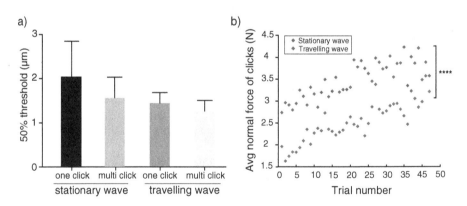

Fig. 5. (a) Comparison of the perceptual thresholds between the multiple clicks and one click conditions for both actuation techniques. The boxplots and error bars show respectively the median values and the interquartile ranges. (b) Scatter plot of the average peak normal force during pressing for a given trial number.

6 Conclusion

Overall, actuation by travelling ultrasonic wave is a promising technique to create tactile feedback on a finger that is not moving laterally. For the keyclick, this method decreases the threshold for perceiving the click by 25–30% compared to actuation with a stationary ultrasonic wave and the normal force exerted by the participants is also significantly reduced compared to the stationary condition. In future applications, one can imagine to vary the speed and direction of a travelling wave at a high frequency to create different types of signal on the unmoving finger such as meaningful interactive cues, force-based vibrations or cues for localizing a screen icon. These applications could be complementary to the textures and renderings already available through stationary ultrasonic friction modulation.

Acknowledgment. The authors would like to thank the CNRS/IRCICA - USR 3380 research center, which hosted the research. This work was funded by the MATRICE project (ERDF/Région Nord-Pas-de-Calais-Picardie, France).

References

1. Buxton, W., Hill, R., Rowley, P.: Issues and techniques in touch-sensitive tablet input. ACM SIGGRAPH Comput. Graph. **19**(3), 215–224 (1985)
2. Chen, H.Y., Park, J., Dai, S., Tan, H.Z.: Design and evaluation of identifiable key-click signals for mobile devices. IEEE Trans. Haptics **4**(4), 229–241 (2011)
3. Ghenna, S., Vezzoli, E., Giraud-Audine, C., Giraud, F., Amberg, M., Lemaire-Semail, B.: Enhancing variable friction tactile display using an ultrasonic travelling wave. IEEE Trans. Haptics **10**(2), 296–301 (2017)
4. Gueorguiev, D., Vezzoli, E., Sednaoui, T., Grisoni, L., Lemaire-Semail, B.: Feeling multiple edges: the tactile perception of short ultrasonic square reductions of the finger-surface friction. In: 2017 IEEE World Haptics Conference (WHC), pp. 125–129 (2017)
5. Gueorguiev, D., Bochereau, S., Mouraux, A., Hayward, V., Thonnard, J.L.: Touch uses frictional cues to discriminate flat materials. Scientific reports 6 (2016)
6. Gueorguiev, D., Vezzoli, E., Mouraux, A., Lemaire-Semail, B., Thonnard, J.L.: The tactile perception of transient changes in friction. J. Royal Soc. Interface **14**(137), 20170641 (2017)
7. Hoggan, E., Brewster, S.A., Johnston, J.: Investigating the effectiveness of tactile feedback for mobile touchscreens. In: Proceedings of the SIGCHI Conference on Human Factors in Computing Systems, pp. 1573–1582. ACM (2008)
8. Koskinen, E., Kaaresoja, T., Laitinen, P.: Feel-good touch: finding the most pleasant tactile feedback for a mobile touch screen button. In: Proceedings of the 10th International Conference on Multimodal Interfaces, ICMI 2008, pp. 297–304. ACM, New York (2008)
9. Kuchenbecker, K.J., Fiene, J., Niemeyer, G.: Improving contact realism through event-based haptic feedback. IEEE Trans. Vis. Comput. Graph. **12**(2), 219–230 (2006)
10. Ma, Z., Edge, D., Findlater, L., Tan, H.Z.: Haptic keyclick feedback improves typing speed and reduces typing errors on a flat keyboard. In: 2015 IEEE World Haptics Conference (WHC), pp. 220–227. IEEE (2015)

11. Meyer, D.J., Peshkin, M.A., Colgate, J.E.: Tactile paintbrush: a procedural method for generating spatial haptic texture. In: 2016 IEEE Haptics Symposium (HAPTICS), pp. 259–264. IEEE (2016)
12. Monnoyer, J., Diaz, E., Bourdin, C., Wiertlewski, M.: Ultrasonic friction modulation while pressing induces a tactile feedback. In: Bello, F., Kajimoto, H., Visell, Y. (eds.) EuroHaptics 2016. LNCS, vol. 9774, pp. 171–179. Springer, Cham (2016). https://doi.org/10.1007/978-3-319-42321-0_16
13. Monnoyer, J., Diaz, E., Bourdin, C., Wiertlewski, M.: Optimal skin impedance promotes perception of ultrasonic switches. In: 2017 IEEE World Haptics Conference (WHC), pp. 130–135. IEEE (2017)
14. Tashiro, K., Shiokawa, Y., Aono, T., Maeno, T.: Realization of button click feeling by use of ultrasonic vibration and force feedback. In: Third Joint Euro Haptics Conference and Symposium on Haptic Interfaces for Virtual Environment and Teleoperator Systems, World Haptics 2009, pp. 1–6. IEEE (2009)
15. Vezzoli, E., Sednaoui, T., Amberg, M., Giraud, F., Lemaire-Semail, B.: Texture rendering strategies with a high fidelity - capacitive visual-haptic friction control device. In: Bello, F., Kajimoto, H., Visell, Y. (eds.) EuroHaptics 2016. LNCS, vol. 9774, pp. 251–260. Springer, Cham (2016). https://doi.org/10.1007/978-3-319-42321-0_23
16. Vezzoli, E., Vidrih, Z., Giamundo, V., Lemaire-Semail, B., Giraud, F., Rodic, T., Peric, D., Adams, M.: Friction reduction through ultrasonic vibration part 1: modelling intermittent contact. IEEE Trans. Haptics 10(2), 196–207 (2017)
17. Von Békésy, G., Wever, E.G.: Experiments in Hearing, vol. 8. McGraw-Hill, New York (1960)
18. Weir, D.W., Peshkin, M., Colgate, J.E., Buttolo, P., Rankin, J., Johnston, M.: The haptic profile: capturing the feel of switches. In: Proceedings of 12th International Symposium on Haptic Interfaces for Virtual Environment and Teleoperator Systems, HAPTICS 2004, pp. 186–193. IEEE (2004)
19. Wiertlewski, M., Friesen, R.F., Colgate, J.E.: Partial squeeze film levitation modulates fingertip friction. Proc. Natl. Acad. Sci. 113(33), 9210–9215 (2016)
20. Wilson, A.D., Izadi, S., Hilliges, O., Garcia-Mendoza, A., Kirk, D.: Bringing physics to the surface. In: Proceedings of the 21st Annual ACM Symposium on User Interface Software and Technology, pp. 67–76. ACM (2008)

A High Performance Thermal Control for Simulation of Different Materials in a Fingertip Haptic Device

Massimiliano Gabardi$^{(\boxtimes)}$, Domenico Chiaradia, Daniele Leonardis,
Massimiliano Solazzi, and Antonio Frisoli

Percro Laboratory, Scuola Superiore Sant'Anna, Pisa, Italy
m.gabardi@santannapisa.it

Abstract. In this work we present an advanced thermal control for a miniaturized fingertip haptic device: the aim is to achieve high fidelity in following temperature references, in order to accurately simulate contact with different materials. The thermal module is designed to be mounted in a wearable device called Haptic Thimble, which is able to render surface orientation and fast contact transition through a linear electromagnetic actuator. The thermal module is expected to simulate the relatively fast thermal transients occurring at the contact with virtual materials. By means of a thin plate design of the device, and of a specific control implementation presented in this paper, we were able to achieve fast and accurate temperature tracking of temperature transients simulating different real materials. The control implementation and algorithm, making use of an inner current control loop and of an asymmetric temperature control loop is presented in this work and experimentally validated, also in presence of disturbance of the user's fingerpad. Particularly good results (comparable to non-portable, bulky thermal stages) have been obtained in terms of dynamics and accuracy of the temperature tracking (1 Hz bandpass frequency). Moreover, a perception experiment with seven subjects involving discrimination of contact with different virtual materials (copper, glass, urethane) has been conducted. The aim of the experiment was to assess the capability of the fully wearable device to properly render thermal transients when virtual contact occurs.

Keywords: Thermal interaction · Wearable haptics
Haptic rendering · Devices · Material simulation

1 Introduction

Relying on the touch sense, human beings can easily recognize objects properties without looking at them. Touch sense provides people with a large amount of information regarding manipulated objects. Thanks to these information a subject can recognize the texture, the shape, the surface curvature, the temperature

© Springer International Publishing AG, part of Springer Nature 2018
D. Prattichizzo et al. (Eds.): EuroHaptics 2018, LNCS 10894, pp. 313–325, 2018.
https://doi.org/10.1007/978-3-319-93399-3_28

and the material the object is made of. Object manipulation in virtual environments is usually felt as unnatural by subjects. This happens also because of the lack of coherent touch information provided to the subjects while performing the task. While performing manipulation or exploration of virtual objects, it is reasonable to think that the use of wearable devices able to coherently trigger both thermo-receptors and mechano-receptors of the skin of the users fingertips can significantly improve the sense of embodiment perceived by the user as well as its dexterity in accomplishing the task. Concerning the thermal properties perception a detailed study about human capability in material discrimination and localization by thermal cues has been presented in [14] by Ho and Jones. In order to understand and reproduce heat exchange perception mechanisms, in the last decades, many studies have been performed with the aim of describing the thermal heat exchange which occurs during the contact between finger and object surface [12,19].

Many research studies have been focused on the thermal perception of people in virtual environments such as the one presented in [17] focused on the perception of dynamic thermal stimulation on the hand. At this purpose computer controlled devices have been developed to trigger the skin thermo-receptors and simulate the thermal flux provoked by the contact with different materials. The results and models derived from the previous studies define the temperature or heat flux profiles used for driving thermal devices while simulating the contact with different materials [13]. Such as in [24] where both a thermal contact model based on thermal effusivity and a device for the simulation of contact with different materials are presented. Whereas in [15] the semi-infinite body in contact model has been used to thermally simulate the early phase of the contact. Over the last decade proposed thermal devices became smaller and multimodal. Tactile modules have been added in order to increase the richness of the feedback provided to the users. Perceptual interactions in thermo-tactile multimodal displays have been investigated in [23]. Different examples of thermo haptic devices are presented in [9,26] where a pin array is used to provide the tactile stimuli, whereas in [20,27] vibro-tactile actuators are used to generate the haptic feedback. Finally, a device able to provide a kinesthetic feedback combined to thermal feedback is presented in [2].

Most of thermal devices find their application in telepresence [11], teleoperation [3] or virtual reality [10]. Thermo-haptic devices can be used for different purposes, for example in [18] an application for blind or visually impaired people is proposed. Although better dynamic performance for the thermal feedback are obtained using a temperature controlled water flow, such as in [6,21], the majority of the devices use peltier cells to generate the thermal feedback. Small dimensions of the peltier cells allow the design of miniaturized interfaces, such as the one described in [7]. Peltier cells are commonly driven using voltage-temperature control loops and linear control algorithms (typically PID), although this might not be the best choice: in a peltier cell with constant thermal gradient between the faces, the heat flow can be considered linearly proportional to the current intensity. Conversely, current intensity is not linearly proportional to the applied voltage [8], since the peltier cell is a non-ohmic conductor. The use of flux sensors (as implemented in some of the devices referenced above) or of internal current control loops is expected to reduce system non-linearities and thus improve performance of the controlled thermal devices.

Even though the most of the mentioned devices have been developed to be portable or wearable, all the experiments reported in literature have been performed by grounding the devices on a ground surface.

Recently, authors have developed a wearable haptic interface for the rendering of virtual shapes and surface features called Haptic Thimble [5] and a powerful thermal module specifically designed to be integrated with the Haptic Thimble [4]. The potential of the novel thermal module is due to its miniaturized design: not only it allows integration in the Haptic Thimble, it also allows fast thermal transients due to thinness of the structure, improving heat propagation and effectiveness of the integrated water cooling. In this paper we present design and implementation of a dedicated control method for the thermal module, making use of an inner current control loop, and of an asymmetric temperature control loop in the heating and cooling phase. It takes advantage of the thermal module design for obtaining a hi-fidelity temperature rendering. Inner current control allows to avoid performance loss due to the non-ohmic behavior of the peltier cells and to obtain performance comparable to performance of bulky and powerful devices (i.e. [6]). The control method has been implemented and experimental validated through step and frequency response, and by means of temperature references that simulate thermal transients of real materials when skin contact occurs. Perception of the obtained temperature rendering in simulation of contact with different virtual materials has been experimentally investigated. It involved discrimination of different materials rendered with the thermal module and with contact - no contact transition provided by the Hapic Thimble.

2   The Thermo-haptic Device

The integrated multimodal interface is composed of the Haptic Thimble [5] and of the miniaturized thermal module (Fig. 1). The Haptic Thimble is a 3-Degrees of Freedom (DoFs) wearable fingertip haptic interface for tactile rendering. It features a serial kinematics, wrapped around the fingertip, composed by two revolute joints and one prismatic joint. The two revolute joints orient a plate around the user's fingertip whereas the prismatic joint pushes the end-effector plate in contact with the user's fingertip. The prismatic joint is actuated by a voice coil: due to its fast dynamics, it is able to render both contact/non-contact fast transitions and low to high frequency tactile stimulation resembling textures and other surface features. The miniaturized thermal module is used to generate thermal feedback. It is placed at the top of the voice coil and modulates temperature of the end-effector plate, which goes in contact with the user's finger. In particular, the module has been designed with two coplanar aluminum plates that are independently thermally controlled. This feature allows to provide the

Fig. 1. Miniaturized thermal module integrated with the Haptic Thimble device. The whole small system can render virtual shapes, textures, surface features and thermal transients in virtual or teleoperated environments.

user with thermal illusions like the thermal grill illusion, also called synthetic heat [1,22]. For each half of the thermal module, the heat flux is generated by a peltier cell and the temperature feedback is provided by a thermistor embedded in the top aluminum plate. The peltier cell is cooled down by means of a miniaturized water heat-sink: proper heat dissipation of the lower face of the peltier cell is fundamental for guaranteeing system performance and stability, as already experimentally evidenced for this thermal module in [4]. A small pump (15,7 × 15,7 × 28,5 mm, 14 g, 650 mL/min) has been used to generate the water flow in the small circuit realized with thin very flexible silicone pipes. No water tank has been necessary for keeping stability of the device, resulting in a very compact and portable solution (Fig. 2).

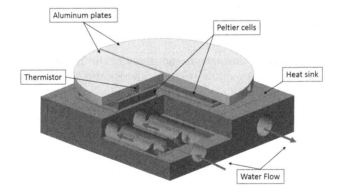

Fig. 2. Section view of the thermal module main components.

2.1   Driving System and Control Strategy

The aim of the control system was to take advantage of the thermal module design to obtain a fast, accurate temperature rendering at the plate in contact with the fingerpad. Such hi-fidelity rendering would allow the simulation of virtual materials by reproducing the heat flow occurring between the finger and the virtual material, as well as other generic thermal feedback including different perception effects and illusions (i.e. the thermal grill). To this purpose, a specific control algorithm was developed, based on asymmetric control for the heating and cooling phases and on an internal current control loop. Moreover, it was implemented on compact and low voltage H-bridge drivers, sensors ICs and microcontroller board, envisaging a compact, wearable haptic-thermal device with embedded electronics.

A compact microcontroller board (PJRC Teensy 3.6, based on a 32 bit 180 MHz ARM Cortex-M4 processor with FPU) has been used to compute the control algorithm of the whole haptic device (including control of the thermal stage and control of the linear stage moving the plate in contact with the finger). Hall-effect current sensors (Allegro MicroSystems ACS712 IC) were connected in series with the peltier cells and read by the microcontroller ADCs. Current sensors output and thermistors embedded in the thin upper aluminum plates of thermal module were read through the ADC of the microcontoller. Analog RC filters (time constant of 1.6 ms) were implemented on each ADC channel to reduce noise introduced by Pulse Width Modulation driving of the Peltier cells and of the linear stage. Compact H-bridges IC (Texas Instruments DRV8835) were used for driving the Peltier cells, the linear voice coil actuating the end-effector plate and the miniaturized water pump used in the cooling system. Electronics operated at low voltage (5V DC) including drivers of the actuators.

Regarding design of the control algorithm, a preliminary evaluation of the thermal module has been shown in [4]. The response to step signals evidenced asymmetry in system behavior between the heating and cooling phases, as expected for a peltier-driven system. In fact, heat generated by joule effect adds to the heat flow generated by the peltier effect, thus requiring less power to render a positive temperature gradient (fingertip temperature higher than environmental one) than a negative temperature gradient. Such behavior led the development of the control strategy toward an asymmetric control approach, implementing two sets of the PID (Proportional, Integral, Derivative) controller parameters, different for the heating and cooling phases. In particular, the heating and cooling phases were defined by the temperature error, computed as the difference between the temperature reference and the current temperature measured by the thermistor embedded in the thermal module. Positive and negative temperature errors switched the PID parameters between the heating phase and cooling phase respectively. In order to tune the PID parameters, two different step responses, one for the heating, the other for the cooling phases, were analyzed. PID was tuned starting from the Ziegler Nichols recommendations and up to achieving an overshoot approximatively about 5%. The temperature control algorithm was computed at 100 Hz on the microcontroller board.

The heat flow generated by the peltier effect can be considered linearly proportional to the current intensity, while the relationship between applied voltage and current intensity is not linear due to the non-ohmic properties of the peltier cell. For this reason an internal current control loop based on a current sensor has been implemented, overcoming the non linear electric behavior of the cell seen by the external temperature control loop. Due to the PWM modulation used for driving the Peltier cells, and to the non-inductive behavior of such elements compared to typical electromagnetic actuators, an additional digital low-pass filter (cutoff frequency of 15 Hz) was used to filter the current sensor signal. A PI controller was implemented and tuned in order to limit the overshoot below 5%. The current control algorithm was computed at 1 KHz on the microcontroller board. Each of the two halves of the thermal module implemented an independent temperature and current controller.

3   Material Simulation in Virtual Environment

In order to properly replicate the typical transient heat-flux of the contact between the skin and different materials by controlling the display temperature, a thermal model for temperature prediction is needed. For this application, display temperature profiles have been derived from the model provided in [16] as shown in [19]. The adopted model is an improved semi-infinite bodies in contact model that takes into consideration the influence of the thermal contact resistance. Accordingly to the cited thermal contact model, after contact occurs Eqs. (1) and (2) show the transient temperature behavior of both the finger and the object surfaces respectively.

$$T_s(t) = \frac{A}{B}\{1 - e^{\alpha_s B^2 t} erfc[B(\alpha_s t)^{1/2}]\} + T_{s,i}, \tag{1}$$

$$A = \frac{-(T_{s,i} - T_{o,i})}{k_s R_{s-o}}, \qquad B = \frac{1}{k_s R_{s-o}}\left[1 + \frac{(k_s \rho_s c_s)^{1/2}}{(k_o \rho_o c_o)^{1/2}}\right].$$

$$T_o(t) = \frac{C}{D}\{1 - e^{\alpha_o D^2 t} erfc[D(\alpha_o t)^{1/2}]\} + T_{o,i}, \tag{2}$$

$$C = \frac{T_{s,i} - T_{o,i}}{k_o R_{s-o}}, \qquad D = \frac{1}{k_o R_{s-o}}\left[1 + \frac{(k_o \rho_o c_o)^{1/2}}{(k_s \rho_s c_s)^{1/2}}\right].$$

where $T_{s,i}$, $T_{o,i}$ and $T_s(t)$, $T_o(t)$ are respectively the initial temperatures and the transient temperatures as functions of time t. R_{s-o} is the thermal contact resistance evaluated as: $R_{s-o} = (0.37 + k_o)/(1870 \cdot k_o)$ [m^{2}K/W]. k_s, k_o represent the thermal conductivity values ρ_s, ρ_o are densities and c_o, c_s are specific heat values. Finally, α_s, α_o are thermal diffusivity coefficients evaluated as: $\alpha_{(s,o)} = k_{(s,o)}/(\rho_{(s,o)} c_{(s,o)})$ [m^2/s]. Subscripts s and o refer to *skin* and *object* respectively.

In the experimental phase three different materials are used: urethane plastic, glass and copper. Property values assumed for the skin and the three materials are listed in Table 1.

Table 1. Values for skin properties from [16]; values for material properties from [25].

Material	Th. conductivity k [W/m·K]	Density ρ [kg/m^3]	Specific heat c [J/kg·K]
Skin	0.37	1000	3770
Urethane	0.026	70	1045
Glass	1.4	2500	750
Copper	401	8933	385

By imposing the equality condition between the real and the simulated heat-flux, relation (3) is derived and the proper transient temperature at the display for simulating the contact thermal transient can be evaluated as shown in eq. (4), by assuming $R_{s-d} = 5,34 \cdot 10^{-4}$ for a display surface made of alumina [19].

$$q'' = \frac{T_s(t) - T_o(t)}{R_{s-o}} = \frac{T_s(t) - T_d(t)}{R_{s-d}}, \tag{3}$$

$$T_d(t) = T_s(t) \cdot \left[1 - \frac{R_{s-d}}{R_{s-o}}\right] + \frac{R_{s-d}}{R_{s-o}} \cdot T_o(t). \tag{4}$$

4   Performance Evaluation Methods

Capabilities of the thermal device, controlled with the presented method, were experimentally evaluated by means of temperature tracking performance and by means of perception experiments involving simulation of virtual materials.

4.1   Temperature Tracking Performance

Regarding performance in temperature tracking, step response was measured for a set of step amplitudes ranging from 12 °C to 32 °C, thus exploring a set of references covering the range of temperatures typically needed for simulation of virtual materials. Bandpass frequency of the closed-loop system was also experimentally measured by using a chirp signal as reference temperature. The chirp signal frequency ranged from 0.1 Hz to 2 Hz with an amplitude of 4 °C. System behavior in tracking specific temperature references simulating different materials was also analyzed in presence of contact with the finger. Temperature references simulating finger contact with three different materials (urethane plastic, glass and copper) were computed using real thermal conductivity coefficients, as explained in Sect. 3. Temperature tracking of these references were then evaluated in presence of finger contact with the plate. In order to synchronize the contact time with the temperature reference, the voice coil actuator was activated for pushing the plate in contact with finger at a precise time. Temperature of the environment and of the fingertip, measured by an external thermistor in free-air grasped by the subject, was measured at the beginning of the experiment.

4.2 Perception Experiment Involving Simulation of Virtual Materials

Finally, a perception experiment was performed to investigate perception of different materials; they were simulated using the HapticThimble device with the proposed thermal control. Seven healthy subjects (male, aged 32 ± 4) were enrolled in the study providing written consent to participate. They were asked to wear the HapticThimble device, integrating the thermal module, and to explore contact with a virtual surface (Fig. 3). An optical position tracker (Optitrack V120 Trio) was used for tracking position of the fingertip and to simulate the contact threshold with a virtual planar surface. A real-time Simulink model, running on a host PC, was used to compute the virtual contact, to compute the temperature transient and to send temperature and position references (100 Hz sample time) to the HapticThimble through USB communication. The simulation of the three materials (copper, glass and urethane plastic) used in the experimental methods described above (Sect. 4.1) were used as stimuli: in particular, each stimulus was computed for each subject depending on the subject's fingertip temperature, the room temperature, and the thermal properties of the simulated material. It finally consisted in a temperature transient to be rendered by the device, in order to reproduce the heat flux transient occurring between the finger and the simulated material. Ambient temperature and subjects' fingertip temperature were measured at the beginning of each experimental session by means of a thermistor sensor left in free air. Stimuli of the three materials were preliminary presented to subjects, then a sequence of five repetitions for each stimuli in random order was presented. Subjects could touch the virtual surface with no limits of time or in the number of exploratory contact - out of contact transients. A resting period of about 30 seconds followed presentation of each stimuli.

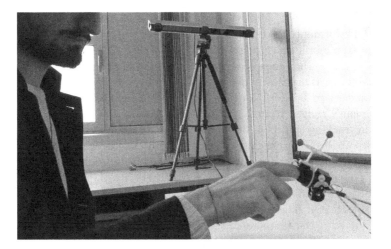

Fig. 3. The experimental setup of the perception experiment involving discrimination of virtual materials differing in thermal conductivity. For rendering the virtual surface, position of the HapticThimble was measured through an optical tracking system

5   Results

This paragraph presents results obtained in terms of temperature tracking of the Haptic Thimble and in terms of response to the perception experiment involving discrimination of different simulated materials.

5.1   Temperature Tracking Results

Graph in Fig. 4a shows system response to the set of step temperature references. It can be noted the noticeably fast rising time of 0.46 ± 0.18 s: The thermal control was tuned in order to take advantage of the fast temperature transients allowed by the thin design of the thermal module. Also the temperature control loop showed to be stable for both the cooling and the heating phases, with average overshoot of $7.25 \pm 3.05\%$. The frequency response of the system in closed loop, measured through a chirp temperature reference, is shown in Fig. 4b. The cut-off frequency of the system was 1.03 Hz, showing relatively fast dynamics for a thermal rendering device.

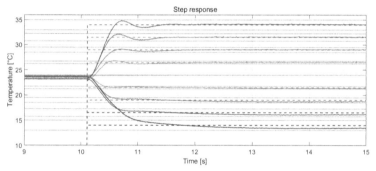

(a) Step response of the temperature controlled closed-loop system

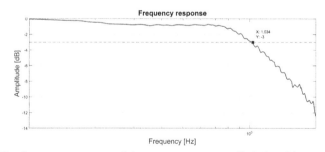

(b) The frequency response of the temperature controlled closed-loop system

Fig. 4. Closed loop system response.

Concerning performance of the system in tracking temperature references that simulated real materials, results are shown in Fig. 5. Importantly, the plate was put in contact with the finger of the subject at the beginning of each transient, thus simulating the real device operation in virtual reality setups. Before starting the experiment, the measurement of the environment temperature was 22 °C, while the temperature of the subject's fingertip was 31 °C. Results show accurate tracking of the computed temperature reference, with mean absolute error (MAE) of 0.03 °C for the reference simulating urethane plastic, 0.15 °C for glass, and 0.02 °C for copper. Maximum measured error was 0.13 °C for the reference simulating urethane plastic, 0.59 °C for glass, and 0.09 °C for copper (grand average 0.27 °C).

5.2   Perception Experiment Results

Results regarding discrimination of three different simulated materials are reported by means of the confusion matrix shown in Fig. 6. Overall, average correct rate was well above the chance level (33.3%), measuring 88.57% for urethane plastic, 62.86% for glass and 77.14% for copper (76.19% grand average). Yet, some dispersion in the confusion matrix can be noted. An additional analysis has been conducted to understand whether different fingertip temperatures might have played a role in discrimination performance. In fact, amplitude of the temperature transient depends on the difference between the simulated material temperature (room temperature) and the temperature of the fingertip. Lower difference between fingertip and room temperature generated a less intense stimulation, thus a lower discrimination performance was expected. The graph in Fig. 6 shows the coefficient of determination that correlates correct rate and fingertip temperature of each subject. A significant correlation was found ($R^2 = 0.72$, $p < 0.015$).

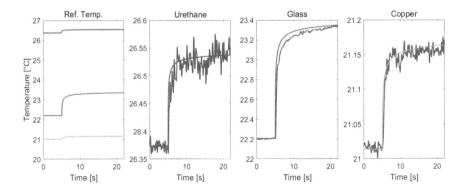

Fig. 5. Modeled temperature references simulating contact transients with the three different materials Urethane, Glass, and Copper (first,left), and temperature tracking of the three temperature references represented with different temperature scales.

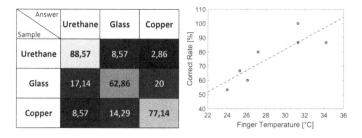

Fig. 6. Results of the virtual material discrimination experiment, showing correct rate for the different materials and relationship between subjects' accuracy and fingertip temperature.

6 Discussions and Conclusion

In this work a temperature control method has been specifically developed for the Haptic Thimble thermal module: the novel device design was potentially capable of fast temperature transients due to the thinness of the structure and due to the integration of a miniaturized water cooling system. In order to take advantage of the module design, the developed control approach tried to cope with non linearities of the system, thus implementing asymmetry between the heating and cooling phases and an internal current control loop for driving the peltier cells. The proposed control method, implemented on the novel thermal module, obtained fast temperature transients that were close to the performance of other bulky and powerful thermal stages presented in literature, and not intended to be portable (i.e. the device presented in [6]). The control approach allowed not only fast transients, but also stable and accurate temperature tracking, as shown by step responses for different temperature references (rising time of 0.46 ± 0.18 s and overshoot of $7.25 \pm 3.05\%$). One of the target applications of the wearable Haptic Thimble is the rich, multimodal rendering of surface contacts in virtual or teleoperated environments (the device renders surface orientation and fast contact - no contact transients with modulation of the normal force), thus experiments involving simulation of virtual materials were specifically performed. Temperature references simulating heat flux with virtual materials were computed and tested through the proposed system, validating accuracy of temperature tracking also in presence of contact with the fingertip (maximum measured error of $0.27\,^{\circ}$C). Perception of the simulated materials was also investigated in a final experimental session with subjects. The experiment integrated the thermal module with the Haptic Thimble, in a typical virtual environment working condition. It showed capability of subjects in discrimination of three different virtual materials (average correct rate 76.19%), although discrimination performance showed to be correlated to the difference between room and subjects' fingertip temperature. Overall, the proposed device and the temperature control method showed very promising results due to the performance in temperature tracking and to the compactness of the device. While performance of the novel thermal module was close to non-portable thermal stages, its miniaturization was suitable for integration in the wearable Haptic Thimble: the whole system reaches novel capabilities of multi-modal surface rendering in VR by means of a compact, wearable device.

Aknowledgments. This work has been funded from the "CENTAURO" project of the European Union Horizon 2020 Programme, Grant Agreement n. 644839.

References

1. Bouhassira, D., Kern, D., Rouaud, J., Pelle-Lancien, E., Morain, F.: Investigation of the paradoxical painful sensation (illusion of pain) produced by a thermal grill. Pain **114**(1), 160–167 (2005)
2. Citérin, J., Pocheville, A., Kheddar, A.: A touch rendering device in a virtual environment with kinesthetic and thermal feedback. In: Proceedings 2006 IEEE International Conference on Robotics and Automation, ICRA 2006, pp. 3923–3928. IEEE (2006)
3. Drif, A., Citérin, J., Kheddar, A.: Thermal bilateral coupling in teleoperators. In: 2005 IEEE/RSJ International Conference on Intelligent Robots and Systems, (IROS 2005), pp. 1301–1306. IEEE (2005)
4. Gabardi, M., Leonardis, D., Solazzi, M., Frisoli, A.: Development of a miniaturized thermal module designed for integration in a wearable haptic device. In: 2018 IEEE Haptic Symposium (HAPTICS), pp. 100–105. IEEE (2018)
5. Gabardi, M., Solazzi, M., Leonardis, D., Frisoli, A.: A new wearable fingertip haptic interface for the rendering of virtual shapes and surface features. In: 2016 IEEE Haptics Symposium (HAPTICS), pp. 140–146. IEEE (2016)
6. Gallo, S., Cucu, L., Thevenaz, N., Sengul, A., Bleuler, H.: Design and control of a novel thermo-tactile multimodal display. In: 2014 IEEE Haptics Symposium (HAPTICS). IEEE (2014)
7. Gallo, S., Rognini, G., Santos-Carreras, L., Vouga, T., Blanke, O., Bleuler, H.: Encoded and crossmodal thermal stimulation through a fingertip-sized haptic display. Front. Robot. AI **2**, 25 (2015)
8. Gallo, S., Santos-Carreras, L., Rognini, G., Hara, M., Yamamoto, A., Higuchi, T.: Towards multimodal haptics for teleoperation: design of a tactile thermal display. In: 2012 12th IEEE International Workshop on Advanced Motion Control (AMC), pp. 1–5. IEEE (2012)
9. Gallo, S., Son, C., Lee, H.J., Bleuler, H., Cho, I.J.: A flexible multimodal tactile display for delivering shape and material information. Sens. Actuators A: Phys. **236**, 180–189 (2015)
10. Guiatni, M., Kheddar, A.: Theoretical and experimental study of a heat transfer model for thermal feedback in virtual environments. In: IEEE/RSJ International Conference on Intelligent Robots and Systems, IROS 2008, pp. 2996–3001. IEEE (2008)
11. Guiatni, M., Kheddar, A.: Modeling identification and control of peltier thermo-electic modules for telepresence. J. Dyn. Syst. Meas. Control **133**(3), 031010 (2011)
12. Ho, H.-N.: Influence of object material properties and geometry on skin temperature responses during contact. In: Bello, F., Kajimoto, H., Visell, Y. (eds.) EuroHaptics 2016. LNCS, vol. 9774, pp. 281–290. Springer, Cham (2016). https://doi.org/10.1007/978-3-319-42321-0_26

13. Ho, H.N.: Material recognition based on thermal cues: mechanisms and applications. In: Temperature, pp. 1–20 (2017)
14. Ho, H.N., Jones, L.A.: Contribution of thermal cues to material discrimination and localization. Attention Percept. Psychophys. **68**(1), 118–128 (2006)
15. Ho, H.N., Jones, L.A.: Development and evaluation of a thermal display for material identification and discrimination. ACM Trans. Appl. Percept. (TAP) **4**(2), 13 (2007)
16. Ho, H.N., Jones, L.A.: Modeling the thermal responses of the skin surface during hand-object interactions. J. Biomech. Eng. **130**(2), 021005 (2008)
17. Ho, H.N., Sato, K., Kuroki, S., Watanabe, J., Maeno, T., Nishida, S.: Physical-perceptual correspondence for dynamic thermal stimulation. IEEE Trans. Haptics **10**(1), 84–93 (2017)
18. Jia, Z., Li, J., Chen, C.: Design and evaluation of a thermal tactile display for colour rendering. Int. J. Adv. Robot. Syst. **12**(11), 162 (2015)
19. Jones, L.A., Ho, H.N.: Warm or cool, large or small? The challenge of thermal displays. IEEE Trans. Haptics **1**(1), 53–70 (2008)
20. Nakatani, M., Sato, K., Sato, K., Kawana, Y., Takai, D., Minamizawa, K., Tachi, S.: A novel multimodal tactile module that can provide vibro-thermal feedback. In: Hasegawa, S., Konyo, M., Kyung, K.-U., Nojima, T., Kajimoto, H. (eds.) AsiaHaptics 2016. LNEE, vol. 432, pp. 437–443. Springer, Singapore (2018). https://doi.org/10.1007/978-981-10-4157-0_73
21. Sakaguchi, M., Imai, K., Hayakawa, K.: Development of high-speed thermal display using water flow. In: Yamamoto, S. (ed.) HCI 2014. LNCS, vol. 8521, pp. 233–240. Springer, Cham (2014). https://doi.org/10.1007/978-3-319-07731-4_24
22. Sato, K., Maeno, T.: Presentation of sudden temperature change using spatially divided warm and cool stimuli. In: Isokoski, P., Springare, J. (eds.) EuroHaptics 2012. LNCS, vol. 7282, pp. 457–468. Springer, Heidelberg (2012). https://doi.org/10.1007/978-3-642-31401-8_41
23. Singhal, A., Jones, L.A.: Perceptual interactions in thermo-tactile displays. In: 2017 IEEE World Haptics Conference (WHC), pp. 90–95. IEEE (2017)
24. Yamamoto, A., Cros, B., Hashimoto, H., Higuchi, T.: Control of thermal tactile display based on prediction of contact temperature. In: 2004 IEEE International Conference on Robotics and Automation, Proceedings, ICRA 2004, vol. 2, pp. 1536–1541. IEEE (2004)
25. Yang, G.H., Jones, L.A., Kwon, D.S.: Use of simulated thermal cues for material discrimination and identification with a multi-fingered display. Presence: Teleoper. Virtual Environ. **17**(1), 29–42 (2008)
26. Yang, G.H., Kwon, D.S.: Thermo-tactile interaction using tactile display device. IFAC Proc. Volumes **41**(2), 14708–14713 (2008)
27. Yang, G.H., Yang, T.H., Kim, S.C., Kwon, D.S., Kang, S.C.: Compact tactile display for fingertips with multiple vibrotactile actuator and thermoelectric module. In: 2007 IEEE International Conference on Robotics and Automation, pp. 491–496. IEEE (2007)

Overcoming the Variability of Fingertip Friction with Surface-Haptic Force-Feedback

Nicolas Huloux[1(✉)], Jocelyn Monnoyer[1,2], Marc Boyron[1],
and Michaël Wiertlewski[1]

[1] Aix Marseille University, CNRS, ISM, Marseille, France
{nicolas.huloux,jocelyn.monnoyer}@etu.univ-amu.fr,
{marc.boyron,michael.wiertlewski}@univ-amu.fr
[2] PSA Groupe, Paris, France

Abstract. Touch screens have pervaded our lives as the most widely used human-machine interface, and much research has focused recently on producing vivid tactile sensations on these flat panels. One of the main methods used for this purpose is based on ultrasonic vibration to controllably reduce the friction experienced by a finger touching a glass plate. Typically, these devices modulate the amplitude of the vibration in order to control the frictional force that the finger experiences without monitoring the actual output. However, since friction is a complex physical process, the open-loop transfer function is not stationary and varies with a wide range of external parameters such as the velocity of exploration or the ambient moisture. The novel interface we present here incorporates a force sensor which measures subtle changes of the frictional force on a wide frequency bandwidth including static forces. This force sensor is the basis for real time control of the frictional force of the finger, which reduces significantly the inherent variability of ultrasonic friction modulation while maintaining a noise level below human perception thresholds. The interface is able to render of precise and sharp frictional patterns directly on the user's fingertip.

Keywords: Surface haptics · Feedback control · Squeeze film
Ultrasonic friction modulation

1 Introduction

Surface-haptic promises to restore the tangibility of virtual interfaces while users are interacting with flat and featureless touchscreens. Virtual bumps, texture, clicks and scrolling effects produce sensations that guide the users' motion and provide them with feedback about their actions. One of the most promising approaches developed to date for generating rich perceptual sensations consists in modulating the friction between the user's finger and the plate via either electrostatic adhesion [1] or ultrasonic squeeze-film levitation [2,3]. The main advantage of these methods over vibrotactile stimulation is that they produce stimuli

© Springer International Publishing AG, part of Springer Nature 2018
D. Prattichizzo et al. (Eds.): EuroHaptics 2018, LNCS 10894, pp. 326–337, 2018.
https://doi.org/10.1007/978-3-319-93399-3_29

which not only include transient events –i.e. texture, impacts or vibrations– but affects continuous forces exerted by a sliding fingertip. Modulating these forces makes it possible to induce of tactile illusions of shape and large features, such as bumps and holes, similar to what could be achieved with robotic force feedback devices [4,5].

In spite of their advantages, friction modulation methods tend to produce signals that are distorted and attenuated [6,7]. The main factor responsible for the signal variance is the complexity of the frictional behavior of a finger sliding over a glass plate. The angle of the finger, the pressure force, and the moisture of the skin all affect the friction force [8]. Worst still, even if the exploration conditions are accounted for, sweating and the subsequent softening of the stratum corneum induce large changes in the friction with time [9].

In addition the fact that they both rely on friction to produce forces to the fingertip, each of the above two technologies has its own drawbacks. Despite the advantages of electro-adhesion methods, such as their large functional bandwidth and their compatibility with strong forces, the occurrence of non-linearities results in the distortion of the signal [1]. Squeeze-film levitation methods based on ultrasonic standing waves make it possible to modulate the friction force in a wider dynamic range, but have disadvantages such as poor frequency responses [10] and large static non-linearities [11]. It has been proposed to combine both methods in order to increase the dynamic range of possible signals [12,13], but this does not solve the variability inherent to friction force modulation processes.

Feedforward filters can be used to counteract the attenuation inherent to ultrasonic friction modulation and provide users with fast and clear signals. Dynamics is improved by temporarily overdriving the actuators in order to quickly reach a given friction force [14]. Distortions due to static non-linearities can also be corrected using a look-up table [15]. Although these feedforward model-based approaches give better performances than those of open-loop systems, the inherent variability prevents to precisely regulate a given force. Ben Messaoud et al. recently proposed to tackle these drawbacks by introducing real-time measurements of the friction force that are fed to a closed-loop feedback control able to reject unknown disturbances [16]. The control strategy relies on a sliding mode strategy to robustly remove static error and improve the dynamic response.

However, like any closed-loop control system, noise from the force sensor was re-injected into the actuators, which resulted in noisy stimulus. In order to overcome the limitations of this approach, we developed a custom built capacitive sensor which is able to resolve the force with a dynamic range ratio of more than 1:50,000. This sensor is used as the backbone of a closed-loop force feedback scheme which is able to produce low noise signal, yet accurately control of the friction force by means of a state-of-the-art proportional-integral controller.

2   Simulations

2.1   Linearized Dynamic Model of Ultrasonic Friction Modulation

In order to account for the stochastic nature of ultrasonic friction modulation and design the most appropriate controller, the relationship between the amplitude set on the plate and the frictional force that is actually produced has to be modeled. We recorded the force and amplitude data of 26 participants while they were sliding there finger on a glass plate excited with a 30 kHz ultrasonic carrier of 2.5 μm amplitude modulated by a 1 Hz sine wave. Participants were free to explore the surface which resulted in a dataset that contained various exploration speed, forces and finger posture. Datapoints showing force as a function of the vibration amplitude are presented in Fig. 1a along with statistics across trials on binned data. Although the individual trials often showed the existence of a clearly negative correlation between the vibration amplitude and the friction force, the relationships observed from trial to trial were not consistent. To account for this behavior in simulations, the non-linear Gaussian model described in [11] was extended by adding an unknown perturbation d, which was bounded so as to prevent the occurrence of negative friction force values. The modified friction force model was therefore:

$$f = f_0 \exp\left(-\frac{a^2}{2\tau^2}\right) + d = g(a) + d \tag{1}$$

where $f_0 = 0.8\,\text{N}$ is the nominal friction force, a is the vibration amplitude, and $\tau = 1.32\,\mu\text{m}$ is the susceptibility to ultrasonic levitation. The deterministic behavior is denoted by the function $g(a)$, and d is taken to be a 1 Hz sine wave with an amplitude of 0.8 N and an offset of 0.4 N.

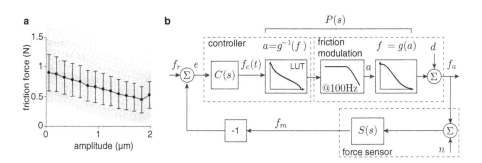

Fig. 1. a. Friction force and amplitude data points recorded in 26 sliding trials are shown in gray. Means and standard deviations are presented in black. b. Block diagram of the control scheme.

2.2   Control Strategy

The block diagram of the control strategy implemented in this study is shown in Fig. 1b. The friction modulation process, in which the amplitude is the input, delivers a friction force. This process is modeled by means of a linear time-invariant function serving as a first order low pass filter with a cutoff frequency of 100 Hz, in line with the attenuation reported in [10]. The filter is followed by the non-linear relationship described by Eq. 1 to complete the model for the friction modulation process.

A lookup table is implemented in the controller to compensate for the non-linearity of the ultrasonic friction modulation captured by Eq. 1. The lookup table and the friction modulation process combines into a single linear time-invariant transfer function called $P(s)$, to which a saturation function is added, where the amplitude of the ultrasonic wave is bounded between 0 and 2.5 μm. The controller $C(s)$ therefore has to compensate for the corrected process $P(s)$, which acts as a first-order low-pass filter, and for a slowly evolving unknown disturbance, d.

A force sensor measures the friction force applied to the finger along with some undesirable noise n. This parameter typically fits a zero-mean random Gaussian process. The dynamics of the sensor are modeled by means of the transfer function $S(s)$, which, to simplify the simulation, is taken to be a low-pass filter with a cutoff frequency of 1 kHz. The force measured f_m is then subtracted from the set-point force f_r in order to compute the error e, which is subsequently fed to the controller.

2.3   Precision and Accuracy Trade-Off

The ideal control scheme would have a fast, effective means of disturbance rejection without having to add any noise to the friction force measured by the system. In practice, these two objectives impose opposite constraints on the controller. In the current implementation, a proportional-integral controller was adopted so that $C(s) = K_p + K_i/s$. A larger set of gains K_p and K_i ensures fast convergence, but results in the amplification of the noise introduced by the sensor. This noise is detrimental to the user's tactile experience because it adds fluctuations that are not part of the original signal. This trade-off between the convergence to a specific value (the accuracy) and the noise injected (the precision) in the closed loop has to be evaluated, giving, the maximum noise that the sensor can generate.

From the block diagram described in Fig. 1, taking only the linear behavior into account, the expression for the force perceived by the finger in the Laplace domain can be expressed as follows:

$$f_a = d\,\frac{1}{1+G} + f_r\,\frac{CP}{1+G} - n\,\frac{G}{1+G} \tag{2}$$

where $G(s) = C(s)P(s)S(s)$. To study the effects of the noise n on the variance of the friction force σ_f^2, the variance of the setpoint and the disturbance can be taken to be null in the steady state. Error propagation analysis therefore gives the following equation:

$$\sigma_f^2 = \left| \frac{G}{1+G} \right|^2 \sigma_n^2 \tag{3}$$

This equation shows that the noise perceived by the user, σ_f^2 is affected by the gain of the controller. A lower gain attenuates the noise originating from the sensors. However, since the disturbance is affected by the sensitivity function $\frac{1}{1+G}$, which favors high gains, an optimum can be found.

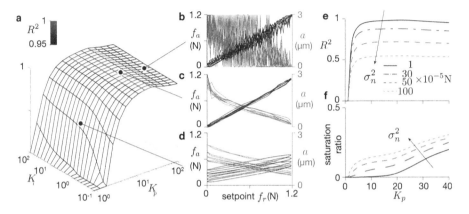

Fig. 2. a. The fidelity of the control given by the R^2 parameter in comparison with $f_a = f_r$ in the case of a set of K_i and K_p coefficients. b. $K_i = 2$ and $K_p = 40$. Over-corrected signal results in noisy signals. c. $K_i = 2$ and $K_p = 10$. The right balance between a high gain and fast convergence. d. $K_i = 2$ and $K_p = 1$. Low gains give unsatisfactory disturbance rejection. e. Effects of greater sensor noise on the precision of the control. f. Greater noise results in significant saturation of the controller.

Figure 2a shows the results of a set of simulations, where the controller's parameters K_p and K_i were varied and the signal fidelity of the control was measured. The fidelity of the system is reflected in the goodness-of-fit R^2 between the input and the output of the simulation in comparison with an ideal transfer function in which $f_a = f_r$. Both the disturbance rejection and the noise attenuation have a positive impact on the fidelity. In this simulation, the setpoint signal was a logarithmically-swept sinusoid ranging from 1 Hz to 100 Hz with an amplitude of 1.2 N, the disturbance was a 1 Hz sine wave with an amplitude of 0.4 N and the noise was a white Gaussian noise with an amplitude of 10^{-5}N. As shown by the graph in Fig. 2, proportional gains K_p ranging between 5 and 20 provide an efficient disturbance rejection while preventing any significant feedback noise. The integral term K_i is responsible for rejecting the static error, but as long as it is above the value of 2, its tuning has fairly little influence. The input-output relationship with three different proportional gains $K_p = [40, 10, 1]$ is shown in Fig. 2b,c and d, respectively. A high gain, as in Fig. 2b, results in a noisy and saturated command, whereas a low gain, as in Fig. 2d, results in a low precision controller. The optimum efficiency was found to occur at values of $K_p = 10$ and $K_i = 2$, as shown in Fig. 2c.

The influence of the noise on the fidelity and the saturation of the actuation is shown in Fig. 2e,f. The saturation index was calculated from the ratio between the number of data points having a saturated input and the total number of data points. Noise levels above 10^{-4} N in the force sensor will significantly decrease the precision and increase the likelihood of saturating the output. We therefore adopted a proportional gain of $K_p = 10$.

Based on the results of the simulation, it is clear that the effectiveness of the controller depends on the noise added by the sensor, and that low noise results in a sharp, untainted tactile stimulation. It has been estimated that the lowest force perceivable by the human somatosensory system is in the 5.10^{-4} N range [14]. The output noise produced by a sensor with a noise level of 5.10^{-5} N remains subliminal.

3 Friction Force Sensor Design

The output of the simulation reveals that the force sensor is the centerpiece of the control strategy, and proper care must be taken in the choice of technology and design to achieve high-fidelity tactile renderings on surface-haptic devices.

3.1 Performance Requirements

To ensure that the force perceived by the user will remain untainted by the noise, while being able to support forces as high as 2.5 N, the sensor noise must be less than 5.10^{-5} N. These requirements lead to a dynamic range figure of 1:50,000 or about 95 dB. The stiffness and frequency bandwidth are also crucial factors, since they directly affect the sensor's response via the transfer function $S(s)$. A softer sensor might have a high signal to noise ratio, but this will be at the expense of a low frequency bandwidth. The glass plate typically weights approximately $m_p = 400$g, and the sensor's first resonance frequency is prescribed by $f_0 = 1/2\pi\sqrt{k/m_p} = 250$ Hz in the case of a sensor stiffness of 1N.µm. This means that in order to resolve 2 N, the sensor will be displaced by 2 µm. Since force sensors are based on the measured displacement of a known elastic structure, the underlying displacement sensor should have a minimum noise of 0.5 pm.

The sensitivity requirements rule out the use of metal and semiconductor strain-gauge sensors, which usually have signal-to-noise ratios of the order of 1:1,000 in rigid load-cells. Piezoelectric sensors, while having an exceptionally high signal-to-noise ratios and high stiffness, are not suitable for closed-loop feedback applications because of the low-frequency drift, which would require frequent resetting of the control loop. All these constraints are within the range of capacitive sensors, which are capable of a dynamic range within the present requirements while remaining impervious to drift [17].

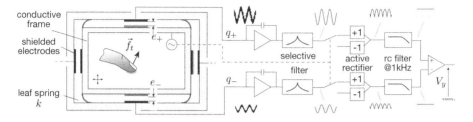

Fig. 3. Mechanical and electrical schematics of the capacitive force sensor, illustrated on one axis

3.2 Implementation

The capacitive force sensor is based on the architecture illustrated in Fig. 3. The ultrasonic plate is fixed to a frame that is suspended by four curved leaf springs grounded to the rest of the device. The curved leaf spring have a relatively high mobility in the plane of the surface, with a lateral stiffness of 6.10^6 N/m, while maintain rigidity three order of magnitude higher along the normal axis which keep it stiff. This structure constrains the motion of the inner frame to two translations collinear with the friction force. The deformation of the leaf spring is determined by four non-contact sensors, each of which measures the distance of each edge of the suspended frame to the grounded frame. The measurements are differential in each dimension, with one sensor experiencing a reduction in the gap, while the one on the opposite side detects an increase. This differential amplification method counteracts the thermal effects and unwanted electromagnetic perturbations. Each sensor is composed of one rectangular active electrode, surrounded by a single trace connected to ground that shields the active electrode from external perturbation. These electrodes are made out of 75 μm-thick copper coated using an electroless nickel immersion gold process which provides a smooth finish and immunity to corrosion (PCB-POOL, Aarbergen, Germany). The copper trace is mounted on a FR4 substrate for a total active area of $40 \times 4.5\text{mm}^2$. An intermediate part maintains these electrodes parallel to the inner frame, which is conductive and excited by a 120 kHz sinusoidal signal V, polarizing the sensing electrode. Charges $q_\pm$ are proportional to the voltage V and inversely proportional to the distance $e_\pm$ such that $q_\pm = V \epsilon_0 A/e_\pm$, where ϵ_0 is the permittivity of the air and A is the active area of the sensors.

The capacitive measurement circuit is adapted from the low-noise topology described in [17]. The charges from the sensing electrodes are transformed into a voltage via a charge amplifier and the signal is then passed through a selective filter with a center frequency matching the excitation of 120 kHz. After the filter, there is no artifacts left in the signal. At that stage, the envelope of the signal, which depends on the distance between the electrode and the outer frame, is recovered using synchronous demodulation followed by a low pass filter with 1 kHz cutoff frequency. The last operation takes the difference between the signal coming from two electrodes to recover the signed voltage V_s that reflects the displacement of the inner frame and therefore the force that is applied by the fingertip.

3.3 Sensor Characterization

The sensor was calibrated under quasi-static conditions, using a set of standard weights which applied to the frame a known gravitational force via a string and pulley system. The results are presented in Fig. 4a, and the linear regression showed a goodness of fit of $R^2 = 0.95$. The frequency bandwidth measurements were performed using an impact hammer. The signal was then normalized and converted into the maximum sensing value. The frequency response showed the occurrence of an initial resonance at 145 Hz owing to the large glass plate. The noise of the sensor studied using a 10 s sample without any external perturbations show the existence of a floor at 5.10^{-5} N in the low frequency and an attenuation above 300 Hz, due to a first order filter. The frequency response and noise spectrum are shown in Fig. 4b. The dynamic range of the sensor before its first resonance is 1:50,000, or about 93 dB.

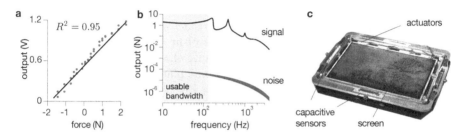

Fig. 4. a. Linearity of the lateral force sensor b. Frequency spectrum of the noise and impulse response c. Picture of the device

4   Friction Force Feedback

4.1   Hardware

A picture of the final device is shown in Fig. 4c. A glass plate measuring $255 \times 140 \times 3 \, mm^3$ vibrating at a frequency of 46 kHz in a 16×0 mode provided the friction modulation. Four piezoelectric actuators are bonded to the plate and provide a maximum displacement of 2.5 μm. The plate is clamped to the inner frame at the end of 3 nodal lines on each side. The inner and outer frame and curved leaf springs were milled out of a block of 2024-grade aluminum alloy.

In addition to the lateral force sensor, the system is equipped with an optical position sensor based on [14], not used in this study, and 4 normal force sensors at each corner to measure the user's finger normal force. Finger position and normal force sensors can drive the production of complex virtual environments. The real-time control is ensured by a low-latency 5 kHz timer implemented on a microcontroller (Teensy 3.1, PRJC, Portland, OR, USA). Every cycle the sensors values are acquired, the PI control and the look-up table are computed and the amplitude of the ultrasonic carrier is modulated. The amplitude modulated ultrasonic carrier is then filtered with a 10 to 50 kHz bandpass filter and amplified before being sent to the piezoelectric actuators. The controller parameters were set at $K_p = 10$ and $K_i = 2$ in accordance with Sect. 2.3.

4.2   Closed-Loop Performance

Comparisons were made between the open-loop and closed-loop modes of operation of the friction modulation using a commanded force f_r matching a 1 Hz sine wave between 0.3 and 0.9 N, which corresponds to a range of reliably achievable forces. This friction range was implemented using three 1 Hz sine waves 0.1 N in amplitude with a mean value of [0.4 0.6 0.8] N as the setpoint to minimize the variations in the friction force. One participant slid his finger along the interface at 20 mm.s^{-1} 5 times with each force signal and 50 periods of the modulation were recorded. As shown in Fig. 5a, the open-loop response poorly matched the commanded force since the linear regression showed a goodness of fit of only $R^2 = 0.22$. The closed loop condition gave satisfactory tracking of the setpoint, since the linear regression yielded a goodness of fit of $R^2 = 0.98$. Low friction values caused most of the errors, partly because the large amplitudes required could not be reached with the present ultrasonic plate.

The step responses recorded are shown in Fig. 5b. The frictional force was tracked with a response time of 37 ± 20 ms (SD) with a decreasing friction step and 32 ± 16 ms with an increasing friction step, with an exploration speed of approximately 20 mm.s^{-1} in both cases. The results shown in this figure can be improved with larger gains in the closed loop at the expense of greater noise. The traces in the figure show that the steady state friction was not as noise-free as one might have expected in view of the signal to noise ratio of the sensor. It seems likely that the additional fluctuations may have been due to friction noise and tremors of the user's hand. Figure 5c gives a close-up view of the control strategy in a single step. In order to achieve fast responses, the controller overshoots in amplitude before converging back to a lower steady-state value to stabilize the output.

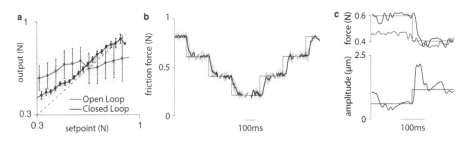

Fig. 5. Friction force feedback control. a. The closed loop limits the variability and compensate for the static non-linearity. b. The system response to successive unit steps shows a response time of around 30 ms. c. During a unit step, the commanded amplitude of the ultrasonic waves overshoots.

5 Discussion

The disturbance rejection of the closed-loop force feedback is on a par with the results obtained by [16], who used a strain gauge sensor and a sliding mode controller. The steady state friction is kept within 20 mN of the set point, which is a substantial improvement over the 0.25 N variations which occur when ultrasonic friction modulation is operating in the open-loop mode. The custom-built force sensor has a noise floor of less than 10^{-4}N, and the gain of the controller is set so as to limit the noise fed back to the actuator, which results in the production of tactile stimuli that are sharp and devoid of artifacts. Yet the traces in Fig. 5b show that the actual friction force undergoes fluctuations in the order of 20 mN. These fluctuations are also present in open loop control [10] and in closed loop control that uses strain-gauge load cells [16]. The remaining fluctuations are probably due to physiological and frictional noise [18], which the feedback system struggles to cancel. A frequency synthesis of the control taking into account the friction noise might help to develop a higher order controller with which these fluctuations could be ironed out.

It is worth noting that the present simulation of the entire system revealed that in order to obtain a specific noise level in the output force, the sensor noise has to be one order of magnitude lower. This particular ratio, which was not predicted by the noise sensitivity function based on linear control theory, may have resulted from the non linearity present in the real-life system. The response time is also reduced from 50 ms to 20 ms with respect to open-loop condition, at slow sliding speeds. These results could be further improved by using a more powerful actuator, since the current dynamics were limited only by the maximum amplitude that the plate can reach.

6 Conclusion

In this paper, we report on the simulation and implementation of a surface-haptic device which can be used to deliver precise and accurate stimuli to a user's sliding finger in the dynamic range of 0.3 to 0.9 N. In particular, it was established that the combination of a force sensor with a wide dynamic range (1:50,000) and a PI controller sufficed to considerably reduce the variability of the stimuli produced by the ultrasonic friction modulation.

The performances of the current device were limited by the power of the ultrasonic plate, and ongoing engineering studies are now focusing on building a more powerful actuator which is compatible with fast, large changes in the amplitude. Thanks to the online regulation of the friction force, frictional stimuli with great precision and accuracy are delivered, and this interface therefore provides a valuable tool for use in psychophysical experiments requiring finely controlled stimuli [19]. The improved sharpness and fidelity are also key assets for simulating unambiguous virtual environments on user interfaces.

Acknowledgments. The authors would like to thank Julien Diperi for his assistance with the mechanical engineering and Stéphane Viollet for his thoughtful comments on the design of the controller. This research was part of the French Research Agency project IOTA (ANR-16-CE33-0002), with some additional support from the Openlab PSA-AMU "Automotive Motion Lab" project.

References

1. Shultz, C.D., Peshkin, M.A., Colgate, J.E.: The application of tactile, audible, and ultrasonic forces to human fingertips using broadband electroadhesion. In: 2017 IEEE World Haptics Conference (WHC), pp. 119–124. IEEE (2017)
2. Biet, M., Giraud, F., Lemaire-Semail, B.: Squeeze film effect for the design of an ultrasonic tactile plate. IEEE Trans. Ultrason. Ferroelectr. Freq. Control **54**(12), 2678–2688 (2007)
3. Winfield, L., Glassmire, J., Colgate, J.E., Peshkin, M.: T-pad: Tactile pattern display through variable friction reduction. In: Proceedings of the Second Joint EuroHaptics Conference 2007 and Symposium on Haptic Interfaces for Virtual Environment and Teleoperator Systems, World Haptics 2007, pp. 421–426. IEEE (2007)
4. Minsky, M., Ming, O.Y., Steele, O., Brooks Jr., F.P., Behensky, M.: Feeling and seeing: issues in force display. In: ACM SIGGRAPH Computer Graphics, vol. 24, pp. 235–241. ACM (1990)
5. Robles-De-La-Torre, G., Hayward, V.: Force can overcome object geometry in the perception of shape through active touch. Nature **412**(6845), 445–448 (2001)
6. Sednaoui, T., Vezzoli, E., Dzidek, B., Lemaire-Semail, B., Chappaz, C., Adams, M.: Experimental evaluation of friction reduction in ultrasonic devices. In: 2015 IEEE World Haptics Conference (WHC), pp. 37–42. IEEE (2015)
7. Monnoyer, J., Diaz, E., Bourdin, C., Wiertlewski, M.: Optimal skin impedance promotes perception of ultrasonic switches. In: 2017 IEEE World Haptics Conference (WHC), pp. 130–135. IEEE (2017)
8. Tomlinson, S., Lewis, R., Carré, M.: The effect of normal force and roughness on friction in human finger contact. Wear **267**(5), 1311–1318 (2009)
9. Pasumarty, S.M., Johnson, S.A., Watson, S.A., Adams, M.J.: Friction of the human finger pad: influence of moisture, occlusion and velocity. Tribol. Lett. **44**(2), 117 (2011)
10. Meyer, D.J., Wiertlewski, M., Peshkin, M.A., Colgate, J.E.: Dynamics of ultrasonic and electrostatic friction modulation for rendering texture on haptic surfaces. In: 2014 IEEE Haptics Symposium (HAPTICS), pp. 63–67. IEEE (2014)
11. Wiertlewski, M., Friesen, R.F., Colgate, J.E.: Partial squeeze film levitation modulates fingertip friction. Proc. Natl. Acad. Sci. **113**(33), 9210–9215 (2016)
12. Vezzoli, E., Messaoud, W.B., Amberg, M., Giraud, F., Lemaire-Semail, B., Bueno, M.A.: Physical and perceptual independence of ultrasonic vibration and electrovibration for friction modulation. IEEE Trans. Haptics **8**(2), 235–239 (2015)
13. Smith, T.A., Gorlewicz, J.L.: HUE: a hybrid ultrasonic and electrostatic variable friction touchscreen. In: 2017 IEEE World Haptics Conference (WHC), pp. 635–640. IEEE (2017)
14. Wiertlewski, M., Leonardis, D., Meyer, D.J., Peshkin, M.A., Colgate, J.E.: A high-fidelity surface-haptic device for texture rendering on bare finger. In: Auvray, M., Duriez, C. (eds.) EUROHAPTICS 2014. LNCS, vol. 8619, pp. 241–248. Springer, Heidelberg (2014). https://doi.org/10.1007/978-3-662-44196-1_30

15. Vezzoli, E., Sednaoui, T., Amberg, M., Giraud, F., Lemaire-Semail, B.: Texture rendering strategies with a high fidelity - capacitive visual-haptic friction control device. In: Bello, F., Kajimoto, H., Visell, Y. (eds.) EuroHaptics 2016. LNCS, vol. 9774, pp. 251–260. Springer, Cham (2016). https://doi.org/10.1007/978-3-319-42321-0_23

16. Messaoud, W.B., Amberg, M., Lemaire-Semail, B., Giraud, F., Bueno, M.A.: High fidelity closed loop controlled friction in smarttac tactile stimulator. In: 2015 17th European Conference on Power Electronics and Applications (EPE 2015 ECCE-Europe), pp. 1–9. IEEE (2015)

17. Lotters, J.C., Olthuis, W., Veltink, P.H., Bergveld, P.: A sensitive differential capacitance to voltage converter for sensor applications. IEEE Trans. Instrum. Meas. **48**(1), 89–96 (1999)

18. Wiertlewski, M., Hudin, C., Hayward, V.: On the 1/f noise and non-integer harmonic decay of the interaction of a finger sliding on flat and sinusoidal surfaces. In: World Haptics Conference (WHC), pp. 25–30. IEEE (2011)

19. Bernard, C., Monnoyer, J., Wiertlewski, M.: Harmonious textures: the perceptual dimensions of synthetic sinusoidal gratings. In: Eurohaptics. Springer (2018, in Press)

Localisation of Vibrotactile Stimuli with Spatio-Temporal Inverse Filtering

Charles Hudin[✉] and Sabrina Panëels

CEA, LIST, Sensory and Ambient Interfaces Laboratory,
91191 Gif-sur-Yvette, France
{charles.hudin,sabrina.paneels}@cea.fr

Abstract. A number of researchers and companies have investigated methods to improve touchscreen interaction through actuators providing vibrotactile stimuli. Wave propagation enables remote actuation but makes such stimuli perceivable all over the surface. In this paper, we report the use of an array of actuators combined with a spatio-temporal inverse filter to produce independent vibrotactile feedback at different positions on a surface. A experimental evaluation showed that this setup successfully corrects for distortion, reverberation and cross talk between piezoelectric actuators glued to a glass surface providing 300 Hz burst vibrations. A user study conducted with 10 participants demonstrated that this filtering not only improved the user's discrimination but also required less concentration when compared to a method without such filtering.

Keywords: Surface haptics · Vibrotactile stimuli
Multifinger interaction · Inverse filter · Localised feedback evaluation

1 Introduction

Tactile displays are now commonly adopted as they provide a more direct and natural user interaction through touch. However, most still lack appropriate haptic feedback for a truly and more complete natural user experience. And yet, haptic feedback offers several benefits: for example, it can enhance performance with feedback closer to real world interactions, like with compliant materials [18] or with a keyboard [6]; it can enable eyes-free interactions in situations where the visual modality is not available or highly demanded for the primary task such as in the automotive domain [16] or for the visually impaired users [13]; or it can be used to enrich the experience, in games for instance or shopping.

Several academics and industrials have investigated methods to provide haptic feedback to touchscreens. In many cases, users do not touch the vibration actuator directly but rather a surface to which actuators are glued. Because mechanical vibrations propagate, the vibration actually experienced by the user is not only affected by the actuator's response but also by the wave propagation

© Springer International Publishing AG, part of Springer Nature 2018
D. Prattichizzo et al. (Eds.): EuroHaptics 2018, LNCS 10894, pp. 338–350, 2018.
https://doi.org/10.1007/978-3-319-93399-3_30

and reverberation in the touched surface. In the absence of appropriate compensation, the spatial and temporal control of the vibrotactile stimuli displayed on a surface is therefore limited and forces designers to assume single touch exploration and replace spatial with temporal modulation [13]. A solution consists in using an array of transducers while stopping wave propagation passively through damping [10, 12] or patterns on the surface [1], but modifying the structure and mechanical properties of the touched surface is not always possible.

Focusing mechanical waves is an alternative but suffers from the diffraction limit. Because of this limit, two points away from the actuators must be distant by at least half a wavelength for their vibrations to be independently controllable. Vibrotactile vibrations, with frequency below 1 kHz have a typical wavelength of hundreds of mm in thin plates (see [4], p. 229 for the calculation of wave velocity in plates). Therefore, it is not possible with standard approaches to achieve, with remote actuators, a localisation at the scale of a finger while working at frequencies within the tactile sensitivity range. Focused approaches are therefore either poorly localised [19] or operate at ultrasonic frequencies [8] where tactile detection relies on non linear phenomenon that are not easily controllable.

The solution explored in this paper consists in using an array of actuators that controls vibrations locally, in their near field, where the diffraction limit does not apply. In this configuration, the ability to control the vibrations of two points is given by the actuators' size rather than the wavelength. For a thin glass surface, like the one used in the experimental validation, the wavelength of a 300 Hz vibration is 150 mm but we demonstrate that we can successfully control the vibrations of points distant by 25 mm $= \lambda/6$. Spatio temporal inverse filtering is a method for wave field shaping employed in medical imaging [17] or spatial audio rendering [9]. It relies on the knowledge and inversion of the transfer function matrix between a set of actuators and a set of control points. This paper investigates the use of such a filter in a near field configuration, i.e. with control points collocated with actuators, to achieve wave control at a sub wavelength scale and produce independent vibrations on top of actuators glued to the same continuous surface. The idea of cancelling the vibration produced by other actuators was also developed in [11] but in our approach relies on a preliminary calibration and does not require any vibration sensor.

This paper first introduces this technique, the Spatio Temporal Inverse Filter (referred to as STIF in the paper) and its implementation. It then focuses on the validation of the method both with experimental and user evaluations. On one hand, the experimental evaluation shows that the filter can successfully correct for distortion, reverberation and cross talk between piezoelectric actuators glued to a glass surface providing 300 Hz sine-burst vibrations. On the other hand, the user study demonstrates that STIF not only improves the user's discrimination but also requires less concentration when compared to the standard method, i.e. without filtering.

2   Spatio Temporal Filtering

An actuator j with a linear response and driven with a signal $s_j(t)$, produces at a position i a displacement $u_i(t)$ given by

$$u_i(t) = s_j \otimes h_{ij}, \tag{1}$$

with $\otimes$ the convolution operator and h_{ij} the impulse response between point i and actuator j. In the frequency domain, this expression writes

$$U_i(\omega) = S_j(\omega)H_{ij}(\omega), \tag{2}$$

with $H_{ij}(\omega)$ the transfer function between point i and actuator j. When several actuators are activated simultaneously, the displacement is simply the addition of individual contributions, that is:

$$U_i(\omega) = \sum_j S_j(\omega)H_{ij}(\omega). \tag{3}$$

If we consider N actuators and N control points on the surface, this equation writes, in matrix form,

$$\begin{bmatrix} U_1 \\ U_2 \\ \vdots \\ U_N \end{bmatrix} = \begin{bmatrix} H_{11} & H_{12} & \dots & H_{1N} \\ H_{21} & H_{22} & \dots & H_{2N} \\ \vdots & \vdots & \ddots & \vdots \\ H_{N1} & H_{N2} & \dots & H_{NN} \end{bmatrix} \begin{bmatrix} S_1 \\ S_2 \\ \vdots \\ S_N \end{bmatrix}, \tag{4}$$

or in condensed form

$$\boldsymbol{U}(\omega) = \boldsymbol{H}(\omega)\boldsymbol{S}(\omega). \tag{5}$$

The idea of inverse filtering is now, for each frequency components, to proceed to a matrix inversion of $\boldsymbol{H}(\omega)$. With this inverted matrix, we then compute the driving signals $\boldsymbol{S}(\omega)$ that will produce the target displacements $\boldsymbol{V}(\omega)$ at the set of control points with the relation

$$\boldsymbol{S} = \boldsymbol{H}^{-1}\boldsymbol{V}. \tag{6}$$

Finally, the filtering can be done in the temporal domain through a convolution operation of the desired displacements $v_j(t)$ with $h_{ij}^{-1}(t)$ the inverse Fourier transform of $H_{ij}^{-1}(\omega)$.

$$s_i(t) = \sum_j v_j \otimes h_{ij}^{-1} \tag{7}$$

This filter is therefore temporal, as it operates on all frequency components, and spatial, as it takes into account the transfer function between all actuators and all control points.

3   Experimental Validation

The experimental validation was carried out on the setup depicted in Fig. 1. Four piezoelectric actuators (Ferroperm Pz27) with a 10 mm radius and 500 μm thickness were glued with epoxy (3M DP490) to the bottom side of a borosilicate glass plate with dimensions $150 \times 105 \times 0.7$ mm. The plate was fixed by a foam tape to a rigid 3D printed plastic support. Actuators were independently driven with arbitrary signals produced by an acquisition card (NI 6363 - National Instrument) and amplified to 200 V_{pp} by piezo haptic drivers (DRV8662 - Texas Instrument). A laser vibrometer (Polytec OFV-534/2570) mounted on a motorised three axis platform measured the surface displacement at the center of each actuator in the calibration and validation steps. The 16 transfer functions between the four actuators and the four positions were estimated with a swept sine technique [15]. All signals were sampled at 25 kHz.

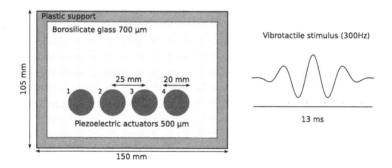

Fig. 1. Left: Setup for the experimental evaluation and user study. Four piezoelectric actuators are glued on a glass plate to produce vibrotactile stimuli. Right: waveform of the vibrotactile stimulus (4 cycles burst at a 300 Hz oscillation).

3.1   Surface Displacement

In both the experimental evaluation and user study, the target vibrotactile stimulus consisted in four cycles of a 300 Hz cosine wave modulated by a hamming window, as depicted in Fig. 1. In the first case, later referred to as the standard method, this signal is sent directly to the actuator where a stimulation is intended. The resulting displacements on top of each actuator are displayed on top of Fig. 2. On this figure, the nth row corresponds to the displacement measured on top of actuators 1 to 4 when the signal is sent to the nth actuator. The displacements on top of the driven actuators exhibit distortion caused by the electromechanical response of the actuator. The reverberation of waves into the plate also makes the actual vibration last longer than the desired waveform. Finally, because of wave propagation into the plate, significant displacements are measured on top of all the other actuators. The stimuli are thus produced

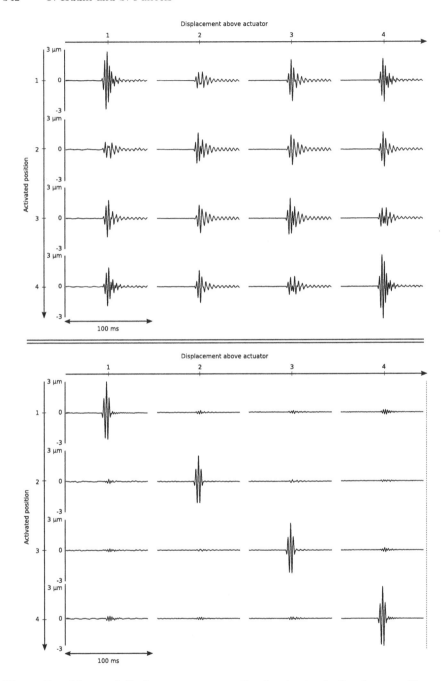

Fig. 2. Top: Measured displacements on top of each actuator in the absence of inverse filtering. The actuator at the activated position is driven directly with the waveform of Fig. 1. Bottom: Measured displacement with an inverse filter applied to the driving signals of all actuators. The filtering cancels the cross talk between activated positions and corrects for signal distortion and reverberation.

not only at the position of the activated actuators but also at any position over the plate.

In the second case, the intended vibrotactile signal is fed into the inverse filter to compute driving signals sent to all actuators. All actuators where the vibration must be controlled or cancelled are thus driven simultaneously. Figure 2 (bottom) shows the resulting displacements that are now localised on top of the desired actuators. The propagation of waves from an actuator position to others was therefore successfully estimated and compensated. The vibration waveform corresponds to the desired stimuli and has the same amplitude for all actuators, thus showing that reverberation effects and non-flat actuator responses were correctly compensated.

The spatio temporal inverse filter is therefore successful at correcting linear signal distortions and at cancelling cross talk between actuators glued to the same surface. It gives a more precise control over the stimuli and enables an independent control at different positions over the surface.

4   User Study

The purpose of this user study was to find out whether the proposed method for improving the localisation of vibrotactile stimuli was more effective in the discrimination of the stimuli and more efficient than the standard method. To that effect, two presentation methods were tested and compared: the STIF method and the standard method.

4.1   Methodology

Participants. The study was conducted with 10 participants (2f–8m), aged between 24 and 54 ($M = 31.5$, $SD = 10.2$), two of which were left-handed. Most of them were recruited within the laboratory and thus had experience with haptics technology but had never tested the prototype device or the STIF method before.

Technical Settings. The prototype device depicted in Fig. 3(a) was used in the experiment, delivering stimuli as described in Sect. 3.1. The device was placed on a table, in front of the participant, with arm rests the participant could use if he/she desired. The participants were instructed to use both the index and middle fingers of each hand and to place them onto the black circles on the device for the trials, as displayed on the figure. The noise generated by the piezoelectric actuators was subtle and could not help localise the feedback, therefore noise-cancelling methods via headphones were not used. The experimenter used a standard Windows laptop both for running the Python application controlling the feedback presentation and for logging the participants' verbal answers (see Fig. 3(b)).

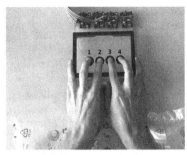 

(a) Prototype device   (b) Python Interface

Fig. 3. Experimental setup with subfigure (a) showing the participant using the prototype device and subfigure (b) depicting the interface used for playing the stimuli and recording the answers and times

Procedure. The experiment was a 2×2 (session x presentation method) within-subject repeated measures design consisting of two sessions. Each session was divided into two blocks, each testing a presentation method. The order of the blocks was counterbalanced between the participants and between the sessions to ensure the methods were tried in a different order (i.e. AB BA or BA AB with A, B standing for the different presentation methods). Each block consisted of 80 trials, accounting for 160 trials per presentation method and 320 trials in total per participant. The experiment lasted one hour on average and the participants were compensated with sweets.

In each block, the task was to identify the position/finger that received the haptic stimulus. The participants were instructed to provide the answer verbally as soon as they recognised the stimulus, which was provided only once, whilst their hands remained on the device. To accustom participants to the feedback and reduce the impact of learning effects, prior to each block, participants were presented with the haptic stimulus three times on each of the finger positions.

After the first session, the participants were asked whether they perceived a difference between the two perception methods. At the end of the last session, the participants were asked to rate on a nine-point bipolar scale which method they preferred, with minus values corresponding to the method referred to the participant as "Technique 1", which is the standard method and the positive values to "Technique 2" or the STIF method. They were also asked to rate their cognitive load for each of the methods on a continuous scale from 0 (none) to 10 (maximum effort) and more open questions about learning effects and general comments.

As for quantitative measures, the interface collected the responses and the response times. The performance was calculated on the basis of a score for correct answers out of 80. The response time was collected to provide trends about a timing difference rather than an absolute value as the answers were provided verbally by the participants and logged by the experimenter. However, as the experimenter was the same across participants, the bias introduced in the time to answer was repeated across the measurements and thus these can be used for general indication. Moreover, the interface was designed so that the answer buttons were equidistant to the play button (see Fig. 3(b)).

4.2 Results

Identification Rates.

Effect of the Method and the Session. Before choosing the appropriate statistical test, the parametric assumptions were tested to determine the normality of the distribution. Both the scores in the first session were significantly non-normal. For the second session, only the scores for the STIF method were significantly non-normal. However, for each session, the distributions of the differences between the scores for each method were normal, with for Session 1 and 2, $D(10) = 0.17$, $p > .05$. As Field [3] (Chap. 9, p. 329) points out, the main assumption for applying dependent t-tests is that "the sampling distribution of the differences between scores should be normal, not the scores themselves". Moreover, t-tests and ANOVA are considered robust for these tests by a number of researchers [2,5,14].

Therefore, a factorial 2×2 (session x presentation method) repeated-measures ANOVA was used to verify the different effects and their interaction. Pairwise Bonferroni corrected t-tests were used for post hoc tests. There were no significant effects of the session or of an interaction between the session and the conditions. However, there was a significant main effect of the type of condition, $F(1,9) = 37.64$, $p < .05$, $r = 0.90$. In fact, on average (see Fig. 4(a)), in both sessions, participants performed significantly better with the STIF method than with the standard method (see the results of the complementary t-tests in Table 1). In both cases the reported effect is very large. Thus, the results support the hypothesis that the STIF method has improved the recognition compared to the standard method.

Table 1. Results from the t-tests for the performance and response time

		Session 1				Session 2			
		Mean	SE	$t(9)$, $p < .05$	Effect	Mean	SE	$t(9)$, $p < .05$	Effect
Performance	STIF	75.80	2.08	−8.44	0.94	75.00	2.66	−3.94	0.80
	Standard	64.40	2.75			62.90	2.73		
Time	STIF	1.84	0.05	2.75	0.68	1.80	0.06	2.92	0.70
	Standard	2.07	0.10			1.98	0.08		

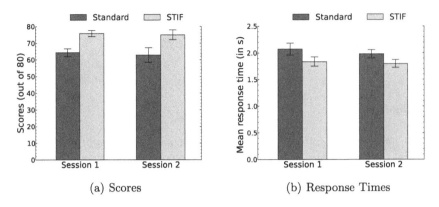

(a) Scores   (b) Response Times

Fig. 4. Performance for each method and each session in terms of correct responses and response times.

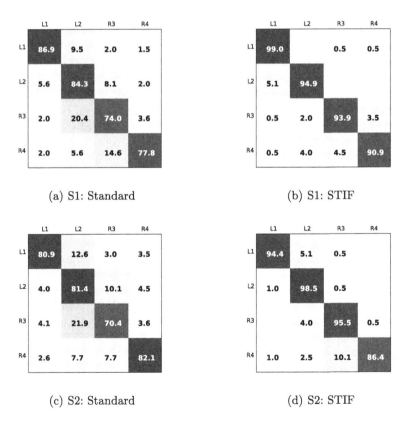

(a) S1: Standard   (b) S1: STIF

(c) S2: Standard   (d) S2: STIF

Fig. 5. Confusion matrices for each of the conditions and for each session, where L and R stands for left and right hands respectively and the numbers are the positions of the actuators.

Effect of the Hand/Fingers. Figure 5 presents the scores for each position as well as the confusion with other positions. As can be seen from Figs. 5(a) and (c), the most important confusion happened with the inner adjacent positions, i.e. for the left hand, the highest confusions were with the adjacent positions on the right side, whereas the opposite can be noticed for the right hand, with the confusions with the left adjacent positions. This can be explained by the signals that are less differentiable when the stimulus is on the inner positions, as can be seen on Fig. 2. As the scores are much improved with the STIF method, this is not observed for that technique (also see Fig. 2).

Response Times. Both the scores in the first session, $D_{Standard}(10) = 0.15$, p > .05 and $D_{STIF}(10) = 0.22$, p > .05, and the scores for the second session, $D_{Standard}(10) = 0.21$, p > .05 and $D_{STIF}(10) = 0.19$, p > .05, did not significantly differ from a normal distribution. Therefore, a factorial 2×2 (session x presentation method) repeated-measures ANOVA was used for the statistical analysis. Pairwise Bonferroni corrected t-tests were used for post hoc tests.

There was no significant interaction effect between the session and the type of condition. However, there was a significant main effect of the session on response times, $F(1,9) = 6.48$, $p < .05$, $r = 0.65$. The response times were significantly lower overall in Session 2, $M = 1.89$, $SE = 0.06$ compared to Session 1, $M = 1.96$, $SE = 0.06$. There was also a significant main effect of the type of condition, $F(1,9) = 9.54$, $p < .05$, $r = 0.72$. The response times were significantly lower overall with the STIF method ($M = 1.82$, $SE = 0.06$) compared to the standard method ($M = 2.03$, $SE = 0.08$). Complementary t-tests revealed that on average (see Fig. 4(b) and Table 1), participants answered faster with the STIF method than with the standard method in each session. In both cases the reported effect is very large. Therefore, the results support the hypothesis that the recognition is faster with the STIF method, most likely because it improves discrimination (see results in Sect. 4.2). Interestingly, participants answered faster in the second session, exhibiting a familiarisation with the process with more confidence in their answers and also possibly fatigue or boredom effects that could have enclined them to answer faster in order to finish faster. Indeed, 5 participants commented they thought they were getting better at answering when inquired about learning effects at the end of the study, while 2 mentioned that the perception remained the same, however the fatigue was increasing towards the end.

Questionnaires

Cognitive Load. At the end of the experiment, participants were asked to rate the perceived cognitive load on a continuous scale from 0-no mental workload to 10-very high mental workload. The ratings for the cognitive load for the STIF method were significantly non-normal, $D(10) = 0.30$, $p < .05$ whereas the ratings for the standard method were not deviating from normality, $D(10) = 0.24$, $p > .05$. However, the difference between the ratings was distributed normally $D(10) = 0.18$, $p > .05$, which is a sufficient condition to perform *t*-tests [3]. A repeated *t*-test showed a significant difference in the ratings for the two methods, with the STIF method demanding significantly less cognitive effort ($M = 4.00$, $SE = 0.80$) than the standard method ($M = 7.30$, $SE = 0.63$), $t(9) = 3.79$, $p < .05$, $r = 0.78$. Participants commented that with the STIF method, as the localisation of the stimuli was improved, it required less concentration.

Perceived Difference and Preferred Technique. All participants except one perceived the difference between the two techniques as soon as the second one was tested in the first block. Participants often commented that the STIF method was more precise and the vibration was more localised spatially whereas with the standard method, the sensation was more "fuzzy". This lack of precision was particularly noted for the inner positions where participants were often unsure about their replies. Funnily, one participant who tried the STIF method first even thought when experiencing the standard method that the device was broken. This is illustrated by the notable preference for the STIF technique with all the ratings on the positive side towards the STIF method, ranging between 2 and 4, except for one participant who remained neutral as he did not feel any difference between the two techniques. The average preference score is 2.9 out of 4 ($SD = 1.37$), with a mode of 4 (half of the participants gave the maximum rating) and a median of 3.5.

5   Conclusion

This paper introduced the use of Spatio Temporal Inverse Filtering (STIF) to provide localised and temporarily controlled haptic feedback through a set of discrete actuators glued to a uniform surface. Experimental measurements validated that arbitrary stimuli could be provided on top of any actuator, with improved temporal definition and without cross talk between actuators positions. The results of a user study with 10 participants support the main hypothesis that the STIF method improves the perception and localisation of the haptic stimulus both quantitatively and qualitatively. Quantitatively, it improved significantly the recognition rates and the response times. Qualitatively, the STIF method was highly preferred and demanded less cognitive effort than the standard method. Participants commented that the standard method was more "fuzzy" than the STIF technique, particularly for the inner positions while the STIF technique provided more localised feedback. The only negative points reported were about the setup which was not optimised in terms of positions of the stimuli for the study.

Although not demonstrated, the same filter could not only cancel cross talk but also produce simultaneous independent tactile feedback. Other types of actuators like coil based actuator could be employed. This method requires an array of actuators but only those at fingers positions, where the vibration must be controlled, need to be driven. Optical transparency could be achieved, despite the array of actuators, by using transparent piezoelectric actuators. An alternative would be to place those actuators behind the screen stack.

Finally, we used the same glass surface and piezoelectric actuators as in [7] for local friction rendering. A future prototype could therefore combine both modalities and provide localised vibrotactile and texture rendering on a same surface.

References

1. Benali-Khoudja, M., Hafez, M., Kheddar, A.: VITAL: an electromagnetic integrated tactile display. Displays **28**(3), 133–144 (2007)
2. Blanca, M.J., Alarcón, R., Arnau, J., Bono, R., Bendayan, R.: Non-normal data: is anova still a valid option? Psicothema **29**(4), 552–557 (2017)
3. Field, A.: Discovering Statistics Using IBM SPSS Statistics, 3rd edn. Sage Publications Ltd., Thousand Oaks (2009)
4. Graff, K.F.: Wave Motion in Elastic Solids. Courier Dover Publications, New York (1975)
5. Harwell, M.R., Rubinstein, E.N., Hayes, W.S., Olds, C.C.: Summarizing monte carlo results in methodological research: the one- and two-factor fixed effects anova cases. J. Educ. Stat. **17**(4), 315–339 (1992)
6. Hoggan, E., Brewster, S.A., Johnston, J.: Investigating the effectiveness of tactile feedback for mobile touchscreens. In: SIGCHI Conference on Human Factors in Computing Systems (CHI 2008), pp. 1573–1582. ACM (2008)
7. Hudin, C.: Local friction modulation using non-radiating ultrasonic vibrations. In: IEEE World Haptics Conference. Fürstenfeldbruck (Munich), Germany (2017)
8. Hudin, C., Lozada, J., Hayward, V.: Localized tactile feedback on a transparent surface through time-reversal wave focusing. IEEE Trans. Haptics **8**(2), 188–198 (2015)
9. Mouchtaris, A., Reveliotis, P., Kyriakakis, C.: Inverse filter design for immersive audio rendering over loudspeakers. IEEE Trans. Multimedia **2**(2), 77–87 (2000)
10. Nicolau, H., Montague, K., Guerreiro, T., Rodrigues, A., Hanson, V.L.: Holibraille: multipoint vibrotactile feedback on mobile devices. In: Web for All Conference (W4A 2015), pp. 30:1–30:4. ACM, New York (2015)
11. Pance, A., Alioshin, P., Bilbrey, B., Amm, D.T.: Method and apparatus for localization of haptic feedback, February 2013
12. Papetti, S., Schiesser, S., Frohlich, M.: Multi-point vibrotactile feedback for an expressive musical interface, Baton rouge, June 2015
13. Rantala, J., Raisamo, R., Lylykangas, J., Surakka, V., Raisamo, J., Salminen, K., Pakkanen, T., Hippula, A.: Methods for presenting braille characters on a mobile device with a touchscreen and tactile feedback. IEEE Trans. Haptics **2**(1), 28–39 (2009)
14. Schmider, E., Ziegler, M., Danay, E., Beyer, L., Bhner, M.: Is it really robust? Methodology **6**(4), 147–151 (2010)
15. Stan, G.B., Embrechts, J.J., Archambeau, D.: Comparison of different impulse response measurement techniques. J. Audio Eng. Soc. **50**(4), 249–262 (2002)
16. Stoklosa, A.: We try boschs haptic-feedback touchscreen, are touched by its effectiveness, January 2016. https://blog.caranddriver.com/we-try-boschs-haptic-feedback-touch-screen-are-touched-by-its-effectiveness/
17. Tanter, M., Aubry, J.F., Gerber, J., Thomas, J.L., Fink, M.: Optimal focusing by spatio-temporal inverse filter. i. basic principles. J. Acoust. Soc. Am. **110**(1), 37–47 (2001)

18. Visell, Y., Duraikkannan, K.A., Hayward, V.: A device and method for multi-modal haptic rendering of volumetric stiffness. In: Auvray, M., Duriez, C. (eds.) EUROHAPTICS 2014. LNCS, vol. 8618, pp. 478–486. Springer, Heidelberg (2014). https://doi.org/10.1007/978-3-662-44193-0_60
19. Woo, J.H., Ih, J.G.: Vibration rendering on a thin plate with actuator array at the periphery. J. Sound Vib. **349**, 150–162 (2015)

Haptic Applications

Reaching and Grasping of Objects by Humanoid Robots Through Visual Servoing

Paola Ardón[1,2,4]($\boxtimes$), Mauro Dragone[3,4], and Mustafa Suphi Erden[3,4]

[1] School of Mathematical and Computer Science,
Heriot-Watt University, Edinburgh, UK
Paola.Ardon@hw.ac.uk
[2] School of Informatics, University of Edinburgh, Edinburgh, UK
[3] School of Engineering and Physical Sciences,
Heriot-Watt University, Edinburgh, UK
[4] Edinburgh Centre for Robotics, Edinburgh, UK

Abstract. Visual servoing allows to control the motion of a robot using information from its visual sensors to achieve manipulation tasks. In this work we design and implement a robust visual servoing framework for reaching and grasping behaviours for a humanoid service robot with limited control capabilities. Our approach successfully exploits a 5-degrees of freedom manipulator, overcoming the control limitations of the robot while avoiding singularities and stereo vision techniques. Using a single camera, we combine a marker-less model based tracker for the target object, a pattern tracking for the end-effector to deal with the robot's inaccurate kinematics, and alternate pose based visual servo technique with eye-in-hand and eye-to-hand configurations to achieve a fully functional grasping system. The overall method shows better results for grasping than conventional motion planing and simple inverse kinematics techniques for this robotic morphology, demonstrating a 48.8% of increment in the grasping success rate.

Keywords: Robotics · Grasping · Visual servoing
Pepper humanoid robot

1 Introduction

Grasping is considered to be simple for humans, yet it is not so simple for robots expected to operate in a dynamic environment. It requires information of the object's position, shape and environment among others. Studies demonstrate that for humans most of this information is obtained through vision [1–3]. Hence, the importance of visual control techniques that allow to handle the motion of a robotic system with the information extracted from the vision sensors.

Thanks to Giovanni Claudio for his help on the use of ViSP and bridging Pepper robot with ROS.

© Springer International Publishing AG, part of Springer Nature 2018
D. Prattichizzo et al. (Eds.): EuroHaptics 2018, LNCS 10894, pp. 353–365, 2018.
https://doi.org/10.1007/978-3-319-93399-3_31

The objective of this work is to enable visual servoing (VS)-based reaching and grasping behaviours for a service robot with limited control capabilities. We demonstrated our system using a Pepper humanoid robot from Softbank Robotics [4,5].

There are many works that apply VS techniques on robots with morphologies that account for greater than 6-degrees-of-freedom (DOF) manipulators and apply stereo vision for target pose calculation such as [6–11]. However, our method uses VS techniques with the purpose of reaching and grasping on a service robot with a limited control system using a single camera [7].

The proposed approach uses Pepper's 5-DOF and a single camera located in its mouth. We combine a marker-less model based tracker (MBT) for the target object, a pattern tracking for the end-effector to deal with the inaccuracy of the robot kinematics and lack of proprioceptive sensing, and alternate posebased- visual-servoing (PBVS) with eye-in-hand-and/eye-to-hand configurations to achieve a fully functional grasping system. The time performance proves it to be suitable for real time applications, being less than a minute to complete the reaching and grasping tasks.

We demonstrate that VS can be effectively used to enable a service robot like Pepper, which has limited range of motion and poor control features, to detect and grasp objects. We test the impact of our VS implementation and demonstrate that the grasping is substantially more successful when we use VS in contrast to the case when we use only motion planning without VS. The code of the implementation is available to download in an open repository along with the guidelines for the installation of the needed modules[1]. Additionally, given the structure of the implementation, it can easily be extended to different objects and other service robots.

This paper is organized as follows: Sect. 2 explains the state-of-the-art methods for VS, Sect. 3 shows the implemented control technique and the software used for the implementation, Sect. 4 details the pattern tracking algorithm to obtain the position of the robot's end-effector and the a marker-less model based tracker that gives the object's position. Finally, Sect. 5 analyses the results and provides suggestions for future work.

2   State of the Art

In order to achieve a successful application that controls the motion of a robot we need to combine VS and robot end-effector control techniques.

Regardless of the chosen control scheme we look to reduce the error over time, $e(t)$, between the actual and desired position of the end effector with respect to the target [3]. This error is defined as:

$$e(t) = s(m(t), a) - s^*, \tag{1}$$

where $m(t)$ represents the set of visual measurements that are used to compute a vector of k visual features $s(m(t), a)$ [3]. a is the set of potential additional

---

[1] https://bitbucket.org/paolaArdon/master_thesis_vs_pepper.

data. This can be the camera intrinsic parameters or the 3D model of the object to track. And s^* is the vector that stores the desired values of the features or desired final position.

2.1   Control and Visual Servoing

VS schemes vary on how to construct s and s^* which influences on the interaction matrix L and the robot end-effector configuration. There are two main configurations for the robot end effector: (i) *eye-in-hand*, which is when the camera is attached to the moving hand, thus moves with the end-effector, and, (ii) *eye-to-hand* which is when the camera observes the target and the moving hand from a fixed position. There are mainly three types of control techniques:

- Image based VS when usually the desired position is composed of the image coordinates of different points belonging to the target.
- Pose based VS extracts the desired position from the 3D model of the object which directly depends on the camera intrinsic parameters [3].
- Hybrid VS combines the advantages of both image based visual servoing (IBVS) and PBVS techniques. However, it is highly sensitive to noise and it is computational expensive [2].

2.2   Related Work

Many approaches have been directed towards the integration and implementation of robust VS techniques for reaching and grasping behaviours. These techniques range from learning [10–13] to VS with marker-less objects using stereo vision and edge detection [14].

One of the first studies on VS [15] used a real-time tracking algorithm in conjunction with a predictive filter to allow a robotic arm to track a moving object. The work [9] proposes a method to align the end effector with the tracking target; [16] proposes new redundancy-based solutions to avoid robot joint limits of a manipulator on virtual humanoid robots, [17] applies this redundancy solution on a walking HRP2-humanoid robot. In [18] the authors present a hybrid visual servoing (HVS) control scheme for grasping that proves to be robust for real-time applications. The paper [18] shows the robustness of the system with ARMAR III arm robot; where the control scheme is based on estimating the hand position, in case of failed visual hand tracking, with the combination of visual, force and motor encoder data sensors. A similar study [19] demonstrates an application which does not rely on force sensors for the reaching and grasping but only on visual data. The paper [20] shows a combination of PBVS with a robust laser scanner that grabs features such as colour in an indoor environment. This is combined with stereo measurements that ensures the efficiency of the grasping action even if the object is unknown.

For this application we achieve a VS method that does not rely on data other than the extracted from the visual sensors and therefore do not need stereo vision for target pose calculation nor a 6-DOF manipulator. Our system can be applied on real time applications using service robots with limited morphologies for the grasping task.

3   Proposed Solution and Architecture

In this section we focus on VS for the humanoid robot Pepper for which we apply a PBVS with eye-in-hand and eye-to-hand configuration. In order to extract the visual information, we use the bottom 2D camera, located in the mouth along with the right end-effector of the robot.

The goal frame $^cM_{h*}$ is equal to the transformation defining the position of the object with respect to the camera, $^{h*}M_c$, multiplied by a constant transformation $^oM_{h*}$ [19]. This constant transformation is learned by placing the hand at the desired position with respect to the object, saving the vector h^*. The transformation defining the desired pose of the hand with respect to the camera is then obtained as:

$$^cM_{h*} = \left(^{h*}M_c \ ^cM_o \right)^{-1} \tag{2}$$

In order to reduce the error of the hand, e_h, we define the transformation matrix of the current pose, h, in relation to the desired pose, h^*, as $^{h*}M_h =^o M_{h*}^{-1} \ ^cM_o^{-1} \ ^cM_h$. The error of the current position of the hand with respect to the target is given as:

$$e_h = \left(^{h*}t_h, {}^{h*}\theta u_h \right), \tag{3}$$

where $^{h*}t_h$ represents the translation and $^{h*}\theta u_h$ the rotation control of the current position h with respect to the desired position $h*$ of the manipulator. The interaction matrix used in our approach is the one defined in [3] as:

$$L = \begin{bmatrix} ^{h*}R_h & 0_3 \\ 0_3 & L_{\theta_u} \end{bmatrix} \tag{4}$$

given that $L_{\theta_u} = I_3 - \frac{\theta}{2}[u]_\times + \left(1 - \frac{sinc\theta}{sinc^2\frac{\theta}{2}}\right)[u]_\times^2$

$^{h*}R_h$ represents the rotation matrix that determines the orientation of the current camera frame with respect to the desired frame. The control scheme is expressed in joint space as [3]:

$$\dot{q}_h = -\lambda \widehat{J_e^+}e + P_\lambda g, \tag{5}$$

where, λ is the gain of the servo, $\widehat{J_e^+}$ is a combination of the interaction matrix and the articular Jacobian of the robot [21]. e is defined as $e = s - s^*$, and J_e depends on the VS task. P_λ is the large projection operator that allows the system to perform a secondary task [21]. It is defined in [3] as: $P_\lambda = \overline{\lambda}(||e||)P_{||e||} + (2 - \overline{\lambda}(||e||))P_e$, where $P_e = (I_n - J_e^+ J_e)$ is the classical projector and $P_{||e||}$ is the new projection operator that imposes the exponential decrease of the norm of the error instead of each term of the error vector. The sigmoid function $\overline{\lambda}(\|e\|)$ is used to switch from $P_{\|e\|}$ to P_e [21]. g is a vector that defines the secondary task [19]. In our case we use it to avoid joint limits so that the velocity controller is more reliable.

This approach produces a straight trajectory in the Cartesian space guaranteeing the exponential decay in the error measurement as seen in Fig. 4a. The implementation of the PBVS for Pepper is represented in Fig. 1 where the features and the desired position are obtained from the MBT. The hand tracker, instead of coming from the robot's odometry, comes from the tracking of the patterns. The joints control in velocity is implemented through a joint velocity control package from visual servoing platform (VISP) called *pepper_control* [22].

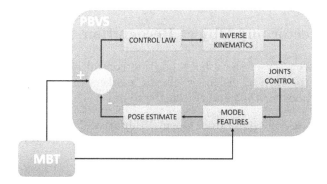

Fig. 1. Closed PBVS control scheme for Pepper humanoid robot.

3.1 System Considerations

Since Pepper's arm has only 5-DOF, in our implementation we decided to use an additional 1-DOF, the base. For the first stage, we apply a combination of PBVS with eye-in-hand configuration, where the current position is defined by the transformation matrix between the torso and the head-pitch joint, and the goal position is the one defined by the box. The second stage consists of a combination of PBVS with an eye-to-hand configuration, where the current position is the one given by the right hand and the desired position is where the hand should arrive to grasp the box. Pepper robot does not account with accurate sensor measurements, thus we added markers on the end manipulator to be tracked by vision, as explained in Sect. 4.

Secondly, a adaptive gain λ is used to reduce the time of convergence in order to speed up the servo. This parameter is manually set in the system. If its value is too high there is a risk of oscillations at the time of convergence, which compromises the precision of the method.

3.2   Software

We use Robotic Operating System (ROS) that facilitates libraries and tools to help the development of robot applications [23]. Some of the third party libraries used for this architecture are:

- **naoqi_driver** is a driver module between Aldebaran's NAOqiOS and ROS. It publishes all sensor and actuator data to handle the behaviour and grasping tasks [24,25].
- **WhyCon** libraries offer a vision-based tracker system specifically for low frame rate cameras, just as Pepper's [26].
- **vision_visp** which is a ROS node that provides VISP algorithms as ROS components [27].

4   End Effector and Object Recognition

Due to the inaccuracy of the robot's position control and sensing this task is achieved with the help of vision by placing markers on the end effector. We tested two methods for the hand tracking system:

1. Quick response code (QR) from OpenCV libraries [28–31].
2. Roundels detection from WhyCon Libraries which is the focus of this section.

Because of the low image resolution the detection and tracking is done with the roundels detection which showed to be more robust, as seen in Fig. 2. This method is solely based on the efficient detection of black and white roundels, such as the ones shown in Fig. 3d. The roundels inner and outer diameter need to be known. The tracking is divided in detections and location of these patterns [32]. The detection combines a flood-fill segmentation algorithm with an efficient thresholding technique [32].

The position of each circle, x_c, is calculated by eigen analysis, which is represented in camera coordinate frame. We are interested on getting the orientation and position of Pepper's hand. To achieve this we use four circular patterns, following the scheme in [33], that helps us define the transformation between a global x and the camera coordinate system x_c, represented as $x = T(x_c - t_0)$, where T is the similarity transformation matrix [32], and t_0 represents the coordinate system origin. In our case we have x_0, x_1, x_2, x_3 to define t_0 as the centre of mass of all the patterns. We calculate the transformation between the vector t_0 (camera coordinate frame) and matrix T (global coordinate system), which is the matrix of interest. We can see in Fig. 2 that both methods have an acceptable time frame performance, under 200 ms. However, the roundels detection update is slightly faster than the QR codes (120 ms vs 160 ms). Figure 2a shows the accuracy rate of both detection methods where the roundels method shows to be 25% higher than the QR codes, meaning that it is less likely to fail at detecting the pattern.

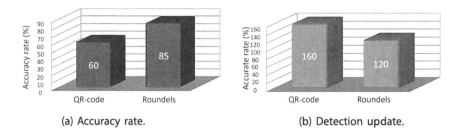

(a) Accuracy rate.   (b) Detection update.

Fig. 2. Comparison of recognition performance for both methods.

To track our object we use a 3D MBT from VISP that allows the tracking of a marker-less object when the computer-aided-design (CAD) model is provided. The MBT is a twofold process [34]: (a) to extract the features of the object we use the Kanadae-Lucas-Tomasi (KLT) method [35,36]; (b) to determine the pose of the camera to match the features [34] we use a virtual VS to match the tracked features with the obtained 3D model.

5   Results and Final Discussion

In this section we present the unified results of combining both tracking methods and the PBVS eye-hand configuration to achieve a grasping application. The system flow is shown in Fig. 3.

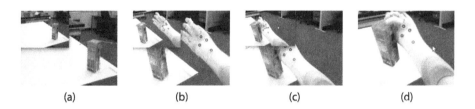

(a)   (b)   (c)   (d)

Fig. 3. PBVS with Pepper humanoid robot. Before starting the servo of the base, the system stores the homogeneous matrix relating the actual position of the robot with the stored desired position, $cMdBox$. (a) Using eye-in-hand configuration: the blue vector shows the desired position. The error e_h is continuously calculated during the servo of the base; (b) using eye-to-hand: the matrix describing the 3D position of the box with respect to the hand, ehM, and the homogeneous matrix relating the actual box position with the desired position, dhM, are calculated; (c) the error e_h for the manipulator is continuously calculated until it reaches approximately 0; and (d) the system decides it is safe to grasp the object and closes the end effector. The calculations are done using the equations of Sect. 3.

The experiments are done on Linux Trusty system using a 5 GHz network to connect to the Naoqi 2.4 version on Pepper robot. We measure the number of successful attempts. Specifically, for our purposes we consider a successful grasp if the box is not dropped by the end-effector during the reaching process and can be lifted-up. We consider a failed attempt whenever the box was dropped in the process or if it was approached correctly but the robot did not lift it up.

Figure 4a shows the exponential decrement of the error measurements in cm and rad. Where:

- $\lambda_0 = \lambda(0)$ is the gain in 0, which is for very small values of $||e||$,
- $\lambda_\infty = \lambda_{||e|| \to \infty} \lambda(||e||)$ is the gain to infinity, which is for high values of $||e||$,
- And, λ_0' is the slope of λ at $||e|| = 0$

We obtain an average error of 1 mm and 5°. In this case, the task error arrives to convergence in 17 s. A detailed image of the decay on the tasks error for the arm VS can be seen on Fig. 4b.

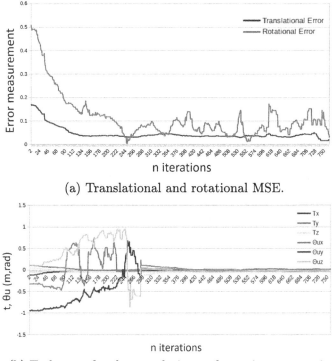

(a) Translational and rotational MSE.

(b) Task error for the translation and rotation at grasping.

Fig. 4. Error measurements for: $\lambda_0 = 0.7$, $\lambda_\infty = 0.08$ and $\lambda_0' = 3$. Convergence for the error $= 17$ s.

We want to know the right value of the parameters so that our approach is as efficient as possible. Given our implementation we care about tuning the adaptive gain values. Figure 5 shows the output of the applied velocities when we vary λ_∞. Table 1 shows a summary of the results from varying the λ_∞ parameter. Where we can compare the threshold values chosen for the translational and rotational errors, $||e_{u_t}||$ and $||e_{u_\theta}||$ respectively and their convergence time.

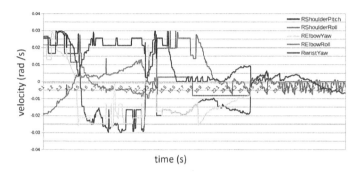

(a) $\lambda_0 = 0.06$, $\lambda_\infty = 0.02$ and $\lambda'_0 = 3$. Convergence: 30 sec.

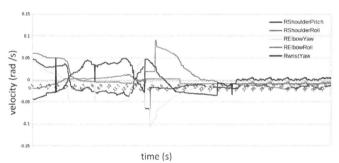

(b) $\lambda_0 = 0.06$, $\lambda_\infty = 0.07$ and $\lambda'_0 = 3$. Convergence: 25 sec.

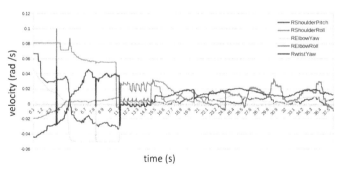

(c) $\lambda_0 = 0.06$, $\lambda_\infty = 0.1$ and $\lambda'_0 = 3$. Convergence: 12 sec.

Fig. 5. Varying λ_∞ on Pepper right hand joints.

Table 1. Summary for tuning parameters

λ_∞	$||e_{u_t}||$	$||e_{u_\theta}||$	Conv. time
0.02	1 mm	1°	30 s
0.07	4 mm	3°	25 s
0.1	6 mm	8°	12 s

From Table 1 we see that the higher the gain the faster the system arrives to convergence, which is the case for $\lambda_\infty = 0.1$ where the convergence time is only 12 s. On the down side for this case, the imprecision is higher. Table 1 is a summary of the error threshold used in the different cases of varying the gain.

In all the cases, changing our adaptive gain the system arrives to the goal position travelling a relative straight line in the Cartesian space.

5.1 Discussion

We see that the combination of the hybrid marker-less MBT for the box, the roundels tracker for Pepper's hand along with an adaptive gain for the control scheme allows for reasonable execution times, as observed on Table 1 where the longest convergence time is 30 s. Given the modularity of the implementation it can easily be adapted to other humanoid robots and objects.

Figure 5 shows the velocities discontinuities and oscillations. From the varying λ_∞ we observe that the applied velocities are high when the error exponential decrement is high and small when the error decrement is small. The oscillations are directly related to the λ_0 or λ_∞ gain value.

The greater the λ_∞ value the faster the system arrives to a convergence time, as observed in Table 1. However, the threshold error also needs to be greater so that the robot does not drop the box during the reaching process. The system achieves a precision of 1 mm and 1° when λ_∞ is really small (0.02), however it takes around half a minute to grasp the box. For our purposes we care more about precision than computational time. Therefore we use a combination of $\lambda_\infty = 0.07$ but a $\lambda_0 = 0.02$ in the final implementation. As a result, we achieve the position quite fast but reducing the oscillations when the error is small so that we have a higher precision when grasping. For this task we take 28 s to complete the arm PBVS task. Out of 25 consecutive trials Pepper successfully grasped the object 17 times. Obtaining a sensitivity rate of 80%. Which means that we rarely miss the target object.

During the different tests it was noticed that the attempts where Pepper miss-predicted the goal position were the ones where the hybrid MBT fails. Either it gets lost because of illumination, miss-calculates the features and/or is not correctly initialized by the user.

5.2   Comparing Methods

As a summary, Table 2 contrasts the reaching task by using *MoveIt!* [37] with our PBVS technique. *MoveIt!* is a state-of-the-art software for manipulation available with ROS which can be connected with Aldebaran [38] software.

Table 2. Comparing *MoveIt!* and PBVS.

	MoveIt	PBVS
Time (sec)	**2.6**	28
Success rate	23.20%	**72%**
Sensitivity rate	1	**0.8**

As observed in Table 2, the final PBVS outperforms *MoveIt!* software in success grasping rate. We demonstrated that VS can be effectively used to enable a service robot like Pepper, which has limited range of motion and low power actuation, to detect and grasp objects. We test the impact of VS in this scheme and demonstrate that the grasping is substantially more successful when we use VS compared to the case when we use only motion planning.

6   Conclusions and Future Work

This work presents a grasping application for service robots with limited range of motion and poor control features, to detect and grasp objects using a single camera for the visual feedback. We consider our application to have potential, giving room to some extensions. Some of them being:

- The biggest setback in terms of processing is the tracking of the target features through the network. Therefore a good improvement would be to integrate this tracker into the robot's central processing unit (CPU) instead of having it running on the external computer.
- Both hands could be integrated into the servo alternating their usage.
- Remove the visual markers on the hand and integrate a MBT to track its position instead.
- To initialize the target it needs to be inside the camera frame. A nice extension would be to add a tracking learning detection (TLD) tracker so that it looks for the box in the room before initializing the MBT.

References

1. Schack, T., Ritter, H.: The cognitive nature of action functional links between cognitive psychology, movement science, and robotics. Prog. Brain Res. **174**, 231–250 (2009)
2. Espiau, B., Chaumette, F., Rives, P.: A new approach to visual servoing in robotics, pp. 313–326. IEEE (1992)
3. Siciliano, B., Khatib, O.: Springer Handbook of Robotics. Springer Science & Business Media, Heidelberg (2008). https://doi.org/10.1007/978-3-540-30301-5
4. Aldebaran cartesian control. http://www.bx.psu.edu/~thanh/naoqi/naoqi/motion/control-cartesian.html. Accessed 03 Feb 2017
5. Aldebaran aldebaran - pepper robot specifications. http://doc.aldebaran.com/2-0/family/juliette_technical/. Accessed 05 May 2017
6. Lippiello, V., Ruggiero, F., Siciliano, B., Villani, L.: Preshaped visual grasp of unknown objects with a multi-fingered hand. In: 2010 IEEE/RSJ International Conference on Intelligent Robots and Systems (IROS), pp. 5894–5899. IEEE (2010)
7. Corke, P., Good, M.: Controller design for high-performance visual servoing. IFAC Proc. **26**(2), 629–632 (1993)
8. Rizzi, A.A., Koditschek, D.E.: An active visual estimator for dexterous manipulation. IEEE Trans. Robot. Autom. **12**(5), 697–713 (1996)
9. Horaud, R., Dornaika, F., Espiau, B.: Visually guided object grasping. IEEE Trans. Rob. Autom. **14**(4), 525–532 (1998)
10. Kraft, D., Detry, R., Pugeault, N., Baseski, E., Piater, J.H., Kruger, N.: Learning objects and grasp affordances through autonomous exploration. In: ICVS (2009)
11. Macura, Z., Cangelosi, A., Ellis, R., Bugmann, D., Fischer, M.H., Myachykov, A.: A cognitive robotic model of grasping (2009)
12. Levine, S., Pastor, P., Krizhevsky, A., Ibarz, J., Quillen, D.: Learning hand-eye coordination for robotic grasping with deep learning and large-scale data collection. Int. J. Rob. Res. 0278364917710318 (2016)
13. Morales, A., Chinellato, E., Fagg, A.H., Pobil, A.P.D.: An active learning approach for assessing robot grasp reliability. In: 2004 IEEE/RSJ International Conference on Intelligent Robots and Systems (IROS) (IEEE Cat. No. 04CH37566) (2004)
14. Vicente, P., Jamone, L., Bernardino, A.: Towards markerless visual servoing of grasping tasks for humanoid robots. In: 2017 IEEE International Conference on Robotics and Automation (ICRA), pp. 3811–3816. IEEE (2017)
15. Allen, P.K., Yoshimi, B., Timcenko, A.: Real-time visual servoing. In: 1991 IEEE International Conference on Robotics and Automation, Proceedings, pp. 851–856. IEEE (1991)
16. Chaumette, F., Marchand, É.: A redundancy-based iterative approach for avoiding joint limits: application to visual servoing. IEEE Trans. Robot. Autom. **17**(5), 719–730 (2001)
17. Mansard, N., Stasse, O., Chaumette, F., Yokoi, K.: Visually-guided grasping while walking on a humanoid robot. In: 2007 IEEE International Conference on Robotics and Automation, pp. 3041–3047. IEEE (2007)
18. Vahrenkamp, N., Wieland, S., Azad, P., Gonzalez-Aguirre, D.I., Asfour, T., Dillmann, R.: Visual servoing for humanoid grasping and manipulation tasks. In: Humanoids (2008)
19. Claudio, G., Spindler, F., Chaumette, F.: Vision-based manipulation with the humanoid robot Romeo. In: Humanoids (2016)
20. Taylor, G., Kleeman, L.: Grasping unknown objects with a humanoid robot (2002)

21. Marey, M., Chaumette, F.: A new large projection operator for the redundancy framework. In: 2010 IEEE International Conference on Robotics and Automation, pp. 3727–3732 (2010)
22. Inria peppercontrol. https://github.com/lagadic/pepper_control. Accessed 03 Feb 2017
23. ROS ros.org. http://wiki.ros.org/. Accessed 02 Feb 2017
24. ROS naoqi driver. http://wiki.ros.org/naoqi_driver. Accessed 03 Feb 2017
25. Inria visp naoqi bridge. http://jokla.me/software/visp_naoqi/. Accessed 01 Feb 2017
26. Irse whycon. https://github.com/lrse/whycon. Accessed 02 Feb 2017
27. ROS vision visp. https://github.com/lagadic/vision_visp. Accessed 03 Feb 2017
28. QRCode optical flow. http://docs.opencv.org/3.2.0/d7/d8b/tutorial_py_lucas_kanade.html. Accessed 03 Feb 2017
29. OpenCV opencv team. http://opencv.org/. Accessed 02 Feb 2017
30. Kato, Y., Deguchi, D., Takahashi, T., Ide, I., Murase, H.: Low resolution QR-code recognition by applying super-resolution using the property of QR-codes. In: ICDAR (2011)
31. Belussi, L., Hirata, N.S.T.: Fast QR code detection in arbitrarily acquired images. In: SIBGRAPI (2011)
32. Nitsche, M., Krajnik, T., vCizek, P., Mejail, M., Duckett, T.: Whycon: an efficient, marker-based localization system (2015)
33. INRIA whycon tracking. https://github.com/lagadic/pepper_hand_pose. Accessed 03 Feb 2017
34. Comport, A.I., Marchand, É., Pressigout, M., Chaumette, F.: Real-time markerless tracking for augmented reality: the virtual visual servoing framework. IEEE Trans. Vis. Comput. Graph. **12**, 615–628 (2006)
35. INRIA visp edge tracking. http://visp-doc.inria.fr/manual/visp-2.6.0-tracking-overview. Accessed 03 Feb 2017
36. Inria visp. https://visp.inria.fr/. Accessed 03 Feb 2017
37. ROS moveit simpple grasps. https://github.com/davetcoleman/moveit_simple_grasps/. Accessed 28 Apr 2017
38. Aldebaran movement detection. http://doc.aldebaran.com/2-4/naoqi/vision/almovementdetection.html#almovementdetection. Accessed 13 Apr 2017

LiquidReality: Wetness Sensations on the Face for Virtual Reality

Roshan Lalintha Peiris[1(✉)], Liwei Chan[2], and Kouta Minamizawa[1]

[1] Keio University Graduate School of Media Design, Yokohama, Japan
{roshan,kouta}@kmd.keio.ac.jp
[2] National Chiao Tung University, Hsin Chu, Taiwan
liwei.name@gmail.com

Abstract. We present LiquidReality, a wearable system that simulates wetness sensations directly on the user's face for immersive virtual reality applications. The LiquidReality system consists of a headmounted display integrated with thermal and vibrotactile modules that provides co-located haptic feedback with the displayed visuals. With this system, we conducted a preliminary study that evaluated nine types of thermal and thermal/vibrotactile stimuli to induce a wetness sensation on the user's face. Our results indicate that thermal only stimuli and low frequency vibrotactile stimuli (combined with thermal) induced better wetness perception. Next, using the results from this preliminary study, we evaluated the immersion enhancement when using the LiquidReality system in combination with related visuals. The results indicate that using the LiquidReality system with related visuals, enhances the level of immersion for the user.

1 Introduction

Virtual reality HMDs (head mounted displays) enable the users to immerse in virtual reality environments through the use of visual stimuli. Furthermore, research has shown that haptically simulating environmental conditions by combining additional multisensory stimuli enhances this immersive experience [6]. As such, recent research has attempted to haptically simulate conditions such as ambient temperature [13,14] and wind [14] for enhanced virtual reality experiences.

Research in neurophysiological sciences have indicated that humans perceive wetness through a combination of thermal and tactile sensations [5]. In LiquidReality, we attempt to haptically simulate wet sensations directly on the user's face, by recreating this effect with a head mounted display integrated with thermal and tactile modules (Fig. 1). The integration of thermal and vibrotactile modules directly on the HMD allows us to co-locate the haptic feedback with the visuals.

With LiquidReality, we enable applications such as enhancing the immersion in underwater virtual environments or enrich the experience of wetness related

© Springer International Publishing AG, part of Springer Nature 2018
D. Prattichizzo et al. (Eds.): EuroHaptics 2018, LNCS 10894, pp. 366–378, 2018.
https://doi.org/10.1007/978-3-319-93399-3_32

visuals such as water splashes. As such, we conducted two user studies: first, to identify the suitable stimuli for wetness perception; and second, to evaluate immersion enhancement when using the LiquidReality system with related visuals.

The main contributions of this work are (1) haptically simulating wetness sensation with thermal modules mounted on a head mounted display (2) Exploration of the thermal and vibrotactile stimuli combinations that produce a wetness sensations (3) Exploration of the enhancement of the immersion and presence when using the LiquidReality system.

1.1 Background

Many fields of research and applications use underwater simulations as a core part of their applications. For example, some virtual reality games [1] use maritime environment simulations that require the player to traverse through an underwater world. In addition, research has focused on presenting more immersive underwater environments using technologies such as cave-like simulators [17]. However, majority of these works focus more on the visual aspects and how they are presented than the haptic simulation of the underwater effects itself. The recent work by Jain et al. [8] presented a scuba diving simulator that combined wide variety of sensations that are experienced underwater. The simulations included kinesthesia, balance, temperature, and audio-visual stimuli. In this work too, the thermal sensation was used to recreate the ambient temperature change at various depths of the ocean.

As another approach, some research has focused on using pools or tanks of water to recreate the underwater effects. In AquaCAVE [17], the authors used walls of the tank for rear projection to provide the swimmer with a stereoscopic underwater environment. In addition, the work by Blum et al. [3], used waterproof head mounted displays to provide an augmented reality environment to enhance the users' experience.

In a more recent study, Shibahara [15] et al. used thermal stimuli in an effort to produce a sensation of wetness on cloths. In this study, the authors controlled the temperature and the softness of the cloth to create and 'illusion' of wetness to the user.

With, LiquidReality, we propose a similar approach based on neurophysiological principles to generate an illusion of wetness on the user's face.

2 LiquidReality

2.1 Wetness Perception

In order for haptic stimulation of wetness, it is important to understand the key aspects of wetness perception. Humans perceive wetness on a daily basis in situations such as during a shower, sweating, swimming, and drinking water. In addition, previous research has shown that, the perception of wetness is important in physiological processes such as maintaining thermal comfort and controlling of sweat glands [12]. However, unlike certain insects who are equipped with humidity receptors, humans lack hygroreceptors in their skin. As such, recent research has shown that the perception of wetness in humans occurs primarily through a combination of other primitive sensations such as thermal and tactile sensations [5].

Research by Filingeri et al. [5], indicated a simple cold-dry stimuli (a cold stimuli) could induce a wetness sensation on a user's skin. That is, when skin temperature is changed (cooled) at rate of approximately $0.5^0C/s$ or above using cold-dry stimuli, the participants perceived wetness sensations. Further research indicated that tactile stimuli such as low pressure stimuli in combination with the cold-dry stimuli further increased this perception. In addition, the research confirmed that warm-dry stimuli or only-tactile stimuli could not induce any wetness perception. An application of this concept was demonstrated recently where, an illusion of wetness was presented on dry cloth by controlling the temperature and softness of the cloth [15].

2.2 LiquidReality System

In LiquidReality, we attempt to explore cold-dry stimuli and tactile stimuli to provide wetness sensations on the user's face. As such we use a head mounted display with five thermal modules (2 cm × 1.5 cm) integrated on to the facial interface of the HMD (Fig. 1) similar to the HMD proposed in ThermoVR [13]. These modules are capable of providing thermal feedback (including hot and cold stimuli) directly on to the user's face. Each peltier module is driven by a full bridge motor controller and all modules are controlled by an Arduino Mega

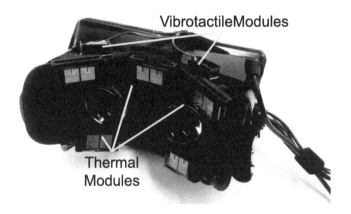

Fig. 1. LiquidReality Head Mounted Display. The Prototype System of LiquidReality that integrates five thermal modules and two vibrotactile modules

microcontroller[1] employing a closed loop PID (proportional, integral, derivative) temperature controller for accurate temperature control.

Our prelimnary investigations indicated that mounting pressure actuators would result in increased weight and the size of the integrated HMD resulting in severe discomfort to the user. As such, for the scope of LiquidReality, we used vibrotactile as the tactile stimuli. In addition, previous research has not fully investigated vibrotactile stimuli for its effects on wetness perception. We integrated two $HAPTIC^{TM} Reactor$ vibrotactile[2] modules on the body of the HMD to provide tactile stimuli to the user. During vibration, the vibrations would propagate effectively through the structure of the facial interface and the thermal modules on to the user's skin. The vibrotactile modules are driven through a tactile signal amplifier (Techtile Toolkit[3] [10]). Having the thermal and tactile stimuli mounted directly on the HMD allows us to provide co-located visual and haptic stimuli to the user.

In addition, for the scope of LiquidReality, we only consider activating *all modules (thermal and vibrotactile)* at the *same time*. Localized stimuli are not considered for the scope of this work.

3   Study 1: Evaluation of Stimuli

In this preliminary study, we evaluated providing different types of thermal and vibrotactile stimuli with LiquidReality system. The main objective of this study was to identify the stimuli or combination of stimuli (thermal and vibrotactile) that would present a high level of wetness perception while using the HMD. Specifically, we explored if the wetness perception on the facial area (with HMDs) would reproduce similar characteristics with different temperature change rates as suggested by previous research on other parts of the body. Secondly, if combining vibrotactile stimuli with thermal stimuli would effect the wetness perception when using the HMD.

Table 1. Stimuli of Study 1. ⑦ is the no stimuli condition. Thermal Stimuli start from the skin temperature. All stimuli are presented simultaneously for 1 s.

		Thermal		
		$3^0 C/s$	$1^0 C/s$	None
Vibro-tactile	175 Hz	①	④	⑧
	64 Hz	②	⑤	⑨
	None	③	⑥	⑦

---

[1] https://www.arduino.cc/en/Main/arduinoBoardMega.
[2] http://www.alps.com/prod/info/E/HTML/Actuator/.
[3] http://www.techtile.org/en/techtiletoolkit/.

Stimuli. For the study 1, we evaluated two types of thermal stimuli and two types of vibrotactile stimuli as shown in Table 1. The thermal stimuli are based on typically used and recommended thermal stimuli [7,9] and start from skin temperature and presented for 1s. Both thermal stimuli are above the wetness perception detection threshold recommended by Filengeri et al. [5]. Similarly, for the vibrotactile stimulation, we used two stimuli: 64 Hz based on recommended comfortable stimulation frequency for the head [11]; 175 Hz, a typical frequency of a typically used LRA[4] (Linear Resonant Actuator) vibrotactile motor.

During each stimulus, a blank screen was displayed in the visuals of the HMD. Based on the condition, all stimuli were provided simultaneously by actuating thermal and vibrotactile actuators at the same time for 1s. As such, in condition ⑦ (No Stimuli) condition, only the blank screen was displayed without any stimuli. The ⑦ condition was to ensure that the color of the blank screen did not influence the wetness perception.

In summary, there were two variables for the study, where THERMO ($3^0C/s$, $1^0C/s$ and None) had three conditions and VIBRO (175 Hz, 64 Hz, and None) has three conditions. The condition *None*. As a result, we provided nine stimuli conditions to the user. Each condition was repeated five times resulting in 45 stimulus presentations. All tasks were randomized for each participant.

Measurements. After each task, participants reported the Wetness Perception and the Comfort Level of the Stimuli using an interface provided in the visuals of the HMD (Fig. 2). Both measures were self-reported by the participants using a semantic differential scale. The scale ranged from -5 to $+5$ where -5 denoted an extremely dry or uncomfortable rating while $+5$ indicated an extremely wet or comfortable rating respectively. Similar scales have been adopted in wetness perception related studies by Filengeri et al. [5] and Shibahara et al. [15]. Participants were allowed to provide a score of "0" if they did not perceive any wetness or comfort level.

Procedure. 13 participants took part in the study (7 female, avg. age 26.2). During the study, the participants wore the LiquidReality system. The visuals in the HMD displayed the visual interface that was used for the study. The interface depicted in Fig. 2 was developed using Unity3D[5]. When the users click the "Start" button, the blank screen was displayed. After 3 s of the blank screen, the stimuli were provided, after which, the interface was re-displayed for the users to rate the Wetness Perception and the Comfort Level. Next, clicking "Confirm" would start a 15 s countdown after which, the process was repeated. Before each experiment, the participants were introduced to the system and went through a training phase where they experienced different conditions while familiarizing with the interface. Each experiment lasted approximately 20 min per participant.

---

[4] https://www.precisionmicrodrives.com/vibration-motors/linear-resonant-actuators-lras.

[5] https://unity3d.com/.

Fig. 2. Interface displayed on the HMD for selecting Wetness Perception and Comfort Level during the evaluation

It should be noted that due to practical reasons, the participant could see the LiquidReality system and they could have been aware that the wetness sensation was artificial. As one of the objectives was to provide wetness sensations while using the HMD, we could not blindfold the participants. However, as a part of our instructions, we indicated that the stimuli could be wet, dry or neutral (none or any other feeling). As such, they could indicate their perception from a negative (dry) to a positive (wet) or 0 (neutral).

3.1 Study 1: Results

As the results indicate, all conditions that included a thermal stimuli (3^0C/s and 1^0C/s) induced a wetness perception. In addition, all conditions that did not include thermal stimuli (⑦, ⑧, ⑨) resulted in negative values for the wetness perception (perceived as dry). There was sphericity for the interaction term, as assessed by Mauchly's test of sphericity ($X^2(2) = 3.808$, $p = 0.149$). There was no significant interaction found between THERMO and VIBRO stimuli (F2, $24 = 1.668$, $p = 0.210$). We ran paired-samples t-tests to independently compare all stimuli conditions with ⑦ (No Stimuli) condition, and found significant differences between all conditions that included thermal stimuli (①, ②, ③, ④, ⑤, ⑥) and no-stimuli conditions (all $p < 0.005$). Main effects analysis revealed a significant effect between THERMO stimuli (F1,12 $= 36.401$, $p < 0.0005$) with participants felt in general two times more wetness with Thermal 3^0C/s than Thermal 1^0C/s (2.949 vs. 1.464) across vibrotactile stimuli (with the thermal stimuli), but no effects between VIBRO stimuli (F1.233, 14.798 $= 3.102$, $p = 0.93$) (Fig. 3).

When comparing all stimuli conditions with ⑦ (No Stimuli) using paired-samples t-tests, we found all stimuli that included thermal stimuli ($p < 0.05$), except the two 175 Hz conditions ① ④ ($p = 0.117, p = 0.464$) were significantly perceived with higher comfort levels than ⑦ (No Stimuli). In other words, participants general felt less comfort with 175 Hz stimuli.

In summary, both thermal stimuli (3^0C/s and 1^0C/s) induced a wetness perception regardless of the vibrotactile stimuli. In addition, the vibrotactile only

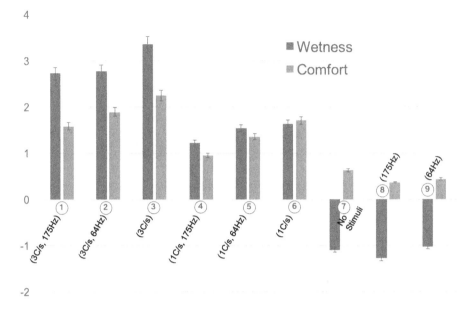

Fig. 3. The Wetenss Perception scores and Comfort Level Scores for the different stimuli conditions.

stimuli could not generate any wetness perception for the users. This result confirms the previous wetness perception results where cold dry stimuli above $0.5^0C/s$ would generate a wetness perception on the user [5]. In addition, it can be observed that while $3^0C/s$ produced higher levels of wetness while $1^0C/s$ produced relatively lower levels of wetness perception. When considering vibrotactile stimuli, it was observed that all conditions except for 175 Hz conditions (①️ and ④️) had significantly high comfort levels.

We conducted an informal interview with the participants following the preliminary study to gain more insights to the observerations. Some of the feedback included one participant mentioning *"Although I felt the stimuli was wet, the vibration at times was confusing"*. Another participant mentioned *"I liked the low frequency vibration. It reminded me of rain. But the high frequency vibration felt more like a new experience rather than a liquid situation"*. Out of the combined stimuli, many participants mentioned that ②️, ⑤️ (lower frequency conditions) conditions felt more relevant to wetness related events.

Thus, from this preliminary study, we observe the following

- Both thermal-only conditions (③️ and ⑥️) induced a wetness perception better than when combined with vibrotactile stimuli.
- The wetness perception was higher for ③️ condition and lower for the ⑥️. Thus, the rate of temperature was found to have influenced the level of wetness perception
- Based on results and participant feedback, the lower frequency vibrotactile stimuli ②️, ⑤️ was preferred for representing wetnessl related events.

4   Study 2: Immersion Experience with LiquidReality

The main objective of this study was to qualitatively evaluate the immersion experience of the presence with the use of the LiquidReality system. Therefore, the stimuli selected from the first study was presented with related visuals in order to identify the immersion experience enhancement with the LiquidReality system.

4.1   Experimental Design

We presented two different visuals (SCENARIO conditions) that could associate the selected stimuli. The visual scenarios were selected to represent a variety of wetness related scenarios such as immersing in a wet environment and impact of water on the skin. The SCENARIO conditions are,

- UNDERWATER Scenario: Here, we presented an underwater environment to the user as seen in Fig. 4(a). In this scenario, the user is able to travel (similar to diving) through the environment. The UNDERWATER scenario represents immersing in a wet environment.
- SPLASH Scenario: In the splash scenario (Fig. 4(b)), we used visuals that simulated water splashing the viewer's face.

Stimuli. Based on the results from the previous study, this study consists of three STIMULI conditions: *THERMAL (Only thermal Stimuli); VIBTHERMAL (Thermal and Vibrotactile Stimuli); NONE (No Stimuli: visuals only)*. The thermal stimuli $3^0C/s$ was presented based on the content of the scenarios. The vibrotactile stimuli was 64 Hz stimuli. The thermal and vibrotactile stimuli were synchronized based on the content of the visuals as listed here.

- UNDERWATER Scenario: In this scenario, the stimuli were provided every three seconds. All modules were actuated simultaneously similar to the previous study. We selected the $3^0C/s$ stimuli as the thermal stimuli for this scenario to represent the fully immersive nature of the scenario.

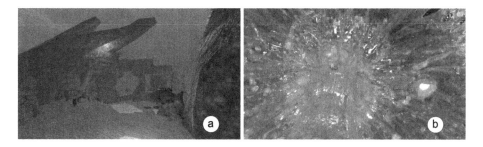

Fig. 4. Usage Scenarios: (a) UNDERWATER senario: user is able to explore virtual underwater environments while feeling the immersive wetness sensations of the underwater environment; (b) SPLASH scenario: user can see and directly feel the splash of water on the face

- SPLASH Scenario: In this scenario, the stimuli were started at the estimated point of impact of the wet splash on the face. All modules were actuated simultaneously similar to the previous study. We selected the $3^0C/s$ stimuli as the thermal stimuli for this scenario.

All the three SCENARIO conditions were presented under the three STIM-ULI conditions. Therefore, this experiment consisted of 6 randomized tasks (3-stimuli conditions, 2-scenarios). All tasks were presented for 15 s.

Measurements. We used a questionnaire consisting of 15 questions adopted from the Presence Questionnaire by Witmer and Singer [16]. The questions in the presence questionnaire are focused on four factors: sensory factors, control factors, realism factors and distraction. However, for the LiquidReality system, we only included questions that related to the scope of our task: sensory and realism (subscale) factors. In addition, we included questions that related to wetness perception to identify the effect of the feedback with the visuals and in addition, to identify if the feedback was perceived as in fact wetness and not ambient temperature. As our task did not contain any action to perform, we did not include questions relating to other factors.

Procedure. 15 participants (different from the previous study) took part in the study (7 female, avg. age 26.6). During the study, the participants wore the LiquidReality system and experienced each task condition. Any instructions relating to the visuals or stimuli were not provided. The participants filled up the questionnaire at the end of each task. The complete study lasted for approximately 15 min per participant.

4.2   Study 2: Results

The results of the Immersion Experience using LiquidReality are shown in Fig. 5. As observed, overall immersion experience is highest under the THERMAL condition.

The results were analyzed using repeated measures ANOVA. All post hoc comparisons used Bonferroni corrected confidence intervals. The overall trend of the data on each factor is displayed in Fig. 5.

There was a significant main effect of STIMULI ($F_{2,28} = 130.360, p < 0.0005$) and pairwise tests show that both THERMAL and VIBTHERMAL were greater than NONE (5.20 vs. 2.49, $p < 0.0005$; 4.9 vs. 2.49, $p < 0.0005$). The difference between THERMAL and VIBTHERMAL was not significant ($p = 0.214$).

There was a significant main effect of STIMULI ($F_{1.283,17.959} = 13.607$, $p < 0.001$) and pairwise tests show that THERMAL was greater than NONE (4.95 vs. 3.66, $p = 0.0005$), and also greater than VIBTHERMAL (4.95 vs. 4.36, $p = 0.005$). No significant difference between NONE and VIBTHERMAL was found ($p = 0.136$).

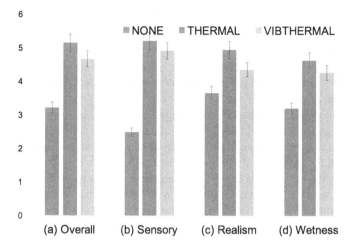

Fig. 5. Participant ratings of the immersion experience study (on a scale 0-7): (a) Overall Immersion Levels (b) Senory Factor Levels (c) Realism Levels (d) Wetness Perception Levels. All results are averaged for UNDERWATER and SPLASH scenarios.

Furthermore, the results showed that the wetness perception was enhanced with under the THERMAL and VIBTHERMAL conditions. As the results indicate (Fig. 5), the THERMAL condition significantly enhanced the presence levels overall under the sensory and realism factors wetness perception compared to the NONE condition. In addition, This was observed in the participant feedback where one participant said that *"I really liked the underwater visual when there was no vibration. It felt like I was moving in there"*. The VIBTHERMAL condition significantly enhanced the presence under the sensory and involvement factors compared to the NONE condition. We received positive and negative feedback for the VIBTHERMAL condition. One participant remarked that *"I really didn't like it. The vibration made me aware that I was wearing your system. It was really nice when you did not have vibration"*. However, four participants mentioned that they enjoyed the SPLASH scenario under the VIBTHERMAL condition. One participant remarked *"How did you spray water on my face?!"*. *"It was like taking a shower while looking at the shower head!"* was one of the comments by one participant. Thus, from this study, we observe that the immersion level is best enhanced under the THERMAL condition when using the LiquidReality system with related visuals. However, although not statistically proven, we recommend that vibrotactile stimuli may be used for visual scenarios where the impact of water on the skin could be simulated.

5   Discussion

The overall results indicate that the LiquidReality system was able to simulate wet sensations and enhance the immersion of the user with related virtual reality content. We confirmed that with the LiquidReality system, cold dry thermal stimuli are required for generating wetness perceptions. That is, vibrotactile stimuli alone could not generate any wetness perceptions for the participants. We also observed that, if vibrotactile feedback is used, lower frequency vibrotactile stimuli were preferred by the users. However, we present few limitations that we wish to address in our future works.

It should be noted that the stimuli selected in the preliminary study are as a starting point and are limited. However, in our next steps we wish to expand the range of the selected stimuli such as lower frequencies for vibration and different thermal ranges for inducing a wetness sensation.

The main task of our 2nd study (Immersion Experience study) was limited to visual and haptic simulations and did not contain any action as a part of the task. As such, we did not consider the control factors for the immersion experience. One participant mentioned this under the VIBTHERMAL condition and UNDERWATER scenario: *"I liked it, but it was like a 4D cinema"*. Therefore, as our immediate next step, we wish to explore the perception of wetness during task performance.

Our current approach did not consider localized wetness stimuli as we actuated all thermal and vibrotactile modules together. Localized actuation could have the benefit of creating simulation effects such as rain and wind with the appropriate visuals. Furthermore, providing temporal stimuli from individual thermal modules has shown to create a moving thermal effect on the skin [4]. Such phenomena could benefit in producing moving wetness effects on the user's skin with the relevant visuals. We wish to implement these localized and moving characteristics with the LiquidReality system in order to simulate effect such as rain and moving droplets on the skin.

Another focus of our future work is to explore other forms of stimuli that can induce wetness sensations. For example, electrotactile stimuli has shown to evoke some wetness sensations [2] as well. As such, combinations of other stimuli such as pressure, thermal, electrotactile have the potential to further simulate other wetness and even liquid properties such as viscosity and density.

6   Conclusion

LiquidReality describes an initial attempt to simulate wetness sensations on the face while using a HMD integrated with thermal and vibrotatile modules. In our first study, we indicate that the thermal only conditions (3^0C/s and 1^0C/s) simulates the best sensations while combined lower frequency vibrotactile stimuli (64 Hz) were preferred for scenarios such as a splash. As such, we demonstrated that when combined with related visuals such as underwater and wet splashes, the LiquidReality system enhanced the immersion of the user.

Acknowledgment. This work was supported by the JSPS Kakenhi (JP18K18094) and the JST ACCEL Embodied Media project (JPMJAC1404), Japan.

References

1. Abzu (2016). http://www.abzugame.com/
2. Bach-y-Rita, P., Kercel, S.W.: Sensory substitution and the human machine interface. Trends Cognit. Sci. **7**(12), 541–546 (2003). http://www.sciencedirect.com/science/article/pii/S1364661303002900
3. Blum, L., Broll, W., Müller, S.: Augmented reality under water. In: SIGGRAPH 2009: Posters, SIGGRAPH 2009, pp. 97:1–97:1. ACM, New York (2009). http://doi.acm.org/10.1145/1599301.1599398
4. Chen, Z., Peiris, R.L., Minamizawa, K.: A thermal pattern design for providing dynamic thermal feedback on the face with head mounted displays. In: Proceedings of the Eleventh International Conference on Tangible, Embedded, and Embodied Interaction, TEI 2017, pp. 381–388. ACM, New York (2017). http://doi.acm.org/10.1145/3024969.3025060
5. Filingeri, D., Fournet, D., Hodder, S., Havenith, G.: Why wet feels wet? a neurophysiological model of human cutaneous wetness sensitivity. J. Neurophysiol. **112**(6), 1457–1469 (2014)
6. Gugenheimer, J., Wolf, D., Eiriksson, E.R., Maes, P., Rukzio, E.: Gyrovr: simulating inertia in virtual reality using head worn flywheels. In: Proceedings of the 29th Annual Symposium on User Interface Software and Technology, UIST 2016, pp. 227–232. ACM, New York (2016). http://doi.acm.org/10.1145/2984511.2984535
7. Halvey, M., Wilson, G., Brewster, S.A., Hughes, S.A.: Perception of thermal stimuli for continuous interaction. In: CHI EA 2013, pp. 1587–1592 (2013)
8. Jain, D., Sra, M., Guo, J., Marques, R., Wu, R., Chiu, J., Schmandt, C.: Immersive scuba diving simulator using virtual reality. In: Proceedings of the 29th Annual Symposium on User Interface Software and Technology, UIST 2016, pp. 729–739. ACM, New York (2016). http://doi.acm.org/10.1145/2984511.2984519
9. Jones, L.A., Ho, H.N.: Warm or cool, large or small? the challenge of thermal displays. IEEE Trans. Haptics **1**(1), 53–70 (2008)
10. Minamizawa, K., Kakehi, Y., Nakatani, M., Mihara, S., Tachi, S.: Techtile toolkit: a prototyping tool for design and education of haptic media. In: Proceedings of the 2012 Virtual Reality International Conference, VRIC 2012, pp. 26:1–26:2. ACM, New York (2012). http://doi.acm.org/10.1145/2331714.2331745
11. Myles, K., Kalb, J.T.: Vibrotactile sensitivity of the head, U.S. Army Research Laboratory (2009)
12. Parsons, K.: Human Thermal Environments: The Effects of Hot, Moderate, and Cold Environments on Human Health, Comfort, and Performance, 3rd edn. CRC Press Inc., Boca Raton (2014)
13. Peiris, R.L., Peng, W., Chen, Z., Chan, L., Minamizawa, K.: Thermovr: exploring integrated thermal haptic feedback with head mounted displays. In: Proceedings of the 2017 CHI Conference on Human Factors in Computing Systems, CHI 2017, pp. 5452–5456. ACM, New York (2017). http://doi.acm.org/10.1145/3025453.3025824
14. Ranasinghe, N., Jain, P., Tolley, D., Karwita, S., Yilei, S., Do, E.Y.L.: Ambiotherm: simulating ambient temperatures and wind conditions in vr environments. In: Proceedings of the 29th Annual Symposium on User Interface Software and Technology, UIST 2016 Adjunct, pp. 85–86. ACM, New York (2016). http://doi.acm.org/10.1145/2984751.2985712
15. Shibahara, M., Sato, K.: Illusion of wet sensation by controlling temperature and softness of dry cloth. In: Bello, F., Kajimoto, H., Visell, Y. (eds.) EuroHaptics 2016. LNCS, vol. 9774, pp. 371–379. Springer, Cham (2016). https://doi.org/10.1007/978-3-319-42321-0_34

16. Witmer, B.G., Singer, M.J.: Measuring presence in virtual environments: A presence questionnaire. Presence: Teleoper. Virtual Environ. **7**(3), 225–240 (1998). https://doi.org/10.1162/105474698565686
17. Yamashita, S., Zhang, X., Rekimoto, J.: Aquacave: Augmented swimming environment with immersive surround-screen virtual reality. In: Proceedings of the 29th Annual Symposium on User Interface Software and Technology, UIST 2016 Adjunct, pp. 183–184. ACM, New York (2016). http://doi.acm.org/10.1145/2984751.2984760

A Classroom Deployment of a Haptic System for Learning Cell Biology

Ozan Tokatli[1]([✉]), Megan Tracey[2], Faustina Hwang[1], Natasha Barrett[3], Chris Jones[3], Ros Johnson[4], Mary Webb[2], and William Harwin[1]

[1] Biomedical Engineering, School of Biological Sciences,
University of Reading, Reading, UK
o.tokatli@reading.ac.uk

[2] School of Education, Communication and Society,
King's College London, London, UK

[3] Biomedical Sciences, School of Biological Sciences,
University of Reading, Reading, UK

[4] The Abbey School, Reading, UK

Abstract. The use of haptic systems in the classroom for enhancing science education is an underexplored area. In the education literature, it has been reported that certain concepts in science education are difficult for students to grasp and, as a result, misconceptions can be formed in the students' knowledge. We conducted a study with 62 Year 8 (typically 12–13 years old) students who used a haptic application to study cell biology, specifically the concept of diffusion across a cell membrane. The preliminary analysis of the feedback from the students suggests opportunities for haptic applications to enhance their learning, and also highlights a number of points to consider in the design of the application, including the choice of haptic interface and the design of the virtual environment.

Keywords: Haptic and education · Haptic diffusion simulation
Haptic rendering

1 Introduction

Education and skills training provide a key application area for haptic technology, yet provides challenge that range from control and stability, through to haptic rendering and pedagogy. Medical, veterinary and dental skills training forms the core of much research in this domain [14,20]. Recently authors have begun to explore the use of haptic devices in engineering education at university level [5,9,15,16,18]. A third group that may benefit from haptic principles in education are students in secondary education (that is in the age range of approximately 11 to 18 years old). Scientific concepts are sometimes particularly difficult to grasp and a haptic approach for this constituency may afford students a chance to use a 'hands-on' approach to learn and test principles across a range of subjects.

© Springer International Publishing AG, part of Springer Nature 2018
D. Prattichizzo et al. (Eds.): EuroHaptics 2018, LNCS 10894, pp. 379–389, 2018.
https://doi.org/10.1007/978-3-319-93399-3_33

2   Background

Technology enhanced learning (TEL) is a general term that is applied widely in secondary school education. A wide range of technologies from mobile computing to virtual reality installations are considered within TEL. However educational content has largely been provided as a two dimensional representation, and interaction when provided to the students has been either touch screen gestures, or mouse and keyboard interactions. But there is a growing interest in visualising 3-D structures, with most work centred on biology ranging from cell structures to the cardiovascular system [3, 10, 11]. Haptic interfaces can offer a natural way to interact and explore this rich 3-D learning environment since it encourages visual and tactile (haptic) interactions and may facilitate student cooperation as well as providing students with opportunities to hypothesise and explore complex scientific concepts.

In science education, hands-on practical work, in which individuals or small groups of students manipulate the objects or materials they are studying, has often been highly-valued by teachers as a pedagogical approach that motivates students and helps to develop their understanding. The benefits of practical work in science education include enhancing the learning of scientific knowledge, challenging students' misconceptions of scientific ideas and processes, teaching laboratory skills, enabling insight into and expertise in scientific method as well as stimulating students' interest and increasing motivation to study science beyond school [13]. In some areas of science a rich multi-sensory learning experience can be achieved using physical objects but many areas involve visualising structures and processes that cannot easily be observed directly, or for which cost or ethical considerations prove prohibitive.

It has long been recognised that the ability to visualise and to manipulate objects in the imagination is a crucial skill for learning science (for example see the review of 3D visualisation in chemistry [21]) but this is not easily achieved through the 2-D representations and static 3-D models frequently used in science classrooms [23]. Technology enhanced learning (TEL) can support the development of visualisation skills [17], the learning of difficult concepts and enable hypothesis testing in areas of science learning where direct manipulation of real-world objects is not possible [19, 23]. However TEL in science has mainly consisted of simulations, animations, modelling, measurement and control devices and online learning environments, where the interaction remains largely one of mouse clicks and windows menus, an interface method that is poorly-suited for 3D interactions [8].

Haptic interfaces are synonymous with the haptic sense, that is a sensory-motor interaction, that underlies natural interactions and helps to calibrate visual cues [7]. Haptic technologies give the learner a sensation of kinaesthetic feedback in conjunction with auditory and visual sensory input while the learner is engaged in the cognitive processing necessary to learn a procedure.

3   Curriculum and Content

The use of visualisation tools in school is a natural consequence of the steady improvement in computers. The Abbey School, Reading introduced 3D stereo projectors into their teaching in 2009 and has since used it at specific points in their biology curriculum [10]. The students are given shutter glasses during their lesson and the software allows the teacher to manipulate 3D models of relevant biological simulations via a 3D mouse, thus allowing students to appreciate the spatial relationships between features.

In a small trial run in 2010, students in their first year at the school (aged 11) were introduced to cell structures either via traditional teaching, or via a lesson that included the chance to use shutter glasses to observe a cell model that the teacher could manipulate. The post test was to construct a cell and the teachers observed a strong correlation between students observing the stereoscopic cell model and their subsequent ability to visualise the cell in three dimensions [10,11].

The complexity, scale and importance of cell biology makes it an interesting domain to introduce better interaction with content via haptic interactions. The problems experienced by students in visualising the three dimensional nature of cells may be a consequence of the difficulty of making direct observation of cell processes. Thus most educational content is in terms of cross sectional schematics, or observations via a light microscope, and although more educational material is now available as interactive websites [2] or high quality animations [4] these still do not allow students to explore on their own terms.

In this paper we are presenting a cell simulation that allows students to observe the particle motion and interact with particles diffusing through the cell membrane. We hypothesise that the proposed haptic learning approach can help to reinforce specific educational concepts and can foster collaborative and active learning.

4   Experimental Setup

4.1   Multi-finger Haptic System

The experimental setup, shown in Fig. 1, supports a pair of students, designated a *pilot* and a *co-pilot*, to work collaboratively. The pilot, who wears a head-mounted display (an Oculus Rift for this study) and is immersed into the virtual world, interacts with the virtual environment using the haptic interface. The co-pilot shares the same view as the pilot but using a computer screen, and uses the keyboard for certain interactions such as application controls.

The haptic interface setup consists of two Phantom robots [12]. The device is controlled by a single hand (either left or right) and the fingers of the user (thumb and index fingers) are attached to the Phantom robots by thimble linkages which allow 3 DoF rotation. The multi-finger haptic interface allows 5 DoF manipulation of objects. The location of each finger in space is calculated using the forward kinematics of the robot. However, there is no orientation sensing for the fingers of the user and so the rotation of virtual objects along the axis connecting the fingers is not possible. The workspace dimensions of the haptic device are 30 cm along the x-axis, 23 cm along the y-axis and 40 cm along the z-axis. When manipulating an object with two fingers, the device allows rotations of 360° about the x-axis, 180° about the y-axis and 180° about the z-axis.

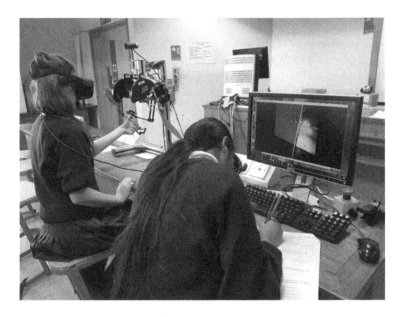

Fig. 1. The multi-finger haptic interface used by the pilot while the co-pilot is working on the worksheet. The device is controlled by a single hand where the fingers of the user (thumb and index fingers) are attached to the robots by a thimble.

One of the mechanical design challenges of the haptic interface is achieving a flexible solution for attaching various sizes of fingers to the robots of the haptic interface. This problem becomes significant as the target group in the experiments is boys and girls of age around 12 who have a wide range of finger and thumb diameters. The thimble design is used in Fig. 1 to attach the student's finger to the haptic interface. This design provides flexibility for a wide range of finger sizes and aims to ensure that the finger is firmly attached while not being uncomfortable to the user.

4.2   The Virtual Environment

In this project, we created a virtual environment to simulate diffusion across the cell membrane and a concentration gradient for particles at cellular level (Fig. 2). In this virtual environment, the planar object dividing the world into two halves represents the cell membrane. The texture of this object depicts the lipid bilayer which is the building blocks of the membrane. White objects embedded into the membrane represent membrane proteins and the channels which are used to transport certain molecules/particles from one side of the membrane to the other. These structures are freely floating within the membrane and the student moving them feels a resistive force in response to movement. The interior of the cell (cytoplasm) and the outside of the cell (extracellular space) are labelled to help the students relate the virtual environment to their prior cell knowledge. The virtual environment contains various particles (Fig. 2 is depicting oxygen (O_2) and carbon dioxide (CO_2). Other particles in the environment are sodium (Na), potassium (K) and glucose ($C_6H_{12}O_6$)) which are moving under a random force to represent the Brownian motion of the particles. The choice of particle types is based on the biology curriculum of Year 8 students, hence other particles are omitted for the virtual environment. While the cell membrane is transparent to O_2 and CO_2, *i.e.* they can pass freely through the membrane, the other particles are not free to pass through the membrane. As a result the particle will bounce back if they are forced by the user. For these particles, specialised channels are embedded into the cell membrane and used for transporting the particles. GLUT, the glucose transporter, as well as sodium/potassium channels are included into the virtual environment. Finally, the red and blue cubes in the virtual environment are the haptic cursors which follow the movement of the user's fingers.

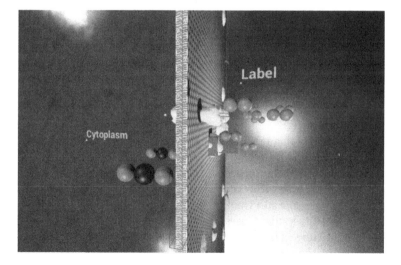

Fig. 2. The virtual environment used in the experiments. The cell membrane divides the world into two halves where the left hand side is the interior of the cell (cytoplasm) and the right hand side is the outside of the cell (extracellular fluid). Oxygen and carbon dioxide molecules are depicted in the figure. Membrane proteins are shown "floating" in the cell membrane. The "Label" shown in the figure is a place holder where the name of the particle grabbed by the user.

The virtual environment was created using Unreal Engine with a Toia add-on developed by Generic Robotics (http://www.genericrobotics.com/). Toia is a haptic add-on that bridges the gap between the graphical capabilities of Unreal Engine and haptic interfaces. It includes drivers for a range of haptic devices including Phantom, Falcon, Omega, W5D. Toia includes a variety of haptic rendering algorithms, including the extended friction cone algorithm for multi-finger haptic rendering. The development environment enables fast prototyping and high quality graphics with high performance graphical rendering.

5   Experimental Procedure

The broad aims of this research are to investigate the impact that virtual environments with haptics have in the classroom and to understand their effectiveness in supporting students' learning. As justified in Sect. 1, this study focuses on biology curriculum, more specifically the concept of diffusion which is taught to Year 8 students.

The preliminary results which is reporting students' responses to interacting with the haptic system (e.g. ease of use, areas for improvement), as this is an important aspect of likely uptake and hence the system's potential to impact learning are presented in this paper. This section describes the procedure for the research study in full, although the following Results section presents findings just from a subset of the data, specifically interviews with the students about their experiences of using the system.

The study consists of three parts. In the first part, the student was given a biology and three psychometric tests. This biology test (*pre-test*), consists of questions on fundamental biology knowledge and diffusion. The aim of the pre-test is to measure the student's knowledge and reveal misconceptions relating to diffusion; moreover the results of the test are used to measure the learning of the student after the second part of the study which is the hands-on session with the haptic interface.

In addition to the biology pre-test, the student is given 3 psychometric tests: block design test [6], fine dexterity test [1] and spatial reasoning test [22]. The block design test requires the subject to match the pattern of the blocks to the reference patter by aligning the correct faces of 9–12 blocks. The aim of this test is to measure the spatial visualisation and motor skills of the student. For the fine dexterity test, student uses his/her fingers to put washers on pegs in a fixed amount of time. This test measures the manipulative dexterity of the student. Finally, in the spatial reasoning test, the student is given the view of a three dimensional object from different angles and asked to select the correct shape/geometry from the given shapes/objects. This test measures the spatial understanding of the student.

In the second part, two students form a pair and work on the virtual environment using the haptic interface described in Sect. 4.1. Instructions about the task and the questions to be answered are given in a worksheet, and students are asked to work through the activity as independently as possible. This format was intended to be similar to how students would typically carry-out experiments in their biology classes. During this part of the study, students interactions with the system and with each other are recorded on video and their voices are additionally captured by a dictaphone. Moreover, the researchers observe each pair and take notes on the interaction of the students with each other, the haptic system and the virtual environment.

In third and the final part of the study, the student is given another biology test, which will be referred to as the *post-test* and the questions are on fundamental biology knowledge and diffusion. After the post test, each pair were interviewed about their experiences with the haptic interface, exploring which aspects they particularly liked, found easy or difficult, which aspects they would change, and ease of collaborating as a pair using the system. The interviews also probed what the students had learned about cell biology during the activity, and how working collaboratively in a pair supported their learning. The interviews are audio recorded.

62 Year 8 students (typically 12–13 years old), 34 boys and 28 girls, participated in the study. Students had experience of conducting traditional biology experiments as a part of their curriculum, however none of the participants had used haptic interfaces before nor had experience of performing virtual experiments on cells. A minority of students had familiarity with head-mounted displays and indicated that they had previously tried the technology.

The study was reviewed according to the research ethics procedures of King's College London, and was given a favourable ethical opinion for conduct. The parents of each student provided written informed consent, including explicit consent for audio and video recording, and each student also provided written assent.

6   Results

The interviews were transcribed, and the parts of the interviews that related to students' interactions with the haptic system were examined for key points.

6.1   Which Aspects of Interaction Did Students Find Easy?

Students reported that they found the system *easy to use* and *easy to control*. Comments on ease of use referred to the usability of the haptic interface, noting that the multi-finger haptic interface in this study allows effortless manipulation of the objects in the virtual environment. On the other hand, comments relating to ease of control referred to the user interface designed for the co-pilot. Students mentioned that application controls such as adding more particles, slowing down and freezing particle motion was easily done with the keyboard short-cuts.

6.2   Which Aspects of Interaction Did Students Find Difficult?

The majority of the students mentioned that the size of the objects in the virtual environment was crucial for manipulation and commented that small objects, like O_2, were not easy to grab especially if the object was dynamic.

Some students noted some discomfort with the thimble design mentioned in Sect. 4.1. They indicated that the thimble would not be very comfortable for use over a longer time period, and also that putting on the thimble, *attaching the finger to the haptic robot*, should be possible without a help from another person.

6.3 What Would Students Change About the VR and Haptic System?

The majority of students stressed two points: a virtual environment which they can walk around and a haptic interface which has greater workspace. These responses reflect students' desire for greater immersion in the virtual environment, without physical (or mechanical) limitations.

The cursor representation was another important point mentioned by the students. Instead of using red and blue cubes, one pair suggested using 3D finger models in the virtual environment, so that the system would look more realistic: *"I think if I was being really pernickety, I would probably go, instead of having like squares for the fingers, I'd maybe have something more finger like, so it was easier to sort of accept that those are your fingers."*

Manipulation with two hands and using more fingers for manipulation were also frequently mentioned in the interviews. One pair mentioned that a glove-like haptic interface might be better-suited for these kind of applications.

6.4 How Easy Was It to Work Collaboratively?

Students mentioned that they found it easy to collaborate using the haptic application. They noted that sharing the same view with the pilot and having the control of the keyboard for interacting with the virtual environment eased collaboration for the co-pilot.

6.5 Were There Any Barriers to Working Together Effectively?

Majority of the students argued that the head-mounted display that the pilot was wearing isolated him/her from the environment; therefore, the communication between the pilot and the co-pilot was harder than face-to-face communication. This is illustrated by the following excerpt of an exchange between the interviewer (IV), and two students (SP1 and SP2):

IV	Okay. Anything else you found easy?
SP2	Yes, probably being a co-pilot is much more less stressful.
IV	Oh really.
SP2	Yes.
IV	Okay. But you do agree with that SP1 ?
SP1	Well, it's quite hard to communicate what you want the guy to do, and when you're co-pilot he's got the headset on.

On the other hand, from the co-pilot's point of view, not being able to point out an object to the pilot, who is wearing the head-mounted display, was considered as a disadvantage in terms of collaboration.

7   Discussion

Haptic interfaces have been shown to be helpful for learning new skills such as training surgeons. However, using a haptic interface in the classroom for supporting the learning of science subjects has not been explored as extensively. In this work, using biology education as the background, we tested a haptic application and observed how it was used by the students.

We have observed that a haptic application for enhancing learning in a classroom has to be designed very carefully. The important parameters for a successful haptic application in the classroom are the mechanical design of the haptic interface, the usability of the user interface, usability of the graphical display components, and the design of the virtual environment.

The mechanical design of the haptic interface is an important parameter for a successful haptic application since it enables the student to discover the environment so that the underlying learning objectives are met. The multi-finger haptic interface used in this study is a competent example for haptic interfaces for classroom environments since it is intuitive to use. The device acts as an extension of the human fingers to the virtual world and requires little cognitive load for manipulation. Getting used to manipulation with the multi-finger haptic interface is easy and we observed that almost all students had no difficulties using the device even on their first use.

For a system like the multi-finger haptic interface, attaching the user to the haptic system is very crucial. A simple linkage design like the thimble that was used in this study, can undermine the haptic experience. Achieving the ultimate design which fits all fingers is challenging. The thimble design used in this study uses a Velcro strap to fix the user's finger to the thimble linkage. Even though the Velcro strap provides flexibility to different finger sizes, it was observed during the trials, and understood from the student interviews, that the robustness of the thimble attachment should be improved.

Usability of the user interface, including the keyboard interactions in this study, is very important for productive collaboration between the pilot and the co-pilot. Especially for situations where the pilot is isolated from the environment due to wearing the head-mounted display, the user interface helps the co-pilot to manipulate and control the virtual environment and hence helps the pilot to complete the given task.

Students found the head-mounted display awe-inspiring. However, it was observed and also noted by the students that wearing the head-mounted display is isolating the pilot from his/her environment. The isolation may be advantageous depending on the application; however, for enhancing learning in a classroom environment and promoting collaboration between students, isolation could potentially be considered as a disadvantage. Therefore, when designing a haptic application with a head-mounted display, researchers have to be attentive on using this powerful graphical display device. The immersion of the user in the virtual environment is readily apparent; however, the classroom environment favours learning over immersion.

8   Conclusion

In this paper, we present observations and feedback from students from a classroom deployment of a haptic system for supporting biology education. We observed that the haptic systems, combined with VR technology, were well-received and easily used by the students, and these results lend support for the further development and investigation of these systems in science education. Our ongoing work includes measuring the impact of the haptic interaction on students' learning of the scientific concepts and support the preliminary results with thorough quantitative analysis.

Acknowledgements. The authors thank the participants for their valuable feedback and are pleased to acknowledge support for this work from The Leverhulme Trust for the project '3D Learning in a Rich, Cooperative Haptic Environment'. We are also pleased to thank our colleagues on this project Jon Rashid, Carleen Houbart, Phil James, Richard Fisher, Simon Bliss, Peter Tolson and Balazs Janko.

References

1. The morrisby fine dexterity test. http://www.morrisby.com/pages/public/dexterity-tests.aspx. Accessed 29 Jan 2018
2. Inside a cell (2016). http://learn.genetics.utah.edu/content/cells/insideacell/
3. Bamford, A.: Evaluation of innovation in learning using emerging technologies. Technical report, Gaia Technologies (2011). http://www.gaia3d.co.uk/wp-content/uploads/2012/11/Evaluation-of-Innovation-in-Learning-using-emerging-technologies-by-Prof-Anne-Bamford-2011.pdf
4. Bolinsky, D.: Visualizing the wonder of a living cell, March 2007. http://www.ted.com/talks/david_bolinsky_animates_a_cell
5. Bowen, K., O'Malley, M.K.: Adaptation of haptic interfaces for a labview-based system dynamics course. In: 2006 14th Symposium on Haptic Interfaces for Virtual Environment and Teleoperator Systems, pp. 147–152. IEEE (2006)
6. Wechsler, D.: Intelligence Scale for Children. NCS Pearson (2014)
7. Ernst, M., Banks, M.: Humans integrate visual and haptic information in a statistically optimal fashion. Nature **415**(6870), 429–433 (2002)
8. Gauldie, D., Wright, M., Shillito, A.: 3D modelling is not for WIMPS part II: stylus/mouse clicks. In: Proceedings of Eurohaptics, pp. 182–189 (2004)
9. Gillespie, R., Hoffinan, M., Freudenberg, J.: Haptic interface for hands-on instruction in system dynamics and embedded control. In: 11th Symposium on Proceedings Haptic Interfaces for Virtual Environment and Teleoperator Systems, HAPTICS 2003, pp. 410–415, March 2003
10. Johnson, R.: 3D at The Abbey. Eng. Technol. Educ., 12–15 (2011)

11. Macaulay, K.: Use of 3D technologies in the classroom. In: international Education and Technology Conference, April 2012. http://www.3deducationconference.org/
12. Melder, N., Harwin, W.: Extending the friction cone algorithm for arbitrary polygon based haptic objects. In: Haptic Interfaces for Virtual Environment and Teleoperator Systems, pp. 234–241. IEEE (2004). http://ieeexplore.ieee.org/iel5/9655/30512/01407005.pdf
13. Millar, R.: Practical work. In: Osborne, J., Dillon, J. (eds.) Good Practice In Science Teaching: What Research Has To Say, 2nd edn., pp. 108–134. Open University Press, Maidenhead (2010)
14. Okamura, A., Basdogan, C., Baillie, S., Harwin, W.: Haptics in medicine and clinical skill acquisition. IEEE Trans. Haptics 4(3), 153–154 (2011)
15. Okamura, A.M., Richard, C., Cutkosky, M., et al.: Feeling is believing: using a force-feedback joystick to teach dynamic systems. J. Eng. Educ. 91(3), 345–349 (2002)
16. Otaran, A., Tokatli, O., Patoglu, V.: Hands-on learning with a series elastic educational robot. In: Bello, F., Kajimoto, H., Visell, Y. (eds.) EuroHaptics 2016. LNCS, vol. 9775, pp. 3–16. Springer, Cham (2016). https://doi.org/10.1007/978-3-319-42324-1_1
17. Piburn, M.D., Reynolds, S.J., McAuliffe, C., Leedy, D.E., Birk, J.P., Johnson, J.K.: The role of visualization in learning from computer-based images. Int. J. Sci. Educ. 27(5), 513–527 (2005)
18. Rose, C.G., French, J., O'Malley, M.K., et al.: Design and characterization of a haptic paddle for dynamics education. In: Haptics Symposium (HAPTICS), pp. 265–270. IEEE (2014)
19. Rutten, N., van Joolingen, W.R., van der Veen, J.T.: The learning effects of computer simulations in science education. Comput. Educ. 58(1), 136–153 (2012)
20. Tse, B., Harwin, W., Barrow, A., Quinn, B., San Diego, J., Cox, M.: Design and development of a haptic dental training system - hapTEL. In: Kappers, A.M.L., van Erp, J.B.F., Bergmann Tiest, W.M., van der Helm, F.C.T. (eds.) EuroHaptics 2010. LNCS, vol. 6192, pp. 101–108. Springer, Heidelberg (2010). https://doi.org/10.1007/978-3-642-14075-4_15. http://www.springerlink.com/content/978-3-642-14074-7#section=726919&page=1
21. Tuckey, H., Selvaratnam, M.: Studies involving three-dimensional visualisation skills in chemistry: a review. Stud. Sci. Educ. 21(1), 99–121 (1993)
22. Levy, J.U., Levy, N.: Mechanical Aptitude and Spatial Relations Tests. Thomson Learning (1999)
23. Webb, M.: Impact of it on science education. In: Voogt, J., Knezek, G. (eds.) International Handbook of Information Technology in Primary and Secondary Education, pp. 133–148. Springer, Boston (2008). https://doi.org/10.1007/978-0-387-73315-9_8

Haptic Rendering of Solid Object Submerged in Flowing Fluid with Environment Dependent Texture

Avirup Mandal$^{(\boxtimes)}$, Dwaipayan Sardar, and Subhasis Chaudhuri

Vision and Image Processing Lab, Department of Electrical Engineering,
Indian Institute of Technology Bombay, Mumbai 400076, India
mandal.avirup@gmail.com, dsnalkel@gmail.com, sc@ee.iitb.ac.in

Abstract. Haptic rendering of complex scenes where interacting materials coexist at different states is a challenging task. In our work, we propose an equal sized, Smoothed Particle Hydrodynamics (SPH) based novel technique to render stable, real-time and realistic haptic force feedback of a dynamic solid-fluid hybrid environment. Along with force feedback, a space varying solid object texture is also rendered using a depth map differencing approach and further improved by mapping custom material friction on the object surface. The setup has been implemented on a single, mid-end GPU achieving a frame rate of 300 frames/second for 65000 particles. The quantitative and qualitative evaluations are done using feedback forces and user study, respectively and compared with state of the art.

Keywords: Haptic rendering · Unified particle model
Position based dynamics · Object texture · Buoyancy

1 Introduction

This work presents a prototype of an interactive touch museum for underwater artefacts where a user can virtually dive into the flowing water and feel different kinds of submerged solid objects. SPH forms the core of fluid rendering and solids are derived as a special case of fluids, as shown in Fig. 1(a). This interactive framework can be used for different kinds of application like interactive scuba gaming, tele-medical system of blood-tissue mixture. Recent works have dealt with haptic rendering for the simulation of multiple states of matter in a unified SPH based framework but are limited to just force rendering. None of these works has considered rendering a proper object texture depending on the surrounding environment. Here we have developed a robust framework using uniformly sized

Electronic supplementary material The online version of this chapter (https://doi.org/10.1007/978-3-319-93399-3_34) contains supplementary material, which is available to authorized users.

particles which is capable of rendering the force as well as the texture feedback in any kind of hybrid environment. As shown in Fig. 1(b), the rendering process is divided into two parallel rendering algorithms, one for solid and other for fluid. Finally depending on the position of proxy, proper haptic force is calculated.

The main contributions of our work are listed below:

- developing an interactive underwater system with an emphasis on rendering small scale details like fluid buoyancy, object texture;
- rendering of texture variation of a solid object depending on the surrounding environment, e.g. part of the object submerged in water will grow a mossy envelop and should feel slippery while the part outside water has a natural object texture;
- voxelization with an appropriate gap closing method to render a dense solid object made of spherical particles;
- simulating a continuous and infinite flow of fluid with a finite number of particles while preserving all the boundary conditions.

The rest of the paper is organized as follows. In Sect. 2, works closely related to haptic rendering of fluid-solid is discussed. Following that in Sect. 3, we discuss existing theories of haptic rendering of fluid. In Sect. 4 we propose the appropriate theory and implementation details for solid object haptic rendering. Section 5 presents the boundary conditions required for this simulation. Finally we present results on performance analysis in Sect. 6 and draw concluding remarks on our work in Sect. 7.

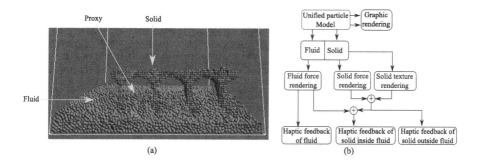

Fig. 1. Illustration of (a) voxel level modeling of both liquid and a partially immersed solid object (a bridge) through a uniform particle size, (b) haptic rendering algorithm.

2 Related Work

In this section we will survey the existing works on three different areas: literatures that presented solutions for physics based fluid simulation, the methods developed by computer graphics community to apply texture to fluids and solids for visual rendering, and finally, works that explored haptic interaction with solids and fluids with specific coupling mechanisms.

2.1   Interactive Fluid Simulation

There exists two broad approaches based on Navier-Stokes (N-S) equations: the Eulerian approach, where the space is divided into small grids and physical quantities get updated at each grid at every time instant, and the Lagrangian approach where the fluid is represented as a set of independent particles interacting with each other. In our present work, we will focus on the Lagrangian approach. SPH is a very popular particle based approach in Lagrangian simulations [1] for mesh-free volumetric rendering. It is shown in [2–4] that using SPH based simulation one can achieve stable and fast interactive rates in fluid simulation. One major drawback of SPH based simulation is computational overhead for rendering complex scenes. However with the development of parallel processing architecture CUDA, the fluid simulation has become more realistic with a very fast interactive frame rate [5].

2.2   Visual Rendering of Fluid

The main problem with fluids simulated through SPH is to render a smooth surface. In case of Eulerian approach the surface is explicit as the space is divided into grids. To render a surface in the particle based model, improved marching cubes and marching tiles based methods are proposed in [6,7]. Although the marching cube based methods are very effective in rendering a proper surface and preserving the finer details, for a large number of particles the frame rate drops making them unacceptable for real time applications. Thus, for a fast surface rendering, a novel technique called screen space fluid rendering was developed by Van der Laan et al. [8]. In this method, first the fluid surface depth is calculated, and then smoothed by minimizing its curvature. Next the per-pixel normals from a view space are computed using the smoothed surface and a proper lighting model is applied using these normals to get a fluid like visual experience.

2.3   Haptic Rendering of Solid-Fluid Interaction

Haptic rendering of fluid is a relatively unexplored area. One preliminary work on fluid resistance map was carried out by Dobashi et al. [9]. Using unified SPH method, Cirio et al. proposed a framework in [10] which renders the total fluid force and torque acting on solid objects and later they further improved their results [11] including state transition of matter e.g. solid to fluid. However the interaction with solid objects inside fluid and buoyancy were not attended to. Feng et al. [14] proposed a fluid deformation control method based on haptic interaction which takes into account the effect of buoyancy. Interaction with underwater solid is developed in [15] but it is limited only to a high amplitude force feedback without any kind of texture mapping. The primary difference between previous works and ours is that while those works rendered solid-fluid interaction by fixing the movement of solid object with a haptic handle thus ignoring haptic feedback for solid object itself, we have simulated an environment where solid and fluid coexist together and rendered force and texture feedback for the entire environment through a proxy. Haptic rendering of multiple fluid is discussed in [17,18].

3   Haptic Rendering of Fluid

In this section we will discuss the simulation of fluid using Navier-Stokes equation and SPH formulation. The dynamics of fluid force feedback through a haptic proxy is presented in the next subsection.

3.1   SPH Based Fluid Simulation

For an incompressible fluid flow, the governing Navier-Stokes equation is

$$\rho \frac{d\vec{v}}{dt} = -\nabla p + \rho \vec{g} + \mu \nabla^2 \vec{v} \tag{1}$$

and the continuity equations is $\dfrac{d\vec{v}}{dt} = -\rho \nabla \cdot \vec{v}$ (1.1)

where ρ is fluid density, μ is dynamic viscosity coefficient, p is pressure, $\vec{g}$ is body/external force and $\vec{v}$ is velocity of fluid.

SPH is a widely used method for Lagrangian based fluid simulation based on N-S equation. In this approach each fluid particle i carries its position $\vec{x}_i$, velocity $\vec{v}_i$, mass m_i, density ρ_i and other attributes A_i. According to SPH, any smoothed attribute $A(\vec{x})$ at a position $\vec{x}$ in the workspace can be computed by interpolating (smoothing) the quantities from its neighboring particles j. In general

$$A(\vec{x}) = \sum_{\forall j \neq i} \frac{m_j}{\rho_j} A_j W(\vec{x} - \vec{x}_j, h) \tag{2}$$

where W is the SPH kernel of support h implying particles lying further than h distance will not contribute. Focused on single particle i, the forces acting on it are pressure force $\vec{F}^{pres}$, viscosity force $\vec{F}^{vis}$, cohesive attraction force $\vec{F}^{atrc}$ and other external forces $\vec{F}^{ext}$ like global damping, gravity. So the resultant force on a fluid particle is

$$\vec{F}_i^{fluid} = \vec{F}_i^{pres} + \vec{F}_i^{vis} + \vec{F}_i^{atrc} + \vec{F}_i^{ext}. \tag{3}$$

Using the SPH model presented in [3,4] density and other forces for each fluid particle can be calculated as

$$\rho(\vec{x}_i) = \sum_{\forall j \neq i} m_j W(\vec{x}_i - \vec{x}_j, h) \tag{4}$$

$$\vec{F}_i^{pres} = -\nabla p(\vec{x}_i) = -\sum_{\forall j \neq i} \frac{m_j}{\rho_j} \left(\frac{p_i + p_j}{2} \right) \nabla W(\vec{x}_i - \vec{x}_j, h) \tag{5}$$

from ideal gas state equation, the pressure follows as $p_i = k(\rho_i - \rho_0)$ where k is gas constant and ρ_0 is rest density of fluid.

$$\vec{F}_i^{vis} = \mu_f \nabla^2 v(\vec{x}_i) = \mu_f \sum_{\forall j \neq i} \frac{m_j}{\rho_j} (\vec{v}_i - \vec{v}_j) \nabla^2 W(\vec{x}_i - \vec{x}_j, h) \tag{6}$$

$$\vec{\mathbf{F}}_i^{atrc} = \sum_{\forall j \neq i} \frac{m_j}{\rho_j} \left(\frac{f_i + f_j}{2} \right) \nabla W(\vec{\mathbf{x}}_i - \vec{\mathbf{x}}_j, h) \tag{7}$$

where attraction between two interacting particles, i and j is defined by

$$f_i = -K_a x_r \tag{8}$$

$$x_r = \begin{cases} |\vec{\mathbf{x}}_i - \vec{\mathbf{x}}_j|, & |\vec{\mathbf{x}}_i - \vec{\mathbf{x}}_j| \leq h \\ 0, & \text{elsewhere} \end{cases} \tag{9}$$

where K_a is an appropriate constant. External force here consists of two components

$$\vec{\mathbf{F}}_i^{ext} = \vec{\mathbf{F}}_i^g + \vec{\mathbf{F}}_i^{gd} \tag{10}$$

where $\vec{\mathbf{F}}_i^g$ is the Gravity force acting upon all the parts of the environment equally. $\vec{\mathbf{F}}_i^{gd}$ is the damping force applied to the moving fluid particles in contact with solid object boundary which is calculated in a similar way as viscosity:

$$\vec{\mathbf{F}}_i^{gd} = \mu_s \sum_{\forall j \neq i} \frac{m_j}{\rho_j} (\vec{\mathbf{v}}_i - \vec{\mathbf{v}}_s) \nabla^2 W(\vec{\mathbf{x}}_i - \vec{\mathbf{x}}_s, h) \tag{11}$$

where $\vec{\mathbf{v}}_s$ is velocity of the solid object in contact.

As used in [14], the following kernels are applied to calculate different parameters: poly6 kernel for density, spiky kernel for pressure and viscosity kernel for viscosity calculation. Spiky and viscosity kernels are used for attraction force and global damping, respectively, as their formulations are similar to pressure and viscosity. After computing pressure and viscosity forces from SPH, acceleration, velocity and position of each particle are calculated through a Leapfrog integration scheme.

3.2   Fluid Force Rendering Through Haptic Proxy

While interacting with fluid by a spherical haptic proxy, the total interaction force rendered is calculated as follows:

$$\vec{\mathbf{F}}_{fluid}^{interact} = \sum_{i=1}^{n} \left(\vec{\mathbf{F}}_i^{buoy} + \vec{\mathbf{F}}_i^{fluid} \right) \tag{12}$$

where n is the number of fluid particles on the contour of haptic proxy, $\vec{\mathbf{F}}_i^{buoy}$ is buoyancy and $\vec{\mathbf{F}}_i^{fluid}$ is the fluid force calculated in Eq. 3.

Buoyant Force. According to the formulation presented in [16] buoyancy is given by

$$\vec{\mathbf{F}}_i^{buoy} = b(\rho_i - \rho_p)\vec{\mathbf{g}}_a \tag{13}$$

where ρ_p is density of the proxy, $\vec{\mathbf{g}}_a$ is gravity and b is a controlling parameter. The size of haptic proxy being small, the number of particles on the contour of proxy is less, resulting low buoyancy. Increasing the value of b leads to sharp, unstable and discontinuous feedback. But to develop an interactive underwater touch museum we need to render the buoyancy of a fully grown human body of volume V_{hu}. For simplicity here we have assumed that whole volume of the body is concentrated at the proxy. To render full body buoyancy, first depending on how far the proxy goes under fluid surface, we have calculated what fraction volume of the human body is submerged and added an extra artificial buoyancy accordingly. So the total interaction force rendered is

$$\vec{\mathbf{F}}_{fluid}^{interact} = \rho_0 l V_{hu} \hat{\mathbf{y}} + \sum_{i=1}^{n} \left(\vec{\mathbf{F}}_i^{buoy} + \vec{\mathbf{F}}_i^{fluid} \right) \tag{14}$$

where $\rho_0 l V_{hu} \hat{\mathbf{y}}$ is added artificial buoyancy with $l V_{hu}$ is the fraction of human body submerged, l is a variable related to depth of submersion of proxy in fluid and ρ_0 is the rest density of fluid. Hence we allow the virtual explorer to get a feel of being submerged in water.

4 Unified SPH Method and Haptic Rendering of Solid

In this section first we delineate on theories related to how SPH can be modified to simulate a solid piece of object partly submerged in a flowing fluid. Later we introduce the theory of position based dynamics to render the proper force feedback for solid objects. At the end we render texture of solid object using a depth map differencing approach. Major emphasis of our work is to get a real feel of the fluid flow with the object rigidity and texture through a single point haptic device.

4.1 Solid Object Construction and Tunneling

Unlike fluid, the solid is composed of closely spaced overlapped spheres. To this end, one must have a 3D model (mesh or point cloud) of the desired object. For experimentation, we have selected a 3D hollow mesh data of an object from www.turbosquid.com, followed by repairing the defects present in that mesh data using MeshLab. This hollow model is then voxelized to get a dense point cloud representation and a particle sphere is fitted at each voxel position. As a result, the sphere fitted object contains a lot of holes as shown in Fig. 2(a). Due to this porous rendering, while interacting with a solid object the proxy or a fluid particle occasionally plunges into the solid object if hit with a high speed as depicted in Fig. 2(c). This is called tunneling and caused due to discrete collision handling. To fill up those holes by tight sphere packing, Fig. 2(b), we have reduced the distance between any two voxels by a factor of 1.5, thus increasing the packing density of particles by a factor of $(1.5^3 - 1) \approx 2.4$. After this gap closing tunneling gets reduced considerably as there are more solid particles per unit volume, so the proxy encounters more particles, resulting more force.

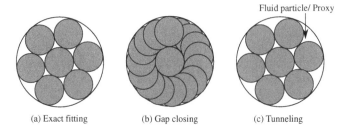

(a) Exact fitting   (b) Gap closing   (c) Tunneling

Fig. 2. Illustration of particle based representation of a solid object, (a) exact fitting and (b) close fitting with spheres as voxels. (c) possibility of proxy tunneling in case of exact fitting.

4.2 Solid Object Interaction with Haptic Proxy Inside and Outside Fluid

Once the solid object is placed inside the fluid, the movements of its particles are frozen. The fluid particles and the haptic proxy will continue to interact with solid particles giving rise to the forces discussed earlier but the position and velocity of the solid particles will not get updated due to rigidity constraint.

Force Feedback for Solid Object. To make the interaction with solid object more realistic and to reduce the chances of tunneling, we have modified the simple discrete collision dynamics to position based dynamics, where the fundamental spring constant varies according to the position. Here we have used a piecewise linear spring constant for collision of proxy with a solid object. As per Fig. 3,

$$\vec{\mathbf{F}}_i^{sol} = \begin{cases} k_1\beta\frac{\vec{\mathbf{P}}_{AB}}{|\vec{\mathbf{P}}_{AB}|}, & 0 \leq \beta < \frac{\beta_{max}}{3} \\ k_2\beta\frac{\vec{\mathbf{P}}_{AB}}{|\vec{\mathbf{P}}_{AB}|}, & \frac{\beta_{max}}{3} \leq \beta < \frac{2\beta_{max}}{3} \\ k_3\beta\frac{\vec{\mathbf{P}}_{AB}}{|\vec{\mathbf{P}}_{AB}|}, & \frac{2\beta_{max}}{3} \leq \beta < \beta_{max} \end{cases} \tag{15}$$

where $\beta_{max} = \min(R_A, R_B)$ and β is the overlap magnitude between i^{th} solid particle and the proxy while k_i's are spring constants with $k_3 > k_2 > k_1$.

Object Texture with Friction Map. For a partially immersed solid object, a proper formulation is needed to render different types of haptic feedback for various parts of the object. The part of the object outside the fluid has a proper object texture while the part inside fluid should feel slippery along with the texture due to a mossy surface.

To render the object texture, first we have generated depth at each point of object by reading the depthbuffer in OpenGL. This depthmap is then smoothed using a Gaussian low-pass filter and the finer texture details are extracted by taking the difference between the original and the smoothed depthmap as presented in [13]

$$\delta z = g_0 - w * g_0 \tag{16}$$

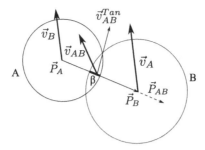

Fig. 3. Illustration of the physical model of collision between two particles (or a particle with the spherical proxy). The attributes of the ith particle are position $\vec{\mathbf{P}}_i$, radius R_i and velocity $\vec{v}_i$. Here $\vec{\mathbf{P}}_{AB} = \vec{\mathbf{P}}_B - \vec{\mathbf{P}}_A$, $\vec{v}_{AB} = \vec{v}_B - \vec{v}_A$. and β is the amount of overlap between two particles.

where g_0 is original depthmap and w is the weights of Gaussian low-pass filter. The haptic feedback of the surface texture is rendered by

$$\vec{\mathbf{F}}_i^{tex} = \vec{\mathbf{F}}_i^{sol} + k_h \delta z_i \tag{17}$$

where k_h is an appropriate constant and δz_i is texture at i^{th} solid particle position.

To make solid object interaction more realistic, material friction is also added over the surface of the object. To this end, we have randomly assigned the free-hand recordings of friction data of a brick [19] to each of the surface particles of the solid object. Therefore the total feedback rendered for a solid object through a haptic proxy is

$$\vec{\mathbf{F}}_{solid}^{outfluid} = \sum_{i=1}^{n} \left(\vec{\mathbf{F}}_i^{sol} + k_h \delta z_i + \vec{\mathbf{F}}_i^{fric} \right) \tag{18}$$

where $\vec{\mathbf{F}}_i^{fric}$ relates to the proper force derived from the recorded friction data, assigned to i^{th} solid particle and n is the number of solid particles interacting with proxy.

Now to detect the portion of the object submerged in fluid, we have applied a three dimensional neighbourhood search algorithm. If position of any solid particle is $\vec{x}_i$, then *count* which signifies the number of surrounding fluid particles, goes as follow

$$count = \sum_{\vec{x}_j \in \mathbf{A}} \mathbb{1}_{\mathbf{A}} \tag{19}$$

where $\mathbf{A} := \left\{ \vec{x}_j \mid ||\vec{x}_i - \vec{x}_j||_2 < \epsilon, \quad \epsilon > 0, \forall j \in Fluid \right\}$. If the *count* $> N_{thres}$ then that particle is assumed to be submerged and in touch with the fluid. To render slipperiness, whenever the haptic proxy collides with these submerged solid particles, an extra tangential force is rendered along with the original solid force defined in Eq. 18. As the proxy goes inside the fluid to feel the submerged object, $\vec{\mathbf{F}}_{fluid}^{interact}$ also starts acting.

$$\vec{\mathbf{F}}_{solid}^{influid} = \left(\vec{\mathbf{F}}_{solid}^{outfluid} + \mu_s \vec{\mathbf{v}}_{rel}^{Tan}\right) + \vec{\mathbf{F}}_{fluid}^{interact} \tag{20}$$

where μ_s is the shear modulus of the material and $\vec{\mathbf{v}}_{rel}^{Tan}$ is the tangential relative velocity of the proxy w.r.t. the solid particle at its point of contact before overlap happens.

5   Boundary Conditions

Two kinds of boundary conditions are encountered in our framework, boundary condition for fluid flow and solid-fluid boundary.

5.1   Fluid Flow Boundary

In this work we have simulated two kinds of fluid flow in x direction, finite circular flow inside a tank and a river like infinite flow, within a cube of length 2 units with the right handed Euclidean coordinate placed at the center of the cube.

Flow in a Tank (Finite Flow). In this type of flow, as shown in Fig. 4(a) we have considered the $x = -0.9$ and $x = 0.9$ planes of the cubical box as inflow and outflow boundaries, respectively. When the particles reach the outflow region, we do not evolve the parameters of those anymore and introduce the same number of particles inside the inflow region with a **pre-defined** velocity and density.

Flow in a River (Infinite Flow). To get this type of flow, the cubical simulation box is replicated throughout the space to create a virtual infinite lattice in the x direction. This kind of flow is simulated by linking the particles of opposite boundaries i.e. whenever a particle leaves the $x = 1$ plane, another particle re-enters $x = -1$ plane immediately with the **exact same** velocity and density, maintaining the continuity of the flow.

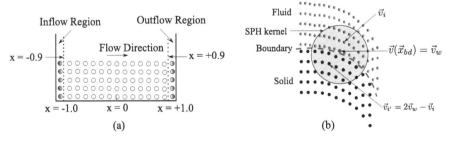

(a)   (b)

Fig. 4. Illustration of (a) boundary conditions for finite and infinite flow, (b) handling kernel truncation problem by introducing dummy velocities $\vec{\mathbf{v}}_{i'}$ for particles belong to the solid object.

5.2 Solid-Fluid Boundary

The main problem in modeling solid-fluid interaction with SPH is that the support domain of the SPH kernel is truncated by the interfacing boundary as shown in Fig. 4(b). Moreover, as per fluid dynamics, a free-slip and a no-slip boundary condition have to be imposed at the boundary [12] to avoid penetration of fluid particles into the solid. The kernel truncation problem can be solved by introducing dummy velocities to the solid particles. By putting the value of viscosity coefficient between fluid and solid particle to zero, the free-slip condition can be achieved. To impose a no-slip condition for a fluid particle at the boundary position $\vec{\mathbf{x}}_{bd}$ (see Fig. 4(b)), first we extrapolate the smoothed velocity field for fluid particle i, within kernel support radius of h, to the solid particle positions by

$$\vec{\mathbf{v}}_i = \sum_j \frac{m_j}{\rho_j} \vec{\mathbf{v}}_j W(\vec{\mathbf{x}}_i - \vec{\mathbf{x}}_j, h) \tag{21}$$

Then corresponding to the fluid particle, a solid particle is assigned the dummy velocity

$$\vec{\mathbf{v}}_{i'} = 2\vec{\mathbf{v}}_w - \vec{\mathbf{v}}_i \tag{22}$$

where $\vec{\mathbf{v}}_w$ is the object velocity at the boundary. It can be proved that with this assumption the no-slip condition gets satisfied at the boundary i.e. $\vec{\mathbf{v}}(\vec{\mathbf{x}}_{bd}) = \vec{\mathbf{v}}_w$.

6 Experimental Results

Our aim was to render a realistic haptic feedback of hybrid environment. The evaluation of the same has been carried out via (a) haptic feedback measurements, (b) user study i.e. subjective evaluation and (c) device parameter measurements. Unlike previous works on SPH solid-fluid interaction, which primarily dealt with simple force and torque feedback, our prime focus is to access the capability of a user to feel the change of solid object texture inside and outside fluid along with buoyancy and drag force of fluid. For our work we have used an Intel i7-4770K CPU at 3.50 GHz, 32.0 GB RAM, a single Geforce GTX TITAN GPU with 5860 MB of graphics memory and a 6-DOF haptic device from Geomagic Touch.

6.1 Force Feedback

We have attached the movement of the user, exploring the virtual scene, with the proxy. Thus moving the proxy, a person can get the feeling of being in an underwater museum interacting with artefacts. The process of exploration is divided into four steps:

1. Pushing the haptic proxy gradually into the fluid. Figure 5(a).
2. Dragging haptic proxy inside fluid without colliding with solid. Figure 5(a).
3. Touching the solid object outside fluid from x direction and dragging the proxy over solid in $y - z$ plane. Figure 5(b).

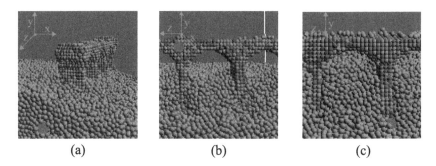

$$\text{(a)} \qquad\qquad \text{(b)} \qquad\qquad \text{(c)}$$

Fig. 5. Illustration of (a) entering and dragging the proxy inside fluid, (b) contact with a solid object outside fluid, and (c) contact with a solid object inside fluid.

4. Interacting with a solid object inside fluid in the same way as mentioned in (3). Figure 5(c).

According to the first phase of Fig. 6(a), the proxy goes deeper into the fluid resulting in a gradual increase of force along y (vertical) direction due to buoyancy. Due to full body buoyancy rendering the magnitude of our buoyancy is more compared to Liang et al.'s method, Fig. 8 in [15]. In the second phase as the proxy is dragged inside the fluid, the resistance force along x and z directions turns up. Finally in the third phase all the forces decrease to zero as the proxy is moved out of fluid. As per Fig. 6(b) the force along x direction increases very sharply while interacting with the solid outside fluid. While dragging the proxy over solid we can notice a vibration in all x, y and z directions rather than a flat line as obtained by Cirio et al.'s method for rigid object, Fig. 4 in [11] and by Liang et al.'s method, Fig. 8 in [15]. This vibration arises due to the texturing and friction modeling on solid as discussed in Sect. 4. Interaction with a solid inside fluid Fig. 6(c) shows less vibration compared to Fig. 6(b) due to slipperiness. But the force values in all directions are higher due to buoyancy and fluid resistance. Figure 6(d) shows a comparative study for haptic rendering of solid object with and without tunneling. As follows from the plot, the sharp dips to zero which arise due to tunneling, are eliminated using our approach i.e. tight sphere packing and position based dynamics. (Please see the supplementary video included with this submission).

6.2   User Study

The experiment was conducted using a 6-DOF haptic device from Geomagic Touch. Ten subjects (8 male, 2 female) of age group 20–30 years participated in the experiment. The subjects were instructed to keep their elbows fixed on an armrest of a chair with haptic stylus in their hand, and explore the virtual scene in the four steps mentioned earlier, starting from roughly the same position.

Depending on how realistic the environment feels, the subjects were asked to rate the experience on a scale of 1 to 5, 1 being very poor and 5 being excellent.

Table 1. Mean opinion score table

Parameter	Mean	Variance
Fluid with buoyancy	4.05	0.191
Solid outside fluid	4.25	0.069
Solid inside fluid	3.95	0.302

For each subject the experiment lasted around 5 min. The mean opinion score is given in Table 1. As we can see from the table that the mean opinion score of all these parameters are high indicating that the haptic interaction is stable and realistic while the small variance implies that most of them have a similar opinion regarding the scenario.

6.3   Device Parameters

We used 65000 particles to simulate the whole scene out of which 6000 particles are used to model the solid object and the rest are used for the fluid. The whole simulation is implemented using the CUDA framework provided by NVIDIA, thus parallelizing the force update of each particle. Using this set up, around 295 − 300 fps can be achieved which is good enough to obtain a smooth haptic interaction.

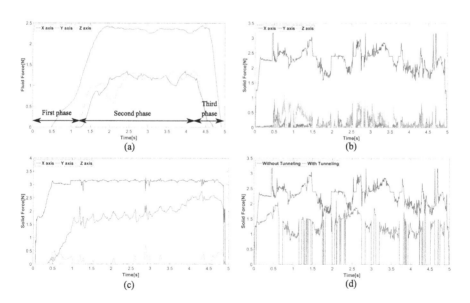

Fig. 6. Feedback force while interacting with (a) fluid (corresponds to Fig. 5(a)), (b) a solid object outside the fluid (corresponds to Fig. 5(b)), (c) a solid object inside the fluid (corresponds to Fig. 5(c)), and (d) a solid object with and without tunneling outside the fluid.

7   Conclusions

In this paper, we have proposed a SPH based framework that simulates interactive hapto-visual rendering of fluid and submerged solid objects. The proposed framework is capable of rendering variable textures of solid inside and outside fluid. No divergence issue is encountered, thus allowing a seamless haptic rendering through an unified physics based particle modeling. Potential applications of our work can range from surgical training to entertainment industry. Future work will involve extending this framework from solid objects to deformable objects. Our major focus will be put on avoiding the tunneling phenomena and developing a full fledged multi-modal rendering system by inclusion of sound feedback in addition to haptic feedback.

References

1. Monaghan, J.J.: Smoothed particle hydrodynamics. Annu. Rev. Astron. Astrophys. **30** (1992)
2. Bridson, R., Müller-Fischer, M.: Fluid simulation. In: ACM SIGGRAPH Courses (2007)
3. Müller, M., Charypar, D., Gross, M.: Particle-based fluid simulation for interactive applications. In: Proceedings of ACM SIGGRAPH (2003)
4. Solenthaler, B., Schläfli, J., Pajarola, R.: A unified particle model for fluid-solid interactions. Comput. Animat. Virt. Worlds. **18** (2007)
5. Macklin, M., Müller, M.: Position based fluids. ACM Trans. Graph. **32** (2013)
6. Williams, B.W.: Fluid surface reconstruction from particles. Master's thesis, The University Of British Columbia (2008)
7. Jihun, Y., Greg, T.: Reconstructing surfaces of particle-based fluids using anisotropic kernels. ACM Trans. Graph. **32** (2013)
8. van der Laan, W.J., Green, S., Sainz, M.: Screen space fluid rendering with curvature flow. In: Proceedings of Symposium on Interactive 3D Graphics and Games (2013)
9. Dobashi, Y., Sato, M., Hasegawa, S., Yamamoto, T., Kato, M., Nishita, T.: A fluid resistance map method for real-time haptic interaction with fluids. In: Proceedings of the ACM Symposium on Virtual Reality Software and Technology (2006)
10. Cirio, G., Marchal, M., Hillaire, S., Lecuyer, A.: Six degrees-of-freedom haptic interaction with fluids. IEEE Trans. Vis. and Comp. Graph. **17** (2011)
11. Cirio, G., Marchal M., Otaduy, M.A., LÃl'cuyer, A.: Six-oof haptic interaction with fluids, solids, and their transitions. In: Proceedings of World Haptics (2013)
12. Adami, S., Hu, X.Y., Adams, N.A.: A generalized wall boundary condition for smoothed particle hydrodynamics. J. Comput. Phys. **231**, 7057–7075 (2012)
13. Sreeni, K.G., Priyadarshini, K., Praseedha, A.K., Chaudhuri, S.: Haptic rendering of cultural heritage objects at different scales. In: Isokoski, P., Springare, J. (eds.) EuroHaptics 2012. LNCS, vol. 7282, pp. 505–516. Springer, Heidelberg (2012). https://doi.org/10.1007/978-3-642-31401-8_45
14. Feng, G., Liu, S.: Haptic interaction based SPH fluid control. In: Proceedings of CASA (2017)
15. Liang, J., Yu, G., Wang, K., Wang, Y., Guo, L.: Realtime haptic rendering in hybrid environment using unified SPH method. In: Proceedings of Soft Computing & Machine Intelligence (2016)

16. Müller, M., Solenthaler, B., Keiser, R., Gross, M.: Particle-based fluid-fluid interaction. In: Proceedings of ACM SIGGRAPH (2005)
17. Mora, J., Lee, W.: Real-time fluid interaction with a haptic device. In: Proceedings of HAVE (2017)
18. Zhang, X., Liu, S.: SPH haptic interaction with multiple-fluid simulation. In: Proceedings of VR (2017)
19. http://www.lmt.ei.tum.de/downloads/texture/

Haptic Guidance with a Soft Exoskeleton Reduces Error in Drone Teleoperation

Carine Rognon[1(✉)], Amy R. Wu[2], Stefano Mintchev[1], Auke Ijspeert[2],
and Dario Floreano[1]

[1] Laboratory of Intelligent Systems, Ecole Polytechnique Fédérale de Lausanne (EPFL),
1015 Lausanne, Switzerland
carine.rognon@epfl.ch
[2] Biorobotics Laboratory, Ecole Polytechnique Fédérale de Lausanne (EPFL),
1015 Lausanne, Switzerland

Abstract. Haptic guidance has been shown to improve performance in many
fields as it can give additional information without overloading other sensory
channels such as vision or audition. Our group is investigating new intuitive ways
to interact with robots, and we developed a suit to control drones with upper body
movement, called the FlyJacket. In this paper, we present the integration of a
cable-driven haptic guidance in the FlyJacket. The aim of the device is to apply
a force relative to the distance between the drone and a predetermined trajectory
to correct user torso orientation and improve the flight precision. Participants (n
= 10) flying a simulated fixed-wing drone controlled with torso movements tested
four different guidance profiles (three linear profiles with different stiffness and
one quadratic). Our results show that a quadratically shaped guidance, which
gives a weak force when the error is small and a strong force when the error
becomes significant, was the most effective guidance to improve the performance.
All participants also reported through questionnaires that the haptic guidance was
useful for flight control.

Keywords: Wearable haptics and exoskeletons · Teleoperation and telepresence
Robotics

1 Introduction

The recent years have witnessed a growing demand for drones in multiple fields such
as agriculture, industrial inspection, logistics, and search and rescue [1]. However,
despite the recent advances in drone design and sensing, their direct teleoperation still
mainly relies on traditional remote controllers. These types of controllers are neither
natural nor intuitive and require long training periods to be mastered [2]. In order to
make drones more accessible to non-expert users and facilitate their direct control in
demanding tasks such as inspection or rescue missions, several studies have investigated
the use of gestures [3, 4]. In a previous study, the authors have identified an intuitive
upper body movement pattern that naïve users exploited to fly a fixed wing drone [5].
This embodied flight style, which allows the user to directly control the pitch and roll

© Springer International Publishing AG, part of Springer Nature 2018
D. Prattichizzo et al. (Eds.): EuroHaptics 2018, LNCS 10894, pp. 404–415, 2018.
https://doi.org/10.1007/978-3-319-93399-3_35

of a drone using torso movements, reduces learning time and increases performance when compared to the use of a traditional remote controllers. In order to record torso gestures, the authors have developed the FlyJacket, a sensorised suit equipped with unobtrusive and removable arm supports, which allow people to fly with their arms spread out without experiencing fatigue or degrading the flight performance [6].

This paper presents the integration and test of a cable-driven haptic guidance in the FlyJacket. This work is motivated by several results showing that haptic feedback improves the task performance in many domains such as for surgery [7], rehabilitation [8] or sports [9, 10]. Haptic feedback has been implemented as a force feedback on joysticks to control flight for obstacles avoidance [11–13]. In those studies, an attractive or resistive corrective force relative to the distance between the drone position and the obstacle increases users' awareness and reduces collision occurrences. The flight immersion can also be enhanced by including the velocity of the drone in the haptic feedback [14, 15].

When the aim of the haptic feedback is to correct a trajectory, linear feedback control laws (e.g. proportional-derivative control) on the error between the robot position and a reference trajectory are typically used [7, 8, 16–18]. The stiffness of the guidance is a very important feature because a too soft guidance may not be effective while a too strong guidance may lead to user passivity [16, 17, 19]. Therefore, the force profile and stiffness play an important role and need to be studied in order to optimize the guidance provided by the haptic feedback.

The kinesthetic feedback proposed in this paper aims to correct and guide the user toward waypoints when flying a simulated fixed-wing drone using torso gestures. We investigated four different force profiles to determine their contribution on the reduction of the error between the drone and the waypoints. We studied how the addition of haptic feedback acts on the performance and on the workload of the user.

2 Haptic Guidance Implementation

2.1 FlyJacket Hardware

The FlyJacket is a soft exosuit developed for gesture based control of drones [6] (Fig. 1). This wearable suit tracks the torso orientation, and converts it into drone commands. The design of the exosuit and its ergonomics are suited for this flight style that has been identified has a natural and intuitive approach that naïve users adopt to fly fixed wing drones [5]. The user sits on a backless stool and bends his torso forward and backward in the sagittal plane, to control the pitch up and down maneuvers respectively. The user bends at the sides in the frontal plane to control the roll angle of the drone. The mapping between torso movements and drone commands is linear and the gains from the torso angle to the drone angle are 2.5 when pitching up, 1.5 when pitching down and 2 when rolling. Torso movements are recorded with an Inertial Measurement Unit (IMU) (Xsens, Enschede, The Netherlands) located in the middle of the back (Fig. 1C). The exosuit is equipped with arm supports that allow the user to fly with the arms spread out without experiencing fatigue (Fig. 1A).

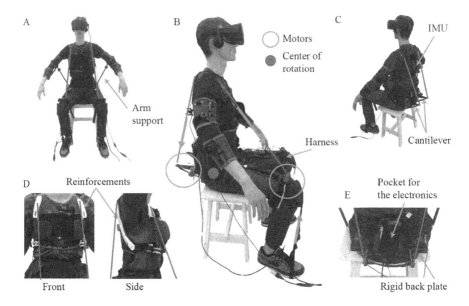

Fig. 1. FlyJacket with haptic guidance device. Cables are highlighted in red and the forces shown in green. (A) Front view. (B) Side view. (C) Back view. (D) Magnification on the torso part to highlight the reinforcements. (E) Magnification of the lower back part to highlight the back motors. (Color figure online)

Haptic guidance to the FlyJacket user was provided by a cable-driven system. With this system, four electrical motors (DC22S, gear ratio 6.6:1, Maxon Motor, Switzerland) pull on cables (Dyneema 0.4 mm, Spiderwire, SC, USA, displayed in red in Fig. 1) attached to the user's upper torso. In order to pull the torso according to the gestures performed by the user during flight, e.g. bending forward and backward with a center of rotation located on the hip (see Fig. 1B), one motor is positioned on the distal part of each leg and two motors on each side of the lower back. With this antagonistic configuration, forces bend the user in both the sagittal and frontal planes. Both front motors are fixed to the legs with a harness system. To prevent the motors from sliding along the legs when pulling on the cables, they are maintained by a non-elastic textile band attached at its extremity to the user's feet by the mean of a loop. Padding on the knee avoids user discomfort due to the force routing. The two back motors are located on the lower back and screwed onto a rigid plate to prevent them from moving (Fig. 1E). Cantilevers made of 3D printed Acrytonitrite Butadiene Styrene (ABS) create a lever arm to induce forces that pull the user backward, instead of downward. Two non-elastic textile bands attached from the extremities of the cantilevers to the leg harness, passing on the back of the thigh, restrain the cantilever tips from moving when the back motors are pulling on cables. As the cables are attached on the torso part made of leather, reinforcements made of polymorph thermoplastic (Thermoworx Ltd, Ayrshire, Scotland, UK) have been inserted to stiffen the structure in order to prevent force losses and transmission delays (see Fig. 1D).

The range of force of the haptic guidance should induce a torque higher than the passive stiffness of the human torso of around 10 Nm [20], in order to be able to move the torso of a fully compliant human. However, the user should also have full control of their body movements at any time. Therefore, we ensure that the maximal torque applied to the torso is much lower than the maximal torque a human can produce, which is around 150 Nm [21, 22]. As a comparison, the X-Arm 2, a rigid arm exoskeleton used to teleoperate a humanoid robot for extra-vehicular space missions, can produce up to $1/20^{th}$ of the maximum human arm torque to deliver force feedback during manipulation [23]. Each motor of the FlyJacket's haptic system can produce up to 30 N of force, which corresponds to a torque of approximately 20 Nm for a 175 cm tall user when both motors of one body side are pulling together.

The four electrical motors are independently controlled by four transistors activated through a control board (Arduino Uno, Arduino, Italy). Thanks to the low gear ratio (6.6:1), motors are back-drivable. They are only activated when a corrective force is required to pull on the cables.

2.2   Guidance Profiles

The haptic guidance is based on the error (Δx) between the drone position and a predetermined trajectory at a predefined time in the future. For ease of visualization, Fig. 2A is showing a 2D schematic of the distances, but the flight trajectories in the tasks are 3D. This error (Δx) is calculated as the scalar product between the vector from the drone to the look ahead point and the vector perpendicular to the direction of flight, pointing to the right for the correction in roll and up for the correction in pitch. The look ahead principle has been shown to enable stable vehicle control using external interfaces (e.g. remote controller) [17, 18]. In this study, participants were asked to follow a trajectory in the sky symbolized by small clouds (see Fig. 3A), called waypoints, spaced apart by approximately 40 m. The look ahead time was set to 3 s, which corresponds to a distance of 36 m as the drone is flying at a constant speed of 12 m/s. The user receives an attractive force relative to their error (Δx), which indicates how they should move their torso to correct the drone position. As the four motors can be actuated separately, combination of forces on the front, back, and sides are achievable in order to correct the drone in pitch, roll or a combination of both. For example, as shown in Fig. 2A, if the drone is positioned too far on the left regarding to the predetermined trajectory, front-right and back-right motors will pull on cables to exert a force to bend the user's torso on the right side. With this torso movement, the drone will roll on the right, and the error (Δx) will be reduced.

Four guidance curves were implemented to investigate which type of feedback could best correct torso movements during a flight task (see Fig. 2B). We used three linear profiles with different levels of stiffness (hard, medium, and soft) and one quadratic profile that transitions from soft to hard guidance. These force profiles have been calibrated based on the Root Mean Square (RMS) and standard deviation (std) of the error (Δx_{wp}) measured at each waypoint from a previous study having a similar flight task but without guidance (see Fig. 2A and C, and [6]). This error was the distance between the center of the waypoint and the point where the trajectory of the drone crosses a plane

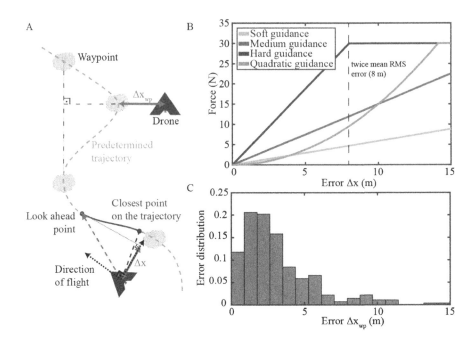

Fig. 2. (A) 2 D schema displaying the error (Δx) for the haptic guidance (measured throughout the task) and the error (Δx$_{wp}$) to measure the performance at each waypoint. (B) Force guidance over the error (Δx). (C) Waypoint error distribution (Δx$_{wp}$) found in previous experiment [6].

drawn perpendicular to the line connecting the previous and next waypoint [24]. The participant's performance was computed as the RMS of these distances over all waypoints of the task. The mean RMS error over all participants was 4.02 ± 1.62 m (mean $\pm$ std).

The hard guidance has the advantage of giving a strong feedback to the user with a stiffness of 3.75 N/m. This guidance imparts the maximum force the motor can produce (30 N) at twice the mean RMS error found in previous experiment (Eq. 1). At more than 30 N, the motor is not able to produce more force, and it saturates as shown in Fig. 2B. Since more than 90% of the errors (Δx$_{wp}$) found in the previous experiment [6] were smaller than twice the mean RMS error (8 m, see Fig. 2B), users seldom reach the saturation limit. This guidance strongly pulls the torso toward the orientation that would correct the drone's trajectory and immediately emphases every small error (Δx). However, this strong force may be unpleasant for the user as they may feel less involved in the control.

$$F_{\text{hard}} = \begin{cases} 3.75 \cdot \Delta x, & |\Delta x| \leq 8 \\ 30, & |\Delta x| > 8 \end{cases} \tag{1}$$

In contrast, the soft guidance aims to hint which movements the user should perform to correct their orientation as the forces are too weak to influence the torso movement. This guidance has a stiffness of 0.59 N/m, which gives the maximal force at the mean error plus 30 times the standard deviation (Eq. 2). For small errors, the guidance force is very weak, which allows the user to make some mistakes without being strongly pushed back towards the reference trajectory as the hard guidance does.

$$F_{soft} = \begin{cases} 0.59 \cdot \Delta x, & |\Delta x| \leq 51 \\ 30, & |\Delta x| > 51 \end{cases} \tag{2}$$

The medium guidance aims to be an intermediate guidance between hard and soft guidance and was designed to give half of the maximal force at the mean error plus 10 times the standard deviation, which corresponds to a stiffness of 1.5 N/m (Eq. 3).

$$F_{medium} = \begin{cases} 1.5 \cdot \Delta x, & |\Delta x| \leq 20 \\ 30, & |\Delta x| > 20 \end{cases} \tag{3}$$

The fourth proposed guidance has a quadratic shape. It combines the advantages of both the soft and the hard guidance. For small errors, it gives a weak correction force; therefore, the participant avoids being strongly perturbed. When the error becomes more significant, this guidance pulls the user strongly towards the reference trajectory. The force intensity was set to match the error of the medium guidance at half of the maximum motor force (15 N) as display in Fig. 2B (Eq. 4).

$$F_{quadratic} = \begin{cases} 0.15 \cdot \Delta x^2, & |\Delta x| \leq 14 \\ 30, & |\Delta x| > 14 \end{cases} \tag{4}$$

2.3 Flight Experiment

In order to evaluate the effectiveness of haptic guidance of the four different guidance profiles, ten participants (six men and four women, age 28.5 ± 4.5 years; mean $\pm$ std) flew a simulated fixed-wing drone using upper body movements. All participants tested the four types of guidance and flew once without guidance. They sat on a stool wearing the FlyJacket with arm support and virtual reality goggles (Oculus Rift, Oculus VR, Menlo Park, USA) that gave a first person view of the flight and wind sound for more immersion. They flew a fixed-wing drone in a simulator developed in Unity3D (Unity Technologies, San Francisco, CA, USA). The simulated drone physics were based on the eBee (SenseFly, Parrot Group, Paris, France), flying at a constant cruise speed of 12 m/s which is the nominal speed of drones during imaging and mapping tasks.

Participants started with a short training without guidance composed of two tasks. At first, they had to follow the direction of an arrow positioned in front of them. The arrow was pointing consecutively "right", "left", "up", and "down" twice. The goal of this task, which lasted one minute, was to make the participants perform every flight control movement at least once. The second task was one and a half minutes of free flight in a 3D reconstruction of our campus. The goal of the training was to enable the participant to feel comfortable with the control of the flight. For the evaluation part, participants were instructed to fly through 42 waypoints represented by small clouds (see Fig. 3A). These waypoints formed a trajectory in the sky and disappeared when they were reached. The

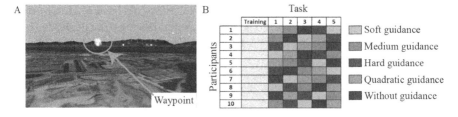

Fig. 3. (A) Flight environment. (B) Task order for each participant.

waypoints sequence was randomized, but the number of maneuvers (up/down/right/left) was the same for every task. Each participant completed five trials, once with each guidance condition and once without guidance. They were not told which type of guidance they were to receive or what type they had received. The order of the guidance conditions presented to the participant was arranged so that each condition was placed twice at every position in the task order (see Fig. 3B). The same succession of conditions was avoided as much as possible in order to remove learning effects. Participants' performance was computed as the RMS of the error (Δx_{wp}) of all waypoints.

At the end of each task, participants completed a Nasa-TLX questionnaire with pairwise comparison [25], which assessed the workload variation between flight conditions. At the end of the experiment, participants completed a final questionnaire asking which kind of guidance condition they enjoyed the most and the least, and which guidance condition they found the most and least useful (Table 1). The EPFL Human Research Ethics Committee approved the study and the participants provided written informed consent. All calculations for the data analysis done in this study were computed in Matlab (MathWorks, Massachusetts, USA). Graphs were also ploted in Matlab and aesthetically enhanced with Adobe Illustrator (Adobe Systems Incorporated, San Jose, CA, USA).

3   Results

3.1   Performance Results

Participant performance was measured as the RMS error reduction obtained by subtracting the RMS error of each task done with haptic guidance from the RMS error in the condition without guidance for each participant. This removes the performance level variation among participants and shows the effect of flying with a haptic guidance with respect to no guidance, i.e. what is the error reduction induced by the haptic guidance comparatively to flying without guidance. Therefore, a positive RMS error reduction means that the haptic guidance increases flight performance.

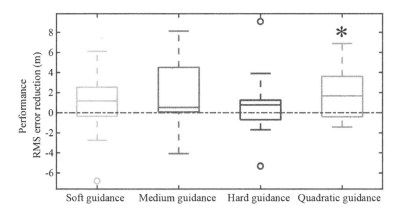

Fig. 4. Participant performance measured by RMS error reduction of each haptic guidance relative to without guidance ($n = 10$). The central mark indicates the median, the bottom edge the 25th percentile and the top edge the 75th percentile. The whiskers show the most extreme data points not considered outliers (open circles). Asterisk (*) denotes $p < 0.05$.

Results of Fig. 4 show that the median RMS errors for all types of haptic guidance are positive; the RMS error of the task was lower when performing the task with any type of haptic guidance than when flying without guidance. To determine if any of the guidance has a statistically significant effect on the error reduction, we ran a Wilcoxon Signed Rank Test using Matlab. The error reduction was significant for the quadratic guidance with a p-value of 0.0488. The three other guidance conditions, i.e. soft guidance (p-value = 0.4922), medium guidance (p-value = 0.0840) and hard guidance (p-value = 0.4316), do not show any statistical significance. However, due to the limited number of samples commonly gathered with human experiments, these results do not have a high statistical power. Therefore, we used a bootstrap metric. This non-parametric method generates the replication of 500 sample means (obtained by sampling with replacement 10 samples from the original dataset), which follow the same distribution as the data recorded during the experiment. This allowed us to obtain the empirical distribution for the sample mean. We then assessed whether the [2.5;97.5] quantile interval covers 0; the negation of the latter implying that the mean is significantly different than 0. We found that the quadratic guidance has a significant p-value of 0.0040, which supports the result found using the Wilcoxon Signed Rank Test done on our ten participants. In addition, the medium guidance also has a significant result with a p-value of 0.0260. The other two guidance conditions, i.e. soft guidance and hard guidance did not show any statistical significance with p-values of 0.2080 and 0.1860 respectively.

3.2 Subjective Assessment of Haptic Guidance

At the end of the experiment, participants filled a questionnaire specific to haptic guidance. The statement "I found the haptic guidance useful" was rated 6.08 out of 7 on the Likert scale from 1 (Strongly disagree) to 7 (Strongly agree). All participants rated between 5 and 7. They reported that it helped them anticipate maneuvers, particularly roll movements.

In the same questionnaire, they had to state which flight condition they found the most and the least enjoyable and the most and the least useful (Table 1). 6/10 participants found the hard guidance the least enjoyable versus 0/10 for the quadratic guidance. Also, half of the participants found the hard guidance the least useful versus 1/10 for the quadratic guidance. Notably, no participants found that the soft guidance, which provides the weakest force, was the least useful guidance.

Results for the most enjoyable and the most useful haptic guidance were more mixed (Table 1). 3/10 participants found the quadratic guidance the most enjoyable and the most useful and three others the soft guidance versus 0/10 for without guidance. As no participants rated the without guidance condition as the most enjoyable or the most useful, this result corroborates the high score of the guidance usefulness.

Table 1. Number of participants selecting the flight task as the most or least enjoyable and most or least useful in the final questionnaire (n = 10).

In which task was haptic feedback:	Soft guidance	Medium guidance	Hard guidance	Quadratic guidance	Without guidance
the least enjoyable	1	2	6	0	1
the least useful	0	1	5	1	3
the most enjoyable	3	3	1	3	0
the most useful	3	2	2	3	0

3.3 Workload Results

As shown in Fig. 5A, there are no statistically significant workload differences between flying with a haptic guidance and flying without guidance. There is also no difference in workload among haptic guidance types. Workload is composed of six different contributions: physical demand, mental demand, effort, temporal demand, frustration and performance, each of which can be analyzed separately [25]. The effort (Fig. 5B) when flying with the medium and the quadratic guidance is significantly lower than when flying without guidance (p = 0.0488 and p = 0.0352 respectively). The same bootstrap metric used for the performance analysis with a replication of 500 sample means was applied. Both guidance show significance with p = 0.0080 for the medium guidance and p = 0.0040 for the quadratic guidance. The contribution of the effort on the general workload is 17%. The other workload contributions did not show any significant difference from zero and between guidance conditions.

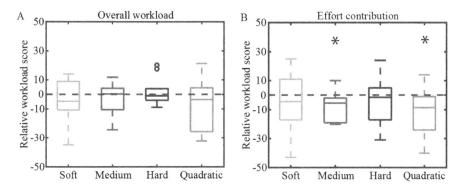

Fig. 5. (A) Overall workload found from the Nasa-TLX questionnaire, which includes contribution from the effort. See Fig. 4 for boxplot explanation. (B) Effort contribution. (*) denotes p < 0.05 (n = 10), (open circles) signify outliers.

4 Discussion

This study demonstrated that receiving quadratically shaped haptic guidance when performing a flight task with the FlyJacket helped improve flight accuracy without increasing the workload. Out of the four force profiles tested, the quadratic profile was found to be the best over three linear profiles of different stiffness. In addition, our results showed that all users found haptic guidance useful when flying.

Having a quadratically shaped guidance, which gives weak force when the error is small and strong force when the error becomes large, is the most effective type of feedback to improve precision but also the one that requires the lowest effort. In comparison, the soft guidance was not only more enjoyable than hard guidance, but participants also found it more useful. Hard guidance was rated least enjoyable because participants felt the force was too strong. This may be because any small deviations from the nominal trajectories trigger large forces from the FlyJacket's haptic system, frequently perturbing the user's body. Consequently, they may not feel fully in control of their torso orientation, leading to the unpleasant feeling of being obstructed or to user passiveness [19]. The medium guidance, which is an intermediate guidance between the hard and soft guidance, had a more meaningful impact on the performance than the two extremes (soft and hard guidance) and significantly reduced user's effort.

Our study had a few limitations. We instructed users to follow waypoints during the evaluation task, and we calculated the performance measure only at these waypoints. However, in order to have a more precise understanding of drone dynamics, error in future studies could be measured by assessing the deviation from an overall trajectory, rather than discrete waypoints. To do so, additional experiments should be designed were the participant is able to see, for example by the mean of a line, the full trajectory in between the waypoints. We also restricted our tests to proportional controllers. Additional experiments could be performed to determine if adding a derivative term of the drone position to the quadratic or medium controller (e.g. PD controller) would further improve the performance.

By identifying an effective profile to reduce the error when following waypoints, this study provides the basis for further investigating the learning rate of the user with guidance in comparison to without guidance. The goal will be to understand if haptic guidance can accelerate the flight learning process and if this knowledge can be better retained by users. If so, having such a haptic guidance included in the FlyJacket could greatly reduce user training time. This could facilitate drone control and, therefore, make their use more accessible to non-expert users. For real world applications, we will also explore the use of haptic guidance for obstacle avoidance. This collision avoidance feedback can also be implemented by having the device pull the user's torso away from obstacles detected by vison or range sensors commonly embedded in commercial drones. While our current study utilized known reference trajectories for guidance, this type of force feedback can also be applied to constrain user motions to prevent maneuvers outside the flight envelope of the drone, for example to avoid stall conditions.

Acknowledgments. The authors would like to acknowledge Alexandre Cherpillod for the implementation of the error calculation in the drone simulator and thanks Claire Donnat for her help with the statistical analysis. This work has been supported by the Swiss National Center of Competence in Research in Robotics (NCCR Robotics).

References

1. Floreano, D., Wood, R.J.: Science, technology and the future of small autonomous drones. Nature **521**(7553), 460–466 (2015)
2. Murphy, R.R., Tadokoro, S., Nardi, D., Jacoff, A., Fiorini, P., Choset, H., Erkmen, A.M.: Search and rescue robotics. In: Siciliano, B., Khatib, O. (eds.) Springer Handbook of Robotics, pp. 1151–1173. Springer, Heidelberg (2008). https://doi.org/10.1007/978-3-540-30301-5_51
3. Sanna, A., Lamberti, F., Paravati, G., Manuri, F.: A Kinect-based natural interface for quadrotor control. Entertain. Comput. **4**(3), 179–186 (2013)
4. Pfeil, K., Koh, S.L., LaViola, J.: Exploring 3D gesture metaphors for interaction with unmanned aerial vehicles. In: Proceedings of the 2013 International Conference on Intelligent User Interfaces, pp. 257–266. ACM, Santa Monica (2013)
5. Miehlbradt, J., Cherpillod, A., Mintchev, S., Coscia, M., Artoni, F., Floreano, D., Micera, S.: A data-driven body-to-machine interface for the effortless control of drones, submitted for publication
6. Rognon, C., Mintchev, S., Dell'Agnola, F., Cherpillod, A., Atienza, D., Floreano, D.: FlyJacket: an upper-body soft exoskeleton for immersive drone control. IEEE Robot. Autom. Lett. **3**(3), 2362–2369 (2018)
7. Coad, M.M., Okamura, A.M., Wren, S., Mintz, Y., Lendvay, T.S., Jarc, A.M., Nisky, I.: Training in divergent and convergent force fields during 6-DOF teleoperation with a robot-assisted surgical system. In: IEEE World Haptics Conference, pp. 195–200. IEEE, Munich (2017)
8. Nef, T., Mihelj, M., Riener, R.: ARMin: a robot for patient-cooperative arm therapy. Med. Biol. Eng. Comput. **45**(9), 887–900 (2007)
9. Rauter, G., von Zitzewitz, J., Duschau-Wicke, A., Vallery, H., Riener, R.: A tendon-based parallel robot applied to motor learning in sports. In: Proceedings of 3rd IEEE RAS and EMBS International Conference on Biomedical Robotics and Biomechatronics (BioRob), pp. 82–87. IEEE, Tokyo (2010)

10. Sigrist, R., Rauter, G., Riener, R., Wolf, P.: Augmented visual, auditory, haptic, and multimodal feedback in motor learning: a review. Psychon. Bull. Rev. **20**(1), 21–53 (2013)
11. Lam, T.M., Mulder, M., van Paassen, M.R.: Haptic interface in UAV tele-operation using force-stiffness feedback. In: International Conference on Systems, Man and Cybernetics, pp. 835–840. IEEE, San Antonio (2009)
12. Son, H.I., Kim, J., Chuang, L., Franchi, A., Giordano, P.R., Lee, D., Bülthoff, H.H.: An evaluation of haptic cues on the tele-operator's perceptual awareness of multiple UAVs' environments. In: World Haptics Conference, pp. 149–154. IEEE, Istanbul (2011)
13. Omari, S., Hua, M.D., Ducard, G., Hamel, T.: Bilateral haptic teleoperation of VTOL UAVs. In: IEEE International Conference on Robotics and Automation, pp. 2393–2399. IEEE, Karlsruhe (2013)
14. Hou, X., Mahony, R., Schill, F.: Comparative study of haptic interfaces for bilateral teleoperation of VTOL aerial robots. IEEE Trans. Syst. Man Cybern. Syst. **46**(10), 1352–1363 (2016)
15. Kanso, A., Elhajj, I.H., Shammas, E., Asmar, D.: Enhanced teleoperation of UAVs with haptic feedback. In: IEEE International Conference on Advanced Intelligent Mechatronics (AIM), pp. 305–310. IEEE, Busan (2015)
16. van Asseldonk, E.H., Wessels, M., Stienen, A.H., van der Helm, F.C., van der Kooij, H.: Influence of haptic guidance in learning a novel visuomotor task. J. Physiol. Paris **103**(3), 276–285 (2009)
17. Mulder, M., Abbink, D.A., Boer, E.R.: The effect of haptic guidance on curve negotiation behavior of young, experienced drivers. In: IEEE International Conference on Systems, Man and Cybernetics, pp. 804–809. IEEE, Singapore (2008)
18. Forsyth, B.A., MacLean, K.E.: Predictive haptic guidance: intelligent user assistance for the control of dynamic tasks. IEEE Trans. Vis. Comput. Graph. **12**(1), 103–113 (2006)
19. Schmidt, R.A., Wrisberg, C.A.: Motor Learning and Performance (2004)
20. McGill, S., Seguin, J., Bennett, G.: Passive stiffness of the lumber torso in flexion, extension, lateral bending, and axial rotation: effect of belt wearing and breath holding. Spine **19**(6), 696–704 (1994)
21. Mcneill, T., Warwick, D., Andersson, G., Schultz, A.: Trunk strengths in attempted flexion, extension, and lateral bending in healthy subjects and patients with low-back disorders. Spine **5**(6), 529–538 (1980)
22. Graves, J.E., Pollock, M.L., Carpenter, D.M., Leggett, S.H., Jones, A., MacMillan, M., Fulton, M.: Quantitative assessment of full range-of-motion isometric lumbar extension strength. Spine **15**(4), 289–294 (1990)
23. Rebelo, J., Sednaoui, T., den Exter, E.B., Krueger, T., Schiele, A.: Bilateral robot teleoperation: a wearable arm exoskeleton featuring an intuitive user interface. IEEE Robot. Autom. Magaz. **21**(4), 62–69 (2014)
24. Cherpillod, A., Mintchev, S., Floreano, D.: Embodied flight with a drone. arXiv preprint arXiv:1707.01788 (2017)
25. Hart, S.G., Staveland, L.E.: Development of NASA-TLX (Task Load Index): results of empirical and theoretical research. Adv. Psychol. **52**, 139–183 (1988)

Human Guidance: Suggesting Walking Pace Under Manual and Cognitive Load

Tommaso Lisini Baldi[1,2(✉)], Gianluca Paolocci[1,2],
and Domenico Prattichizzo[1,2]

[1] Department of Information Engineering and Mathematics,
University of Siena, Via Roma 56, 53100 Siena, Italy
{lisini,paolocci,prattichizzo}@diism.unisi.it
[2] Department of Advanced Robotics, Istituto Italiano di Tecnologia,
Via Morego 30, 16163 Genova, Italy

Abstract. This paper presents a comparison between two different approaches to control human walking cadence, with the further aim to assess if the users can synchronize to the suggested rhythm with low efforts while performing other tasks. Elastic haptic bands are used to suggest walking-pace during an exercise aimed at reproducing real industrial or human-robot cooperation task. The proposed system consists of two wearable interfaces for providing timing information to the users, and a pressure sensor to estimate the real gait pattern, thus resulting in a combination of walking-state monitoring and vibro-tactile stimuli to regulate the walking pace. Vibrational stimuli with a constant presentation interval are alternately and repeatedly given to the right and left side of the human body, in accordance with the desired walking cadence. We tested two different interface placements: wrists and ankles. The guidance system has been evaluated under mental and manual workload using an additional task: balancing a small sphere in the center of a flat surface. Experimental results revealed that subjects prefer the ankle position for what concerns wearability, comfort and easiness in task execution. Examples of the proposed approach in daily use are training and coaching in sports, rehabilitation, and human-robot cooperation and interaction.

1 Introduction

Nowadays there is growing interest in technologies and methods to assist people during daily activities; despite many attempts, research on navigation aids is still in its infancy. Most of them rely on vision or hearing as primary communication channels, which could be overloaded in many multi-tasking scenarios. We investigated the opportunity of controlling pedestrian cadence at non-attentional level.

The research leading to these results has received funding from the European Union Horizon 2020 research and innovation programme - Societal Challenge 1 (DG CONNECT/H) under grant agreement n. 643644 of the project "ACANTO: A CyberphysicAl social NeTwOrk using robot friends".

The original version of this chapter was revised: The title of this chapter was corrected. The erratum to this chapter is available at https://doi.org/10.1007/978-3-319-93399-3_60

D. Prattichizzo et al. (Eds.): EuroHaptics 2018, LNCS 10894, pp. 416–427, 2018.
https://doi.org/10.1007/978-3-319-93399-3_36

Related works demonstrated that walkers are able to synchronize to auditory and visual cues [5], but this approach demands more attention and may conflict with daily tasks due to the limited resources availability [22]. The interaction with electronics and mechanical devices may arise interference due to the dependency on visual and auditory channels, contributing to overload, thus reduce, sensory perceptions [13,19]. A clear way to reduce cognitive load consists in replacing the audiovisual cues with stimuli involving other senses. This prevents channels from saturating and lowers the overall mental efforts [3].

Our method exploits a feature of the human sensory-motor system, called sensory-motor entrainment, to suggest a specific walking cadence [6,14]. It is known that the frequency of a cyclic movement, such as walking and running, can be affected by rhythmic sensory inputs and can smoothly converge to the input rhythm. For example, when people walk while listening to music, their step cycle gradually conforms to the rhythm of the music. Recent works highlighted how haptic stimuli can be used to deliver walking cadence with minimal interference to other sensory channels, which might lead to better user safety or task execution. In this paper we outline how, given a desired walking pace, users can adjust their gait cadence to match it with little error and minimal effort by means of vibro-tactile cues. The coordination of a team of humans for sport training and the cooperation between humans and robots, represent two examples among the numerous guidance scenarios. Haptic communication offers an effective, yet non-intrusive, way for providing cues to the users when visual modality is temporarily impaired or the audio modality is overloaded by background noise. The underlying idea is that audio or visual systems do not represent the right solutions to guide the walking velocity of a subject while hands are involved in a task, such as assembling parts in an industrial environment or writing on a touch display. By freeing cognitive and attentional resources, the users can carry out their tasks with improved safety and quality.

Recently, several systems based on haptics have been developed, most of which focus on providing stimuli mainly via bracelets and waist belts. More in detail, a torso-mounted vibro-tactile display was used to provide cues for improving situational awareness of soldiers in a simulated building-clearing exercise [10]. In [4,20], a vibro-tactile belt was used for human guidance in indoor and outdoor environments, respectively. In [17], the authors used vibro-tactile armbands to guide users along a predefined path, assisted by a mobile robot. In addition, in [3] the authors exploited the use of haptic stimuli for indoors pedestrian guidance using two wrist-worn interfaces. Vibro-tactile armbands were used to navigate subjects along fixed and dynamic paths [2,11], where three basic haptic cues were sent to the user to steer the locomotion. Adame *et al.* in [1] proposed a comparison among different vibro-tactile devices for guidance of visually impaired users. Most of the contributions in literature focused on how to suggest a given rotation to the human body, or how to steer humans along a certain trajectory. An often undervalued important parameter to guide locomotion is the time to reach the target *i.e.*, the steps cadence. Haptic interfaces placed at the subjects feet were used to regulate gait frequency through vibrations in [21]. In [8] the authors presented an interesting vibro-tactile guidance method to suggest cadence to users by means of haptics. An exemplar application is guiding subjects toward the closest bus stop at the optimal walking speed. Also post-stroke rehabilitation benefits from periodic vibro-tactile cues, in terms of increase in subjects' step length and synchronization to the provided rhythm, compared to audio and visual signals [7].

With this work, we present results concerning the idea of using haptic interfaces to suggest walking pace when users are asked to accomplish additional tasks. We tried to replicate the traits of a real scenario, such as human-robot cooperation and industrial tasks. In particular we concentrate on applications where the operator use her/his hands to perform manipulation tasks while walking towards a target.

Two different solutions to provide the periodic vibro-tactile guidance have been tested and compared with the approach proposed in [8], to extend it under cognitive and manual load.

2 Human Pace Suggestion via Haptic Feedback

In this Section we analyze the gait synchronization strategy developed to control the user gait cadence. The principles of our guidance approach are based on the step cycle schema proposed by Philippson in [15]. A step consists of a limb movement performed from heel strike to next heel strike of the same foot. The step cycle and length are defined as temporal duration and spatial distance of a single step.

In our method, haptic stimuli, *i.e.*, vibrations, are periodically provided to different left/right body parts to assess which is the most suitable haptic input location. The user mean gait cadence is measured using a pressure sensor placed under the right foot, and is compared with the suggested cadence.

In this paper we want to investigate whether it is more beneficial to place the haptic interface on the wrists or the ankles while humans are performing additional tasks. To identify which is the best location for the haptic stimulation in a work environment, we asked participants to perform additional tasks, which purpose was to increase the manual and mental workload to verify differences in performances related to the haptic bands locations. Synchronization capability and comfort are the metrics used to evaluate the best body location.

2.1 System Overview

The proposed system is composed of two parts: the former is in charge of providing haptic cues to the user, whereas the latter, used only for experimental testing and validation, detects contacts between the foot and the ground, thus to compute the user cadence. In what follows we describe the two components of the system.

Haptic Bands. The desired cadence is suggested to the users through rhythmic vibrations provided by remotely controlled elastic haptic bands. Each wearable haptic interface is composed by two water-proof vibro-motors, which can be independently controlled (Fig. 1). Whenever a trigger is sent to a haptic device, the motors vibrate providing a vibro-tactile stimulus to the wearer. In order not to overload the user's tactile channel and reduce the recognition time, we do not modulate the frequency of the signal, but we use a simple on/off mechanism, similar to the one used in [18]. We activate alternatively the two devices in accordance with the desired gait cycle. An additional stimulus to *stop* the user by activating both the haptic devices is implemented. When an interface is activated, its motors vibrate for 0.1 s at a frequency of 250 Hz. Subjects wear one haptic bracelet on each ankle or wrist in order to maximize the stimuli separation, keeping the discrimination process as intuitive as possible.

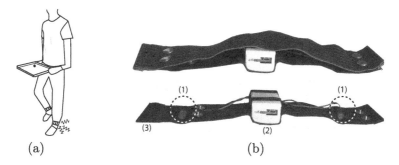

(a)   (b)

Fig. 1. Cadence cues are provided to the users via two vibro-tactile elastic bands placed on the wrists or on the ankles (a) of the user during a task with manual and cognitive load. The haptic bands (b) are composed of two vibrating motors (1) attached to an elastic wristband (3). A Li-Ion battery is in charge of power and an Arduino board controls the interface (2).

The communication is realized with an RN-42 Bluetooth antenna connected to a 3.3 V Arduino pro-mini. The wireless connection baud rate is 57600 bps. The microcontroller installed on the board is used to independently control the activation of each motor and receiving data from an external PC. Note that the proposed vibro-motors are controlled by applying a certain amount of voltage which determines both frequency and amplitude. Thus, we can not change frequency and amplitude independently. As the user's maximal sensitivity is achieved around 200–300 Hz [16] (the human perceptibility range is between 20 Hz and 400 Hz), two Precision Microdrives Pico Vibe vibration motors are placed into two fabric pockets inside the bracelet (the width of the wristband is about 60 mm), with vertically aligned shafts. The motors have a vibration frequency range of 100–300 Hz, lag time of about 20 ms, rise and stop time of 35 ms. The bracelet guarantees about 4 h of battery life with one motor always turned on. Each bracelet weights about 90 g.

Pressure Sensor. The second component has been developed to capture the walking pattern, with the aim to extract the step timing. Its function is the heel strike detection and it is composed by a flexible force sensor (FSR 400, manufactured by Interlink Electronics, Inc.) and a XBee radio module. The force sensing resistor measures the force applied through the deformation of the active surface, which produces a resistance variation. We use this component as unobtrusive and comfortable switch to detect the contact of the shoe with the ground. The XBee module is used to convert an analog signal into a digital signal and send it wirelessly to another module, connected to the laptop. The pressure value is converted into a 10 bit digital signal. The step extraction procedure exploits a single-threshold value, defined as the double of the standard deviation of the data, measured during the initialization phase (see Sect. 3). The sensor records the pressure under the heel at 100 Hz. Thus, we are able to measure the step cycle and monitor the walking state from the obtained data. The step-detection procedure consists of three phases. In the first step, raw pressure data are acquired by the system and normalized (Fig. 2(a), then it is transformed into a two-levels signal using a custom threshold (Fig. 2(b)). The square wave indicates whether the foot is in contact or not with the ground, assuming value 1 or 0, respectively. Then, the algorithm extracts positive edges matching the contact of the heel with the floor, identifying the step as the interval between two consecutive edges. Let the number of steps per minute be the *stride-frequency* and the space between two subsequent steps the *stride-length*. *Walking velocity* can be thus computed as the product of *stride-frequency* and *stride-lenght*. Even if the walking speed seems to be controlled by two parameters, Laurent *et al.* in [9] demonstrated that the gait can be controlled acting on only one of the two parameters. We decide to control the stride-frequency.

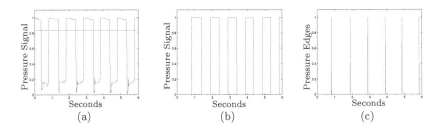

Fig. 2. The pressure values are recorded by a flexible force sensor (FSR 400) and sent wireless through a XBee radio module. The raw signal showed in (a) is normalized between 0 and 1. Steps are extracted by thresholding the raw signal (b), and only considering the positive edges (c). The threshold is set at $2*STD$ (Standard Deviation).

3   Experimental Validation

We validated the proposed walking-pace suggestion technique using two different body locations for the haptic interfaces, wrist and ankle.

Preliminary Test. We started the experimental validation of our system by exploiting the results presented in [8]. We performed preliminary tests using haptic interfaces either as bracelets or anklets. Eight healthy subjects walked for 220 m. Three step duration values were tested for each configuration. Each test S_i was labeled according to the suggested walking pace ($i = \{1, 2, 3\}$ corresponding to the desired step cycles of 0.8, 1.0, and 1.2 s, respectively). We selected these values to test the system since we observed in preparatory experiments that 0.8–1.2 s is a suitable range considering the standard human comfortable cadence. The aim of this test was to verify the attitude of our system in suggesting walking speed and computing a rough estimation of users' response. Users, step duration and body location were pseudo-randomly selected. We discarded the first 4 s of data, where the participant is transitioning from stationary to walking state. During task execution, participants wore headphones reproducing white noise to be acoustically insulated from the environment and avoid cues generated from the motors vibrations. The metric is the error in adapting to the proposed rhythm. We defined the error as the average of the difference between subjects' and desired stride duration per each step, normalized and expressed in percentage (with respect to the suggested cadence):

$$error = \frac{1}{N} \sum_{k=1}^{N} \left| \frac{u(k) - d(k)}{d(k)} \right| \times 100\%. \tag{1}$$

Where N is the number of steps walked during the test, u_k and d_k are the duration of the $k - th$ step and the desired time, respectively. The standard deviation of the error, calculated for each subject, is considered the user synchronization capability. In fact, the higher is the standard deviation the bigger is the difference in step duration. In Sect. 4.1 we report and discuss results with statistical tests.

3.1   Cognitive Load

The main objective of this work is to compare the performance of the haptic guidance method for users performing tasks requiring cognitive load. In line with the aim of the paper, two conditions were considered: vibrations provided on wrists and ankles.

Once the capability of suggesting walking pace using vibrations was established, and a candidate interface location was determined in absence of secondary tasks, we studied the potential of the proposed system in association with manual and cognitive tasks. To increase the subject cognitive load during the synchronized walk a balancing ball-plate game has been designed in a preparatory phase. This task involved the use of both hands, to simulate a real work situation, and required a discrete effort to successfully accomplish the trial.

The aim of the task was to maintain a ball inside a plate avoiding contacts with the edges. It can be considered very close to a real task: maintaining a ball in the center of a plate involves hands, eyes, and it is not excessively immersive. Moreover, we can score and rate how the user is performing the tasks. The plate is equipped with a touch sensor on the border, thus the number of hits (i.e. errors in execution) gives a score on the accomplishment.

The evaluation of the system with additional cognitive load was performed on 16 healthy subjects (10 males, age range 23–35): one of them had experience with the proposed vibro-tactile device, the remaining users had less or no experience with our haptic interfaces. None of the participants reported any deficiencies in perception abilities or physical impairments. To enrich the discussion after the trials and to better understand the results, we estimated the user's physiological cadence at the beginning of the experiment. We asked users to walk for the entire pathway without haptic suggestions. In the first 20 m we checked and calibrated the pressure sensor, whereas in the remaining we evaluate the most comfortable walking cadence while the user acquainted with the pathway. Then, subjects were asked to synchronize the gait cadence to the vibrations provided by the haptic devices. Two values of cadence were tested: ±10% with respect to the comfortable one (previously estimated). We adopted user-dependent cadences to preserve uniformity in testing an heterogeneous set of volunteer with variegated ages, heights, and walking habits. Each participant performed 5 trials: the comfortable gait cycle was estimated during the first trial, then the 4 remaining trials were haptic-guided. Subjects and desired walking pace were sorted in a pseudo-random order. Our setup was not designed to measure the step length, so we refer to the mean cadence, which is the inverse of the mean step duration. During task execution, participants wore headphones reproducing white noise to acoustically insulate them from the environment and avoid cues generated from the motors vibrations. As the primary hypothesis was to provide a purely tactile stimulus, the white noise was designed to cover the motor vibration noise. Each subject was followed by a ghost operator equipped with a laptop for data acquisition, walking at distance of about 5 m behind. This distance was selected not to disturb the task execution, while keeping the communication active between the wireless devices. Furthermore, vibrations parameters were manually set by the operator via an ad-hoc software. The operator was also in charge of starting the pressure data recording, using the same software. The pressure sensor was placed in the same position of the previous experimental setup. The pressure sensor placement has proven critical for the success of the measurement: the optimal place was the posterior part of the sole, where there was no contact with the foot during the swing phase. We selected this location after numerous prior tests.

4   Results and Discussion

In this section we analyse the data collected in the experimental phase (see Sect. 3) by means of statistical tests to give a more accurate and reliable interpretation, then we proceed with a discussion on the users questionnaire responses.

4.1   Results and Statistical Analysis

Preliminary Test. Regarding the preparatory test, for each user we compared the gait cycle error (mean and standard deviation) in trials with different haptic

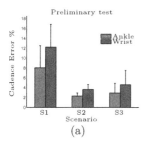
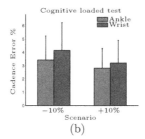
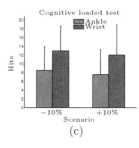

(a)   (b)   (c)

Fig. 3. Results of the experimental validation, divided by scenario. Blue bars represent data where haptic cues were provided to the wrist, whereas red bars represent data where information was displayed at ankle location. (a) Preliminary test. In S1 users were asked to follow a 0.8 s step cycle, 1.0 and 1.2 s were asked in S2 and S3 respectively. (b–c) Cognitive test. Two values of step cycle were tested: ±10% with respect to the comfortable pace. In (b) we report error in maintaining the suggested cadence, whereas in (c) bars depict error in performing the task (*i.e.*, number of hits). (Color figure online)

interface body locations. We calculated the difference between the synchronization error while performing the "ankle "trials and the error in the "wrist" trials of the same subjects, at the same desired cadence, and then we ran statistical analysis on that data. Visual representation is summarized in Fig. 3. Experimental results revealed an average error among all trials of $6.62 \pm 2.16\%$ and $4.19 \pm 2.33\%$ in the case of interfaces worn as bracelets and anklets, respectively. Since we were interested in selecting the optimal location, we performed statistical analysis tests to assess if the difference in error was significant or not. Resulting errors were normally distributed, as assessed by Shapiro-Wilk's test ($p = 0.365 > 0.05$). Statistical tests revealed a mean gait cycle error reduction of $2.43 \pm 0.85\%$ while wearing haptic interfaces as anklet with respect to the wrist placement. The paired samples t-test underlined a statistically significant decrement of the mean error using anklets ($t(23) = 2.829$, $p = 0.012 < 0.05$). Then we ran statistics on the subjects error standard deviation. The Shapiro-Wilk's test assessed the normality of the distribution ($p = 0.770 > 0.05$).

Additionally, three paired-samples t-tests were conducted, to check whether in the three different scenarios (S1, S2, and S3) the metric of interest proved more statistically significant in ankle stimulation with respect to the wrist positioning. For each test, we computed the error percent between the real and desired cadence (cfr. Eq. (1)) and then performed statistical analyses to assert differences in performance between the proposed haptic bands locations. We verified the absence of significant outliers, and the possibility to approximate the dependent variable distributions of the two groups (trials with bracelets and anklets) as normal distributions. None of the tests showed outliers, and the assumption of normality was not violated in any test, as assessed by Shapiro-Wilk's test ($p_1 = 0.366$, $p_2 = 0.312$, $p_3 = 0.646$ for the error mean, and $p_1 = 0.807$, $p_2 = 0.532$, $p_3 = 0.288$ for the error standard deviation). Participants were found to align with the desired cadence more often (*i.e.*, the average error is lower) when the elastic haptic bands were positioned on ankles: outcomes of data analysis showed an error percent reduction of $4.09 \pm 1.69\%$, $1.31 \pm 0.41\%$, and $1.70 \pm 0.55\%$ in scenario S1, S2, and S3 ($t_1(7) = 2.418$, $p < 0.05$, $t_2(7) = 3.160$, $p < 0.05$, $t_3(7) = 3.101$, $p < 0.05$). The mean difference in standard deviation indicated that subjects were able to synchronize more consistently using the haptic interfaces as anklets: values obtained were $1.48 \pm 0.33\%$, $0.75 \pm 0.27\%$, and $1.09 \pm 0.35\%$, respectively in scenario S1, S2, and S3 ($t_1(7) = 3.424$, $p < 0.05$, $t_2(7) = 2.706$, $p < 0.05$, $t_3(7) = 3.072$, $p < 0.05$).

Cognitive Test. For what concerns the test executed with a not-negligible cognitive load task, we evaluated the results through two different metrics: the error in following the suggested step frequency and the number of times the ball hit the tray margin during the task execution. In Fig. 3(b) and 3(c) we pictorially summarize the experimental evaluation results. On both metrics of interest we carried out statistical tests to validate the results. As we did for the preparatory experiment, we analysed errors on trials with different gait cadence both separately and together. For what concerns all the trial, the wrist location elicited a statistically significant average error increasing of $0.54 \pm 0.17\%$ compared to the ankle. Statistical significance was established using paired-sample t-test ($t(31) = 3.132, p < 0.05$). Values satisfied the Shapiro-Wilk test ensuring a normal distribution of the mean error differences ($p > 0.05$). Additionally, statistical analysis was used to infer about the subjects synchronization. Users maintained a more uniform pace using the haptic bands as anklets. Difference between error standard deviations using bracelets and anklets resulted to be $0.22 \pm 0.06\%$. The Shapiro-Wilk test verified the distribution normality ($p > 0.05$) and the paired-sample t-test confirmed the statistical significance ($t(31) = 3.768, p < 0.05$). Moreover, we performed single paired-sample t-test for each condition, investigating whether the increasing in performance is related to the position of the haptic bands for each scenario. For both gait cycle conditions we compared the error mean values. The ankle solution, compared to the wrist location, elicited an average error reduction of $0.26 \pm 0.11\%$ ($t(15) = 2.339$, $p < 0.05$) in following the slower rhythm and $0.80 \pm 0.31\%$ ($t(15) = 2.607$, $p < 0.05$) for the faster one. The error standard deviation reduction is $0.20 \pm 0.08\%$ ($t(15) = 2.335$, $p < 0.05$) in following the slower rhythm and $0.25 \pm 0.08\%$ ($t(15) = 2.903$, $p < 0.05$) for the faster one. Error are expressed as percentage of the trial requested cadence.

Data from participants were analysed to understand the correlation of haptic suggestions and task performance. Number of errors (hits against the touch sensor) was used as a metric. Of the 32 trials (2 for each participant to the study), the wrist location elicited an increase in mistakes in 26 trials compared to the ankle position, whereas two trials saw no change. Moreover, results in accomplishing the requested task were analysed to further understand the correlation of haptic suggestions and task performance. Of the 16 participants recruited to the study, the anklet position elicited a reduction in hits in 12 participants compared to the wrist position, whereas one participant saw no improvement and 2 performed better with the bracelets. We performed Wilcoxon signed-rank tests considering both separating trials by gait cycle ($+10\%$, and -10% with respect to the physiological), and together. Trials with higher cadence (-10%) showed a statistically significant median reduction in hits (4 hits) when subjects wore anklets (7 hits) compared to the bracelets (11 hits), $z = 2.051$, $p < 0.05$. Also outputs of the test conducted on the slowed pace ($+10\%$) confirmed an improvement in executing the task with the anklets. The median number of hits wearing haptic interfaces in the ankles drew from 11 to 8, resulting in a median reduction of 3 hits ($z = 3.087$, $p < 0.05$).

Qualitative User Feedback. In addition to the statistical results, we take into account also the users' point of view. The aim of this paper is to compare different haptic guidance strategies for real applications. Thus, not only numbers but also personal experiences represent a key value. At the end of the trials, a survey based on the Usability and User Experience (USE) [12] in the form of a bipolar Likert-type was proposed to the subjects. The USE questionnaire evaluates three dimensions of usability: comfort, ease of use, and wearability. Each feature is evaluated using a number of items: subjects must select a mark on a seven-point scale (1 = *strongly prefer Wrist*, 7 = *strongly prefer Ankle*). Results are shown in Table 1.

Table 1. Questionnaire factors and relative marks.

Questionnaire factors	Mean (SD)
Comfort	6.33 (0.88)
Ease of use	3.82 (0.90)
Wearability	5.67 (1.10)

Marks range from "*1 = strongly prefer Wrist*" to "*7 = strongly prefer Ankle*". Mean and standard deviation (Mean (SD)) are reported

4.2 Discussion

Based on the results explained and detailed in the previous section, and from Table 1, we can assert that the ankle is the most suitable location for suggesting walking pace under mental and manual load. The test revealed that wearing the haptic interfaces in the ankles slightly increased the capability of guiding the walking pace. Several subjects stated to prefer the ankle position because they had an immediate feedback on the prediction of the next vibration thanks to the contact with the ground at the heel strike. Observing both the result graphs (Fig. 3) and the statistical test outputs, we observed that the farther the required cadence was from the comfortable one (in average 1 s per step cycle), the greater was the difference in performances between the two adopted guiding policies. Moreover, from the outcomes of these trials we noticed that the higher was the required cadence, the higher was the error.

In addition to the improvement of the performance highlighted by statistical analysis, subjects rated positively the ankle version of the system. For what concerns the easy of use, since the working principle is the same for both anklets and bracelets, results outline the equivalence of the two approaches. Without any doubt, we can affirm that the subjects strictly prefer the anklets from the comfort point of view. Users motivated this choice since the vibration in the arm was considered at the same time both a pace suggestion and a disturbance to the task. They were using their hands to balance a ball; a vibrations represented an interference in the task execution. For what concerns the last factor, the wearability feature, the questionnaire results revealed that users prefer the anklets with respect to the bracelets. This answer can be attributed to the subjects often wearing bracelets, watches and other accessories on their forearm. Despite the haptic device being lightweight (89.3 g), subjects preferred wearing it on their legs because it felt less constraining and tiring. A further suggestion users gave us after the experimental session was the possibility to hide more easily the haptic interface under their clothes in the case of anklet.

5 Conclusions

In this paper, we report preliminary results regarding the problem of guiding humans by modifying their step duration *i.e.*, the linear velocity. Haptic stimulation is used as an interesting way to provide velocity information when audio or visual channels are not available or overloaded. We consider two different location for displaying vibrations and suggesting walking pace, the wrist and the ankle. A task requiring a not negligible cognitive load was assigned to users. Experimental evaluation and subjects usage feedback showed a preference for the ankle location. Such body position resulted in a smaller error regarding rhythm synchronization and better performances in executing a real task; it also was preferred by the users for usability, wearability and comfort.

References

1. Adame, M.R., Yu, J., Moller, K., Seemann, E.: A wearable navigation aid for blind people using a vibrotactile information transfer system. In: Proceedings International Conference on Complex Medical Engineering, pp. 13–18 (2013)
2. Aggravi, M., Scheggi, S., Prattichizzo, D.: Evaluation of a predictive approach in steering the human locomotion via haptic feedback. In: Proceedings IEEE/RSJ International Conference Intelligent Robots and Systems, Hamburg, Germany (2015)
3. Bosman, S., Groenendaal, B., Findlater, J.W., Visser, T., de Graaf, M., Markopoulos, P.: GentleGuide: an exploration of haptic output for indoors pedestrian guidance. In: Chittaro, L. (ed.) Mobile HCI 2003. LNCS, vol. 2795, pp. 358–362. Springer, Heidelberg (2003). https://doi.org/10.1007/978-3-540-45233-1_28
4. Cosgun, A., Sisbot, E., Christensen, H.: Guidance for human navigation using a vibro-tactile belt interface and robot-like motion planning. In: Proceedings IEEE International Conference on Robotics and Automation, ICRA. pp. 6350–6355 (2014)

5. Danion, F., Varraine, E., Bonnard, M., Pailhous, J.: Stride variability in human gait: the effect of stride frequency and stride length. Gait & Posture **18**(1), 69–77 (2003)
6. Delcomyn, F.: Neural basis of rhythmic behavior in animals. Science **210**(4469), 492–498 (1980)
7. Georgiou, T., Holland, S., van der Linden, J.: A blended user centred design study for wearable haptic gait rehabilitation following hemiparetic stroke. Pervasive (2015)
8. Karuei, I., MacLean, K.E.: Susceptibility to periodic vibrotactile guidance of human cadence. In: Haptics Symposium (HAPTICS), 2014 IEEE, pp. 141–146. IEEE (2014)
9. Laurent, M., Pailhous, J.: A note on modulation of gait in man: effects of constraining stride length and frequency. Hum. Mov. Sci. **5**(4), 333–343 (1986)
10. Lindeman, R., Sibert, J., Mendez-Mendez, R., Patil, S., Phifer, D.: Effectiveness of directional vibrotactile cuing on a building-clearing task. In: Proceedings SIGCHI Conference on Human Factors in Computing Systems, pp. 271–280 (2005)
11. Lisini Baldi, T., Scheggi, S., Aggravii, M., Prattichizzo, D.: Haptic guidance in dynamic environments using optimal reciprocal collision avoidance. IEEE Rob. Autom. Lett. (2017)
12. Lund, A.: Measuring usability with the use questionnaire. STC usability SIG newsletter (2001)
13. MacLean, K.E.: Putting haptics into the ambience. IEEE Trans. Haptics **2**(3), 123–135 (2009)
14. Miyake, Y., Miyagawa, T.: Internal observation and co-generative interface. In: 1999 IEEE International Conference on Systems, Man, and Cybernetics, IEEE SMC 1999 Conference Proceedings, vol. 1, pp. 229–237. IEEE (1999)
15. Philippson, M.: L'autonomie et la centralisation dans le système nerveux des animaux: étude de physiologie expérimentale et comparée. Falk (1905)
16. Riener, A.: Sensor-Actuator Supported Implicit Interaction in Driver Assistance Systems. Springer, Wiesbaden (2010). https://doi.org/10.1007/978-3-8348-9777-0
17. Scheggi, S., Aggravi, M., Prattichizzo, D.: Cooperative navigation for mixed human-robot teams using haptic feedback. IEEE Trans. Hum. Mach. Syst. **47**(4), 462–473 (2017)
18. Scheggi, S., Aggravi, M., Morbidi, F., Prattichizzo, D.: Cooperative human-robot haptic navigation. In: Proceedings IEEE International Conference on Robotics and Automation, ICRA, pp. 2693–2698 (2014)
19. Traylor, R., Tan, H.Z.: Development of a wearable haptic display for situation awareness in altered-gravity environment: some initial findings. In: 10th Symposium on Haptic Interfaces for Virtual Environment and Teleoperator Systems, HAPTICS 2002, Proceedings, pp. 159–164. IEEE (2002)
20. Van Erp, J.B., Van Veen, H.A., Jansen, C., Dobbins, T.: Waypoint navigation with a vibrotactile waist belt. ACM Trans. Appl. Percept. (TAP) **2**(2), 106–117 (2005)
21. Watanabe, J., Ando, H.: Pace-sync shoes: intuitive walking-pace guidance based on cyclic vibro-tactile stimulation for the foot. Virtual Reality **14**(3), 213–219 (2010)
22. Wickens, C.D.: Multiple resources and mental workload. Hum. Factors **50**(3), 449–455 (2008)

Haptics of Screwing and Unscrewing for Its Application in Smart Factories for Disassembly

Dima Mironov[✉], Miguel Altamirano, Hasan Zabihifar, Alina Liviniuk, Viktor Liviniuk, and Dzmitry Tsetserukou

Skolkovo Institute of Science and Technology (Skoltech), 127055 Moscow, Russia
dima.mironov@skoltech.ru

Abstract. Reconstruction of the skilled human sensations and design of related control system is important for robust control of the robots. We are developing an unscrewing robot with a comprehensive control system for the automated disassembly of electronic devices. Experiments involve screwing and unscrewing, and since humans typically have a broad range of screwing experiences and sensations throughout their lives, we conducted a series of experiments to find out these haptic patterns. Results show that people apply axial force to the screws to avoid screwdriver slippage (cam-outs), which is one of the key problems during screwing and unscrewing, and this axial force is proportional to the torque which is required for screwing. We have found that type of the screw head influences the amount of axial force applied. Using this knowledge an unscrewing robot for the smart disassembly factory RecyBot is being developed, and experiments confirm the optimality of the strategy used by humans. Finally, a methodology for robust unscrewing algorithm design is presented as a generalization of the findings. It can speed up the development of the screwing and unscrewing robots and tools.

Keywords: Haptics · Screwing · Automated disassembly

1 Introduction

The importance of e-waste recycling is rapidly increasing due to the need for energy conservation material resources, and landfill capacity. For example, Apple corporation recently developed a disassembly line for iPhone 6 [9] with a high material recovery potential. A Skoltech-MIT project RecyBot has the goal to develop a universal high-speed intelligent robotic system for electronics recycling. RecyBot consists of several robots, each tailored to perform a specific task, whose joined target is to disassemble smart-phones at the component level and enable material recovery. Previous attempts of mobile phone disassembly automation have been primarily focused on the disassembly system design [6,7], yet are outdated due to the changes in a typical phone from 2006 to 2017, which obstruct

© Springer International Publishing AG, part of Springer Nature 2018
D. Prattichizzo et al. (Eds.): EuroHaptics 2018, LNCS 10894, pp. 428–439, 2018.
https://doi.org/10.1007/978-3-319-93399-3_37

milling and recent advantages in computer vision techniques, which potentially bring system autonomy issues to a new level [12]. Therefore, RecyBot focuses on the development of the series of smart robots with computer vision to automate operations often performed during electronic waste disassembly. The unscrewing operation is an essential part of the RecyBot project because screws are a central category of fasteners and are found in the majority of electronic products [11]. Screw removal has to be performed via non-destructive means, since it often precedes the battery removal, which, if broken, may cause more environmental damage, than the ecological benefits of recycling. The previous attempt to build an unscrewing robot was described by Chen et al. [4], who built a robot to assist humans in electric vehicle batteries disassembly. The paper focuses on the tool change procedure, and it omits the details of the unscrewing itself. An extensive analysis and detection of common errors during automatic unscrewing are done by Apley et al. [2]. They use a screwdriver, attached to a DC motor with a potentiometer to read the screwdriver head rotation angle, and continuously estimate the torque from the motor current. They successfully detect normal unscrewing, cam-out (slippage between the screwdriver and the screw), the situation, when the screwdriver missed the screw, and the situation, when their system cannot provide enough torque. However, they do not suggest how to overcome these problems.

Fig. 1. The experimental setup. The disposable plastic prism (2) with a 3 mm hole for the M3 screw is fixed inside the prism holder (3). The prism holder is attached to a 6 DOF force and torque sensor (4), which is fixed to a heavy table using an acrylic fixture (5). The screw is unscrewed by a participant with a corresponding screwdriver (1). The center line of the screw is positioned along the Z-axis, which points up. Force and torque along Z-axis are recorded with the frequency of 100 Hz.

The cam-out is an important issue during osteosynthesis procedures in medicine. Majewicz et al. built a simulator to teach surgeons to screw using the torque data gathered by an automated screwdriver, and validated the teaching with the help of more experienced surgeons [8]. The cam-out in the same medical context was studied in [3], where screws were intentionally damaged, and this damaging torque was measured, but the paper does not describe a way to prevent slippage which occurs not from metal deformations, but from the screwdriver coming out of the screw.

It is assumed that screwing and unscrewing patterns of humans, who incorporate their broad experiences in the patterns which they use, may lead us to insights into robotic screwing and unscrewing. Two critical characteristics of the process have been measured: force applied along the screwdriver and screwing/ unscrewing torque. Then it is observed how humans prevent cam-out (screwdriver slippage), which is one of the most common failures [2], and how they decide, when to stop. This paper presents a methodology for robust robotic unscrewing development to decrease the cam-out occurrence, using skilled humans data. The experiment on human screwing and unscrewing is presented in Sect. 2 and a description of the application of its results to an unscrewing robot is given in Sect. 3. First, experimental setup and procedure are described in Sect. 2.1, where it is measured how humans perform screwing and unscrewing operations in different conditions. The conclusions from the human experiment are presented in Sect. 2.2.

In the second part, an unscrewing robot is described, and the results of the first part are applied. First, mechanical design is described in Sect. 3.1, then the control system, which is inspired by the experiment from the first part, is elaborated on in Sect. 3.2. The experiments with the robot are further described in Sect. 3.3. The overall approach is discussed and summarized in Sect. 4.

2   Human Experiment

The principal approach of this paper is to design robot control algorithms based on the coefficients which are obtained from humans. Screwing and unscrewing are rather complex procedures, and humans integrate their past experiences into their behavior and pattern. Human screwing and unscrewing are classified, their important characteristics are measured, and then these parameters are transferred to robotic unscrewing. The experiment is designed to get a thorough and broad view of the patterns human use.

2.1   Experimental Design

The principal factors to measure and control in the screwing and unscrewing operation are the force and the torque which are applied perpendicular to the direction of the surface and along the axis of the screw (axial force). However, the torque applied during the interaction with the real smart-phone screws was too low to measure with the available sensors. To measure the human patterns of screwing and unscrewing, an experimental setup has been built as shown in Fig. 1. A plastic holder (3) was designed to keep the pilot holes and nuts object, where the screwing process happened. The object, where the participants screwed and unscrewed, was designed as a disposable triangular prism (2) with a pilot hole in the center of it of 3 mm diameter. These prisms were fixed in the center of the holder and replaced after being used. To reproduce the presence of a nut in some smart-phones, an M3 nut was added to some prisms during the 3D printing 5 mm below the end of the prism. During all the experiment were used M3 x 8 mm screws with two different heads: Phillips and internal Hex, with their corresponding screwdriver (1). The Phillips head was chosen, because it was observed that the 65.4% of the screws present in a set of 6 smart-phones of different brands are of this type. The Internal Hex head was chosen because his application is different than the Phillips type. In the Fig. 2 both the disposable plastic prisms and the heads of the two different screws used during the experiment are shown.

The holder was attached to a Robotiq 6 DOF force and torque sensor FT300 (4) and the pilot hole in the prism was aligned with a sensor along Z-axis. This sensor was chosen because of its frequency of 100 Hz for data output and the low noise signal of 0.1 N and 0.003 N · m in F_z and in M_z respectively [1], that allowed getting enough data for the purposes of this experiment. The sensor was fixed to a massive and stiff table (Siegmund Professional S4 welding table) using an acrylic base (5).

(a) Disposable plastic prism with a 3 mm pilot hole.

(b) Disposable plastic prism with an M3 nut added during the 3D printing.

(c) Phillips screw head

(d) Internal Hex screw head, also called Allen screw

Fig. 2. Disposable plastic prisms, where the participants screw and unscrew. Two types of screws were used, Phillips and Internal Hex.

Ten participants, who used screwdrivers at least occasionally for their duties, were recruited for the experiment, seven men, and three women, in an age range from 22 to 40 years. They were asked to screw the screw in the prism, holding the screwdriver only with one hand during all the process, and, if it was necessary, to hold the screw with the other hand. After that, they were asked to unscrew the same screw. The experiment consisted of 9 screwing and 9 unscrewing operations in 6 different conditions as shown in the Table 1. The condition is called "exceptional" when a screwdriver was used that did not correspond with the screw (Phillips 2), and the others" are called "typical" conditions. The disposable prism has been replaced after each unscrewing, to avoid the influence of the thread, which appeared in the plastic. Four of the participants were also asked to screw and unscrew the screw into the disposable plastic prism without applying any force in the direction of the screw.

Table 1. The experiment conditions imposed on the subjects.

Repetitions	Operation	Screw type	Orientation of the screwdriver	Prism type	Screwdriver type
2	Screwing	Phillips	Horizontal	Pilot hole	Phillips 0
2	Unscrewing	Phillips	Horizontal	Pilot hole	Phillips 0
1	Screwing	Internal Hex	Horizontal	Pilot hole	Internal Hex 2.5
1	Unscrewing	Internal Hex	Horizontal	Pilot hole	Internal Hex 2.5
3	Screwing	Phillips	Horizontal	With M3 nut	Phillips 0
3	Unscrewing	Phillips	Horizontal	With M3 nut	Phillips 0
1	Screwing	Phillips	Horizontal	Pilot hole	Phillips 2
1	Unscrewing	Phillips	Horizontal	Pilot hole	Phillips 2
1	Screwing	Phillips	Vertical	Pilot hole	Phillips 0
1	Unscrewing	Phillips	Vertical	Pilot hole	Phillips 0
1	Screwing	Internal Hex	Vertical	Pilot hole	Internal Hex 2.5
1	Unscrewing	Internal Hex	Vertical	Pilot hole	Internal Hex 2.5

2.2   Experimental Results

The typical patterns of force and torque during unscrewing of Phillips screws in plastic disposable prism are shown in Fig. 3. The oscillatory pattern with the frequency of (1.3 ± 0.4) Hz is observed in every operation plot. The average period of oscillations was calculated for all experiments using periods between local maximums. The deviation of max and min length of cycle from the average is used as an amendment. It is observed in all the measurements from all the participants both in torque and in force and is independent of age or gender. It is caused by the need for humans to regrasp the screwdriver due to lack of joints with limitless rotation.

The pattern of local maximums of torque and force represents the moments when real screwing and unscrewing were happening. The torque required to rotate the screw is defined by the friction, which is defined by the environment: it depends on the state of the thread in the plastic and weakly depends on the rotation speed in a wide range of speeds (see Sect. 3.3). During unscrewing from a disposable plastic prism (see Fig. 3a), the maximal torque is applied at the beginning of the procedure, and then it decreases gradually, which is defined by the decrease of the length of the screw inside the plastic and thus the friction decrease. In Fig. 3c a typical screwing pattern is shown. The torque is gradually increasing in the first seconds while the screw is dipping into the plastic. Then it remains constant indicating, that most friction is occurring due to the need to cut a new treading in the plastic. Final torque increase indicates the reach of the plastic surface with a screw head. Humans feel the torque increase and stop screwing.

A correlation between force and torque applied simultaneously is observed, which can be seen in Fig. 3b. For all of the measured conditions the absolute value of the correlation coefficient $r = (0.75 \pm 0.13)$, which indicates a significant rela-

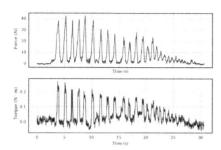

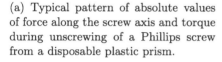

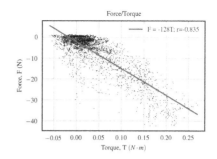

(a) Typical pattern of absolute values of force along the screw axis and torque during unscrewing of a Phillips screw from a disposable plastic prism.

(b) Relationship between force and torque for the time series from (a). Points represent individual measurements and the red line is the least squares approximation.

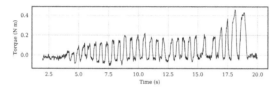

(c) Typical pattern of absolute values of torque during screwing of a Phillips screw into a disposable plastic prism.

Fig. 3. Typical patterns of force along the screw axis and torque during screwing and unscrewing an M3 Phillips screw in the disposable plastic prism.

tion. We than denote the Force/Torque ratio γ and take it as a characteristic of the screwing or unscrewing procedure in the specific conditions. Two reasons to apply force simultaneously with torque are, first, the need to avoid screw slippage and, second, the nature of human arm, which uses muscles to produce torque via forces [10]. To estimate the importance of the first factor, we compare the Phillips screws and screws with internal Hex. The average γ for screwing the Phillips screw operations is $\gamma = (106\pm37)$ m^{-1} which is significantly higher than $\gamma = (57\pm25)$ m^{-1} for screwing of the screws with internal Hex. Since the second factor does not depend on the screw, the difference is contributed to only by the slippage avoidance. Thus, the screws with internal hex are less affected by slippage, than the Phillips screws, being screwed or unscrewed with the same force.

In Fig. 4, a typical pattern of screwing a screw in the nut is shown. During the first seconds the torque is hardly distinguishable from noise, but when the screw head touches the surface, the torque increases, human feel it and stop screwing. The typical unscrewing pattern is very similar, but inverted in time and requires smaller maximum torque, than the maximum torque which was applied during screwing.

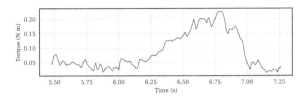

Fig. 4. Typical pattern of absolute values of torque during screwing of a Phillips screw into a disposable plastic prism with a nut. The black line represents the measurements.

In Fig. 5 a box plot of the γ coefficient is shown for all the typical conditions. The γ for the exceptional condition when the screwdriver does not match the screw is much larger, in the order of 300 ± 250 m^{-1} and was omitted to keep the scale sensible. The large γ is reasonable, since it was very hard for the participants to apply any significant torque, because of continuous slippage. Moreover, during operations of participants, when explicitly asked not to apply any force, and only apply torque, the slippage was also constantly occurring. This confirms the hypothesis, that the function of the typically applied force is to avoid slippage. The mean values of γ differ between screwing and unscrewing. For the taken conditions γ is typically in the range from 25 to 140.

The difference between horizontal and vertical operations could be introduced with the need to press the screwdriver in the screw in the horizontal position even during regrasp, to avoid its fall and caused by the relative comfort of force application in different orientations.

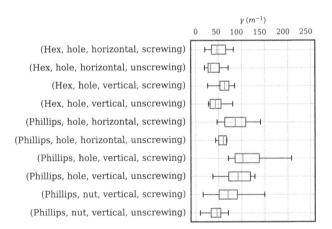

Fig. 5. Bar plot of Force/Torque ratio γ (m^{-1}) in different conditions. The conditions in the brackets represent (the screw type, "hole" is for the disposable plastic prism and "nut" is for a prism with a nut, the orientation of the screw, screwing or unscrewing).

We analyze the results of our user experiment using one-way ANOVA without replications, in order to see if the differences between conditions are real or due to chance. The chosen significance level is set to $p < 0.05$. According to the test findings, the Participant and Sex conditions have significance value p = 0.909 and p = 0.104 respectively, which are above 0.05, therefore we could conclude that this two conditions do not have any effect for the screwing and unscrewing processes: Force/Torque ratio didn't significantly change over experiments. Type of screw (hexagonal/Phillips) $(p = 5.3 \times 10^{-8} < 0.05)$, prism type (pilot hole/M3 nut) $(p = 9.0 \times 10^{-11} < 0.05)$, orientation of the screwdriver (horizontal/vertical) $(p = 1.5 \times 10^{-4} < 0.05)$, operation (screwing/unscrewing) $(p = 4.7 \times 10^{-2} < 0.05)$, and the physical condition of the users (physical performance, if they have a particular training or not) $(p = 7.1 \times 10^{-17} < 0.05)$ are important parameters for screwing and unscrewing processes.

2.3   Discussion

The discovery of the linear relationship between applied torque and force is a key to designing a robust screwing or unscrewing system. Since the target torque is defined by the environment (see Sect. 3.3), the robust algorithm should use force control and define the force from torque, using the coefficient, obtained from humans for the exact conditions.

3   Unscrewing Robot

An unscrewing robot is being developed as a part of the RecyBot project. It is equipped with computer vision to detect screws and a gripper to unscrew them. To perform unscrewing well, the force applied to the screw has to be controlled. Analyzing data from human experiment helps to define appropriate pattern and thresholds for force and torque in robotic implementation. Maximum force, maximum torque, and force-torque relation are the important parameters that are used. The setup diagram is shown in Fig. 6.

3.1   Mechanical Design

A collaborative robot UR3 from Universal Robots was used to move the gripper. The design of the gripper, endowed with passive compliance, was done with the objective to increase the force feedback precision in the compliant direction of Z-axis [5]. The passive compliance is implemented by a linear bearing, a spring system, and a linear potentiometer. The relative position of the potentiometer indicates the force applied to the screw as defined by the spring system. The design of the gripper is shown in Fig. 7. The linear potentiometer was calibrated using a Robotiq 6 DOF force and torque sensor FT150 to allow the force measurement. The screwdriver in the gripper is attached to a brushed DC motor from Maxon, the current from which is measured and used to determine the torque applied during the operation in regular mode, but is ignored during this

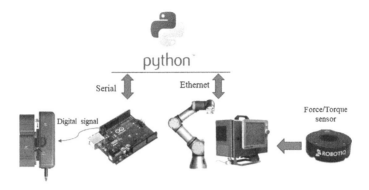

Fig. 6. The general scheme of communication in the testbed for robotic unscrewing.

experiment. Both force and torque could be measured by the internal gripper sources, and used in the real unscrewing. For the propose described in this paper, the force and torque feedback applied from the gripper was obtained by the same 6 DOF Robotiq sensor used in the Human Experiment in Sect. 2.

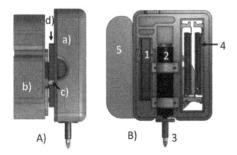

Fig. 7. The Gripper design used in the Unscrewing Robot. The lateral view A shows the cover of the gripper (a), the connection with the UR (b), the connection with the linear potentiometer (c), and the linear bearing. The internal parts of the gripper are shown in the front view B, the linear potentiometer (1), the motor (2), the screw driver (3), the spring system (4) and the connection with the UR (5)

3.2   Screwing and Unscrewing with Slippage Avoidance

Unscrewing procedure is controlled using a force control algorithm. The PID force controller with feed-forward signal was designed, and in Fig. 8 the structure of the control system is shown. The control output signal is a position command which is applied to the robot end-effector. The force feedback is received from the 6 DOF sensor.

In addition, to prevent cam-out, which is one of the most common failures [2], the force is applied according to the torque multiplied by the Force/Torque ratio γ, which is obtained from human experiment data. When the robot senses the slippage of the screwdriver (with a sharp drop in torque, see Fig. 9), the force is increased to prevent it. In fact, when the force, which is applied during the unscrewing is controlled, one can make the robot's activity closer to human activity as a clever actor.

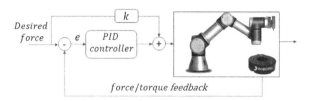

Fig. 8. Structure of the control scheme. Position is controlled using the force feedback.

3.3 Robot Screwing and Unscrewing Results

The robot was programmed with an algorithm, close to the proposed. The difference is in cam-out detection and increase of the force as a response. In Fig. 9 the obtained force and torque are shown. The cam-outs are clearly visible as drops in the torque. Their detection was implemented using a threshold. The force was being gradually increased, with higher increase speed, when slippage was detected. The frequency of the cam-outs notably drops with the increase of the force from 5 to 25 s. This means sufficiently large force has been reached to avoid cam-outs. The head of the screw touched the plastic at 40 s. The torque started to grow rapidly. When the Force/Torque ratio γ lowered due to the increase in torque, the slippage started to occur again after 43 s. Then the thread is overturned since no torque limit has been implemented in the prototype algorithm.

To check the hypothesis that the torque does not depend on the speed of the screw rotation, one experiment has been performed with the robot. The unscrewing speed was changed in a range from 22.5 to 360 degrees per second and the measured unscrewing torque in the same conditions was $T = (0.19 \pm 0.03)$ N· m. This confirms the hypothesis of the independence of the friction on the speed.

3.4 Discussion

The novel end-effector has been designed, which is able to screw or unscrew the screws with precise force feedback. The main feature of the robot is the desired Force/Torque relationship γ of the robot unscrewing, which is gathered from the human experiments. The results of the robotic unscrewing agree with the results of the human experiments and demonstrate the universality of the conditions of the successful unscrewing found in the previous part. The human experiment data helps us to find out the well-performing desired force pattern.

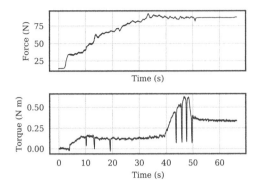

Fig. 9. Force and torque values obtained from a robot, screwing thew screw into a disposable plastic prism. The robot is set to gradually increase the force until the maximum value is reached. Cam-outs correspond to sharp drops in torque. Their frequency is decreasing from 5 s to 22 s when the force reaches the value twice higher than the one, computed from γ, the Force/Torque ratio in humans.

4 Discussion and Conclusions

A typical frequency of human screwing and unscrewing is reported here to be (1.3 ± 0.4) Hz without any dependence on age and gender. It seems to correlate more with the strength of the participants, but we did not measure this variable directly. A significant correlation between applied torque and force during screwing and unscrewing is discovered in this paper, and it should be a reasonable assumption for any screwing and unscrewing procedures design.

In this paper, a new approach for robotic screwing and unscrewing procedure has been proposed. To choose the constants for the robot screwing and unscrewing algorithm, one has to, first, measure the Force/Torque ratio γ humans typically apply in the exact conditions, and then implement the force control, based on the continually measured torque and obtained γ. One can increase the coefficient to introduce a safe margin but should consider the fragility of the environment. Also, the maximum torque humans use has to be chosen as a threshold for screwing condition detection. The γ depends on the type of the screw, and is higher for Phillips screws, which are more prone to cam-outs than internal Hex screws.

This methodology can speed up the development of the screwing and unscrewing robots and tools. For example, it can help in direct transfer of the haptic knowledge from the more knowledgeable experts to the novices in the simulators for surgeons and other professionals, where a required γ can be measured and taught. Likewise, in the RecyBot project it can reduce the slippage and increase the unscrewing process efficiency.

References

1. Robotiq FT300 specifications. https://assets.robotiq.com/production/support_documents/document/specsheet-FT300-Nov-08-V3_20171116.pdf?_ga=2.252630985.1712588583.1517308561-1050351704.1509722697
2. Apley, D.W., Seliger, G., Voit, L., Shi, J.: Diagnostics in disassembly unscrewing operations. Int. J. Flex. Manuf. Syst. **10**(2), 111–128 (1998). https://doi.org/10.1023/A:1008089230047
3. Behring, J.K., Gjerdet, N.R., Mlster, A.: Slippage between screwdriver and bone screw. Clin. Orthop. Relat. Res. **404**, 368–372 (2002)
4. Chen, W.H., Wegener, K., Dietrich, F.: A robot assistant for unscrewing in hybrid human-robot disassembly. In: 2014 IEEE International Conference on Robotics and Biomimetics (ROBIO), pp. 536–541. IEEE (2014). http://ieeexplore.ieee.org/abstract/document/7090386/
5. Ham, R., Sugar, T., Vanderborght, B., Hollander, K., Lefeber, D.: Compliant actuator designs. IEEE Rob. Autom. Mag. **16**(3), 81–94 (2009). http://ieeexplore.ieee.org/document/5233419/
6. Kopacek, P., Kopacek, B.: Robotized disassembly of mobile phones. IFAC Proc. Vol. **36**(23), 103–105 (2003). http://linkinghub.elsevier.com/retrieve/pii/S1474667017376693
7. Kopacek, P., Kopacek, B.: Intelligent, flexible disassembly. Int. J. Adv. Manuf. Technol. **30**(5–6), 554–560 (2006). https://doi.org/10.1007/s00170-005-0042-9
8. Majewicz, A., Glasser, J., Bauer, R., Belkoff, S.M., Mears, S.C., Okamura, A.M.: Design of a haptic simulator for osteosynthesis screw insertion. In: Haptics Symposium, 2010 IEEE, pp. 497–500. IEEE (2010)
9. Rujaevich, C., Lessard, J., Chandler, S., Shannon, S., Dahmus, J., Guzzo, R.: Liam - an innovation story (2016). https://www.apple.com/environment/pdf/Liam_white_paper_Sept2016.pdf. Bibtex: liam_2016
10. Tsetserukou, D., Sato, K., Tachi, S.: Exointerfaces: novel exosceleton haptic interfaces for virtual reality, augmented sport and rehabilitation. In: Proceedings of the 1st Augmented Human International Conference, AH 2010, pp. 1:1–1:6. ACM, New York, NY, USA (2010). https://doi.org/10.1145/1785455.1785456
11. Vongbunyong, S., Chen, W.H.: Disassembly Automation. SPLCEM. Springer, Cham (2015). https://doi.org/10.1007/978-3-319-15183-0
12. Vongbunyong, S., Kara, S., Pagnucco, M.: Basic behaviour control of the vision based cognitive robotic disassembly automation. Assembly Autom. **33**(1), 38–56 (2013). https://doi.org/10.1108/01445151311294694

Towards a Test Battery to Benchmark Dexterous Performance in Teleoperated Systems

Milène Catoire[1], Bouke N. Krom[2], and Jan B. F. van Erp[3,4(✉)]

[1] Training and Performance Innovations, TNO, Soesterberg, The Netherlands
milene.catoire@tno.nl
[2] Distributed Sensor Systems, TNO, The Hague, The Netherlands
bouke.krom@tno.nl
[3] Human Media Interaction, University of Twente, Enschede, The Netherlands
jan.vanerp@utwente.nl
[4] Perceptual and Cognitive Systems, TNO, Soesterberg, The Netherlands

Abstract. A high level of dexterity is becoming increasingly important for tele-operated inspection, maintenance and repair robots. A standard test to benchmark system dexterity can advance the design, quantify possible improvements, and increase the effectiveness of such systems. Because of the wide variety of tasks and application domains ranging from dismantling explosives from a safe distance to maintenance of deep sea oil rigs, we defined a library of basic, generic tasks and selected five tests that reflect these basic tasks and for which benchmark data already exist or are easy to gather: the Box & Block test, the Purdue Pegboard test, the Minnesota Manual Dexterity test, the ISO 9382 trajectory test (based on the ISO 9382:1998 standard) and the adapted version of the screwing subtest of the IROS 2017 service robots challenge.

Keywords: Haptic · Dexterity · Teleoperation · Test battery · Standards
Benchmarking

1 Introduction

Successful robot operation in for instance unpredictable environments relies on optimal integration of human (motor) intelligence, flexibility and creativity and robot precision, power and endurance. Therefore human (motor) intelligence will be needed for remotely operated robots in ever changing situations with unpredictable task constraints, perhaps for decades to come. With recent advances in technology, a high level of dexterity is becoming increasingly viable for teleoperated Inspection, Maintenance and Repair robots (IRM), the use case we employ in this paper. Currently, there is no standard test or instrument available to benchmark system dexterity, while such a benchmark is important to advance system design, quantify possible improvements (like adding certain feedback modalities), and increase the effective application of such systems. Our aim is to come to a simple and generic test set to benchmark dexterity of teleoperated systems. Our approach is to define a library of basic tasks and re-use or adopt existing tests (for instance from the rehabilitation domain) to benchmark task performance.

© Springer International Publishing AG, part of Springer Nature 2018
D. Prattichizzo et al. (Eds.): EuroHaptics 2018, LNCS 10894, pp. 440–451, 2018.
https://doi.org/10.1007/978-3-319-93399-3_38

1.1 Background

Traditionally, robots are used to perform tasks that are dull, dirty or dangerous (the 3 D's) for humans. Although the application of robots nowadays expands into many more fields (e.g. service-oriented or time-critical), the 3 D's, as they are known, remain key driving factors for many robotics systems. Especially the robots doing "dull" jobs have a high degree of autonomy, which is still increasing thanks to increased techno-logical capability. Autonomous robots can plan and to some degree adapt tasks in reaction to changing circumstances without human interference. Although the advances in autonomy are rapid, autonomous robots will not be a viable option in all ("dirty" or "dangerous") cases for the foreseeable future (SPARC 2017). Autonomous robots are often designed to perform a specific task, in a specific type of environment. If the tasks of a robotic system are diverse, the environments unpredictable and the stakes of successfully performing the task are high, autonomy will not be relied upon. This is the case in for example explosive ordnance disposal, and maintenance and disaster response on petrochemical sites. In these applications, robots will not be able to carry out all necessary tasks with sufficient reliability without human involvement.

The common solution in these use cases is teleoperation (Van Erp et al. 2006). In teleoperation the task is performed by an operator controlling the robot remotely, typically in a master-slave setup. Since the cognitive part of the task still remains with the human operator, a wider array of (unexpected) tasks can be performed – given sufficient sensory, movement and manipulation abilities of the robot. Teleoperated robots are often used for collecting data about the environment, in order to decide on further courses of action (i.e., *telesensing*). With increasingly advanced robots, manipulation of the environment becomes a possibility as well: *telemanipulation*. Telemanipulation can be used in order to reach certain areas (e.g. opening doors or bags), or to perform a critical part of the task (e.g. sampling a fluid, closing a valve, cutting a wire).

This paper concerns the manipulation of the direct environment of a robot (i.e. the telemanipulation part of teleoperation), with one or more robotic arms and end effectors. Using IRM as use case, we define a library of basic tasks (Sect. 2) and describe relevant dexterity tests in Sect. 3. Sections 4 and 5 present the selection criteria and the final test selection, respectively. In Sect. 6, we discuss the results and way forward.

1.2 Definitions of Dexterity

Dexterity is often considered as a mechanical property of the robot itself. Several authors propose different definitions (Ma and Dollar 2011). Bicchi (2000) and Li et al. (1989) stress the importance of being able to move an object to any arbitrary position and orientation within the workspace, while other authors limit dexterity to in-hand manipulation only (e.g. Bullock et al. 2013). What all definitions have in common though is: (a) that the robot has to be able to perform in-hand (or in-effector) manipulations using different ways of gripping, and (b) that the manipulator typically needs a redundant number of degrees of freedom. An example of an effector with a high level of dexterity is a hand-shaped gripper with four independently moveable 'fingers', allowing manipulation within the effector, while an example of an effector with a low level of dexterity would be a two-finger parallel gripper. The use of more than one effector appendage or arm, or combining several types of effectors will increase the level of dexterity.

We adopt the definition of Okamura et al. (2000): "Cooperation of multiple manipulators, or fingers, to grasp and manipulate objects,". For the purpose of this paper, we extend that definition to include the complete teleoperated system, including the robot, communication channel, human interface and human operator, not just the (isolated) end effector. For instance, adding haptic feedback does not change the dexterity of the end effector but may increase dexterous performance of the teleoperated system as a whole.

2   Library of Basic Tasks

Defining basic tasks is required since the number of possible movements is virtually infinite (Bullock et al. 2013) and the number of tests and evaluations is also very large, even for a single application domain. To be able to select the appropriate tests, we defined a library of basic tasks for our IRM use case. Additional libraries may be developed for other domains like surgery. Based on inspection, maintenance, and repair activities, a library of basic tasks was created. The basic tasks can be considered as basic building blocks and can also be combined to form more complex tasks. A basic task is a simple task that can be performed in a variety of contexts, goals, and restraints, but consist of the same movements when the context is removed. The basic tasks that were defined are: (a) screwing an object off another object; (b) screwing an object on another object; (c) placing a constrained object; (d) removing a constrained object; (e) placing a freely movable object; (f) removing a freely movable object; (g) following the external structure of an object; and (h) following a visual trajectory. All basic tasks are depicted in Fig. 1.

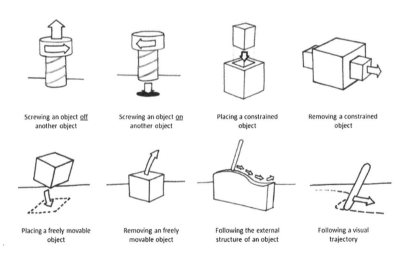

Fig. 1. Basic tasks included in our library for the remote Inspection, Repair and Maintenance use case.

The basic tasks cover most (but not all) movements made during IRM activities. This combination of tasks covers both translational and rotational movements. Tasks a through f can be done with either visual or haptic feedback, while the trajectory following tasks explicitly require tactile (task g) or visual (task h) information. The constrained object tasks (a through d) prompt a level of precision and subtleness from the system, while the freely movable tasks (e through h) can assess the speed of grosser movements.

3 Existing Dexterity Tests

Our approach is to adopt and where needed adapt already existing dexterous performance test from the relevant domains: robotics, rehabilitation, and occupational health.

3.1 Dexterity Assessment in Robotics Research

In the context of robotics, dexterity assessment is often done related to the isolated robotic system, or even only the end effector. This can be done by e.g. classifying kinematic properties of the system (Gosselin 1990), ticking off a dexterous manipulation taxonomy (Bullock et al. 2013) or a grasp taxonomy (Cutkosky 1989, Ruehl et al. 2014). Since we are developing a benchmark of the system as a whole, task-centric tests are more suitable. Most robotic systems in literature are tested using a custom test with specialized metrics for the system or use case at hand. Outside of academic literature, there are two ways in which the performance of robotic systems is contrasted and compared: standards and competitions.

Standards. A well-known robotics standard is ISO 9283 (1998), which considers manipulation with industrial robots in terms of precision, speed, repeatability and maximum load. Although this is an assessment of the robot's mechanics and not about the dexterous capabilities of the robot, we will adapt one of the patterns recommended by this standard for our tests (see Sect. 5). A more systems approach to haptic and tactile system evaluation (i.e. including the user and user experience) is advocated by ISO through ISO 9241 WG 9 (Van Erp and Kern 2008) but guidance for this topic is still under construction.

More domain-specific standardized tests can be found in the Standard Test Methods for Response Robots as formulated by the DHS-NIST-ASTM (Messina et al. 2009). This expansive array of tests includes mobility, safety, communications, sensors, underwater and aerial tests. The tests for manipulator dexterity are still under development, and not standardized yet. These tests are explicitly focused on EOD tasks: several for package-sized Improvised Explosive Devices (IEDs) and some for Personnel- and Vehicle-borne IEDs. The tests include aiming (touching an object in the right spot) and removing a cap, either by grasping it or pulling a wire. These tasks are part of our library of basic tasks.

Competitions. The robotics community has a long tradition of demonstrating robot capabilities in a competitive environment. Using tests from competitions would have the added value of some population data already being available. Two recent competitions that are specific to our field of application are the Argos Challenge (remote inspection and maintenance: http://www.argos-challenge.com/) and the ELROB 2016 (explosive ordnance disposal robots: http://www.elrob.org/). Unfortunately, the Argos challenge did not include manipulation tasks, and the ELROB does not publicly describe detailed tasks and results, underlining the importance to establish benchmark tests.

In more general applications there are two interesting competitions. The DARPA robotics challenge, which ended in 2015 (http://archive.darpa.mil/roboticschallenge/), included relevant and challenging tasks like opening a valve and cutting through drywall with a tool made for humans. The robots participating in this challenge can hardly be called teleoperated however, since their communications were deliberately limited and regularly cut off completely. This necessitated semi-autonomous solutions for all tasks. Secondly, the IROS 2017 Robotic Grasping and Manipulation Competition (http://www.rhgm.org/activities/competition_iros2017/) featured all sorts of tasks related to dexterous manipulation, including pouring water into a cup, placing connectors and assembling a set of gears. These tasks were supposed to be performed autonomously however, so there is no data on teleoperation performance. Although most tasks are more specific versions of our general basic tasks and only applied in (semi-) autonomous systems so far, we will use one task due to a lack of alternatives.

3.2 Dexterity Assessment in Rehabilitation and Human Factors Research

Besides robotics, dexterity is a common term in rehabilitation and other human related research fields (Yancosek and Howell 2009). Dexterity from a human perspective is also referred to as fine motor skills or the ability to make skillful, controlled arm-hand manipulations of objects (Makofske 2011). Dexterity in humans can be defined, taking a systems perspective, as the coordination of movements of lower arm and hand based on input from the visual system, the proprioceptive system and/or the haptic system. Various types of diseases can impair dexterity in humans, such as stroke, Parkinson's disease, cerebral palsy, other neurological disorders and trauma. The diminished dexterity in these patients is caused by impaired motor control and/or decreased sensory feedback, which has some overlap with the 'handicap' experienced in telemanipulation and caused by lack of transparency and sub-optimal control. This makes test to quantify reductions in fine motor skills also relevant for our goals.

Rehabilitation. Since dexterity and sensory integration (De Dieuleveult et al. 2017) are crucial for so-called 'activities of daily living (ADLs)', many tests are available from the rehabilitation domain. In patients with a sudden decrease in dexterity (for example following a stroke) it can be very valuable to know the extent of dexterity decrease, and possible increase during rehabilitation. Examples of dexterity tests are the Wolf Motor Function Test (WMFT, Wolf et al. 2001), the Chedoke Arm and Hand Activity Inventory (CAHAI, Barreca et al. 2005) and the Action Research Arm Test (ARAT, Yozbatiran et al. 2008). All three tests consist of several subtests and/or subscales testing grasp, grip, pinch and gross arm movements. Some subtests are ADLs, such as dialing 911, while other subtests are simple movements, such as placing the hand behind the head. The ARAT focusses on tasks can that be described as more basic movements, while the

CAHAI only consists of ADLs. The WMFT combines both types of tasks. The subtests included in the tests largely consist of movements that match the basic tasks in our library. The disadvantage is that they have to be performed by a (trained) physical therapist and are based on observer scoring. For the ARAT for example participants are scored between 0 and 3, where 0 is that the subject is not able to complete the task, while 3 is that the subject is able to perform the task in 5 s. Reference data are available for the WMFT, CAHAI and ARAT, however, the current way of scoring lacks sensitivity to discriminate current robot systems. Teleoperated robots are in general slower when performing a task compared to humans and the robots will perform the task less fluently/correctly. In the ARAT test, most robots will therefore score a 1 (able to partially perform the subtest in sixty seconds) or a 2 (able to perform the subtest, but slow), making it very hard to distinguish between the performance of different robots/robot modalities. To increase the discriminative power, scoring time needed or the number of repetitions in a certain timespan would be more suitable, but this reduces the usefulness of the reference data.

Occupational Research. Several dexterity tests were developed for dexterity assessment in occupational settings. Examples of such tests are the nine peg hole test (NPHT, Mathiowetz et al. 1985a), the Purdue pegboard test (PPT, Tiffin and Asher 1948), the box & block test (B&BT, Mathiowetz et al. 1985b) and the Minnesota rate of manipulation test (MRMT, Surrey et al. 2003). All these tests were developed at least 30 years ago to test dexterous performance of factory workers or dexterous performance of the general population. They all use rather abstract tasks (with good fits to our library), compared to the ADL inspired tasks used in rehabilitation. The advantage of occupational tests is that they are standardized, validated, have norms for a variety of populations, are commercially available and have a fine granularity in scoring (i.e. the number of pegs/blocks that can be moved in a certain timespan, or time to complete a task). This makes them also interesting for usage in robotics, allowing a unique way of benchmarking robotic dexterous performance.

4   Criteria for Subtest Selection

We used the criteria below to select the preferred test for each basic task in our library.

- Covers a basic task. A test should reflect one or more basic tasks. One basic task can be tested by more than one test.
- Has objective scores and sufficient discriminative power. The scoring of dexterous performance of teleoperated systems should preferably be objective and independent of observer (training). The sensitivity is high in the relevant range for teleoperated systems.
- Is clearly prescribed. This means that the methods of the test are simple and described in detail (preferably in literature), and the materials needed are easy to reproduce or obtain.
- Has population data/norms. Since we are striving for a benchmark test, comparison between systems or with specific populations is important.

5   Selected (Sub-)tests

Based on the criteria in Sect. 4, we selected the tests described and discussed below.

- Minnesota test. The Minnesota test (MT) has two versions that are very similar: the Minnesota rate of manipulation test (MRMT; 1969) and the Minnesota manual dexterity test (MMDT; 1991). The newer MMDT is most commonly used, although the MRMT standardization is better. Both MT's are produced by the Lafayette Instrument Company and both have boards with have 60 holes and feature the same instruction and scoring system. The MT consist of five subtests: placing, turning, displacing, one-hand turning and placing, and two-hand turning and placing test, all based on removing and placing blocks as fast as possible. The basic tasks performed in the MT are: (c) placing of a constrained object, (d) removing of a constrained object, and (f) removing a freely movable object. The MT also matches all the other criteria as described in Sect. 4. The MT is used in rehabilitation to establish baseline values for patients, and as a screening and selection tool in occupational health. Populations studied include stroke patients, children with cerebral palsy, COPD patients and upper-extremity amputees.
- Purdue pegboard test. The Purdue Pegboard test (PPT) was developed to select employees in industrial jobs such as assembly, packing and operation of certain machines. The PPT is produced by Lafayette Instruments Company and consist of four subtests, testing right hand, left hand, both hands and assembly performance. The first three test gross movements of hand and fingers, the forth also tests in-hand dexterity. In all subtests the subject has to place as many pegs as possible into (small) holes in a pegboard within a set time. The PPT is highly standardized and is used extensively in research and occupational practice. The basic tasks covered are included are: (c) placing a constrained object, and (f) removing a freely movable object. These basic tasks are also covered by the MT, but the objects that have to be grasped and the holes that the objects have to be placed in are significantly smaller with the PPT which makes it a valuable addition. The norm data available from the PPT is largely based on a relatively healthy and young population, but other populations include children, patients with Parkinson's disease, Huntington's disease and other types of brain injuries, patient with hand injuries and patients with a visual impairment.
- Box & block test. The Box & Block test (B&BT) was developed to fill the gap between the PPT and the MT. The B&BT requires a lower level of dexterity compared to the PPT, allowing also patient with a lower functioning level to be tested. Compared to the MMDT is the B&BT easier to perform, since its duration is shorter and the restrictions for the environment and subjects are less demanding. The aim of the B&BT is to move as many blocks as possible over an elevation (i.e. a standing board) in 60 s. The number of moved blocks is counted and represents the tests core. The test is not used in an occupational setting. Norms for the B&BT are available for the normal adult population, elderly, adults with neuromuscular problems and young school children. The basic tasks covered by this test are: (e) placing a freely movable object and (f) removing a freely movable object.

- ISO 9382 trajectory test. The ISO 9382 standard published in 1998 includes a pattern to assess the accuracy of a robot to follow a (pre-planned) trajectory as depicted in Fig. 2, and is an interesting option to test the basic tasks g) following the external structure of an object, and (h) following a visual trajectory. The deviations from the trajectory (maximum and average) for each part of the trajectory are monitored and represent the scores. The trajectory test based on the ISO 9382 pattern is not standardized to a degree such as the B&BT, MMDT and PPT and norms and population data are lacking.
- IROS subtest 10 (screwing test). For the basic tasks (a) screwing an object off another object and (b) screwing an object on another object, no standardized test is currently available meeting all our criteria. Our current plan is to adapt subtest 10 from the IROS 2017 challenge for service robots: open a bottle with a safety locking cap but with the bottle anchored onto a flat surface. The time to complete the task will be measured, resulting in an objective measure of performance. No norms are available for this test.

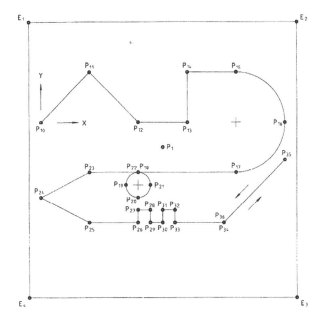

Fig. 2. The pattern as depicted in the ISO 9382 standard.

6   Discussion and Future Directions

One of the uses of the test battery is to assess which modalities of haptic feedback improve the system. The addition of haptic feedback to a teleoperated system likely aims at improving dexterous performance and this test battery will enable us to structurally and thoroughly test the added value of haptic feedback modalities. Haptic feedback that is too intense, or combinations of feedback that are too complicated may lead to decreased dexterous performance. Some forms of feedback on the other hand may be superfluous. The test battery will allow us to find the most useful modalities and level of haptic feedback for optimal dexterous performance. Our approach to define a library of basic tasks and select existing (sub-) tests turned out to work reasonably well, but several issues need attention.

Disturbing Effects of the Operator's Skill Level. The focus is of this paper is on dexterous performance of a complete teleoperated system, including the robot, the communication link and the operator. One of the difficulties that arise is the influence of the skill level and training of the operator on the system performance. Usually this is approached by either using operators that have no training or within-experiment training only (academic studies), or by using expert operators to get the best performance possible (industrial evaluations). Inter-operator differences can be bypassed by comparing an operator only with himself, attributing all differences in performance to the teleoperated system. This defeats one of the primary purposes of our tests however: comparing the test scores to norm data. We therefore suggest that each operator performs the task manually (without the teleoperated system) first as baseline, which will then be used as a normalizing value to estimate the performance of the teleoperated system on the task. Furthermore the difference between operators can also be minimized by including a homogenous group of participants with similar experiences with teleoperated systems. Finally, several tests (PPT, MT, B&BT) are repetitive. By analyzing the variation in performance of a single operation throughout the test, we can establish when a subject has finished training and improving.

From Unimanual to Bimanual. Most current teleoperated systems are unimanual (having a single effector), and our current library consists of unimanual basic tasks only. There may be good reasons to employ a bimanual robot (Smith et al. 2012), although the operation is more complicated. An interesting question is whether the increased mechanical capabilities of the robot can be sufficiently utilized by an operator to justify the addition of a second arm. Although not specifically designed towards this question, the proposed test battery may be suitable. There are three tests that can be performed in an uni- and bimanual mode (MT, PPT, and B&BT), allowing a comparison in perform- ance of uni- and bimanual teleoperated systems for the current library. In addition, specific bimanual basic tasks may be added to the library, or current basic tasks may be modified into a bimanual version, for instance, screwing something of an object holding the object.

Calculate a Single Dexterity Measure. We selected five subtests of tasks, each with its own scoring method and procedure. It is not yet clear how these tests can be combined together to create a single dexterity measure. Calculating a general score for each test (like percentile) and establishing weightings over tests ultimately allows to calculate a single dexterity score.

Extending the Basic Task Library. Future extensions of the basic task library may include bi-manual tasks (as argued above), in-hand manipulation tasks, and other use- cases than the current IRM use case). In-hand manipulation is more common in human dexterity research than in robotics research, but may be useful to include for specific use cases and advanced robotic systems.

Scaling. The implicit assumption made in our approach is that we can transfer (human) dexterity tests to teleoperated robotic systems without scaling. However, the size and range of the robotic system does not necessarily have to be in the 'human' range but may be considerably smaller or larger. Although the basic tasks can be scaled accordingly, it is not a priori clear if and how the test protocols, norms, etc. should be adjusted. This requires further research.

Super-human Skills. A second implicit assumption is that the teleoperation test scores will be at best that of a healthy human but more likely in the range of that of children or even patients after a stroke or neuromuscular disease. However, there is no reason to restrict the performance of teleoperated systems to the normal human range, and robot speed, accuracy and stamina may (when combined with human dexterity and motor intelligence) ultimately result "super-human skills" that are outside the test range and norms. This may in the future force us to adjust the tests, the scoring, and the norms.

Restrictions. One skill that is not typically part of the definition of dexterity is the fine control of exerted force. This skill is reflected in the basic tasks, but specific tests may result in clearer insight in its role in dexterous performance. Lack of accurate force control may hamper dexterous performance, for instance through dropping objects. The second restriction is that we focus on the telemanipulation part of teleoperation, while teleoperation performance also depends on the telesensing part. For instance, better situational awareness (view on the workspace), better self-awareness (proprioception, localization, eye-hand coordination), and better platform movement (positioning for the task), may all contribute to the teleoperation performance. Finally, for telemanipulation, there is more to dexterity than pure object manipulation. Discovery of an object's texture, weight, size and/or temperature may be valuable in some cases, and is not tested for by our benchmark.

7   Conclusions

This paper describes the first step towards benchmarking the performance of teleoperated systems. After surveying the literature in the research fields of robotics, rehabilitation, occupational research and haptics a set of five subtests was selected. All subtests met at least three out of four of the defined criteria: (1) testing one or more basic tasks, (2) objectively measured, (3) described in detail and (4) norm data being available. The selected subtests are the Box & Block test, the Purdue Pegboard test, the Minnesota Manual Dexterity test, the ISO 9382 trajectory test (based on the ISO 9382:1998 standard) and the adapted version of the screwing subtest of the IROS 2017 service robots challenge.

Acknowledgements. We would like to thank our colleague Wietse van Dijk (TNO) for preparing Fig. 1.

References

Barreca, S.R., Stratford, P.W., Lambert, C.L., Masters, L.M., Streiner, D.L.: Test-retest reliability, validity, and sensitivity of the chedoke arm and hand activity inventory: a new measure of upper-limb function for survivors of stroke. Arch. Phys. Med. Rehabil. **86**(8), 1616–1622 (2005)

Bicchi, A.: Hands for dexterous manipulation and powerful grasping: a difficult road toward simplicity. IEEE Trans. Robot. Autom. **16**(6), 2–15 (2000)

Bullock, I.M., Ma, R.R., Dollar, A.M.: A hand-centric classification of human and robot dexterous manipulation. IEEE Trans. Haptics **6**(2), 129–144 (2013)

Cutkosky, M.R.: On grasp choice, grasp models, and the design of hands for manufacturing tasks. IEEE Trans. Robot. Autom. **5**(3), 269–279 (1989)

De Dieuleveult, A.L., Siemonsma, P.C., Van Erp, J.B.F., Brouwer, A.-M.: Multisensory integration: a systematic review on age related changes and activities of daily life. Front. Aging Neurosci. (2017). https://doi.org/10.3389/fnagi.2017.00080

Gosselin, C.M.: Dexterity indices for planar and spatial robotic manipulators. In: IEEE International Conference on Robotics and Automation (1990)

ISO, NEN-EN-ISO 9283 (1998)

Li, Z., Canny, J.F., Sastry, S.: On motion planning for dexterous manipulation. I. The problem formulation. In: IEEE International Conference on Robotics and Automation (1989)

Ma, R.R., Dollar, A.M.: On dexterity and dexterous manipulation. In: The 15th International Conference on Advanced Robotics, Tallinn (2011)

Makofske, B.: Manual dexterity. In: Kreutzer, J.S., DeLuca, J., Caplan, B. (eds.) Encyclopedia of Clinical Neuropsychology, pp. 1522–1523. Springer, New York (2011). https://doi.org/10.1007/978-0-387-79948-3_1460

Mathiowetz, V., Volland, G., Kashman, N., Weber, K.: Adult norms for the box and block test of manual dexterity. Am. J. Occup. Ther. **39**(6), 387–391 (1985a)

Mathiowetz, V., Weber, K., Kashman, N., Volland, G.: Adult norms for the nine hole peg test of finger dexterity. Occup. Ther. J. Res. **5**(1), 24–38 (1985b)

Messina, E., Huang, H.-M., Virts, A., Downs, A., Norcross, R., Sheh, R., Jacoff, A.: Standard Test Methods For Response Robots: Guide for Evaluating, Purchasing, and Training with Response Robots Using DHS-NIST-ASTM International Standard Test Methods (2009)

Okamura, A., Smaby, N., Cutkosky, M.: An overview of dexterous manipulation. In: IEEE International Conference on Robotics and Automation (2000)

Ruehl, S.W., Parlitz, C., Heppner, G., Hermann, A., Roennau, A., Dillmann, R.: Experimental evaluation of the schunk 5-finger gripping hand for grasping tasks. In: IEEE International Conference on Robotics and Biomimetics, pp. 2465–2470, December 2014

Smith, C., Karayiannidis, Y., Nalpantidis, L., Gratal, X., Qi, P., Dimarogonas, D.V., Kragic, D.: Dual arm manipulation - a survey. Robot. Autonom. Syst. **60**(10), 1340–1353 (2012)

SPARC: Robotics 2020 Multi-Annual Roadmap For Robotics in Europe (2017)

Surrey, L.R., Nelson, K., Delelio, C., Mathie-Majors, D., Omel-Edwards, N., Shumaker, J., Thurber, G.: A Comparison of Performance Outcomes Between the Minnesota Rate of Manipulation Test and the Minnesota Manual Dexterity Test. Work (Reading, Mass.), vol. 20, no. 2, pp. 97–102 (2003)

Tiffin, J., Asher, E.J.: The purdue pegboard: norms and studies of reliability and validity. J. Appl. Psychol. **32**(3), 234–247 (1948)

van Erp, J.B.F., Kern, T.A.: ISO's work on guidance for haptic and tactile interactions. In: Ferre, M. (ed.) EuroHaptics 2008. LNCS, vol. 5024, pp. 936–940. Springer, Heidelberg (2008). https://doi.org/10.1007/978-3-540-69057-3_118

Van Erp, J.B.F., Duistermaat, M., Jansen, C., Groen, E., Hoedemaeker, M.: Tele presence: bringing the operator back in the loop. In: NATO RTO Workshop on Virtual Media for Military Applications (2006)

Wolf, S.L., Catlin, P.A., Ellis, M., Archer, A.L., Morgan, B., Piacentino, A.: Assessing wolf motor function test as outcome measure for research in patients after stroke. Stroke **32**(7), 1635–1639 (2001)

Yancosek, K.E., Howell, D.: A narrative review of dexterity assessments. J. Hand Ther. **22**(3), 258–270 (2009)

Yozbatiran, N., Der-Yeghiaian, L., Cramer, S.C.: A standardized approach to performing the action research arm test. Neurorehabil. Neural Repair **22**(1), 78–90 (2008)

Evaluation of Sensory Feedback
from a Robotic Hand: A Preliminary Study

İpek Karakuş[1], Hasan Şahin[2], Ahmet Atasoy[1], Erkan Kaplanoğlu[2], Mehmed Özkan[1],
and Burak Güçlü[1(✉)]

[1] Institute of Biomedical Engineering, Boğaziçi University, Istanbul, Turkey
{ipek.toker,ahmet.atasoy,mehmed,burak.guclu}@boun.edu.tr
[2] Department of Mechatronics Engineering, Marmara University, Istanbul, Turkey
hasansahin13@marun.edu.tr, ekaplanoglu@marmara.edu.tr

Abstract. In this study, a robotic hand was equipped with force and bend sensors. Sensors were modified to fit the robotic hand and for more efficient utilization. A cylindrical grasping task was performed for three conditions, namely no object, soft object and hard object. Features were formed using the outputs of the sensors and their first and second derivatives. A multinomial logistic regression model was fitted to the data. Classification was done according to both object type (no object, soft object and hard object classes) and movement type (no movement, flexion, contact/release and extension classes). Results have shown that the information from the force sensors do not adequately contribute to the feature space because of poor coupling and this affects discrimination of soft object and contact/release classes. More sensors and a better actuation protocol need to be used in future work.

Keywords: Prosthesis · Sensory feedback · Force sensing resistor · Bend sensor
Classification · Multinomial logistic regression

1 Introduction

Human hand has complex sensory and motor functions during daily life activities. Therefore, loss of limb/hand can cause impairment in both functions. The motor functions of the hand such as holding, supporting and stabilizing actions can be replaced by using prosthetic hands, but lack of sensory function would result in difficulties for control of the hand and embodiment. A prosthetic hand with sensory feedback is expected to be controlled easier than the traditional myoelectric hands and increase the acceptance rate of the hand by the user [1]. By transmitting reaction forces of the mechanism, body-powered prostheses provide some feedback to the user but externally powered (myoelectric) prostheses mostly lack sensory feedback. That is why body-powered prostheses are still preferred by amputees, despite improved capabilities of myoelectric prostheses. Design and validation of sensory feedback systems for prosthetic hands is a relatively new topic in haptics literature. The published studies can be grouped depending on the stimulation method (invasive methods, non-invasive methods) and decoded information (grasp force, hand aperture). Invasive methods require direct stimulation of nerves in

© Springer International Publishing AG, part of Springer Nature 2018
D. Prattichizzo et al. (Eds.): EuroHaptics 2018, LNCS 10894, pp. 452–463, 2018.
https://doi.org/10.1007/978-3-319-93399-3_39

peripheral or central nervous system [2, 3]. Non-invasive methods provide non-natural sensation compared to invasive methods; however, they have the advantage of no need for surgical operation [4, 5]. Recently, a comprehensive review on non-invasive sensory feedback methods was published [6]. Vibrotactile and electrotactile stimulation are the most common non-invasive stimulation methods in the literature [4, 5]. Although modality matched sensations (e.g. mechanotactile stimulation) result in better performance [7], electrotactile or vibrotactile stimulation is preferred in most of the studies because of small stimulator dimensions, ease of implementation and low power consumption [6]. In terms of feedback parameters, grasp force and hand aperture feedback are used frequently [8–10], since these parameters are crucial for object manipulation. Grasp force should be carefully adjusted while picking up delicate objects and there is no way to directly estimate it during action. Prosthesis user may follow the hand movements during grasping, but this has two drawbacks. First, use of prosthesis becomes dependent on visual cues and increases cognitive load. Second, it may be too late to adjust grasping force after observing contact.

Non-invasive stimulation methods generally depend on continuously modulating one or multiple stimulation parameters proportional to change of sensor outputs [11, 12]. This procedure increases signal processing load and also requires a long learning phase for the user. In contrast to continuous modulation, Discrete Event-Driven Sensory Feedback Control (DESC) policy seems promising in some applications [13]. DESC policy states that, manipulation of an object mostly depends on discrete sensory events [14, 15]. Thus, the same task can be facilitated by applying discrete sensory feedback signals related to events, rather than continuous stimulation. As a result, both signal processing load may be decreased and the learning phase may be shortened. Clemente et al. designed a device, called DESC-glove, including sensorized thimbles and a vibrotactile feedback unit. Making or breaking contact of the thimble with the objects are coded as discrete events and the vibration motors are activated for each event. They tested the success of the device in a virtual eggs test and have shown that the performance of the users was improved [13].

Our study was inspired by the same hypothesis; however, the device used is different. We equipped a robotic hand with joint angle measurement, in addition to force measurement. Thus, more detailed discrete events, comprising information on the movement direction and hand position, can be signaled to the user. This study is the preliminary application of our DESC-based sensory feedback system for prosthetic hands. We collected data from sensors during a predefined grasp pattern (labeled by video analysis) and fitted the sensor training data to a model using multinomial logistic regression algorithm. Both grasp force and joint angles were measured simultaneously and formed the features of the training and the test data. Using regression model coefficients, we classified the test data. Thus, we aimed to predict object hardness and movement type during manipulation. At this time, there is no real time human involvement in the system, and it runs on programmed control. The system is relatively novel in terms of the sensors being used and sensor placement. The bend sensor is commonly used with glove systems which are designed for robotic arm control, rehabilitation, gaming or virtual reality applications [16, 17]. To our knowledge, the bend sensor used in this study was utilized only in one previous prosthesis study for supplying joint angle feedback [18]. Our study differs from theirs in terms of sensor placement. In the work presented here, we placed a bend sensor for each joint of the finger. For this purpose, the bend sensors were modified and shortened to fit the joint lengths.

2   Materials and Methods

2.1   Robotic Hand

The robotic hand which is used in this study (Fig. 1-a) was originally designed at Robotic Laboratory, Institute of Biomedical Engineering, Boğaziçi University [19]. It is dimensionally modeled similar to the human hand. Each finger, except the thumb, is formed by three phalanges, and has three degrees of freedom (DOF) and one degree of mobility (DOM) which is flexion/extension. The thumb has two DOFs and two DOMs (one additional DOM for abduction/adduction). The original hand is controlled by DC motors and shape-memory-alloy (SMA) actuators. Here, the fingers were actuated through a single tendon system; the finger is flexed by motors, but the extension occurs with the help of tensile forces. The motion of the fingers was controlled by six servo motors (Goteck, GS-9025MG) (one for each finger, one additional for thumb), and the motors were commanded by Arduino Mega. A nylon thread was attached to the tip of the distal phalanx of each finger. The other end of the thread was fixed to the servo motor shaft. When the motor is activated, the nylon thread wraps around the shaft and the tension causes the finger to flex. When the motor shaft rotates back to its initial position, the finger extends, with the help of the tensile force in an elastic thread passing through the joints. For easy integration of sensors, the fingers were modified without changing the mechanical properties of the hand. For mounting of bend sensors, sliding sockets were added on the dorsal surface of the fingers. Additionally, the fingertips were flattened for proper integration of force sensors. The naturally curved shape was provided with the help of a dome-shaped silicon rubber glued on the sensors (Fig. 1-c).

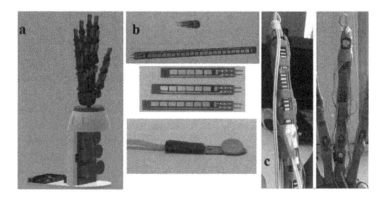

Fig. 1.   (a) Robotic hand. (b) Bend sensors were cut and modified for correct size. Dome-shaped silicon rubber was glued on force sensors. (c) Fingers with attached sensors.

2.2   Sensors, Signal Conditioning, and Characterization

Feedback in neuroprosthetic applications is used either for automatic control of the hand or for providing sensory feedback to the user. For both, grasp force and joint angle information are of primary importance. Joint angle sensors provide proprioceptive information, and tactile information can be obtained by force sensors. For this purpose, various types of force and position sensors were used in the literature [20]. Although each sensor has advantages and disadvantages over the others, a sensor should have some minimum required properties to be used in prosthetic applications. It should be low powered, light, thin, and easy to mount. Considering these requirements, piezoresistive sensors were used for grasping force and joint angle measurements in this study (Fig. 1-b).

For joint angle measurements, piezoresistive bend sensor (FlexSensor, Spectra-Symbol) was preferred. Its technology is based on resistive carbon elements. When the sensor is bent, resistive carbon elements are separated and the resistance increases. Conversely, when the sensor is straight, the resistive carbon elements get closer and the resistance decreases. The increase in resistance is inversely related to the bend radius. When it is straight, the resistance is around 15 kΩ and it reaches 50 kΩ for 90° of bending. In this study, since a distinct sensor is used for each joint, the sensors were shortened to fit joint lengths (Fig. 1-b, c). The electrical continuity was ensured by coating the cut end with conductive glue (Nickel Print) [21].

The force sensors were force sensing resistors (FSR400-Short, Interlink Electronics) which are commonly used in the literature [22–24]. They are fabricated in different sizes and shapes. In this study, FSR400-Short was used, with 0.2" diameter of active area and short tails. It consists of two layers, separated by a spacer adhesive. One of the layers has two sets of interdigitated patterns that are electrically distinct. The other layer has conductive polyetherimide film (FSR ink). When pressure is applied, the two layers are merged and the FSR ink shorts the patterns. Thus, the electrical resistance changes depending on the applied pressure. The sensor has very large resistance ($\gg$MΩs) when no force is applied, and it decreases to approximately 3–5 kΩ when 1 kg force is applied. In order to distribute force homogeneously over the active area, a dome-shaped silicon structure was designed and glued on the sensor (Fig. 1-b, c), similar to the studies in the literature [24, 25]. Thus, the applied force was focused on the active area of the sensor, independent of actual contact area with the object. The dome-shaped structure also increased the friction between the object and robotic hand, thus ensured more stable grasping.

In this study, only the thumb and the middle finger of the robotic hand were equipped with sensors (Fig. 1-c). There was a distinct bend sensor for each joint to provide proprioceptive information. To obtain tactile information by measuring contact forces, force sensors were placed at both fingertips. Another force sensor was placed on the distal end of the middle finger's metacarpal. The change in resistance of the sensors was converted to voltage by using op-amp circuits. The first stage of the circuit consisted of a voltage divider. Since the direction of resistance change is opposite, the force sensor is connected as a pull-up resistor (Fig. 2), while the bend sensor as a pull-down resistor (Fig. 3). To use the full span of the data acquisition card for all sensors with different sensitivity ranges, a gain adjustable amplifier is used as the next stage. The last stage of the interface circuit is a second-order Butterworth low-pass filter with cut-off frequency of 10 Hz. For the bend sensors, an additional offset adjustment stage was included (Fig. 3), which was not needed for force sensors because of their very high nominal resistance.

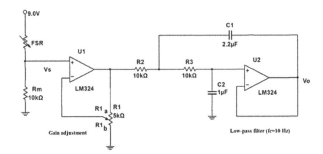

Fig. 2. Force sensor interface circuit. Subscripts represents the resistance values after adjustment of multiturn trimpots. The output of the circuit is given as $V_o = \dfrac{R_1}{R_{1b}} V_s$.

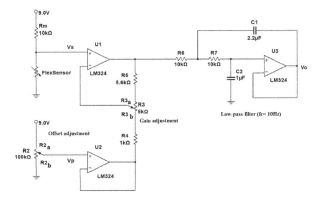

Fig. 3. Bend sensor interface circuit. Subscripts represents the resistance values after adjustment of multiturn trimpots. The output of the circuit is given as $V_0 = \left(1 + \dfrac{R_5 + R_{3a}}{R_{3b} + R_4}\right) V_s - \left(\dfrac{R_5 + R_{3a}}{R_{3b} + R_4}\right) V_p$.

The force sensing resistors were calibrated by using a digital precision balance. The circuit gain was adjusted to use the full span of the data acquisition card (Fig. 2). The sensor was first fixed on the scale and the force was changed gradually using a micro-manipulator. The force in grams and circuit output were recorded during loading and unloading cycles. Characterization of the bend sensors was performed on the robotic hand in order to have the same bending radius as in the classification experiments. The circuit output when the sensor is straight was set to zero by an offset adjustment trimpot. The gain was also adjusted to use the full span (Fig. 3). The servo motor position of the finger was changed gradually and bending angles of all sensors were measured by using a goniometer.

2.3   Data Acquisition and Grasping Experiment

The experimental data was acquired using a data acquisition card (NI-USB6259) at a sampling frequency of 1 kHz. The card has 16 analog inputs (voltage range of –10 V to 10 V), 4 analog outputs and 48 digital I/O's. Two cylindrical objects (diameter: 9 cm, length: 12 cm) differing in stiffness were used for experiments. The soft object (1029 N/m) was made of rolled sponge. The hard object (1225 N/m) had additional cardboard layers within the sponge. The stiffness constants were measured with flat indenters by using the sensor characterization setup.

According to the Cutkosky grasp taxonomy and the activities of daily living (ADL), not all grasp patters are needed for prosthesis users [25]. Additionally, some finger postures are impossible to attain because of anatomical limitations. Therefore, prosthetic hands are generally designed to implement limited grasp types. In this study, the under-actuated (fewer actuators than DOFs) mechanism of the robotic hand did not allow us to implement precision grasps, since it was impossible to control each phalanx independently. Only power grasps could be performed. As a preliminary work, we only tested the cylindrical power grasp. The target motor positions were set to 180° for both objects and the data from the sensors were recorded during periodical flexion and extension movements of the fingers. The same recording was also performed without any object. Each movement cycle lasted approximately 6 s. The overall data included 264 cycles, with 83 for the no object condition, 94 and 87 for the hard and soft object conditions, respectively. The movements of the robotic hand were also captured on video (by a simple webcam) for labeling.

2.4   Classification

The experimental sensor data was analyzed in MATLAB. It was initially low-pass filtered (second-order Butterworth, fc = 0.5 Hz); and the first and second derivatives of the filtered data were calculated. Since the movement of the thumb was not stable during the experiment, only the sensor data from the middle finger was included in the classification. Additionally the data from the metacarpal force sensor was discarded, because it did not establish any contact with the objects. The filtered sensor data (3 bend sensors + 1 force sensor) and their derivatives were segmented into non-overlapping 30-ms windows (corresponding to one video frame) and time-averaged within each window. For every 30-ms window, the time-averaged values established the two feature matrices. The first one consisted of 8 features (4 sensor data and the first derivatives), and the second one also included the second derivatives (12 features).

Four classifications were performed: for object type (no object, soft object and hard object classes) and for movement type (no movement, flexion, contact/release and extension classes) with two feature sets each. The class labeling of the data were performed manually by analyzing the video frames of the movements. The motor on/off commands were taken as reference for transition times of flexion and extension phases. The labeled data were randomly divided into training and test data sets, with 169 and 95 grasp cycles respectively. The training data was used to fit a multinomial logistic regression model. The classes of the test dataset were predicted using the model coefficients.

3 Results

3.1 Sensor Characterization

Two parameter power equation was fitted to the data with the parameters (a, b, and c) given in Table 1. Characterization results of each sensor type are given in Figs. 4 and 5. Sensors show non-linear behavior and low hysteresis. The hysteresis can be tolerated by using their different calibration coefficients for loading and unloading cycles.

Table 1. Parameters of the calibration equation: $V = ax^b + c$ (averages of loading and unloading cycles). V: measured circuit output, x: force for force sensors or the angle for bend sensors, IP: interphalangeal, MCP: metacarpophalangeal, DIP: distal interphalangeal, PIP: proximal interphalangeal, FSR: force sensor, Flex: bend sensor.

	a	b	c
FSR-thumb-fingertip	−55.3466	−0.4756	9.7394
FSR-middle-fingertip	−87.7424	−0.6230	9.3373
FSR-middle-metacarpal	−54.1629	−0.4520	10.8738
Flex-thumb-IP	0.5956	0.5953	−1.3370
Flex-thumb-MCP	1.4614	0.4064	−2.0537
Flex-middle-DIP	0.0421	1.1325	0.9450
Flex-middle-PIP	0.0090	1.4924	3.8003
Flex-middle-MCP	0.0879	0.9406	−0.1557

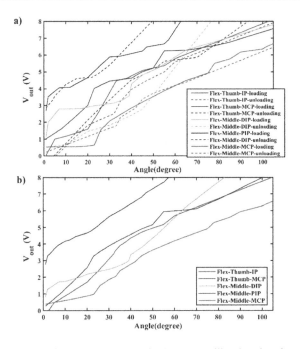

Fig. 4. a) Calibration cycles of bend sensors. b) Average calibration data from bend sensors.

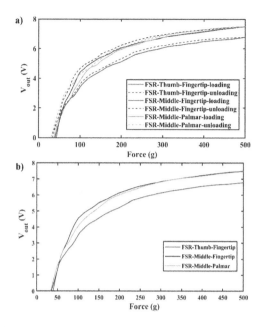

Fig. 5. a) Calibration cycles of force sensors. b) Average calibration data from force sensors.

3.2 Cylindrical Grasping Data

Using coefficients of the calibration curves, a look-up table was composed for each sensor. The estimated joint angle and force values were calculated for the circuit outputs recorded during the cylindrical grasping experiment. The filtered data and the derivatives from exemplary sensors are given in Figs. 6 and 7. Sensor output changed depending on each object condition.

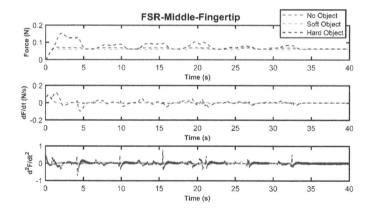

Fig. 6. Force sensor output from the grasping experiment.

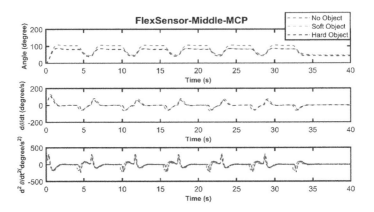

Fig. 7. Bend sensor output from the grasping experiment.

3.3 Classification Results

For object type classification, no object and hard object conditions were discriminated better than the soft objects class (Table 2). The confusion matrix for object type classification results are also given in Fig. 8. It can be seen that mostly soft object and hard object classes were confused with no object condition. This is due to the lack of adequate information from the force sensor. However, the hard object condition was classified much better than the soft object condition.

Table 2. Classification results

		Recall	Precision	F1 Score
8 features	No object	0.892	0.748	0.813
	Soft object	0.084	0.174	0.113
	Hard object	0.429	0.569	0.489
12 features	No object	0.918	0.728	0.812
	Soft object	0.042	0.113	0.062
	Hard object	0.409	0.678	0.510
8 features	No movement	0.793	0.710	0.749
	Flexion	0.689	0.764	0.724
	Contact/ Release	0.012	0.143	0.021
	Extension	0.497	0.561	0.527
12 features	No movement	0.813	0.708	0.757
	Flexion	0.694	0.801	0.744
	Contact/ Release	0.197	0.548	0.289
	Extension	0.483	0.592	0.532

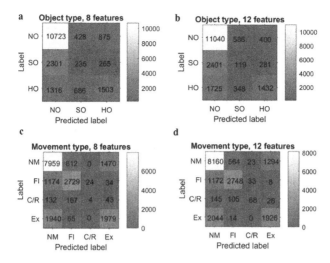

Fig. 8. Confusion matrices for the classification results. Numbers indicate counts for each prediction (NO: no object, SO: soft object, HO: hard object, NM: no movement, Fl: flexion: C/R: contact/release, Ex: extension).

Movement classification results show that, no movement, flexion and extension classes were classified much better than the contact/release class. This is due to the insufficient information about contact and release events. The contact and/or release durations were very low compared to other classes. As a preliminary study, only one force sensor was used; more sensors would improve the results. It can also be deduced from contact/release results that, recall of the classification increased when 12 features were used. This implies that acceleration information, represented by second derivative of the bend sensors and the second derivative of forces had a positive effect on movement type discrimination.

4   Conclusion and Discussion

This study was a preliminary evaluation of a sensory feedback system for prosthetic hands. We equipped two fingers of a robotic hand with sensors and conducted a pilot cylindrical grasping experiment. The sensor data and its derivatives were used for classification according to object type (no object, soft object, hard object) and movement type (no movement, flexion, contact/release, extension). However, because of poor coupling with the objects and instability of the thumb, only data from one force sensor and three bend sensors were used in the classification algorithm (multinomical logistic regression). The results were satisfactory for classes which did not depend on information from the force sensor. For example, F_1 scores were about 0.81 and 0.51 for no object and hard object conditions; 0.76, 0.74, 0.53 for no movement, flexion, and extension conditions, respectively. It was concluded that the force sensor data did not have much contribution to the classification. That is why soft object and contact/release classes could not be classified. To solve this problem, the number of force sensors should be increased, and the coupling should be improved. As such, contact/release data from multiple points can be processes together.

Another drawback of the system is the simplicity of the particular robotic hand and actuation. Due to the control mechanism of the hand, the phalanges were flexed/extended in conjunction with each other. Consequently, stable contact could not be maintained for some grasp cycles. For working with this hand, object size and type should be chosen carefully, in order to guarantee stable contact and maximize the contact points between the object and the fingers. If the actuator mechanism is improved in the future, tendon forces can also be measured as an additional type of proprioceptive input.

Additionally, transition requirements and the physical movement model were not included in the classification. Only trained by static labels, the algorithm provided an output as a 'worst-case' scenario, but nevertheless with some decent predictions about the grasping experiment. We plan to include the transition requirements and an adaptive window size in the real-time implementation of the system.

References

1. D'Alonzo, M., Clemente, F., Cipriani, C.: Vibrotactile stimulation promotes embodiment of an alien hand in amputees with phantom sensations. IEEE Trans. Neural Syst. Rehabil. Eng. **23**(3), 450–457 (2014)
2. Kim, S.S., Sripati, A.P., Vogelstein, R.J., Armiger, R.S., Russell, A.F., Bensmaia, S.J.: Conveying tactile feedback in sensorized hand neuroprostheses using a biofidelic model of mechanotransduction. IEEE Trans. Biomed. Circ. Syst. **3**(6), 398–404 (2009)
3. Dhillon, G.S., Horch, K.W.: Direct neural sensory feedback and control of a prosthetic arm. IEEE Trans. Neural Syst. Rehabil. Eng. **13**(4), 468–472 (2005)
4. Witteveen, H.J.B., Droog, E.A., Rietman, J.S., Veltink, P.H.: Vibro- and electrotactile user feedback on hand opening for myoelectric forearm prostheses. IEEE Trans. Biomed. Eng. **59**(8), 2219–2226 (2012)
5. D'Alonzo, M., Dosen, S., Cipriani, C., Farina, D.: HyVE — hybrid vibro-electrotactile stimulation — is an efficient approach to multi-channel sensory feedback. IEEE Trans. Haptics **7**(2), 181–190 (2014)
6. Stephens-Fripp, B., Alici, G., Mutlu, R.: A review of non-invasive sensory feedback methods for transradial prosthetic hands. IEEE Access. **PP**(99), 6878–6899 (2018)
7. Antfolk, C., D'Alonzo, M., Controzzi, M., Lundborg, G., Rosén, B., Sebelius, F., Cipriani, C.: Artificial redirection of sensation from prosthetic fingers to the phantom hand map on transradial amputees: vibrotactile versus mechanotactile sensory feedback. IEEE Trans. Neural Syst. Rehabil. Eng. **21**(1), 112–120 (2013)
8. Dosen, S., Markovic, M., Strbac, M., Belić, M., Kojić, V., Bijelić, G., Keller, T., Farina, D.: Multichannel electrotactile feedback with spatial and mixed coding for closed-loop control of grasping force in hand prostheses. IEEE Trans. Neural Syst. Rehabil. Eng. **25**(3), 183–195 (2017)
9. Brown, J.D., Kunz, T.S., Gardner, D., Shelley, M.K., Davis, A.J., Gillespie, R.B.: An empirical evaluation of force feedback in body-powered prostheses. IEEE Trans. Neural Syst. Rehabil. Eng. **25**(3), 215–226 (2017)
10. Witteveen, H.J.B., Luft, F., Rietman, J.S., Veltink, P.H.: Stiffness feedback for myoelectric forearm prostheses using vibrotactile stimulation. IEEE Trans. Neural Syst. Rehabil. Eng. **22**(1), 53–61 (2014)

11. Chatterjee, A., Chaubey, P., Martin, J., Thakor, N.: Testing a prosthetic haptic feedback simulator with an interactive force matching task. JPO J. Prosthetics Orthot. **20**(2), 27–34 (2008)
12. Antfolk, C., Björkman, A., Frank, S.-O., Sebelius, F., Lundborg, G., Rosen, B.: Sensory feedback from a prosthetic hand based on air- mediated pressure from the hand to the forearm skin. J. Rehabil. Med. **44**, 702–707 (2012)
13. Clemente, F., D'Alonzo, M., Controzzi, M., Edin, B.B., Cipriani, C.: Non-invasive, temporally discrete feedback of object contact and release improves grasp control of closed-loop myoelectric transradial prostheses. IEEE Trans. Neural Syst. Rehabil. Eng. **24**(12), 1314–1322 (2016)
14. Johansson, R.S., Flanagan, J.R.: Coding and use of tactile signals from the fingertips in object manipulation tasks. Nat. Rev. **10**, 345–359 (2009)
15. Flanagan, J.R., Bowman, M.C., Johansson, R.S.: Control strategies in object manipulation tasks. Curr. Opin. Neurobiol. **16**, 650–659 (2006)
16. Gücüyener, A., Kaplanoğlu, E.: Wireless hand rehabilitation system (WHRS). Balk J. Electr. Comput. Eng. **5**(1), 9–13 (2017)
17. Syed, A., Agasbal, Z.T.H., Melligeri, T., Gudur, B.: Flex sensor based robotic arm controller using micro controller. J. Softw. Eng. Appl. **5**, 364–366 (2012)
18. Bundhoo, V., Haslam, E., Birch, B., Park, E.J.: A shape memory alloy-based tendon-driven actuation system for biomimetic artificial fingers, part I: design and evaluation. Robotica. **27**, 131–146 (2009)
19. Atasoy, A., Kaya, E., Toptas, E., Kuchimov, S., Kaplanoglu, E., Ozkan, M.: 24 DOF EMG controlled hybrid actuated prosthetic hand. In: Proceedings of IEEE EMBC, pp. 5059–5062, Orlando-USA (2016)
20. Saudabayev, A., Varol, H.A.: Sensors for robotic hands: a survey of state of the art. IEEE Access. **3**, 1765–1782 (2015)
21. Karakuş, İ., Kaplanoğlu, E., Özkan, M., Güçlü, B.: Characterization of a bend sensor for neuroprosthetic applications. In: Proceedings of EBBT, İstanbul-Turkey (2017)
22. Castro, M.C.F., Cliquet, A.: A low-cost instrumented glove for monitoring forces during object manipulation. IEEE Trans. Rehabil. Eng. **5**(2), 140–147 (1997)
23. Flórez, J.A., Velásquez, A.: Calibration of force sensing resistors (fsr) for static and dynamic applications. In: Proceedings of ANDESCON, pp. 2–7, Bogota-Colombia (2010)
24. Hall, R.S., Desmoulin, G.T., Milner, T.E.: A technique for conditioning and calibrating force-sensing resistors for repeatable and reliable measurement of compressive force. J. Biomech. **41**, 3492–3495 (2008)
25. Cutkosky, M.R.: On grasp choice, grasp models, and the design of hands for manufacturing tasks. IEEE Trans. Robot. Autom. **5**(3), 269–279 (1989)

Suitability of a Tool-Speed-Dependent Force Model for VR-Based Soft-Tissue Dissection

Fernando Trejo and Yaoping Hu[✉]

Department of Electrical and Computer Engineering, University of Calgary,
Calgary, AB, Canada
{fjtrejot,huy}@ucalgary.ca

Abstract. Models of tool-tissue interaction forces find a potential application in Virtual Reality (VR) based simulators for surgical training. What remains unclear is the effect of such force models on user performance of surgical tasks with different tool speeds. Since soft-tissue dissection accounts for about 35% of surgical time, we herein conducted a preliminary study on user performance of the 1 degree-of-freedom dissection under an analytic force model for various tool speeds. Derived from empirical force-displacement data, the model had averagely a computation time of 2.5 µs to ensure force rendering via a haptic device. On a VR-based simulator featuring the force model, the user's hand holding a virtual scalpel via the haptic device executed the dissection at the tool speed of 0.10, 1.27, or 2.54 cm/s. User hand movements were recorded by the simulator to compute objective performance metrics of tracing accuracy, speed accuracy, motion quality and damage reduction. User perceived workload was measured using NASA-TLX. One-way ANOVA analyses revealed significantly lower user performance for the tool speed of 0.10 cm/s, compared to both higher speeds. Nonetheless, there were no differences in perceived workload among these speeds. Agreeing with the convention that a low tool speed demands refined hand movements in the dissection, these findings validate the suitability of the force model for VR-based soft-tissue dissection at various tool speeds.

Keywords: Analytic model · Objective metrics · Dissection
Tool-tissue interaction forces · Tool speeds
Virtual reality based simulation · Workload

1 Introduction

In-vivo measurement of soft-tissue responses to external forces has been an active research field in biomechanics since many years. This leads to some understanding of complex tool-tissue interactions exhibited in surgical tasks such as indentation, insertion, cutting, and dissection. Indentation is soft-tissue deformation, inflicted by the forces of a surgical tool normal to the surface of a tissue [1]. Once these forces surpass the stiffness threshold of the tissue surface, insertion occurs as the tool pierces into the tissue and traverses vertically within the tissue [2]. Tissue fractures after the insertion are propagated through different layers of the tissue, yielding tissue cutting [3]. Being more complex than cutting, dissection consists of two alternated tool motions. As the first motion, the tool travels vertically to be perpendicular to the tissue surface, yielding

© Springer International Publishing AG, part of Springer Nature 2018
D. Prattichizzo et al. (Eds.): EuroHaptics 2018, LNCS 10894, pp. 464–475, 2018.
https://doi.org/10.1007/978-3-319-93399-3_40

indentation, insertion, and cutting. As the second motion, the tool then moves horizontally in parallel to the tissue surface, causing tissue friction and fracture. Both motions alternate during dissection, resembling the use of the tool to trace a predefined path on the tissue surface. The analysis of these tool-tissue interactions conveys insights for planning and execution of surgical procedures on soft-tissues such as the brain [1, 4] and the liver [1, 2]. The analysis also enables the formulation of force models and their haptic implementation to serve virtual reality (VR) based surgical simulators [5] and/or robot-assisted surgical systems [6].

Tool-tissue interaction forces are modeled using finite element method (FEM) for indentation [1, 7, 8], insertion [3], and cutting [8]; mass-spring configuration (MSC) for indentation [9] and dissection [10]; or analytic modeling for indentation [11], insertion [2, 12, 13], cutting [14], and dissection [15]. Force models that rely on FEM or MSC are mostly confined to VR-based simulators for an integrated visuo-haptic display of soft-tissue biomechanical responses. Although FEM is more robust than MSC, both FEM and MSC are computationally expensive and struggle to meet real-time force rendering at 1.0 kHz (= 1.0 ms) [16]. The computation of FEM models is more than 2.0 ms [7], while the computation of MSC models may reduce to 1.5 ms [10].

Analytic models are an alternative for modeling realistic tool-tissue interaction forces. In mathematic formulations, analytic models comprise three categories including viscoelastic tissue models [11–13]; tissue fracture mechanics [13, 14]; and observation-based empirical methods [2, 15]. The advantage of analytic models is fast computation over FEM and MSC. The computation time of analytic models is less than 1.0 ms [12, 14]. This ensures the models to be adequate for real-time force rendering. In turn, analytic models find applications in both surgical simulators and robot-assisted surgery, which requires recreating tool-tissue interaction forces in real time. Nonetheless, there are a few reports on the ability of analytic models to estimate tool-tissue interaction forces at different tool speeds [11, 13, 15]. This includes indentation with quasi-static tool speeds of 0.08, 0.15, and 0.30 cm/s [11]; insertion at tool speeds from 0.10 cm/s to 25.00 cm/s [13]; and dissection following tool speeds of 0.10 and 1.27 cm/s [15]. The key of devising analytic models is the characteristics of soft-tissue responses at different tool speeds. In insertion [3] and dissection [17], it is known that the lower a tool speed is, the larger soft-tissue resistance to the tool motion becomes and, the more abrupt changes in tool-tissue interaction forces arise.

Despite the efforts of modeling tool-tissue interaction forces, a few models have been integrated in VR-based simulators to validate their suitability for surgical tasks. A study on a VR simulator that incorporated a FEM model reported improved performance of surgical residents over medical students for removing brain tumors [8]. Another study indicated outperformance of force feedback derived from an analytic model of needle-tissue interactions during simulated suturing tasks over no-force feedback [12]. Although those studies support the usefulness of force models for surgical simulation, tool-tissue interactions at different tool speeds remain unexamined.

To our knowledge, there is a lack of validation on force models, as a function of tool speeds, for their suitability for VR-based surgical tasks. The outcomes from such validations may underlie training feedback to trainees. This becomes of particular interest in neurosurgery during interacting jelly-like brain tissues [18]. High dexterity is needed to minimize tissue damage by maintaining precise motion of a surgical tool in very slow and constant speed. Among diverse surgical tasks, dissection accounts for ∼35% of surgery time [19]. Hence, we conducted a user study to investigate the suitability of a force model for VR-based soft-tissue dissection.

In the study, the dissection took place on the brain tissues alike in neurosurgery. The dissection was undertaken on different tool speeds along a predefined path with 1 degree-of-freedom (DOF), which facilitated comparison of user performance among the tool speeds. Using an existing modeling framework [15], we formulated dissection forces as an analytic model based on an empirical force-displacement dataset [17]. The formulation obeyed to the adequateness of analytic models for real-time force rendering. The model captures force-displacement characteristics of dissecting the brain tissue at prescript tool speeds of 0.10 cm/s, 1.27 cm/s, and 2.54 cm/s. While the speed of 0.10 cm/s is commonly observed in neurosurgery [18], the speeds of 1.27 cm/s and 2.54 cm/s are intermediate and conventional, respectively, for performing liver biopsy [17]. In agreement with the convention that a low tool speed demands refined hand movements in dissection, the observations of our study validated the suitability of the model for VR-based dissection. The validation might serve towards the development and acquisition of surgical skills in soft-tissue dissection.

2   Analytic Force Model

A force arises when a surgical tool dissects a soft tissue to cause its deformation, friction, and fracture. The dissection force has nonlinear and zigzag characteristics with respect to tool displacements along the soft-tissue surface. An analytic model can approximate these characteristics using the following formulation [15]:

$$\hat{y} = f(x, \hat{\alpha}) = f_1(x, \hat{\alpha}_a) + f_2(x, \hat{\alpha}_b) f_3(x, \hat{\alpha}_{(A+B+2)}), \tag{1}$$

where x indicates the tool displacement; $\hat{y}$ is the estimated dissection force; and $\hat{\alpha}$ is a vector-set of estimated parameters $\begin{bmatrix} \hat{\alpha}_a & \hat{\alpha}_b & \hat{\alpha}_{(A+B+2)} \end{bmatrix}^T$ with the vectors $\hat{\alpha}_a = [\hat{\alpha}_0, \ldots, \hat{\alpha}_A]^T$ and $\hat{\alpha}_b = \begin{bmatrix} \hat{\alpha}_{(A+1)}, \hat{\alpha}_{(A+2)}, \ldots, \hat{\alpha}_{(A+B+1)} \end{bmatrix}^T$. The $f_1(x, \hat{\alpha}_a)$ component in Eq. (1) represents the exponential growth of the dissection force due to tissue deformation; while the $f_2(x, \hat{\alpha}_b) f_3(x, \hat{\alpha}_{(A+B+2)})$ component portrays the abrupt changes in the force due to tissue friction and fracture. The function $f_3(x, \hat{\alpha}_{(A+B+2)})$ filters the changes caused by $f_2(x, \hat{\alpha}_b)$ within a range, $x \in [0, \hat{\alpha}_{(A+B+2)}]$, transits gradually during a band, $x \in (\hat{\alpha}_{(A+B+2)}, w\hat{\alpha}_{(A+B+2)})$, and maintains the changes for an interval, $x \in [w\hat{\alpha}_{(A+B+2)}, \infty)$. The factor w is greater than 1.0 to signify a transiting slope from the range to the interval. Details of the analytic model in Eq. (1) and its modeling framework for computing $\hat{\alpha}$ and determining w are presented in the existing work [15].

An empirical force-displacement dataset of soft-tissue dissection is essential for computing $\hat{\alpha}$ and estimating a dissection force. Inputting the force-displacement dataset along with the pre-determined factor, the modeling framework outputs the corresponding $\hat{\alpha}$ in Eq. (1). We formulated three analytic force models based on three empirical force-displacement datasets at the tool speeds of 0.10, 1.27, and 2.54 cm/s

[17], respectively. The datasets were correspondingly comprised of 106, 73, and 57 data points. Due to the lack of empirical measures for dissecting the brain, the datasets were scaled from a maximum force of 4.3 N for dissecting the liver to 0.6 N as observed in neurosurgery [20]. The scaling resulted from different stiffness between the liver and brain, since both tissues exhibit hyper-viscoelasticity under a surgical tool [1, 2]. Table 1 shows 11 parameters of the model for each tool speed with A = 2 and B = 6, and using w = 1.1 for all speeds.

Table 1. Parameters of the analytic force model for each tool speed of dissection.

Parameters		Tool speeds		
		0.10 cm/s	1.27 cm/s	2.54 cm/s
$\hat{\alpha}_a$	$\hat{\alpha}_0\,[N]$	4.4147e−01	4.3158e−01	4.7122e−01
	$\hat{\alpha}_1\,[cm^{-1}]$	2.1968e−01	2.7117e−01	9.5242e−01
	$\hat{\alpha}_2\,[-]$	1.8641	2.4423	1.1385
$\hat{\alpha}_b$	$\hat{\alpha}_3\,[N]$	3.2960e−02	3.4217e−02	3.5026e−02
	$\hat{\alpha}_4\,[cm]$	9.5340	7.7333	4.4139e−01
	$\hat{\alpha}_5\,[cm]$	4.5426	4.8231	5.4369e−01
	$\hat{\alpha}_6\,[cm]$	3.2906	2.9807	3.6505
	$\hat{\alpha}_7\,[cm]$	2.1438e−01	7.7278	2.8440
	$\hat{\alpha}_8\,[cm]$	4.5429	2.7536e−01	1.4199
	$\hat{\alpha}_9\,[cm]$	1.6000	2.6181e−01	7.0622
$\hat{\alpha}_{(A+B+2)}$	$\hat{\alpha}_{10}\,[cm]$	2.2366	6.3089e−01	2.0303

Figure 1(a) plots the estimated force of the analytic model and the empirical force-displacement dataset at the tool speed of 0.10 cm/s. The model gave a close estimation of the empirical dataset with a coefficient of determination $R^2 = 0.93$ ($0 \leq R^2 \leq 1$). The analytic models derived from the empirical datasets at the speeds of 1.27 and 2.54 cm/s achieved comparable levels of estimation for $R^2 = 0.91$ and $R^2 = 0.81$, respectively, as shown in Fig. 1(b). The lower the tool speed is, the more abrupt changes the dissection force has. A lower tool speed of dissection warrants more

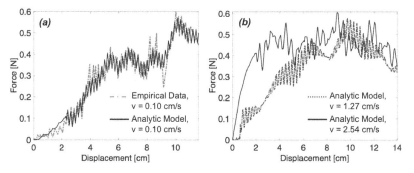

Fig. 1. The estimated forces of the analytic model: (a) an empirical force-displacement dataset for the tool speed of 0.10 cm/s and the corresponding counterpart of the analytic model; and (b) forces of the analytic model for the tool speeds of 1.27 cm/s and 2.54 cm/s.

completion of tissue deformation, fracture, and relaxation than a higher speed. This agrees with tool-speed-dependent hyper-viscoelastic responses of soft tissues [17].

Figure 2 depicts comparisons between the forces of the analytic model computed within the simulator as inputs to the haptic device and the corresponding forces rendered by the device. The rendered forces were acquired within the rendering loop of the device via OpenHaptics library. In the spatial domain, Fig. 2(a) depicts the force-displacement profiles computed within the simulator and inputted to the haptic device. These profiles matched well with their rendered counterparts in Fig. 2(b), delivered by a haptic device (PHANToM Premium 1.5/6DOF). Similar correspondence levels existed in the frequency domain, as shown in Figs. 2(c, d). These outcomes confirm proper implementation and force rendering of the analytic model for each tool speed. To assess the suitability of the analytic model for VR-based dissection, we conducted a study on user performance of the 1-DOF dissection.

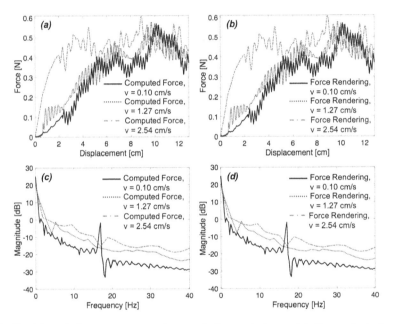

Fig. 2. Spatial and frequency comparisons of the analytic model for each tool speed: (a) computed force-displacement profiles of the analytic model; (b) corresponding rendered profiles acquired via OpenHaptics; (c) computed magnitude-frequency responses of the analytic model; and (d) corresponding rendered responses acquired via OpenHaptics.

3   User Study

3.1   VR Simulator

Our VR simulator was based on a workstation (DELL Precision T5500 with a 64-bit windows 7 operating system, dual-quadro core Intel Xeon processors at 2.53 GHz, and

12 GB RAM). The workstation had a graphic card NVDIA Quadro FX 4800; an ASUS VG248 24″ 3D LED monitor with a maximum refresh rate of 144 Hz for active stereoscopic vision; a NVIDIA 3D vision 2 kit with an infrared emitter and wireless stereoscopic shutter glasses; and a Geomagic PHANToM Premium 1.5/6DOF haptic device. The simulator was developed with C++, OpenGL 3.3, and OpenHaptics 3.2.

Figure 3 shows the configuration of the simulator. Each participant sat on a height-adjustable chair in front the configuration as exemplified in Fig. 3(a). For his/her interaction with virtual objects, the participant placed his/her chin on a chin-rest to ensure a consistent view of the objects on the monitor. The participant rested his/her right elbow on the chair armrest and handled the stylus of the haptic device to execute soft-tissue dissection by tracing a 1-DOF path. As depicted in Fig. 3(b), the base center of the haptic device was placed at 30.0 cm and 40.0 cm away from the center of the chin-rest and the front edge of the configuration, respectively. The configuration with the dimensions of 100.0 (depth) × 125.0 (width) × 89.0 (height) cm^3 encased the VR simulator to remove ambient lights and augment user immersion.

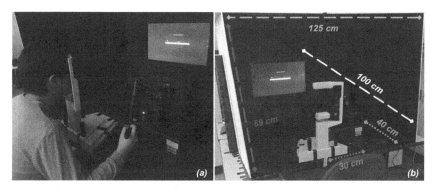

Fig. 3. VR-based dissection simulator: (a) participant performing a dissection task; and (b) setup of the human-computer interaction.

3.2 Participants

Ten participants (4 male and 6 female, 23.6 ± 5.9 years old) were recruited for the study. This participant number was greater than the minimally required number by Lehr's formula [21]. All participants were naïve to the purpose of the study. Each of them passed a pre-screening and then undertook the 1-DOF dissection. The outcomes of the pre-screening indicated that all participants were right-handed, had regular color vision, possessed normal or corrected-to-normal vision with stereo acuity of at least 40″ of arc, and exhibited no cyber-sickness symptoms [22]. The study had an ethics approval from our university under its ethics guidelines.

3.3 User Interaction

On the VR simulator, each participant utilized the pen-like stylus of the haptic device to move a virtual scalpel (i.e., a tool) along a virtual blood-vessel-like pipe (0.6 cm in radius and 21.8 cm long). As shown in Fig. 4, this mimics the act of dissecting diseased tissue near the vessel. The direction of the tracing was horizontal from left to right, being adequate for the right hand of the participant to actuate the tool and minimize his/her hand tiredness. The path of the dissection was exemplified by a 17.8 cm line located on the pipe. A motion scaling was 1:1 between the stylus and the tool. The stylus also conveyed force feedback onto the participant's hand.

Each trial of the VR-based dissection had four stages. The first two stages ensured a consistent initiation of the dissection, while the third stage executed the dissection. The last stage allowed the participant's hand to transit comfortably from the dissection to the endpoint of the trial. In the first stage, the scalpel was moved to a blue sphere at the right edge of the simulator shown in Fig. 4(a). The sphere served as a starting location of user interaction. Once the tip of the scalpel was placed within a radius of 2.0 cm from the sphere's center, an attraction force of 0.4 N was delivered by the stylus to facilitate aligning the scalpel tip to the sphere. An arrow pointed to the sphere assisted visually the alignment. Once the tip met the sphere, the arrow and sphere disappeared to signal the end of the first stage.

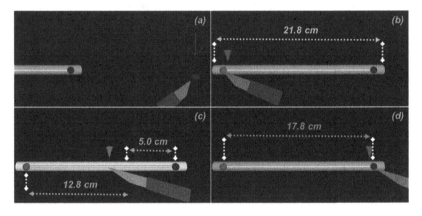

Fig. 4. Four stages of the VR-based dissection: (a) first stage; (b) second stage; (c) third stage; and (d) fourth stage. (Color figure online)

As shown in Fig. 4(b), a red and a blue sphere on the pipe (in yellow) encased a 1-DOF dissection path. The red and blue spheres indicated the beginning and the end of the path, respectively. In the second stage, an attraction force of 0.2 N assisted the scalpel tip to pierce the red sphere when the tip was within a radius of 1.0 cm from the sphere's center. The pipe then changed from yellow to green and a cone above the red sphere altered from blue to magenta indicating the occurrence of the third stage.

During the third stage, the magenta cone traveled towards the blue sphere on the pipe at a prescript speed of 0.10, 1.27, or 2.54 cm/s as depicted in Fig. 4(c). While the cone travelled, the participant moved the scalpel tip along the dissection path. In his/her efforts, the tip followed the position/speed of the cone; and avoided piercing the pipe or moving away from the path. The end of the third stage occurred when the scalpel tip reached a radius of 1.0 cm from the center of the blue sphere.

The fourth stage began by delivering an attraction force of 0.2 N to aid placing the scalpel tip in the blue sphere. The cone changed from magenta back to blue, once it reached the blue sphere as shown in Fig. 4(d). The end of the dissection took place when the scalpel tip touched the blue sphere and the pipe switched back to yellow.

In the third stage, the VR simulator recorded the movements of the scalpel tip; and rendered a dissection force according to the analytic model of the prescript tool speed. The direction of the force was rendered horizontally against the cone motion, mimicking soft-tissue resistance to the displacement of a surgical tool [17]. As shown in Fig. 4(c), the dissection force was rendered within the 12.8 cm segment of the path from the red sphere. The segment was deemed the effective length of the dissection. The force was then ramped down to 0.2 N within the next 4.0 cm segment of the path. The 0.2 N force became an attraction force to align the scalpel tip within the blue sphere. This permitted a smooth force transition from the end of the effective length to the end of the dissection. No dissection force was rendered during the first 2 stages.

Each participant completed 3 blocks corresponding to the tool speeds of 0.10, 1.27, and 2.54 cm/s, respectively. The sequence of the blocks was in a descending order of the tool speeds, to minimize fatigue. Each block had a practice prior to a test. The practice varied from 1 to 3 trials based on the learning curve of the participant, while the test had 4 trials. After completing each trial with a prescript speed of 0.10, 1.27, or 2.54 cm/s, the participant had a break of 60, 10, or 5 s, respectively. The different lengths of the break permitted the participant to have an adequate rest after his/her exposure to each tool speed. Once a practice or test was completed, the participant was administered an NASA Task Load Index (TLX) questionnaire [23] and a Simulator Sickness Questionnaire (SSQ) [22]. The NASA-TLX measured workload perceived by the participant, and the SSQ monitored cyber-sickness symptoms. The participant took ∼1.0 h for the study, including the pre-screening and the 3 blocks.

3.4   Data Collection and Analysis

For each test block, four objective metrics were devised from the recorded movements (kinematic data) of the scalpel tip within the effective length of dissection. The metrics included tracing accuracy (TA), speed accuracy (SA), motion quality (MQ), and damage reduction (DR). The computation of each metric took a normalization on the kinematic data. Thus, all metrics were unit-less for comparison. In addition, a subjective metric – workload (WL) – was derived from the responses to the NASA-TLX. Table 2 gives brief descriptions of these metrics.

On the data of each metric, we conducted a one-way repeated-measure analysis of variance (ANOVA). The ANOVA had its independent factor of "tool speeds" for 0.10, 1.27, and 2.54 cm/s. Prior to the ANOVA, normal distribution of the data was verified through the Anderson-Darling normality test. Significant differences found by the ANOVA were further examined using the Bonferroni post-hoc test.

Table 2. Description of the metrics that measure user performance of VR-based dissection.

Metrics	Description
Tracing Accuracy (TA)	The measure of precision of user hand tracing
Speed Accuracy (SA)	The measure of agreement between the mean speed of user hand and prescript tool speed
Motion Quality (MQ)	The degree of smoothness of user hand movements
Damage Reduction (DR)	The level of damage eluded on healthy tissue
Workload (WL)	Cognitive workload based on NASA-TXL [23]

3.5   Results

None of the participants exhibited cyber-sickness symptoms, confirmed by their responses to the SSQ administered before and after each block. Thus, the data of all participants were used for the ANOVA and Bonferroni post-hoc tests. Table 3 listed the outcomes of the ANOVA for each metric. Significant differences (with $p < 0.01$) were found among the tool speeds of 0.10, 1.27, and 2.54 cm/s for all objective metrics. As indicated by $p > 0.05$, the subjective metrics of WL had no significant difference among the tool speeds. Bonferroni post-hoc tests for each objective metric provided further insights as shown in Table 4. With $p < 0.01$, the tool speed of 0.10 cm/s conveyed a statistically lower performance of tracing accuracy (TA), speed accuracy (SA), and motion quality (MQ) than the speeds of 1.27 and 2.54 cm/s. Likewise, the lowest speed also yielded a statistically poorer performance of damage reduction (DR) than the speed of 1.27 cm/s. There was however no statistical difference of DR between the lowest and highest speeds, as shown by $p > 0.05$. Moreover, no significant difference existed for each objective metric between the speeds of 1.27 and 2.54 cm/s.

The above results indicate that the performance of the naïve participants was dependent of the tool speeds. Although varied dexterity was needed to maintain the tool speeds, all participants completed the dissection under the forces rendered according to the analytic models. The force model of the lowest tool speed constrained considerably the dissection performance of the participants, compared to those of the higher speeds. This might aid to achieve high dexterity required to move a surgical tool at 0.10 cm/s, reasserting the convention that neurosurgical procedures are performed by experienced surgeons, who have mastered to maintain a tool speed close to 0.10 cm/s [18]. The reassertion validates the suitability of the analytic model for dissection.

Moreover, there was no noticeable effect of the tool speeds on the workload (WL) metric. This suggests that dissection forces of all 3 tool speeds caused no sever fatigue or discomfort for the participants. This might result from the good correspondence of dissection forces between the analytic models and the empirical datasets.

Table 3. Results of one-way ANOVA for all subjective and objective metrics.

Metrics	Tool speeds [cm/s]			ANOVA $F_{(2, 18)}$	
	0.10	1.27	2.54	F	p
TA	2.26 ± 1.89e−01	2.65 ± 7.22e−02	2.58 ± 1.71e−01	19.32	<0.01
SA	3.07e−01 ± 1.21e−01	9.30e−01 ± 4.54e−02	9.65e−01 ± 3.57e−02	308.25	<0.01
MQ	1.14 ± 1.68e−01	1.93 ± 2.61e−02	1.94 ± 2.23e−02	216.25	<0.01
DR	3.60 ± 1.30e−01	3.75 ± 1.32e−01	3.67 ± 1.15e−01	6.18	<0.01
WL	103.19 ± 42.58	86.79 ± 46.83	93.34 ± 45.46	1.20	>0.05

Table 4. Bonferroni post-hoc tests for the objective metrics.

Tool speeds [cm/s]	Metrics			
	TA	SA	MQ	DR
0.10 *vs.* 1.27	$p < 0.01$	$p < 0.01$	$p < 0.01$	$p < 0.01$
0.10 *vs.* 2.54	$p < 0.01$	$p < 0.01$	$p < 0.01$	$p > 0.05$
1.27 *vs.* 2.54	$p > 0.05$	$p > 0.05$	$p > 0.05$	$p > 0.05$

4   Discussion

Two aspects underlie the results found in the study. One aspect is related to the force-displacement characteristics of soft-tissue dissection. The characteristics become less evenly zigzag from the tool speed of 0.10 cm/s to that of 2.54 cm/s, as exemplified in Figs. 1(a, b). The lower the speed is, the more abrupt changes the dissection force has, which signifies more tissue deformations and fractures. This is due to the fast responsiveness of soft tissues (such as the brain and liver) to resist the slow displacements of a tool [17]. Predominant and abrupt changes in dissection forces at a low tool speed hinder the execution of slow-paced dissection and demand high dexterity to maintain the speed. Another aspect is tool speeds accustomed by the human hand. The speeds of 1.27 cm/s and 2.54 cm/s are commonly applied by the hand to perform daily tasks such as pen-writing [24]. As we observed, the participants on average underwent less number of trials during the practice and needed less rest time in the blocks of these speeds. Consequently, the human hand is used to the movements at these speeds than at the speed of 0.10 cm/s, as in neurosurgery [18].

The realism of the analytic force model at each tool speed is supported by the following considerations. At first, each parameter-set in Table 1 permitted its analytic model to estimate reasonably well a corresponding empirical force-displacement dataset. This was supported by a coefficient of determination ($0 \leq R^2 \leq 1$), which ranged from 0.81 to 0.93 by using about 81% to 93% data of the datasets for the 3 tool speeds. Secondly, the dissection force yielded by the analytic model of each tool speed uncompromised the workload perceived by the participants. There was no report on discomfort/fatigue in dissection; neither significant difference of the perceived workload among the 3 tool speeds. This might reveal that each analytic model estimates adequately the dissection force under the prescript speed. Lastly, a mean computation time of each analytic model was about 2.5 µs, allowing stable force rendering at 1.0 kHz via the haptic device (PHANToM Premium 1.5/6DOF) [12, 14]. Moreover, the force yielded by the analytic model was within a frequency bandwidth of ∼30 Hz [25], permitting distortionless force rendering via the haptic device as confirmed in Fig. 2. No noise/jolt was generated by the haptic device or reported by the participants during force rendering. Thus, the analytic model is deemed a realistic representation of dissection forces to be rendered adequately via the haptic device.

Our findings indicate that the analytic model is tool-speed dependent and suitable for VR-based dissection. This was validated by the convention that surgical procedures of soft tissues (such as the brain) are performed by experienced surgeons, who are masters to keep a constant tool speed close to 0.10 cm/s [18]. The validation would be crucial for VR-based simulators to train dexterity needed in dissection.

5 Conclusion

We developed a tool-speed-dependent force model using empirical force-displacement datasets and conducted a user study to verify the suitability of the model for VR-based dissection. In agreement with the convention that a low tool speed demands refined hand movements in soft-tissue dissection, our findings validate the suitability of the force model for VR-based dissection at various tool speeds. Future work will be to extend the analytic model to multiple DOFs and to assess the effect of the analytic model on VR-based training of soft-tissue dissection.

References

1. Miller, K.: Biomechanics of soft tissue. Med. Sci. Monit. **6**, 158–167 (2000)
2. Okamura, A.M., Simone, C., O'Leary, M.D.: Force modeling for needle insertion into soft tissue. IEEE TBME **51**, 1707–1716 (2004)
3. Hing, J.T., Brooks, A.D., Desai, J.P.: A biplanar fluoroscopic approach for the measurement, modeling, and simulation of needle and soft-tissue interaction. Med. Image Anal. **11**, 62–78 (2007)
4. Marcus, H.J. (et al.): Forces exerted during microneurosurgery: a cadaver study. Int. J. Med. Robotics Comput. Assist. Surg. **10**, 251–256 (2014)
5. Misra, S., Ramesh, K.T., Okamura, A.M.: Modeling of tool-tissue interactions for computer-based surgical simulation: a literature review. Presence Teleop. Virt. **17**, 463–491 (2008)
6. Okamura, A.M.: Haptic feedback in robot-assisted minimally invasive surgery. Cure. Opin. Urol. **19**, 102–107 (2009)
7. Basdogan, C., De, S., Kim, J., Muniyandi, M., Kim, H., Srinivasan, M.A.: Haptics in minimally invasive surgical simulation and training. IEEE CG&A **24**, 56–64 (2004)
8. Delorme, S., Laroche, D., DiRaddo, R., Del Maestro, R.F.: NeuroTouch: a physics-based virtual simulator for cranial microneurosurgery training. Neurosurg. **71**, 32–42 (2012)
9. Basafa, E., Farahmand, F.: Real-time simulation of the nonlinear visco-elastic deformations of soft tissues. Int. J. CARS **6**, 297–307 (2011)

10. Vafai, N.M., Payandeh, S.: Toward the development of interactive virtual dissection with haptic feedback. VR **14**, 85–103 (2010)
11. Wang, Z., Sun, Z., Phee, S.J.: Haptic feedback and control of a flexible surgical endoscopic robot. Comput. Methods Programs Biomed. **112**, 260–271 (2013)
12. Santos-Carreras, L., Beira, R., Sengul, A., Gassert, R., Bleuler, H.: Influence of force and torque feedback on operator performance in a VR-based suturing task. Appl. Bionics Biomech. **7**, 217–230 (2010)
13. Mahvash, M., Dupont, P.E.: Mechanics of dynamic needle insertion into biological material. IEEE TBME **57**, 934–943 (2010)
14. Mahvash, M., Hayward, V.: Haptic rendering of cutting: a fracture mechanics approach. Haptics-e **2**, 1–12 (2001)
15. Trejo, F., Hu, Y.: Towards an analytic haptic model for force rendering of soft-tissue dissection. In: Proceedings of the IEEE International Conference SMC, pp. 1098–1103 (2016)
16. Gokgol, C., Basdogan, C., Canadinc, D.: Estimation of fracture toughness of liver tissue: experiments and validation. Med. Eng. Phys. **34**, 882–891 (2012)
17. Chanthasopeephan, T., Desai, J.P., Lau, A.C.W.: Modeling soft-tissue deformation prior to cutting for surgical simulation: finite element analysis and study of cutting parameters. IEEE TBME **54**, 349–359 (2007)
18. Miller, K., Chinzei, K., Orssengo, G., Bednarz, P.: Mechanical properties of brain tissue in-vivo: experiment and computer simulation. J. Biomech. **33**, 1369–1376 (2000)
19. Wagner, C.R., Stylopoulos, N., Jackson, P.G., Howe, R.D.: The benefit of force feedback in surgery: examination of blunt Dissection. Presence **16**, 252–262 (2007)
20. Sutherland, G.R., Maddahi, Y., Gan, L.S., Lama, S., Zareinia, K.: Robotics in the neurosurgical treatment of glioma. Surg. Neurol. Int. **6**, S1–S8 (2015)
21. Van Belle, G.: Statistical Rules of Thumb. Wiley, New Jersey (2011)
22. Kennedy, R.S., Lane, N.E., Berbaum, K.S., Lilienthal, M.G.: Simulator sickness questionnaire: an enhanced method for quantifying simulator sickness. Int. J. Aviat. Psychol. **3**, 203–220 (1993)
23. Hart, S.G.: NASA-Task load index (NASA-TLX); 20 years later. In: Proceedings of the Human Factors and Ergonomics Society Annual Meeting, pp. 904–908 (2006)
24. Prunty, M., Barnett, A.L.: Understanding handwriting difficulties: a comparison of children with and without motor impairment. Cogn. Neuropsychol. **34**, 205–218 (2017)
25. Cavusoglu, M.C., Feygin, D., Tendick, F.: A critical study of the mechanical and electrical properties of the phantom haptic interface and improvements for high-performance control. Presence **11**, 555–568 (2002)

Making a Socially Assistive Robot Companion Touch Sensitive

Steffen Müller[✉] and Horst-Michael Gross

Neuroinformatics and Cognitive Robotics Lab, Technische Universität Ilmenau,
98693 Ilmenau, Germany
steffen.mueller@tu-ilmenau.de
http://www.tu-ilmenau.de/neurob

Abstract. Socially assistive robots are in the focus of research for a while. These robots are to be in close interaction with humans and try to communicate in a natural way. One intuitive modality for interaction is touch. This paper describes the design of our service robot intended for use in private homes of elderly people. We combined capacitive touch sensors at the stiff parts of the robot's shell with a pressure sensitive textile array sensor on the flexible back of our robot. A detailed description of the construction and properties of our pressure sensitive matrix sensor is presented. Furthermore, a maximum likelihood classification algorithm is presented, which is capable of online classification without explicit segmentation of touch gesture events in before.

Keywords: Resistive pressure sensor · Mobile robot
Capacitive sensor

1 Introduction

The work presented here is part of the SYMPARTNER[1] project, which aims at developing a service robot intended to live together with elderly people in their private homes [1]. This project continues our previous work on socially assistive robots [5,6,14]. Like its predecessors, the new designed robot is capable of autonomous navigation in the apartment and, therefore, can bring specially designed services to the user. These services comprise calendar management with active reminders, communication via video telephony, encouraging people, entertaining by means of presenting various media and social companionship. One function, which is also relevant for the interaction in a sitting position is the ability to stop the robot's autonomous navigation in order to allow the users to position the robot manually according to their demands. For that purpose, it

This work has received funding from the German Federal Ministry of Education and Research (BMBF) to the project SYMPARTNER (grant agreement no. 16SV7218).

[1] SYMbiosis of PAul and RoboT companion for Emotion sensitive caRe (www.sympartner.de).

D. Prattichizzo et al. (Eds.): EuroHaptics 2018, LNCS 10894, pp. 476–488, 2018.
https://doi.org/10.1007/978-3-319-93399-3_41

is necessary to enable the robot to notice when people push or grab it, which has been realized by means of capacitive touch sensors. A pressure sensitive patch on the back of the robot additionally can be used for receiving unspecific feedback to the robot in form of petting gestures or small slaps. The robot will show an emotional reaction expressed by means of facial animations and sound outputs in that case. This functions is intended to reinforce the relationship of the user and the robot. In our ongoing work the feedback via touch gestures will be used for adaptation of the robot's interaction behavior.

The remainder of this paper is structured as follows: First, related work in the field of haptic human robot interaction will be discussed. Then, the robot and the tactile sensor hardware will be described in detail followed by an introduction to our real-time classification approach for touch gestures on the sensitive patch on the back of the robot.

2   Related Work

Tactile sensors have a wide range of application and come along with different qualities of the signal gained. On the one hand, there are systems providing only a touch signal (capacitive sensors), and on the other hand there are force or pressure sensors. Detectable forces thereby can be in perpendicular direction only or the amount of shearing forces at the surface is detectable as well. Furthermore, the position of a touch event can be distinguished more or less accurate, whereby the amount of independent touch areas is of interest for a system designer. Similarly, there is a variety of physical measurement principles available like optical, capacitive, and resistive effects as possible sources for information [16]. Additionally, [2] proposed a method for using changes in the magnetic field generated by bending small magnetized fibers on a surface. Also acoustic surface waves have been used for recognizing changes in the transmission characteristics, if an object (e.g. a hand) gets in contact with the surface. An important aspect for practical application of such systems in a robotic prototyping application is the manufacturing process. Commercially available touch sensor systems often are not suitable for the curvy shape of a robot or can only be adapted with high costs. Nevertheless, there are several projects explicitly dealing with the development of complex artificial skin [9]. For application at a human hand prosthesis, these systems comprise a variety of modalities like pressure, temperature, and humidity. On mobile assistive robots these modalities would be interesting too, but at the moment these techniques may break the budget of many robotics projects. A survey on artificial skin and tactile sensing for socially interactive robots can be found in [15].

A popular approach to overcome the shape restrictions is the usage of a flexible textile material, able to cover non-planar and even flexible surfaces [13]. Especially for recognition of social touch gestures on artificial creatures, such low cost solutions are widely used [3,4].

With the availability of pressure array sensors a competition for gesture classification and recognition methods emerged [7,8]. Open questions here are: What is a useful set of distinguishable gestures? and Which features and classifier are best suited for the data? In a former project, we also developed a pressure sensitive patch of fur [11], that could be mounted on the convex head of our service robots Max and Tweety. With a simple Bayesian classifier, we were able to classify chunks of pressure data. This approach and also other popular methods [4] have the problem, that touch signals first have to be segmented before a classification, which leads to a delay for the recognition depending on the size of the window to be classified.

In this paper, we propose a sliding window classifier, which is able to overcome that drawback and is able to detect an event as soon as the pattern makes a distinction from other classes possible.

In addition to the pressure array sensor for touch gesture recognition, a capacitive touch technique has been used on our previous robots as well [10] in order to enable them for motor assisted pushing of the robot. In contrast to that, our new platform can be moved with ease, and a simple binary signal for stopping the robot's autonomous movements is sufficient.

3   Robot Hardware

Figure 1 shows our robot platform with the sensors available. The robot has been designed by University of Siegen [17] and was manufactured by Metralabs GmbH Ilmenau. Its mobility is based on a differential drive, and the robot has battery capacity for about 4 h of mobile operation, where two dual core mobile PCs and a variety of active sensors have to be provided with power. Together with its charging station, the robot is able to autonomously recharge itself. With this capability, an around-the-clock operation can be guaranteed. The footprint of approximately 45×55 cm is chosen to be as small as possible in order to allow for navigation in narrow indoor environments. For navigation purposes, the system is equipped with a SICK laser range scanner at a height of 20 cm, two ASUS Xtion RGB-D cameras on the back and on the head facing downwards. For people detection, a Kinect2 RGB-D sensor is mounted at a tiltable head. Interaction is mainly supported by a 15' touch display and sound outputs. Head animations using a second display and two movable ears are used to communicate emotions and internal states of the robot. To complete the human interface, the robot has capacitive touch sensors at the base and a pressure sensitive textile sensor array at the back side of the neck (see Fig. 1 right side). Both of these sensors are controlled by a circuit board (see Sect. 5.2) connected to the robot's PC via USB. In the following, these sensor systems will be described in more detail.

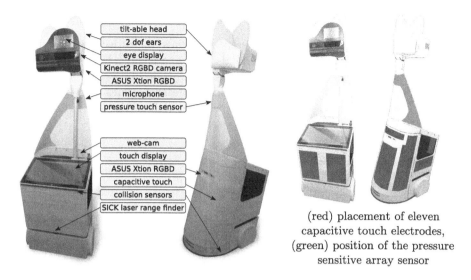

tilt-able head
2 dof ears
eye display
Kinect2 RGBD camera
ASUS Xtion RGBD
microphone
pressure touch sensor

web-cam
touch display
ASUS Xtion RGBD
capacitive touch
collision sensors
SICK laser range finder

(red) placement of eleven
capacitive touch electrodes,
(green) position of the pressure
sensitive array sensor

Fig. 1. Overview on the robot's sensor systems mainly used for autonomous navigation and interaction with a user. (Color figure online)

4   Capacitive Touch Sensors

First part of the robot's tactile interface is a set of capacitive touch sensors, which are mounted at the inner side of the 3d printed outer shell. As mentioned before, we only need a binary signal to stop the robot's movement, if a contact is detected. Therefore, the low spatial resolution of only eleven panels (see red faces in Fig. 1 right side) is sufficient. The sensitive areas are on the back, on the front, on both sides, and in the inner sides of the compartment beneath the display, which is the first choice for grabbing the robot to pull it from a sitting position. The sensor panels are made from a self adhesive copper foil directly attached to the plastic parts. The subdivision of the sensitive surface helps to keep the areas of the individual sensors small, which is necessary, since the relative change of capacitance when touched by a human hand gets smaller if the area of the electrode is large (see Fig. 2). By means of that, we could apply a standard IC (AT42QT1111) for reading the capacitance values into the microcontroller for evaluation.

In software, there is a continuously working calibration implemented. This allows to find the individual quiescent values for each of the panels by means of a moving average filter. The sensors are quite sensitive, such that the robot also gets signals when it is moving close to obstacles depending on the material (see next subsection and Fig. 2). For recognizing a touch event, we introduced a simple threshold for the difference of the actual signal and the average, that is high enough to avoid false detections in a normal home environment.

4.1   Properties of the Capacitive Sensors

The capacitive sensors respond to different materials and objects with specific characteristics. An experiment, where hands, legs, and a couch have been placed in different distances to the sensor surfaces, shows this property (see Fig. 2). This makes it difficult to derive the actual distance or pressure values from the sensor readings. The curves also show, that after contact (left of the dotted line) the pressure or contact area increases the signal further.

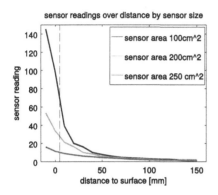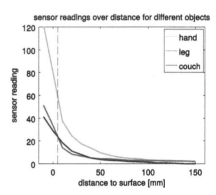

Fig. 2. Characteristics of capacitive sensors regarding material of the interacting object (right) and size of the electrodes (left); Values left of the dashed line are after contact with increasing pressure and thus increasing contact area.

The comparison of the sensor responses at the various electrodes of different size shows that smaller electrodes give larger signals since the huge electrodes already have a higher capacitance even in untouched conditions. Differences in electrode size and sensitivity can be individually adjusted by means of the values of the reference capacitors on the circuit board.

The graphs of Fig. 2 shows, that it is possible to find a threshold for recognizing contact with a hand without reacting to close by situated furniture and legs, which is very important for all autonomous navigation tasks.

5   Pressure Sensor Array

The more interesting part of the tactile interface is the pressure sensitive matrix sensor. Like [13] and others we used textile materials for building the pressure sensor, since the treatment of such material is relatively easy and does not require any special equipment. Regarding the construction of resistive matrix sensors, we already had some experience from former projects [11], but for this robot we tried new materials and increased the number of channels and thus the spatial resolution of the sensor.

The layered structure of the matrix sensor basically consists of two conductive electrode layers one implementing the rows and the other one for the columns (see Fig. 3). The conductive material for these layers is an emf shielding fleece (100dB RF Shielding-Fleece Aaronia X-Dream^{TM} by AARONIA AG), which has a coating with conductive adhesive at the back. In between these electrodes, a piezoresistive layer of Eeontex^{TM} stretch fabric forms the sensitive elements at the crossing points of the rows and columns. The Eeontex^{TM} material has a surface resistivity of $20\,k\Omega/cm^2$. In addition to these active layers, the matrix consists of two layers of iron fleece to give the sensor its structure and the wiring by means of enamelled copper wire. The sensor is wrapped in a cover from cotton fabric to realize the haptics and color specified by the designers. The completed sensor finally is sewed onto the 2 mm thick back piece made from flexible transparent plastic.

5.1   Manufacturing the Sensor

In our former approach [11], the electrodes were made from copper coated nylon fabric sewed at a carrier layer of fabric. For the much smaller electrodes of our new construction, manual sewing was not a useful option anymore. Therefore, we have chosen a bonding solution. The electrodes were cut out, and the matrix layout can easily be arranged by fixating the strips at a sticky worktop with the adhesive side facing upwards. The electrodes have a width of about 13 mm with a gap of 4–5 mm (see Fig. 3). This gap is necessary to limit the crosstalk in the matrix, since there are no diodes that would allow to address individual cells. There also exists a fabric material, which already has a stripe pattern of conductive and insulating regions. Unfortunately, for our layout parallel stripes were not suitable, and the bonding of wires to that stretchy material is also not easy. In other setups of resistive textile matrix sensors, a spacer layer can be found between the electrodes and the piezoresistive material [4]. This exists to completely disconnect cells that are not touched. Unfortunately, this spacer increases the minimum pressure that is recognizable by the sensor, so we left that out accepting the resulting cross talk effects.

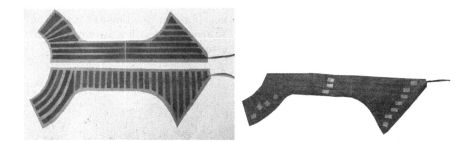

Fig. 3. (left) inner sides of the electrodes assemblies of the pressure sensitive matrix sensor, (right) sensor array sewed together.

After laying out the electrodes, the wiring bond to the electrodes by means of self adhesive copper foil. After the wiring, a patch of iron fleece can be sticked to the arranged electrodes and the layout gets finalized by ironing. Figure 3 on the left shows the row and column electrodes bond to the carrier. Figure 3 on the right side shows the resulting sensor matrix with the piezoresistive layer in between.

5.2   Electronic Circuit

The electronics for reading out the sensors is based on an ATMEGA328P microcontroller. The resistive matrix is addressed via two analog multiplexers (74HD4067), one for the columns and one for the rows (see Fig. 4). This allows for 16 by 16 cells of spatial resolution, whereby only a part of this amount is used due to the irregular shape of the sensor area on the robot. A reference resistor is used to get a varying signal at the analog digital converter of the microcontroller. The microcontroller also communicates to the capacitive touch controller (AT42QT1111) via SPI and sends out the captured and preprocessed sensor values to the PC via USB.

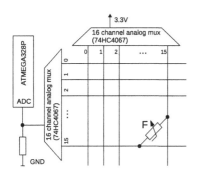

Fig. 4. Principle of measuring the pressure sensitive array.

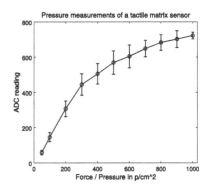

Fig. 5. Characteristics of the pressure matrix sensor resulting ADC values for 10 repetitions with a force on a $1\,cm^2$ area.

5.3   Properties of the Matrix Sensor

We did a series of experiments with a prototype of the matrix sensor to find out the characteristics of the specific materials. Figure 5 shows the dependency of voltage at the adc input over the force (simple weight) put on a 1 by 1 cm patch on the matrix sensor. The graph shows that the sensor has its best resolution in the region below $400p$, which corresponds well to the forces occurring during natural touch gestures. According to [15], these are in a range from 0.3 N to 10 N.

The sensor also shows correlating signals at very low forces below $50p/cm^2$, but they are difficult to distinguish from the changing quiescent value. That leads to a drawback of the setup using loose layers of flexible materials. After a pressure event, the sensor needs some time to get back to its resting state, which additionally can change in a limited range. That is the reason for the necessity of a run-time calibration that can deal with such unsteady signals. Alternatively, classification working on the temporal derivatives of the sensor values can be applied.

One further effect of a resistive matrix is a crosstalk between cells in the rows and columns of active cells. Because of the high resistance of unpressed matrix cells ($\approx 1\,M\Omega$) compared to the values of a pressed cell ($\approx 30\,k\Omega$), the amount of crosstalk activations can be neglected for our application.

6 Signal Processing and Online Gesture Classification

6.1 Calibration and Preprocessing

The microcontroller is programmed to read out each of the 256 matrix elements $\hat{a}_{i,j}$ at an internal rate of 100 Hz with 10bit resolution. These raw signals at first are low pass filtered using a moving average filter in order to reduce the noise. Afterwards, they get sub-sampled and transmitted to the PC with a rate of 20 Hz (now called $a^t_{i,j}$). As mentioned before, the resting state of the array sensor can change over time. Therefore, the individual minimum values $m_{i,j}$ are tracked over time using the following equation for temporal smoothing/low-pass filtering:

$$m^t = min\{a^t, m^{t-1} + \tau(a^t - m^{t-1})\} \tag{1}$$

Here the time constant τ defines the adaptation speed. Knowing the individual minimum values, for each sensor cell a normalized activation value $r^t_{i,j}$ is computed by subtracting the minimum and scaling it by a constant gain $g_{i,j}$.

$$r^t_{i,j} = min\{max\{g_{i,j}(a^t_{i,j} - m^t_{i,j}), k\}, 1\} \tag{2}$$

This simple scaling is reasonable, since the characteristic is nearly linear in the region below $300p/cm^2$. The values finally are cropped to $[k, 1]$ range and get further processed in the classification algorithm. The lower limit $k = 0.08$ is to cancel out noise and crosstalk activations.

6.2 Gesture Classification

To enable the recognition of touch gestures, in our previous approach [11] an event detection was employed, that captured fixed size sequences of the signals (4 s) starting with excitation of an activity threshold. Because of this, the classification was always a bit delayed especially for short gestures (slap). This approach had been used to ensure that the pattern is always aligned to the window in the same way, and thus the variance in the data was reduced.

In order to overcome this delay problem, we now apply a sliding window classifier, which therefore has to deal with more variance in the patterns, because they are not longer aligned to the boundaries of the segmented classification window. An event detection is realized on a sample-based decision. We have chosen a probabilistic classifier that can provide a posterior probability distribution of the actual gesture classes given the features $\mathbf{f}^t$ of the current window of the signals. Only if one class has a significant probability, the event is triggered. The advantage of this approach is, that gestures can be recognized as soon as the patterns are significantly different to the other classes independent of the length of the gestures. For the evaluation in this paper, we used a window length of 3 s, which equals 60 samples to be processed.

As shown by [8], Bayesian classifier and more complex classifiers like SVMs can reach similar results. Therefore, we expect reasonable results despite the usage of such simple methods like Gaussian Mixture Models (GMM). Simpler models additionally have the advantage of requiring less data for training compared to complex models.

For each of the gesture classes $c \in C$, a Mixture of Gaussians model $p(\mathbf{f}|C = c)$ $\propto \sum_{k=1}^{n} w_k \mathcal{N}(\mathbf{f}|\mu_k^c, \Sigma_k^c)$ is learned from a training dataset by means of the Expectation Maximization (EM) algorithm in order to implement a maximum likelihood classifier. In our application, the inference of $p(C|\mathbf{f}^t)$ is done at the rate of the incoming pressure values (20 Hz), where the a-priori probability of the gestures $p(C)$ was supposed to be uniform. If the probability of one class raises above a threshold and the class id did change, a gesture event is send to the application.

Social interaction gestures could successfully be classified based on the area, pressure, and their dynamics [12]. Also [4] defined a sliding window and extracted statistical features min, max, median, mean, and variance of pressure, and centroid position. Therefore, we also rely on a set of statistical features of the pressure signals. For computing features for a time window, at first basic feature values are extracted from the activation matrix of each time step $r_{i,j}^t$ in the window:

- the maximum activation $f_1^t = max_{i,j}\{r_{i,j}^t\}$
- the sum of the cells activations $f_2^t = \sum_{i,j}\{r_{i,j}^t\}$
- the number of active cells (which corresponds to the area) $f_3^t = |\{r_{i,j}^t > k\}|$
- the center of activation in the two dimensions of the sensor surface $f_4^t = (\sum_{i,j} i\ r_{i,j}^t)/f_2^t$ and $f_5^t = (\sum_{i,j} j\ r_{i,j}^t)/f_2^t$

To derive a feature vector for a time window $t \in \{t_0, \ldots t_{59}\}$ the maximum, mean and variance of the raw features f_1^t, f_2^t and f_3^t over all time steps in the window are computed. This provides the first nine features. Additionally, the number of time steps with at least one active cell is used as a feature describing the duration of a gesture. To encode the movement of the contact area, the distance of the activation centers of consecutive time steps is accumulated as a further feature followed by the variance of the 2d center of activation. One drawback of this approach is that the features do not describe where in the time window the patterns take place. This can be improved in future, e.g. by subdividing the window. Unfortunately, this would increase the dimensionality of the feature vector. Concluding, we have twelve features describing the signals in the sliding time window with a length of 3 s.

6.3 Evaluation and Results

For the scenario of our application, four gesture classes should be distinguished. These are (i) a **stroke** gesture that is used for praising the robot, (ii) a **tickling** gesture to provoke an emotional reaction, (iii) a **pushing** gesture, which actually is not intended for communication but occurs when the robot is positioned manually, and (iv) a **slapping** used to objurgate the robot for its behavior. There are other datasets having much more classes [8], but [7] showed, that fine granular gestures are not to distinguish robustly e.g. scratch and tickling.

Since touch gesture data depends on the actual sensor and its configuration on the robot, we captured an own gesture datasets with gestures performed by 8 persons. During the recording, the desired class was given in before, and there had to be a break of at least 4 s between consecutive gesture events. All the dataset comprises 200 events in 88,800 samples. For the training, the demanded class label simply is assigned to the feature vectors of all timestamps of a session also including silence intervals in between. By means of that, all class models contain the silence and transition features and, therefore, a balanced probability distribution will result in the classification process, if there are not characteristic features for one particular gesture (see Fig. 7 in between the events). For validation, the actual events have been segmented by means of an activity threshold on the raw pressure data to yield a ground truth (see bottom line of Fig. 7). For all further evaluations, a cross-validation was used, where each time the data of one person was used for validation and the other 7 datasets for training.

per sample cross-validation results

	stroke	tickle	push	slap	si-lence
stroke	**5822**	**101**	**93**	**53**	6
tickle	**34**	**1761**	**19**	**68**	97
push	**93**	**3**	**5931**	**89**	0
slap	**0**	**99**	**26**	**773**	49
not rec-ognized	17171	12882	9490	19839	14285

TPR of all samples: 0.32
TPR of detected samples: 0.95
(bold faced submatrix)

confusion matrix
of detected events

ground truth	detection			
	stroke	tickle	push	slap
stroke	34	4	2	1
tickle	6	52	7	8
push	6	1	37	3
slap	0	13	1	25

Correct: 148/200 = 0.74
False detections: 52/200 = 0.26
Misses: 51/200 = 0.25

Fig. 6. Confusion matrices for cross-validation results.

First, a parameter grid search was done, where the number of components and the probability threshold have been optimized. Best performance for

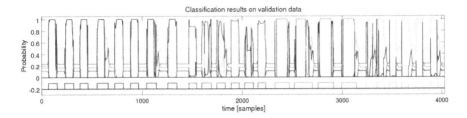

Fig. 7. Output probabilities for the classes stroke (blue), tickling (red), pushing (green), and slapping (magenta) over a validation dataset, the ground truth events are shown below. (Color figure online)

event detection was found at a threshold of 0.99 and $n = 5$ mixture components. Figure 6 (left) shows the resulting confusion matrix for a sample based classification. When the probability threshold was not exceeded by any of the classes, samples got count as not recognized. The true positive rate for sample-based classification is rather low with only 32%. Nevertheless, the correct classification rate of all samples with a significant probability is 95%, which seems promising for the event detection, because for the duration of a gesture not every sample needs to be classified, but one needs to have a high probability and the correct class. An evaluation based on the events showed satisfactory results (see Fig. 6 right). 74% of the 200 events could be detected correctly, while 25% were not detected at all. Additionally, 26% false detections occurred. Figure 7 shows the classifier results for a part of the data. It can be seen, that the tickling and slapping gestures often do not reach high significance, which is due to the short and weak activation, which also can be part of the other gestures, too.

The actual classification results on unrestricted gesture datasets containing a variety of people seem to be too insufficient in terms of absolute numbers, which is caused by the inherent inter-personal variance of the data. Nevertheless, in a real application on a robot, which directly gives a feedback to touch gestures, a learning effect can be observed at the users. People change their touch patterns until the robot shows the intended reaction. This is similar to a human-human or human-pet situation. Therefore, we do not try to collect a huge dataset that covers a great variance of gestures. Such training data would reduce the distinctness of the gesture classes. Instead, we successfully applied the model containing only a limited but consistent set of samples, that gives the robot a character in terms of specific patterns that lead to an appropriate and consistent reaction.

7   Conclusion

With our experiments we showed, that it is possible to realize a multi-modal touch interface for a mobile assistance robot with very inexpensive materials and construction processes. Furthermore, we found that the classification of touch gestures in practice is acceptable. The pressure matrix system is able to distinguish coarse classes of different gestures independent of the position they are performed.

In future robotic projects, we plan to apply the pressure matrix solution again, while we will benefit from the easy production process and the high configurability of the approach. One further aspect of interest is the crosstalk effect in resistive matrix sensors in multi-touch situations. We currently work on an efficient computationally compensation but also try to combining the capacitive sensors and the pressure sensors to mask out the phantom activations in the pressure matrix.

References

1. http://www.sympartner.de. Accessed Apr 2018
2. Alfadhel, A., Khan, M.A., Cardoso, S., Leitao, D., Kosel, J.: A magnetoresistive tactile sensor for harsh environment applications. Sensors **16**(5), 650 (2016)
3. Cang, L., Bucci, P., MacLean, K.E.: CuddleBits: friendly, low-cost furballs that respond to touch. In: Proceedings of the 2015 ACM on International Conference on Multimodal Interaction, pp. 365–366. ACM (2015)
4. Cang, X.L., Bucci, P., Strang, A., Allen, J., MacLean, K., Liu, H.: Different strokes and different folks: economical dynamic surface sensing and affect-related touch recognition. In: Proceedings of the 2015 ACM on International Conference on Multimodal Interaction, pp. 147–154. ACM (2015)
5. Gross, H.M., Mueller, St., Schroeter, Ch., Volkhardt, M., Scheidig, A., Debes, K., Richter, K., Doering, N.: Robot companion for domestic health assistance: implementation, test and case study under everyday conditions in private apartments. In: IEEE/RSJ International Conference on Intelligent Robots and Systems (IROS), pp. 5992–5999. IEEE (2015)
6. Gross, H.M., Schroeter, Ch., Mueller, St., Volkhardt, M., Einhorn, E., Bley, A., Langner, T., Merten, M., Huijnen, C., van den Heuvel, H., van Berlo, A.: Further progress towards a home robot companion for people with mild cognitive impairment. In: IEEE International Conference on Systems, Man, and Cybernetics (SMC), pp. 637–644. IEEE (2012)
7. Jung, M.M., Cang, X.L., Poel, M., MacLean, K.E.: Touch Challenge'15: recognizing social touch gestures. In: Proceedings of the 2015 ACM on International Conference on Multimodal Interaction, pp. 387–390. ACM (2015)
8. Jung, M.M., Poppe, R., Poel, M., Heylen, D.K.: Touching the void-introducing cost: corpus of social touch. In: Proceedings of the 16th International Conference on Multimodal Interaction, pp. 120–127. ACM (2014)
9. Kim, J., Lee, M., Shim, H.J., Ghaffari, R., Cho, H.R., Son, D., Jung, Y.H., Soh, M., Choi, C., Jung, S., et al.: Stretchable silicon nanoribbon electronics for skin prosthesis. Nat. Commun. **5**, 5747 (2014)
10. Müller, St., Schröter, Ch., Gross, H.-M.: Low-cost whole-body touch interaction for manual motion control of a mobile service robot. In: Herrmann, G., Pearson, M.J., Lenz, A., Bremner, P., Spiers, A., Leonards, U. (eds.) ICSR 2013. LNCS (LNAI), vol. 8239, pp. 229–238. Springer, Cham (2013). https://doi.org/10.1007/978-3-319-02675-6_23
11. Müller, St., Schröter, Ch., Gross, H.-M.: Smart fur tactile sensor for a socially assistive mobile robot. In: Liu, H., Kubota, N., Zhu, X., Dillmann, R., Zhou, D. (eds.) ICIRA 2015. LNCS (LNAI), vol. 9245, pp. 49–60. Springer, Cham (2015). https://doi.org/10.1007/978-3-319-22876-1_5

12. Naya, F., Yamato, J., Shinozawa, K.: Recognizing human touching behaviors using a haptic interface for a pet-robot. In: 1999 IEEE International Conference on Systems, Man, and Cybernetics, IEEE SMC 1999 Conference Proceedings, vol. 2, pp. 1030–1034. IEEE (1999)
13. Pan, Z., Cui, H., Zhu, Z.: A flexible full-body tactile sensor of low cost and minimal connections. In: 2003 IEEE International Conference on Systems, Man and Cybernetics, vol. 3, pp. 2368–2373. IEEE (2003)
14. Schroeter, Ch., Mueller, St., Volkhardt, M., Einhorn, E., Huijnen, C., van den Heuvel, H., van Berlo, A., Bley, A., Gross, H.M.: Realization and user evaluation of a companion robot for people with mild cognitive impairments. In: IEEE International Conference on Robotics and Automation (ICRA), pp. 1145–1151. IEEE (2013)
15. Silvera-Tawil, D., Rye, D., Velonaki, M.: Artificial skin and tactile sensing for socially interactive robots: a review. Rob. Auton. Syst. **63**, 230–243 (2015)
16. Weiss, K., Worn, H.: Resistive tactile sensor matrices using inter-electrode sampling. In: 31st Annual Conference of IEEE Industrial Electronics Society, IECON 2005, 6 p. IEEE (2005)
17. Welge, J., Hassenzahl, M.: Better than human: about the psychological superpowers of robots. In: Agah, A., Cabibihan, J.-J., Howard, A.M., Salichs, M.A., He, H. (eds.) ICSR 2016. LNCS (LNAI), vol. 9979, pp. 993–1002. Springer, Cham (2016). https://doi.org/10.1007/978-3-319-47437-3_97

Design and Evaluation of Mid-Air Haptic Interactions in an Augmented Reality Environment

Brygida Dzidek[1(✉)], William Frier[2], Adam Harwood[1], and Richard Hayden[1]

[1] Ultrahaptics, Glass Wharf, Bristol BS20EL, UK
brygida.dzidek@ultrahaptics.com
[2] Department of Informatics, University of Sussex, Brighton, UK

Abstract. Augmented Reality mid-air environments are currently re-evaluating the interaction principles of the objects rendered in space. The surface, texture complexity, compliances and dynamics can be represented through volumetric rendering, comprised of shape, size and/or volume. Haptic representation of the graphical content and the dynamics of the interface can be tailored to the application requirements. The solution, however, is highly dependent on the tasks and the need for tactile feedback. The ideal system must blend the right level of factors and attributes to maximize user performance and satisfaction. The mechanics and perceptual correlation of mid-air haptics are still unresolved. Based on human tactile limitations, the prime classification of the tactile interactions was proposed, based on spatial and temporal requirements and limitations. Proposed classes are intuitive and proved to be easily adapted to many interactions, as well as compatible with gesture recognition. This paper discusses the haptic design criteria for mid-air, tactile-enhanced interactions suitable for interface AR applications. Design evaluation involved a sequence of six scenes, directed to engage user attention and strengthen performance. Proposed solution and its influence on ergonomics and efficiency, were subjected to user cognitive evaluation. A non-contact, interactive demo, blending cross modal stimulations, combining vision, auditory and tactile sensations was produced, and user studies were discussed.

Keywords: Mid-air haptics · Augmented reality interface
AR control and interaction design

1 Introduction

The success of a variety of Virtual and Augmented Reality applications has been enabled by efforts in the electronics industry since the 80 s. As an emerging and powerful technology, Augmented Reality (AR) integrates images of virtual objects into the real world in a variety of applications. The virtual elements can overlay existing physical elements, appearing to change their properties e.g. change physical properties such colour, shape or texture, represent 3D objects or maps in GPS apps [1]. Alternatively, virtual content can provide additional information to help in specific tasks (e.g. assembly [2]).

Augmented Reality presents the information in a context-sensitive way that is appropriate for a specific task and, typically, relative to the user's physical location.

© Springer International Publishing AG, part of Springer Nature 2018
D. Prattichizzo et al. (Eds.): EuroHaptics 2018, LNCS 10894, pp. 489–499, 2018.
https://doi.org/10.1007/978-3-319-93399-3_42

Traditionally user inputs were executed through hand held controllers, however Head Mounted Displays (HMD) (either for VR or AR), focus on visual output and temporal hand gesture recognition. To take better advantage of the 3D interaction space available, hand-tracking technology was developed (e.g. Leap Motion or Microsoft Kinect).

In a typical AR system, a video camera is used to capture the physical world. Using one or more markers placed in the scene, fast image-processing techniques can determine the user, as well as strategic element, location compare to the camera. Knowing these locations, allows the user to manipulate virtual content in a more natural way using hand gestures. Previous studies have determined which are users' preferred gestures out of an almost infinite array of possibilities [3]. However, to make interaction with virtual content feel comprehensive and seamless, one important component is still neglected: tactile feedback.

Mid-air haptics is a branch of haptics that is concerned with conveying haptic stimuli in air, without the user requiring any apparatus (such as a glove). There are different kind of mid-air haptic devices, including ones that utilise air-jets [4], air-vortices [5] and ultrasound arrays [6, 7].

An ultrasound phased-array uses a collection of ultrasonic speakers to focus the sound pressure in a point (Focal Point; FP) of space thanks to a precise phase shift between the different speakers. The pressure points hence obtained are strong enough to displace the skin on the hands and induce a tactile sensation [6]. To increase the perceived sensation strength, the pressure point is often modulated at a given frequency, hence creating a vibrotactile stimuli. Furthermore, the creation of several pressure points at once can give the illusion of volumetric shapes [8].

One of the most important challenges of three-dimensional, multi-component interactions is user perception. To satisfy spatial, ergonomic and technological limitations, interactive content of the application must be adapted. Components of the design, such as active/passive exploration, haptic feedback projection or graphical alignment, influence the user's attention. In the real world, passive touch tends to focus the observer's attention on its subjective bodily sensations, whereas contact resulting from active exploration tends to guide the observer's attention to properties of the external environment [9]. However, AR challenges the understanding of classical interactions due to unlimited spatial exploration.

HMD, gesture recognition and mid-air haptic technologies can be combined to produce engaging applications (e.g. a piano application [10] or interacting with holograms [11]). However, the nature and influence of generated sensations is still not clear. Several mechanically different haptic primitives (parametric equation defining the path of the FP displacement in x, y, z dimensions) can represent the same sensation (due to human-tactile limitations). On the other hand, one may also find, a single haptic primitive rendered in several scenarios that could be perceived as different due to pseudo-haptic effects [12].

In the current study we propose the first design and classifications of non-contact haptic effects, implemented in AR environment interactions. We define 5 classes of haptic sensations based on the spatial FP rendering and their possible adaptations to visual input implemented in the demo. In total, we defined five haptified interactions: (a) Validation Interaction; (b) Menu Interaction; (c) Sound Interaction; (d) Presence

Interaction; (e) Dynamics Interaction. Finally, we present results of the demo LTX evaluations test, where we defined a user's preference and level of the demands that AR interactions request from future inexperienced users.

2 Experimental Design and Evaluation

2.1 AR Mid-Air Interface Design

The user interactions, an important part of Augmented Reality design, constitute how users can efficiently and effectively interact in spatial 3D computer-generated environments. While the use of spatial cues and three-dimensional object manipulation are common in face-to-face communication, tools for three-dimensional mid-air tactile stimulations are still rare.

Non-contact haptics can be adapted to many physical features of the rendered objects. The size and volume can be represented by rendering a single or several focal points over *haptic primitives/*continuous paths (e.g. simple geometrical shapes like squares or circles, or more complex like Lissajous or Rose Curves), moreover modulation of the rendering frequency might enhance the strength of the haptics or create a new sensation. Therefore, visual context plays a prior role in the haptic sensation design. The graphical environment and type of the hand gestures directly predefine parameters available, like haptic size, position on the palm or precision of the rendered details.

Primary Classification of FP Rendering. To leverage mid-air haptic stimuli capabilities in an AR-based pseudo-three-dimensional environment, five spatial classifiers, representing the most distinguishable sensations, were proposed (Fig. 1). This classification comprised the perceptual limitations of spatial resolution of the human hand [13, 14], general cognitive interaction classification derived from [15], and the most common geometrical properties of haptified objects (like edges and shapes).

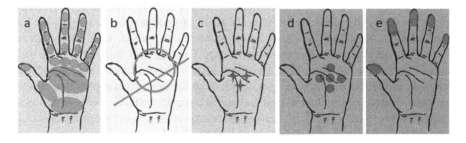

Fig. 1. Haptic sensations spatial classification. Schematic representation of the hand sensation groups generated by mid-air haptics.

The first class, *Field sensations*, represents the intensive sensations clearly distinguishable on each unit of the palm (Fig. 1a). This class focuses on user ability to distinguish the location of the rendered object, its shape and size. It combines the variety of the FP's rendering paths, independently of their size, frequency or dynamics.

The second class, *Edge detection* (Fig. 1b), combines the types of sensations which give the illusion of defined edges or borders between rendered sensations. Most of sensations in this class are determined and limited by shape and size of the rendered haptic primitive. Therefore, by increasing the size, the sensations remain the same or become more distinctive. This class is insensitive to frequency fluctuations.

The third class, *Focused sensations* (Fig. 1c) describes a strong perception of the "sharp contact point". This group comprises the haptics rendering which can be described as a sharp and pointy (a sensation that users describe as needles "poking"), independently of the location on the hand. Haptics in this class may be rendered by a single as well as many separate focal points at the same time. This class is very sensitive to rendered frequency and size of the haptic primitives.

The fourth class is based on a blunt bulky *Spherical sensation* (Fig. 1d). This class interprets the contact point as a blunt spot (derived from FP natural shape). Sensations in this class describe a strong perception of contact with a spherical-like (bubbly/bumpy) rendered object (or possibly many separate ones), regardless of the position on the hand. Class three and four should not be interpreted as opposite to each other. Both classes share a FP rendering dependency on size and trajectory (like in e.g. Rose or Lissajous curve types). Their common appearance in the same sensation is rare, however it's common that one can transition into the second (e.g. while resizing or frequency deviation).

The fifth class represents *Fingertip sensations* (Fig. 1e). Limitations of the size of a single fingertip and its detection are a challenge to reliable sensation design. The class describes a strong perception of the haptics, on the fingertip(s). This class combines all types of FP trajectories where their parameters like shape, size and frequency matches the fidelity and perceptual limitations of the fingertips. This allows not only the ability to detect the presence of the rendered stimuli but opens the range of details possible to detect (like textures or details of the objects).

Active and Passive Touch in Mid-Air. The AR interface mid-air interactions were designed using two types of tactile exploration: active and passive. Furthermore, each type can be further divided into two states of haptic projection (play "on object" or "on palm"). Unlike traditional in-contact haptic stimulations, mid-air tactile stimulations rely on constant physical engagement by the user. The users are required to place their hands in air, above the ultrasound array and are not constrained by any physical or ergonomic limitations e.g. screen edges, wires, direction or depth of exploration. Therefore, classification of the interactions and applied haptic feedback, were designed to enhance the free hands movement. Active hand(s) exploration type corresponds to tactile stimulation, dynamically dependent on the user's hand position, while the passive exploration type describes the interactions where the hand does not influence rendered stimuli. While the position of the hands might change, tactile stimulation can remain constant or evolve independently. The haptic projection depends on the tracking software to support and recognise spatial exposition on the palm or on the object.

Intensity of Tactile Stimuli. Spatial displacement of the FP generates the variety of haptic sensations. However, to perceptually influence the strength of the tactile stimulations, the frequency of the FP rendering was also considered. We observed that the rendering frequency suggested positive correlation with "smoothing" the haptic sensation. Therefore, three ranges of the frequencies based on the available update rate and size of the rendered haptics were proposed: low frequencies (0 to 40 Hz), medium (40–80 Hz), high (80–120 Hz). These frequencies satisfied the hands' perceptual abilities [9] and generated a wide range of possible sensations. Frequencies higher than 120 Hz were not sufficient to generate any significant stimulation and were excluded.

2.2 Evaluation Design and Interactions

Setup. The general approach to realize AR is to merge the physical and virtual worlds by exploiting rapid video processing, precise tracking, and computer graphics. The evaluation setup is presented on Fig. 2B. The user was asked to sit on a chair opposite the TouchBase and wear the Meta Headset. The Ultrahaptics TouchBase was placed at 30 cm from the edge of the table, to provide its best performance (the highest strength of the focal point rendering is ~15–60 cm from the surface of the board) and an ergonomic interaction zone. To support the tracking system and minimize possible occlusion, four markers were placed on the additional black "halo" background around the board.

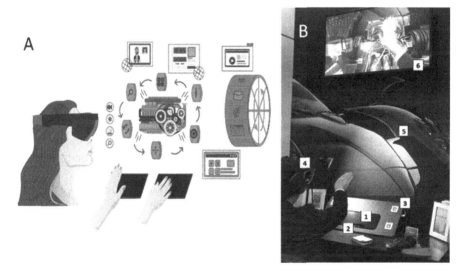

Fig. 2. A(left): The image represents modelled workspace prime design. All conventional elements such as a monitor, keyboard or mouse will be replaced by an AR headset that will project holograms in front of the user. Moreover, additional hardware (e.g. an ultrasound phased array) will generate mid-air haptic feedback, which allows users to interact with holograms and feel their edges, shapes and textures. The user will be working in an environment where three senses will be engaged: vision – holograms (grey/blue in image); touch – haptic sensations (red in image); sound (green in image). B(right): Demo setup: (1) Ultrahaptics TouchBase (2) Leap Motion Controller (3) Square Markers (4) Meta Headset (5) Background (6) Spectator screen (above the user field of vision, only for spectators to see what is happening in the headset). (Color figure online)

In front of the user, a dark poster was hung to improve the visibility and colour saturation of the AR objects.

Hardware and Software. The Ultrahaptics TouchBase and the Meta2 Headset were used. Both platforms were connected to an Intel i7 4.2 GHz machine running Windows 10 combined with two NVIDIA GeForce GTX 1080Ti graphic cards. The TouchBase platform consists of a board of 252 piezoelectric transducers (focusing ultrasound at 40 kHz to create up to 4 pressure focal points (FP), ~8 mm in diameter) integrated with a Leap Motion camera module (two monochromatic infrared cameras and three infrared LEDs) combined with computer vision algorithms to perform accurate hand tracking. The Ultrahaptics TouchBase is angled at 40° for better hand recognition within the interaction zone. The Meta Headset 2 is an AR device with 2550 × 1440 pixel resolution, 90° top/80° bottom horizontal FOV and 50° vertical FOV. Meta headset software can identify features of the surroundings to map the environment.

Software. The demonstrator used in the current study was developed in Unity 2017.1. The graphics of the demo, including a detailed model of a Pagani Huayra Roadster, were created and integrated by ZeroLight[1]. Moreover, to avoid the slight space drifting that accumulates over running time as well as unexpected hardware displacements, a multimarker technique combined with outlier elimination, moving average and Slerp, were performed. The markers were recognised using ARToolKit 5 connected with the Meta Headset RGB camera stream. The palm position was estimated either by the Meta headset or by the Leap Motion camera module. When any part of the estimated hand collided with the collision area (applied on the specific object in the scene), the corresponding haptic was activated.

Demo Flow. The demo presented a hypothetical car designer AR work environment. It consisted of 6 different scenes with 5 types of haptified interactions (mimics the Fig. 2A), which the supposed AR user/designer might require. The scene sequence was ordered in increasing complexity and immersion, to help the user become smoothly accustomed to the AR experience.

As the demo starts, a holographic button is presented, floating 40 cm above the array (Fig. 3, Scene 1). A virtual hand is displayed touching the button from the top, thus inviting the user to place the hand onto the button. After the user holds the position for 2.5 s, the next scene is triggered. If the user's hand moves away from the button, it slowly dims and eventually stops glowing with no action resulting. This simple scene is used to get the user accustomed to the holographic representation (navigation).

In the second scene, the user has the chance to change the colour of the luxury sports car through a spinner, represented as a set of 8 petals of different colours placed on a circular setup above the array (Fig. 3, Scene 2). At the beginning, a virtual hand is also displayed, passing horizontally across the petal circle, prompting the user to perform a swipe movement. This interaction causes the petal circle to rotate with a force proportional to the speed of the hand during the interaction. After the first spin, the swiping virtual hand disappears and another virtual hand, tapping on one petal, appears. When

---

[1] ZeroLight: https://zerolight.com/.

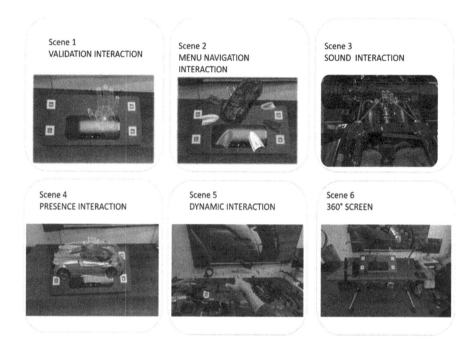

Fig. 3. Sequence of the demo interactions. Interactions were composed of up to three modalities (visual, tactile, acoustic) to maximise user performance and satisfaction.

the user performs tap/selection on one petal, the car's colour changes into the petal's colour. The user can change the colour multiple times according to personal preference. After any colour selection, a validation button, to move onto the next scene, is shown, on the side of the spinner.

During the third scene, the user interacts with a haptified sound controller. The car gets bigger and rotates so that the engine bay faces the user. The bay opens to reveal the engine in detail as well as a virtual hand hovering around the engine (Fig. 3, Scene 3). The user's hand is expected to be placed on any part of the engine. The user can feel and hear the car revving. The haptic feeling was synchronised with the sound (*Sound Interaction*). On the side of the car, a validation button leads the user to the next scene.

In the fourth and fifth scene, the car goes back to its initial size and position. A virtual hand is placed on the roof of the car, inviting the user to explore the car presence. The user in navigated by virtual hand until the first correct hand adjustment (Fig. 3, Scene 4).

The fifth scene is merged into fourth and relay on interaction with the exploding engine. The user hand, once placed on the roof of the car is triggering the dynamic count (~5 s) finalising the changes of the scene (sensation of the circle opening (increasing radius) and closing (decreasing radius)). The explosion is accompanied with a sound effect (Fig. 3, Scene 5).

In the final scene, the car 'explodes' into its component parts, and these float around the user at around 50–100 cm (Fig. 3, Scene 6). A virtual hand appears, prompting the user to raise their hand to eye level. This gesture initialises the spinning of the floating car elements around the user, mimicking a holographic 360-degree screen (see dynamics interaction). The scene lasts 40 s, after which the car goes back to its original state and the demo ends.

2.3 Interactions

Validation Interaction. To mimic the classical validation interface controller, a button-like hologram was designed, as a way for the user seamlessly proceed to the next scene. The button was presented as a 3-dimensional, semi-transparent disc-like object of 10 centimetres radius and 5 centimetres depth. The haptic feedback was projected in the centre of the button. Due to the active exploration condition, the sensation had to be clearly distinctive and unified across the whole palm. The sensation was based on a hand size sphere approximation and low frequency of the FP rendering at 40 Hz. Therefore, the spatial design of the rendered FP consists of two focal points, with a pi(π) separation distance in between, moving along a 4 cm radius sphere. The dynamics of the visual and auditory sensations were combined (Table 1).

Table 1. Summary of the five, evaluated demo tactile interactions: Enter, Select, Sound, Presence and Dynamics. These were characterised based on spatial design, temporal design and most efficient rendering frequency; [*]Audio file tactile feedback was rendered by using band pass filter (see *Sound Interaction*).

	Validation Interaction	Menu navigation Interaction	Sound Interaction	Presence Interaction	Dynamics Interaction
Spatial design	*Tap:* Field Sensation	*Swipe:* Edge detection *Tap:* Field Sensation	*Hold:* Focused Sensation	*Hold:* Field Sensation	*Hold:* Focused Sensations
Temporal design	Passive Touch Play "in object"	Passive Touch Play "on object"	Active Exploration Play "on object"	Passive Touch Play "on object"	Active Exploration Play "on palm"
Rendered frequency	Low (bumpy, intense sensation)	High (Smooth sensation)	Band pass filter input from audio source[*]	High (Smooth sensation)	Low (Sharp, vibrating sensations)

Virtual Hand. All the interactions were prompted without the use of text, as reading floating holograms was potentially too demanding for the user. To encourage the user to interact with the holograms, we used a virtual hand that was presented as a transparent human-like hand (Fig. 3, Scene 1). The virtual hand animation looped until the user had done the prompted gesture, whereupon the virtual hand would disappear.

Menu Navigation Interaction. We represented the menu interaction using an adaptation of a horizontal spinner. Using a swipe gesture, users could navigate through the menu and then select with a tap the desired option (the colour of the car). The interaction was anchored to a graphical representation of the controller (coloured petals) and gestures were performed with an open palm facing the array surface. The petals were enhanced with haptic feedback in two stages, firstly for the swipe gesture and secondly for the tap gesture. While *Swipe* gesture, menu's dynamics (spinning speed and direction) were dependent on the hand movement, therefore haptics were designed to follow and mimic dynamic movement of the spinner (two FPs rendering 10 cm line at 90 Hz). Haptic feedback was positioned on the top surface of the petals and rendered a line along the petals, perpendicular to the spinning axis. The second stage, a *Tap*, was designed to enhance the selection confirmation, while the spinner was static. FP was rendered on the inner edge of the petal (~10% smaller size) at frequency of 90 Hz, mimic the soft and smooth petal's volume. Haptics were displayed on the top of the petal, while the hand collided with the virtual object. The visual and tactile components were combined with acoustic feedback ("spinning" and "click" sound) dependent on the scene dynamics.

Sound Interaction. An audio file was used to create immersive audio-tactile sensations. The band pass filter was at 85–90 Hz (the chosen band must avoid peak-to-peak distance lower than 30 ms, due to perceptual resolution), Hilbert transformation and normalisation were applied on the mono .wav file, to create the base envelope file used as a FP's intensity threshold. Four separate FP (in parallel) were rendered semi-randomly covering internal field of the 10 × 10 cm square, displayed on the object surface, during the hand and the object collision. Tactile components were combined with acoustic feedback in the scene.

Presence Interaction. Two FPs, in parallel, were rendered at 90 Hz, within the close approximation of the geometry, of the haptified object (in demo: square roof of the car). Haptics were aligned with the virtual object's surface. Additional visual stimuli were applied, around the collision. The collider's glow was adjusted depending on the distance between the hand and the object surface. Its intensity gradually increased (while approaching) or decreased (while moving away).

Dynamics Interaction. Focused sensation type haptics was rendered at 40 Hz and applied on the palm. An anticipatory haptics sensation was also created by moving single FP on the concentric spiral path (hand sized; 10 cm radius) with increased velocity over each of 7 cycles, leading to a dynamics state change (the fifth scene). The haptic sensations were combined with acoustic input.

2.4 Questionnaire and User Evaluation

The proposed design implemented into a demonstration was subjected to user evaluation. The evaluation group included 40 participants (total: 30 males, 10 females; age 21–60) with no or very limited knowledge of AR applications or previous experience with their headsets. Following a short introduction to the test, the participant then began the experiment, which consisted of a single try of the demonstrator. During evaluation, participants were given unlimited time to test the proposed application content, without the additional requirements of using a specific hand. The experimental trial was followed by the widely-used NASA-TLX subjective assessment: (i) Mental Demand, (ii) Physical Demand, (iii) Temporal Demand, (iv) Performance, (v) Effort and (vi) Frustration. The standard form was expanded by additional preference selection of the most attractive interaction segment and a voluntary comments section.

3   Results and Discussion of the Design Evaluation

The user evaluation presented high interest and satisfaction. The TLX assessment (in scale from 1 to 10) suggested low mental, temporal and physical demand, at an average of 3.6 ($\pm$0.1), 3.4 ($\pm$0.1) and 3.4 ($\pm$0.1) respectively. Users assessed performance and effort both to be at a medium level of 5 ($\pm$0.1) suggesting rather low complexity level and seamless navigation, considering users' very little previous experience with AR applications. They assessed frustration as 4.4($\pm$0.1) what stand in agreement with several comments on unprecise gesture tracking respond either low inability to perform interactions by the first time.

Additional questions on personal preference showed that the Select Interactions were the most interesting and immersive (38%), followed by Sound and Dynamic interactions at 19% both. Least interesting interaction was Validation (only 5%). This might be explained by two factors: low attention to constant elements in the scene (user simply get used to it and did not recognise it as most engaging) either lower graphical satisfaction, where user exposed to least colour and detailed element, does not perceive it as most attractive. The voluntary comments emphasised the lack of previous experience and need for prime adjustments ("More explanation needed during demo, over all a good experience.", "I wasn't sure how to activate the petals at first", "Some extra instruction best required."). However, compare to average time of the completion >3 min and zero disruptive interactions, we can assume the system (on such early stage) is promising.

User evaluation, also showed that although each interaction was composed of multiple sensory feedbacks, prime and most memorable, while self-assessment, were the graphical components enhanced by "on object" haptic rendering ("Colour Picker" and "Engine Row" interactions). This may suggest the exploratory rather than merely receptive way of rendering the interface interactions.

4   Conclusions

In the current study, we present primary design and evaluation of the, dedicated to workspace, AR demonstrator, which combines visual, auditory and mid-air tactile feedback. User test demonstrated that mid-air haptic design, could be effectively used in AR interactions also by users with limited experience. Prime classification, based on the spatial and temporal FP rendering, allows create many compelling and intuitive AR interactions. The designed haptic sensations allow user to understand the primary visual context and satisfy need for fully immersive experience. Further evaluations based on the user feedback, are necessary.

Acknowledgments. The authors would like to acknowledge the substantial input of the ZeroLight company, especially Chris O'Connor and Andrew Ayre in the demo graphic design and demo integration. Special thank you to Meta for the hardware support and assistance in hand gesture recognition as well as Ultrahaptic's Tools Team for technical support.

References

1. Laurinavicius, T.: 10 Hot Augmented Reality Apps To Watch. Forbes (2017). https://www.forbes.com/sites/tomaslaurinavicius/2017/10/19/augmented-reality-apps-to-watch/#504f9e8a3a36
2. Nolle, S., Klinker, G.: Augmented reality as a comparison tool in automotive industry. In: 2006 IEEE/ACM International Symposium on Mixed and Augmented Reality, vol. 3, no. 1, pp. 249–250 (2006)
3. Piumsomboon, T., Clark, A., Billinghurst, M., Cockburn, A.: User-defined gestures for augmented reality. In: Kotzé, P., Marsden, G., Lindgaard, G., Wesson, J., Winckler, M. (eds.) INTERACT 2013. LNCS, vol. 8118, pp. 282–299. Springer, Heidelberg (2013). https://doi.org/10.1007/978-3-642-40480-1_18
4. Tsalamlal, M.Y., Issartel, P., Ouarti, N., Ammi, M.: HAIR: HAptic feedback with a mobile AIR jet. In: Proceedings of the IEEE International Conference on Robotics and Automation, pp. 2699–2706 (2014)
5. Sodhi, R., Poupyrev, I., Glisson, M., Israr, A.: AIREAL: interactive tactile experiences in free air. In: SIGGRAPH (2013)
6. Carter, T., Seah, S.A., Long, B., Drinkwater, B., Subramanian, S.: UltraHaptics: multi-point mid-air haptic feedback for touch surfaces (2013)
7. Iwamoto, T., Tatezono, M., Shinoda, H.: Non-contact method for producing tactile sensation using airborne ultrasound. In: Ferre, M. (ed.) EuroHaptics 2008. LNCS, vol. 5024, pp. 504–513. Springer, Heidelberg (2008). https://doi.org/10.1007/978-3-540-69057-3_64
8. Long, B., Seah, S.A., Carter, T., Subramanian, S.: Rendering volumetric haptic shapes in mid-air using ultrasound. ACM Trans. Graph. 33(6), 1–10 (2014)
9. Lederman, S.J., Klatzky, R.L.: Haptic perception: a tutorial. Atten. Percept. Psychophys. **71**(7), 1439–1459 (2009)
10. Hwang, I., Son, H., Kim, J.R.: AirPiano: enhancing music playing experience in virtual reality with mid-air haptic feedback, pp. 213–218, June 2017
11. Kervegant, C., Raymond, F., Graeff, D., Castet, J.: Touch hologram in mid-air. In: ACM SIGGRAPH 2017 Emerging Technologies - SIGGRAPH 2017, pp. 1–2 (2017)
12. Lecuyer, A., Coquillart, S., Kheddar, A., Richard, P., Coiffet, P.: Pseudo-haptic feedback: can isometric input devices simulate force feedback? In: Proceedings of the IEEE Virtual Real 2000 (Cat. No. 00CB37048), pp. 83–90 (2000)
13. Klatzky, R.L., Pawluk, D., Peer, A.: Haptic perception of material properties and implications for applications. Proc. IEEE **101**(9), 2081–2092 (2013)
14. Hincapié-Ramos, J.D., Guo, X., Moghadasian, P., Irani, P.: Consumed endurance: a metric to quantify arm fatigue of mid-air interactions. In: Proceedings of the 32nd Annual ACM CHI Conference on Human Factors in Computing Systems - CHI 2014, pp. 1063–1072 (2014)
15. Gibson, J.J.: Observations on active touch. Psychol. Rev. **69**(6), 477–491 (1962)

Anti-Veering Vibrotactile HMD
for Assistance of Blind Pedestrians

Victor Adriel de Jesus Oliveira[1](✉), Luciana Nedel[1](✉), Anderson Maciel[1](✉),
and Luca Brayda[2](✉)

[1] INF, Universidade Federal do Rio Grande do Sul (UFRGS), Porto Alegre, Brazil
{vajoliveira,nedel,amaciel}@inf.ufrgs.br
[2] RBCS, Fondazione Istituto Italiano di Tecnologia (IIT), Genoa, Italy
luca.brayda@iit.it

Abstract. Veering is a common experience for blind pedestrians and
for individuals walking in unfamiliar spaces. In this paper, we assess a
vibrotactile Head-Mounted Display to assist blind individuals to walk
straight from a point to another. Our goal was to assess such device
for both assistance and self-Orientation and Mobility (O&M) training
to provide more autonomy to blind pedestrians. Blind and blindfolded
subjects performed a series of assisted and non-assisted sessions to verify
how deviation errors are modulated according to the use of the device.
Moreover, the vibrotactile feedback was compared to audible walking
signals commonly present in many road-cross scenarios, as well as in
traditional O&M sessions. Performance and subjective measures were
assessed as a function of stimulus modality and group profile. Results
show that the vibrotactile feedback significantly reduces the veering for
both sighted and blind subjects.

Keywords: Tactile guidance · Anti-veering · Vibrotactile display

1 Introduction

Humans tend to veer when trying to perform a straight walk through environments that lack reliable orienting cues [21] (see Fig. 1). For impaired pedestrians, it represents a critical problem in everyday life [28]. When crossing the street, for instance, blind pedestrians may veer from the ideal path and end up in the middle of a busy street. To minimize the risk, audible pedestrian signals are commonly used to assist visually impaired individuals when crossing the street [30]. However, such cues are not always available or can be confusing in a noisy setting such as busy intersections in a city [29]. Without the assistance of pedestrian signals, blind people often rely on sighted people to help them navigate unknown spaces [6]. This dependency on others reduces their autonomy and so their mobility [14]. To avoid this, visually impaired pedestrians can recur to both orientation and mobility (O&M) training and to assistive devices.

When blind, walking requires extensive training lasting several years. Nonetheless, studies show that training can, in fact, reduce blind pedestrians'

© Springer International Publishing AG, part of Springer Nature 2018
D. Prattichizzo et al. (Eds.): EuroHaptics 2018, LNCS 10894, pp. 500–512, 2018.
https://doi.org/10.1007/978-3-319-93399-3_43

Fig. 1. Veering is the tendency to depart from linearity in locomotion.

veering [8]. Almost no technological aid is available at the training stage and the ones available are limited to turn-by-turn, audio-based cues that rely on GPS and odometric data. Thus, blind pedestrians have to work closely with O&M instructors to improve their performance when trying to walk a straight line without assistance. Most navigation and anti-veering systems are designed to assist visually impaired pedestrians during the walk and not for training. However, autonomy is essential for blind pedestrians. Thus, a navigational and anti-veering device could be used for training the straight walking task at home or in familiar open spaces (e.g. gyms, courtyards) to optimize the time that the blind individuals spend at their O&M sessions. In addition, it could provide assistance during the walking task, minimizing the risks of veering anytime pedestrians feel necessary even after being trained [8].

Navigational aids are commonly made to convey information through the auditory or tactile sense [2,17]. In this context, the tactile feedback has the main advantage of not blocking the auditory sense, which is the most important perceptual input source for a visually impaired user in large spaces [1]. In addition, vibrotactile devices are wearable which also allows a free-hands interaction. In the human body, the skin around the head is known to be one of the most sensitive regions to mechanical stimulation [25]. That motivates the design of tactile devices that can be worn around the head to aid locomotion, orientation, obstacle detection and attentional redirection [13,15]. However, even though the existing literature on head stimulation reinforces the feasibility and advantages of the so-called tactile Head-Mounted Displays (HMDs) [25], it is still unknown whether it can be used as an anti-veering device.

In this paper, we propose the design of a vibrotactile HMD to be used as an anti-veering device for the assistance of blind pedestrians. Deviation errors are assessed while the subjects perform a straight walking task in a series of assisted and non-assisted sessions. For the assisted conditions, the vibrotactile HMD is also compared to a conventional O&M session using ambient audible walking signals. Both blind and blindfolded sighted subjects participated in the experiments. Learning effects, trajectories, anxiety levels, workload, and easiness are assessed as a function of the stimulus modality and group profile. Our main contribution is on the assessment and adjustment of a haptic guidance technique based on head stimulation to support the straight walking assistance.

2   Related Work

2.1   Anti-Veering Devices

Electronic travel aids should accomplish four basic requirements: be free-hands, free-ears, wearable, and simple [2]. That places tactile devices ahead auditory assistance as its free-ears aspect is essential for blind pedestrians. Vibrotactile guidance is also preferred when it comes to performance. For instance, Ross and Blasch [26] assessed two auditory modalities and a vibrotactile modality. The one that gave the best results in terms of subject performance and preference was the vibrotactile interface. In a study made by Flores et al. [7], it was found that the haptic guidance resulted in closer path-following compared to the auditory feedback. In addition, Martinez et al. [13] found that the workload was lower with haptic feedback compared to audio for blind participants.

Most comparisons made between vibrotactile devices and auditory assistance devices encode both stimuli in a comparable way (e.g. the auditory devices produce beeps on the left and right ears of the subject to indicate a turn) [6,15,26]. It shows that, as assistive devices, these vibrotactile implementations are more suitable in design and performance than the auditory ones. However, when it comes to O&M sessions, ambient audible pedestrian signals are still a common used resource [30]. These signals are composed by intermittent beeps and rendered by a non-wearable source instead. In this paper, we aim to implement a vibrotactile device that can be both an assistive and a self-training device. Therefore, we compare our vibrotactile anti-veering device to an audio condition that is more similar to the audible pedestrian signals.

2.2   Head Stimulation

Contrarily to handheld anti-veering devices [31], a multivibrator display mounted on the head or on the torso is more suitable to render directional cues. In addition, a multivibrator display can indicate how much the pedestrian deviated, decreasing the search time. Even though head stimulation is not conventionally applied for anti-veering, the position of the head is usually tracked to estimate the pedestrian's heading direction [19]. Thus, with a vibrotactile HMD, we can have a single piece for acquiring the user position and to trigger directional cues from an egocentric perspective. Using a vibrotactile HMD, Kaul et al. [13] found that haptic feedback was faster and more precise than auditory feedback for object finding. In addition, Kerdegari et al. [15] showed that the haptic modality leads to a lower route deviation compared to auditory feedback. However, these studies implemented vibrotactile HMDs for guidance, not dealing with the veering tendency.

A number of studies have been performed on vibrotactile localization [3,16] and spatial acuity [11] to produce guidelines for head stimulation. In a more recent study, a technique called Tactile Fovea is proposed to increase accuracy during target detection and support directional cueing of gaze [10,24]. In this paper, we implement the Tactile Fovea technique for an unobtrusive guidance and to support a straight walking task.

3   Methods

We designed and assessed a vibrotactile HMD to provide anti-veering assistance. Deviation errors were assessed across five sessions of assisted and non-assisted walk (three non-assisted sessions, one audio-assisted, and one vibration-assisted). Blind and blindfolded subjects participated in this evaluation. We also assessed the subject anxiety, the task workload, and easiness as dependent variables.

We hypothesize that the vibrotactile HMD might aid subjects to deviate less from their intended path than their baseline veering; We also hypothesize that a short training session should be enough to show some learning effect after using audio and/or vibration [22].

3.1   Subjects

Fourteen subjects (9 female, 5 male) participated in the experiment with ages varying from 11 to 38 years old (M = 22, SD = 9.62). Seven were blind and seven were sighted. From the blind group, three were severely blind (from childhood) and four were moderately blind (seeing some shadows and light).

The sample was selected by the Rehabilitation Institute for Blind People *Istituto David Chiossone onlus* in Genoa, Italy, which also hosted the experiments. The recruitment was accomplished according to the local Ethical Committee. Six blind subjects reported having constant O&M instruction in the Institute about how to get aligned (head, shoulders, and feet) and perform a straight walk across the room. The other subjects reported never having done the mentioned training before. We applied an Edinburgh Handedness Inventory [4] and two subjects were shown to be left-handed.

3.2   Experimental Setup

Venue. The walking task concerned the subject walking across the room from point A to point B, then from point B to point A. Figure 2 shows a top-view of the room and the setup.

Continuous acquisition of subject position and orientation was made using a Vicon MX motion capture system with 10 cameras. Three reflective spherical VICON markers of 12.5 mm each were attached to the subject's head to compose a trackable *head template* (see Fig. 2(left)). The head template was automatically labeled in real-time by VICON Nexus (version 1.8.5). Its position was acquired in real-time via the VICON DataStream SDK (version 1.5) by a laptop placed inside a frontal bag. The bag was placed in the front of the subjects so they could align their back with the starting points (a very common practice in O&M training) and to not induce a veering to the right or to the left [21].

Instead of observing when subjects cross checkpoints on the floor, we use a motion capture system for more precision. Due to the volume that could be sensed by the motion capture system, the distance between points A and B was 5 m. A 5-m long path might be enough to detect subjects with severe veering [8] as some crossings measure about the same length.

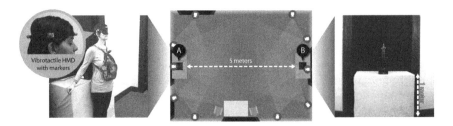

Fig. 2. The walking straight task was performed in a room with 10 cameras of a motion capture system. (left) Subjects wore the vibrotactile display with three reflective markers and a bag with a small computer in the front. (right) Loudspeakers were placed on both sides of the room for the audio-assisted session.

Vibrotactile Feedback. We assembled a vibrotactile headband according to the literature on head stimulation [10,11] (see Fig. 3). Accordingly, seven electromechanical tactors - 10 mm Linear Resonant Actuator, 4 mm type (C10-100 Precision Microdrives) - were attached to a piece of Velcro to be worn around the head. The tactors were controlled with an Arduino Mega ADK board and Adafruit DRV2605L haptic controllers, vibrating at 175 Hz.

Fig. 3. Vibrotactile headband based on a Tactile Fovea technique [10].

The deviation error was measured as the distance between the center of the head template and the intended path [19], while the vibrotactile warning was triggered according to the rotation from the target direction [8,22] (see Fig. 4). Then, the location of the vibrating stimuli was dynamically updated in function of head motion and used by the subjects to align their whole body accordingly (head, then shoulders and feet). As subjects walked a straight line, the central motor would indicate that the target was still in front of them, at the end of the intended path. If the subject veered, the actuator corresponding to the direction of the target would vibrate until the subject returns to the intended path.

Studies show that the absence of feedback when walking straight is considered more natural and preferred by blind participants [23]. Thus, no stimulus was delivered if the subject kept heading the target. However, when the subject was off-target by the threshold of $7.5°$ [22,26], then the corresponding tactor would vibrate indicating that there was a veering. Finally, as vibrations are only triggered when the subject goes out of the intended path, vibrations should be less felt as subjects improve in the task (for the sake of learning).

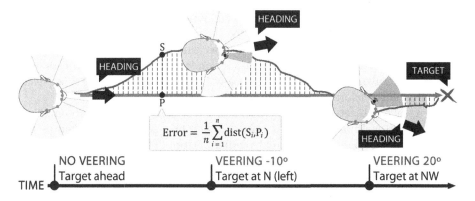

$$\text{Error} = \frac{1}{n}\sum_{i=1}^{n}\text{dist}(S_i, P_i)$$

NO VEERING	VEERING -10°	VEERING 20°
Target ahead	Target at N (left)	Target at NW

TIME

Fig. 4. Vibrotactile cues were provided only when the veering was detected. So, if the pedestrian turns $-10°$, the right motor on the forehead vibrates. If the pedestrian turns $20°$ instead, the motor facing NW would vibrate, and so on. The distance from the subject (S) to the planned straight path (P) was acquired every 3 cm to calculate the mean deviation.

Auditory Feedback. Auditory stimuli were sent through two ADAM5 speakers placed on each side of the room exactly on the target position (see Fig. 2). Only one speaker, at the opposite side of the room, would be activated during the assisted walk. The speakers were placed at 1 m from the ground to account for the different heights of the underage participants.

The audible signals were produced with 880 Hz, following the American Manual on Uniform Traffic Control Devices (MUTCD, Sect. 4E.11, P7 & P8 [5]). In a conventional O&M session, auditory feedback is systematically reduced during the assisted walk. Therefore, different walk signals were composed by beeps of 200 ms with a variable inter-stimulus duration, from 500 ms up to 1700 ms. These walking signals varied across trials. The room was also covered with a carpet to limit acoustic feedback and the sound of the subject steps.

3.3   Protocol

Each subject performed *five blocks* of assisted (by audio or vibration) and non-assisted sessions (see Fig. 5).

Fig. 5. Experimental protocol.

Each subject answered a demographic questionnaire before starting the experiment. While wearing the prototype device (headband and bag with the computer) and a blindfold, each subject was guided to walk across the room and feel the start and end points with their hands. Even the blind subjects were blindfolded to avoid receiving cues from any light or shadows. Sighted subjects were blindfolded before entering the room.

Then, each subject performed a non-assisted walking across the room. They were asked to walk as straight as possible. The first session was taken as the baseline as it registered their normal veering pattern. Then, subjects performed *two blocks* of an assisted session (audio or vibration) and *two blocks* of non-assisted sessions, counterbalanced across subjects. Each session has six trials. All sessions were performed on the same day. Subjects could ask for a break at any moment. The whole participation took on average 1 hour for each subject.

After each session, subjects answered to a six-item short-form of the State-Trait Anxiety Inventory (STAI-6) [20], a 20-point Single Easy Question (SEQ) [27], and a non-weighted NASA Task Load Index (NASA-TLX) questionnaire [9] with two tangible scales carved in hard foam.

4   Results

4.1   Performance

Figure 6 shows the results of blind and blindfolded subjects for each session.

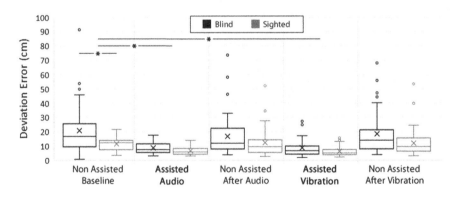

Fig. 6. Mean deviation errors for the five sessions: First Non assisted for Blind (M = 21 cm, SD = 17.5) and Sighted (M = 11 cm, SD = 4.7), Audio-Assisted for Blind (M = 9 cm, SD = 3.9) and Sighted (M = 7 cm, SD = 2.6), Non assisted after Audio for Blind (M = 17 cm, SD = 14.6) and Sighted (M = 12 cm, SD = 10.0), Vibration-Assisted for Blind (M = 9 cm, SD = 6.7) and Sighted (M = 6 cm, SD = 3.4), Non assisted after Vibration for Blind (M = 18 cm, SD = 14.6) and Sighted (M = 12 cm, SD = 9.5). The baseline veering error for blind subjects was higher than for sighted subjects. Assisted conditions reduced the veering error for both blind and sighted (blindfolded) subjects.

A Two-way analysis of variance was conducted on the influence of condition and sight on the deviation errors. Condition included the five sessions and sight consisted of two levels (blind and sighted). All effects were statistically significant at the .05 significance level.

There was a significant difference between the mean deviation (error) for the conditions ($F(4,410) = 15.011$, $p < .001$). There was also an effect of sight on mean deviation ($F(1,410) = 24.727$, $p < .001$). The interaction effect was not significant though ($p = .134$).

Post hoc tests using the Bonferroni correction revealed that both the audio-assisted and the vibration-assisted conditions yielded fewer errors than the non-assisted baseline condition for both blind ($p < .001$) and sighted subjects ($p < .01$). Overall, blind subjects deviated more from the intended path than sighted subjects. The baseline veer of blind subjects was already higher than the baseline veer of sighted subjects ($p < .01$). However, there was no difference between sighted and blind subjects when assisted by audio or vibration ($p = .99$).

The non-assisted sessions after audio and after vibration were also compared to the non-assisted baseline to observe whether there was a learning effect coming from the previous assisted sessions. There was no significant difference between the conditions concerning the mean deviation from the planned path.

Figure 7 shows the trajectories of a blind subject across the five experimental conditions. The veering tendency registered in the non-assisted baseline is clearly reduced on the audio and vibration assistance. In addition, it is possible to see the course changes caused by the directional cues received during the session assisted by vibration. These trajectories are representative of both groups of blind and sighted subjects.

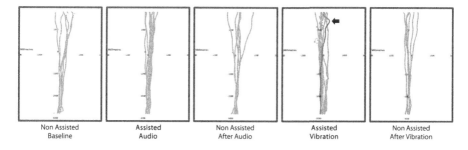

| Non Assisted Baseline | Assisted Audio | Non Assisted After Audio | Assisted Vibration | Non Assisted After Vibration |

Fig. 7. Trajectories of a blind subject across the five experimental conditions. The arrow points to a course change induced by the vibrotactile cue.

4.2 Subjective Measures

A Wilcoxon Signed-Ranks Test indicated that the workload for the audio-assisted condition (Mdn = 5.8) was statistically significantly higher than the vibration-assisted (Mdn = 8.0) for blind subjects ($Z = 2.3664$, $p < .009$). Audio-assisted

(Mdn = 8.5) and vibration-assisted (Mdn = 7.8) did not vary significantly for the sighted subjects though (see Fig. 8(left)).

In addition, the audio-assisted condition (Mdn = 19) was shown to be easier to perform compared to the vibration-assisted (Mdn = 12) for blind subjects (Z = 1.5724, p = .05). Again, audio-assisted (Mdn = 17) and vibration-assisted (Mdn = 16) did not vary significantly for the sighted subjects (see Fig. 8(right)).

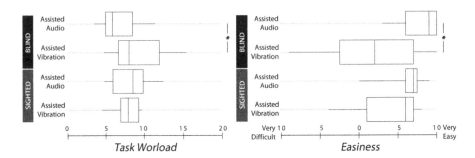

Fig. 8. (left) Scores of NASA-TLX (20-point scale, non-weighted). (right) Easiness across modalities (SEQ with a 20-point scale).

The anxiety levels did not increase according to the specific use of tactile or audio assistance though. Overall, subjects yielded low scores for the STAI questionnaire. Thus, subjects presented low levels of anxiety during the experiment. Levels of anxiety dropped after the first assisted session, which was lower than the levels reported in the beginning of the experiment (Z = 2.00, p < 0.05). The scores kept low throughout the subsequent sessions.

5   Discussion and Conclusion

We designed and assessed a vibrotactile HMD to be used as an anti-veering device. Subjects performed a straight walking task on a series of non-assisted and assisted sessions. For the assisted sessions, audible walking signals conventionally used in O&M sessions were compared to vibrotactile cues rendered by our device on the subject's head. As hypothesized, results show that the deviation errors were reduced in average 11% from the baseline veering when using the vibrotactile HMD. When it comes to the baseline deviation, subjects could arrive even at 1 m far from the target. However, the veering tendency was significantly reduced with vibration for both blind and blindfolded subjects. With the vibration assistance, the deviation was of only 11 cm on average.

To attenuate the effect of some basic sources of veering, such as initial orientation and biases in step direction [12], O&M instructors guide blind pedestrians to keep their head, shoulders and feet always aligned during the initial positioning and while walking. A change in the head direction might affect the pedestrians moving direction [8]. Thus, the vibrotactile HMD notifies the pedestrian about changes in the head positioning and how far it deviated from the intended path. Trajectories of the subjects using the vibrotactile HMD show the points in which subjects deviate beyond the threshold (see Fig. 7). At these points, the vibrotactile feedback is perceived and, then, the subjects can change their routes to recover from veering. Thus, the vibrotactile HMD works by restricting the pedestrian to a virtual corridor. Such corridor might be translated later to a crosswalk, a sidewalk or a platform, for instance.

The main advantage of the vibrotactile device is to be worn and carried around. The vibrotactile actuators might be attached to hats, helmets, or even a headband. Thus, pedestrians may use our device for assistance anytime they need to. Unless the pedestrian is making a turn or engaged in communication with another pedestrian, the stimuli can be activated to support anti-veering support. Since vibration is not attached to a traffic light, as it is with audible walking signals, our stimulation mode can be used in different venues with arbitrary landmarks, possibly chosen by rehabilitation practitioners or by the blind person. Then, for larger distances, landmarks can be fixed to predefined GPS locations and rendered on the user's head, so that a blind person can be trained or even self-train with autonomy. In addition, by using different environmental sensors (such as GPS, sonars, and cameras), the vibrotactile HMD can also point the position of other pedestrians, vehicles, and different obstacles in the street and sidewalks. Results also show that the vibrotactile feedback can be useful for sighted subjects as well. Sighted subjects can use the vibrotactile guidance in different contexts, such as for display-free navigation, navigating unknown spaces, guidance in dark environments or in the fog, for instance.

We also have hypothesized that a short training session could lead to a better performance in a subsequent session without assistance as reported in the literature [22]. However, such effect was not shown for the non-assisted sessions after audio nor after vibration. The deviation errors did not vary significantly between the non-assisted sessions and the baseline. As pointed by Maclean [18], subjects have been using audition for the kinds of tasks we test since early childhood, and they've been using the tactile version for a short training period. Thus, as the vibrotactile feedback is an unconventional modality, blind subjects had to be more attentive during the walk which might have increased task workload. Future studies should also consider the use of the vibrotactile HMD across time, which is likely to more firmly set the advantages of vibrational cues. Moreover, since rehabilitation sessions may last years, future studies should also verify how vibrational cues correct veering tendency (with no assistance) after several sessions. Finally, the vibrotactile HMD should also be assessed for guidance in more complex trajectories, including piecewise straight lines (typical in O&M scenarios) or even curved paths.

Acknowledgments. The authors thank the rehabilitation operators of the Istituto David Chiossone, Claudia Vigini and Serena Portacci. Thanks to Elena Cocchi and Elisabetta Capris for the support and the recruitment of our sample. Special thanks to the subjects who made this study possible. This study is partly supported by the Ligurian PAR-FAS grant Glassense (CUP G35C13001360001) and EU FP7 grant BLIND-PAD (grant number 611621). We also acknowledge FAPERGS (17/2551-0001192-9) and CNPq-Brazil (311353/2017-7).

References

1. Cardin, S., Thalmann, D., Vexo, F.: A wearable system for mobility improvement of visually impaired people. Vis. Comput. **23**(2), 109–118 (2006)
2. Dakopoulos, D., Bourbakis, N.G.: Wearable obstacle avoidance electronic travel aids for blind: a survey. IEEE Trans. Syst. Man. Cybern. Part C (Appl. Rev.) **40**(1), 25–35 (2010)
3. Dobrzynski, M.K., Mejri, S., Wischmann, S., Floreano, D.: Quantifying information transfer through a head-attached vibrotactile display: principles for design and control. IEEE Trans. Biomed. Eng. **59**(7), 2011–2018 (2012)
4. Dragovic, M.: Towards an improved measure of the edinburgh handedness inventory: a one-factor congeneric measurement model using confirmatory factor analysis. Laterality Asymmetries Body Brain Cogn. **9**(4), 411–419 (2004)
5. Federal Highway Administration, U.S. Department of Transportation: Manual on uniform traffic control devices (MUTCD) (2017). http://mutcd.fhwa.dot.gov/. Accessed 17 Jan 2017
6. Fiannaca, A., Apostolopoulous, I., Folmer, E.: Headlock: a wearable navigation aid that helps blind cane users traverse large open spaces. In: Proceedings of the 16th International ACM SIGACCESS Conference on Computers & Accessibility, ASSETS 2014, pp. 323–324. ACM, New York (2014)
7. Flores, G., Kurniawan, S., Manduchi, R., Martinson, E., Morales, L.M., Sisbot, E.A.: Vibrotactile guidance for wayfinding of blind walkers. IEEE Trans. Haptics **8**(3), 306–317 (2015)
8. Guth, D.: Why does training reduce blind pedestrians veering. In: Blindness and Brain Plasticity in Navigation and Object Perception, pp. 353–365. Taylor & Francis (2008)
9. Hart, S.G.: Nasa-task load index (NASA-TLX); 20 years later. In: Proceedings of the Human Factors and Ergonomics Society Annual Meeting, vol. 50, pp. 904–908 (2006)
10. de Jesus Oliveira, V.A., Nedel, L., Maciel, A., Brayda, L.: Localized magnification in vibrotactile HMDs for accurate spatial awareness. In: Bello, F., Kajimoto, H., Visell, Y. (eds.) EuroHaptics 2016. LNCS, vol. 9775, pp. 55–64. Springer, Cham (2016). https://doi.org/10.1007/978-3-319-42324-1_6
11. de Jesus Oliveira, V.A., Nedel, L., Maciel, A., Brayda, L.: Spatial discrimination of vibrotactile stimuli around the head. In: 2016 IEEE Haptics Symposium (HAPTICS), pp. 1–6. IEEE (2016)
12. Kallie, C.S., Schrater, P.R., Legge, G.E.: Variability in stepping direction explains the veering behavior of blind walkers. J. Exp. Psychol. Hum. Percept. Perform. **33**(1), 183 (2007)
13. Kaul, O.B., Rohs, M.: Haptichead: 3D guidance and target acquisition through a vibrotactile grid. In: Proceedings of the 2016 CHI Conference Extended Abstracts on Human Factors in Computing Systems, CHI EA 2016, pp. 2533–2539. ACM, New York(2016)
14. Kempen, G.I., Ballemans, J., Ranchor, A.V., van Rens, G.H., Zijlstra, G.R.: The impact of low vision on activities of daily living, symptoms of depression, feelings of anxiety and social support in community-living older adults seeking vision rehabilitation services. Qual. Life Res. **21**(8), 1405–1411 (2012)

15. Kerdegari, H., Kim, Y., Prescott, T.J.: Head-mounted sensory augmentation device: comparing haptic and audio modality. In: Lepora, N.F.F., Mura, A., Mangan, M., Verschure, P.F.M.J.F.M.J., Desmulliez, M., Prescott, T.J.J. (eds.) Living Machines 2016. LNCS (LNAI), vol. 9793, pp. 107–118. Springer, Cham (2016). https://doi.org/10.1007/978-3-319-42417-0_11

16. Kerdegari, H., Kim, Y., Stafford, T., Prescott, T.J.: Centralizing bias and the vibrotactile funneling illusion on the forehead. In: Auvray, M., Duriez, C. (eds.) EUROHAPTICS 2014. LNCS, vol. 8619, pp. 55–62. Springer, Heidelberg (2014). https://doi.org/10.1007/978-3-662-44196-1_8

17. Loomis, J.M., Golledge, R.G., Klatzky, R.L., Marston, J.R.: Assisting wayfinding in visually impaired travelers. In: Applied Spatial Cognition: From Research to Cognitive Technology. Lawrence Erlbaum Associates Mahwah, NJ (2007)

18. MacLean, K.E., Hayward, V.: Do it yourself haptics: Part II. IEEE Rob. Autom. Mag. 15(1), 104–119 (2008)

19. Marston, J.R., Loomis, J.M., Klatzky, R.L., Golledge, R.G.: Nonvisual route following with guidance from a simple haptic or auditory display. J. Vis. Impairment Blindness 101(4), 203 (2007)

20. Marteau, T.M., Bekker, H.: The development of a six-item short-form of the state scale of the spielberger state-trait anxiety inventory (STAI). Br. J. Clin. Psychol. 31(3), 301–306 (1992)

21. Millar, S.: Veering re-visited: noise and posture cues in walking without sight. Perception 28(6), 765–780 (1999)

22. Nagy, H., Wersényi, G.: Comparative evaluation of sighted and visually impaired subjects using a mobile application for reducing veering during blindfolded walking. Acta Technica Jaurinensis 9(2), 140–157 (2016)

23. Panëels, S.A., Varenne, D., Blum, J.R., Cooperstock, J.R.: The walking straight mobile application: Helping the visually impaired avoid veering. In: ICAD 2013: Proceedings of the International Conference on Autoditory Display, ICAD 2013, pp. 25–32. Lodz University of Technology Press (2013)

24. Rantala, J., Kangas, J., Raisamo, R.: Directional cueing of gaze with a vibrotactile headband. In: Proceedings of the 8th Augmented Human International Conference, AH 2017, pp. 7:1–7:7. ACM, New York (2017)

25. Rash, C.E., Russo, M.B., Letowski, T.R., Schmeisser, E.T.: Helmet-mounted displays: sensation, perception and cognition issues. Technical report, DTIC Document (2009)

26. Ross, D.A., Blasch, B.B.: Wearable interfaces for orientation and wayfinding. In: Proceedings of the Fourth International ACM Conference on Assistive Technologies, Assets 2000, pp. 193–200, ACM, New York (2000)

27. Sauro, J., Dumas, J.S.: Comparison of three one-question, post-task usability questionnaires. In: Proceedings of the SIGCHI Conference on Human Factors in Computing Systems, CHI 2009, pp. 1599–1608. ACM, New York (2009)

28. Shangguan, L., Yang, Z., Zhou, Z., Zheng, X., Wu, C., Liu, Y.: CrossNavi: enabling real-time crossroad navigation for the blind with commodity phones. In: Proceedings of the 2014 ACM International Joint Conference on Pervasive and Ubiquitous Computing, UbiComp 2014, pp. 787–798. ACM, New York (2014)

29. Uematsu, A., Inoue, K., Hobara, H., Kobayashi, H., Iwamoto, Y., Hortobágyi, T., Suzuki, S.: Preferred step frequency minimizes veering during natural human walking. Neurosci. Lett. 505(3), 291–293 (2011)

30. Wall, R.S., Ashmead, D.H., Bentzen, B.L., Barlow, J.: Directional guidance from audible pedestrian signals for street crossing. Ergonomics **47**(12), 1318–1338 (2004)
31. Zeng, L., Weber, G.: Building augmented you-are-here maps through collaborative annotations for the visually impaired. In: Proceedings SKALID, p. 7 (2012)

An Improved Adaptive Robotic Assistance Methodology for Upper-Limb Rehabilitation

Fabio Stroppa[1]($\boxtimes$), Claudio Loconsole[2], Simone Marcheschi[1],
Nicola Mastronicola[1], and Antonio Frisoli[1]

[1] PERCRO, TeCIP Scuola Superiore Sant'Anna, Pisa, Italy
f.stroppa@santannapisa.it
[2] Dipartimento di Ingegneria Elettrica e dell'Informazione (DEI),
Politecnico di Bari, Bari, Italy

Abstract. In this work, we propose an improved version of our algorithm for real-time robotic assistance tuning in robot-based therapy with any kind of active device for upper-limb rehabilitation. In particular, the work describes in detail how to extract accurate performance indices from the subject's execution, and how to correlate them with the amount of assistance to be correspondingly provided over time. The algorithm also aims at enhancing subject's efforts for a more effective recovery, tailoring the therapy to the patient without prior knowledge of his/her clinical status. Finally, an assessment phase illustrates the effectiveness of the procedure, showing how the system tunes the assistance required by the subjects to perform specific tasks.

1 Introduction

Millions of patients around the world suffer from stroke and other long-term disabilities. In this case, neurorehabilitation is an indispensable solution to treat them. Clinical studies have shown that a proper therapy should be repetitive [1], intense [2], long term [3], and task specific [4].

In particular, when the rehabilitation is assisted by robots, the aforementioned features are joined by higher precision, subject involvement and entertainment, as well as a reduction of the therapist physical burden [5]. Clinical trials have proved the effectiveness of robotic rehabilitation [6], especially with active robots implementing the "assist-as-needed" paradigm [7,8]: robotic devices can be driven to help the subject properly perform the task based on his/her actual physical abilities. However, a disproportionate amount of assistance might induce a reduction of voluntary control, resulting in a task where the subject does not lead the execution.

Previously, we proposed a real-time assist-as-needed procedure for robotic rehabilitation of the human upper limb [9]. This algorithm aimed at obtaining the proper robotic assistance required to improve subjects' performance and, at the same time, enhance their efforts. The adaptive regulation of assistance was

D. Prattichizzo et al. (Eds.): EuroHaptics 2018, LNCS 10894, pp. 513–525, 2018.
https://doi.org/10.1007/978-3-319-93399-3_44

proposed among a continuous set of difficulty levels. The strengths of this approach relied on *(i)* formulating an "assistance-performance" relationship, differently from other statistical inference studies [10], and *(ii)* exploiting geometrical information rather than kinematic errors [11].

In this work, we improve the previous algorithm by addressing the non-linearity of the human behavior with an online learning procedure, such that the system automatically adapts to different subjects, relying exclusively on the performance achieved during the execution.

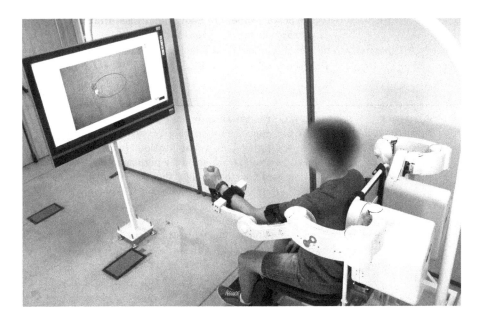

Fig. 1. A subject wearing the ALEx robot and performing the pursuing task.

The algorithm operates on the same pursuing exercise we introduced in [9], in which the subject is asked to follow a target in a 2D virtual environment along a predefined polygonal or elliptical trajectory; yet, it could be exploited in any kind of repetitive trajectory-based task. The robotic assistance is realized as a virtual coupling between the end effector and the target, where the value of the stiffness coefficient modulates the degree of attraction to the target (the more the stiffness, the easier the task).

The evaluation of subject's performance was previously based on fitted shapes retrieved by a metaheuristic research algorithm, which however provided highly unstable indices resulting in different solutions from the same input. In this work, we will introduce a new strategy for the performance evaluation, based on simpler geometric aspects and providing more reliable results (Sect. 2.1).

The assistance tuning algorithm has been completely revised, and it is the main topic discussed in Sect. 2.2. Previously, the strategy was based on knowing the relationship between assistance and performance, so that the amount of assistance required could be calculated straightforwardly. However, this app-roach presented some anomalies, especially if the subject remained still without reacting to the exercise. The new strategy is based on the assumption that this relationship cannot be described by a linear function when the human factor is added to the system. We propose an online learning procedure, rather than exploiting a training phase that would be too long and repetitive to be used in a clinical context. The therapy can start right after the patient has worn the device; on the other hand, this requires a transitional phase to reach the target.

The algorithm has been developed and tested on ALEx Rehab System [12], shown in Fig. 1; and it could be exploited with other different active haptic devices on similar repetitive tasks. Section 3 will present a pilot experiment with healthy subjects, showing how the algorithm reacts.

2   Proposed Methodology

The proposed methodology consists of: *(i)* a performance evaluator, which pro-vides the achievements of the subjects during the execution in real time; and *(ii)* a tuning assistance algorithm, setting the correct amount of assistance to be provided by the robot based on the performance previously calculated.

2.1   Performance Evaluation

The evaluation of subjects' performance takes into account several aspects of the task execution, and collect them in a global unique index to be correlated with the assistance. In particular, it considers: *(i)* the trajectory to be followed, described as a geometric shape S_{ref}; *(ii)* the movements of the subject, sampled and collected in m points $p \in P$; and *(iii)* the positions of the moving target, sampled and collected in m points $t \in T^1$. From these features, the performance is then identified by the two following values:

– j_1, or *Distance From Geometric Shape* index, the mean error occurring between P and the reference trajectory S_{ref} (1);

$$j_1 = \frac{\sum_{i=1}^{m} \mathtt{distance}(p_i, S_{ref})}{m} \tag{1}$$

– j_2, or *Distance From Target* index, the mean spatial difference between P and T (2).

$$j_2 = \frac{\sum_{i=1}^{m} \sqrt{(p_i - t_i)^2}}{m} \tag{2}$$

---

[1] It is worth pointing out that both P and T are stored at the same sample frequency, resulting in having the same number of points.

The values of these indices get lower as the subject's abilities improve. More in detail, index j_1 considers the geometric aspects of the performance, taking into account the size of the patient's trajectory and its orientation in the space; whereas j_2 considers the evolution of the execution during time. Figure 2 shows a graphical representation of the indices. The final index j, which is correlated to the change of assistance, is given by the arithmetic average of j_1 and j_2, as reported in (3).

$$j = \frac{j_1 + j_2}{2} \tag{3}$$

It is worth to point out that index j_2 alone could represent a good performance descriptor. Nevertheless, during the evaluation it is joined by j_1 to distinguish the geometrical aspect from the time execution.

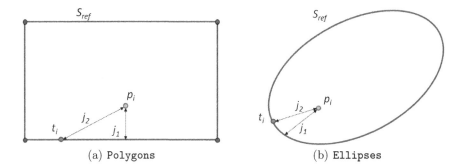

(a) Polygons   (b) Ellipses

Fig. 2. Evaluation of performance indices at time i.

2.2   Assistance Tuning Algorithm

The algorithm herein described adapts in real time the assistance provided by the robot aiming at achieving an appropriate target of performance. This results in a system that changes the dynamics and strength of the assistance based on the difficulties experienced by the subject.

In particular, the change of assistance must follow three requirements: *(i)* it must improve subject's performance; *(ii)* it must complement subject's effort; and *(iii)* it must be performed in real time. The first aspect is required to help the subject perform the task correctly: achieving a more efficient performance motivates the patient and significantly increases the power of shoulder and elbow muscles. Furthermore, realizing that the task is performed more precisely may raise patients' morale, especially if integrated with visual feedback as in the case of virtual serious games. The second aspect ensures that the robot allows the patient to lead the execution, such that the task would not be a passive exercise for the subject. Finally, the third aspect requires that the evaluation is performed during the task execution to adjust the assistance while the subject is still performing the therapy.

The main parameters involved in the procedure are:

- j, the performance achieved by the subject in the current lap (expressed in cm as the error in the performance, and reported in (3)); and
- k, the assistance to be provided by the robot in the next lap, in response to the performance obtained (defined as a stiffness constant[2] and therefore expressed in N/m).

Real-Time Execution. The algorithm for performance evaluation described in Sect. 2.1 can be executed at the end of the session to provide an overall evaluation of the subject's performance and an estimation of the assistance required for following therapies. However, in order to adapt the assistance to the subject during the therapy, the performance evaluation algorithm must be executed online at a regular interval of time. According to the type of exercise proposed, this requirement is correctly fulfilled by running the evaluation every time the moving target performs a lap around the trajectory. This strategy allows the algorithm to perform the evaluation on the entire task, so that every part of the analysis processes the same type of information.

Complementing Subject's Effort and Improving the Performance. Complementing subject's effort requires the identification of an appropriate target of performance to be reached, which is directly related to the subject's execution in absence of assistance. To obtain this value, let's define the following:

- j_B as the baseline behavior, which is the performance achieved by the subject when the robot is not providing any assistance; and
- j_T as the performance target, which is the goal to be achieved for the therapy to be effective.

In particular, the relationship between the two parameters is:

$$j_T = f \cdot j_B \qquad (4)$$
$$f \in (0,1) \Rightarrow j_B > j_T$$

The rule $j_B > j_T$ must always be true to improve subject's performances, which means that the error committed at the end of the session must be smaller than the one done at the beginning. More in detail, j_T is related with j_B by a multiplying factor f, which varies in the range $(0,1)$. The effort experienced by the subject depends on the value of this factor: the difference between j_T and j_B must be *small* enough to allow gradual improvements over several sessions. For example, $f = 0.7$ may be an efficient value, so that the subject will be asked to

---

[2] It is worth to point out that despite this is a resistance element, it is actually used as an assistive feature: the force of attraction towards the target increases with higher value of the stiffness, making the task easier.

perform 30% better than his/her baseline. On the other hand, if f had a null value, j_T would push the system to achieve a perfect performance, which would consequently lead the robot to do all the work without any interaction from the subject. However, the final decision is left to the therapist.

Algorithm 1. Overall Processing

---

    input : j_B, j_T, J, i, n, f
    output: j_B, j_T, ΔK

1 **begin**
2    $\Delta K[i] \leftarrow 0$;
3   **if** $i \leq n$ **then**
4   **if** $i = 1$ **then**
5        $j_B \leftarrow 0$;
6      $j_B \leftarrow j_B + J[i]$;
7   **if** $lap = n$ **then**
8      $j_B \leftarrow j_B/n$;
9      $j_T \leftarrow f \cdot j_B$;
10   **if** $i \geq n$ **then**
11      $\Delta K[i] \leftarrow$ tuningStiffness$(J[i], j_T)$;

The evaluation is detailed in Algorithm 1. The procedure includes a series of n laps performed without any assistance, or *familiarization phase*. The baseline j_B is calculated as the average value of j obtained during this phase (lines 3–9).

$$j_B = \frac{\sum_{i=1}^{n} J[i]}{n} \tag{5}$$

During the following laps, the increment of assistance Δk is evaluated based on j and j_T (lines 10–11)[3].

Algorithm 1 is executed every lap to retrieve the increment of stiffness Δk required to reach j_T. In addition to the aforementioned variables, the algorithm also takes as input the array of performance indices J and the number of the current lap i; and provides as output the array of assistance increments ΔK, as well as the updated terms j_B and j_T. Note that Algorithm 1 refers to the term Δk as $\Delta K[i]$ and j as $J[i]$, being the i-th value of arrays ΔK and J, respectively.

Assistance Calculation. The function tuningStiffness, executed at line 11 of Algorithm 1, is the procedure aiming at retrieving Δk. As previously mentioned, if the relationship between assistance and performance was known, then the calculation of Δk would be straightforward once defined the increment of

---

[3] It is worth to point out that Δk may also assume negative values, indicating a decrement of assistance.

performance desired. The strategy herein described proposes an online learning process based on the proportion in (6):

$$\frac{\Delta k}{\Delta j_{des}} = \frac{\Delta k_{prev}}{\Delta j_{mes}} \tag{6}$$

where:

- Δj_{des} is the desired increment of performance $J[i] - j_T$,
- Δj_{mes} is the measured increment of performance $J[i-1] - J[i]$ as result of
- Δk_{prev}, the increment of assistance performed at the end of the previous lap $\Delta K[i-1]$.

Note that both Δj_{des} and Δj_{mes} are calculated such that if the performance improves their values are positive.

More in detail, the proportion aims at calculating Δk based on the increment/decrement of performance achieved during the previous laps. Δj_{des} is multiplied by the ratio r between Δk_{prev} and Δj_{mes}, to obtain the required amount of assistance from the previous trend of the system. The term r can then be considered as a learning factor.

At the first lap with assistance ($i = n$), the amount $\Delta K[n-1]$ will be equal to zero (Algorithm 1, line 2), which means that r requires a start value to let the assistance start. This value is set at 250 by default, considering the maximum amount of stiffness required against a significant error in performance. In particular, $1000\,\text{N/m}$ are provided for an error of $4\,\text{cm}$, which is considered as the value indicating high impairments and poor performance.

$$\Delta K[i] = \Delta j_{des} \cdot \frac{\Delta K[i-1]}{\Delta j_{mes}} = \Delta j_{des} \cdot r \tag{7}$$

It is worth to point out that j_{des} will always be different from j_{mes}. Therefore, the evaluation is based on the amount of performance actually measured as a result of a change in assistance, rather than a fixed multiplying factor.

Filtering Strategies. It is possible to find some anomalies during the evaluation of Δk that make the process incorrect. The following paragraphs will illustrate a series of strategies to solve all the problems that may arise from the formula reported in (7). All the following cases were implemented by observing the response of the system with real subjects wearing the device.

Case 1 - Assumption. The algorithm is based on the following assumption:

"If the assistance increases, the performance improves"

which means that if Δk_{prev} is positive, then also Δj_{mes} is. This assumption can be expressed as in (8), and if it was always true than the control algorithm would be complete. However, this is not always correct: it is possible to obtain oscillatory values of performance when the change in assistance is small. When this anomaly is found, r is set to zero, so that k will not change. The evaluation is then left to the next lap.

$$\frac{\Delta j_{mes}}{|\Delta j_{mes}|} = \frac{\Delta K[i-1]}{|\Delta K[i-1]|} \Rightarrow \frac{\Delta K[i-1]}{\Delta j_{mes}} > 0 \tag{8}$$

Case 2 - Infinite Value. In the case in which Δk is set to a small or null value, then it is possible that the resulting change in performance will be null. If Δj_{mes} is null, then the ratio r is infinite, as shown in (9). When this anomaly is found, r is set to the default value, such that the learning can continue. It is obvious that when the required difference in performance is small, then Δj_{des} will lead to a small Δk even if the value of r is high.

$$\Delta j_{mes} = 0 \Rightarrow r = \frac{\Delta K[i-1]}{\Delta j_{mes}} = \infty \tag{9}$$

Case 3 - Target Achieved. When the target j_T is achieved, no further Δk is required. The expression in (10) shows that, once Δj_{des} is zero, the learning stops and Δk will assume a null value for all the following iterations. With the same motivations of *case 2*, when this anomaly is found, r is set to the default value. However, in practice, the value of j will not be precisely equal to j_T for the rest of the session, due to the oscillatory trend of the performance.

$$\Delta j_{des} = 0 \Rightarrow \Delta K[i] = 0 \Rightarrow \frac{\Delta K[i]}{\Delta j_{mes}} = 0 \Rightarrow \frac{\Delta K[i+1]}{\Delta j_{mes}} = 0 \Rightarrow \dots \tag{10}$$

Case 4 - Assistance Overestimation. If j is lower than j_T for several consecutive laps, then the amount of k provided is too high; a reduction of assistance is required. In this case, it may happen that j remains constant, resulting in a $\Delta j_{mes} \approx 0$. This leads to the following situation: a high value of r pushes k to zero if $|\Delta K[i]| > k \wedge \Delta K[i] < 0$. Whenever the assistance goes to zero, the impairment compensation is canceled; this may cause a sudden movement during the execution, worsening the performance as in (11). In this case, the value of Δk is filtered not to remove the assistance completely. The processing is shown in Algorithm 2 and it simply halves the value required to reach $0\,\text{N/m}$ (lines 6–7). Furthermore, the algorithm also shows the filtering on the upper bound: Δk can not exceed the limit of $1000\,\text{N/m}$ (lines 2–3).

$$\Delta j_{mes} \approx 0 \Rightarrow r = \frac{\Delta K[i-1]}{\Delta j_{mes}} \approx \infty \Rightarrow |\Delta K[i]| \approx \infty \tag{11}$$

On lines 4–5, the algorithm deals with another problem coming from assistance overestimation. In the case in which the subject remains still during the baseline laps, the algorithm will set the assistance at $1000\,\text{N/m}$, which will lead the subject to have a completely passive behavior during the execution. Since the value of j_{i+1} will probably be lower then j_t (enhancing effort), Δk will be higher than required, and the system will take several laps to converge. Whenever k goes from 0 to 1000, Algorithm 2 filters Δk to be halved.

This submodule is executed every lap.

Algorithm 2. Δk Filtering

---

    input : k, Δk
    output: Δk

1 **begin**
2   **if** $k + \Delta k \geq 1000$ **then**
3         $\Delta k \leftarrow 1000 - k$;
4   **if** $k = 0 \wedge \Delta k = 1000$ **then**
5            $\Delta k \leftarrow \Delta k / 2$;
6   **else if** $k + \Delta k \leq 0$ **then**
7         $\Delta k \leftarrow (0 - k)/2$;

Case 5 - Steady Region. As mentioned for *case 3*, it is hard for the user to remain precisely stable on j_T, so adopting the same tuning strategy for any value of j may cause undesired behavior due to this oscillatory trend. Even though the value of Δk is contained by the small value of Δj_{des}, a further control might help the algorithm to stabilize k.

$$|\Delta j_{des}| \leq c_{th} \tag{12}$$

In particular, if the value Δj_{des} ranges within a *Steady Region* defined by the threshold c_{th} (empirically set at 0.15 cm), then $|\Delta k|$ can not exceed 10 N/m; this ensures that the performance will not undergo major changes when the user is close to the target. Algorithm 3 illustrates the filtering process. It is worth to point out that the value 10 N/m can be changed based on it significance.

Algorithm 3. Steady Region Filtering

---

    input : r, Δj_{des}, c_{th}
    output: r

1 **begin**
2   **if** $(|\Delta j_{des}| \leq c_{th}) \wedge (|r \cdot \Delta j_{des}| > 10)$ **then**
3         $r \leftarrow 10/|\Delta j_{des}|$;

Case 6 - Sudden Change. After the algorithm has learned how to obtain the correct amount of assistance for the subject, a sudden change in the execution may deceive the learning process; this can include a situation where the subject gets stuck and resists the robotic force. Such an event is defined in (13), so that the algorithm recognizes this case whenever Δj_{des} exceeds the threshold e_{th}, empirically set to 0.4 cm.

$$|\Delta j_{des}| \geq e_{th} \tag{13}$$

When this anomaly is found, r is set to the default value, so that a fast response will be provided against a high error.

Case 7 - Assistance Transitory Phase. The Sudden Change event does not need to be managed at every lap. It is safe to assume that the value of j will be high during the first laps, since the algorithm will not have performed any evaluation yet about the assistance required. In this situation, *case 6* will always be true during the first laps. To prevent this problem, the first laps of the session are considered as part of a Transitory Phase.

More in detail, this phase ends the first time j enters the Steady Region, so when (12) becomes true; and it starts again every time a Sudden Change takes place, so when (13) was true in the previous lap. It is obvious that the Steady Region and the Transitory Phase are mutually exclusive.

Case 8 - Recording Transitory Phase. Robot control strategies mostly ensure that the device moves smoother whenever a high force is suddenly applied. This could be the case in which the therapy starts with no assistance, the patient is not able to move the arm alone, and the tuning algorithm sets a high Δk. However, this kind of precaution let another problem arise. Assuming that the therapy starts without any assistance ($K[n] = 0$ N/m), at lap $i = n + 1$ the algorithm will provide a certain value of Δk aiming at reaching Δj_{des}. The errors committed during the time required to reach the target will cause the next lap to have a value of Δj_{mes} significantly higher than Δj_{des}, mostly because these errors will be aggravated by the device reaction time. This high value of Δj_{mes} will deceive the algorithm, since j will be higher than the value one could expect from the given Δk. Consequently, at lap $i = n + 2$, the ratio r will be calculated on erroneous results, will produce a high Δk, and will hinder the algorithm convergence.

A second Transitory Phase is thus introduced: whenever the stiffness goes from 0 N/m to any other value, all the points recorded from the robot are discarded until the end effector gets close to the target.

3   Experimental Validation

A preliminary experiment has been carried out to show the algorithm's potential and its reaction to the human behavior.

3.1   Experiment Description

The algorithm has been tested with fifteen healthy subjects with no known neuromuscular disorder affecting their upper limbs (thirteen males, 33 ± 5 yrs old; and two females, 30 ± 1 yrs old). The subjects were asked to wear ALEx exoskeleton and perform 30 laps around an elliptical trajectory (9×16 cm) placed on the subject's coronal plane, with the target moving at the constant angular speed of 0.60 rad/s.

The assessment was composed of two phases:

– a *Familiarization* phase, where the algorithm retrieves j_B during the first 5 laps; and
– a *Motor Adaptation* phase, where the algorithm provides the assistance required to reach j_T, during the rest of the session.

The relationship between j_B and j_T has been set at $f = 0.6$.

To simulate arm impairment, a disturbance factor has been introduced on the end effector for all the duration of the experiment, such that the robot pushes the arm of the subjects slightly away from the trajectory.

3.2   Results and Discussion

Figure 3(a) shows the results for a single subject, while 3(b) shows the results averaged over fifteen subjects. The plot presents the trend of both assistance and performance (in average and standard deviation for Fig. 3(b)).

During the first five laps, the plot shows a high error due to the disturbance effect, defining the baseline behavior of the subjects without assistance. At lap 6, when the algorithm provides the assistance value to the robot, the system does not fall into the Transitory Phase, since the subjects were performing a restrained error with respect to a subject that would not move the robot at all (0.8 cm on average against the 4.0 cm limit set on Sect. 2.2). Therefore, in the following laps until the end of the execution, the trend is always within the Steady Region, being the difference between j and j_T always lower than $c_{th} = 0.15$ cm.

The amount of assistance varies from 77 to 290 N/m among the fifteen subjects, a low value when compared to the maximum allowed (1000 N/m). This indicates that the algorithm is able to cope with artificial disturbance without taking control of the execution, but allowing the subjects to lead the game. Disturbances derived from impaired limbs may behave differently, according to subjects' physical situation. However, it is likely to assume that for minor disabilities the trend will not differ dramatically. Furthermore, the assistance trend also shows that the system always reaches the target for all the subjects having different degrees of performance, highlighting its adaptability.

Finally, the case of the subject presented in Fig. 3(a) shows that, the assistance provided by the robot decreases while the performance remains slightly stationary. As discussed in our previous work [9], this might be evidence of facilitation in the acquisition of motor learning skills.

To sum up, the findings of this test have shown that the tuning algorithm meets the target in a reasonable time, and remains slightly stable during the following iterations. This indicates that the algorithm fits the requirements and it might be considered as a good strategy for clinical usage.

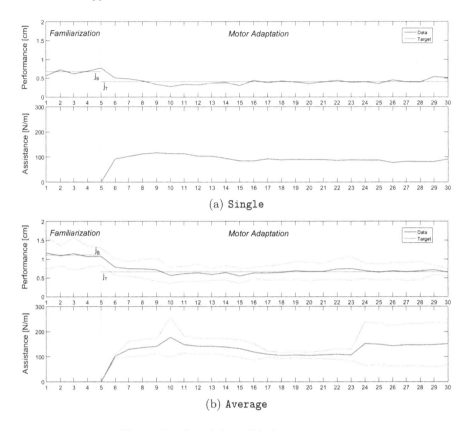

(a) Single

(b) Average

Fig. 3. Results of the validation assessment.

4 Conclusion

We proposed an improved version of our algorithm for real-time assistance tuning, to be exploited in neurorehabilitation scenarios involving upper limb mobility. The procedure can be used with any kind of active exoskeleton and without prior knowledge about the patients' abilities. Results showed that the system fits the requirements, providing real-time assist-as-needed in accordance with subjects' performance. Such a system can be used to promote motor skill learning and neuro-motor recovery, motivating the patients efficiently.

Future plans will include a clinical assessment on real post-stroke patients to attest whether the system promotes efficient motor recovery.

Acknowledgment. This work has been partially supported by RONDA project, code 4042.16092014. 066000065, funded by Regione Toscana, Italy, within the FAS 'Salute' 2014 program.

References

1. Bütefisch, C., Hummelsheim, H., Denzler, P., Mauritz, K.-H.: Repetitive training of isolated movements improves the outcome of motor rehabilitation of the centrally paretic hand. J. Neurol. Sci. **130**(1), 59–68 (1995)
2. Kwakkel, G., Wagenaar, R.C., Twisk, J.W., Lankhorst, G.J., Koetsier, J.C.: Intensity of leg and arm training after primary middle-cerebral-artery stroke: a randomised trial. Lancet **354**(9174), 191–196 (1999)
3. Sunderland, A., Tinson, D., Bradley, E., Fletcher, D., Hewer, R.L., Wade, D.: Enhanced physical therapy improves recovery of arm function after stroke. A randomised controlled trial. J. Neurol. Neurosurg. Psychiatry **55**(7), 530–535 (1992)
4. Bayona, N.A., Bitensky, J., Salter, K., Teasell, R.: The role of task-specific training in rehabilitation therapies. Top. Stroke Rehabil. **12**(3), 58–65 (2005)
5. Norouzi-Gheidari, N., Archambault, P.S., Fung, J.: Effects of robot-assisted therapy on stroke rehabilitation in upper limbs: systematic review and meta-analysis of the literature. J. Rehabil. Res. Dev. **49**(4), 479 (2012)
6. Nykanen, K.: The effectiveness of robot-aided upper limb therapy in stroke rehabilitation: a systematic review of randomized controlled studies. Master's thesis, University of Jyvaskyla, Institute of Health Sciences, Physiotherapy (2010)
7. Colombo, R., Sterpi, I., Mazzone, A., Delconte, C., Pisano, F.: Taking a lesson from patients' recovery strategies to optimize training during robot-aided rehabilitation. IEEE Trans. Neural Syst. Rehabil. Eng. **20**(3), 276–285 (2012)
8. Casadio, M., Sanguineti, V.: Learning, retention, and slacking: a model of the dynamics of recovery in robot therapy. IEEE Trans. Neural Syst. Rehabil. Eng. **20**(3), 286–296 (2012)
9. Stroppa, F., Marcheschi, S., Mastronicola, N., Loconsole, C., Frisoli, A.: Online adaptive assistance control in robot-based neurorehabilitation therapy. In: 2017 International Conference on Rehabilitation Robotics (ICORR), pp. 628–633. IEEE (2017)
10. Squeri, V., Basteris, A., Sanguineti, V.: Adaptive regulation of assistance 'as needed' in robot-assisted motor skill learning and neuro-rehabilitation. In: 2011 IEEE International Conference on Rehabilitation Robotics, pp. 1–6. IEEE (2011)
11. Guidali, M., Schlink, P., Duschau-Wicke, A., Riener, R.: Online learning and adaptation of patient support during ADL training. In: 2011 IEEE International Conference on Rehabilitation Robotics (ICORR), pp. 1–6. IEEE (2011)
12. Pirondini, E., Coscia, M., Marcheschi, S., Roas, G., Salsedo, F., Frisoli, A., Bergamasco, M., Micera, S.: Evaluation of the effects of the arm light exoskeleton on movement execution and muscle activities: a pilot study on healthy subjects. J. NeuroEng. Rehabil. **13**(1), 1 (2016)

Assessing Articulatory Modalities for Intercommunication Using Vibrotactile HMDs

Victor Adriel de Jesus Oliveira$^{(\boxtimes)}$, Luciana Nedel$^{(\boxtimes)}$, and Anderson Maciel$^{(\boxtimes)}$

INF, Universidade Federal do Rio Grande do Sul (UFRGS), Porto Alegre, Brazil
{vajoliveira,nedel,amaciel}@inf.ufrgs.br

Abstract. In computer-mediated tactile intercommunication, users not only have to perceive tactile cues but also have to articulate them to carry a two-way interaction. By pressing buttons or performing specific gestures, interlocutors can exchange tactile signals but are not able to extrapolate the given vocabulary. When more access to hardware parameters is provided instead, interlocutors can have more autonomy. Yet, changes in articulation might produce tactile signals that are not perceptually suitable, hindering mutual understanding during intercommunication. In this paper, we explore the trade-off between freedom of articulation and mutual understanding by comparing three articulatory approaches. Dyads performed a collaborative task using their vibrotactile HMDs to communicate. Their performance during the task, as well as mutual understanding, workload and easiness, were assessed as a function of each articulatory condition. Results show that static and mediating conditions support higher performance and mutual understanding compared to a dynamic articulation.

Keywords: Haptic articulation · Tactile communication
Vibrotactile HMD

1 Introduction

Touch is our most social sense. However, despite its importance to interpersonal interaction, tactile communication across a distance is not well supported by current technology [13,14,33]. To mitigate such deficiency, a number of systems have been proposed to mechanically simulate interpersonal touch [17,35]. Force-feedback and cutaneous stimulation are applied to enhance the sense of presence in virtual environments [1,30], to support collaborative manipulation of virtual objects [19,20], for remote training [8], and to provide a multisensory interaction [3,28]. However, only a handful of previous works applies touch in a way that teams can use expressive tactile signals to intercommunicate [5–7].

When it comes to tactile communication, vibrating stimuli are broadly used. That is because a range of different parameters can be used for encoding information with vibration [4,34]. In addition, it is easy to construct tactile displays

© Springer International Publishing AG, part of Springer Nature 2018
D. Prattichizzo et al. (Eds.): EuroHaptics 2018, LNCS 10894, pp. 526–538, 2018.
https://doi.org/10.1007/978-3-319-93399-3_45

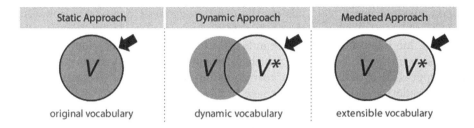

Fig. 1. A Static approach preserves the original tactile vocabulary (V), while a Dynamic approach allows interlocutors to express it in different ways and even to include new signals to it (V*). A Mediated approach though can preserve the given vocabulary and still allows the addition of new signals.

that can be worn in different parts of the body by using vibration motors [9]. As the skin around the head is known to be one of the regions of the human body most sensitive to mechanical stimulation [29], a number of recent studies have been proposed in which tactile actuators are embedded to virtual reality headsets [22,25,27] to provide warning and guidance cues on the user's head. The so-called tactile Head-Mounted Displays [26,29] allow for the conventional VR headset to be transformed into a complete item for multisensory interaction. However, when interacting with peers in a collaborative scenario, people are still not able to use haptics as a way to exchange information.

To solve this, we propose a device that is built on the back of a vibrotactile HMD (i.e. at the opposed side to the lenses) to capture touch gestures and translate them into tactile feedback. Back-of-HMD interfaces were proposed before to support interaction with VR content [15,16] but never for the articulation of tactile signals[1]. By having the articulatory device integrated with the tactile display, the user would be interacting with the environment and other users by touching on the same body area where the tactile feedback is delivered in a direct and intuitive way [23]. Such on-body interaction offers the advantage of leveraging human proprioception as an extra feedback mechanism [32]. Yet, the impact of the interface on the communication process it is still unknown. For instance, how the translation between articulatory gestures and tactile signals must be performed.

In previous works, users could trigger tactile cues by pressing buttons [6], performing specific gestures [5,7], or even selecting graphical icons on a display [21]. However, since the interface delimitates the articulation of the signals, it hinders the users' autonomy. As a consequence, the given tactile vocabulary may become stagnant and restrictive in two-way interactions (this can be called a *static approach*). Instead, users can have more freedom to articulate tactile cues by receiving more access to the hardware parameters. Such approach increases user's autonomy and allows users to adapt the tactile signals according to their

---

[1] As our utterances are related to our control over our vocal apparatus, tactile articulation should be related to our control over tactile parameters [23].

communication needs [23] (this can be called a *dynamic approach*). However, variability in articulation might produce tactile signals that are not perceptually suitable, hindering mutual understanding during intercommunication. Here, we propose a *mediated approach* in which small variations of articulatory gestures are suppressed to not affect the corresponding tactile signals, but completely new articulations still can produce new tactile signals (see Fig. 1).

In this paper, we explore the trade-off between freedom of articulation and mutual understanding by comparing three articulatory approaches: static, dynamic, and mediated articulation. Each articulatory condition varies in how much the articulatory gesture affects the final tactile signal. First, we designed and assessed a set of vibrotactile signals to support tactile guidance. Then, subjects were paired to perform a collaborative task in an immersive virtual setup using a vibrotactile HMD and the given tactile vocabulary to guide each other. We assessed their performance during the task as a function of each articulatory condition. In addition, we assessed subjective measures, such as workload, easiness, and mutual understanding during the task for each condition.

2   Methods

2.1   Subjects

Twenty subjects participated voluntarily in the study (14 males and 6 females). Their ages ranged from 17 to 26 years (M = 21, SD = 2.5). They participated in pairs (i.e. 10 dyads) and each pair knew each other before the experiment. All subjects read and agreed with an Informed Consent Form before the experiment as required by the Helsinki declaration.

Handedness was assessed with an Edinburgh Handedness Inventory [12] and fifteen subjects were shown to be right-handed, while the remaining were marked as mixed-handed. Three subjects reported that they never used a VR headset or any tracking device before. In addition, eleven subjects reported having some visual problem, namely eight cases of Myopia (one of them also presented Keratoconus) and three cases of Astigmatism (one of them with Hyperopia). No correlation was found between the subject condition and their performance during the experiment.

2.2   Apparatus

Vibrotactile Display. Two vibrotactile headbands were built according to the literature on head stimulation [24]. Each headband had seven electromechanical tactors. The tactors are controlled with an Arduino Mega ADK board and Adafruit DRV2605L haptic controllers (see Fig. 2 (left)). Each tactor - 10 mm Linear Resonant Actuator, 4 mm type (C10-100 Precision Microdrives) - was attached to a piece of Velcro to be easily worn around the head.

For each headband, five tactors were placed at equal distance from the center of the forehead over the Cardinal and Collateral points (with no tactor in the back of the head). Two extra tactors were set 5 mm apart from the central tactor to provide additional resolution around the sagittal plane. Each headband was combined with an Oculus Rift. Movements of the head were used for updating the vibration parameters in the headband. Stimuli were delivered at 175 Hz.

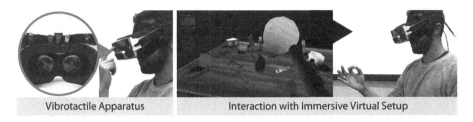

| Vibrotactile Apparatus | Interaction with Immersive Virtual Setup |

Fig. 2. (left) Vibrotactile HMD with articulatory screen. (right) Subjects use their hands to manipulate objects and articulate vibrotactile cues.

Back-of-Device Touch Screen. We have attached a Leap Motion device and a smartphone Samsung Galaxy S6 SM-G920F (143.4 × 70.5 × 6.8 mm) to the back of each Oculus Rift to serve as an input device. The multitouch screen has 5.1 in. with a resolution of 1440 × 2560 pixels and weighted 138 g.

An application was developed to capture touch gestures on the smartphone and it was connected to the server through TCP (Transmission Control Protocol) channel to avoid packet loss. Each packet carried touch coordinates, touch duration, and the offset from the previous touch. As the smartphone has a Super AMOLED capacitive touchscreen, a black screen allowed long hours of use without recharging the phone.

The overall latency of the wireless network was about 97 ms (SD = 137.8). Considering the network latency and the haptic apparatus, with the typical rise time for the actuator of 35 ms and a typical lag time of 12 ms, the overall latency was about 144 ms. For the Leap Motion, the render time was 16 ms.

2.3 Collaborative Task

To understand how the articulatory freedom would affect tactile communication, we designed a collaborative haptic guidance task (see Fig. 3). Every two subjects had to collaborate to prepare a recipe by taking ingredients in a given order. Either partner knows which ingredient the other has to select and throw into the cauldron in a given moment, but the only way to communicate such information is by activating vibrotactile cues on the other user.

During the collaborative task, subjects could use their hands to manipulate the ingredients placed on their own table. They also could see which ingredient was grabbed by the other, but they could not talk with the other so we could see how they would interact using only the haptic channel.

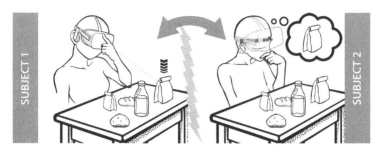

Fig. 3. Subjects had to communicate only with vibrotactile cues to guide each other during the collaborative task.

2.4   Stimuli Set and Conditions

The index finger on the back of a mobile device may be better suited to simple 1D movements (particularly horizontal ones) [36]. When it comes to on-body interaction, 1D gestures (e.g. flicking) are better suited than 2D ones (e.g. pinching) [32]. Thus, simple gestures (e.g. tap, double tap, long tap, and swipe) were chosen for articulation and an initial set of five vibrotactile signals were proposed according to the actions required by the task. After a perceptual adjustment, the final vibrotactile vocabulary was composed of only three sets of signals: Positive signal, Direction signals, and Right/Left signals (see Fig. 4).

The *Direction* of an ingredient is given from an egocentric perspective. If the subject performs a long tap anywhere on the screen while facing an ingredient, the tactor facing the ingredient position starts to vibrate indicating its position. The other subject feels a vibration and turns the face towards the target felt until the vibration is perceived on the center of the forehead, indicating that the subject is now facing the proper ingredient. Such stimulus is conventionally used for guidance [24]. When a subject grabs an ingredient, the partner can confirm the selection with a *Positive* signal using a double tap. The subject can also say that an ingredient is more on the left or more on the right of the table with a swipe towards the correspondent direction. This *Left/Right* signal was also used before for guidance using a vibrotactile HMD [26]. The burst duration for all signals has 200 ms as well as the interval between two bursts. Sequences are activated without interval between bursts. To make sure subjects are aware of the stimuli they produce on their team partners, they also receive the same vibrating feedback.

In the *Static articulation*, the system only recognizes the three predefined gestures (double tap, long tap, and swipe). Even swipe gestures of different lengths always trigger the same Left/Right signal. Any other gesture (e.g. short taps) are suppressed[2]. In the *Dynamic articulation*, every signal is produced according to the articulated gesture, and it can change in position and duration. Thus, the position of vibration, length of a sequence, and burst/interburst duration are

---

[2] Suppressed signals are not rendered and the person who articulated the gesture is aware that the gesture was not recognized by the system.

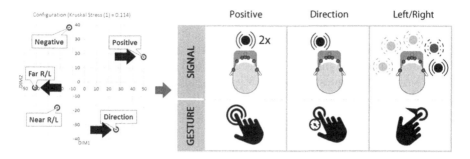

Fig. 4. (left) MDS solution for the adjustment of an initial vocabulary in 2 dimensions. The stress is a measure of the fitness of the space's dimension based on perceived distances between stimuli [34]; (right) Gestures and resulting vibrotactile feedback.

modified as a function of the articulatory gesture (e.g. a slow swipe will result in a slow sequence of actuation). When it comes to the *Mediated condition*, the system also recognizes variations of the three predefined gestures. However, other gestures are not suppressed (e.g. a slow swipe will not slow down the sequence of actuation, but short taps are triggered according to the tapped position).

2.5   Experimental Protocol

Each subject filled out a demographic questionnaire and read instructions before starting the experiment. Then, each subject had to perform an Interpretation test, where the subject had to feel a vibrotactile signal and answer what is the meaning of that signal. Ten signals were presented in a randomized order. Subjects did not practice before the task, so it served to reinforce the learning of the vibrotactile vocabulary as well.

Finally, subjects had to perform the collaborative task in dyads. Tests were done in a dedicated room. Each subject was set in a swivel chair at one of the sides of the room. Each one of them was wearing a VR headset with the vibrotactile headband, the articulatory screen, and a Leap Motion mounted on the headset. Subjects had an ambient sound (music) played on their Oculus headphones and were instructed to not talk to each other.

Every subject had ten ingredients each (total of twenty) to select in a given order. The selection order was randomized across sessions. They could not see each other, but they viewed the table from the same perspective. They selected ingredients by gazing towards the object and grabbing with a pinch gesture (captured by the Leap Motion, as shown in Fig. 2 (right)). A small reticle was shown at the center of the field of view to provide a reference for selection. Subjects performed a practice session to understand the elements of the virtual scene. Then they performed three sessions of the collaborative task. Each session corresponded to an articulatory condition and the sessions were counterbalanced across dyads. The whole experiment took in average 50 min.

The performance was assessed as the number of correct ingredients selected during the task, duration, and use of tactile signals. After each session, subjects filled out a Mutual Understanding questionnaire [2] and a Single Easy Question (SEQ) [31] as usability measure. Subjects also had to fill out a NASA Task Load Index (NASA TLX) questionnaire [18] to self-judge their task load.

3   Results

3.1   Interpretation of Tactile Signals

Table 1 shows the confusion matrix for the interpretation task. Without having experienced the stimuli before, subjects were able to properly interpret the meaning of more than 80% of each tactile signal. The Direction Signal, which corresponds to a long vibration towards a given direction, was the most mistaken with 83% of right answers. In this case, 10% of the trials were marked as a Left/Right signal that corresponds to a sequence of actuation moving to the left or to the right.

Table 1. Signal interpretation confusion Matrix, N = 3 [Response (%)]

	"Positive"	"Direction"	"Left/Right"	" "
Positive signal	**96.67**	0.00	0.00	3.33
Direction signal	3.33	**83.33**	10.00	3.33
Left/Right signal	0.00	3.75	**92.50**	3.75

3.2   Performance and Behavior

Figure 5 shows the average performance of dyads for each articulatory condition.

An One-Way ANOVA test shows that the articulatory modality has an effect on the amount of items selected by mistake during the task [$F(2,27) = 4.7339$, $p = 0.017$] (see Fig. 5 (left)). Post-hoc comparisons with Student's t-test indicated that with the Dynamic articulation dyads mistake more items compared to the use of Static ($p < 0.05$) and Mediated articulation ($p < 0.01$).

When it comes to the total time for performing each task, there was no significant difference between conditions (see Fig. 5 (center-second axis)). However, the articulatory conditions presented an effect on the time it took to select the correct item [$F(2,27) = 4.7588$, $p = 0.0166$] (see Fig. 5 (center-first axis)). When using the Dynamic condition, dyads take more time to find the correct item compared to Static ($p < 0.05$) and Mediated modalities ($p < 0.01$).

In average, dyads exchange more tactile signals per second using Mediated and Dynamic articulation than the Static modality, with no significant difference between the amount of articulated signals for each condition (see Fig. 5 (right-second axis)). Yet, there is an effect of the articulatory modality on the amount

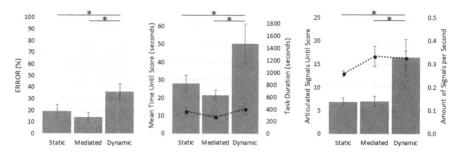

Fig. 5. Bar plots represent left axis and line plots represent right axis. (left) Dynamic articulation yields more errors (M = 36%; SE = 6.3) than Static (M = 19%; SE = 5.5) and Mediated (M = 14%; SE = 4.1); (center) It takes more time to select a correct item with Dynamic articulation (M = 50 s; SE = 10.8) compared to Static (M = 28 s; SE = 4.5) and Mediated (M = 21 s; SE = 2.8). Mean time for each task was of 348 s; (right) It takes more signals to indicate the correct item with Dynamic articulation (M = 16; SE = 3.8) compared to Static (M = 6; SE = 0.9) and Mediated (M = 7; SE = 1.1). Subjects expressed less signals per second with Static condition.

of signals exchanged to select an item correctly [F(2,27) = 5.3676, p = 0.0109] (see Fig. 5 (right-first axis)). Post-hoc comparisons indicated that, to choose the correct item, dyads have to articulate more signals with the Dynamic modality compared to both Static and Mediated modalities (p < 0.01).

3.3   User Experience

Figure 6 shows the subjects' evaluation for mutual understanding and usability during the collaborative task for each articulatory condition.

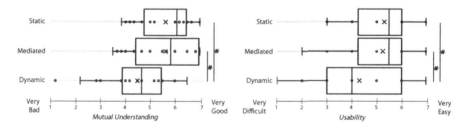

Fig. 6. (left) Mutual Understanding was better for Static (M = 5.6; SE = 0.3) and Mediated (M = 5.6; SE = 0.4) compared to Dynamic articulation (M = 4.5; SE = 0.4); (right). It was also easier to perform the task with Static (M = 5.3; SE = 0.4) and Mediated (M = 5.3; SE = 0.4) conditions compared to Dynamic (M = 4.3; SE = 0.5) condition according to the SEQ scale.

Figure 6 (left) shows that the articulatory modality has an effect on mutual understanding [F(2,57) = 5.6857, p = 0.0059]. Post-hoc comparisons indicated that understanding a partner during the collaborative task is more difficult when using the Dynamic modality compared to the remaining modalities ($p < 0.01$).

Figure 6 (right) shows that there is also an effect of the articulatory modality on usability [$F(2,57) = 3.1708$, $p = 0.0481$]. It is harder to perform the task using the Dynamic modality over both Static and Mediated modalities ($p < 0.05$).

The overall workload did not vary significantly across conditions (see Fig. 7). However, articulatory conditions had an effect on the Performance dimension for the NASA-TLX [$F(2,57) = 4.7991$, $p = 0.0118$]. The perceived performance when using the Dynamic articulation was more affected than the performance for Static ($p < 0.05$) and Mediated modalities ($p < 0.01$).

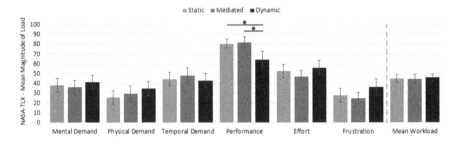

Fig. 7. Mean scores from NASA-TLX. Mean workload did not vary significantly between Static (M = 44.7; SE = 3.8), Mediated (M = 44.5; SE = 4.4), and Dynamic (M = 45.8; SE = 3.6) conditions. The perceived performance, though, was worse for Dynamic condition (M = 64; SE = 8.5) compared to Static (M = 80; SE = 4.6) and Mediated (M = 82; SE = 5.5).

4   Discussion and Conclusion

The literature on tactile communication supports the clear understanding of how people perceive and process vibrotactile signals [4,34] and how to construct and validate vibrotactile vocabularies to support different tasks [6,23,26]. However, there is still a lot to understand about computer-mediated interpersonal touch [13,14,33]. For instance, tactile cues are usually rendered reactively by the system, while an important part of social interaction is to perceive the others' needs and intentions and *proactively* act on these perceptions [11]. Therefore, it is important to understand not only how people perceive tactile cues but how people articulate signals in order to communicate with others. In this paper, we proposed an interface for tactile articulation and assessed how the differences in articulation can affect communication between partners in a virtual setup. Our contribution is to validate approaches that can be applied for tactile intercommunication in both physical or virtual applications, for close or remote tasks, with or without the assistance of other sensory modalities.

In this paper, we show that a dynamic vocabulary, that has position and duration transformed according to the articulatory gesture, is more difficult to understand during a collaborative task. The changes in the given stimuli set affect communication, and therefore the performance of the dyad during the task. Like in any conversation, the participants try to establish whether what has been said has been understood (in a grounding process [10]). For the tactile intercommunication, the grounding process can be expressed in terms of the time and the number of signals necessary to establish what is a correct item to be selected. Thus, the Dynamic condition was shown to take more time and more signals in the grounding process. It was also more difficult to understand and to perform when using such modality.

Previous work has shown that interlocutors are able to modify a tactile vocabulary according to their needs using a dynamic approach [23]. With the Dynamic approach, subjects might reproduce signals in different ways or even create new ones. Thus, the tactile vocabulary that emerges during the tactile communication might differ from the original. However, in our experiment, dyads did not have the time or the complementary channels to agree with variations of a given signal or to the addition of new signals.

Tactile feedback is especially useful when other senses are overloaded or unavailable. With the ability to articulate tactile signals, subjects can receive feedback from peers (e.g. a specialist from distance) instead of receiving feedback only from a machine. For that, a Static articulation is well suited. Yet, results show that a Mediated condition did not vary significantly in performance, usability, and mutual understanding compared to the Static condition. Moreover, the Mediated condition allowed subjects to vary a few parameters and to express more signals than the given stimuli set. Therefore, it is reasonable to assume that there is an advantage in preserving the given vocabulary to some extent and still allow users to extrapolate the given vocabulary to some extent to provide flexibility during the conversation.

Future works should address the interaction between time and position on perception due to the transformations during articulation. Future works would also involve making the Mediated condition smarter. By using tools such as machine learning it is possible to build an interface that corrects articulatory gestures to preserve the tactile signals and guarantee its perceptual adjustment. In addition, the interface can learn new articulatory gestures and add the corresponding signals to the vocabulary. Future works should also verify how peers can apply tactile communication to support each other in different tasks, such as remote guidance, triggering warnings, and exchanging affective information.

Acknowledgments. The authors thank CAPES and CNPq-Brazil for the financial support to the provision of post-graduate scholarship. The authors also thank the subjects whose participation made this study possible. We also acknowledge FAPERGS (project 17/2551-0001192-9) and CNPq-Brazil (project 311353/2017-7).

References

1. Ansar, A., Rodrigues, D., Desai, J.P., Daniilidis, K., Kumar, V., Campos, M.F.: Visual and haptic collaborative tele-presence. Comput. Graph. **25**(5), 789–798 (2001)
2. Biocca, F., Harms, C., Gregg, J.: The networked minds measure of social presence: Pilot test of the factor structure and concurrent validity. In: 4th Annual International Workshop on Presence, Philadelphia, PA, pp. 1–9 (2001)
3. Brave, S., Dahley, A.: inTouch: a medium for Haptic interpersonal communication. In: CHI 1997 Extended Abstracts on Human Factors in Computing Systems, pp. 363–364. ACM (1997)
4. Brewster, S., Brown, L.M.: Tactons: structured tactile messages for non-visual information display. In: Proceedings of the Fifth Conference on Australasian User Interface, vol. 28, pp. 15–23. Australian Computer Society, Inc. (2004)
5. Brown, L.M., Williamson, J.: Shake2Talk: multimodal messaging for interpersonal communication. In: Oakley, I., Brewster, S. (eds.) HAID 2007. LNCS, vol. 4813, pp. 44–55. Springer, Heidelberg (2007). https://doi.org/10.1007/978-3-540-76702-2_6
6. Chan, A., MacLean, K., McGrenere, J.: Designing haptic icons to support collaborative turn-taking. Int. J. Hum.-Comput. Stud. **66**(5), 333–355 (2008)
7. Chang, A., O'Modhrain, S., Jacob, R., Gunther, E., Ishii, H.: ComTouch: design of a vibrotactile communication device. In: Proceedings of the 4th Conference on Designing Interactive Systems: Processes, Practices, Methods, and Techniques, DIS 2002, pp. 312–320. ACM, New York (2002)
8. Chebbi, B., Lazaroff, D., Bogsany, F., Liu, P.X., Niy, L., Rossi, M.: Design and implementation of a collaborative virtual Haptic surgical training system. In: 2005 IEEE International Conference on Mechatronics and Automation, vol. 1, pp. 315–320. IEEE (2005)
9. Cholewiak, R., Brill, J., Schwab, A.: Vibrotactile localization on the abdomen: effects of place and space. Percept. Psychophysics **66**(6), 970–987 (2004)
10. Clark, H.H., Brennan, S.E., et al.: Grounding in communication. Perspect. Socially Shared Cogn. **13**(1991), 127–149 (1991)
11. Cramer, H., Kemper, N., Amin, A., Wielinga, B., Evers, V.: give me a hug: the effects of touch and autonomy on people's responses to embodied social agents. Comput. Anim. Virtual Worlds **20**(2–3), 437–445 (2009)
12. Dragovic, M.: Towards an improved measure of the edinburgh handedness inventory: a one-factor congeneric measurement model using confirmatory factor analysis. Laterality Asymmetries Body Brain Cogn. **9**(4), 411–419 (2004)
13. Field, T.: Touch, 2nd edn. MIT Press, Cambridge (2001)
14. Gallace, A., Spence, C.: The science of interpersonal touch: an overview. Neurosci. Biobehav. Rev. **34**(2), 246–259 (2010)
15. Gugenheimer, J., Dobbelstein, D., Winkler, C., Haas, G., Rukzio, E.: FaceTouch: enabling touch interaction in display fixed UIs for mobile virtual reality. In: Proceedings of the 29th Annual Symposium on User Interface Software and Technology, UIST 2016, pp. 49–60. ACM, New York (2016)
16. Gugenheimer, J., Stemasov, E., Sareen, H., Rukzio, E.: FaceDisplay: enabling multi-user interaction for mobile virtual reality. In: Proceedings of the 2017 CHI Conference Extended Abstracts on Human Factors in Computing Systems, pp. 369–372. ACM (2017)

17. Haans, A., IJsselsteijn, W.: Mediated social touch: a review of current research and future directions. Virtual Reality **9**(2–3), 149–159 (2006)
18. Hart, S.G.: NASA-task load index (NASA-TLX); 20 years later. In: Proceedings of the Human Factors and Ergonomics Society Annual Meeting, vol. 50, pp. 904–908. Sage Publications (2006)
19. Hashimoto, T., Ishibashi, Y.: Group synchronization control over Haptic media in a networked real-time game with collaborative work. In: Proceedings of 5th ACM SIGCOMM Workshop on Network and System Support for Games, p. 8. ACM (2006)
20. Iglesias, R., Prada, E., Uribe, A., Garcia-Alonso, A., Casado, S., Gutierrez, T.: Assembly simulation on collaborative haptic virtual environments (2007)
21. Israr, A., Zhao, S., Schneider, O.: Exploring embedded Haptics for social networking and interactions. In: Proceedings of the 33rd Annual ACM Conference Extended Abstracts on Human Factors in Computing Systems, pp. 1899–1904. ACM (2015)
22. de Jesus Oliveira, V.A., Brayda, L., Nedel, L., Maciel, A.: Designing a vibrotactile head-mounted display for spatial awareness in 3D spaces. IEEE Trans. Vis. Comput. Graph. **23**(4), 1409–1417 (2017)
23. de Jesus Oliveira, V.A., Nedel, L., Maciel, A.: Proactive Haptic articulation for intercommunication in collaborative virtual environments. In: 2016 IEEE Symposium on 3D User Interfaces (3DUI), pp. 91–94. IEEE (2016)
24. de Jesus Oliveira, V.A., Nedel, L., Maciel, A., Brayda, L.: Localized magnification in vibrotactile HMDs for accurate spatial awareness. In: Bello, F., Kajimoto, H., Visell, Y. (eds.) EuroHaptics 2016. LNCS, vol. 9775, pp. 55–64. Springer, Cham (2016). https://doi.org/10.1007/978-3-319-42324-1_6
25. Kaul, O.B., Rohs, M.: HapticHead: 3D guidance and target acquisition through a vibrotactile grid. In: Proceedings of the 2016 CHI Conference Extended Abstracts on Human Factors in Computing Systems, pp. 2533–2539. ACM (2016)
26. Kerdegari, H., Kim, Y., Prescott, T.J.: Head-mounted sensory augmentation device: designing a tactile language. IEEE Trans. Haptics **9**(3), 376–386 (2016)
27. Núñez, O.J.A., Lange, M., Steinicke, F., Bruder, G.: Vibrotactile assistance for user guidance towards selection targets in VR and the cognitive resources involved. In: 2017 IEEE Symposium on 3D User Interfaces (3DUI), pp. 95–98, March 2017
28. Oakley, I., Brewster, S., Gray, P.: Can you feel the force? an investigation of Haptic collaboration in shared editors. In: proceedings of EuroHaptics, pp. 54–59 (2001)
29. Rash, C.E., Russo, M.B., Letowski, T.R., Schmeisser, E.T.: Helmet-mounted displays: sensation, perception and cognition issues. Technical report, DTIC Document (2009)
30. Sallnäs, E.L., Rassmus-Gröhn, K., Sjöström, C.: Supporting presence in collaborative environments by haptic force feedback. ACM Trans. Comput.-Hum. Interact. (TOCHI) **7**(4), 461–476 (2000)
31. Sauro, J., Dumas, J.S.: Comparison of three one-question, post-task usability questionnaires. In: Proceedings of the SIGCHI Conference on Human Factors in Computing Systems. ACM (2009)
32. Serrano, M., Ens, B.M., Irani, P.P.: Exploring the use of hand-to-face input for interacting with head-worn displays. In: Proceedings of the 32nd Annual ACM Conference on Human Factors in Computing Systems, pp. 3181–3190. ACM (2014)
33. Smith, J., MacLean, K.: Communicating emotion through a haptic link: design space and methodology. Int. J. Hum.-Comput. Stud. **65**(4), 376–387 (2007)

34. Ternes, D., MacLean, K.E.: Designing large sets of Haptic icons with rhythm. In: Ferre, M. (ed.) EuroHaptics 2008. LNCS, vol. 5024, pp. 199–208. Springer, Heidelberg (2008). https://doi.org/10.1007/978-3-540-69057-3_24
35. Van Erp, J.B., Toet, A.: Social touch in human-computer interaction. Front. Dig. Humanit. **2**, 2 (2015)
36. Wobbrock, J.O., Myers, B.A., Aung, H.H.: The performance of hand postures in front-and back-of-device interaction for mobile computing. Int. J. Hum.-Comput. Stud. **66**(12), 857–875 (2008)

Operation Guidance Method for Touch Devices by Direction Presentation Using Anisotropic Roughness

Masato Kobayashi[✉], Takahiro Shitara[✉], Seitaro Kaneko[✉], and Hiroyuki Kajimoto[✉]

The University of Electro-Communications, 1-5-1 Chofugaoka, Chofu, Tokyo 182-8585, Japan
{kobayashi,shitara,kaneko,kajimoto}@kaji-lab.jp

Abstract. Most previous studies of tactile presentation for touch devices have presented tactile cues as a function of the position of the finger. In the current study, we examined whether directional information could be presented by modulating tactile cues depending on the direction of motion of the finger, using a new method called "anisotropic tactile presentation". Preliminary experiments confirmed that direction presentation and navigation to a goal could be achieved by decreasing the presentation of roughness when moving in the designated direction. In addition, we conducted two experiments comparing the proposed system with a conventional position-based guidance method. The results revealed that the proposed method enabled participants to search for the target more quickly and accurately compared with the conventional tactile presentation method.

Keywords: Anisotropic roughness · Direction presentation · Navigation Touch device

1 Introduction

Devices equipped with touchpad or touch panels have become widely used in recent years. The lack of haptic feedback, such as a clicking sensation, can lead to operational errors with these devices [1, 2], and many tactile presentation methods for touch devices have been proposed. Fukumoto et al. developed a system called ActiveClick [3], which vibrates the entire surface using a transducer, enabling the presentation of a clicking sensation when an icon is pressed. In addition to this type of tapping operation, a method has been developed for providing tactile feedback while swiping the surface of a touch device. Bau et al. developed TeslaTouch [4], in which the frictional force between the touch device and the finger is changed using electrostatic attraction to modify the texture of the display surface. Several methods have proposed systems utilizing the manipulation friction and roughness via the ultrasonic vibration squeeze effect [5–7] or vibro-tactile cues [8, 9].

The methods for the presentation of tactile stimulation for touch devices discussed above have largely aimed to convey the properties of the contact object, such as hardness, roughness and friction. However, some applications for touch devices require finger movement in a specific direction. For example, guidance systems that involve limiting

© Springer International Publishing AG, part of Springer Nature 2018
D. Prattichizzo et al. (Eds.): EuroHaptics 2018, LNCS 10894, pp. 539–550, 2018.
https://doi.org/10.1007/978-3-319-93399-3_46

movement to a single direction may be suitable for the operation of a scroll bar or volume control. In alphabet-learning applications for children, tactile stimulation may be useful for guiding fingers in a specific direction. In such situations, haptic feedback is required to move the finger in a specific direction. Many texture presentation displays provide texture feedback corresponding to the coordinates of the finger (i.e., position). However, in applications in which users are instructed to move a finger in a specific direction, texture feedback according to the direction of movement of the finger may be more suitable. Such a method could be used to indicate that one direction is the correct direction for moving the finger whereas another direction is incorrect. In the current study, we tested a direction-dependent texture presentation method called anisotropic texture presentation, and compared it with a conventional position-dependent texture presentation method called isotropic texture presentation.

We first describe our proposed navigation method using anisotropic texture presentation. We then tested participants' ability to move the cursor of the touch device to a specific point by using the proposed method, and compared navigation performance with the conventional isotropic texture presentation method. Third, a practical task was carried out, requiring participants to unlock the screen of a smartphone using a specific motion pattern, enabling a comparison between the proposed system and the conventional method.

2   Related Work

Several studies have presented directional cues to fingers. Ho et al. developed a system called Slip-Pad [10], which presents directions by providing a shearing force to the fingers using a two degrees of freedom belt mechanism. A method for directly driving the fingertip has also been proposed [11, 12]. Jung et al. developed Pinpad [13], which uses a pin array touchpad to assist the operation of a device by restricting the direction of finger movement. However, these approaches require additional hardware, and are difficult to apply in small devices, such as smartphones.

Klatzky et al. tested a system using a one-dimensional gradient on an electrostatic tactile display by gradually changing the concentration of the roughness of the electrostatic friction, and reported that the gradient direction was recognizable [14], which they suggested could be applied to navigation. However, this method has not been tested in two-dimensional space.

3   Method

3.1   Navigation Method Using Roughness

In the current study, we considered a situation requiring finger movement in a specific direction, such as a tracing task in an alphabet-learning application. We used the change of the roughness of the surface of the touch device to correct the movement of the finger and guide it in the correct direction. We call this method anisotropic roughness presentation, because the presented roughness is dependent on the instantaneous velocity vector.

When a finger is moved on the touch device, roughness is presented to the finger to correct the direction of movement. Thus, the user can reach the destination by continuously perceiving the correction signals, as shown in Fig. 1.

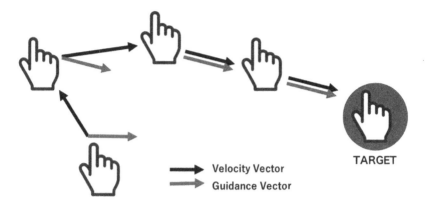

Fig. 1. Finger movement navigation method using direction presentation. The velocity vector indicates the correct movement direction of the finger, and the guidance vector indicates the direction of the target.

3.2 Direction Presentation Using Anisotropic Roughness

When the finger moves on the touch device, an angular difference is generated between the velocity vector indicating the movement direction and the guidance vector indicating the guidance direction (Fig. 2). The direction-dependent texture is presented by modulating the magnitude of roughness corresponding to this angular difference. We speculated that it would be physically or mentally difficult to move in the direction in which the roughness becomes stronger, meaning that direction could be indicated naturally by presenting the lowest level of roughness when the finger moves in the designated correct direction, and the greatest level of roughness when moving in the opposite direction.

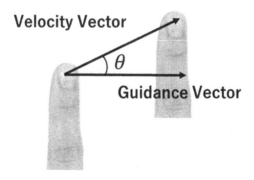

Fig. 2. Angle between the velocity vector and guidance vector.

We propose an anisotropic texture method suitable for guiding in one direction, as shown in Fig. 3. Roughness is not generated when moving the finger in the direction along the background arrow of the figure, but increases when the finger moves against the flow of the background arrow. We used an anisotropic texture that mimics a texture flowing in a certain direction, similar to the sensation of touching animal fur. The magnitude $R(\theta)$ of the generated roughness is given by the following Eq. (1).

$$R(\theta) \propto |\sin(\theta/2)| \tag{1}$$

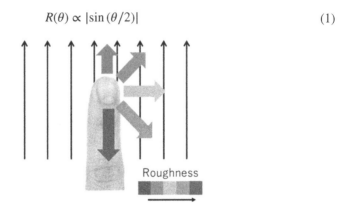

Fig. 3. Anisotropic texture suitable for guiding in one direction.

4   Hardware

4.1   Overview of the Roughness Presentation Touchpad System

Figure 4(a) shows an overview of the experimental device. The device comprised a disassembled commercial touchpad (PERIPAD-501, Perixx Computer), audio speaker (NSW 1-205-8 A (2), AURASOUND), audio amplifier (M50, MUSE), texture signal source (Xperia arcS, SONY) and texture modulation circuit (MCP4018T-103E/LT and

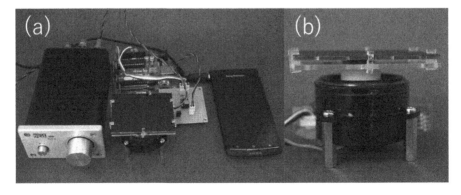

Fig. 4. Roughness presentation touchpad system: (a) Overview of the device; (b) Side view of the touchpad.

Arduino UNO, Arduino). Figure 4(b) shows a side view of the touchpad. The audio speaker was attached below the touchpad, and the surface of the touchpad was vibrated by the speaker to present texture to the finger.

4.2   System Configuration

The system configuration of the device is shown in Fig. 5. The touch pad is connected to a PC via USB, and operates as a normal external connection touch pad. Using software running on the PC, the magnitude of the roughness for presenting the direction could be calculated and transmitted to the amplitude modulation circuit as a control signal. By inputting the control signal and the texture signal to the amplitude modulation circuit, the amplitude-modulated texture signal is then output. The original texture signal was band-limited white noise with its upper limit set to 200 Hz. Preliminary testing revealed that there was a latency of approximately 50 ms between the actual motion of the finger and the presentation of vibration.

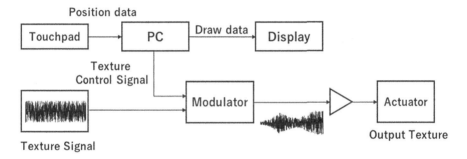

Fig. 5.   System configuration of the roughness presentation touchpad.

5   Experiment

5.1   Preliminary Experiment: Comparison of Increase and Decrease in Roughness

Procedures and Tasks.   In the proposed method, we hypothesized that it would be difficult to move the fingers physically or mentally under conditions of high roughness, and that natural guidance can be performed by setting the direction with low roughness as the guidance direction. To test this hypothesis, we conducted an experiment comparing a direction presentation method using two types of anisotropic roughness: the method of minimizing roughness and the method of maximizing roughness when the guidance direction and motion direction matched.

Participants performed a task involving searching for a correct target using direction information based on anisotropic roughness. Participants were required to find one target among four potential targets, arranged as shown in Fig. 6(b) (Fig. 6(a) was used in a subsequent experiment described below). We measured the time spent searching and the correct response rate.

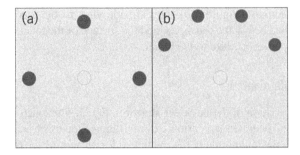

Fig. 6. Arrangement of the target point; in both position conditions, the target was located equidistant from the starting point (red circle): (a) CROSS; (b) SPREAD (Color figure online)

The process of starting the movement and selecting the target constituted one trial. A total of 20 trials (five trials for each of the four targets) was considered to constitute one measurement period. The trials were performed in a random order, and each participant performed a total of two measurement periods (i.e., one for each method).

We recruited four participants (right-handed males, 21–25 years old). Participants were divided into two groups. The first group was first presented with the condition in which roughness decreased when the direction matched, then the condition in which roughness increased when the direction matched. The second group experienced the conditions in the reverse order. Three exercise tasks were performed before each measurement period, and experiments were conducted after the method was explained in detail. Participants performed the experiments with their hearing blocked, to prevent them hearing the sound generated by the device.

Result. Figure 7 shows the results of the preliminary experiment. The horizontal axis shows two types of presentation methods of anisotropic roughness. In the DECREASE method, roughness decreases in the guidance direction. In the INCREASE method, roughness increases in the guidance direction.

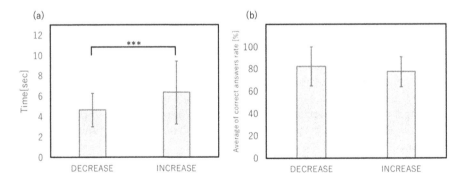

Fig. 7. Measurement result of preliminary experiment: (a) answer time for each guidance direction presentation method; (b) correct answer rate for each guidance direction presentation method. (*** $p < .001$)

The response times are shown in Fig. 7(a). The vertical axis shows the time taken to respond, and the horizontal axis shows the two types of presentation method for anisotropic roughness. Error bars indicate the standard deviation. The search time was shorter when searching with the DECREASE method compared with the INCREASE method ($p < .001$, t-test).

Participants' response accuracy is shown in Fig. 7(b). The vertical axis shows the average correct response rate, and the horizontal axis shows the two kinds of presentation methods of anisotropic roughness. The results revealed that the DECREASE method resulted in a higher correct answer rate, but the difference did not reach statistical significance.

The results described above confirmed that the method in which the roughness decreased towards the guidance direction was more appropriate. Based on these findings, we used this method in subsequent experiments.

5.2 Experiment 1: Comparison of Isotropic Roughness and Anisotropic Roughness

Procedures and Tasks. We conducted experiments comparing our proposed anisotropic roughness presentation method with an isotropic roughness presentation method, which depends on positional information. As in the preliminary experiments, participants were required to search for one correct target among four targets, as shown in Fig. 6. For isotropic (position-based) roughness presentation, we used a method that was dependent on the distance to the target. In this method, roughness decreases as the cursor approaches the correct target, and increases as the cursor gets farther away. In other words, by searching for a position with low roughness, it is possible to identify the correct target. The vibration is presented only while the finger moves, because continuous vibration is impractical.

In this experiment, we tested a CROSS (Fig. 6(a)) configuration, in which the targets were placed at the four sides, and a SPREAD (Fig. 6(b)) configuration, in which the targets are gathered in a narrower configuration than the CROSS. The SPREAD configuration is assumed to be more difficult to navigate. In both target arrangement conditions, the targets were equidistant from the starting point (red circle).

As in the preliminary experiment, each trial was defined as the selection of one target from the starting point. Each measurement period involved 20 trials (five trials for each of the four targets). Participants performed four measurements involving two types of arrangement conditions × two types of induction methods, in a random order.

We recruited seven participants (seven right-handed males, 21–25 years old). Three exercise tasks were performed before each measurement, and experiments were conducted after the method was explained in detail.

Result. Figure 8 shows the results of Experiment 1. The response times in each measurement condition are shown in Fig. 8(a). The vertical axis shows time, and the horizontal axis shows the condition. Error bars indicate standard deviation. The results of a two-factor analysis of variance (two target arrangement conditions × two guidance methods) revealed a significant main effect of arrangement condition ($F[1, 1] = 21.472$,

$p < .001$). In addition, we found a significant main effect of guidance method (F [1, 1] = 8.258, $p < .01$), indicating that anisotropic roughness presentation enabled participants to respond in a shorter time than isotropic roughness presentation.

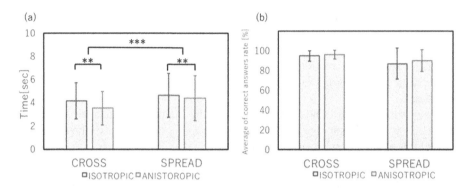

Fig. 8. Results of Experiment 1: (a) response times in each measurement condition; (b) correct response rate for each measurement condition. (** $p < .01$, *** $p < .001$)

Figure 8(b) shows the average correct response rate in each measurement condition. The vertical axis shows the average correct response rate, and the horizontal axis shows each measurement condition. The results of a two-factor analysis of variance (two target arrangement conditions × 2 derivation method conditions) revealed no main effects in any condition.

5.3   Experiment 2: Comparison in Complex Guided Tasks

Procedure and Tasks. As an advanced version of the experiment described in Sect. 5.2, we conducted an experiment requiring participants to unlock a pattern formula lock on a smartphone lock screen using roughness guidance. As shown in Fig. 9(a), one of the nine targets was set as the starting point. The measurement began when the participant tapped the starting point. In the search phase, the two types of roughness change were used to guide the finger (Fig. 9(b)). By tapping the target, the target was registered as a passing point, and the route was drawn. At this time, if an erroneous target was tapped, it was not registered, but was recorded as a miss tap, and search was restarted. This process was repeated in four trials. When a pattern was drawn by four routes, the trial ended (Fig. 9(c)). The whole duration and the number of miss taps were recorded. The starting point and the route were generated randomly for each trial.

In each measurement period, the unlocking task was performed 20 times. Participants performed two measurements under two conditions: isotropic roughness and anisotropic roughness. We recruited six participants (three males and three females, 21–24 years old, five right-handed and one left handed). Participants were divided into two groups. The first group was presented with the isotropic roughness condition first, followed by the anisotropic roughness condition. The second group was presented with the conditions in the reverse order. Participants performed three practice trials before each

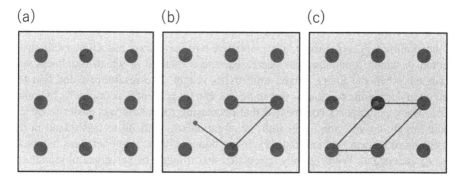

Fig. 9. Pattern formula unlocking task: (a) Standby phase: the starting point (red circle) is set to a random position; (b) Search phase: participants search for the target according to guidance cues; (c) Exit phase: The fourth target is selected, and the participant exits the task. (Color figure online)

measurement period, and began the experiment after a full explanation of the method. In addition, participants performed experiments while their hearing was blocked so they could not hear the sound generated by the device.

Result. Figure 10 shows the results of Experiment 2. Figure 10(a) shows the response time for one task. The vertical axis shows time, and the horizontal axis shows the guidance method condition. Error bars indicate standard deviation. It was confirmed that using anisotropic roughness required a shorter time compared with isotropic roughness ($p < .001$, t-test).

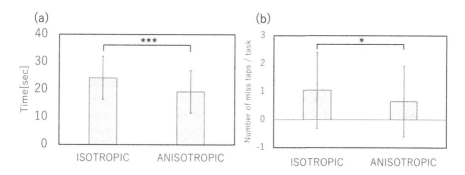

Fig. 10. Results of Experiment 2: (a) Response time for each guidance method condition; (b) Number of miss taps per task in each guidance method condition. (* $p < .05$, *** $p < .001$)

Figure 10(b) shows the number of miss taps per trial. The vertical axis shows the number of miss taps that occurred per trial, and the horizontal axis shows the guidance method. The results confirmed that the number of miss taps was lower when anisotropic roughness presentation was used ($p < .05$, t-test).

6   Discussion

In the preliminary experiment, we compared two roughness reduction methods: a method in which roughness was decreased, and a method in which roughness was increased, when the finger moved towards the target. The results revealed that the method of decreasing roughness was more suitable for guidance, as originally hypothesized. Many participants commented that decreasing roughness was easier to understand, largely because the upper limit of vibration was difficult to understand in the increasing roughness method; thus, the lower bound with no roughness was relatively easy to understand. We originally speculated that it might be perceived physically or mentally more difficult to move in a direction if roughness increased. However, no participant mentioned difficulty in finger movement. Rather, participants appeared to perceive the tactile presentation as a simple symbolic tactile cue.

In Experiment 1, the cursor was haptically guided to the correct target among several candidates, using two methods: the proposed anisotropic texture presentation method, and the isotropic texture presentation method. It should be noted that isotropic texture presentation is easier to implement, because it only requires positional information. In contrast, anisotropic texture presentation requires a velocity vector, which necessitates fast-response touch sensing. In the present case, this was achieved using a stable 50 ms latency in our system configuration. The experimental results revealed that the method using anisotropic roughness presentation resulted in shorter response times than the conventional distance-dependent isotropic method. Isotropic roughness presentation requires searching around each target, whereas anisotropic roughness presentation can provide guidance direction with less movement. Furthermore, because isotropic roughness presentation depends on the location, many participants searched exhaustively for the target and were unable to search using the optimal route. In contrast, there was no significant difference in the correct response rate, and both methods can be considered sufficient for guiding search.

Experiment 2 was an advanced version of Experiment 1, with a task involving unlocking a pattern formula lock. As in Experiment 1, the response time was shorter when guidance was provided via anisotropic roughness. Similar to Experiment 1, some participants used brute-force search in the isotropic roughness presentation condition. This tendency was not observed when anisotropic roughness was presented, and most participants connected the targets with straight lines. These results indicate that the anisotropic roughness method was able to present the route by limiting the movement direction.

The number of miss taps was also reduced when the anisotropic roughness method was used, which may have also contributed to the decreased response time.

7   Conclusion

In the current study, we developed a system to guide a finger in a specific direction on a touch device by presenting tactile cues, named anisotropic roughness presentation. This method was achieved by vibrotactile presentation that depended on the direction of motion of the finger with respect to the designated direction. We initially hypothesized that increasing the roughness of a surface would make it more difficult for users to move. Our preliminary experiment showed, however, that while decreasing roughness presentation along the designated direction was effective, users comprehended the stimuli symbolically. Subsequently, in Experiments 1 and 2, we compared isotropic roughness presentation with our proposed direction-dependent anisotropic roughness presentation. In both experiments, anisotropic roughness presentation significantly shortened the response time.

In Experiment 2, participants were required to search for an unknown unlocking-pattern. When anisotropic roughness presentation was used, many participants searched along the path of the pattern. This result suggests that the proposed method could be used not only for presenting a target destination, but also for presenting a route (i.e., navigation).

All experiments in the present study were conducted under conditions in which the route was invisible. However, in some applications it is appropriate for the route to be visible, such as in alphabet-learning for infants. In future experiments, we plan to test our method in such applications.

Acknowledgement. This work was supported by JSPS KAKENHI Grant Number 15H05923 (Grant-in-Aid for Scientific Research on Innovative Areas, "Innovative SHITSUKSAN Science and Technology").

References

1. Sears, A.: Improving touchscreen keyboards: design issues and a comparison with other devices. Interact. Comput. **3**, 253–269 (1991)
2. Hasegawa, A., Yamazumi, T., Hasegawa, S., Miyano, M.: Evaluating the input of characters using software keyboards in a mobile learning environment. Wireless, Mobile and Ubiquitous Technology in Education, pp. 214–217 (2012)
3. Fukumoto, M., Sugimura, T.: Active click tactile feedback for touch panels. In: SIGCHI Conference on Human Factors in computing Systems, pp. 121–122 (2001)
4. Bau, O., Poupyrev, I., Harrison, C.: TeslaTouch: electrovibration for touch surfaces. In: UIST 2010 Proceedings of the 23nd Annual ACM Symposium on User Interface Software and Technology, pp. 283–292 (2010)
5. Watanabe, T., Fukui, S.: A method for controlling tactile sensation of surface roughness using ultrasonic vibration. In: IEEE International Conference on Robotics and Automation, pp. 1134–1139 (1995)
6. Takasaki, M., Kotani, H., Mizuno, T., Nara, T.: Transparent surface acoustic wave tactile display. In: Intelligent Robots and Systems (IROS), pp. 3354–3359 (2005)
7. Winfield, L., Glassmire, J., Colgate, J.E., Peshkin, M.: T-Pad: tactile pattern display through variable friction reduction. In: EuroHaptics Conference 2007 and Symposium on Haptic Interfaces for Virtual Environment and Teleoperator Systems, IEEE World Haptics Conference, pp. 421–426 (2007)
8. Asano, S., Okamoto, S., Yamada, Y.: Toward quality texture display: vibrotactile stimuli to modify material roughness sensations. Adv. Rob. **28**, 1079–1089 (2014)

9. Yamauchi, T., Okamoto, S., Konyo, M., Tadokoro, S.: Realtime remote transmission of multiple tactile properties through master-slave robot system. In: Proceedings of IEEE International Conference on Robotics and Automation, pp. 1753–1760 (2010)

10. Ho, C., Kim, J., Patil, S., Goldberg, K.: The Slip-Pad: a haptic display using interleaved belts to simulate lateral and rotational slip. In: IEEE World Haptics Conference, pp. 189–195 (2016)

11. Roudaut, A., Rau, A., Strez, C., Plauth, M., Lopes, P., Baudisch, P.: Gesture output: eyes-free output using a force feedback touch surface. In: SIGCHI Conference on Human Factors in Computing Systems, pp. 2547–2556 (2013)

12. Saga, S., Deguchi, K.: Lateral-force-based 2.5-dimensional tactile display for touch screen. In: IEEE Haptics Symposium, pp. 15–22 (2012)

13. Jung, J., Youn, E., Lee, G.: PinPad: touchpad interaction with fast and high-resolution tactile output. In: SIGCHI Conference on Human Factors in Computing Systems, pp. 2416–2425 (2017)

14. Klatzky, R.L., Adkins, S., Bodas, P., Haghighi Osgouei, R., Choi, S., Tan, H.Z.: Perceiving texture gradients on an electrostatic friction display. In: IEEE World Haptics Conference, pp. 154–158 (2017)

Effect of Pseudo-Haptic Feedback on Touchscreens on Visual Memory During Image Browsing

Takeru Hashimoto[1(✉)], Takuji Narumi[1,2], Ryohei Nagao[1],
Tomohiro Tanikawa[1], and Michitaka Hirose[1]

[1] Graduate School of Information Science and Technology,
The University of Tokyo, 7-3-1 Hongo Bunkyo-Ku, Tokyo, Japan
{hashimoto,narumi,nagao,tani,
hirose}@cyber.t.u-tokyo.ac.jp
[2] JST PRESTO, Tokyo, Japan

Abstract. This study investigated the effect of pseudo-haptic feedback that is rendered based on visuo–haptic interaction with a touchscreen, on a visual memory task during image browsing. Pseudo-haptic feedback on a touchscreen is rendered by changing the control/display ratio (C/D ratio), which is the ratio of the movement of the user's finger (control) to the movement of the background image on the display (display). By using this method, we compared the performances of the visual memory task under two visual modification conditions (i.e., with and without dynamic C/D ratio modification) and two interactivity conditions (i.e., with an interactive system and with an autonomous system). The experimental results showed that the figures associated with the pseudo-haptic feedback significantly remained in memory, and the participants showed the best performance of the visual memory task when using interactive scrolling with dynamic C/D ratio modification. These results show that pseudo-haptic feedback on touchscreens affects a user's memory during image browsing.

Keywords: Pseudo-haptics · Memory · Attention · Touch screens

1 Introduction

Touch-sensitive interfaces ranging from small handheld devices to large interactive tabletop surfaces are widely used nowadays. Many people routinely use smartphones or tablets having touchscreens to perform various tasks such as reading e-mails, browsing the web, and accessing social networking sites. Touchscreen interactions offer a sensation of direct physical manipulation of objects, enabling us to handle information shown on the screen as we intend to.

On the other hand, a significant drawback of touch interfaces is that they provide poor haptic feedback, producing a sensation of a flat glass surface and relying on visual feedback to display information and realistic interactive effects. The need for a better haptic feedback was recognized in a previous research. Several studies have focused on rendering haptic sensation by physical stimulation. For example, the haptic simulation

© Springer International Publishing AG, part of Springer Nature 2018
D. Prattichizzo et al. (Eds.): EuroHaptics 2018, LNCS 10894, pp. 551–563, 2018.
https://doi.org/10.1007/978-3-319-93399-3_47

of a user touching buttons on monitors, induced through touch-panel vibration [1, 2] or electrical stimulation [3], enables the generation of haptic feedback. In terms of accuracy, power consumption, and size, however, tangible add-ons for touchscreens are often impractical. Thus, creating haptic feedback without any additional equipment is preferable for handheld devices. To address this requirement, the resistive swipe feature, which renders haptic perceptions with a touchscreen based on visuo–haptic interaction, has been proposed [4]. This feature evokes the feeling of resistive force by creating a discrepancy between the movement of the finger during swiping the screen and a background image shown on the screen. This approach uses a pseudo-haptic illusion that presents haptic sensation with appropriate visual feedback [5].

This approach enables us to design pseudo-haptic feedback via ordinary smartphones/tablets by modulating the visual feedback of the movement of the image shown in the background. At the same time, pseudo-haptic feedback occurring during information browsing may affect our attention consciously or unconsciously because it modifies physical and cognitive efforts to extract information [6]. In this study, we investigated the effect of pseudo-haptic sensation that is rendered based on the visuo–haptic interaction with a touchscreen, on a visual memory task during image browsing. We investigated whether the pseudo-haptic feedback can be used to draw our attention to particular information during information browsing. If the method used to design pseudo-haptic feedback via touchscreens also enables us to effectively control attention on the screen, it can be used for advertisements, education, and supportive user interface development. Especially, we focused on the effect on a user's memory after information browsing with pseudo-haptic feedback. Short-term memory of the user is directly affected by attention [7]. What the user remembers after browsing depends on how they paid attention during browsing. To explore this, we performed an experiment to investigate the effect of pseudo-haptic feedback during information browsing on memory.

2   Related Work

2.1   Pseudo-Haptic Feedback on Touchscreens

Studies have increasingly focused on illusional haptic perceptions evoked by vision. In particular, a pseudo-haptic illusion is expected to induce haptic illusions without the need for complex, bulky, and expensive haptic interfaces. Pseudo-haptic illusion occurs when the physical movement of our body differs from the observed movement of a virtual pointer [5]. This illusion succeeds in simulating haptic sensations by using dynamically changing control/display (C/D) ratios. The C/D ratio is a unit-free coefficient that maps the movement of a pointing device to the movement of the pointer on the display [8]. When the C/D ratio is 1.0, the pointer moves exactly at the same speed as the control device. When the C/D ratio is greater than 1.0, the pointer moves at a faster rate and farther compared with the control device. When the C/D ratio is less than 1.0, the pointer moves slower and covers a lesser distance than the control device. The C/D ratio can be treated as a sensitivity measure of the input device and is a key parameter when evoking pseudo-haptic illusion [5].

This technique has been mainly implemented in standard desktop environments and used for presenting various haptic properties (mass [9], shape [10], size [11], and texture [12]). However, an overly large discrepancy between proprioceptive and visual information makes the users feel something "odd" in the cross-modal feedback [13]. Thus, evoking a pseudo-haptic illusion is difficult in conventional touch interfaces because of the noticeable difference in the movement between finger input and the pointer [14]. To avoid this problem, Kokubun et al. proposed a handheld system where users could feel pseudo-stiffness when pushing or pinching a deformable virtual object on a separate rear-touch interface [14]. The main idea of this method is separating the input area and display. The visual image on the front display was warped relative to the user input. In this system, the users could not directly see their fingers, and a virtual finger was displayed on the screen. Meanwhile, Narumi et al. recently proposed a method to render haptic perceptions by using a touchscreen based on visuo–haptic interaction by using a background image instead of a pointer [4]. To avoid recognizing the large discrepancy, this method evokes the feeling of resistive force by creating a discrepancy between the movement of the finger during swiping the screen and a background image shown on the screen.' This method is easy to implement and applicable to ordinary smartphone/tablet applications that use swipe gestures to scroll an image or a page on the screen. Therefore, we applied this technique in our study.

2.2   Attention, Memory, and Haptic Feedback

Attracting the attention of users to a predefined region in the content is a part of guidance. Some methods have been proposed to guide viewers' attention toward predefined regions of an image and text, such as modifying the color, contrast, or resolution of the regions [15–17]. However, these methods require modification of the original form.

Meanwhile, Tanaka et al. proposed a method to induce users to look at a predefined point in a spherical image by redirecting a virtual camera under virtual reality settings [18]. The direction of the user's virtual camera is shifted to look at a point closer to a target. Therefore, when users look around the virtual environment, the time they spend looking at the target becomes longer according to the shift strength. They applied the method to a virtual museum environment and set important exhibits as the targets and showed that the time users spent looking at the target exhibits became considerable longer than the additional exposure time by mediating the direction of the virtual camera. It is considered that more users get interested in the exhibits by visual modification. Tanaka et al. further extended their method and realized another method to implicitly affect the walking direction in virtual environments based on the approach [19]. Imura et al. used a similar effect to induce a user's movement in augmented reality environments [20]. In these cases, it is not required to modify the contents to draw the user's attention. The algorithm employed for redirecting the virtual camera is similar to the one of "snapping" [21]. Snapping provides aligned positions with an attraction behavior, and users feel a "pseudo-haptic" feeling described as "magnetism" [21] or "gravity" [22] when they use snapping. Recent computer applications often use snapping to help users perform tasks such as aligning objects and searching for specific objects.

Two possible reasons exist why these interactive view modification methods can draw a user's attention and induce a user's interest to a predefined point: exposure duration, and haptic feedback. First, these methods modify the duration when the target point is shown on the screen. This evokes a mere exposure effect [23], and users were interested in what they saw for a long time. Simion et al. have researched preference bias by gaze manipulation. They discovered that the gaze of participants is biased toward a face that they will prefer finally in advance of subjective judgment (the gaze cascade effect) in an experiment that assessed preferred faces. Further, they found that preference could be manipulated by gaze manipulation [24]. Such effects might be evoked by modified visual feedback. Second, their method provides a pseudo-haptic feedback during interactive browsing, and this feedback affects the user's attention and interest consciously or unconsciously. Research on tangible interfaces have revealed that haptic feedback enhances a user's interest and helps in learning and memorizing as perception and cognition are closely interlinked [25, 26]. Moreover, recent research on embodied cognition revealed that haptic sensations implicitly influence higher cognitive processing and change our attention and preferences [27, 28]. For example, heavy objects made job candidates appear more important, rough objects made social interactions appear more difficult, and hard objects increased rigidity in negotiations. If users make efforts to browse information in a certain area by pseudo-haptic resistive feedback, users could consider the information in that area as important. Then, pseudo-haptic feedback elicited by visual feedback could strongly affect our attention and impression separately from the exposure duration. Considering these, we investigated whether pseudo-haptic feedback can be used to draw a user's attention toward particular information during information browsing.

3   Design of Pseudo-Haptic Feedback on Touchscreens

In the present study, we use the pseudo-haptic approach proposed by Narumi et al. [4] to present haptic feedback during information browsing on a touch panel. The system was developed on an iPad Air 2. The application was written in the language Swift, considering a stable frame rate of 60 fps. The user can browse a web page by scrolling up/down. The ratio of the displacement of the finger (control) to the amount of scroll of the page (display) changes according to Eq. (1).

$$C\,/\,D\,Ratio = \begin{cases} minCD + (1 - minCD)\cos\left(\frac{Pt - window}{Ps - window} * 2\pi\right) & if\,|Ps - Pt| < \frac{window}{2} \\ 1 & otherwise \end{cases} \quad (1)$$

In Eq. (1), $minCD$ is the minimum value of the C/D ratio, $window$ is the height of the target area to which we aim to draw the user's attention, Ps is the current position of the screen center, and Pt is the position of the center of the target area (Fig. 1(a)). Figure 1(b) illustrates the change in the C/D ratio. Equation (1) is a continuous function differentiable at any point; thus, the C/D ratio smoothly changes according to the current position. Based on the results of a previous work [4] and a preliminary user study, we set the value of $minCD$ as 0.3, which can present strong resistance and also avoid losing the feeling that the page moves synchronously with the user's movement.

To investigate the effect of pseudo-haptic feedback during information browsing on memory separately from the effect of exposure duration, we also developed a non-interactive system. On this system, the screen scrolls autonomously. We first recorded the movement of the screen when the participants used the interactive system, and then made the movement reappear on the non-interactive system in another trial. By doing so, the presentation duration of each part of the page was made identical to that when using an interactive system. By comparing these two systems (interactive vs autonomous), we can purely investigate the effect of pseudo-haptic feedback.

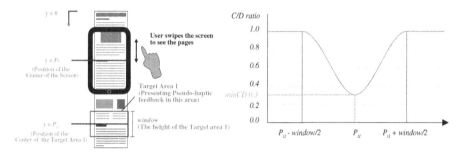

Fig. 1. Definition of parameters and change in C/D ratio according to screen position

4 Experiment: Investigating the Effect of Pseudo-Haptic Feedback During Swipe Gestures on Memory

To investigate the effect of pseudo-haptic feedback via a touchscreen during information browsing on visual memory tasks, separately from the effect of exposure duration, we conducted a laboratory experiment.

4.1 Design, Apparatus, and Participants

We used a 2 × 2 within-subjects experimental design. We tested two visual modification conditions (i.e., *with dynamic C/D ratio modification based on Eq. (1)* and *with static C/D ratio* (always equals to 1)), two interactivity conditions (i.e., *with an interactive system* and *with an autonomous system*) and three repetitions for each of the four combined conditions. The reason why we used 2 × 2 conditions including two interactivity conditions is to investigate the effect of pseudo-haptic feedback on memory separately from the effect of exposure duration. Because visual feedback under the *autonomous condition* is generated based on the results obtained using the interactive system, performing the *interactive condition* earlier than the *autonomous condition* is necessary. Then, to make it difficult for the participants to associate scrolling actions that the subject performed in the past with the behavior of auto-scrolling, the presentation of the conditions was set in the following order: *(with the interactive system* × 2 *visual modification conditions* → *with the autonomous system* × 2 *visual modification conditions)* × 3 *repetitions*. To avoid the ordering effect as much as possible, the order of the visual modification conditions was randomized.

In this experiment, we asked participants to browse web pages with an iPad Air 2. Twelve figures were arranged vertically in each web page. The figures were arranged such that the screen always showed one figure. *With the interactive system*, the participants could browse all figures by swiping the screen. *With the autonomous system*, the participants could start auto-scrolling by tapping a button at the center of the screen. Under the *dynamic C/D ratio condition*, the C/D ratio was modified when four figures (target figures) were randomly selected from twelve figures shown on the screen (*window* was set to the height of the screen, and the center of the selected figures was set as *Pt.*) (Fig. 2(b)). The page included four target figures and eight nontarget figures. Under the *static C/D ratio condition*, the C/D ratio was always set to 1.0. To reduce the difference in memorability of each figure, we used simple abstract figures, as shown in Fig. 2. We prepared 204 figures (Fig. 2(a)), and 12 completely different figures were used for each session.

The participants were 12 university students (8 men and 4 women between the ages of 20 and 23 years (mean: 21.9 years)). All participants had used touch panel interfaces such as smartphones and tablets and had normal or corrected-to-normal vision.

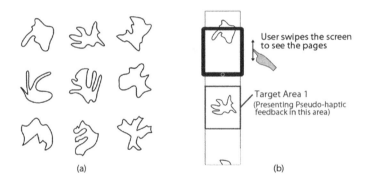

Fig. 2. (a) Examples of figures used in the experiment and (b) how to display them.

4.2   Procedure

The experiment was conducted in a quiet laboratory room. Before the experiment, all participants signed an informed consent form and were given a brief description of the purpose. Then, participants completed a background survey (i.e., age, sex, experience of using touch panels, and visual acuity) and were explained the procedure of the experiment.

After that, each participant underwent an information browsing trial to become used to the interface before the experiment was conducted. In the trial session, participants were asked to browse a list of figures using an iPad Air 2 on the table for 45 s and remember the figures. They browsed the figures at a static C/D ratio using an interactive system and an autonomous system during the trial. After each trial, the participants took a test to examine the memorized figures and answered questionnaires about the perceived resistance and uncomfortable feeling felt during the session. They also answered a questionnaire on the perceived difficulty of the task. After the trial, the participants had experimental sessions. All sessions were conducted in the same procedure as the trial session. Participants took 1-min breaks every session. Twelve sessions were conducted as mentioned in 4.1. Each participant took about 45 min to complete the experiment, and this duration also included explanation about the experiment. All participants did not know the true purpose of the experiment until the experiment was finished.

4.3 Materials

Exposure Time: The system measured the amount of time each figure was *shown* on the screen (if any part of the figure is in the display, it is considered to be *shown* here). As stated above, the system was designed so that only one figure is shown on the screen at a time. Therefore, this display time of each figure can be thought of as the exposure time when the participants were watching it.

Correct Answer Rate: The participants took a test to examine the memorized figures after each session. In the test, they selected the figures seen when browsing the list of figures by choosing from nine figures shown on the screen. We calculated the rate of questions answered correctly. Participants saw four figures with dynamic C/D ratio modifications and eight figures without modification under *dynamic C/D ratio conditions*. We randomly selected two to four figures from four figures with dynamic C/D ratio modification and two to four figures from eight figures without dynamic C/D ratio modification. Under *static C/D ratio conditions*, we randomly selected two to four figures from twelve figures. Then, we randomly selected from figures not used in the session so that the total number of figures would be nine. The reason why we randomized the number of the selected figures in each test is to avoid fixing a user's strategy to answer by changing the total number of the correct figures. If the number of the shown figures with the *dynamic C/D ratio condition* is three and the participant chose two of them, the correct answer rate for this condition is 0.66.

Perceived Resistance, Uncomfortable Feeling, and Difficulty of the Task: In the questionnaire used to investigate the perceived resistance, uncomfortable feeling, and perceived difficulty of the task, each response was scored on a 7-point Likert Scale, with 1 meaning "totally disagree" and 7 indicating "totally agree."

4.4 Results

Exposure Time: Figure 3 shows the mean of the measured exposure time under *interactive conditions* with and without dynamic C/D ratio modification. Especially, it includes the measured exposure time for target figures (with dynamic C/D ratio modification) and others (without dynamic C/D ratio modification) under *C/D ratio modification conditions*. We ran a Shapiro–Wilk normality test to check the assumption of normality. There was no violation in the assumption of normality. Then, we conducted a one-way repeated ANOVA and did not find any significant effect of the C/D ratio modification ($F(2, 22) = 2.46$, $p = 0.11$). Surprisingly, the exposure time did not significantly change with C/D ratio modification.

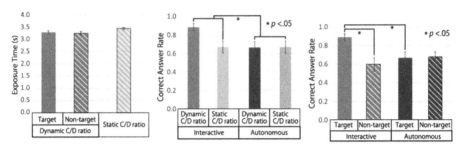

Fig. 3. Exposure time (Mean ± SE).

Fig. 4. Correct answer rate by each condition (Mean ± SE).

Fig. 5. Correct answer rate under "with dynamic C/D ratio condition (Mean ± SE)."

Comparison of Correct Answer Rate Between Conditions: Figure 4 shows the correct answer rate under each condition. We ran a Shapiro–Wilk normality test to check the assumption of normality. There was no violation in the assumption of normality. The two-way repeated measures ANOVA revealed significant effects of the visual modification method (*dynamic C/D ratio modification* vs *static C/D ratio*) ($F(1, 11) = 4.95$, $p = 0.048$, $f = 0.67$). The ANOVA also revealed no significant effects of interactivity (*the interactive system* vs *the autonomous system*) and interaction. However, large effect sizes were found in both; (interactivity: $F(1,11) = 2.95$, $p = 0.11$, $f = 0.51$; interaction: $F(1,11) = 2.61$, $p = 0.13$, $f = 0.48$). A multiple comparison using the Holm method showed that significant differences exist between the correct answer rates with and without dynamic C/D ratio modification under the interactive condition ($t = 3.43$, $p = 0.03$, $r = 0.72$). It also revealed that marginally significant differences exist between the correct answer rates with dynamic C/D ratio modification under the interactive condition and with static C/D ratio modification under the autonomous condition ($t = 2.87$, $p = 0.08$, $r = 0.65$).

Comparison of Correct Answer Rate Between Target and Non-target Figures under *with Dynamic C/D Ratio Condition*: Figure 5 shows the correct answer rate for target and non-target figures under each condition. We ran a Shapiro–Wilk normality test to check the assumption of normality. There was no violation in the assumption of normality. The ANOVA revealed that significant effects of visual modification (*target* vs *non-target*) and interaction exist (visual modification: $F(1, 11) = 4.96$, $p = 0.048$, f = 0.67; interaction: F(1, 11) = 5.05, p = 0.046 f = 0.67). There were no significant effects of interactivity (*the interactive system* vs *the autonomous system*) (F(1, 11) = 0.84, p = 0.38, f = 0.27). The main effect of visual modification is superseded by the visual modification × interactivity interaction. This interaction was investigated further by exam- ining the visual modification. The simple main effects test revealed that significant differences exist between the correct answer rate of target and non-target figures under the interactive condition (F(1, 11) = 6.24, p = 0.030), and one of the target figures under the interactive and autonomous conditions (F(1, 11) = 7.72, p = 0.018).

Perceived Resistance, Uncomfortable Feeling, and Difficulty of the Test: Figure 6 shows the perceived resistance during swiping under each condition. We ran a Shapiro–Wilk normality test to check the assumption of normality. There was no violation in the assumption of normality. The ANOVA revealed significant effects of the visual modification method (*dynamic C/D ratio modification* vs *static C/D ratio*) and interaction (visual modification: F(1, 11) = 28.2, p < 0.01, f = 1.60; interaction: F (1, 11) = 17.5, p < 0.01, f = 1.40). There were no significant effects of interactivity (*the interactive system* vs *the autonomous system*) (F(1, 11) = 0.009, p = 0.493, f = 0.02). The simple main effects test revealed significant differences between the perceived resistance under the *interactive* and *autonomous conditions with dynamic C/D ratio modification* (F(1, 11) = 32.7, p < 0.01), and that *with and without dynamic C/D ratio modification* under *the interactive condition* (F(1, 11) = 11.7, p < 0.01).

Figure 7 shows the perceived uncomfortable feeling during swiping under each condition. We ran a Shapiro–Wilk normality test to check the assumption of normality. There was violation in the assumption of normality (with dynamic C/D ratio modifi- cation under the interactive condition: W = 0.83, p = 0.02). We conducted a non-parametric Friedman rank sum test of differences among repeated measures. The result showed significant differences (χ^2 = 13.4, p < 0.01). A multiple comparison using the Wilcoxon signed-rank test showed that significant differences exist between the perceived uncomfortable feeling with and without dynamic C/D ratio modification under the interactive condition (V = 65, p = 0.030).

Figure 8 shows the perceived difficulty of the task during swiping under each condition. We ran a Shapiro–Wilk normality test to check the assumption of normality. There was no violation in the assumption of normality. The ANOVA revealed no significant effects of the visual modification method (*dynamic C/D ratio modification* vs *static C/D ratio*) and interactivity (*the interactive system* vs *the autonomous system*) (visual modification: F(1, 11) = 3.32, p = 0.96 f = 0.54; interactivity: F(1, 11) = 1.08, p = 0.42 f = 0.31). There were significant effects of interaction (F(1, 11) = 5.30, p = 0.042 f = 0.69). The simple main effects test revealed significant differences between the perceived difficulty of the task with and without dynamic C/D ratio modification under the interactive condition (F(1, 11) = 11.1, p < 0.01).

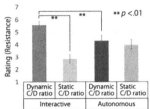

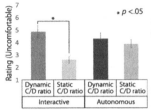

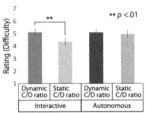

Fig. 6. Perceived resistance (Mean ± SE).

Fig. 7. Perceived uncomfortable feeling (Mean ± SE).

Fig. 8. Perceived difficulty of task (Mean ± SE).

4.5   Discussion

First, although we assumed that the exposure time for the target figures increased, the results showed that it did not change with C/D ratio modification. It is considered that when the participants felt the resistive pseudo-haptic feedback, they reflexively modified their scrolling speed. Moreover, the results showed that no significant differences exist in the correct answer rate between the target and non-target figures under the autonomous condition. This result supported that the exposure time is similar under each condition and it does not affect the materials in this experiment. Therefore, it is reasonable to consider that the effect observed in the experiment was not due to the exposure time, but it was purely the effect of pseudo-haptic feedback. Moreover, this also indicates that the pseudo-haptic feedback did not reduce the total amount of information browsing.

The results showed that the correct answer rate of the target figures under the interactive condition was significantly higher than that of the non-target figures, and the correct answer rate of the target figures under the interactive condition was significantly higher than that under the non-interactive condition. The results also showed that the correct answer rate of the target figures with dynamic C/D ratio modification was significantly higher than that without dynamic C/D ratio modification. These results showed that interactive pseudo-haptic feedback can be used to draw attention and is important for retaining memory. Although the correct answer rate for the non-target figures with dynamic C/D ratio modification was significantly lower than that with dynamic C/D ratio modification, there is no significant difference between the correct answer rate for the non-target figures and those of both the target and non-target figures with the autonomous system. This result indicates that pseudo-haptic feedback does not interfere with a user browsing and remembering the information without feedback, and just helps users to remember the information with feedback.

The participants perceived a stronger resistance with the interactive system and dynamic C/D ratio modification compared with other conditions. At the same time, when they used the interactive system, they felt more uncomfortable with dynamic C/D ratio modification than with static C/D ratio. The participants perceived that performing the task with the interactive system and without dynamic C/D ratio modification was easier compared with those under other conditions. It is considered that this result is linked with the result of uncomfortable feeling. These possible negative effects could be due to the parameter setting of the C/D ratio. Future research should investigate an appropriate C/D ratio to avoid making users uncomfortable. On the other hand, the best performance was achieved when using the interactive system. Therefore, these negative effects in subjective feeling might be negligible from the viewpoint of performance.

5 Conclusion

This study investigated the effect of pseudo-haptic sensation, which is rendered based on visuo–haptic interaction with a touchscreen, on a visual memory task during image browsing. We used two visual modification conditions (i.e., *with dynamic C/D ratio modification* and *with static C/D ratio*) and two interactivity conditions (i.e., *with the interactive system* and *with the autonomous system*), and evaluated the effect of each condition on the visual memory task. The main findings of this study are as follows.

- The duration for which the participants looked at each figure did not change with C/D ratio modification, although it modified the amount of scroll per swipe gesture.
- The figure associated with the pseudo-haptic feedback significantly remains in memory.
- The participants showed the best performance on the visual memory task when using the interactive scrolling with dynamic C/D ratio modification.

These results showed that the pseudo-haptic feedback on touchscreens affects our memory during image browsing. Because this method supports users to remember particular things, it can be used for education, mental care, advertisements, and supportive user interfaces. We believe that this study is the first step to open a new field that supports human cognitive functions with pseudo-haptic feedback. It is considered that the pseudo-haptic feedback affects various cognitions as well as memory. Therefore, the effect of pseudo-haptic feedback on other cognitive functions such as impression and preference formation should be investigated in future research.

Acknowledgement. This study is partially supported by Grant-in-Aid for Scientific Research on Innovative Areas (16H01668) and Grant-in-Aid for Scientific Research (A) (17H00753).

References

1. Brewster, S., Chohan, F., Brown, L.: Tactile feedback for mobile interactions. In: Proceeding of the SIGCHI Conference on Human Factors in Computing Systems, pp. 159–162 (2007)
2. Levesque, V., Oram, L., MacLean, K., Cockburn, A., Marchuk, N.D., Johnson, D., Colgate, J.E., Peshkin. M.A.: Enhancing physicality in touch interaction with programmable friction. In: Proceeding of the SIGCHI Conference on Human Factors in Computing Systems, pp. 2481–2490 (2011)
3. Bau, O., Poupyrev, I., Israr, A., Harrison, C.: TeslaTouch. In: Proceeding of the 23rd Annual ACM Symposium on User Interface Software and Technology, p. 283 (2010)
4. Narumi, T., Ujitoko, Y., Ban, Y., Tanikawa, T., Hirota, K., Hirose, M.: Resistive swipe: visuo-haptic interaction during swipe gestures to scroll background images on touch interfaces. In: Proceeding of the 2017 IEEE World Haptics Conference, pp. 334–339 (2017)

5. Lecuyer, A., Coquillart, S., Kheddar, A., Richard, P., Coiffet, P.: Pseudo-haptic feedback: can isometric input devices simulate force feedback? In: Proceeding of the IEEE Virtual Reality, pp. 83–90 (2000)

6. Tyler, S.W., Hertel, P.T., McCallum, M.C., Ellis, H.C.: Cognitive effort and memory. J. Exp. Psychol.: Hum. Learn. Mem. **5**(6), 607–617 (1979)

7. Norman, D.A.: Memory and attention (1976)

8. Blanch, R., Guiard, Y., Beaudouin-Lafon, M.: Semantic pointing. In: Proceeding of the SIGCHI Conference on Human Factors in Computing Systems, vol. 6, no. 1, pp. 519–526 (2004)

9. Taima, Y., Ban, Y., Narumi, T., Tanikawa, T., Hirose, M.: Controlling fatigue while lifting objects using pseudo-haptics in a mixed reality space. In: Proceeding of the IEEE Haptics Symposium, pp. 175–180 (2014)

10. Ban, Y., Kajinami, T., Narumi, T., Tanikawa, T., Hirose, M.: Modifying an identified curved surface shape using pseudo-haptic effect. In: Proceeding of the IEEE Haptics Symposium, pp. 211–216 (2012)

11. Ban, Y., Narumi, T., Tanikawa, T., Hirose, M.: Modifying perceived size of a handled object through hand image deformation. Presence: Teleoperators Virtual Environ. **22**(3), 255–270 (2013)

12. Lecuyer, A., Burkhardt, J.M., Etienne, L.: Feeling bumps and holes without a haptic interface: the perception of pseudo-haptic textures. In: Proceeding of the SIGCHI Conference on Human Factors in Computing Systems, vol. 6, pp. 239–246 (2004)

13. Pusch, A., Lecuyer, A.: Pseudo-haptics: from the theoretical foundations to practical system design guidelines. In: Proceeding of ICMI 2011, pp. 57–64 (2011)

14. Kokubun, A., Ban, Y., Narumi, T., Tanikawa, T., Hirose, M.: Representing normal and shearing forces on the mobile device with visuo-haptic interaction and a rear touch interface. In: Proceeding of Haptics Symposium, pp. 415–420 (2014)

15. Hagiwara, A., Sugimoto, A., Kawamoto, K.: Saliency-based image editing for guiding visual attention. In: Proceeding of the 1st International Workshop on Pervasive Eye Tracking and Mobile Eye-Based Interaction, pp. 43–48 (2011)

16. Parkhurst, D.J., Niebur, E.: Texture contrast attracts overt visual attention in natural scenes. Eur. J. Neurosci. **19**(3), 783–789 (2004)

17. Kadaba, N.R., Yang, X.D., Irani, P.P.: Facilitating multiple target tracking using semantic depth of field (SDOF). In: Proceeding of CHI 2009 Extended Abstracts on Human Factors in Computing Systems, pp. 4375–4380 (2009)

18. Tanaka, R., Narumi, T., Tanikawa, T., Hirose, M.: Attracting user's attention in spherical image by angular shift of virtual camera direction. In: Proceeding of the 3rd ACM Symposium on Spatial User Interaction, pp. 61–64 (2015)

19. Tanaka, R., Narumi, T., Tanikawa, T., Hirose, M.: Guidance field: potential field to guide users to target locations in virtual environments. In: Proceeding of the IEEE Symposium on 3D User Interfaces, pp. 39–48 (2016)

20. Imura, J., Kasada, K., Narumi, T., Tanikawa, T., Hirose, M.: Reliving past scene experience system by inducing a video-camera operator's motion with overlaying a video-sequence onto real environment. ITE Trans. Media Technol. Appl. **2**(3), 225–235 (2014)

21. Bier, R., Stone, M.: Snap dragging. In: Proceeding of SIGGRAPH 1986, pp. 233–240 (1986)

22. Beaudouin-Lafon, M., Mackay, W.: Reification, polymorphism and reuse: three principles for designing visual interfaces. In: Proceeding of AVI 2000, pp. 102–109 (2000)

23. Gordon, P.C., Holyoak, K.J.: Implicit learning and generalization of the mere exposure" effect. J. Pers. Soc. Psychol. **45**(3), 492 (1983)

24. Simion, C., Shimojo, S.: Interrupting the cascade-orienting contributes to decision making even in the absence of visual stimulation. Percept. Psychophys. **69**(4), 591–595 (2007)
25. Triona, L.M., Klahr, D., Williams, C.: Point and click or build by hand: comparing the effects of physical vs. virtual materials on middle school students' ability to optimize an engineering design. In: Proceeding of CogSci (2005)
26. Barsalou, L.W., Wiemer-Hastings, K.: Situating abstract concepts. In: Pecher, D., Zwaan, R., (eds.) Grounding Cognition: the Role of Perception and Action in Memory, Language, and Thought. Cambridge University Press (2005)
27. Jostmann, N.B., Lakens, D., Schubert, T.W.: Weight as an embodiment of importance. Psychol. Sci. **20**(9), 1169–1174 (2009)
28. Ackerman, J.M., Nocera, C.C., Bargh, J.A.: Incidental haptic sensations influence social judgments and decisions. Science **328**(5986), 1712–1715 (2010)

HandsOn-Computing: Promoting Algorithmic Thinking Through Haptic Educational Robots

Ata Otaran, Ozan Tokatli, and Volkan Patoglu[✉]

Faculty of Engineering and Natural Sciences, Sabanci University, Istanbul, Turkey
{ataotaran,otokatli,vpatoglu}@sabanciuniv.edu

Abstract. *Computational thinking* lies at the intellectual core of computing. Promoting computational thinking ability requires that students are provided with a clear understanding of the fundamental principles and concepts of computer science, including abstraction, logic, algorithms, and data representation. We propose to use force-feedback educational robotic devices for *hands-on* teaching of computational thinking. The addition of haptic feedback for teaching abstract concepts of computer science offers several advantages, as haptic feedback (i) enables an effective means of data hiding, (ii) ensures a high level of student engagement by adding another pathway for perception and enabling active physical interaction, and (iii) improves student motivation through the novelty effect. Moreover, visually impaired students may benefit from replacement of visualization with haptic feedback. We present a force-feedback application for teaching sorting algorithms and report initial student evaluations of integrating haptics to promote computational thinking.

Keywords: Computational thinking · Sorting algorithms
Series elastic actuation · Educational robots · Force control

1 Introduction

As computational thinking and strong foundation in computing have been identified as defining features that are likely to shape the future, computer science has been rapidly expanding into K12 education. Major research and development efforts have been put together in programs like STEM-C (Science, Technology, Engineering and Mathematics, including Computing) to promote computing and computational thinking at the high school level.

Even though programming has been highly promoted and adapted into K12 curricula, *computational thinking*—the ability to formulate precisely a sequence of instructions, or a set of rules, for performing a specific task—that lies at the intellectual core of computing has received less attention. Promoting computational thinking ability requires that students are provided with a clear understanding of the fundamental principles and concepts of computer science, including abstraction, logic, algorithms, and data representation. These core principles are

© Springer International Publishing AG, part of Springer Nature 2018
D. Prattichizzo et al. (Eds.): EuroHaptics 2018, LNCS 10894, pp. 564–574, 2018.
https://doi.org/10.1007/978-3-319-93399-3_48

technology independent and can be illustrated without relying on computers or programming.

Algorithmic thinking is one such key ability that can be developed independently from programming. In fact, earliest known algorithms for factorization and finding square roots have been developed by Babylonians at around 1600 BC. It is emphasized in ACM Computing Curricula that the understanding of the essential algorithmic models transcends the particular programming languages and should be taught separately to avoid distractions of syntax and other requirements and create a solid foundation.

In this study, we propose to use force-feedback educational robotic devices for *hands-on* teaching of abstract concepts of computer science, mainly to high school students and early undergraduates. There exists many educational tools to promote algorithmic thinking, most of which rely highly on visualization of basic algorithms. The addition of haptic feedback for teaching of algorithmic thinking offers several unique advantages: (i) haptic feedback enables an effective means of data hiding, a key component in explaining several core concepts, such as systematic pairwise comparisons during sorting, (ii) haptic feedback ensures a high level of student engagement as it not only adds another pathway to the student perception, but also ensures active physical interactions, and (iii) haptic feedback may improve student engagement as physical interaction with virtual environments are novel and interesting. Furthermore, visually impaired students may benefit from complete replacement of visualization with haptic and auditory feedback.

2   Related Work

In this section, we review related works on methods for teaching computational thinking and uses of educational force-feedback robots.

2.1   Teaching Computational Thinking

The computational thinking is an imperative skill that can be gained in school and how to teach this skill effectively is an open question [16]. With the recent technological developments, there has been a shift from the traditional approach of using blackboards, chalks and verbal analogies, to purposefully designed interactive graphical illustrations, auditory cues and serious games to teach abstract concepts.

Utilizing computer animations is a commonly used approach to teach computational thinking through stimulation of visual cues. [1] presents an early examples of using animations to teach sorting algorithms. Similarly, [5] presents an interactive animation to stimulate the auditory cues of students. It is claimed that this application increases the engagement and immersion, resulting in more effective learning of algorithms. In [3], a mobile interactive animation is developed to teach sorting algorithms to college students. The primary objective of the application is to increase the engagement of students. This animation is designed to be location independent so that the students can also work on the application out of the classroom.

Another approach is to use serious games in classroom to improve student engagement. In [11], three card games and a game that can be implemented on blackboard are designed for teaching sorting algorithms. After the evaluation of the games with students, it is observed that utilizing games for teaching concepts of computing is effective in improving student learning. Similarly, in [2], a board game is designed to teach quick sort and heap sort algorithms. The human subject trials indicate that thanks to the game, remembering, comprehension and ability to apply the sorting algorithms are increased, compared to the traditional education methods.

In this paper, we propose a force-feedback application to help students learn algorithmic thinking through active use of their haptic channel. Up to date, the use of haptic feedback for education has been mostly limited to delivering interaction forces from a virtual environment to help teach physical concepts, such as forces, vibrations, and impedances. To the best of authors' knowledge, force feedback devices have not been used to demonstrate abstract concepts of computer science. Recent developments on affordable haptic interfaces present an opportunity to take advantage of force-feedback as a different modality to teach abstract concepts, to increase student engagement, and to improve learning efficacy.

2.2   Educational Haptic Interfaces

As hands-on experience has been shown to be crucial in strengthening the understanding of basic engineering concepts [6,7], force-feedback devices have been successfully utilized as teaching platforms for various system dynamics and controls classes in many universities around the world [15].

The first investigation of a low-cost force feedback devices (the haptic paddle) in classroom/laboratory environment is conducted in [13]. In this work, the device is used for an undergraduate course with laboratory exercises, including motor spin down test for observing the damping effect, bifilar pendulum test for understanding the components of the dynamic system, sensor calibration and motor constant determination, impedance control and virtual environment implementations. The educational effectiveness of the haptic paddle is measured by student surveys and it has been observed that the device helped students to better grasp engineering concepts.

Similarly, low-cost force-feedback devices iTouch and the Box are used in undergraduate engineering courses at the University of Michigan [9] to support students learning of concepts such as frequency domain representations, dynamical system modeling and haptic interactions. In the laboratory sessions, students implement virtual mass, spring, damper dynamics using an analog computer, experimentally verify the resonant frequency of the device and compare it with the theoretical predictions.

At Rice University, haptic paddles are used in an undergraduate system dynamics course to improve the effectiveness of the laboratory sessions and to introduce students to haptic systems [4]. Motor spin down tests, system component measurements, motor constant determination, sensor calibration and open- and closed-loop impedance control experiments are performed as a part of the laboratory exercises.

A systematic analysis of using haptic paddles in an undergraduate level pHRI course is conducted in [8]. The concepts covered in this course include the effect of having a human in the loop, the design methodology for pHRI systems, system identification for the robotic devices, force controller design and assessment of the robot performance in terms of psychophysical metrics. The effectiveness of using haptic paddles is measured by student surveys, using Structure of Observed Learning Outcomes method. Results indicate that hands-on learning is beneficial for pHRI and can help students learn theoretical concepts more efficiently.

Haptic paddles are also used in an undergraduate system dynamics course at Vanderbilt University [10]. The laboratory sessions include analyzing first and second order system models, determining equivalent mass, damping and stiffness of these system, exploring friction/damping and other external disturbances and observing their effects on the output of the system, experiencing the forced responses of vibratory systems and implementing several closed-loop controllers. The efficacy of haptic paddle integration to the course is also measured by student surveys. The students have higher cumulative scores and better retention rates when the device is used as a part of the course.

The most recent version of Stanford haptic paddle, named Hapkit, has been integrated as the main experimental setup in a massive open online course (MOOC) on haptics [12].

Recently, a low cost, single degree-of-freedom, force-controlled educational robot with series elastic actuation, HANDSON-SEA [14], has been integrated to pHRI education, to allow students to experience the performance trade-offs inherent in force control systems, due to the non-collocation between the force sensor and the actuator. The efficacy of the device is evaluated in an introduction to robotics course and the device is found to be effective in instilling in intuition about fundamental trade-offs in the design and control of force-feedback devices.

3 HANDSON-COMPUTING

Sorting algorithms provide a rich set of approaches that can be used to effectively demonstrate the fundamentals of algorithmic thinking. Along these lines, several sorting algorithms have been developed to use with force-feedback educational interfaces.

HANDSON-COMPUTING application consists of a visual interface (GUI developed using Matlab) and a single degree-of-freedom haptic interface. Even though any haptic interface can be adapted to use with the application, we have preferred to use HANDSON-SEA—a low-cost, open-hardware/software admittance-type haptic interface developed at HMI Laboratory of Sabanci University—as this interface features a large force output capability. Force output capability may be critical for the application, as the human perceptual capabilities can significantly limit the number of objects that can be used for sorting when devices with low force capabilities need to be utilized.

The sorting applications input a certain number of identical looking springs with different spring ratios. The goal is to systematically sort the springs according to their stiffness. A single iteration of sorting algorithms includes the steps of selection of elements, comparison, and decision. GUI systematically guides the user to perform pairwise comparisons and swapping between relevant springs as necessitated by the algorithm. The use of haptic feedback for comparisons provides an effective means of data hiding, as the stiffness of each spring becomes available only during/after physical interaction with that spring. GUI also provides visual feedback about the current status of the algorithm by displaying the iteration count, the progress during each iteration, and termination condition. Figures 1 and 2 present sample GUI snapshots and HANDSON-SEA, respectively.

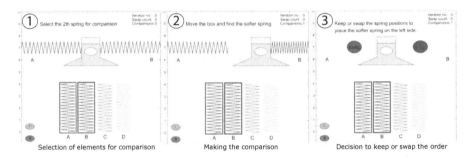

Fig. 1. A single iteration includes the steps of (1) selection of elements, (2) comparison, and (3) decision.

4   Hardware and Software

HANDSON-SEA is a single degree of freedom educational robot that features series elastic actuation and relies on closed loop force control to achieve the desired level of safety and transparency during physical interactions. This device complements the impedance-type haptic paddle designs. HANDSON-SEA is a low cost, easy to build, and open source haptic interface, whose manufacturing files, along with many other instructions are available at http://hmi.sabanciuniv.edu/?page_id=992. Video demonstrations of HANDSON-SEA and HANDSON-COMPUTING are also available at this link.

A TI F28069M type board is used as the micro-controller and programmed via Simulink. The Simulink model is deployed to the micro-controller to set up a virtual environment in real-time. The virtual environment is rendered as a massless handle attached to two virtual springs from both sides. This model receives the stiffness coefficients of the springs that are being compared online from GUI, using serial communication bus. The model outputs the motor positions for use in visualization.

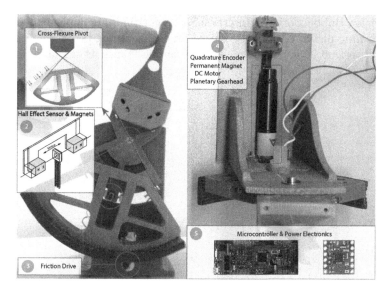

Fig. 2. HANDSON-SEA—A single degree-of-freedom educational robot with series elastic actuation

5   Teaching with HANDSON-COMPUTING

Three phases of operation are implemented for HANDSON-COMPUTING: *exploration* phase, *guided learning* phase, and *retention* phase.

Exploration Phase: In the *exploration* phase, students are only informed about how to select, compare and swap elements. Then, they are asked to create an ordered list of elements. Students are free to choose any element from the list to perform comparisons. Once they are set to compare the elements, they are asked to feel the stiffness of the virtual walls created on both sides of the handle. A stronger wall refers to an element with higher stiffness. Upon understanding this relationship, students decide to swap or keep the positions of the elements. Students are free to compare elements as many times as they would like, but they are also informed that their performance in this level relies on how few comparisons they require. They notify the program by clicking a button, when they believe that they have accomplished the sorting task.

Guided Learning Phase: In the *guided learning* phase, students are supervised by the computer in choosing which elements to compare at each iteration. This supervision is carried out according to the sorting algorithm that has been explained to the students before starting this phase. Students observe the sequence of comparisons and perform the comparisons themselves, so that they can track the relationship among elements at each step of the algorithm. During this phase, students are prompted with questions that test their understanding of the algorithm.

Currently, Bubble Sort and Insertion Sort algorithms are implemented for the *guided learning* phase. GUI is customized for each learning task for an improved learning experience. Figure 3 demonstrates sample snapshots of Bubble Sort and Insertion Sort algorithms.

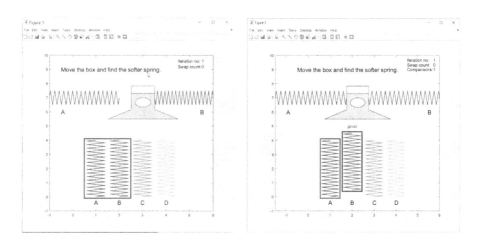

Fig. 3. Snapshots of *guided learning* phase: Bubble Sort algorithm (left) and Insertion Sort algorithm (right)

Retention Phase: In the *retention* phase, students are asked to test their understanding of an algorithm by implementing it without any supervision. This phase essentially shares a similar implementation with the exploration phase, with an additional indicator that signifies whether students are complying with the targeted algorithm or not. Any movement that diverges that from the algorithm is notified to students, at which case students can decide to continue or restart the operation until they get it right. They can also go back to the *guided learning* phase to understand their mistakes.

An ideal training session takes place as follows:

Students are first asked to familiarize themselves with the haptic interface and provided with a general set of instructions such that they have a common understanding of the main goals the task and means to achieve them.

Then, the students are asked to test themselves with an *exploration* phase, during which they are free to select any two springs they want to compare and proceed with sorting as they wish. *Exploration* phase is repeated several times with increasing number of springs to sort. With this phase, it is aimed that the students gradually get a better appreciation for the importance of having a systematic strategy to accomplish the sorting task in a systematic and efficient way.

Next, students are asked to perform *guided learning* phase, during which an interactive GUI guides them through several sorting algorithms, including Bubble Sort and Insertion Sort. Before each such *guided learning* phase, students are informed about the underlying idea of the algorithm by a set of instructions.

During the *guided learning* phase, students are expected to closely observe the order of comparisons that are performed, such that they learn how to make these comparison decisions by themselves. During *guided learning* phase, students are provided with visual feedback that highlights the important features of the underlying sorting algorithm, as well as several performance metrics related to the strategy.

Table 1. Survey questions and summary statistics

Q1: How would you rate the importance of using the haptic interface/feedback for this application?	Frequency	
Data hiding while demonstrating pairwise comparisons		87.5
Addition of another pathway to student perception		87.5
The novelty affecting/providing motivation		82.5
Enabling visually impaired students		87.5
For quantitative tracking learning performance		85.0
Q2: Overall, how do you rate the usefulness of each phase of HandsOn-Computing?	Frequency	
Exploration Phase		68.2
Guided Learning Phase - Bubble sort		84.1
Guided Learning Phase - Insertion sort		82.1
Retention Phase		81.8
Q3: How would you rate the usefulness of HandsOn-Computing for the following groups?	Mean	σ^2
Elementary school students (First five year)	3.54	1.36
Middle school students (6th to 8th year)	4.18	0.75
High school students	4.18	1.25
University students	3.63	1.62
Q4: Please rate the following	Mean	σ^2
Difficulty of sorting in exploration phase		
(i) with 4 elements	1.09	0.30
(ii) with 8 elements	3.72	1.36
Distinguishability of the stiffness of compared springs	4.72	0.38
Importance of using algorithms for higher number of elements	4.00	0.72
Usefulness of guided learning phase for retention phase	4.27	0.56
Importance of adjustability of number of elements	4.20	0.56
Overall usefulness haptic feedback	3.91	1.72
Q5: Please rate following aspects of HandsOn-Computing	Mean	σ^2
Realism of the virtual environment	4.27	1.01
GUI and ease of use	4.18	0.75
Idea of teaching algorithmic thinking via HandsOn-Computing	4.55	0.69

After completing the *guided learning* phase, students are asked to perform the algorithms by themselves in a *retention* phase.

6 Evaluation

Educational effectiveness of HANDSON-COMPUTING has been evaluated through student surveys. In particular, HANDSON-COMPUTING is used at a workshop for teaching different sorting methods to 11 sophomore level students. Almost all of the students have taken an introduction to computer science course, and none of them were familiar with the sorting algorithms at the beginning of the workshop. Throughout the workshop the students interacted with the device and were instructed to fulfill the requirements of the sorting task. Although it has taken more time for some students, all of the student were successful at acquiring the presented knowledge in the *guided learning* phase and apply it in the *retention* phase. At the end of the workshop, the students filled in a questionnaire.

The statistical analysis of the student responses revealed that the factor of major was not statistically significant at the 0.05 level for any of the survey questions; hence, all responses are aggregated for reporting. The Cronbach's α values have been calculated for the whole survey, and the α value is evaluated to be greater than 0.8, indicating high reliability of the survey.

The survey includes 5 questions: Q1 is assessing the importance of using haptic interaction, Q2 is for rating the usefulness of each phase, Q3 is for determination of target population, Q4 aims to reveal the extent to which basic features of the application are useful, and Q5 is for assessing essential aspects of HANDSON-COMPUTING. For all of the questions, the five-point Likert scale, ranging from "1" *not at all* to "5" *very strongly* is used to measure agreement level of the participants.

Questionnaire together with the summary statistics are presented in Table 1.

The main results of the survey can be summarized as follows:

- Responses to Q1 demonstrate that students find the addition of haptic feedback as beneficial for all of the proposed aspects listed in the question.
- From answers given to Q2, we can deduce that students find the *guided learning* and *retention* phases very useful.
- Responses to Q3 reveal that students regard the application to be most useful for middle and high school students. Furthermore, there also exists considerable support to use the application at the elementary school and university level.
- Answers to Q4 indicate that increasing the number of elements are effective in instilling the requirement of using algorithms, the stiffness levels of springs are sufficiently distinguishable, and the *guided learning* phase can effectively prepare students for the *retention* phase.
- For Q5, the mean scores of individual features indicate that students *strongly appreciate* the idea of teaching algorithmic thinking via HANDSON-COMPUTING. They also find the aspects related to performance of the device and visualization successful.

7   Conclusions and Discussions

During testing and verification, it has been observed that certain pre-determined high and low stiffness values can be assigned to the two springs that are being compared, instead of reflecting their real stiffness values. This version of the sorting application has been evaluated to feature three advantages: (i) it matches better with the logic behind sorting algorithms, where the level of difference between elements is of no use, (ii) it enables the application to be scaled as much as desired with ease, and (iii) it can be implemented with many haptic interfaces, even with devices that have relatively low force output capabilities.

However, rendering exact stiffness levels is also valuable, since data hiding through haptic modality has been found very effective in preventing people from planning ahead. Additionally, exact stiffness levels may provide visually impaired students with a better understanding of the algorithm, since such a rendering provides them with a means to evaluate exact feel of the elements during *guided learning* phases. Note that for non-impaired students, this information can be provided visually.

As part of our ongoing works, the force-feedback application is being extended to several other sorting and search algorithms, including the ones that can make effective use of multi degrees-of-freedom haptic interfaces. Furthermore, haptic feedback within the application is being generalized from comparisons to other aspects of the algorithms, such as swapping and listing, that are currently displayed visually.

Future works include collecting feedback from K12 level students who are systematically exposed to HandsOn-Computing. In particular, extensive evaluations will be undertaken where proposed force-feedback approach is compared with a visual only control group and an alternative tactile feedback condition. Another user study is planned to assess the effectiveness of the generalized application when visual cues are completely unavailable, as in the case of visually impaired participants.

References

1. Baecker, R.: Sorting out sorting: a case study of software visualization for teaching computer science. Softw. Vis. Programm. Multimedia Experience **1**, 369–381 (1998)
2. Battistella, P.E., von Wangenheim, C.G., von Wangenheim, A., Martine, J.E.: Design and large-scale evaluation of educational games for teaching sorting algorithms. Inform. Educ. Int. J. **16**(2), 141–164 (2017)
3. Boticki, I., Barisic, A., Martin, S., Drljevic, N.: Teaching and learning computer science sorting algorithms with mobile devices: a case study. Comput. Appl. Eng. Educ. **21**(S1), E41–E50 (2013)
4. Bowen, K., O'Malley, M.: Adaptation of Haptic interfaces for a labview-based system dynamics course. In: Symposium on Haptic Interfaces for Virtual Environment and Teleoperator Systems, pp. 147–152 (2006)
5. Carson, E., Parberry, I., Jensen, B.: Algorithm explorer: visualizing algorithms in a 3D multimedia environment. ACM SIGCSE Bull. **39**, 155–159 (2007)

6. Dogmus, Z., Erdem, E., Patoglu, V.: ReAct!: an interactive educational tool for AI planning for robotics. IEEE Trans. Educ. **58**(1), 15–24 (2014)
7. Ferri, B.H., Ahmed, S., Michaels, J.E., Dean, E., Garyet, C., Shearman, S.: Signal processing experiments with the Lego Mindstorms NXT kit for use in signals and systems courses. In: American Control Conference (2009)
8. Gassert, R., Metzger, J., Leuenberger, K., Popp, W., Tucker, M., Vigaru, B., Zimmermann, R., Lambercy, O.: Physical student-robot interaction with the ETHZ Haptic Paddle. IEEE Trans. Educ. **56**(1), 9–17 (2013)
9. Gillespie, R., Hoffman, M., Freudenberg, J.: Haptic interface for hands-on instruction in system dynamics and embedded control. In: Haptic Symposium, pp. 410–415 (2003)
10. Gorlewicz, J.L.: The efficacy of surface Haptics and force feedback in education. Ph.D. thesis, Vanderbilt University (2013)
11. Hakulinen, L.: Using serious games in computer science education. In: Proceedings of the Koli Calling International Conference on Computing Education Research, pp. 83–88 (2011)
12. Morimoto, T., Blikstein, P., Okamura, A.: Hapkit: an open-hardware Haptic device for online education. In: IEEE Haptics Symposium, p. 1 (2014)
13. Okamura, A.M., Richard, C., Cutkosky, M.R.: Feeling is believing: using a force-feedback joystick to teach dynamic systems. J. Eng. Educ. **91**(3), 345–349 (2002)
14. Otaran, A., Tokatli, O., Patoglu, V.: Hands-on learning with a series elastic educational robot. In: Bello, F., Kajimoto, H., Visell, Y. (eds.) EuroHaptics 2016. LNCS, vol. 9775, pp. 3–16. Springer, Cham (2016). https://doi.org/10.1007/978-3-319-42324-1_1
15. Provancher, W.: Eduhaptics.org (2012). http://eduhaptics.org
16. Yadav, A., Stephenson, C., Hong, H.: Computational thinking for teacher education. Commun. ACM **60**(4), 55–62 (2017)

Experimental Evaluation of Vibrotactile Training Mappings for Dual-Joystick Directional Guidance

Lorenzo Scalera[1(✉)], Stefano Seriani[2], Paolo Gallina[2], Massimiliano Di Luca[3], and Alessandro Gasparetto[1]

[1] Polytechnic Department of Engineering and Architecture, University of Udine, Udine, Italy
scalera.lorenzo@spes.uniud.it, alessandro.gasparetto@uniud.it
[2] Department of Engineering and Architecture, University of Trieste, Trieste, Italy
{sseriani,pgallina}@units.it
[3] School of Psychology, University of Birmingham, Birmingham, UK
m.diluca@bham.ac.uk

Abstract. Two joystick-based teleoperation is a common method for controlling a remote machine or a robot. Their use could be counter-intuitive and could require a heavy mental workload. The goal of this paper is to investigate whether vibrotactile prompts could be used to trigger dual-joystick responses quickly and intuitively, so to possibly employ them for training. In particular, we investigate the effects of: (1) stimuli delivered either on the palm or on the back of the hand, (2) with attractive and repulsive mappings, (3) with single and sequential stimuli. We find that 38 participants responded quicker and more accurately when stimuli were delivered on the back of the hand, preferred to move towards the vibration. Sequential stimuli led to intermediate responses in terms of speed and accuracy.

1 Introduction

Teleoperation is a renown method for remotely controlling robots in difficult or extreme conditions that could either endanger the operator or that could not be physically possible for the operator. Since the half of the 20th century, when the first master-slave manipulator was built by Goertz, teleoperation has proved to be invaluable in several different field of application. In particular, the capability of operating at a distance covers cases which could be dangerous or impossible for humans. These are, for example, radioactive environments [21], space missions [3], planetary explorations [20] and disaster areas [4,32]. Furthermore, teleoperation is applied when motion scaling, dexterity and enhanced visualization lead to better results compared to direct manual operation: above all in robot-assisted surgery [7].

The capability of manipulating objects remotely is always achieved thanks to a human-machine interface, which, in the majority of cases, relies on joysticks,

© Springer International Publishing AG, part of Springer Nature 2018
D. Prattichizzo et al. (Eds.): EuroHaptics 2018, LNCS 10894, pp. 575–586, 2018.
https://doi.org/10.1007/978-3-319-93399-3_49

especially in heavy and industrial applications. Joysticks are reliable, ergonomic, cost-affordable and, to certain extensions, intuitive to be controlled. In fact, in a large number of applications, each joystick degree of freedom (DoF) is mapped to each joint position or velocity of the slave manipulator. Therefore, a heavy mental workload is needed to calculate the inverse kinematics from the DoFs of the slave robot to the DoFs of the joystick [18,25,28,29]. Due to the counter-intuitive and mentally heavy mapping process, subjects operating remote systems by means of joysticks require long training in order to make the telemanipulation system transparent to them. In recent years, several training simulators, especially in the field of excavators and cranes [23,26], have been designed to shorten the learning period of unskilled operators. The training is usually performed with trial-and-errors sessions where an instructor verbally guides the user. At present, vibrotactile stimuli have not been used for training in dual-joystick directional guidance.

The aim of this paper is to investigate effective methods for training subjects in the guidance of two handled joysticks, using vibrotactile prompts. Starting from the results obtained in previously published works [28,29], our motivation to continue the investigation was given by the introduction of the sequential stimulation, already applied in the wrist rotational guidance [16,19]. In particular, we investigate the effects of: (1) stimuli delivered either on the palm or on the back of the hand, (2) with attractive and repulsive prompts, (3) with single and sequential stimuli.

The paper is organised as follows: in Sect. 2 a background is provided for a number of related works, in Sect. 3 a detailed exposition of materials and methods is reported and in Sect. 4 the experimental results are presented. Finally, Sect. 5 gives the conclusions of this work.

2   Background

In the recent years, vibrotactile stimuli have been applied for directional guidance to improve motor learning and to reduce mental workload [2,30]. Applications of vibrotactile displays can be found in sports: soccer, skating and cycling [34], dancing [8], boat rowing [27], snowboarding [31] and karate [5]. A vibrotactile feedback system has been adopted also in the field of music to teach violin bowing [33]. Moreover, vibrotactile guidance has been studied and applied in the field of rehabilitation, especially for stroke [9] and Parkinson's disease patients [17] as well in gait retraining [1]. Vibrotactile displays have also been implemented to enhance navigation and orientation in both real [35] and virtual environments [15,22].

In order to provide an instructional prompt, different stimulation mappings have been studied: attractive/repulsive (pull/push), in which a single vibration is meant either to pull the body toward the signal or to push it away, and "follow me" [19], which consists in a sequence of stimuli that directs the user toward a direction. Attractive and repulsive instructional cues have been compared in the study of torso balance performance [12], in anterior-posterior trunk movements [13] and in wrist guidance [10,16]. On the other hand, a "follow me" mapping has been applied to give a feeling of rotational signal and to guide the user wrist and forearm in 2D space [6,14,16,19].

To the best of Authors' knowledge, no studies on the effects of single and sequential stimuli for dual-joystick directional guidance have been performed until now. Results of this work could, in the future, lead to the development of a practical training protocol for operators involved in joystick-based telemanipulation.

3   Materials and Methods

3.1   Participants

Data were collected from a total of 38 healthy participants (aged 20–45, ten females). They were recruited at the University of Trieste and their academic level was mixed, from undergraduate to associate professor. Before starting the tests, all participants have been subjected to the Handedness Questionnaire [24], which permits the calculation of the Laterality Index (LI); thirty-six of them result to be mainly right-handed, the other two left-handed. All participants were volunteers and signed an informed consent form before the experiment, which was approved by the University of Trieste Ethics Committee.

3.2   Experimental Set-Up

The experiments have been performed using two 2-DoFs joysticks and two gloves, reported in Fig. 1. Each joystick is equipped with 4 vibrating motors along the cardinal directions, whereas each glove with 5 actuators of the same type located in a cross configuration when the user grasps the joystick. These electric actuators, by Precision Microdrives, operate at 3 V and have a diameter equal to 10 mm and a thickness of 3 mm. They have a typical rise time of 92 ms, a stop time of 116 ms and operate at a frequency of 200 Hz, drawing less than 90 mA and providing a vibe force with an amplitude of almost 1 g. The joysticks, by Speedlink, have been modified by substituting the original handle

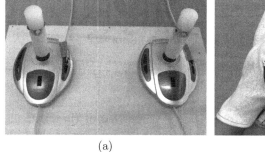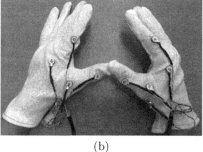

(a)   (b)

Fig. 1. Experimental set-up: joysticks (a) and gloves (b).

with one in teflon, which presents a rubber ring thanks to which the vibrations are not transmitted to the whole stick during the tests. Inside each joystick, two potentiometers detect the motion of the stick in the four directions.

During the tests, the activation of vibrating motors is controlled by a myRio-1900, a portable data acquisition device by National Instruments that is also used to log the data recorded by the potentiometers at a sampling rate of 1 kHz. For this purpose, an ad-hoc real-time software has been developed in LabView™.

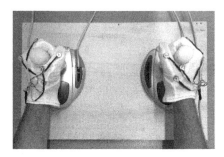

Fig. 2. A subject performing the experimental test using the two 2 DoFs joysticks.

3.3   Vibrotactile Training Mappings

With respect to the results obtained in previous works [28,29], where only single stimuli have been applied to test dual-joystick directional responses, the main overall aim of this case study is to investigate whether a sequential stimulation could lead to more accurate responses with respect to a single prompt. For this purpose, six different vibrotactile training mappings have been completed by the 38 subjects involved in the experiments:

- two tests stimulating the palm of the hand from the actuators placed on joysticks, with attractive (move the joystick toward the vibration) and repulsive (move the joystick in the opposite direction with respect to the vibration felt) single 200 ms vibrotactile stimuli (respectively called *Attractive* and *Repulsive Joystick*);
- two tests stimulating the back of the hand from the vibrating motors placed on gloves, with attractive and repulsive single 200 ms vibrotactile stimuli (*Attractive* and *Repulsive Glove*);
- two tests stimulating the back of the hand with a sequence of three vibrotactile prompts that induce the motion along the direction indicated by the saltatory pattern. One condition is composed of three stimuli of 200 ms each separated by 20 ms (*Slow Follow me*), the other one is comprised of three stimuli of 150 ms one right after the other (*Fast Follow me*).

In Fig. 2 a subject performing the experimental test using the two 2 DoFs joystick is shown, whereas in Fig. 3 examples of vibrotactile training mapping are

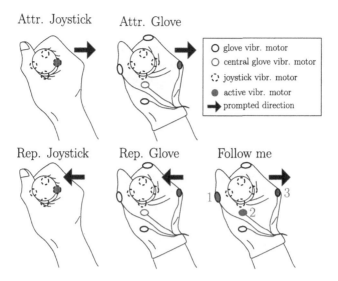

Fig. 3. Examples of vibrotactile training mappings: the red dots indicate the vibrations whereas the arrows the prompted directions. (Color figure online)

reported for the different tests; the Follow me mapping is the same in both Fast and Slow modalities. Each test consists of 16 stimuli delivered in random order, two for each joystick DoF (Forward, Backward, Rightward and Leftward). In particular, the attractive prompts are intended to induce the motion of the joystick in the direction of the vibration prompt, whereas the repulsive mode induces the motion in the opposite direction to the one from which the vibration is delivered. Moreover, a sequential stimulus induces the motion in the direction provided by the saltatory pattern. The 16 prompts are delivered one at a time for each hand every 3000 ms, lasting a total of 48 s for each test. The different tests are completed by participants in random order, so as to avoid the effects of a possible progressive learning.

The experimental protocol was the following: each subject was instructed to handle the joysticks with both hands and to listen which test will be provided. Then, each participant was asked to move the joystick related to the prompted hand in the direction indicated by the stimuli as soon as it was felt. After the motion, the joystick had to be brought back in its central position. No training sessions have been performed before the experiments and the vibrotactile stimuli were the only feedback that the subject received. This experiment could be seen as a particular case of the One-Interval, Two-Alternatives, Forced-Choice decision model (1I-2AFC) [11], in which eight stimulus alternatives are presented on each trial instead of two (1I-8AFC). Indeed, each subject expects one of eight possible stimulations (four for each hand) and has to choose only one response direction within the time interval.

3.4   Performance Metrics

Data logged during the experiments were elaborated and analysed in Matlab™ in order to extract the information about accuracy and reaction times performed by participants during the experiment. Accuracy is computed as the percentage of correct responses for each of the six tests. Reaction times are calculated as the time elapsed between the beginning of the stimulation and the time at which one of the two joysticks potentiometers reached the 75% of its range. This particular threshold was determined with pilot tests as it could trigger the response before the end of the joystick workspace, but it also prevented the system to record small unintentional motions. In Attractive mappings, the response is considered right if the potentiometer that reached the threshold is in the direction of the vibration, whereas in Repulsive conditions in the opposite way. Finally, in Follow me test, the potentiometer that is taken into account is the one related to the direction of the third stimulus out of three. To better visualize how reaction times are computed, an Attractive, a Repulsive, a Fast and a Slow Follow me prompt are depicted in Fig. 4. The joystick position is ranged between 1 and −1.

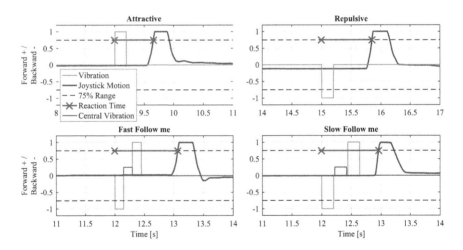

Fig. 4. Computation of reaction times in the different tests. The y-axis for the vibrations is only qualitative: we have assigned a value equal to 1 for the attractive prompt, to −1 for the repulsive one and to 0.25 for the central vibration.

4   Experimental Results

4.1   Accuracy

Figure 5(a) reports the box-plot representation of the proportional number of correct responses, whereas in Table 1 the percentage values are reported as median and interquartile range. Results for a Kolmogorov-Smirnov test for normality indicated that correct responses are not normally distributed ($p < 0.001$ for all the six conditions). A non-parametric Friedman test was conducted to test differences between each condition leading to a Chi-square of $\chi^2(5, 185) = 59.3$, which was statistically significant $p < 0.001$. Furthermore, in order to test differences between every couple of conditions a Bonferroni corrected Wilcoxon matched-pairs signed-ranks test has been applied. Results are reported in Table 2, where significant differences ($p < 0.05$) have been highlighted. Participants responded more frequently in the correct direction with both Glove and Follow me conditions with respect to the Joystick ones. No coherent differences in the number of correct responses have been obtained due to the attractive/repulsive task demand as well as due to the fast/slow mapping.

4.2   Reaction Times

The statistical distribution of reaction times does not deviate significantly from a normal distribution (K.-S. test for the six conditions: Attr. Glove $p = 0.822$, Rep. Glove $p = 0.664$, Attr. Joystick $p = 0.534$, Rep. Joystick $p = 0.847$, Fast Follow me $p = 0.313$, Slow Follow me $p = 0.666$). Figures 5(b) and (c) report the box-plot representation of reaction times for right and wrong responses respectively in the six conditions, whereas in Table 1 mean and standard deviation values are reported in milliseconds. The repeated measures one-way ANOVA between reaction times of the different conditions resulted statistically

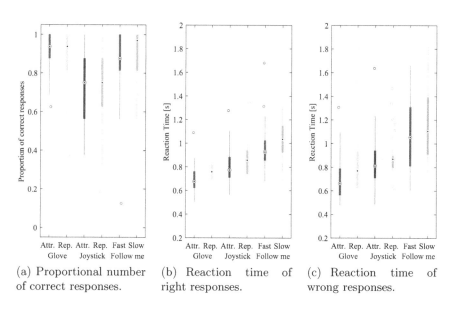

(a) Proportional number of correct responses.

(b) Reaction time of right responses.

(c) Reaction time of wrong responses.

Fig. 5. Experimental results: box-plot representation. The central mark indicates the median, the bottom and top of each box represent the first and third quartiles, the whiskers extend to the most extreme data points not considered outliers (the empty circles).

Table 1. Accuracy [%] and reaction times [ms] of right and wrong responses.

Test		Accuracy Median	Int. Range	Right responses Mean	St. Dev.	Wrong responses Mean	St. Dev.
Glove	Attractive	93.8	12.5	692	111	707	201
	Repulsive	93.8	18.8	773	136	822	295
Joystick	Attractive	75.0	31.3	803	148	848	217
	Repulsive	75.0	25.0	862	153	895	183
Follow me	Fast	87.5	18.8	959	184	1099	357
	Slow	96.9	18.8	1028	162	1181	351

Table 2. Comparison between accuracy results for each couple of conditions: Bonferroni corrected p-values of Wilcoxon matched-pairs signed rank-test (significance at $p < 0.05$).

		Glove Attr.	Rep.	Joystick Attr.	Rep.	Follow me Fast	Slow
Glove	Attr.		> 0.99	< 0.001	< 0.001	> 0.99	> 0.99
	Rep.			0.0020	< 0.001	> 0.99	> 0.99
Joystick	Attr.				> 0.99	0.0061	< 0.001
	Rep.					0.0051	< 0.001
Follow me	Fast						> 0.99
	Slow						

significant $F(5, 227) = 59.9$, $p < 0.001$, $\eta_p = 61.8$. A series of Bonferroni corrected paired-sample t-tests has been applied on the right responses reaction times for each couple of conditions (Table 3). From the table it can be seen that participants responded faster in the glove condition rather then in the joystick one. Furthermore, in the Glove condition, faster responses were given with attractive modality rather than with repulsive one. In the Follow me condition, reaction times are higher than in both Glove and Joystick mappings but no significant differences have been found between Fast and Slow conditions.

4.3 Relation Between Accuracy and Reaction Times

In order to analyse the relationship between accuracy and reaction times, a linear mixed-effects analysis has been performed for the different conditions. We have adopted the following model: $y \sim x_1 + x_2 + (z_{11}|g_1)$, where the dependent variable y is the proportion of correct responses, the fixed effects x_1 and x_2 are the conditions and the reaction times, whereas z_{11} and g_1 represents the random effects covariance parameters and the grouping variables, respectively. We have obtained a value of the Log-Likelihood test equal to 95.625.

Table 3. Comparison between reaction times for each couple of conditions: Bonferroni corrected paired-sample t-test (significance at $p < 0.05$).

			Glove		Joystick		Follow me	
			Attr.	Rep.	Attr.	Rep.	Fast	Slow
Glove	Attr.	t		-6.4239	-5.8862	-10.1079	-9.5810	-15.5401
		p		< 0.001	< 0.001	< 0.001	< 0.001	< 0.001
	Rep.	t			-1.5598	-5.9210	-6.4843	-12.4896
		p			> 0.99	< 0.001	< 0.001	< 0.001
Joystick	Attr.	t				-2.4924	-5.8414	-8.3457
		p				0.2594	< 0.001	< 0.001
	Rep.	t					-3.4845	-8.2684
		p					0.0193	< 0.001
Follow me	Fast	t						-2.7501
		p						0.1374
	Slow	t						
		p						

In Fig. 6 the interpolating lines of the predicted responses together with the 95% confidence intervals for the predictions are reported. From the figure it can be seen that, across participants, reaction times increase as the proportion of correct responses decreases. This trend could be due to a higher sensibility of skilled subjects, who respond with fewer errors. By analysing the interpolating lines, differences between Glove and Joystick conditions can be clearly seen. Moreover, the lines associated to the Fast and Slow Follow me condition are higher than both the Joystick and Glove, suggesting that a sequential stimulation led to better performances in terms of proportion of correct responses with respect to a single stimulation, on equal reaction times.

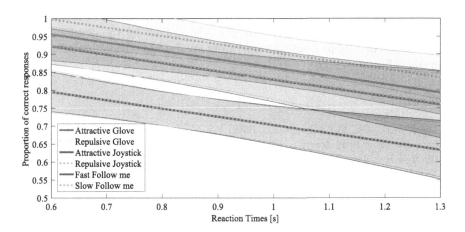

Fig. 6. Linear mixed-effects analysis between accuracy and reaction times for the six different conditions: interpolating lines and 95% confidence intervals.

5   Conclusion

In this work we investigated effective methods for the training of subjects in the guidance of two handled joysticks, using vibrotactile prompts. In particular, we studied the effects of: stimuli delivered either on the palm or on the back of the hand, with attractive and repulsive mappings, and with single and sequential stimuli. Experimental tests, consisting in six different tests each composed by 16 random stimuli, have been performed on 38 healthy subjects and the results have been analysed in terms of accuracy and reaction times. With respect to previously published works [28,29], the experiments here presented confirmed that a stimulation on the back of the hand could lead to better results with respect to a stimulation on the palm and that an attractive mapping gives better performance with respect to a repulsive one. Furthermore, the main overall result of this novel study is given by the differences between single and sequential stimuli (Follow me condition): it has been revealed that a slow saltatory pattern could give better results in terms of proportion of correct responses compared to the other tested conditions. Reaction times could be slower in the Follow me condition due to the longer pattern of stimulation. Furthermore, the sequential presentation of the stimuli could require higher level processing to interpret the vibration pattern as a whole and the subjects could have spread attention on a large area of the hand over the course of stimulation. Finally, a linear mixed-effects analysis suggests that the Follow me condition could lead to better results in terms of proportion of correct responses with respect to both Glove and Joystick ones on equal reaction time.

In the future, we plan to further investigate vibrotactile training mappings for dual-joystick directional guidance. In particular, we will start from the results of this study to better analyse the progressive co-adaptation of subjects responses to vibrotactile prompts in a dual-joystick guidance. Furthermore, because of the relative low-cost of the experimental hardware and of the overall easy practical implementation of the tests, this research holds promise for the development of new practical training protocols for operators involved in telemanipulation tasks in several different fields.

References

1. Afzal, M.R., Oh, M.K., Lee, C.H., Park, Y.S., Yoon, J.: A portable gait asymmetry rehabilitation system for individuals with stroke using a vibrotactile feedback. BioMed Res. Int. **2015** (2015). https://doi.org/10.1155/2015/375638. Article ID 375638, 16 pages
2. Alahakone, A., Senanayake, S.A.: Vibrotactile feedback systems: current trends in rehabilitation, sports and information display. In: 2009 IEEE/ASME International Conference on Advanced Intelligent Mechatronics, AIM 2009, pp. 1148–1153. IEEE (2009)
3. Artigas, J., Balachandran, R., Riecke, C., Stelzer, M., Weber, B., Ryu, J.H., Albu-Schaeffer, A.: KONTUR-2: force-feedback teleoperation from the international space station. In: 2016 IEEE International Conference on Robotics and Automation (ICRA), pp. 1166–1173. IEEE (2016)

4. Bimbo, J., Pacchierotti, C., Aggravi, M., Tsagarakis, N., Prattichizzo, D.: Teleoperation in cluttered environments using wearable Haptic feedback. In: IEEE/RSJ International Conference on Intelligent Robots and Systems, IROS 2017 (2017)
5. Bloomfield, A., Badler, N.I.: Virtual training via vibrotactile arrays. Presence Teleoperators Virtual Environ. **17**(2), 103–120 (2008)
6. Chinello, F., Pacchierotti, C., Bimbo, J., Tsagarakis, N.G., Prattichizzo, D.: Design and evaluation of a wearable skin stretch device for Haptic guidance. IEEE Robot. Autom. Lett. **3**(1), 524–531 (2018)
7. Coad, M.M., Okamura, A.M., Wren, S., Mintz, Y., Lendvay, T.S., Jarc, A.M., Nisky, I.: Training in divergent and convergent force fields during 6-DOF teleoperation with a robot-assisted surgical system. In: 2017 IEEE World Haptics Conference (WHC), pp. 195–200. IEEE (2017)
8. Drobny, D., Borchers, J.: Learning basic dance choreographies with different augmented feedback modalities. In: CHI 2010 Extended Abstracts on Human Factors in Computing Systems, pp. 3793–3798. ACM (2010)
9. Hung, C.T., Croft, E.A., Van der Loos, H.M.: A wearable vibrotactile device for upper-limb bilateral motion training in stroke rehabilitation: a case study. In: 2015 37th Annual International Conference of the IEEE Engineering in Medicine and Biology Society (EMBC), pp. 3480–3483. IEEE (2015)
10. Janssen, L.J., Verhoeff, L.L., Horlings, C.G., Allum, J.H.: Directional effects of biofeedback on trunk sway during gait tasks in healthy young subjects. Gait Posture **29**(4), 575–581 (2009)
11. Jones, L.A., Tan, H.Z.: Application of psychophysical techniques to Haptic research. IEEE Trans. Haptics **6**(3), 268–284 (2013)
12. Kinnaird, C., Lee, J., Carender, W.J., Kabeto, M., Martin, B., Sienko, K.H.: The effects of attractive vs. repulsive instructional cuing on balance performance. J. Neuroeng. Rehabil. **13**(1), 1 (2016)
13. Lee, B.C., Sienko, K.H.: Effects of attractive versus repulsive vibrotactile instructional cues during motion replication tasks. In: 2011 Annual International Conference of the IEEE Engineering in Medicine and Biology Society, pp. 3533–3536. IEEE (2011)
14. Lieberman, J., Breazeal, C.: Development of a wearable vibrotactile feedback suit for accelerated human motor learning. In: 2007 IEEE International Conference on Robotics and Automation, pp. 4001–4006. IEEE (2007)
15. Lindeman, R.W., Sibert, J.L., Mendez-Mendez, E., Patil, S., Phifer, D.: Effectiveness of directional vibrotactile cuing on a building-clearing task. In: Proceedings of the SIGCHI Conference on Human Factors in Computing Systems, pp. 271–280. ACM (2005)
16. Luces, J.V.S., Okabe, K., Murao, Y., Hirata, Y.: A phantom-sensation based paradigm for continuous vibrotactile wrist guidance in two-dimensional space. IEEE Robot. Autom. Lett. **3**(1), 163–170 (2018)
17. Maculewicz, J., Kofoed, L.B., Serafin, S.: A technological review of the instrumented footwear for rehabilitation with a focus on Parkinson's disease patients. Front. Neurol. **7**, 1 (2016)
18. Mavridis, N., Pierris, G., Gallina, P., Papamitsiou, Z., Saad, U.: On the subjective difficulty of joystick-based robot arm teleoperation with auditory feedback. In: 2015 IEEE 8th GCC Conference and Exhibition (GCCCE), pp. 1–6. IEEE (2015)
19. McDaniel, T., Goldberg, M., Villanueva, D., Viswanathan, L.N., Panchanathan, S.: Motor learning using a kinematic-vibrotactile mapping targeting fundamental movements. In: Proceedings of the 19th ACM International Conference on Multimedia, pp. 543–552. ACM (2011)

20. Mellinkoff, B., Spydell, M., Bailey, W., Burns, J.O.: Investigation of minimum frame rate for low-latency planetary surface teleoperations. arXiv preprint arXiv:1706.03752 (2017)
21. Micconi, G., Aleotti, J., Caselli, S.: Evaluation of a Haptic interface for UAV teleoperation in detection of radiation sources. In: 2016 18th Mediterranean Electrotechnical Conference (MELECON), pp. 1–6. IEEE (2016)
22. Montecchiari, G., Gallina, P., Bulian, G., Scalera, L.: The effects of a vibrotactile interface on evacuation simulation with virtual reality. IEEE Trans. Hum. Mach. Syst. (2018, in press)
23. Ni, T., Zhang, H., Yu, C., Zhao, D., Liu, S.: Design of highly realistic virtual environment for excavator simulator. Comput. Electr. Eng. **39**(7), 2112–2123 (2013)
24. Oldfield, R.C.: The assessment and analysis of handedness: the edinburgh inventory. Neuropsychologia **9**(1), 97–113 (1971)
25. Pervez, A., Ali, A., Ryu, J.H., Lee, D.: Novel learning from demonstration approach for repetitive teleoperation tasks. In: 2017 IEEE World Haptics Conference (WHC), pp. 60–65. IEEE (2017)
26. Rezazadeh, I.M., Wang, X., Firoozabadi, M., Golpayegani, M.R.H.: Using affective human-machine interface to increase the operation performance in virtual construction crane training system: a novel approach. Autom. Constr. **20**(3), 289–298 (2011)
27. Ruffaldi, E., Filippeschi, A.: Structuring a virtual environment for sport training: a case study on rowing technique. Robot. Autonom. Syst. **61**(4), 390–397 (2013)
28. Scalera, L., Seriani, S., Gallina, P., Di Luca, M., Gasparetto, A.: An experimental setup to test dual-joystick directional responses to vibrotactile stimuli. In: 2017 IEEE World Haptics Conference (WHC), pp. 72–77. IEEE (2017)
29. Scalera, L., Seriani, S., Gallina, P., Di Luca, M., Gasparetto, A.: An experimental setup to test dual-joystick directional responses to vibrotactile stimuli. IEEE Trans. Haptics (2018, in press)
30. Sigrist, R., Rauter, G., Riener, R., Wolf, P.: Augmented visual, auditory, haptic, and multimodal feedback in motor learning: a review. Psychon. Bull. Rev. **20**(1), 21–53 (2013)
31. Spelmezan, D., Jacobs, M., Hilgers, A., Borchers, J.: Tactile motion instructions for physical activities. In: Proceedings of the SIGCHI Conference on Human Factors in Computing Systems, pp. 2243–2252. ACM (2009)
32. Sulaiman, H., Saadun, M.N.A., Yusof, A.A.: Modern manned, unmanned and teleoperated excavator system. J. Mech. Eng. Technol. (JMET) **7**(1), 57–68 (2015)
33. Van Der Linden, J., Schoonderwaldt, E., Bird, J., Johnson, R.: Musicjacket-combining motion capture and vibrotactile feedback to teach violin bowing. IEEE Trans. Instrum. Measur. **60**(1), 104–113 (2011)
34. Van Erp, J.B., Saturday, I., Jansen, C.: Application of tactile displays in sports: where to, how and when to move. In: Proceedings of Eurohaptics, pp. 105–109. Springer (2006)
35. Van Erp, J.B., Van Veen, H.A., Jansen, C., Dobbins, T.: Waypoint navigation with a vibrotactile waist belt. ACM Trans. Appl. Percept. (TAP) **2**(2), 106–117 (2005)

A Novel Pneumatic Force Sensor
for Robot-Assisted Surgery

Chiara Gaudeni[1(✉)], Leonardo Meli[1], and Domenico Prattichizzo[1,2]

[1] Department of Information Engineering and Mathematics,
University of Siena, Via Roma 56, 53100 Siena, Italy
{gaudeni,meli,prattichizzo}@diism.unisi.it
[2] Department of Advanced Robotics, Istituto Italiano di Tecnologia,
Via Morego 30, 16163 Genoa, Italy

Abstract. This paper presents a pneumatic-based force sensor, used to measure the force generated at the tip of a surgical instrument during robot-assisted minimally invasive surgery (RMIS). Despite the achievements of the robotic surgery, the lack of haptic feedback to the surgeon is still a great limitation, since through palpation the physician can distinguish consistency of tissues and determine the occurrence of an abnormal mass. Although a great effort has been made by researchers to develop novel haptic interfaces able to provide force feedback to the operator, far fewer works exist regarding the design of sensing systems for robotic surgery. In this respect, we propose a new force measurement method based on the relation between the air pressure variation inside a pneumatic balloon and the interaction force due to the contact between the balloon and an object. A performance comparison with a very-fine resolution commercial force sensor proves the feasibility and effectiveness of the proposed approach.

1 Introduction

Robot-assisted minimally invasive surgery (RMIS) is increasingly becoming a fundamental component of the state-of-the-art operating room. It might be considered the evolution of the manual minimally invasive surgery (MIS). Its success is due to several different reasons, e.g., improved precision, enhanced visualization, reduced instruments tremor, error-free and timely repetitive tasks execution, reduced incision size, and shorter hospitalization [6]. On the other hand, there are still a few disadvantages with respect to MIS, in which surgeons feel the interaction between the surgical instrument and the patient via a long shaft, although tactile cues and force feedback result deprived compared with open surgery [20]. In RMIS any natural haptic feedback is generally absent and the lack of effective haptic feedback is often reported as one of the main limitations of robot-assisted surgery [10].

The research leading to these results has received funding from the European Union's Horizon 2020 Research and Innovation Programme under Grant Agreement n°688857 of the project "SoftPro".

© Springer International Publishing AG, part of Springer Nature 2018
D. Prattichizzo et al. (Eds.): EuroHaptics 2018, LNCS 10894, pp. 587–599, 2018.
https://doi.org/10.1007/978-3-319-93399-3_50

Wagner et al. [21] have been among the first to systematically assess the benefits led by force feedback on blunt dissection using robotic surgery: the absence of haptic feedback increased errors causing tissue damage by a mere factor of 3. It is well-known that haptic feedback can complement other sensory modalities and for instance counterbalance the narrow camera view available in minimally invasive surgery.

(a)   (b)

Fig. 1. Working principle of the proposed pneumatic force sensor. (a) A pneumatic elastic membrane is hosted deflated inside the surgical instrument when it is not needed. (b) When a measurement of the interaction force is required, the membrane is inflated and comes into contact with the human tissue. The subsequent change of pressure of the internal gas is then related to instrument/tissue interaction.

Among the several applications present in the literature, robot-assisted palpation seems to be particularly favored by the addition of haptic signals and without them excessive forces might be applied by the surgeon causing complications, such as accidental puncturing of blood vessels. Meli et al. [11] proved that haptic feedback (even magnified) enhances the performance of a teleoperation framework during robot-assisted needle insertion and palpation tasks. Pacchierotti et al. [16] tested different types of tactile feedback in a teleoperation framework in which eighteen subjects used a da Vinci robot (Intuitive Surgical Inc. USA) to palpate a heart model. Fingertip deformation feedback significantly improved palpation performance by reducing the task completion time, the pressure exerted on the heart model, and the subject's absolute error in detecting the orientation of an embedded plastic stick. Mahvash et al. [9] exploited again a da Vinci Surgical System (a customized version) to prove that direct force feedback is superior to graphical force displays in a palpation task of both a heart and a prostate models.

Although a great effort has been made by researchers to develop novel haptic interfaces able to provide force feedback to the operator, far fewer works exist regarding the design of sensing systems for robotic surgery. In any teleoperation scenario the force applied on the slave side needs to be measured, or at least estimated, in order to be fed back to the operator. The main goal of tactile sensing in RMIS is to detect local mechanical properties of tissue such as compliance, viscosity, and surface texture, that can indicate the current status of the tissue, i.e., healthy and non-healthy [15]. Commercially available force/torque sensors are very effective to measure such interaction forces in many teleoperation applications, but the operating theater sets several constraints in terms of biocompatibility, size, cost, and sterilizability [14]. For example a biomimetic tactile sensor is presented in [22]. Deformations of its skin can be detected by displacing a conductive fluid from the vicinity of electrodes on a rigid core. While the sensor is promising in providing human-like haptic capability for surgical robots, it is still not compatible with robot-assisted surgical operations due to its on-board electronics and poor possibility of sterilization.

The easiest way to match all the operating theater constraints consists in using vision to track tissue deformation and consequently estimate its mechanical properties and interaction forces. No add-on sensors are needed, standard endoscopic cameras might be used for this. Different approaches have been studied to model tissue deformations. One among all uses deformable active contours, also called snakes, to observe changes over time [8]. The minimization of the energy function, depending on contour smoothness, image forces, and external constraint forces, has been fused with a prior knowledge from finite-element models of nonlinear elastic materials. However, physical parameters of human organs are not always available [13]. Aviles et al. [1] used again energy functional minimization to measure the tissue surface displacement, but they exploited also a neuro approach to establish a geometric-visual relation and estimate the applied force.

Even though most of the surgical tools were not designed to host sensors, some researchers have had success in integrating them to existing jaws or to the tip of grasping forceps [12]. For sterilizability reasons, sensors should not be mounted directly on the jaws because it is desirable to use tips that can be detached and disposed of after use. In this regard, Tavakoli et al. [19] placed several strain gauges on the base of an endoscopic end-effector far enough from the tip to non-invasively measure interactions with the tissue. A different approach can be to re-design surgical equipment. In this direction, Gonenc et al. [4] presented one of the first micro-forceps that can sense 3-DOF forces at the tool tip to be used in retinal microsurgery. Puangmali et al. [17] developed a miniature 3-axis distal force sensor based on a optical sensing scheme and capable of measuring tissue interaction forces at the tip of a surgical instrument.

In this paper, we present the idea of using a tiny pneumatic balloon to estimate the interaction forces playing on the slave side during robot-assisted surgery. The balloon can be placed in a cavity of either the surgical instrument or the endoscopic camera as sketched in Fig. 1. Due to the contact between the balloon and patient's body, a change in the air pressure inside the balloon occurs. This difference in pressure can be related to the interaction force. While several tactile displays using pneumatic balloons have been developed for RMSI applications [5,18], to the best of our knowledge, such an approach is totally underexploited on the sensing side.

2 Pneumatic Force Sensor

Due to the strict constraints of the operating room, it is not trivial to measure forces occurring during instrument/tissue interactions. In this work, we propose an innovative approach to evaluate those interaction forces, taking advantage of a tiny pneumatic balloon hidden inside the cavity of a surgical tool when not used. By inflating the elastic membrane with a gas, e.g., air, it comes out very close to the tip of the surgical instrument and can be used to palpate the human tissue of interest.

Main advantages of this approach can be appreciated from different points of view. First of all, the elastic membrane can be made of biocompatible material already widespread in surgery, such as latex, polyurethane, or silicone, in order to prevent any kind of inflammation or immune response against the material itself [2]. Secondly, all the parts that need to be embedded in the surgical tool and that enter the human body are simple and very inexpensive. Since most of the surgical tools, e.g., da Vinci tools, are disposable because of sterilizability reasons, the sensing system must not represent a further significant cost. Indeed, in the proposed sensing apparatus, the electronic sensors and boards are not located in the operational workspace, mechanical information are transferred by means of a gas to the sensitive components. A further advantage is that the pneumatic balloon comes out from its housing in the proximity of the end-effector tip only when the elastic membrane is inflated, without limiting or constraining the tool workspace when it is not needed. The balloon acts as the remote surgeon's fingerpad permitting those palpation tasks often essential in open surgical procedures, e.g., locating arteries. Finally, the elastic membrane, because of its nature, adapts to any curvilinear surfaces of the body: this represents a further advantage, because human tissues have an irregular shape and different stiffness. A sensor that can passively adapt to the body part being touched avoids unreliable and non-continuous signals that might be delivered by standard single-point contact sensors. When all the force information is successfully collected by the surgeon, the balloon can be deflated again to avoid limiting surgical instrument tip motions. The surgeon can repeat the aforementioned palpation action anytime it is deemed necessary.

2.1 Device Description

In this paper, we present a proof of concept in which the pneumatic force sensor is composed of a 3D-printed part made of ABSPlus (Stratasys Inc., USA), a latex pneumatic balloon, an air compressor Ciao 25/185 (FNA S.p.A., IT), two solenoid valves L172 2/2 G1/8 (Asco Numatics Sirai S.r.l., IT), a differential pressure sensor MPXV5050DP (Freescale Semiconductor, Inc), an Arduino UNO board, and some pipes and airtight fittings to connect the different components. The tank air compressor equipped with a pneumatic pressure regulator prevents the occurrence of blast waves in the air inside the circuit. The addition of two solenoid valves, whose control is managed by the Arduino board, enables the operator to control the air flow, inflating and deflating the circuit according to the desired pressure value. The opening/closing time of the valves is 10 ms. It is essential that all the hoses and couplings are leakproof to avoid undesired pressure variations that might severely affect sensor readings. The exploited differential pressure sensor has a pressure range of $(0, 50)$ kPa and an accuracy of 2.5% of full scale. The use of our pneumatic force sensor does not present the limitations shared among most of the commercial force sensors and mentioned in Sect. 1: the pressure sensor can be positioned even far from the contact site, as long as in the same pneumatic circuit, since the pressure is uniformly distributed. This can avoid the disposal of the sensor at the end of any surgical intervention.

2.2   Pneumatic System Control

We herein report a brief description of how the micro-controller Arduino Uno, combined with the Arduino 4 Relays Shield, manages the opening and closing of the solenoid valves and induces different system conditions: (i) inflating, (ii) deflating, and (iii) locking.

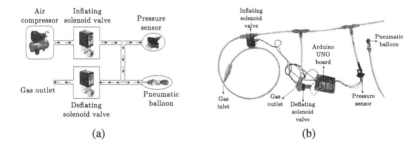

Fig. 2. Pneumatic system control: (a) diagram and (b) real implementation.

Inflating and deflating procedures open the inflating and deflating valves (see Fig. 2), respectively, keeping close the other one. While during both these policies the amount of air present inside the system changes, in the locking condition the two solenoid valves are closed and the amount of air inside the system is constant. The operator can arbitrarily choose in any moment to start the inflating or deflating actions or change the desired pressure value. In the latter case, an automatic procedure will open/close the valves to reach the preset air pressure inside the system and keep it constant. To prevent the chattering of the internal pressure when close to the preset value, that might lead to a malfunction of the whole measuring system, we introduced hysteresis adopting two different thresholds equal to the desired pressure ± 0.1 kPa.

3   Experimental Evaluation

In order to characterize the usability of the proposed sensing system, we conducted three experiments. The first one evaluated the relation between the variation of the internal pneumatic pressure and the applied force; the second and the third experiments validated the proposed system comparing the estimation of the force performed by the pneumatic balloon with the one measured by a commercial force sensor, considered as ground truth, in two different tasks.

Experimental Setup. All the experiments shared the same experimental setup. The pneumatic balloon housing was attached to the end-effector of an industrial robot KR3 (KUKA Robotics, Germany). In front of the robotic manipulator, within its workspace, there was a flat wall, the balloon was supposed to come into contact with. Interaction forces were measured by a ATI Nano17 six-axis force/torque sensor (ATI Industrial Automation, USA) placed on the wall at the contact site (see Fig. 3). Its main features are the small size (17 mm diameter) and a very high resolution (0.00312 N), with a measurement range of ±17 N for the normal direction and ±12 N for the others.

The motion of the robotic arm was constrained along its y-axis, i.e., the normal direction with respect to the balloon exit wound and the force sensor, thus the wall. This particular experimental setup permits to carry out the same experiments an arbitrary number of time in the same condition, i.e., a high degree of repeatability is granted.

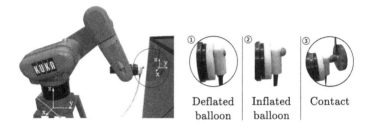

| | Deflated balloon | Inflated balloon | Contact |

Fig. 3. Experimental setup. *Phase 1*: the housing, mounted on the end-effector of a Kuka KR3 robot, hosts the pneumatic balloon deflated. *Phase 2*: the pneumatic balloon is inflated according to the desired pressure value. *Phase 3*: the pneumatic balloon comes into contact with the ATI sensor attached to a wall.

3.1 Experiment #1: Estimation of the Relation Between Applied Force and Pneumatic Pressure

To find the relation between the pressure variation in the circuit, due to the contact between the pneumatic balloon and an object, and the subsequent exerted force, there are two main methods: (i) making a physical model of the system; (ii) estimating an empirical evaluation. We decided to discard the first option because it might be very hard to accurately model the elastic deformation of the pneumatic balloon, in particular when you do not have a full characterization of the material that might significantly affect the behavior of the elastic membrane. Thus, we conducted a preliminary experiment simulating a robot-assisted palpation task to gather data about our system and find an empirical force-pressure relation that implicitly contains also the nonlinear behavior of the elastic balloon. It is worth underlying that the ranges of pressure and force of interest in surgical palpation are small and this facilitates the empirical characterization and evaluation.

Methods. During each palpation task the robotic end-effector, not in contact with the sensor initially, gradually moved towards the wall. Once it came into contact with the force sensor, an increasing force was exerted through the pneumatic balloon. Then it stopped. We considered six different initial pressure ranges for the pneumatic balloon defined according to a pilot experiment and reported in the left column of Fig. 5b. Within each range, we tested multiple values of initial pressure. In particular, starting from the first value of the range, the initial pressure was increased by 0.12 kPa each time. For each pressure value we carried out two palpation tasks in which the displacement of the robotic end-effector was 3 mm and 6 mm, respectively. So, following this procedure we carried out 20 trials for each pressure range, 10 with the end-effector displacement of 3 mm and 10 with the one of 6 mm, for a total of 120 trials. The zero position was considered the one in which the elastic membrane came into contact with the sensor. This moment was detected by the sensor itself with a very small change of the measured force. The maximum robot motion was set so that the pneumatic balloon housing did not hit the ATI, preventing measurements alteration.

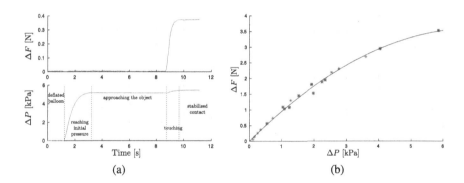

Fig. 4. On the left, the norm of the force measured by the ATI Nano 17 (upper part) and the pressure measured by Freescale MPXV5050DP (lower part). Except for the increasing pressure due to the inflating air, they have constant trends till the impact between the pneumatic balloon and the force sensor. On the right, the relation between ΔP and ΔF collected throughout the whole experiment for the initial pneumatic pressure range $[5.2, 6.4)$ kPa. (Color figure online)

Results. For each experimental trial, when the robotic arm stopped moving, we measured the pressure value of the proposed pneumatic system and the force registered by the ATI sensor. Because of the aim of the evaluation and the way we carried out the experiment, i.e., the robotic manipulator was moving along a normal direction with respect to the sensitive surface of the sensor (y-axis in

Fig. 3), torque components were neglected. Moreover, our pneumatic force sensor cannot give any information about the direction of the applied force: its single value output can be related to the norm of the force measured by the commercial force sensor.

Figure 4a shows the norm of the force measured by the ATI sensor on the top and the pressure measured by the Freescale MPXV5050DP on the bottom during a representative trial. At $t = 0\,$s, the pneumatic balloon is completely deflated and no contact force is present $F_i = 0\,$N. At about $t = 3\,$s, it reaches the initial pressure, i.e., $P_i = 5.2\,$kPa for the considered task, but there is still no contact force playing. At about $t = 8.6\,$s, the balloon applies a force on the ATI sensor, that corresponds to a change of the pneumatic system pressure. The difference in terms of force $\Delta F = F_f - F_i$, where F_f is the value of the force registered by the ATI sensor when the robotic arm stopped moving, needs to be related with $\Delta P = P_f - P_i$, where P_f is the pressure inside the pneumatic system due to the contact with the sensor.

Figure 4b shows with blue stars each couple (ΔP, ΔF) collected throughout the whole experiment for the specific initial pneumatic pressure range [5.2, 6.4) kPa. Data do not result equally distributed on the pressure range because higher contact forces cannot be reached with lower initial pressures. The purple line represents a quadratic fitting of data obtained with a least squares method to estimate the empirical relation between ΔP and ΔF. The different equations estimated this way for any considered initial pressure range are graphically depicted in Fig. 5a and reported in Fig. 5b.

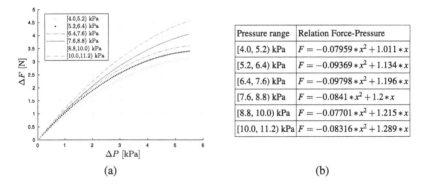

Pressure range	Relation Force-Pressure
[4.0, 5.2) kPa	$F = -0.07959 * x^2 + 1.011 * x$
[5.2, 6.4) kPa	$F = -0.09369 * x^2 + 1.134 * x$
[6.4, 7.6) kPa	$F = -0.09798 * x^2 + 1.196 * x$
[7.6, 8.8) kPa	$F = -0.0841 * x^2 + 1.2 * x$
[8.8, 10.0) kPa	$F = -0.07701 * x^2 + 1.215 * x$
[10.0, 11.2) kPa	$F = -0.08316 * x^2 + 1.289 * x$

(a)   (b)

Fig. 5. Empirical force-pressure relations for the six considered initial pressure ranges.

3.2 Experiment #2: Pneumatic Sensor Validation (Making Contact)

The aim of the second experiment was to validate the previously defined force-pressure relation in a single and maintained contact task, in which it was easier to compute the final estimation error since at the end of each trial the interaction force was constant.

Methods. Similarly to the first experiment, the task consisted in the robotic end-effector, not in contact with the sensor at the beginning, that gradually moved towards the wall and applied an increasing force on the sensor by means of the pneumatic balloon and then stopped. We carried out 10 trials for each initial pressure range depicted on the left side of Fig. 5b, for a total of 60 trials. In any trial both the pressure and the displacement of the robotic end-effector were pseudo randomly picked out in the considered relative range. Regarding the displacement of the robotic end-effector, we selected the range [2, 7] mm to consider a larger number of interactions with the ATI sensor. Again, the zero position was the one in which the elastic membrane came in contact with the ATI and any contact between the ATI and the pneumatic balloon housing was avoided.

Results. For each experimental trial, when the robotic arm stopped moving, we measured the interaction force with both our pneumatic sensor (following the relation force-pressure detailed in Sect. 3.1) and the ATI sensor. Figure 6 shows aggregated information about the error computed by the force estimation performed through the pneumatic sensor with respect to the one measured with the ATI (the ground-truth). Such an error has been normalized over the force ground-truth value and split among the six different initial pressure ranges. The resulting mean of the normalized error is 9.81%. We tested the means of the error normalized over the force measurements for the six considered initial pressure ranges. The collected data passed the Shapiro-Wilk normality test. To determine whether the means of the error are statistically equivalent, we performed a two one-sided t-test (TOST), whose null hypothesis (two groups are different) states that the groups must differ by at most θ to be rejected. In this work we evaluated θ as suggested in [7], where the authors provide a useful step-by-step process for performing equivalence testing with commonly available computational software packages. The tests revealed statistical equivalence for any couple of means.

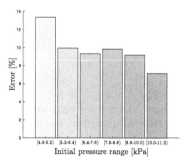

Fig. 6. Estimation error divided among the considered initial pressure ranges comparing data retrieved by the pneumatic sensor and the ATI force sensor. Errors have been normalized over ATI sensor force values.

3.3 Experiment #3: Pneumatic Sensor Validation (Repeated Making/Breaking Contact)

The goal of the third experiment was to validate the empirical relation described in Sect. 3.1 in a more realistic, though repeatable, palpation task. The task consisted in three different and subsequent making/breaking contact actions with the ATI sensor.

Methods. Likewise previous experiments, the robotic end-effector, not in contact with the sensor at the beginning, gradually moved towards the wall and applied an increasing force on the sensor by means of the pneumatic balloon. As soon as it reached a predetermined displacement, it started moving backward, thus decreasing the interaction force, and eventually broke the contact. Then, a similar trial started again and then again, for a total number of three subsequent making/breaking contact actions. Finally, the robot came into contact with the stationary object and stopped after moving for a certain displacement. While the initial pressure the balloon was inflated with was kept the same throughout the task, the robot displacement changed each trial and it was 5.0 mm, 5.5 mm, 6.0 mm, and 6.5 mm for the first, the second, the third, and the fourth trial, respectively. Again, the zero position was considered the one in which the elastic membrane came into contact with the ATI sensor and any contact between the sensor and the pneumatic balloon housing was avoided.

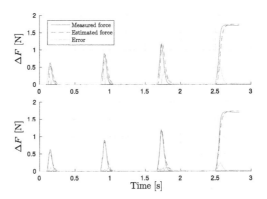

Fig. 7. Repeated making/breaking contact. The solid blue line shows the interaction force measured by the ATI sensor along the y-axis (see Fig. 3). The dashed magenta line represents the interaction force estimated by the proposed pneumatic sensor. The dotted green line indicates the absolute error between the two aforementioned forces. On the top figure it is possible to see a delay between the developed sensor and the commercial one. On the bottom, a time shift of -0.015 s has been introduced to realign the two plots and compute a more meaningful error. (Color figure online)

Results. With respect to the previous experiment of Sect. 3.2, this test aimed at investigating the performance of the proposed sensor throughout a complete palpation task, analyzing the final steady-state interaction force as well as the transient one. During the task we measured the interaction force with the ATI force sensor, considered as ground truth, and we estimated the same force using the proposed pneumatic sensor following the proper equation characterized in Sect. 3.1. Figure 7 shows the force profiles gathered by both the ATI sensor (solid blue line) and our pneumatic sensor (dashed magenta line). During this run the initial pressure was set to 8.15 kPa. On the top, data are reported as recorded and it is worth noting the presence of a time delay between the blue and magenta force profiles due to the different dynamics of the two sensors. On the bottom, this delay has been artificially corrected introducing a constant time shift of -0.015 s to the force estimated by the pneumatic sensor. The green dotted line represents sample by sample the absolute value of the difference between the two gathered forces and can be considered a significant metric to measure the accuracy of our sensor. For the sake of fairness, the error is shown on both the subplots. It has a maximum value of 0.5757 N when the time delay is present and 0.2417 N where it is not.

3.4 Discussion, Conclusion, and Future Work

This paper introduces the design of a novel pneumatic force sensor for robot-assisted surgery, that takes advantage of the measure of a pressure change inside an elastic membrane to estimate the interaction force between the surgical tool and the patient's tissue. The balloon can be inflated only when required, without constraining the surgeon's workspace during the standard medical procedures. Moreover, the delocalization of the electronics with respect to the elastic membrane, makes this surgical tool inexpensive and easily disposable because of sterilizability reasons. Firstly, to characterize the usability of the proposed sensing system, we empirically evaluated the relation between the variation of the pressure inside the elastic membrane and the applied force, considering six different ranges of the initial pneumatic pressure. Then, we validated the computed functions exploiting a commercial F/T sensor as ground-truth twofolds: (i) during a single and maintained contact; (ii) during four subsequent interactions with an object that mimic a complete palpation task. The force-pressure relation shown in Fig. 5 strictly depends on the elastic membrane material and on the system size so, with a view to future applications, the system needs to be calibrated when any main component changes. The use of a gas as a means to estimate interaction forces allows one to change the initial balloon pressure, thus the stiffness of the tool, according to the tissue to be touched and the amount of force to exert. It is clear how the same pressure change leads to different interactions forces, when the initial pneumatic pressure varies. Although the aggregated results depicted in Fig. 6 were declared statistically equivalent, it is worth noting that the pneumatic sensor appears less accurate with a lower initial pressure. This might be due to the fact that measured forces at low initial pressure are lower and a small absolute error might result in a higher error ratio. This trend is also confirmed for the highest pressure range, in which the error ratio is the lowest. Even though Fig. 7 shows a slightly slower dynamics of the proposed pneumatic system with respect to a high-bandwidth very-fine resolution commercial sensor (constant time delay of 0.015 s), the two force profiles result almost overlapped no matter the continuous change of interaction forces. This proves a high reliability of the system both in the transient and in the steady-state interaction. However, the nature of this delay will be further investigated in future works together with its relation to the pneumatic system hoses length and diameter. Faragasso et al. [3] developed in 2014 a system combining vision and a spring mechanism to measure interaction forces in MIS. They proposed two different models, a mathematical and an experimental one, with a RMSE of 0.1535 N and 0.1355 N, respectively, in the range [0, 1.96] N. Computing the RMSE on the data collected during the experiment of Sect. 3.2 and considering the same force range, we found a value of 0.1121 N, comparable, if not lower, to the ones calculated by Faragasso et al. The major advantage of our system, with respect to the aforementioned one, is the possibility of changing online the compliance of the sensing part according to the tissue to touch. In the other system the compliance strictly depends on the structure of the device and the stiffness of the spring used. Despite the simple and intuitive technology exploited to design the proposed pneumatic system, the presented preliminary results appear very promising and, in our opinion, this working principle represents a valuable contribution for the development of inexpensive sensors to be used in RMIS scenarios. Future work will be focused on the reduction of the prototype size and on the actual integration with surgical tools. Surgeons' opinion will be asked how to improve device ergonomics and feasibility in practical usage will be explored. Also a different set of elastic biocompatible materials will be tested to understand which one might be the best for different specific surgical tasks. Besides the application in RMIS that represents the main goal, the proposed system might be used also for different purposes. For instance a set of these pneumatic sensors can also be seen as the fingerpads of a robotic hand, whose compliance of the grasp can be real-time tuned.

References

1. Aviles, A.I., Alsaleh, S., Sobrevilla, P., Casals, A.: Sensorless force estimation using a neuro-vision-based approach for robotic-assisted surgery. In: IEEE/EMBS International Conference on Neural Engineering, pp. 86–89 (2015)
2. Black, J.: Biological Performance of Materials: Fundamentals of Biocompatibility. CRC Press, Boca Raton (2005)
3. Faragasso, A., Stilli, A., Bimbo, J., Noh, Y., Liu, H., Nanayakkara, T., Dasgupta, P., Wurdemann, H., Althoefer, K.: Endoscopic add-on stiffness probe for real-time soft surface characterisation in MIS. In: Proceedings of IEEE International Confeence on Engineering in Medicine and Biology Society, pp. 6517–6520 (2014)
4. Gonenc, B., Chamani, A., Handa, J., Gehlbach, P., Taylor, R.H., Iordachita, I.: 3-dof force-sensing motorized micro-forceps for robot-assisted vitreoretinal surgery. IEEE Sens. J. **17**(11), 3526–3541 (2017)

5. Hwang, Y., Paydar, O.H., Candler, R.N.: Pneumatic microfinger with balloon fins for linear motion using 3D printed molds. Sens. Actuators A Phys. **234**, 65–71 (2015)
6. Lanfranco, A.R., Castellanos, A.E., Desai, J.P., Meyers, W.C.: Robotic surgery: a current perspective. Ann. Surg. **239**(1), 14 (2004)
7. Limentani, G.B., Ringo, M.C., Ye, F., Bergquist, M.L., McSorley, E.O.: Beyond the t-test: statistical equivalence testing. Anal. Chem. **77**(11), 221–226 (2005)
8. Luo, Y., Nelson, B.J.: Fusing force and vision feedback for manipulating deformable objects. J. Field Robot. **18**(3), 103–117 (2001)
9. Mahvash, M., Gwilliam, J., Agarwal, R., Vagvolgyi, B., Su, L.M., Yuh, D.D., Okamura, A.M.: Force-feedback surgical teleoperator: controller design and palpation experiments. In: Proceedings of Symposium on Haptic Interfaces for Virtual Environment and Teleoperator Systems, pp. 465–471 (2008)
10. Van der Meijden, O.A.J., Schijven, M.P.: The value of haptic feedback in conventional and robot-assisted minimal invasive surgery and virtual reality training: a current review. Surg. Endosc. **23**(6), 1180–1190 (2009)
11. Meli, L., Pacchierotti, C., Prattichizzo, D.: Experimental evaluation of magnified haptic feedback for robot-assisted needle insertion and palpation. Int. J. Med. Robot. Comput. Assist. Surg. **13**(4), e1809 (2017). https://doi.org/10.1002/rcs.1809
12. Nakai, A., Kuwana, K., Saito, K., Dohi, T., Kumagai, A., Shimoyama, I.: Mems 6-axis force-torque sensor attached to the tip of grasping forceps for identification of tumor in thoracoscopic surgery. In: Proceedings of IEEE International Conference on Micro Electro Mechanical Systems, pp. 546–548 (2017)
13. Noohi, E., Parastegari, S., Žefran, M.: Using monocular images to estimate interaction forces during minimally invasive surgery. In: Proceedings of IEEE/RSJ International Conference on Intelligent Robots and Systems, pp. 4297–4302 (2014)
14. Okamura, A.M.: Methods for haptic feedback in teleoperated robot-assisted surgery. Ind. Robot Int. J. **31**(6), 499–508 (2004)
15. Okamura, A.M.: Haptic feedback in robot-assisted minimally invasive surgery. Curr. Opin. Urol. **19**(1), 102 (2009)
16. Pacchierotti, C., Prattichizzo, D., Kuchenbecker, K.J.: Cutaneous feedback of fingertip deformation and vibration for palpation in robotic surgery. IEEE Trans. Biomed. Eng. **63**(2), 278–287 (2016)
17. Puangmali, P., Liu, H., Seneviratne, L.D., Dasgupta, P., Althoefer, K.: Miniature 3-axis distal force sensor for minimally invasive surgical palpation. IEEE/ASME Trans. Mechatron. **17**(4), 646–656 (2012)
18. Stanley, A.A., Gwilliam, J.C., Okamura, A.M.: Haptic jamming: a deformable geometry, variable stiffness tactile display using pneumatics and particle jamming. In: Proceedings of IEEE World Haptics Conference, pp. 25–30 (2013)
19. Tavakoli, M., Patel, R., Moallem, M.: Haptic interaction in robot-assisted endoscopic surgery: a sensorized end-effector. Int. J. Med. Robot. Comput. Assist. Surg. **1**(2), 53–63 (2005)
20. Tholey, G., Desai, J.P., Castellanos, A.E.: Force feedback plays a significant role in minimally invasive surgery: results and analysis. Ann. Surg. **241**(1), 102 (2005)
21. Wagner, C., Stylopoulos, N., Howe, R.: Force feedback in surgery: analysis of blunt dissection. In: Proceedings of Symposium on Haptic Interfaces for Virtual Environment and Teleoperator Systems (2002)
22. Wettels, N., Smith, L.M., Santos, V.J., Loeb, G.E.: Deformable skin design to enhance response of a biomimetic tactile sensor. In: Proceedings of IEEE International Conference on Biomedical Robotics and Biomechatronics, pp. 132–137 (2008)

Efficient Evaluation of Coding Strategies for Transcutaneous Language Communication

Robert Turcott, Jennifer Chen, Pablo Castillo, Brian Knott, Wahyudinata Setiawan, Forrest Briggs, Keith Klumb, Freddy Abnousi, Prasad Chakka, Frances Lau, and Ali Israr[✉]

Facebook, Inc., Menlo Park, CA 94025, USA
rturcott@fb.com, jenniferchen@fb.com, pablocastillo@fb.com, brianknott@fb.com, wahyudinata@fb.com, fbriggs@fb.com, kklumb@fb.com, abnousi@fb.com, prasad@fb.com, flau@fb.com, aliisrar@fb.com

Abstract. Communication of natural language via the skin has seen renewed interest with the advent of mobile devices and wearable technology. Efficient evaluation of candidate haptic encoding algorithms remains a significant challenge. We present 4 algorithms along with our methods for evaluation, which are based on discriminability, learnability, and generalizability. Advantageously, mastery of an extensive vocabulary is not required. Haptic displays used 16 or 32 vibrotactile actuators arranged linearly or as a grid on the arm. In Study 1, a two-alternative, forced-choice protocol tested the ability of 10 participants to detect differences in word pairs encoded by 3 acoustic algorithms: Frequency Decomposition (FD), Dominant Spectral Peaks (DSP), and Autoencoder (AE). Detection specificity was not different among the algorithms, but sensitivity was significantly worse with AE than with FD or DSP. Study 2 compared the performance of 16 participants randomized to DSP vs a phoneme-based algorithm (PH) using a custom video game for training and testing. The PH group performed significantly better at all test stages, and showed better recognition and retention of words along with evidence of generalizability to new words.

Keywords: Haptic communication · Speech to touch · Vibrotactile display Learning · Phoneme · Frequency Decomposition · Vocoder

1 Introduction

Transcutaneous language communication (TLC) allows the user to perceive and understand a tactile representation of spoken or written language [1–4]. In contrast to abstracted semantic content (e.g., emojis), TLC provides an unabbreviated, 1:1 translation between language and haptic stimulation, thereby preserving the richness and complexity of natural language.

TLC was an active area of research through the 1980s with a focus on aiding communication for the hearing impaired [5]. Momentum in the field waned with the development of the cochlear implant [6], but TLC has seen a renewed interest with the proliferation of mobile devices and wearable technology. By using the skin, TLC avoids

© Springer International Publishing AG, part of Springer Nature 2018
D. Prattichizzo et al. (Eds.): EuroHaptics 2018, LNCS 10894, pp. 600–611, 2018.
https://doi.org/10.1007/978-3-319-93399-3_51

competing with traditional visual and acoustic communication tools. In addition, it has the potential to provide a discreet, unobtrusive channel for receiving information.

Developing a successful TLC system faces several challenges, including matching mechanical stimulation to the psychophysical properties of the sensory system, designing a display that is sufficiently miniaturized and comfortable to be practical for extended use, establishing a learning process that is rapid and effective, and developing methods to translate language into stimulus patterns that allow real-time interpretation without an undue cognitive burden.

Even when translation algorithms are informed by psychophysics, the task of empirically evaluating candidate algorithms remains, and is particularly challenging because the intended applications typically require extensive training [6, 7]. The development of efficient methods of algorithm evaluation is a focus of this paper. Discriminability, learnability, and generalizability are identified as key criteria that can be evaluated without requiring mastery of a complex and extensive haptic vocabulary. These criteria were applied to 4 candidate algorithms, and provide an empirical basis for selecting the Phonemic algorithm for subsequent development.

The paper is organized as follows: Sect. 2 (Methods) presents a description of the haptic displays, translation algorithms, evaluation criteria, and protocols for Study 1 (discriminability) and Study 2 (learning). Section 3 presents the results of the studies and Sect. 4 discusses them. Finally, the conclusions are summarized in Sect. 5.

2   Methods

2.1   Haptic Display and Control

Each haptic display used 8 voice coils (VCs) (Tectonic Elements TEAX13C02-8/RH) in either a linear arrangement (25 mm between centers) or a 2x4 grid pattern (approximately 50 mm between centers). The VCs were secured to a 23-cm long thermoformed arced surface that served as a rigid backer. They were tailored for arm placement because of the convenience, relatively large surface area, and reasonable discrimination and sensitivity to vibration of this area (Fig. 1).

Fig. 1.   Voice coil actuators were arranged linearly for the acoustic algorithms (left-hand panel) or in a grid pattern for the phonemic algorithm (middle panel). Displays were secured to one or both arms, depending on the protocol, using Velcro straps (right-hand panel).

The VCs were driven using audio .wav files via daisy-chained Motu 24Ao USB audio interfaces (Mark of the Unicorn, Cambridge, USA) with custom amplifier boards using the MAX98306 Stereo Amplifier (Adafruit Industries, New York).

2.2 Algorithms

We studied algorithms that convert language to haptic stimuli from 2 broad classes. Acoustic algorithms process recordings of spoken language to yield haptic control signals [2, 4]. The input is fundamentally acoustic, so changes in speech rate or pitch, for example, result in changes in the haptic stimuli. In contrast, phonemic algorithms first convert language to a sequence of phonemes, then map the phonemes to pre-defined haptic patterns. Features such as pitch, rate, and prosody are not intrinsic to the encoding, but can be conveyed as metadata and used as modifiers to the patterns. The algorithms we investigated are described below. The first 3 are acoustic, and the 4th is phonemic.

Frequency Decomposition (FD). The speech waveform was digitally sampled at 44.1 kHz for Study 1 and 22.05 kHz for Study 2. It was passed through a pre-emphasis filter with = 0.97 before being partitioned into frames of 1024 samples (23.2 ms) with 50% overlap [8]. After multiplication by a Hamming window, the magnitude spectrum was obtained using the fast Fourier transform (FFT). 32 triangular-shaped filters with 50% overlap and unity area were created as follows: the spectrum between 100 Hz and 1 kHz was divided into 3 linearly spaced bands, and between 1 kHz and 8 kHz was divided into 29 mel-frequency-spaced bands [8]. The scaler product of the spectrum and each filter modulated a 200 Hz sine wave at the corresponding haptic actuator. The output was normalized such that the peak amplitude over the duration of the recording corresponded to 25–30 dB sensation level. Frequencies were mapped progressively from left wrist (low) to left shoulder, and from right wrist to right shoulder (high).

Dominant Spectral Peaks (DSP). This algorithm was identical to FD, except that for each frame, only the 5 largest filter outputs were used; all others were set to zero. For phonemes with a prominent formant structure (vowels) this yielded stimulation by actuators that corresponded to the frequency location of the dominant formants. For phonemes lacking formants (e.g., fricatives) this typically resulted in stimulation that migrated in location over the duration of the phoneme.

Autoencoder (AE). An autoencoder is an artificial neural network architecture that uses unsupervised learning to develop an efficient (compressed) representation of the input data [9]. Our embodiment used 128-unit input and output layers, and a bottleneck layer of 32 units, implemented in collaboration with Scyfer B.V. (Amsterdam, NL). Complex 128-point FFTs of recorded speech (down sampled from 22.05 to 16 kHz) with 25% overlap served as input data.

To improve the recognizability of the haptic patterns by humans, the following constraints were incorporated into the training cost function: sparsity (minimize the number of active actuators), discreteness (quantize outputs to 1 of 3 states), and ordinality (sequence output levels rather than treat as categorical). The encodings represented in compressed form by the 32 trinary units of the hidden layer were used to drive the actuators, which were off, or driven with 100 Hz or 250 Hz sinusoidal activation at 25–30 dB sensation level, depending on the state of the unit.

Phonemic (PH). Motivated by findings of previous work [10], we implemented custom haptic patterns that were as simple as possible while still allowing discriminability. Sequences of phonemes were manually transcribed. Encoding rules included assigning dynamic, longer duration patterns to vowels, and approximating place of articulation for consonants with location on the arm (Fig. 2). Active actuators were implemented with voice coils driven at 250 Hz with amplitude 25–30 dB sensation level. Static patterns (consonants) and dynamic patterns (vowels) had durations of 120 and 220 ms, respectively. For dynamic patterns, individual actuators were on for 97 ms, with successive activations offset by 62 ms to enhance the illusion of continuous motion [11]. Activation onset and offset were ramped over a duration that was 10% of the on-time. A 200 ms inter-stimulus interval was used between phonemes.

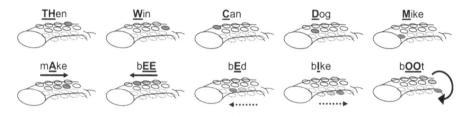

Fig. 2. Custom haptic patterns and associated phonemes used for training and testing.

2.3 Evaluation Criteria

We evaluated the quality of the algorithms according to discriminability, learnability, and generalizability. 'Discriminability' refers to the ability to detect differences in haptic patterns that represent phonetically different words, and to recognize as identical haptic patterns that represent phonetically identical words. Evaluation of discriminability is rapid since learning is not required. In contrast, 'learnability' allows the correct identification of a word, represented by a haptic pattern, some period (minutes-days) after exposure. Finally, 'generalizability' allows the identification of novel patterns by drawing on learned associations between components of the haptic pattern and lexical information. By comparing performance on a subset of phonemes and words, we can gain insight into the quality of the coding algorithms without requiring the arduous process of first learning an entire vocabulary.

2.4 Study 1: Discriminability

The 3 acoustic algorithms were compared in terms of *sensitivity* (fraction of pairs of different words that are correctly identified as different) and *specificity* (fraction of pairs of identical words that are correctly identified as not different). The PH algorithm was not included because its custom patterns were thought to be sufficiently discriminable

by design. Four 8-actuator displays were used with actuators placed in a linear configuration on the dorsal forearms and lateral upper arms, as shown in Fig. 1.

Custom recordings from a single male native speaker of American English were used
to form test pairs of monosyllabic words that differ in a single phoneme: beat/but, bet/
debt, bet/met, bet/pet, bet/vet, bird/bud, book/bought, bought/but, boy/buy, fat/vat, heat/
hit, lit/wit, met/net, pet/tet, sat/shat, and that/vat. These were selected to (1) give good
representation of the different phonemic groups, (2) provide comparison phonemes that
are similar in production and hence perceptually close (e.g., 'b' and 'd' in bet/debt are
both plosives that are produced toward the front of the mouth), and (3) minimize the
number of distinct phonemes. Negative (beat/beat) and positive (boy/sat; differs in all
phonemes) controls were included. Haptic patterns lasted 200–300 ms with an inter-
word interval of 350 ms. A 500 ms delay was imposed between response and subsequent
trial. For each of the 3 algorithms, the 18 pairs were repeated 6 times for a total of 324
trials, with the participant tasked with indicating whether the pairs were "same" or
"different". The order of presentation of each pair was randomized over all repetitions
and algorithms, as was the word order within pairs.

The null hypothesis, that responses associated with different algorithms are governed
by the same underlying statistics, was evaluated with permutation testing, which, advantageously, makes no assumptions about the properties of the data [12]. Briefly, the
response data was randomly relabeled and the test statistic (difference in sensitivity) was
recalculated based on the new labeling. The process was repeated 50,000 times, and a
distribution of the permutation test statistic was generated. The probability that the actual
test statistic arose from this distribution was estimated. If the probability was less than
0.0167 ($p = 0.05$ with Bonferroni correction for 3 comparisons) the null hypothesis was
rejected. An ANOVA with the algorithms as within-subject factors was a pre-specified
secondary analysis.

2.5   Study 2: Learning

The learnability and generalizability of haptic patterns encoded from single words were
tested using the PH and DSP algorithms (results of Study 1 suggested DSP yielded the
best discriminability). 32-channel actuators arranged linearly over both arms were used
for DSP. PH used two 8-channel displays arranged as a 4x4 grid on the left forearm,
with 2x4 grids on the dorsal and volar surfaces.

Training for a practical TLC system would, ideally, be rapid, engaging, and fun. The
potential for implicit learning in the context of video games has previously been demonstrated [13]. In addition, the ability of video games to engage the user is well known [14].
We therefore designed a game-based training paradigm with the goals of incorporating
implicit, explicit, incidental, and adaptive learning approaches; and to reinforce haptic-
audio cross-modal association. The implementation of the game, called RoboRecycle,
was performed by Coatsink Software (Sunderland, UK) using the Unity game engine
(Unity Technologies SF, San Francisco) with haptic controls stored as .wav files and
delivered through a USB audio interface using Max 7 (Cycling '74, San Francisco).

RoboRecycle had 3 modes (Fig. 3). In *Explore* mode, the user initiated haptic playback by selecting from a menu of words to gain familiarity with the stimuli that would

be delivered during gameplay, and to begin to form associations between words and haptic patterns. In *Game* mode, the user attempted to rescue robots before they were consumed by a recycler. A haptic pattern was repeatedly delivered as a conveyor belt carried the robot toward its fate. The player was cued with the associated spoken word, which was delayed to avoid cross-modal masking. As levels progressed, the number of cued words decreased, so at the highest level there were no spoken cues. The player selected an answer from a menu. If correct, the robot was rescued. If incorrect, or if the robot reached the end of the conveyor belt, it fell to its doom. In both cases the correct answer was shown. The player progressed to the next level if >70% of responses were correct. If <50% were correct then the player dropped back to the previous level. If accuracy was between 50 and 70% then the player repeated the level. In *Test* mode, the player received a single presentation of each haptic pattern, and selected an answer from a menu of possibilities. No feedback was provided.

Fig. 3. Screenshots from RoboRecyle Explore, Game, and Test modes

24 words with 2–3 phonemes/word were used in 3 sets as follows: List 0: ace, aid, same, sue; List A: cake, die, make, mime, mood, me, they, weed, wide, woo; List B: deed, dime, do, doom, key, may, meek, wake, why, womb. Words were selected to be representative of the main features of articulation. Lists A and B were derived from the 10 distinct phonemes shown in Fig. 2. Recordings were made by a single male native speaker of American English. List 0 was for demonstration only. The order in which Lists A and B were used in the study was counterbalanced among participants.

The study design is illustrated in Fig. 4. The study began with a demonstration of the RoboRecycle game using List 0. This consisted of a brief guided tour of each game mode with the participant able to activate controls and experience the haptic stimuli.

Training occurred in 2 phases. In the first, the participant was allowed 5 min to initiate haptic playback using Explore mode with List A or B ("List 1"). During this phase, participants in the PH algorithm group had access to a visual representation of patterns associated with each phoneme. Participants in the DSP group received the following description of coding rule: "The algorithm maps frequencies in the speech signal to locations on the arm. Frequencies increase progressively up the arms, with lowest mapped to the left wrist, low-medium to the left shoulder, high-medium to the right wrist, and highest to the right shoulder." The second training phase used Game mode, which was stopped after 20 min or when the participant reached at least 90% correct at the highest level.

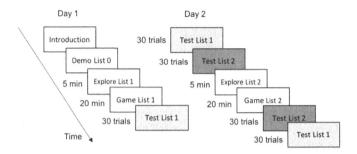

Fig. 4. Learning study design

The participant was tested immediately after completing the Game phase. Each of the 10 haptic patterns was presented 3 times, for a total of 30 trials in random order. At each trial, the haptic pattern was delivered once, and the participant selected an answer from a menu of the 10 words. No feedback was provided.

The second day began with testing the 10 haptic patterns from the previous day (List 1) to evaluate retention. This was followed by a test of 10 new haptic patterns (List 2) to test generalization. The testing protocol was identical to that used on the first day. After testing, the participant again underwent training using RoboRecycle's Explore and Game modes with the previously unused word list (List 2), using the same protocol as Day 1. After the training, the participant was tested on the 10 current words first (List 2), and then on the words that were learned the previous day (List 1).

To evaluate learnability and generalizability, mixed 2x5 ANOVA was conducted on test accuracy with the 2 algorithms and 5 time points (post-training of List 1 on Day 1; and retention of List 1, pre-training of List 2, post-training of List 2, and 2nd retention of List 1 on Day 2) as within-subject factors, followed by post hoc analyses on any significant effects with Bonferroni adjustment. In addition, the test accuracy at 5 different points was compared against 10% chance level using one-sample t-tests with Bonferroni adjustments for multiple comparisons. ANOVA rather than permutation testing was used because of its ability to support multiple comparisons across multiple dimensions. Moreover, the rates of level progression during Game (training) mode across time for different algorithms and on different days were estimated using linear regression.

3   Results

3.1   Study 1: Discriminability

10 participants were recruited from our group after providing informed consent (2 female; ages 34.9 ± 9.2, range 24–54). Previous haptic experience varied from limited to extensive.

Detection sensitivity for FD, DSP, and AE was 0.58 ± 0.20, 0.60 ± 0.19, and 0.38 ± 0.23, respectively (ave $\pm$ SD) (Fig. 5). Permutation testing revealed no significant difference between FD and DSP ($p = 0.37$), but the differences between FD and AE ($p < 0.001$) and between DSP and AE ($p < 0.001$) were significant with Bonferroni correction. These findings were confirmed with ANOVA, which showed no significant differences for specificity ($p = 0.87$) but did for sensitivity ($p < 0.01$) as a result of significantly lower sensitivity of AE than both FD and DSP ($p = 0.02$).

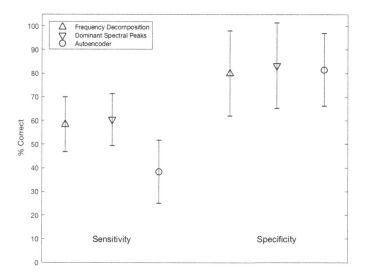

Fig. 5. Sensitivity and specificity (ave ± SEM) for FD, DSP and AE. Specificity was not significantly different among the algorithms, but AE yielded significantly worse sensitivity.

3.2 Study 2: Learning

16 participants without previous haptic experience were enrolled in the learning study after providing informed consent, with 8 randomized to the DSP group (age 31.3 ± 12.3, range 23–57; 4 females), and 8 to the PH group (age 28.8 ± 7.3, range 22–44; 2 females).

Test performance is shown in Fig. 6. Mixed ANOVA analysis revealed a significant main effect of algorithms ($p = 0.01$), with omnibus test accuracy higher in PH than DSP group. There was a significant main effects of time points ($p < .001$), as well as time points by algorithms interaction ($p = 0.01$).

Post-hoc analyses showed that the PH group significantly outperformed the DSP group at pre-training of List 2 (p < 0.01), which was also the only time that a group's test accuracy (DSP) was not significantly different from 10% chance level (PH: $p = 0.01, 0.01, 0.03, 0.025,$ and <0.001; DSP: $p = 0.01, < 0.001, 1.0, 0.01,$ and 0.01; for post 1 on Day 1, and retention 1, pre 2, post 2, and 2nd retention 1 on Day 2, respectively). PH performance was also significantly better on post-training of List 2 ($p = 0.01$) and the 2nd retention test of List 1 on Day 2 ($ps < 0.01$). There were no significant differences among the 3 tests of List 1 for either group ($p > 0.05$), indicating that a decrease (or increase) in retention with the passage of time and acquisition of new material could not be detected. Critically, the recall test result immediately after training was significantly better in List 2 than List 1 for the PH group ($p = 0.01$), but not for the DSP group ($p = 1.0$), suggesting better

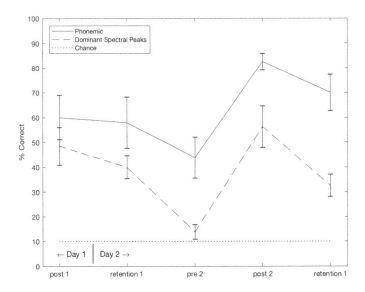

Fig. 6. Test performance (ave ± SEM) for PH (solid), for DSP (dashed), and expected from chance (dotted).

generalizability in the PH group. There was no significant difference in test performance on List A vs B for either algorithm at any test point.

The rate of level progression was not significantly different between PH and DSP groups on Day 1 ($p = 0.17$), but was significantly faster for PH on Day 2 both when compared to DSP on Day 2 ($p < 0.001$), and when compared to itself on Day 1 ($p < 0.001$), indicating improved learnability with the PH algorithm with additional exposure. In contrast, rate of progression was slower for DSP on Day 2 compared to Day 1 ($p = 0.01$), suggesting additional exposure interfered with learning.

Combining word lists, the PH group demonstrated $76.3 \pm 14.7\%$ (ave ± SD) accuracy on the 20 words after 50 min of focused training (excluding learning effects of introduction and test taking). For DSP accuracy was $44.4 \pm 16.2\%$.

4 Discussion

This work presents 4 candidate algorithms for translating natural language to haptic stimuli for transcutaneous communication, along with evaluation methodology based on discriminability, learnability, and generalizability.

The three acoustic algorithms we tested were not significantly different in specificity, however, the ability to detect single phoneme differences in word pairs was significantly worse using AE compared to both FD and DSP. Using a set of 20 words composed of 10 phonemes, learning was possible with both DSP and PH, but participants using the PH algorithm showed significantly better recall, and demonstrated an ability to generalize learned phoneme associations to new words. Overall, the PH group demonstrated 76.3 ± 14.7 accuracy on 20 haptic words after 50 min of focused training.

The AE algorithm represents an instantiation of a well-known class of unsupervised machine learning algorithms that has demonstrated success with data compression. However, the encodings are not readily interpretable by humans due to the high entropy that results from elimination of redundancy during compression. We sought to mitigate this by imposing constraints during training that would facilitate interpretation of haptic stimuli. Despite this, performance in discrimination was inferior to frequency-to-spatial mapping algorithms. Study participants described the AE stimuli as an unstructured, random buzzing, which suggests that entropy remained unacceptably high. More aggressive implementation of constraints was subsequently explored, including adding temporal stability (infrequent changes in state are preferred) and spatial stability (spatial correlation among nearby actuators is preferred). However, reduced entropy came at the expense of lower information capacity to an extent that precluded an acceptable compromise between high entropy and low information content. Further improvement may be possible by incorporating a more refined psychophysical model in network training based on user testing.

Phoneme-based algorithms have several attractive features. Discriminability is guaranteed by design, and mnemonic aids can be incorporated, such as mechanics of articulation [10] or qualitative features of the sound [3]. Furthermore, the language is broken down into a relatively small number of fundamental units (building blocks) with which speakers are intimately familiar, and which form a basis of spoken language acquisition. At the most basic level, once the phoneme/haptic symbol association is learned, comprehension is guaranteed provided the delivery rate is sufficiently slow. Analogous to natural language acquisition, we expect decreased cognitive load along with increased fluency and delivery rate as users master phonetic components and start to recognize longer lexical structures in a 'chunking' process [15]. In contrast, lack of generalization with the DSP algorithm and degradation of performance when new words were added suggest a rote learning process in which acoustic mappings, while discriminable, lacked sufficient perceptual or semantic congruency to the lexical information.

Discriminability, learnability, and generalizability are useful criteria for rapid and effective initial screening of candidate algorithms. Regarding discriminability of word pairs: the algorithm, the haptic display, and the participant together comprise a detection test, which makes analysis amenable to the tools of signal detection theory [16]. In this context, an earlier version of the protocol called for a continuous graded response to reflect the participant's perception of the degree to which the two stimuli differed. However, several drawbacks became apparent: interpretation of the task varied greatly among participants, cognitive demand was greater resulting in longer response times and greater participant fatigue, and while responses were consistent when word pairs were identical or very different, intermediate pairs yielded inconsistent, highly variable responses. For these reasons we adopted the two-alternative, forced-choice protocol presented here.

Viewing the algorithm, haptic display, and participant as an integrated unit also highlights the challenge of evaluating an individual component of the triad. A display that does not reliably deliver the intended stimulus intensity (for example, due to excessive sensitivity to backing pressure) will make it more difficult to detect differences in algorithm performance. Similarly, poor participant motivation, including skepticism of the premise that transcutaneous communication is possible, can mask differences in algorithms or displays. The location for the display was chosen primarily for convenience. The two halves of the display covered both glabrous and hairy skin, and included regions near and far from anchors (wrist, elbow). Different performance can be expected using a display at locations that have greater or lesser sensitivity.

Learnability and generalizability imply discriminability. They more directly reflect the target task but are more demanding and time consuming to test. We minimized these drawbacks by testing a subset of phonemes with a small number of words. Despite the small word set, statistically significant differences in algorithm performance were apparent.

There are several limitations to this work. We take as a premise that discriminability, learnability, and generalizability, as defined here, reveal features of algorithm performance that predict success in the target use case, but this has not been validated. Candidate algorithms were tested on small subsets of phonemes and vocabularies with a modest number of participants, and learning and retention were tested over relatively short time scales. The criteria were applied to isolated words without context, rather than phrases or sentences as would be used in a practical system, and which might aid in interpretation of individual words. The tested algorithms represent specific implementations of their classes; better performance may be possible with further parameter optimization. Future studies will seek to address these limitations.

5   Conclusion

Discriminability, learnability, and generalizability are useful criteria for the efficient evaluation of candidate language-to-haptic translation algorithms. The acoustic algorithms we tested did not differ significantly in specificity, but AE was significantly worse than FD and DSP in sensitivity. Individual words could be learned with both the PH and DSP algorithms, but for PH test performance was significantly better and there was evidence of an ability to generalize learning to previously unseen words. Participants in the PH group demonstrated $76.3 \pm 14.7\%$ (ave $\pm$ SD) correct on 20 haptic words after 50 min of focused training.

Acknowledgements. This work was supported by Facebook, Inc.

References

1. Reed, C.M., Rabinowitz, W.M., Durlach, N.I., Braida, L.D., Conway-Fithian, S., Schultz, M.C.: Research on the Tadoma method of speech communication. J. Acoust. Soc. Am. **77**, 247–257 (1985). https://doi.org/10.1121/1.392266
2. Brooks, P.L., Frost, B.J., Mason, J.L., Gibson, D.M.: Continuing evaluation of the Queen's University tactile vocoder II: identification of open set sentences and tracking narrative. J. Rehabil. Res. Dev. **23**, 129–138 (1986)
3. Israr, A., Meckl, P.H., Reed, C.M., Tan, H.Z.: Controller design and consonantal contrast coding using a multi-finger tactual display. J. Acoust. Soc. Am. **125**, 3925–3935 (2009). https://doi.org/10.1121/1.3124771

4. Galvin, K.L., Mavrias, G., Moore, A., Cowan, R.S.C., Blamey, P.J., Clark, G.M.: A comparison of Tactaid II+ and Tactaid 7 use by adults with a profound hearing impairment. Ear Hear. **20**, 471–482 (1999). https://doi.org/10.1097/00003446-199912000-00003
5. Oller, D.K.: Tactile AIDS for the hearing impaired: an overview. Semin. Hear. **16**, 289–295 (1995). https://doi.org/10.1055/s-0028-1083726
6. Miyamoto, R.T., Robbins, A.M., Osberger, M.J., Todd, S.L., Riley, A.I., Kirk, K.I.: Comparison of multichannel tactile AIDS and multichannel cochlear implants in children with profound hearing impairments. Am. J. Otol. **16**, 8–13 (1995). https://doi.org/10.1016/0165-5876(95)97416-6
7. Brooks, P.L., Frost, B.J.: Evaluation of a tactile vocoder for word recognition. J. Acoust. Soc. Am. **74**, 34–39 (1983). https://doi.org/10.1121/1.389685
8. Muda, L., Begam, M., Elamvazuthi, I.: Voice recognition algorithms using mel frequency cepstral coefficient (MFCC) and dynamic time warping (DTW). Techniques **2**, 138–143 (2010). https://doi.org/10.5815/ijigsp.2016.09.03
9. Hinton, G.E., Salakhutdinov, R.R.: Reducing the dimensionality of data with neural networks. Science **313**, 504–507 (2006). https://doi.org/10.1126/science.1127647
10. Zhao, S., Israr, A., Lau, F., Abnousi, F.: Coding tactile symbols for phonemic communication. In: Proceedings of CHI 2018 (2018). https://doi.org/10.1145/3173574.3173966
11. Israr, A., Poupyrev, I.: Tactile brush: drawing on skin with a tactile grid display. In: Proceedings of CHI 2011, pp. 2019–2028 (2011). https://doi.org/10.1145/1978942.1979235
12. Pesarin, F., Salmaso, L.: The permutation testing approach: a review. Statistica **70**, 481–509 (2010). https://doi.org/10.6092/issn.1973-2201/3599
13. Lim, S.J., Holt, L.L.: Learning foreign sounds in an alien world: videogame training improves non-native speech categorization. Cogn. Sci. **35**, 1390–1405 (2011). https://doi.org/10.1111/j.1551-6709.2011.01192.x
14. Przybylski, A.K., Rigby, C.S., Ryan, R.M.: A motivational model of video game engagement. Rev. Gen. Psychol. **14**, 154–166 (2010). https://doi.org/10.1037/a0019440
15. Hewlett, D., Cohen, P.: Word segmentation as general chunking. In: Proceedings of Fifteenth Conference on Computational Natural Language Learning, pp. 39–47 (2011)
16. MacMillan, N.A.: Signal detection theory. In: Stevens' Handbook of Experimental Psychology (2002)

A Novel Haptic Glove (ExoTen-Glove) Based on Twisted String Actuation (TSA) System for Virtual Reality

Mohssen Hosseini[1](✉), Yudha Pane[1], Ali Sengül[2], Joris De Schutter[1], and Herman Bruyninckx[1,3]

[1] Robotics Research Group, Department of Mechanical Engineering,
KU LEUVEN, Leuven, Belgium
{mohssen.hosseini,yudha.pane,joris.deschutter,
herman.bruyninckx}@kuleuven.be
[2] Helbling Technik AG, Aarau, Switzerland
ali.senguel@helbling.ch
[3] Department of Mechanical Engineering, TU/e, Eindhoven, The Netherlands

Abstract. A compact and light-weight wearable haptic glove (ExoTen-Glove) based on Twisted String Actuation (TSA) system is presented in this paper. The proposed system uses two actuators with small size DC motors and an integrated force sensor based on optoelectronic components. ExoTen-Glove can provide force feedback to the thumb on one side, and to the other fingers grouped together on the other side. This configuration has been selected to provide the user force feedback during the execution of grasping tasks by means of a virtual reality environment to feel the stiffness of different objects. Thus for the first evaluation of the ExoTen-Glove, we only focus on the feedback from thumb and index finger. The paper reports the design of the haptic glove, the description of the actuation system, the embedded controller, and the preliminary experimental evaluation of the device. The ExoTen-Glove has been evaluated by means of a simple experiment in virtual environment with 2-DOF grasping activities of rigid and compliant virtual object (spring) using thumb and index finger to show the applicability of the system for rehabilitation and haptic feedback purposes. Results of the experiments showed that the haptic ExoTen-Glove improved stiffness evaluation significantly for the high and low spring stiffness and users were able to distinguish virtual spring stiffness differences easily with high accuracy.

Keywords: Force feedback · Twisted String Actuation system
Wearable · Virtual reality · Stiffness discrimination
Tendon transmission system

Robotics Research Group—The Robotics Research Group is a university core lab of Flanders Make.

© Springer International Publishing AG, part of Springer Nature 2018
D. Prattichizzo et al. (Eds.): EuroHaptics 2018, LNCS 10894, pp. 612–622, 2018.
https://doi.org/10.1007/978-3-319-93399-3_52

1   Introduction

Over the past years various robotic systems conceived to be directly interfaced with the human hand have been developed, mainly utilized as haptic interfaces for telemanipulation [1,2], or for medical training [3,4], and for interaction with nano and micro scale phenomenon [5,6]. A five-fingered Haptic interface consists of a 6-DOF arm and a 15-DOF hand has been implemented in [7,8] that allow the user to interact with the virtual object without imposing any weight and providing 3D fingertip force display.

One of the main functionality of the robotic hands is haptic interfaces that are conceived to drive teleoperated systems, both virtual and real, therefore the main purpose is to follow the user movements, minimizing or controlling the interface dynamics during free motion, and providing proper feedback to the user in case of contact with virtual or real objects on the teleoperated system. Haptic interfaces can provide various feedback, such has force [9,10], pressure feedback [11,12] or vibro-tactile [13,14]. Wearable haptic devices with the force feedback not only allow the user to grasp and feel the virtual objects in a natural way during interaction with the environment but also allow the user to manipulate virtual objects in a more natural way. The CyberGrasp ^{TM} [15] is a grounded force feedback system which can provide an individual force (up to 12 N) roughly perpendicular to the fingertip of each finger that can be combined with a separately available CyberGlove $^{®}$ dataglove that provides joint angle information of the hand and fingers. The Rutgers Master II-ND glove [16] is a haptic interface designed for dextrous interactions with virtual environments that provides up to 16 N force feedback to each finger using pneumatic actuators. Most of the wearable haptic gloves have substantial number of actuators and hence they are bulk and heavy. If the haptic gloves are made lighter, smaller, easier to wear and cheaper via a new actuation method, such as twisted string actuation (TSA) system, they would become common human-machine interaction interfaces for the interaction in virtual reality.

The robotic system design requirements present many common aspects, such as the adaptability to different users, the mobility of the device that should not interfere the user's movements and the capability of controlling the feedback provided to the user. In this paper, the development of a haptic ExoTen-Glove driven by twisted string actuation (TSA) system [17–19] is reported. The TSA system allow the implementation of low-cost, light-weight and powerful tendon-based driving systems, based on small DC motors characterized by low torque, high speed and very limited inertia that makes it suitable to be used in highly integrated mechatronic devices, e.g. robotic hands and exoskeletons. Also, the slender structure of TSA system makes it particularly suitable to be used in wearable robotic devices. The TSA system has been used in different applications such as DEXMART hand [20] and a 6-DOF cable-driven haptic interface [21].

The proposed ExoTen-Glove is able to provide the user a force feedback during the execution of grasping tasks in a virtual reality environment. The design of the haptic gloves is oriented to the maximum simplicity, therefore it is implemented as a wearable system without any external bulky mechanism to guide the finger movements and support the actuation used to provide the force feedback, but relying on the skeleton structure of the hand itself as supporting mechanism for the tendon-based actuation system.

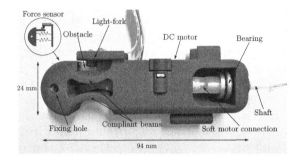

Fig. 1. Detailed view of the TSA module prototype.

The paper is organized as follow. In Sect. 2 the overall device is described, focusing on the design, the actuation system and the controller. Section 3 reports the testing environment and the experimental activity carried out to evaluated the device functionality. In the final Sect. 4 the outcomes of the works are summarized and comments on future work are given.

2   System Description

2.1   Actuation Design

The TSA module design and its integrated force sensor has been described in details in [22–24] and therefore here only a brief summary of its main features is reported. The TSA module structure (see Fig. 1) is made of Polyamide (PA 12) manufactured by Laser Sintering (SLS) and it is composed of:

(i) a frame hosting the DC motor (maxon DCX) and the encoder (maxon ENX), sensor electronic components, with a dimension of (94 mm length, 24 mm height, 19 mm width),

(ii) a fixing hole to connect the module to the supporting frame;

(iii) a force sensor based on optoelectronic component (Omron EE-SX1108) to measure the load applied to the string;

(iv) a pair of axial-symmetric compliant beams that function as a linear spring granting a certain compliance to the structure as well as the implementation of the force sensor;

(v) a shaft supported by an axial bearing at the point of the twisted string connection to both reduce the friction and prevent the transmission force from damaging the motor;

(vi) and a silicon tube for coupling the motor and transmission shafts to provide ample flexibility in order to solve problems due to misalignment of the rotational axes of the motor and the transmission shaft;

(vii) the string (Dyneema with a diameter of 0.16 mm) itself connects the motor module with the linear moving element.

This particular structure allows the transmission force to be completely supported by the output shaft through a combined bearing while the motor is only used to transmit the necessary torque for driving the twisted string actuation to the output shaft. The weight of an ExoTen-Glove actuator, including force sensor, DC motor, encoder and mechanical component like shaft and bearing is 40 g.

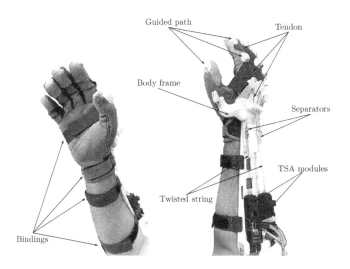

Fig. 2. Overview of the ExoTen-Glove.

2.2 Design of the ExoTen-Glove

Figure 2 demonstrates a simple and light-weight haptic ExoTen-Glove that has been designed to be worn comfortably without any external bulky mechanism to drive the fingers by tendon-based actuation using the skeleton structure of the fingers that fully supports the full motion of the human fingers. It consists of a rigid supporting frame with anatomical shape of forearm made of Polyamide (PA 12) by Laser Sintering (SLS), a soft glove, two independent TSA module to drive a group of fingers from index to little finger and the thumb separately for grasping tasks and tendon guided path. A comfortable soft glove have been used to be worn by user and the fingers are connected to the TSA module by means of tendons (Dyneema 0.26 mm) that are guided through a path made of semi-soft material 3D printed (EFLEX) attached on the glove and a linear guide to prevent the twisting of the strings itself and with a separator to guide the tendons trough each finger. The path is designed with a curved shape to allow the tendons follow the finger movement with its anatomical shape and prevent the shear forces to the attachment points. In order to prevent the slack in top of the fingers, we used binding structure for tightening the glove on top of the fingers. Since the users have different finger length, we can adjust the length of the tendons by twisting the tendon on each finger. The total weight of the ExoTen-Glove is approximately 360 g.

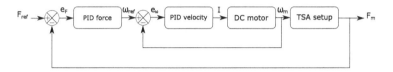

Fig. 3. Block diagram of the TSA's force and velocity control loop. Subscripts ref and m denotes reference and measured, respectively. Meanwhile F, ω, I and e represents force, velocity, current, and error respectively.

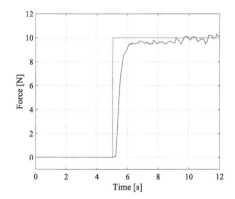

Fig. 4. The step response of the TSA force controller. The control bandwidth is approximately 2 rad/s.

2.3   Electronics

The electronics unit consists of a STM32F4 32-bit microcontroller and an L298-based Arduino motor driver. The design choice was made by considering the performance of the overall system while keeping the cost affordable. The microcontroller performs signal processing and control algorithm calculation including the ADC measurements as well as velocity and force control. Communication between the microcontroller and the PC is established through a serial USB communication.

Fig. 5. The experimental setup. In this experiment participants were asked to wear the ExoTen-Glove and squeeze a set of virtual springs with different stiffness by their thumb and index finger while the ExoTen-Glove were covered.

2.4   Controller

The TSA is controlled with a cascaded PID controller structure whose diagram is shown in Fig. 3. The outer loop regulates the force with a slower frequency of 1 kHz. Meanwhile the inner loop controls the DC motor velocity with a faster 5 kHz frequency. To reduce the ADC noise, the measured force is filtered with a low pass filter. Its parameter is chosen such that the trade-off between delay and noise level is balanced.

The PID gains are tuned by examining the dynamic responses upon applying step force references. For a satisfactory force tracking, a time constant of at least 0.5 s is desired. The step response of the controller is shown in Fig. 4. As evident from the plot, there is still some oscillatory behavior during the steady state phase. This is mostly due to the force sensor noise which is not filtered out entirely. Nevertheless, the noise level is still within tolerance and the rise time satisfies our requirement.

3   Experimental Evaluation

3.1   Subjects

A total of 8 healthy right-handed participants (6 males and 2 females) took a part in the experiment with an average age of 30 years (ranging from 24 to 36 years old) with normal or corrected to normal vision, no disorder of touch and no history of neurological or psychiatric condition. Each experiment took around 30 min for each participant and he/she was informed about the general goal of the research. Each participant was fully debriefed and was given the opportunity to ask questions and to comment on the research after the experiment.

3.2   Material and Apparatus

We employed the TSA based ExoTen-Glove for the experiments. This novel device is the first test-bed for twisted string based haptic glove. The tracking of the finger movement and force feedback are provided through TSA system. It provides one Degrees of Freedom (DOF) motion for each finger and it can render high forces in grasping without instability. The system is lightweight and enable transparent interactions with virtual reality making realistic grasping manipulations possible. The participants were seated at a table and wore the glove in their right hands. The fingers were positioned in the ExoTen-Glove as shown in Fig. 5 and finger movements and interactions with virtual objects were presented on a computer screen. In order to increase the immersion during the experiment, subjects real hands were covered and subjects were informed to focus on the virtual hand. The experiments were done using a desktop PC (Intel i7-6820 HQ Quad-Core CPU with 2.7 GHz, 16 GB of Ram, with Intel HD Graphics 530 processor). An open source platform, CHAI3D, and a set of C++ libraries were used for the modeling and for simulating the haptics, and for visualization of the virtual world. A virtual world with a virtual hand and spring was developed, see Fig. 6. CHAI3D platform supports several commercial haptic devices and it is possible to extend it to support new custom force feedback devices. We have extended this platform by adding the drivers and libraries of our custom-made haptic glove.

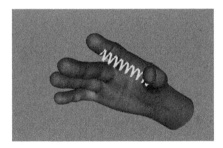

Fig. 6. The virtual hand and spring which was used in this experiment. (Color figure online)

3.3   Experiment Procedure

In this experiment participants were asked to wear the ExoTen-Glove and squeeze a virtual spring with different stiffness by their index and thumb finger aiming to distinguish the stiffness of different virtual springs. The participants were instructed to maintain their right arm on a fixed position. They were asked to complete a task for which instructions were given prior to testing. We implemented eight sets of experimental tasks [26]. In each sets we introduced two spring with different stiffness identifying with color of red and yellow and in each sets stiffness of the springs was chosen randomly. The chosen pair of spring's stiffness are as follow: 2–3, 2–4, 2–5, 2–6, 6–7, 6–8, 6–9, 6–10 N/mm (The order of the stiffness sets during the experiment was chosen randomly for all users). As it was expected, the users would have higher difficulty in distinguishing spring stiffness as their differences become smaller. In the stiffness experiments, the index finger started from a fully open position to a predefined closed position. This enabled the virtual spring between the fingers to be compressed the same amount. Participants presented with a virtual spring and allowed to squeeze it until they are sure about their response.

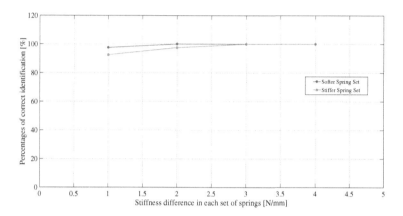

Fig. 7. Percentage of correct identification with respect to stiffness differences for two sets of stiffness.

3.4   Analysis and Results

For stiffness evaluation different experiments are used in the literature [25]. One the commonly used method is Weber Fraction for the characterization of human perception of stiffness. As Weber Fraction is dimensionless; individual performance can be compared with different quantities of force (N) or stiffness (N/m) [25]. In this experiment, a similar experiment design of two-alternative forced choice method is implemented as in Blake et al. [26] rather than Weber Fractions due to forced choice methods simplicity in the design and analysis.

3.5   Discussion

In the present study, a light-weight and compact wearable haptic glove (ExoTen-Glove) based on TSA was presented. The ExoTen-Glove was evaluated by a stiffness difference evaluation experiment. In this experiment, the subjects squeezed two virtual springs with their thumb and index finger. The aim was to find out how well they could differentiate the stiffness differences of two springs with a TSA based ExoTen-Glove. We expected that the users would have difficulty in distinguishing when the stiffness difference got smaller. Our results showed that ExoTen-Glove based on TSA system improved stiffness differentiation task significantly for the high and low spring stiffness and users were able to distinguish virtual spring stiffness differences easily with high accuracy.

Previous studies showed that small stiffness difference cases reported to be near the limit of perception. As the probability of a correct answer by simply guessing is 50%, Blake et al. [26] concluded that in the cases of small difference of soft stiff springs, the users did not receive clear enough information from the haptic glove to be able to distinguish the virtual springs. The result of the present study illustrated that users were able to distinguish small stiffness differences such as 2 and 3 N/mm easily and significantly higher than the previous studies (See Fig. 7). Furthermore, participants percentage of correct responses for the softer spring and the stiffer spring are high. Thereby, the present study extended the previous study [26] and illustrated the advantage of TSA system in stiffness evaluation.

4   Conclusions

This paper presented a compact haptic glove based on TSA system for virtual reality. One of the main challenge in wearable haptic glove research is to design an actuator that is small and compact enough to be worn and at the same time powerful enough for enabling stable and high force feedback to the fingers during grasping virtual objects. Haptic glove based on TSA system has the advantage of a simple design and light-weight actuators in comparison with other tendon-based haptic gloves. Even though using TSA system has many advantages such as low-cost, compact design and high force output, it has a main disadvantages, that is its lifetime. Our presented ExoTen-Glove uses Dyneema tendon for the twisted string actuators and also as a tendon guide through a path made of a semi-soft material (EFLEX) for the finger movements. In the future, different tendon's materials with higher lifetime and lubrication at the tendon could be used to increase its lifetime.

The ExoTen-Glove is evaluated by stiffness experiments. In this experiment, users squeezed a virtual spring with their thumb and index fingers. The aim of the study is to illustrate the benefit of using TSA system in distinguishing stiffness of a pair of virtual springs. As illustrated in the previous studies [26] it is expected the users would have higher difficulty in distinguishing spring stiffness as their differences become smaller. Our results confirmed and extended previous findings. Users were able to identify the spring stiffness with higher percentage of accuracy compared to the previous studies [26]. In the current ExoTen-Glove, grasping a simple object, spring with different stiffness, using index and thumb was demonstrated and experimental results show the advantages of TSA system in stiffness perception and grasping tasks.

Currently, we are working on the next version of the ExoTen-Glove to reduce its weight and cost with implementing a smaller actuation module and using lower cost DC motors and custom-made encoders, adding composite linkages for increasing realism of haptic feedback instead of using a glove. Additionally, we are integrating HTC VIVE headset and Unity game engine into CHAI3D platform for complex hand animations with haptic feedback to increase the realism and immersion of the VR and advanced model based controls. In the future, the haptic glove will be extended for more complex grasping tasks by adding independent actuators for each fingers and controlling them separately for rehabilitation (ExoTen-Hand) and haptic purposes (ExoTen-Glove).

Acknowledgment. The support from VLAIO/Flanders Make Project FIN-ROP_ICON is gratefully acknowledged.

References

1. Ivanisevic, I., Lumelsky, V.J.: Configuration space as a means for augmenting human performance in teleoperation tasks. Trans. Syst. Man Cyber. Part B **30**(3), 471–484 (2000)
2. Dubey, R.V., Everett, S.E., Pernalete, N., Manocha, K.A.: Teleoperation assistance through variable velocity mapping. IEEE Trans. Robot. Autom. **17**(5), 761–766 (2001)
3. Bardorfer, A., Munih, M., Zupan, A., Primozic, A.: Upper limb motion analysis using haptic interface. IEEE/ASME Trans. Mechatron. **6**(3), 253–260 (2001)
4. Basdogan, C., Ho, C.H., Srinivasan, M.A.: Virtual environments for medical training: graphical and haptic simulation of laparoscopic common bile duct exploration. IEEE/ASME Trans. Mechatron. **6**(3), 269–285 (2001)
5. Guthold, M., Falvo, M.R., Matthews, W.G., Paulson, S., Washburn, S., Erie, D.A., Superfine, R., Brooks, F.P., Taylor, R.M.: Controlled manipulation of molecular samples with the nanomanipulator. IEEE/ASME Trans. Mechatron. **5**(2), 189–198 (2000)
6. Marlière, S., Urma, D., Florens, J.-L., Marchi, F.: Multi-sensorial interaction with a nano-scale phenomenon: the force curve. In: Proceedings of EuroHaptics, pp. 246–253 (2004)
7. Kawasaki, H., Doi, Y., Koide, S., Endo, T., Mouri, T.: Hand haptic interface incorporating 1D finger pad and 3D fingertip force display devices. In: Proceedings of International Symposium on Industrial Electronics, pp. 1869–1874 (2010)
8. Kawasaki, H., Mouri, T.: Design and control of five-fingered haptic interface opposite to human hand. IEEE Trans. Robot. **23**(5), 909–918 (2007)
9. Avizzano, C.A., Bargagli, F., Frisoli, A., Bergamasco, M.: The hand force feedback: analysis and control of a haptic device for the human-hand. In: 2000 IEEE International Conference on Systems, Man, and Cybernetics, vol. 2, pp. 989–994 (2000)
10. Achibet, M., Casiez, G., Marchal., M.: DesktopGlove: a multi-finger force feedback interface separating degrees of freedom between hands. In: IEEE Computer Society (ed.) 3DUI 2016, The 11th Symposium on 3D User Interfaces, Proceedings of the Symposium on 3D User Interfaces, Greenville, United States, p. 10 (2016)
11. Tejeiro, C., Stepp, C.E., Malhotra, M., Rombokas, E., Matsuoka, Y.: Comparison of remote pressure and vibrotactile feedback for prosthetic hand control. In: 2012 4th IEEE RAS EMBS International Conference on Biomedical Robotics and Biomechatronics (BioRob), pp. 521–525 (2012)

12. Tabot, G.A., Dammann, J.F., Berg, J.A., Tenore, F.V., Boback, J.L., Vogelstein, R.J., Bensmaia, S.J.: Restoring the sense of touch with a prosthetic hand through a brain interface. Proc. Natl. Acad. Sci. **110**(45), 18279–18284 (2013)
13. Montaño-Murillo, R., Posada-Gómez, R., Martínez-Sibaja, A., Gonzalez-Sanchez, B.E., Aguilar-Lasserre, A.A., Cornelio-Martńez, P.: Design and assessment of a remote vibrotactile biofeedback system for neuromotor rehabilitation using active markers. Procedia Technol. **7**, 96–102 (2013)
14. Olsson, P., Johansson, S., Nysjö, F., Carlbom, I.: Rendering stiffness with a prototype haptic glove actuated by an integrated piezoelectric motor. In: Isokoski, P., Springare, J. (eds.) EuroHaptics 2012. LNCS, vol. 7282, pp. 361–372. Springer, Heidelberg (2012). https://doi.org/10.1007/978-3-642-31401-8_33
15. CyberGrasp. http://www.cyberglovesystems.com. Accessed 3 Apr 2018
16. Bouzit, M., Burdea, G., Popescu, G., Boian, R.: The rutgers master ii-new design force-feedback glove. IEEE/ASME Trans. Mechatron. **7**(2), 256–263 (2002)
17. Palli, G., Natale, C., May, C., Melchiorri, C., Würtz, T.: Modeling and control of the twisted string actuation system. IEEE/ASME Trans. Mechatron. **18**(2), 664–673 (2013)
18. Moshe, S.: Twisting wire actuator. J. Mech. Des. **127**(3), 441–445 (2004)
19. Würtz, T., May, C., Holz, B., Natale, C., Palli, G., Melchiorri, C.: The twisted string actuation system: modeling and control. In: 2010 IEEE/ASME International Conference on Advanced Intelligent Mechatronics (AIM), pp. 1215–1220. IEEE (2010)
20. Palli, G., Melchiorri, C., Vassura, G., Scarcia, U., Moriello, L., Berselli, G., Cavallo, A., De Maria, G., Natale, C., Pirozzi, S., May, C., Ficuciello, F., Siciliano, B.: The DEXMART hand: mechatronic design and experimental evaluation of synergy-based control for human-like grasping. Int. J. Robot. Res. **33**(5), 799–824 (2014)
21. Pepe, A., Hosseini, M., Scarcia, U., Palli, G., Melchiorri, C.: Development of an haptic interface based on twisted string actuators. In: 2017 IEEE International Conference on Advanced Intelligent Mechatronics (AIM), pp. 28–33. IEEE (2017)
22. Hosseini, M., Palli, G., Melchiorri, C.: Design and implementation of a simple and low-cost optoelectronic force sensor for robotic applications. In: 2016 IEEE International Conference on Advanced Intelligent Mechatronics (AIM), pp. 1011–1016. IEEE (2016)
23. Hosseini, M., Meattini, R., Palli, G., Melchiorri, C.: A wearable robotic device based on twisted string actuation for rehabilitation and assistive applications. J. Robot. **2017**, 11 (2017)
24. Palli, G., Hosseini, M., Melchiorri, C.: A simple and easy-to-build optoelectronics force sensor based on light fork: design comparison and experimental evaluation. Sens. Actuators A Phys. **269**, 369–381 (2018)
25. Netta, G., Okamura, A.M., Kuchenbecker, K.J.: Perception of force and stiffness in the presence of low-frequency haptic noise. PloS one **12**(6), e0178605 (2017)
26. Blake, J., Gurocak, H.B.: Haptic glove with MR brakes for virtual reality. IEEE/ASME Trans. Mechatron. **14**(5), 606–615 (2009)

A Comparative Study of Phoneme- and Word-Based Learning of English Words Presented to the Skin

Yang Jiao[1(✉)], Frederico M. Severgnini[1], Juan Sebastian Martinez[1], Jaehong Jung[1], Hong Z. Tan[1], Charlotte M. Reed[2], E. Courtenay Wilson[2], Frances Lau[3], Ali Israr[3], Robert Turcott[3], Keith Klumb[3], and Freddy Abnousi[3]

[1] Haptic Interface Research Lab, Purdue University, West Lafayette, IN 47907, USA
{jiao12,fmarcoli,mart1304,jung137,hongtan}@purdue.edu
[2] Research Lab of Electronics, Massachusetts Institute of Technology, Cambridge, MA 02139, USA
{cmreed,ecwilson}@mit.edu
[3] Facebook Inc., Menlo Park, CA 94025, USA
{flau,aliisrar,rturcott,kklumb,abnousi}@fb.com

Abstract. Past research has demonstrated that speech communication on the skin is entirely achievable. However, there is still no definitive conclusion on the best training method that minimizes the time it takes for users to reach a prescribed performance level with a speech communication device. The present study reports the design and testing of two learning approaches with a system that translates English phonemes to haptic stimulation patterns (haptic symbols). With the phoneme-based learning approach, users learned the haptic symbols associated with the phonemes before attempting to acquire words made up of the phonemes. With the word-based approach, users learned words on day one. Two experiments were conducted with the two learning approaches, each employing twelve participants who spent 100 min each learning 100 English words made up of 39 phonemes. Results in terms of the total number of words learned show that performance levels vary greatly among the individuals tested (with the best learners in both methods achieving word-recognition scores > 90%-correct on a 100-word vocabulary), both approaches are feasible for successful acquisition of word through the skin, and the phoneme-based approach provides a more consistent path for learning across users in a shorter period of time.

Keywords: Haptic speech communication · Language acquisition
Phoneme-based learning · Word-based learning · Haptic symbols for phonemes

1 Introduction

The sense of touch offers rich information about the world around us and past research has demonstrated that it is possible to communicate speech through touch. For example, the Tadoma method, where the listener places the hand on the speaker's face to feel the articulatory processes and associate the sensations with speech production [1], provides an existence proof that speech communication through the skin alone is entirely achievable [2]. Compared with this natural method, several man-made systems have been

© Springer International Publishing AG, part of Springer Nature 2018
D. Prattichizzo et al. (Eds.): EuroHaptics 2018, LNCS 10894, pp. 623–635, 2018.
https://doi.org/10.1007/978-3-319-93399-3_53

developed to display spectral properties of speech on the skin by relying on the principle of frequency-to-place transformation to convey speech information, or by extracting speech features before encoding on the skin (e.g., see reviews [3–8]).

In the current study, a phonemic-based approach to tactual speech communication was selected for several reasons. Because the phoneme is a basic unit of speech, it is more efficient to encode speech with phonemes than alphabets [9] in terms of the number of units needed per speech sound. In addition, once the phoneme set has been established, it can be used to encode any possible word or message in the language, as opposed to the use of tactile metaphors or semantics which must be developed to suit particular situations. Although other approaches to encoding tactile signals are also worthy of consideration (e.g., those based on tactile implementation of sign languages or other types of linguistic features), there is evidence to suggest that the information transfer rates that can be achieved with phonemic codes are at least as good as those of other coding methods [10]. Our initial findings demonstrate that, with sufficient exposure to the tactual display, users are capable of identifying phonemes at a high level of recognition rate [11, 12]. The next goal of our research plan is the exploration of effective approaches to training for minimizing the time required for users to reach a prescribed level of performance.

Previous studies have explored the role of training in the use of haptic devices. For example, a study concerned with the acquisition of Braille by sighted learners has demonstrated that a corresponding visual display was beneficial for the acquisition of haptic Braille [13]. This result suggests the use of a visual display in the current study, corresponding to the activation of vibrators on the tactual display. In addition, the efficacy of correct-answer feedback for perceptual learning tasks is well-established [14], indicating that correct-answer feedback should be employed in the learning procedure. With the phonemic-based tactual display designed for conveying English words, we consider two training approaches to training: phoneme-based and word-based [15]. The phoneme-based approach, which operates on a "bottom-up" theory of learning, concentrates on maximizing the individual's ability to discriminate between and identify the individual sound patterns of speech [15]. The word-based approach is based on a "top-down" theory of learning. It bypasses the training of basic phoneme patterns and starts with words directly [15]. Previous studies of speech training have employed single or combined approaches [16–18]; however, these studies have not led to definitive conclusions for choosing one approach over another.

The present study compares phoneme-based and word-based training approaches for learning 100 English words. To the extent possible, we have kept the learning environment and time similar for both approaches in order to examine outcomes under comparable conditions. In the remainder of this paper, we present the general methods, followed by two experiments with each of the two learning approaches, and compare their results. We conclude the paper with a discussion that includes a comparison of word-learning performance through our phonemic-based haptic display with that obtained in other recent studies of haptic displays for speech communication.

2   General Methods Common to Both Experiments

2.1   Learning Materials

One-hundred common English words were selected for the present study (see Table 1; the 8 groups are explained later in Sect. 4.1). They consisted of 50 CV (consonant-vowel) or VC words and 50 CVC or VCV words. The 100 words were transcribed into the 39 English phonemes [19]. Table 2 shows the 24 consonants and 15 vowels making up the phonemes and example words containing the corresponding phonemes. It follows that the phoneme transcription for "ace" would be "AY" and "S," etc. Each phoneme was mapped to a haptic symbol, as described in Sect. 2.2 below.

Table 1.   The one hundred English words used in the present study

Group 1	Group 2	Group 3	Group 4	Group 5	Group 6	Group 7	Group 8
Ace	Key	Ray	Low	Chow	Jay	Gay	All
Aid	My	She	Oath	Cow	Joy	Go	Fee
Day	Sigh	Shy	Row	How	Knee	Guy	Off
May	They	Shoe	Show	Vow	No	Tie	On
Me	Way	Us	So	Wow	Now	Toe	Ought
Moo	Why	Come	The	Cheese	Pay	Too	You
Sue	Woo	Rock	Though	Choose	Join	Toy	Fought
Doom	Dime	Rum	Base	Hatch	Keep	Azure	Pawn
Dude	Make	Shave	Dome	Him	Noise	Book	Ring
Moose	Seek	Shock	Like	Loud	Pen	Gun	Thing
Same	Side	Vase	Thumb	Mad	Them	Put	Young
Seam	Wake	Wash	Will	Maze	Then	Shirt	Your
Seed	Weed		Wish			Should	

Table 2.   The thirty-nine English phonemes used in the present study

Symbol	Example word	Symbol	Example word	Symbol	Example word	Symbol	Example word
EE	Meet	UU	Hood	K	Key	ZH	Azure
AY	Mate	UH	Hut	P	Pay	CH	Chew
OO	Mood	OE	Boat	T	Tea	J	Jeep
I	Might	OY	Boy	B	Bee	H	He
AE	Mat	OW	Pouch	G	Guy	R	Ray
AH	Father	D	Do	F	Fee	L	Lie
AW	Bought	M	Me	SH	She	Y	You
EH	Met	S	See	TH	Think	N	New
ER	Bird	W	We	V	Voice	NG	Sing
IH	Bid	DH	The	Z	Zoo		

2.2   Haptic Symbols for Phonemes and Words

The experimental apparatus consisted of a 4-by-6 tactor array worn on the non-dominant forearm. The 24 tactors form four rows in the longitudinal direction (elbow to wrist) and six columns (rings) in the transversal direction (around the forearm). As shown in Fig. 1, two rows (i and ii) reside on the dorsal side of the forearm and the other two (iii and iv) on the volar side. A wide-bandwidth tactor (Tectonic Elements, Model TEAX13C02-8/RH, Part #297-214, sourced from Parts Express International, Inc.) was used as the actuator. A MOTU 24Ao audio device (MOTU, Cambridge, MA, USA) was used for delivering 24 channels of audio waveforms to the 24 tactors through custom-built stereo audio amplifiers. A Matlab program running on a desktop computer generated the multi-channel waveforms and ran the learning experiments. With this setup, the tactors can be driven independently with programmable waveforms.

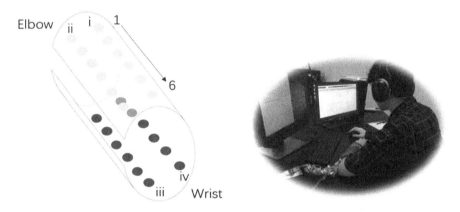

Fig. 1. Illustrations of tactor layout   **Fig. 2.** Experimental setup

Haptic symbols for phonemes consisted of vibrotactile patterns using one or more of the 4-by-6 tactors. The mapping of the phonemes to haptic symbols incorporated the articulatory features of the sounds, balanced by the need to maintain the distinctiveness of the 39 haptic symbols. The stimulus properties included *amplitude* (in dB sensation level, or dB above individually-measured detection thresholds), *frequency* (single or multiple sinusoidal components), *waveform* (sinusoids with or without modulation), *duration, location, numerosity* (single tactor activation or multiple tactors turned on simultaneously or sequentially), and *movement* (smooth apparent motion or discrete saltatory motion varying in direction, spatial extent, and/or trajectory). Examples of the use of articulatory features to construct the phonemes include the use of location on the array to map place of articulation (e.g., front sounds are presented near the wrist and back sounds near the elbow) and the use of unmodulated versus modulated waveforms to distinguish voiceless and voiced cognate pairs. Signal duration was also used as a cue, e.g., as in distinguishing brief plosive bursts from longer fricative noises. The individual haptic symbols ranged in duration from 100 to 480 ms. Details of the phoneme mapping strategies and the resultant haptic symbols can be found in [11].

To display a word, the haptic symbols corresponding to the phonemes making up the word were delivered in sequence, with a 300-ms gap inserted between phonemes. For the words used in the present study, the word duration varied from roughly 1 to 2 s.

The participants sat comfortably in front of a computer monitor and wore noise-reduction earphones (see Fig. 2). The non-dominant forearm was placed on the table with the volar side facing down. The elbow-to-wrist direction was adjusted to be roughly parallel to the torso. To ensure that the haptic symbols were presented at 30 dB sensation level (SL) for all participants, a two-step calibration procedure was carried out for each participant prior to the experiments. First, detection thresholds at 60 and 300 Hz were estimated with one tactor (the "reference tactor") using a one-up two-down adaptive procedure [20]. Second, the intensities of all 24 tactors were adjusted to match that of the reference tactor using the method of adjustment [20].

2.3 Learning with Time Constraints

Our earlier study showed evidence of memory consolidation [21] meaning that learning took place even when the participants weren't being trained or tested [12]. This motivated us to design a 10-day curriculum where learning time was capped at 10 min per day, for a total of 100 min, for either phoneme- or word-based learning. In order to assess learning progress, a phoneme or word identification test without feedback was conducted after the 10-min learning period on some days. The test typically took less than 10 min and did not count towards learning time since no correct-answer feedback was provided. The combined experiment time, excluding the pre-experiment calibration time, reached 80 h (12 participants × 2 learning approaches × 10 days × 1/3 h per day).

3 Experiment I: Phoneme-Based Learning

3.1 Methods

A total of 12 participants (P01–P12; 6 females; age range 18–26 years old, 21.9 ± 1.7 years old) took part in the phoneme-based learning experiment. All were right handed with no known sensory or motor impairments. Six of the participants are native English speakers. The other 6 participants speak English fluently and their first languages include Bulgarian, Chinese and Korean. Most of the participants received early childhood music training including piano, violin, guitar, flute, and cello.

The 10-day curriculum for phoneme-based learning was as follows:

- Day 1: 6 Cs (consonants) – P T K B D G
- Day 2: 12 Cs – Day 1 + F V TH DH S Z
- Day 3: 18 Cs – Day 2 + SH ZH CH J H W
- Day 4: all 24 Cs – Day 3 + M N NG R L Y
- Day 5: 8 Vs (vowels) – EE IH AH OO UU AE AW ER
- Day 6: 15 Vs – Day 5 + AY I OW OE OY UH EH
- Day 7: all 39 phonemes (>90% correct required before learning words)

- Day 8: 50 VC/CV words if >90% correct achieved with 39 phonemes
- Day 9–10: all 100 words, after 1 day with 50 VC/CV words

With the phoneme-based learning approach, the participants learned the haptic symbols associated with the 39 phonemes before learning the 100 words presented as sequences of phonemes. As shown above, the 24 consonants were divided evenly into 4 groups and learned during Days 1 to 4. The 15 vowels were divided into two groups and learned during Days 5 and 6. On Day 7, all 39 phonemes were available for learning and each participant had to achieve at least 90% correct on a phoneme identification test before proceeding to learning words. Therefore, all 12 participants had the same learning tasks from Day 1 to 7. The 100 words were divided into two groups: the first 50 words contained only CV/VC words and the rest included CVC/VCV words. After reaching the 90% criterion for phoneme learning, each participant learned the 50 CV/VC words for one day, and then all 100 words afterwards until 10 days were reached. It follows that the participants proceeded at different paces from Day 8 to 10.

During Days 1 to 7, the 10-min learning time per day included two activities: free play and practice test. During free play (see Fig. 3), the participant could either "Play" a phoneme selected from the left panel or "Show" its visual representation in the right panel. During the practice test, the participant would feel a haptic symbol and then respond by selecting a phoneme button on the computer screen. A trial-by-trial correct-answer feedback was provided. The participants were encouraged to spend time with both activities during the 10-min learning period, and could decide how much time to spend on each task. After the 10 min were up, each participant completed a closed-set phoneme identification test without any feedback.

From Day 8, the participants who had successfully passed the 90%-correct phoneme identification criterion spent their 10-min learning time on free play and practice test, this time with words instead of phonemes. The user interface for word free play was similar to that shown in Fig. 3 except that the phonemes in the left panel were replaced by words. Again, the participant completed a word identification test without any feedback after the 10-min learning period was over.

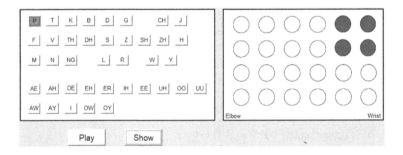

Fig. 3. User interface for phoneme free play. The phoneme highlighted in the left panel shows the phoneme being learned ("P"). The 4 red circles in the right panel represent the 4 activated tactors on the dorsal side and near the wrist of the forearm. (Color figure online)

3.2   Results

The results of phoneme-based learning are summarized in terms of the time taken to reach performance criteria and the performance levels reached. Figure 4 shows the individual progress of the twelve participants in the order of their performance levels. For example, the best learners P06 and P08 reached 90% correct phoneme identification on Day 7, 90% correct word recognition with 50 words on Day 8, and learned the 100 words on Day 9 and Day 10. The percent-correct scores on the right of individual progress bars show that these two participants achieved 95% correct word recognition with the 100 English words used in the present study. The next group of six participants (P02, P03, P04, P09, P11 and P12) passed phoneme identification on Day 8, learned 50 words on Day 9, and tried all 100 words on Day 10. Their word recognition rate with 100 words ranged from 50% to 90% correct. The next two participants (P01 and P05) took longer to reach the phoneme identification criterion on Day 9, and tried 50 words on Day 10. The last two participants (P07 and P10) learned the 39 phonemes by Day 10 but never progressed to words. For the top eight participants who progressed to 100 words, their word recognition accuracy on Day 10 was 80.0% ± 5.9% correct.

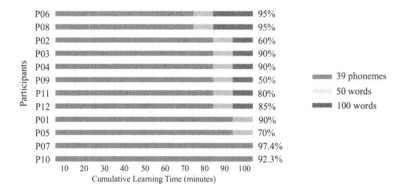

Fig. 4. Individual progress of participants P01 to P12 over the 10-day learning period with the phoneme-based approach. Shown on the right are their final performance levels on Day 10. (Color figure online)

A more detailed look at the percent-correct scores per learning day is shown in Fig. 5. Since all 12 participants performed the same phoneme learning tasks during Day 1 to 7, their individual percent-correct phoneme identification scores for each 10-min learning period can be compared directly (left panel of Fig. 5). Also shown as the solid line is the daily average which remained above 80% correct. The right panel shows the word recognition performance levels for the 10 and 8 participants who learned 50 and 100 words, respectively. The average word recognition scores were 79.5% and 80.6% correct for 50 and 100 words, respectively.

The results obtained with the phoneme-based learning approach demonstrate that all the participants were able to learn the haptic symbols associated with the 39 English phonemes with a >92% accuracy within 100 min. Individual learning outcomes vary,

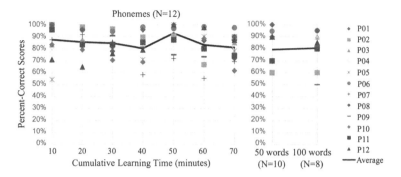

Fig. 5. Individual phoneme identification scores on Days 1 to 7 (left panel) and word recognition scores for some of the participants (right panel). (Color figure online)

and half of the twelve participants were able to learn the 100 English words with a >80% correct score by the end of the 100-min learning period.

4 Experiment II: Word-Based Learning

4.1 Methods

Twelve new participants (P13–P24; 6 females; age range 19–39 years old, 25.0 ± 5.7 years old) took part in the word-based learning experiment. They were similar to P01–P12 in terms of handedness, language background and early childhood musical training.

With the word-based learning approach, all participants started with the learning of words on Day 1. To gradually increase the difficulty levels, the 100 words were divided into 8 groups with increasing number of phonemes contained in each group (see the grouping in Table 1). For example, the 13 words in Group 1 were made up of 6 phonemes: D, M, S, AY, EE and OO. Each successive group contained 12 to 13 additional words with 4 to 5 additional phonemes, as shown below.

- Group 1: 13 words (6 phonemes)
- Group 2: Group 1 + 13 words = 26 words (10 phonemes)
- Group 3: Group 2 + 12 words = 38 words (15 phonemes)
- Group 4: Group 3 + 13 words = 51 words (20 phonemes)
- Group 5: Group 4 + 12 words = 63 words (25 phonemes)
- Group 6: Group 5 + 12 words = 75 words (30 phonemes)
- Group 7: Group 6 + 13 words = 88 words (35 phonemes)
- Group 8: Group 7 + 12 words = 100 words (39 phonemes)

The participants split each 10-min learning period between free play and practice test with the word group for the day. Afterwards, a word identification test was conducted without any feedback. The word test was conducted with a closed set of words shown on the computer screen and the participant responded by typing the word that was just felt on the forearm. A performance level of 80% correct had to be reached before a participant could move onto the next word group. This criterion was based on the average performance level of the 8 participants in Exp. I who reached all 100 words by Day 10. The process continued until 10 learning days were completed. If a participant reached Group 8 before Day 10, then s/he continued with Group 8 until Day 10.

4.2 Results

Figure 6 shows the individual progress of participants P13-P24 over the 10 learning days. The cross "×" marks the day that the participant reached the 80% correct performance criterion and was qualified to move to the next word group. Of the twelve participants, 2 participants (P17 and P13) were able to reach the 80% correct word recognition rate with Group 8 (all 100 words), 5 participants (P19, P22, P18, P15, and P14) with Group 5 (63 words), 4 participants (P20, P23, P16, P21) with Group 4 (51 words), and 1 participant (P24) with Group 3 (38 words). It thus appears that there is a large gap in performance between the top 2 participants and the other 10 participants. On average, it took 21.5 min to learn and pass each group for the 12 participants.

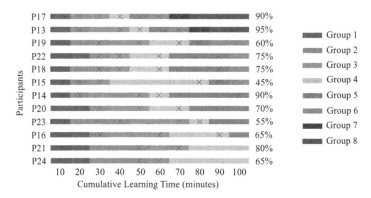

Fig. 6. Individual progress of P13 to P24 over the 10-day period with the word-based approach. Shown on the right are the percent-correct scores for the respective word lists on Day 10. (Color figure online)

Figure 7 compares the 12 participants' performance with the word-based learning approach. Since the participants could be learning a different number of words on any learning day, we derived a new performance metric called the "equivalent number of words correctly identified" by multiplying each percent-correct score with the number of words in the word list that was used in the word recognition test. This metric provided a common basis against which the participants' performance could be compared. It can be seen that the top two participants (P13 and P17) learned English words at a rate of roughly 1 word per minute until they reached 95 and 90 words, respectively. The remaining ten participants started to lag behind the two top performers after about 30 min of learning and their performance plateaued at 57 or fewer words (about half the number of words learned by P13 and P17) at the end of 100 min.

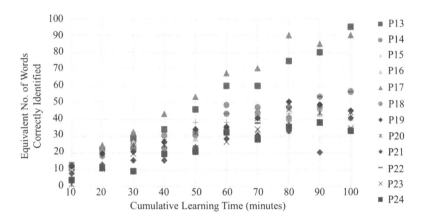

Fig. 7. Performance with word-based learning approach. See text for details. (Color figure online)

5 Discussion

Both experiments demonstrated that participants were able to distinguish vibrotactile patterns and learn English phonemes or words presented to the skin. It is difficult to compare the two approaches during the initial stages of learning because one group learned phonemes first and the other learned words. Thus, our comparisons focus on word learning using the derived measure of "equivalent number of words correctly identified" (Fig. 8). Recall that the participants in the phoneme-based learning experiment did not reach word learning until at least Day 8 of the 10-day learning period. Therefore, the data from the two experiments are plotted for the last 30 min only for each learner. For the learners trained with the phoneme-based approach (left panel of Fig. 8), the equivalent number of words correctly identified was calculated for the 10 participants who were tested with 50 CV/VC words and the 8 participants who were tested with all 100 words (see Fig. 4). It can be seen in the left panel of Fig. 8 that two participants (P06, P08) learned 47.5 and 50 words on Day 8, respectively, jumped to 80 and 95 words on Day 9, respectively, and both ended at 95 words by Day 10. Six participants joined on Day 9 and two more on Day 10. The dashed lines demonstrate a clear upward trend for each participant, especially the four participants in the middle (P03, P04, P11 and P12) whose performance jumped from about 39 words on Day 9 to about 86 words on Day 10. Although to a lesser extent, the two remaining participants (P02 and P09) clearly improved from Day 9 to 10. It is therefore conceivable that given more learning time, the participants in the phoneme-based learning experiment would continue to improve and eventually learn the 100 English words. Data for the learners trained with the word-based approach (right panel of Fig. 8) show a different pattern. There are clearly two groups of learners, with the 2 participants P13 and P17 significantly outperforming the remaining 10 participants. More critically, all participants appear to be reaching plateaus from Day 8 to Day 10, leaving it unclear whether the 10 participants in the lower group would ever reach 100 words.

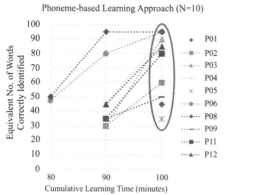
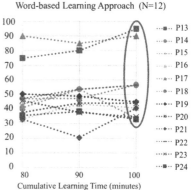

Fig. 8. Performance comparison of (left) phoneme-based and (right) word-based approaches. (Color figure online)

Focusing on the last day of performance for both learning approaches (see encircled data points in Fig. 8), it is apparent that word acquisition levels at 100 min vary significantly among the participants in each group. On the one hand, both approaches are feasible in that there are examples of highly-performing participants with scores above 90% correct for 100 words in either approach. On the other hand, the distributions for the two approaches suggest that the phoneme-based approach would be a safer and more reliable choice. With the phoneme-based approach, half of the 12 participants learned 80 or more words in 100 min. In contrast, only 2 of the 12 participants with the word-based learning approach learned more than 80 words.[1] The comparatively poorer performance of the word-based learners may be considered in light of the phoneme-based approach taken in constructing the words, which may have introduced a bias in favor of the participants who were introduced to the phonemes.

The current study demonstrated that 10 of the 24 participants were able to achieve proficiency on a 100-word haptic vocabulary composed of 39 phonemes within 100 min of training. These results may be compared to other recent studies also concerned with the acquisition of words through haptic displays. Zhao et al. [22] mapped 9 phonemic symbols to 6 tactors on the arm and trained participants to recognize words composed of these symbols. After roughly 30 min of training, participants could recognize 20 words at an accuracy of around 83%. Turcott et al. [8] also included a phonemic approach to encode 10 symbols using 16 tactors on the arm. The participants achieved an accuracy of 76% correct on 20 words after 50 min of training. Novich developed and tested a

---

[1] Debriefing with participants after the experiments revealed that even though 8 of the 12 participants with the word-based approach noticed on Day 1 the repeating haptic symbols associated with the phonemes making up the words, only 2 of them were able to "decode" the phonemes successfully. These two top performers then focused on the learning of new phonemes on subsequent learning days and contrasted them with the old phonemes learned on previous days. The other participants appeared to be less efficient at learning the haptic symbols for phonemes. As more phonemes and words were added to the task, learning became even more challenging since confusions with similar haptic symbols remained unresolved.

spectral-based haptic vest containing 27 tactors to present 50 words in a 4-alternative forced-choice identification paradigm [7]. After 11 to 12 days of training with 300 trials per day, participants achieved scores of 35–65% correct (chance = 25%). Thus the results obtained in the present study in which 39 phonemes were used for word construction compare favorably to these other studies. For the phoneme-based learners in the present study, 10 of 12 were successful at identifying 50 words with an average score of 80% correct (chance = 2%) and 8 of 12 achieved an average score of 80% correct with 100 words (chance = 1%).

The results reported here provide insight for future work on improved training protocols that minimize the amount of time required to achieve criterion levels of performance on word recognition. Our ultimate goal is to develop a haptic speech communication system for people with all levels of sensory capabilities.

Acknowledgments. This work was partially supported by a research grant from Facebook Inc. The authors thank Emily Fredette for her assistance with data collection.

References

1. Reed, C.M., Rabinowitz, W.M., Durlach, N.I., Braida, L.D., Conway-Fithian, S., Schultz, M.C.: Research on the Tadoma method of speech communication. J. Acoust. Soc. Am. **77**(1), 247–257 (1985)
2. Reed, C.M., Durlach, N.I., Braida, L.D.: Research on tactile communication of speech: a review. American Speech-Language-Hearing Association Monographs, no. 20 (1982)
3. Reed, C.M., Durlach, N.I., Delhorne, L.A., Rabinowitz, W.M.: Research on tactual communication of speech: ideas, issues, and findings. Volta Rev. **91**, 65–78 (1989)
4. Tan, H.Z., Pentland, A.: Tactual displays for sensory substitution and wearable computers. In: Barfield, W., Caudell, T. (eds.) Fundamentals of Wearable Computers and Augmented Reality, pp. 579–598. Lawrence Erlbaum Associates, Mahwah (2001)
5. Plant, G.: The selection and training of tactile aid users. In: Summers, I.R. (ed.) Tactile Aids for the Hearing Impaired, pp. 146–166. Whurr Publishers, London (1992)
6. Novich, S.D., Eagleman, D.M.: Using space and time to encode vibrotactile information: toward an estimate of the skin's achievable throughput. Exp. Brain Res. **233**(10), 2777–2788 (2015)
7. Novich, S.D.: Sound-to-Touch Sensory Substitution and Beyond. Doctoral Dissertation, Department of Electrical and Computer Engineering, Rice University (2015)
8. Turcott, R., Chen, J., Castillo, P., Knott, B., Setiawan, W., Briggs, F., Klumb, K., Abnousi, F., Chakka, P.: Efficient evaluation of coding strategies for transcutaneous language communication. In: Proceedings of EuroHaptics 2018, Pisa, Italy, 13–16 June 2018 (2018, to appear)
9. Luzhnica, G., Veas, E., Pammer, V.: Skin reading: encoding text in a 6-channel haptic display. In: Proceedings of the 2016 ACM International Symposium on Wearable Computers (ISWC 2016), pp. 148–155 (2016)
10. Reed, C.M., Durlach, N.I.: Note on information transfer rates in human communication. Presence Teleoperators Virtual Environ. **7**(5), 509–518 (1998)
11. Reed, C.M., Tan, H.Z., Perez, Z.D., Wilson, E.C., Severgnini, F.M., Jung, J., Martinez, J.S., Jiao, Y., Israr, A., Lau, F., Klumb, K., Abnousi, F.: A phonemic-based tactual display for speech communication. IEEE Trans. Haptics (submitted)

12. Jung, J., Jiao, Y., Severgnini, F.M., Tan, H.Z., Reed, C.M., Israr, A., Lau, F., Abnousi, F.: Speech communication through the skin: design of learning protocols and initial findings. In: Proceedings of HCI International, 15–20 July 2018 (2018, to appear)
13. Hall, A.D., Newman, S.E.: Braille learning: relative importance of seven variables. Appl. Cognit. Psychol. **1**(2), 133–141 (1987)
14. Herzog, M.H., Fahle, M.: The role of feedback in learning a vernier discrimination task. Vis. Res. **37**(15), 2133–2141 (1997)
15. Henshaw, H., Ferguson, M.A.: Efficacy of individual computer-based auditory training for people with hearing loss: a systematic review of the evidence. PLoS ONE **8**(5), e62836 (2013)
16. Nitchie, E.: Lipreading, an art. Volta Rev. **15**, 276–278 (1913)
17. Walden, B.E., Erdman, S.A., Montgomery, A.A., Schwartz, D.M., Prosek, R.A.: Some effects of training on speech recognition by hearing-impaired adults. J. Speech Hear. Res. **24**(2), 207–216 (1981)
18. Rubinstein, A., Boothroyd, A.: Effect of two approaches to auditory training on speech recognition by hearing-impaired adults. J. Speech Lang. Hear. Res. **30**(2), 153–160 (1987)
19. Ecroyd, D.H.: Voice and Articulation: A Handbook, pp. 63–87. Scott Foresman & Co Publisher, Glenview (1966)
20. Jones, L.A., Tan, H.Z.: Application of psychophysical techniques to haptic research. IEEE Trans. Haptics **6**(3), 268–284 (2013)
21. Dudai, Y., Karni, A., Born, J.: The consolidation and transformation of memory. Neuron **88**(1), 20–32 (2015)
22. Zhao, S., Israr, A., Lau, F., Abnousi, F.: Coding tactile symbols for phonemic communication. In: Proceedings of CHI 2018, 21–26 April 2018 (2018, to appear)

Vibrotactile Feedback Improves Collision Detection in Fast Playback of First-Person View Videos

Daniel Gongora[✉], Hikaru Nagano, Masashi Konyo, and Satoshi Tadokoro

Graduate School of Information Sciences, Tohoku University,
6-6-01 Aramaki Aza Aoba, Aoba-ku, Sendai, Miyagi, Japan
{daniel,nagano,konyo,tadokoro}@rm.is.tohoku.ac.jp

Abstract. Fast playback of First-Person View (FPV) videos reduces watching time but it also increases the perceived intensity of camera trembling and makes transient events, such as collisions, less evident. Here we propose using camera vibrations as vibrotactile feedback to support collision detection in fast video playback. To preserve camera vibrations *pitch* during fast playback, we use Time-Scale Modification (TSM) methods developed for audio. We show that camera vibrations delivered to the palm of the dominant hand improved collision detection performance in a pilot study. We found that reducing the levels of terrain vibrations is beneficial for collision detection. Furthermore, we found that without vibrotactile feedback participants are likely to underestimate the number of collisions in a video. Our results suggest that vibrotactile feedback has potential to support the detection of transient events during fast playback of FPV videos.

1 Introduction

Fast video playback helps in optimizing video browsing time. To create informative summaries of lengthy videos, playback speed can be set in proportion to image features allowing viewers to skim low activity parts of a video and explore in detail those with high activity. For instance, Peker et al. [1] propose to adjust the playback speed in inverse proportion to motion activity levels in a video. Similarly, in a follow-up study, Peker and Divakaran [2] propose to use estimates of visual complexity in a video along with estimates of motion activity to set the playback speed at levels that do not overload the eyes of the viewer. Fast video playback as proposed in these studies has been successfully applied to sports and surveillance videos.

However, in videos with prominent shake, as the ones obtained in robot teleoperation or in First-Person View (FPV) videos, fast playback poses additional challenges. For instance, increasing the playback speed could result in *unwatchable* videos due to an apparent intensification of the shaking. To address this issue, Kopf et al. [3] and Poleg et al. [4] introduce methods for creating smooth summaries of FPV videos at high playback speed. On the down side,

© Springer International Publishing AG, part of Springer Nature 2018
D. Prattichizzo et al. (Eds.): EuroHaptics 2018, LNCS 10894, pp. 636–647, 2018.
https://doi.org/10.1007/978-3-319-93399-3_54

smooth video summaries might deprive viewers from information pertaining to collisions and other transient events.

Rescue robot teleoperation is one scenario where fast video playback is desirable, and camera vibrations are informative rather than a nuisance. Videos recorded with rescue robots are likely to show considerable amounts of trembling caused by terrain irregularities and they are often recorded under poor lighting conditions. In these circumstances, fast video playback is useful during and after teleoperation. First, during teleoperation the operator might need to playback the last few minutes of video footage to understand the highly unstructured environment that follows a disaster. Fast video playback is important because the success of a search and rescue mission depends on the promptness of the response. Second, after teleoperation, videos obtained during rescue robot teleoperation serve to identify operational problems [5,6], but conventional examination can be time consuming. A team of robots produces several hours of video if we consider that a ground rescue robot is deployed for 20 min in 3 or 4 occasions during one shift according to [7]. In sum, fast video playback is valuable during and after a mission with a rescue robot but conventional adjustments of playback speed via increasing the frame rate produce videos that are uncomfortable to watch, and smooth video summaries even out informative transient events such as collisions.

Here we put forward the idea of using camera vibrations as vibrotactile feedback to prevent viewers from missing transient events in fast video playback. We consider camera vibrations instead of audio recordings because we focus on local events experienced by the camera as opposed to environmental events picked up as background sounds, and we use vibrotactile feedback instead of auditory feedback to preserve regular oral communication channels between viewers. Furthermore, during fast video playback visual cues related to transient events become less noticeable but haptic feedback has proven to be a useful support in tasks with degraded or limited visual cues. Consider for instance the work by Gerovich et al. [8] where participants used force feedback to perceive transitions between tissues in a needle insertion task with limited visual information. Moreover, a meta-analysis of vibrotactile displays and task performance [9] shows that integrating vibrotactile alerts to visual tasks improves performance as measured by the reaction time, completion time, or the number of errors. For example, Van der Burg et al. [10] report that non-spatial vibrotactile feedback enables faster search of visual stimulus in a cluttered environment. The authors argue that synchronization between tactile and visual events augments the saliency of the visual event. This effect was initially observed with auditory cues [11]. All in all, camera vibrations used as vibrotactile feedback are likely to support the detection of transient events during fast video playback without obstructing oral communication channels among viewers.

In this paper, we investigate the combination of visual and vibrotactile feedback to preserve the perception of transient events during fast video playback. To achieve this, we consider a collision detection task to evaluate transient perception during fast video playback, and we use videos and vibrations recorded with a platform cart as case study (Sect. 3). To increase the playback speed of camera vibrations while preserving its *pitch*, we use Time-Scale Modification (TSM) techniques developed for audio. In addition, to study the contribution of terrain vibrations to collision detection, we separate terrain and collision vibrations using a method for Harmonic-Percussive Separation (HPS) of audio. We report the results of a pilot user study in Sect. 4.

2   Related Research

Audio signal processing methods are applicable to vibrotactile feedback. Fast playback of vibrations can be addressed with Time-Scale Modification (TSM) techniques developed for audio. Such techniques permit changes in playback speed while keeping the pitch unaffected (For a comprehensive review of TSM techniques see [12]). Consider for example [13] where TSM is used to preserve the pitch during fast playback of lectures for a video-based learning system. Similarly, terrain and collision vibrations can be separated using Harmonic-Percussive Separation (HPS) of audio [14]. HPS is commonly used for remixing music or as preprocessing for other tasks such as TSM [15].

Haptic feedback provides intuitive ways for controlling media in general, and for adjusting the playback speed in particular. In [17], continuous modification of the playback speed is achieved via knobs. These knobs consist of a single wheel but they present to the hand the dynamics of two concentric wheels that touch each other as the pressure exerted by the user increases. Users advance through the frames of a video by spinning the wheel, and they *feel* features of the video encoded as the contact between wheels.

Fast playback finds applications beyond video browsing. By way of example, in [16] fast playback of seismic signals was used as means for quickly reviewing seismic records. To make seismic signals audible, the authors increased the sampling frequency by a factor of 150 from 40 Hz to 6000 Hz. The results of a user study indicate that *sonified* seismograms enabled participants to group together seismograms that shared some physical parameters.

While fast playback permits a reduction in browsing time, slow playback permits detailed exploration of short events. For instance, slow playback might be used to tap into the information contained in collisions. According to [18], in absence of visual feedback, the categorization of objects (e.g. grains of rice, screw nuts) falling on a flat surface improves after reducing the playback speed of impact vibrations delivered to the skin.

3   Time-Scale Modification of Camera Vibrations

Here we describe the nature of the videos recorded for the collision detection task, as well as the signal processing applied on camera vibrations to preserve its characteristics during fast playback.

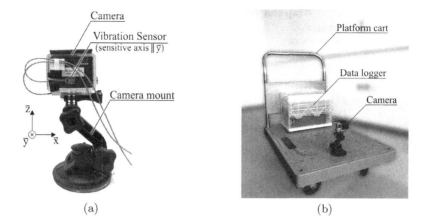

Fig. 1. (a) Vibration sensor mounted on the back of the camera with a thin layer of hot-melt adhesive. (b) Platform cart carrying a datalogger and a camera.

3.1 Video and Vibration Collection

We recorded eight 5 min videos with a camera (GoPro Hero 4) mounted on a platform cart, capturing a vantage point of approximately 38 cm above the ground at 30 fps, Fig. 1. A data logger (Keyence NR-600) recorded at 50 kHz the output of a single-axis vibration sensor (NEC TOKIN VS-BV203) mounted on the back of the camera with its sensitive axis parallel to the viewing axis of the camera. The vibration sensor has a frequency range spanning from 10 Hz to 15 000 Hz, and a sensitivity of 20 mV/m/s^2.

The cart moved following an 8-shaped path around four concrete blocks placed at the corners of a rectangle of 7 m × 3.5 m, Fig. 2. We recorded collisions exclusively during rotations, when the obstacle was out of the field of view of the camera. Collisions had varying intensities that produced varying degrees of camera trembling. The videos depict from 6 to 15 collisions each ($M = 9.12$, $STD = 2.93$).

3.2 Harmonic-Percussive Separation

Collisions bring the cart to a halt and terrain vibrations die out since they are proportional to the speed of the cart. To determine if these changes in terrain vibrations intensity are useful in a collision detection task, we use a Harmonic-Percussive Separation (HPS) procedure to split the vibrations obtained in Sect. 3.1 into terrain and collision vibrations.

First, we decimate the vibrations by a factor of 2 to reduce computation time, this results in a sampling frequency of 25 kHz. Then, we use the MATLAB TSM toolbox [15] to perform the separation. This toolbox implements the HPS method discussed in [14] that consists in applying a mask to the magnitude spectrogram of a signal so that the reconstructed signal corresponds to either

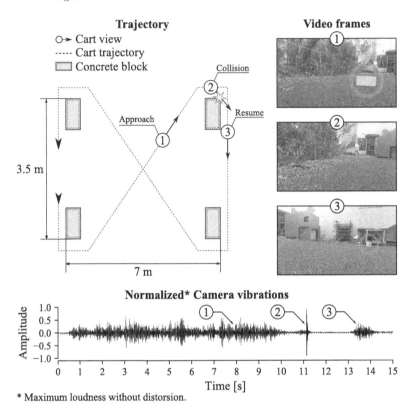

Fig. 2. Video and Vibration Collection. The cart moved around four concrete blocks (shown within red circles in the video frames). The blocks were in sight during approach (1) but out of sight when rotating (2). The cart approaches a different block after turning (3). (Color figure online)

the harmonic or percussive component of the signal. The masks are obtained by applying a running median filter to the time and frequency axes of the magnitude spectrogram. The frame size N used to compute the spectrogram is the most important parameter for harmonic-percussive separation [15]. We settled on $N = 4800$ after several experiments. A systematic investigation to find an optimal N will be addressed in a future study.

3.3 Time-Scale Modification

To preserve terrain and collision vibrations' *pitch* during fast playback we use Time-Scale Modification (TSM) methods developed for audio. A TSM can be conducted in the time domain or in the frequency domain. In both cases, at a fundamental level, TSM algorithms divide the signal into several overlapping segments that are later combined using a different amount of overlap. The signal is compressed in time if the amount of overlap increases from analysis to

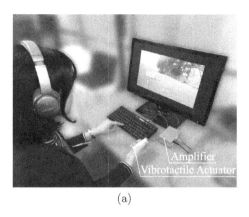
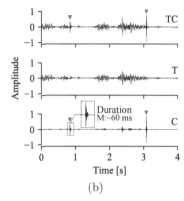

(a)   (b)

Fig. 3. (a) User experiment setup. Linear Resonant Actuator connected to the stereo output of a PC via an amplifier. Note: videos were shown in full screen during the user study. (b) Sample of the vibrations employed in the user study. Red markers indicate collisions. Vibrations were normalized for maximum loudness without distortion and stored as WAV files. (T: Terrain, C: Collision, TC: Terrain and collision.) (Color figure online)

synthesis, and vice versa. Concretely, we used the MATLAB TSM toolbox [15], and we applied the Overlap-Add (OLA) method on collision vibrations, and the Phase Vocoder method on terrain vibrations. We stored the vibrations in 32-bit WAV files at 25 kHz.

4   User Experiment

The goal of this pilot experiment is to evaluate participants capacity to detect collisions in a video under different feedback conditions.

4.1   Stimuli

The stimuli consist of a video played by itself (V) or accompanied by either of the following three types of vibrations: Terrain (T), Collision (C), Terrain and Collision (TC). We consider condition T to determine if changes in terrain vibrations overall intensity help in the collision detection task. We use the videos and vibrations described in Sect. 3. Sample vibrations are shown in Fig. 3b.

We used a Linear Resonant Actuator (Haptuator - Tactile Labs) enclosed by a 3D printed cylinder to deliver the tactile feedback to the palm of participants' dominant hand. The actuator was connected to the stereo output of a PC via an amplifier, and the cylinders vibrated parallel to the skin of the palm. The gain of the amplifier was the same for all participants and it was set to achieve maximum loudness without distortion.

4.2   Participants and Procedure

From thirteen subjects recruited for this pilot user study, one participant could not complete the experiment due to motion sickness and two participants could not stay awake the entire duration of the experiment. We report data from ten right-handed subjects aged 20 to 33 years ($M = 24.1$, $SD = 3.27$) including one female and nine males.

Participants sat down at a viewing distance between 60 cm to 65 cm of a 23.6 in full HD (1920×1080) display, resting their forearms on the arms of the chair, Fig. 3a. The relative viewing distance was 2.03 to 2.20 times the screen height. Participants watched 5 min long videos at $1\times$ or $2\times$ the original playback speed and they were instructed to hold a vibrotactile actuator with the dominant hand when watching the videos. The sound produced by the vibrators was masked by pink noise delivered to the participants through headphones. Prior to the experiment, we used four 30 s video clips to illustrate the difference between turns with and without collision. Afterwards, we used a 1 min video to let participants become familiar with all vibrotactile and visual feedback conditions. During the experiment, participants reported a collision by pressing the space key. Each key press was recorded as a timestamp on the video. Once a video was over, participants were required to take a break of 2 min and a half. However, longer breaks were available on request should participants experience symptoms of motion sickness. In total, each participant watched 8 videos. The presentation order was randomized for each participant at the beginning of the experiment. A complete experiment lasted about 1 h including breaks and briefing.

4.3   Performance Metrics

We used three performance metrics: collision detection performance, reaction time, and the ratio between the number of collisions reported in a video versus the actual number of collisions for that video.

We considered the F_1 score as collision detection performance metric. The F_1 score, also known as Sørensen-Dice coefficient [19,20], ranges from 0 to 1 and it is a measure of binary classification performance that considers both precision and recall. Precision represents the fraction of actual collisions detected from all collisions reported, and recall represents the fraction of actual collisions detected over the total number of collisions in a video. The performance of an ideal observer would show high precision and high recall and consequently an F_1 score near or equal to 1. The F_1 score is defined as:

$$F_1 = \frac{2TP}{2TP + FP + FN},\qquad(1)$$

where TP, FP, and FN stand for true positives, false positives, and false negatives, respectively.

We estimated the reaction time from the timestamps on the videos. For each collision, we defined the reference collision time using the largest excursion in camera vibrations during a collision. For videos played at $2\times$, we accounted for the playback speed by dividing the estimated reaction time over two.

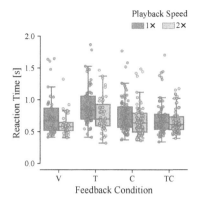

Fig. 4. Reaction time in seconds grouped by feedback type. (V: Video only, T: Terrain, C: Collision, TC: Terrain and collision.)

4.4   Results

We analyzed the effects of feedback type and playback speed with a significance level of $\alpha = .05$. We used the Aligned Rank Transform method [21] with a mixed effects model because Shapiro-Wilk tests revealed a significant departure from normality in the results. To test for order effects, we conducted an analysis using presentation order and subject as fixed and random effects, respectively. We observed non-significant effects of presentation order in the number of impacts reported ($F_{7,63} = 1.20$, $p = .316$, $\eta^2 = .118$) and in participants' F_1 score ($F_{7,63} = 1.21$, $p = .310$, $\eta^2 = .11856$).

To analyze the effects of playback speed and feedback condition on the performance metrics (reaction time, F_1 score, number of collisions reported), we considered a mixed model with playback speed, feedback condition and their interaction as fixed effects, and subject as random effect to account for the repeated measures procedure.

Average reaction times grouped by condition are shown in Fig. 4. We excluded data of one participant due to the lack of correct answers at 2× with conditions V and TC. We observed non-significant effects of feedback condition ($F_{3,56} = 1.96$, $p = .131$, $\eta^2 = .095$), playback speed ($F_{1,56} = 2.851$, $p = .097$, $\eta^2 = .048$), and their interaction ($F_{3,56} = 0.54$, $p = .656$, $\eta^2 = .028$) in participants' reaction time. The average reaction time at 1× was 0.70 s for V, 0.81 s for T, 0.74 s for C, and 0.67 s for TC. At 2×, 0.64 s for V, 0.70 s for T, 0.66 s for C, and 0.68 s for TC.

The total number of collisions reported grouped by condition are shown in Fig. 5a where the vertical axis represents the ratio between the number of collisions reported for a video and the actual number of collisions for that video. We observed a significant effect of playback speed ($F_{1,63} = 6.52$, $p = .013$, $\eta^2 = .094$) and feedback condition ($F_{3,63} = 5.34$, $p = .002$, $\eta^2 = .203$) in the number of impacts reported. Since interaction effects were not significant ($F_{3,63} = 2.27$,

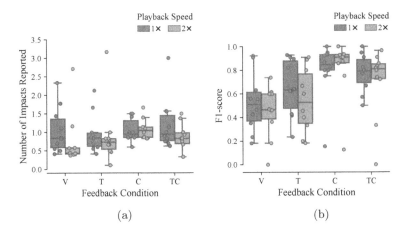

Fig. 5. (a) Total number impacts reported by condition. Values below one indicate fewer answers than collisions in a video and vice versa. (b) Detection performance by condition. F_1 scores range from 0 (worst) to 1 (best). (V: Video only, T: Terrain, C: Collision, TC: Terrain and collision.)

$p = .088$, $\eta^2 = .098$), we report pairwise comparisons within factors. Pairwise comparisons suggest a significant difference (p-values adjusted using Tukey method) in the number of impacts reported between T-C ($t_{63} = -3.12, p = .014$), and C-V ($t_{63} = 3.63, p = .003$).

Detection performance results (as measured by the F_1 score) are shown in Fig. 5b. We observed a significant effect of feedback condition ($F_{3,63} = 19.48$, $p < .0001$, $\eta^2 = .481$) and a non-significant effect of playback speed ($F_{1,63} = 1.15$, $p = .288$, $\eta^2 = .018$) in participants' F_1 score. Since interaction effects were not significant ($F_{3,63} = 1.04$, $p = .380$, $\eta^2 = .047$), we report pairwise comparisons within factors. Pairwise comparisons suggest a significant difference (p-values adjusted using Tukey method) in participants' F_1 score between T-TC ($t_{63} = -2.83$, $p = .031$), T-C ($t_{63} = -5.00$, $p < .0001$), V-TC ($t_{63} = 4.93$, $p < .0001$), and V-C ($t_{63} = 7.10$, $p < .0001$).

Finally, classification performance results are shown in Fig. 6 on a Precision-Recall plot. In absence of collision vibrations (feedback conditions V and T), classification performance spreads broadly on the precision-recall plot. Whereas when collisions vibrations are available (feedback conditions C and TC), results concentrate on the upper right corner showing high recall and high precision.

5   Discussion

The results of the pilot user study suggest that terrain vibrations are dispensable in the collision detection task described in Sect. 4. Although there are reports indicating that noise can enhance the perception of subthreshold stimulus and affect negatively the perception of suprathreshold stimuli [22], the target stimulus (collision) in this study was not concurrent with noise (terrain vibrations).

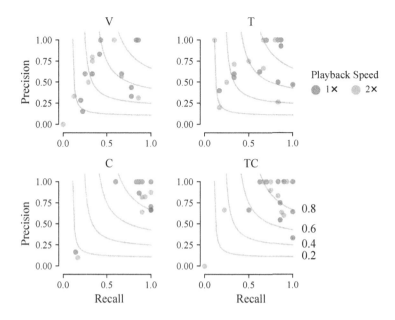

Fig. 6. Detection performance in a Precision-Recall plot. Gray contour lines represent F_1 scores that span from 0 (worst) to 1 (best). (V: Video only, T: Terrain, C: Collision, TC: Terrain and collision.)

In fact, terrain vibrations during rotation were not as intense as during the approach stage. Nevertheless, the potential of terrain vibrations when viewers adjust the playback speed remains to be studied. Terrain vibrations might help in adjusting the playback speed by informing about the speed of the robot. Furthermore, in post-experiment interviews, some participants reported that decreasing terrain vibrations signaled that the cart was about to turn and they used this information to adjust their attention levels to the video.

We asked participants to evaluate task complexity and comfort after the experiment. On task complexity, most of the participants indicated that performing the task with feedback conditions C (collision vibrations) and TC (terrain and collision vibrations) was *easy*, and that performing the task with the feedback condition T (terrain vibrations) was more challenging than completing the task with no vibrations at all. The lack of collision vibrations in feedback condition T confused participants about collisions' occurrence, especially when in the video the camera trembling after a collision was not intense. Furthermore, participants predicted that condition T would impact negatively their reaction time but we did not find evidence at a significance level $\alpha = .05$ to support this observation. On comfort, several participants indicated that completing the task with feedback conditions T (terrain vibrations) and V (no haptic feedback) demanded higher levels of attention in detriment of their comfort.

The results of the pilot user study are promising but further experiments are required to evaluate transient event detection with different videos. For instance, motion in FPV videos recorded with action cameras does not follow a regular pattern as in the videos employed in our user study. Similarly, further studies are necessary to expose constraints due to adaptation. In our user study participants took breaks between videos which might have prevented adaptation. However, temporal constraints to prevent adaptation would affect the user interaction in a practical scenario.

6   Conclusions

In this paper, we proposed using camera vibrations as vibrotactile feedback to preserve the perception of transient events during fast video playback of FPV videos. We demonstrated the feasibility of this proposal by using TSM techniques developed for audio to preserve camera vibrations characteristics during fast playback in a collision detection task. We observed that participants report significantly fewer collisions without vibrotactile feedback than with collision vibrations. Furthermore, we observed that collision vibrations improve collision detection performance (as measured by the F_1 score), and that vibrotactile feedback had no significant effect on participants' reaction time to collisions. Incidentally, comfort and perceived task complexity benefited from the addition of vibrotactile feedback as per participants' accounts. Altogether, we have shown that camera vibrations delivered to the hand can be used to inform about transient events during fast video playback of FPV videos.

Acknowledgments. This research was partially supported by ImPACT Program "Tough Robotics Challenge".

References

1. Peker, K.A., Divakaran, A., Sun, H.: Constant pace skimming and temporal subsampling of video using motion activity. In: 2001 International Conference on Image Processing, Proceedings, vol. 3, pp. 414–417. IEEE (2001)
2. Peker, K.A., Divakaran, A.: Adaptive fast playback-based video skimming using a compressed-domain visual complexity measure. In: 2004 IEEE International Conference on Multimedia and Expo, ICME 2004, vol. 3, pp. 2055–2058. IEEE (2004)
3. Kopf, J., Cohen, M.F., Szeliski, R.: First-person hyper-lapse videos. ACM Trans. Graph. (TOG) **33**(4), 78 (2014)
4. Poleg, Y., Halperin, T., Arora, C., Peleg, S.: Egosampling: fast-forward and stereo for egocentric videos. In: Proceedings of the IEEE Conference on Computer Vision and Pattern Recognition, pp. 4768–4776 (2015)
5. Riley, J.M., Endsley, M.R.: The hunt for situation awareness: human-robot interaction in search and rescue. In: Proceedings of the Human Factors and Ergonomics Society Annual Meeting, vol. 48, pp. 693–697. SAGE Publications, Los Angeles, CA (2004)

6. Kadous, M.W., Sheh, R.K.-M., Sammut, C.: Effective user interface design for rescue robotics. In: Proceedings of the 1st ACM SIGCHI/SIGART Conference on Human-Robot Interaction, pp. 250–257. ACM (2006)
7. Murphy, R.R., Tadokoro, S., Nardi, D., Jacoff, A., Fiorini, P., Choset, H., Erkmen, A.M.: Search and rescue robotics. In: Siciliano, B., Khatib, O. (eds.) Springer Handbook of Robotics, pp. 1151–1173. Springer, Heidelberg (2008). https://doi.org/10.1007/978-3-540-30301-5_51
8. Gerovich, O., Marayong, P., Okamura, A.M.: The effect of visual and haptic feedback on computer-assisted needle insertion. Comput. Aided Surg. **9**(6), 243–249 (2004)
9. Prewett, M.S., Elliott, L.R., Walvoord, A.G., Coovert, M.D.: A meta-analysis of vibrotactile and visual information displays for improving task performance. IEEE Trans. Syst. Man Cybern. Part C (Appl. Rev.) **42**(1), 123–132 (2012)
10. Van der Burg, E., Olivers, C.N., Bronkhorst, A.W., Theeuwes, J.: Poke and pop: tactile-visual synchrony increases visual saliency. Neurosci. Lett. **450**(1), 60–64 (2009)
11. Van der Burg, E., Olivers, C.N., Bronkhorst, A.W., Theeuwes, J.: Pip and pop: nonspatial auditory signals improve spatial visual search. J. Exp. Psychol. Hum. Percept. Perform. **34**(5), 1053 (2008)
12. Driedger, J., Müller, M.: A review of time-scale modification of music signals. Appl. Sci. **6**(2), 57 (2016)
13. Amir, A., Ponceleon, D., Blanchard, B., Petkovic, D., Srinivasan, S., Cohen, G.: Using audio time scale modification for video browsing. In: Proceedings of the 33rd Annual Hawaii International Conference on System Sciences, p. 9-pp. IEEE (2000)
14. Fitzgerald, D.: Harmonic/percussive separation using median filtering. In: Proceedings of the 13th International Conference on Digital Audio Effects, DAFX10, Graz, Austria, pp. 246–253, September 2010
15. Driedger, J., Muller, M., Ewert, S.: Improving time-scale modification of music signals using harmonic-percussive separation. IEEE Signal Process. Lett. **21**(1), 105–109 (2014)
16. Paté, A., Boschi, L., Le Carrou, J.-L., Holtzman, B.: Categorization of seismic sources by auditory display: a blind test. Int. J. Hum. Comput. Stud. **85**, 57–67 (2016)
17. Snibbe, S.S., MacLean, K.E., Shaw, R., Roderick, J., Verplank, W.L., Scheeff, M.: Haptic techniques for media control. In: Proceedings of the 14th Annual ACM Symposium on User Interface Software and Technology, pp. 199–208. ACM (2001)
18. Hashimoto, Y., Kajimoto, H.: Slow motion replay of tactile sensation. In: Proceeding of IEEE ICAT, pp. 51–56 (2010)
19. Dice, L.R.: Measures of the amount of ecologic association between species. Ecology **26**(3), 297–302 (1945)
20. Sørensen, T.: A method of establishing groups of equal amplitude in plant sociology based on similarity of species and its application to analyses of the vegetation on danish commons. Biol. Skr. **5**, 1–34 (1948)
21. Wobbrock, J.O., Findlater, L., Gergle, D., Higgins, J.J.: The aligned rank transform for nonparametric factorial analyses using only anova procedures. In: Proceedings of the SIGCHI Conference on Human Factors in Computing Systems, pp. 143–146. ACM (2011)
22. Collins, J., Imhoff, T.T., Grigg, P.: Noise-mediated enhancements and decrements in human tactile sensation. Phys. Rev. E **56**(1), 923 (1997)

Preliminary Study on Real-Time Interactive Virtual Fixture Generation Method for Shared Teleoperation in Unstructured Environments

Vitalii Pruks[1(✉)], Ildar Farkhatdinov[2], and Jee-Hwan Ryu[1]

[1] Department of Mechanical Engineering, KOREATECH,
1600, Chungjeol-ro, Byeongcheon-myeon, Dongnam-gu,
Cheonan-si, Chungcheongnam-do 31253, Republic of Korea
vprooks@koreatech.ac.kr, jhryu@kut.ac.kr
[2] School of Electronic Engineering and Computer Science,
Queen Mary University of London, London, UK
i.farkhatdinov@qmul.ac.uk
http://robot.kut.ac.kr

Abstract. We present a method for interactively generating virtual fixtures for shared teleoperation in unstructured remote environments. The proposed method allows a human operator to intuitively assign various types of virtual fixtures on-the-fly to provide virtual guidance forces helping the operator to accomplish a given task while minimizing the cognitive workload. The proposed method augments the visual feedback image from the slave's robot video camera with automatically extracted geometric features (shapes, surfaces, etc.) computed from both depth and color video sensor attached next to the slave robot's base. The human operator can select a feature on the computer screen which is then automatically associated with a virtual haptic fixture. The performance of the proposed method was evaluated with a peg-in-hole task and the experiment showed improvements in teleoperation performance.

Keywords: Virtual fixture · Bilateral teleoperation
Unstructured environment · Virtual fixture generation
Computer vision

1 Introduction

In teleoperation, it is well-known that virtual fixtures can assist human operators to improve task performance and safety [1, 10, 11, 14]. Generally, virtual fixtures can be of two categories: (1) guidance fixtures which provide assistive forces to guide a human operator to a target motion and (2) forbidden region virtual fixtures which define resistive force fields to prevent a human operator to work in certain areas of the workspace [2, 4].

© Springer International Publishing AG, part of Springer Nature 2018
D. Prattichizzo et al. (Eds.): EuroHaptics 2018, LNCS 10894, pp. 648–659, 2018.
https://doi.org/10.1007/978-3-319-93399-3_55

Most of the research works on virtual fixtures assume that the fixtures are already present in the environment, or are associated with certain models in a structured environment. The pioneering works on virtual fixtures used material fixtures made of plastic sheets [14,15]. Such fixtures are installed at the master device and provide assistive guidance and forbidden region effects via direct contact with the master device. Assistance and avoidance fixtures are computed automatically with edge or blob detection algorithms in a sufficiently structured environment [3,9]. An environment-specific knowledge embodied into the system allows generating virtual fixtures for more complex scenarios like surgery on a beating heart [16]. Computer vision algorithms using a 3D model [12] or a machine learning algorithm [18] to detect objects and their spatial poses in the visual scene can also be used for automatic fixture definition. In mobile robot teleoperation forbidden region virtual fixtures are defined with respect to the remote environment's objects and help to avoid collisions [5,6]. But, it is not always possible to pre-define virtual fixtures, especially in unstructured and uncertain remote environments, which are the most common cases in teleoperation. Therefore, there has been a necessity of real-time virtual fixture generation method in teleoperation scenarios where no prior knowledge about the remote environment is given. For instance, in disaster scenarios, debris can have arbitrary shapes, and common equipment might be damaged and deformed. In addition, the method should also be intuitive and easy to use on-the-fly. Spending extra time on the generation of virtual fixtures might result in less benefit compared to direct teleoperation without the help of virtual fixtures.

Surprisingly, there has been not much discussion on generating virtual fixtures in real-time during the teleoperation. In [17] an initial trial for interactive virtual fixture generation was presented. The objects of the remote environment were defined as single points which enabled to associate them with virtual fixtures implemented with potential force fields. In [13], the authors proposed a method to specify a point-based path on a surface using a 2D image. In that approach, a human operator picked a set of multiple points on a surface shown from the remote video camera. These points were then used to define the path-based virtual fixtures for robot guidance. Both approaches presented in [13,17] were based on point-based interaction with the environment. Unlike in previous works, in the present paper we propose surface-based virtual fixture generation method. Our approach enables interactive and efficient virtual fixture assignment based on the geometrical shapes recognized from the three-dimensional image acquired from camera at the slave side. The proposed system includes a depth video camera at the slave side and a graphical user interface (GUI) at the master side. A 3D image from the slave robot's camera is used by a human operator to select the objects of interest and associate them with guidance or forbidden region virtual fixtures. These virtual fixtures can be defined and modified by a human operator interactively during the teleoperation.

The paper is organized as follows. The proposed virtual fixture generation method is described in details in Sect. 2. A user evaluation study with master-slave teleoperation system and its results are presented in Sects. 3 and 4. Discussion and conclusion can be found in the Sect. 5.

2   Proposed Interactive Real-Time Virtual Fixture Generation Framework

2.1   General Framework

One of the main challenges of virtual fixture generation is that the virtual fixture has to be specified in the context of the teleoperation task. The context could be extracted automatically by setting logical rules and by providing 3D models prior to the actual teleoperation, but this might be tedious or even not possible if the environment is unstructured. In this paper, we propose to use human cognitive abilities to define the context manually from the two-dimensional projected view from the slave robot's camera and augmented reality GUI. The augmented reality GUI highlights a set of geometrical features of remote objects by graphically overlaying them in the camera view image in order to define the associated force field of virtual fixture.

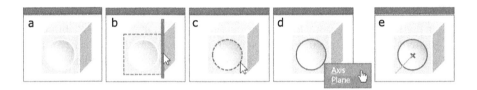

Fig. 1. Virtual fixture generation procedure for the peg in hole task. **a** the remote environment's objects are shown in the user interface. **b, c** the user hovers the mouse cursor over the object and its features are highlighted; if there are multiple features at the same cursor position, all of them will be displayed. **d** right mouse click on a desired feature reveals a pop-up menu that allows to generate the necessary fixture. **e** fixture is placed into the 3d environment for haptic rendering.

In the proposed framework, a human operator can interactively select features (using a computer mouse or a touch screen) on the image coming from the depth camera. With the help of dedicated computer vision algorithms which identify geometrical features of remote objects and overlay them on the video stream from the remote environment, human operator can intuitively select features for assigning virtual fixture following the given teleoperation task context.

The process of fixture generation for the peg-in-hole task can be visualized as follows (Fig. 1). First, operator observes the user interface where an image of the remote environment is displayed. Then, by hovering computer mouse, various features are highlighted, e.g. connected components, line segments, and circles. A virtual guidance that can be used for the peg in hole task is an axis of the hole. To find this axis, it is sufficient for the user to find the circular edge of the hole, and then the pose of the virtual fixture can be computed automatically by computing the center of the hole and normal axis of the center. All the necessary computations are done in the background, and the overall process is intuitive and fast to execute.

2.2   Interactive Generation of Virtual Fixtures

This subsection describes how virtual fixtures are interactively generated based on the assigned features and their properties by a human operator.

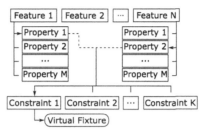

Fig. 2. The process of virtual fixture generation using features from 2D image: human operator selects *Feature 1* and *Property 1* of the tool in the user interface; then, he or she selects *Feature N* and *Property 2* describing the teleoperation target; finally, two properties are constrained together with *Constraint 1* which will define the virtual fixture. A *line with an arrow* shows the choice of the human operator, while *a line not touching an item* is the possibility of a choice.

Figure 2 introduces the process of interactive virtual fixture generation. Three components are used to generate virtual fixtures: a *feature* is a set of pixels highlighted in the user interface on mouse hover; a *property* is the corresponding 3D geometry of each feature, which is necessary to register the virtual fixture in 3D space; a *constraint* is a geometrical relation between two *properties*. First, human operator selects a feature of the tool (i.e., end effector or tool of the slave robot), and selects a property of the feature. Second, human operator selects a feature of the target object in remote environments, and selects the property of the chosen feature. Once two properties are selected, the operator can assign a constraint, which defines the geometrical relationship between two properties, and this is sufficient for the definition of the virtual fixture.

The diagram in Fig. 3 shows the pipeline that computes features and their respective properties from RGB-d camera. Image features such as edges, line segments, and ellipses are detected in the image from the RGB camera and then presented to the user in the GUI. Pixels of the 2D features selected by the user are then transformed into 3D points using corresponding pixels of the depth image and sensor's intrinsic and extrinsic parameters. The user is able to choose a property that is the most useful for task-specific virtual fixture definition, like central point and normal to a surface composed of feature's points. Then, the user chooses an effect the fixture should produce: attraction or repulsion force. The pose of the fixture and its effect is transferred to the shared control system providing haptic assistance to the user through the master device.

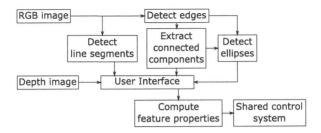

Fig. 3. Feature computation pipeline. Features and their properties from the RGB and Depth image streams are being computed in the real-time and stored in the User Interface. The human operator interacts with the User Interface to define a virtual fixture which is then added to the shared control system.

Dedicated algorithms should be used for geometrical surfaces recognition. Circle/ellipse detection algorithm was developed for the teleoperation task presented in this paper (peg-in-hole). This algorithm is described in details in the next subsection.

2.3   Detecting Basic Geometrical Features: Circle/Ellipse

In order to provide an intuitive tool to human operator for assigning the virtual fixture, automatic feature and property detection algorithm running in the background is important. There are many different type of features and detection algorithms, but in this paper, we introduce a circle/ellipse detection algorithm only for briefly showing feasibility of the proposed framework.

The ellipse classification algorithm is described in Algorithm 1. The algorithm takes a set of 3D points as an input and tells if the points belong to an ellipse, or not. We use the following notations: $\mathbf{P}$ is a set of vectors or scalars, or a matrix; $\{\cdot\}$ is a set, $\boldsymbol{p}$ is a vector, p is a scalar, $\|\cdot\|$ is euclidean norm, $\overline{\cdot}$ is mean of a set.

The idea of the ellipse classification algorithm is to compute the distance d from the given set of points $\mathbf{P}$ of the connected component to the points of an ellipse $\mathbf{E}$ having the same major and minor axes obtained from principal component analysis (PCA) applied to $\mathbf{P}$. To apply PCA, we need to centralize the values of the pixels (steps 1 and 2); on step 3 obtain projection $\hat{\mathbf{P}}$ of $\mathbf{P}$ on principal component vectors. We can find minor and major axes of $\hat{\mathbf{P}}$ as minimum and maximum distance from points of $\hat{\mathbf{P}}$ to the origin. On steps 5 and 6 we then compute points of the ideal ellipse E matching angles and axes of $\hat{\mathbf{P}}$. On step 7 we compute distance d between points of $\mathbf{E}$ and $\hat{\mathbf{P}}$. The resulting distance value is then compared with the threshold ε. If $d < \varepsilon$ then we can say the points belong to an ellipse, otherwise they don't. We set the threshold value ε to be equal to 1 which means that the accumulated error from the image points to the corresponding ellipse should not exceed 1 pixel. In our usage experiments this algorithm is accurate enough as long as the edge detection algorithm extracts consistent edges.

Algorithm 1. Ellipse Classification Algorithm

Output:

    Coordinates of points in a connected component: $\mathbf{P} = \{\boldsymbol{p}_i\}$, $\mathbf{P} \subset \mathbb{R}^2$ $i = 1, 2, \ldots, n$,
n is a matrix of points

    Threshold : ε

Ensure:

    The classification result: true or false

1: $c = \sum_i^n \boldsymbol{p}_i / n$ ▷ compute center of $\mathbf{P}$

2: $\tilde{\mathbf{P}} = \mathbf{P} - c = \{\boldsymbol{p}_i - c\}$ ▷ shift $\mathbf{P}$ towards the center c

3: $\hat{\mathbf{P}} = \tilde{\mathbf{P}}\mathbf{W}$ ▷ Apply PCA to $\tilde{\mathbf{P}}$; $\mathbf{W}$ is a n-by-n matrix whose columns are
    eigenvalues of $\tilde{\mathbf{P}}^T\tilde{\mathbf{P}}$

4: $a = \min_i \|\hat{\boldsymbol{p}}_i\|$, $b = \max_i \|\hat{\boldsymbol{p}}_i\|$ ▷ find major a and minor b axes of $\hat{\mathbf{P}}$

5: $\boldsymbol{\Phi} = \{\phi_i\} = \{\arctan 2(\frac{\hat{p}_{iy}}{a}, \frac{\hat{p}_{ix}}{b})\}$ ▷ compute polar angles of $\hat{\mathbf{P}}$

6: $\mathbf{E} = \{\boldsymbol{e}_i\} = \{(a\cos\phi_i, b\sin\phi_i)\}$ ▷ compute points of ellipse with axes a, b for
    angles $\boldsymbol{\Phi}$

7: $d = \left\|\mathbf{E} - \hat{\mathbf{P}}\right\| = \frac{\sum_i^n \|e_i - \hat{p}_i\|}{n}$ ▷ compute mean distance d of ideal ellipse points $\mathbf{E}$
    and projected values $\hat{\mathbf{P}}$

8: **return** $d < \varepsilon$ ▷ if holds true, then points in P belong to an ellipse, otherwise not

---

3 Experiment

3.1 Experimental Setup

Our bilateral teleoperation system was composed of a UR5 universal robotic manipulator (slave) equipped with a Delta force/torque sensor and CMU Cam 5 video camera at the end effector; Omega 6 haptic interface (master); Microsoft Kinect RGB-d camera installed at the slave side; control computer with the proposed interactive virtual fixture definition GUI. The overall experimental setup can be seen in Fig. 4.

The peg-in-hole task was evaluated during the experiment. The 3D printed peg was rigidly attached to the slave's end-effector. The diameter of the peg was 30 mm and diameter of the hole was 30.5 mm. The setup is based in the KoreaTech Biorobotics lab. Slave and master subsystems were located away from each other and were connected through an Ethernet network and it was assumed to be time delay free. We have also evaluated that there was no packet loss within the network. Force feedback from the slave side was based on direct force measurements from the end-effector's force-torque sensors. Direct position-to-position mapping was used to control the slave robot with the master device. Stability of the bilateral teleoperator was guaranteed by the PO/PC approach (passivity observer and passivity controller [8]). The controller was running at 4 kHz sampling rate.

The ArUco augmented reality marker [7] was used to localize the slave manipulator in the Kinect camera's frame of reference. As a result, the teleoperation controller and virtual fixture definition GUI were operating in the same frame of reference.

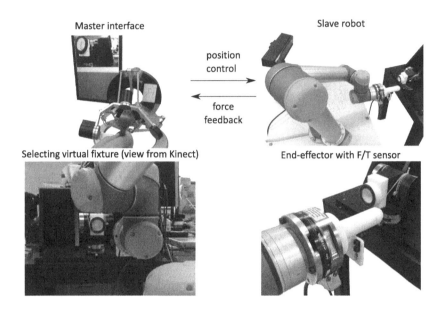

Master interface

Slave robot

position
control

force
feedback

Selecting virtual fixture (view from Kinect)

End-effector with F/T sensor

Fig. 4. Experimental setup for bilateral teleoperation with virtual fixtures

3.2 Generation of Virtual Fixtures

The process of the fixture generation for the peg-in-hole task with the proposed GUI consists of 9 steps (as illustrated in Fig. 5):

1. The human operator enables the *feature selection mode*; in this mode hovering the mouse over the camera view reveals *features*.
2. The human operator finds the necessary feature.
3. Clicking on the found feature selects its type (*ellipse*).
4. The ellipse appears in the *detected features* section (the human operator can select multiple features before proceeding to next step.
5. Clicking on *apply* combines the selected features into one.
6. The combined feature appears in the *combined features* menu; the human operator clicks on the *combined feature*.
7. The geometrical *properties* of the feature appear in a drop-down menu.
8. Clicking on the necessary *property* of the *combined feature*, the user selects a *geometrical constraint*, e.g. *Align*.
9. The *align with the hole's axis* feature is displayed in the user interface and placed in the virtual environment to provide guidance to the human operator.

Current implementation supports *features*: connected components, line segments, ellipses. These features on a 2d image, projected to the depth image from the Kinect sensor, allow to restore 3d positions of the image points; the 3d positions are then used to compute the center of the set of points, normal to the plane fitting the set of points, and spatial orientation of asymmetric planar

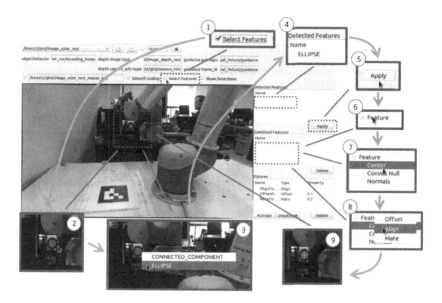

Fig. 5. User interface with description of the virtual fixture generation process.

geometrical objects. The fixtures that can be generated using these features and their properties are *offset, align,* and *mate.*

The user interface supports combining of multiple features into one (Fig. 5 *3–5*). For example, if the edges of the circle for the peg-in-hole task cannot be detected using a single edge contour, then multiple pieces of the contour can be selected.

The whole procedure of the fixture generation consists of 9 actions that are performed by moving the computer mouse and clicking. As most of the features are computed and highlighted automatically, the user doesn't need to perform precise mouse movements. During the experiments, it has been shown that subjects got used to the user interface quickly, and the process of fixture generation takes very short time.

3.3 Protocol and Participants

The goal of the study was to demonstrate that the proposed virtual fixture definition method can be efficiently used in a simple teleoperation scenario. The task of a participant was to complete the peg-in-hole task as fast and as accurate as possible based on limited visual feedback from the end-effector's camera and force feedback from the force-torque sensor. Through the end-effector's camera the participants could see the tip of the peg and the target environment. Additionally, the participants had access to the virtual fixture GUI, so that they could define a guidance fixture for the hole's position in the peg-in-hole task. Two conditions were tested: (1) teleoperation without virtual fixtures and

(2) teleoperation with virtual fixtures. Ten participants took part in the evaluation tests (all male, age 23–35), nine of them were right-handed, one - left-handed. They were instructed how to perform the peg-in-hole task as fast as possible and were given an opportunity to perform several familiarization trials with and without haptic guidance. This was then followed by a set of experimental trials with guidance (5 trials) and without guidance (5 trials). The trials with and without guidance were mixed in order to prevent the adaptation effects. During the experiments, the participants could not see the slave robot as it was intentionally hidden from the field of view.

For each trial, we have recorded the master's and slave's position, measured slave's end-effector force and haptic guidance force if it was used. Time to the first contact with the hole, total completion time, smoothness of master and slave movements, and magnitude of interaction forces were used as performance indicators.

4   Results

All human-subjects were able to complete the trials successfully. Figure 6 presents the total completion time and time to the first contact for all subjects with and without haptic guidance for 10 participants (mean and standard deviation of measured time in all trials). Virtual fixture selection time was not included in the total task completion time. For all participants, average task completion time with a virtual guidance was 15.22 ± 5.55 s (mean±standard deviation) which is less when the virtual guidance was not used 21.09 ± 6.10 s. Time to the first contact was also reduced for all participants when haptic guidance was used: 12.44 ± 3.57 s against 15.61 ± 4.23 s.

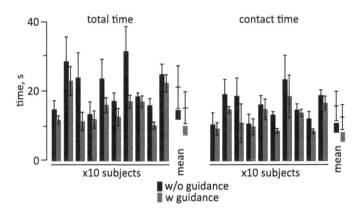

Fig. 6. Results for task completion time per subject with and without virtual fixtures.

Figure 7 presents time series plot with and without guidance for a typical subject (master/slave position, force feedback from the force-torque sensor, and force rendered at master side). Figures 7a–c show the plots for master/slave position, end-effector force measurements, and rendered force at the master side for the case when no virtual fixtures were used. Figures 7d–f show the plots for master/slave position, end-effector force measurements, and rendered force at the slave side for the case when the virtual guidance was enabled. The positions of master and slave devices (Fig. 7a, d) drop to 0 occasionally, this happens when the human operator releases the button at the master device to perform indexing. We can observe that the magnitudes of the measured end-effector force when the peg was inside the hole were smaller for the case when the virtual guidance was enabled. The motion trajectory with virtual guidance enabled was also smoother. These results allow to conclude that the virtual fixture generated in real-time by the operator provided a better quality of motion; it enabled the human operator to move more safely and precisely. Finally, both plots demonstrate that the task execution time was smaller for enabled virtual guidance as it is also visualized in the Fig. 6.

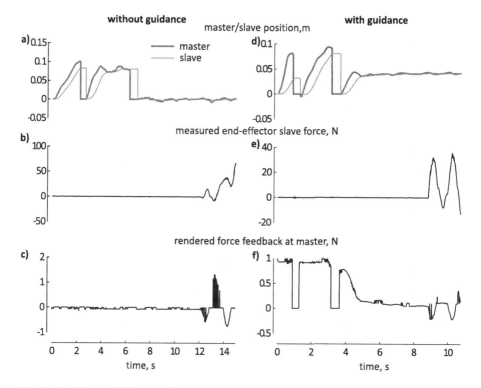

Fig. 7. Position and force profile without (**a, b, c**) and with (**d, e, f**) virtual guidance. Plots: **a, d** - the master's and slave's positions; **b, e** - measured force at the slave's end-effector; **c, f** - rendered force at the master.

5 Conclusion and Future Works

This paper presents a novel interactive virtual fixture generation method for shared teleoperation in unstructured remote environments. The proposed method allows human operator to easily assign and register virtual fixtures on the remote target objects on-the-fly with only several mouse button clicks. The easiness of the virtual fixture generation as well as the effectiveness of the real-time generated virtual fixture was tested with a peg-in-hole task. The human subject study shows improved performance of the peg-in-hole teleoperation task with real-time generated virtual fixture.

As a future work, we are currently generalizing the proposed framework including diverse type of features, properties and constraints, and planning to test the performance and effectiveness of the proposed method with more complicated unstructured teleoperation tasks.

Acknowledgements. This research is supported by the project "Toward the Next Generation of Robotic Humanitarian Assistance and Disaster Relief: Fundamental Enabling Technologies (10069072)" and by the project "Development of core teleoperation technologies for maintaining and repairing tasks in nuclear power plants" funded by the Ministry of Trade, Industry & Energy of S. Korea.

I. Farkhatdinov was partially supported by the UK EPSRC in the framework of the National Centre for Nuclear Robotics project (EP/R02572X/1).

References

1. Aarno, D., Ekvall, S., Kragic, D.: Adaptive virtual fixtures for machine-assisted teleoperation tasks. In: Proceedings of the 2005 IEEE International Conference on Robotics and Automation, ICRA 2005, pp. 1139–1144 (2005)
2. Abbott, J.J., Panadda, M., Allison, O., Marayong, P., Okamura, A.M.: Haptic virtual fixtures for robot-assisted manipulation. In: Robotics Research, pp. 49–64 (2007)
3. Bettini, A., Lang, S., Okamura, A., Hager, G.: Vision assisted control for manipulation using virtual fixtures: experiments at macro and micro scales. In: Proceedings of 2002 IEEE International Conference on Robotics and Automation, vol. 4, pp. 3354–3361 (2002)
4. Bowyer, S.A., Davies, B.L., Rodriguez, Y., Baena, F.: Active constraints/virtual fixtures: a survey. IEEE Trans. Rob. **30**(1), 138–157 (2014)
5. Farkhatdinov, I., Ryu, J.H.: Improving mobile robot bilateral teleoperation by introducing variable force feedback gain. In: 2010 IEEE/RSJ International Conference on Intelligent Robots and Systems, pp. 5812–5817 (2010)
6. Farkhatdinov, I., Ryu, J.H., Poduraev, J.: A user study of command strategies for mobile robot teleoperation. Intel. Serv. Robot. **2**(2), 95–104 (2009)
7. Garrido-Jurado, S., noz Salinas, R.M., Madrid-Cuevas, F., Marín-Jiménez, M.: Automatic generation and detection of highly reliable fiducial markers under occlusion. Pattern Recogn. **47**(6), 2280–2292 (2014)
8. Hannaford, B., Ryu, J.H.: Time-domain passivity control of haptic interfaces. IEEE Trans. Robot. Autom. **18**(1), 1–10 (2002)

9. Jiang, Z., Liu, Y., Liu, H., Zou, J.: Flexible virtual fixture enhanced by vision and haptics for unstructured environment teleoperation. In: 2013 IEEE International Conference on Robotics and Biomimetics (ROBIO), pp. 2643–2648 (2013)
10. Li, M., Taylor, R.H.: Spatial motion constraints in medical robot using virtual fixtures generated by anatomy. In: 2004 IEEE International Conference on Robotics and Automation, Proceedings, ICRA 2004, vol. 2, pp. 1270–1275 (2004)
11. Lin, H.C., Mills, K., Kazanzides, P., Hager, G.D., Marayong, P., Okamura, A.M., Karam, R.: Portability and applicability of virtual fixtures across medical and manufacturing tasks. In: Proceedings 2006 IEEE International Conference on Robotics and Automation, ICRA 2006, pp. 225–230 (2006)
12. Li, M., Kapoor, A., Taylor, R.: A constrained optimization approach to virtual fixtures. In: IEEE/RSJ International Conference on Intelligent Robots and Systems 2015, pp. 1408–1413 (2015)
13. Quintero, C.P., Dehghan, M., Ramirez, O., Ang, M.H., Jagersand, M.: Flexible virtual fixture interface for path specification in tele-manipulation. In: 2017 IEEE International Conference on Robotics and Automation (ICRA), pp. 5363–5368, May 2017
14. Rosenberg, L.: Virtual fixtures: perceptual tools for telerobotic manipulation. In: Proceedings of IEEE Virtual Reality Annual International Symposium. pp. 76–82 (1993)
15. Rosenberg, L.B.: The Use of Virtual Fixtures as Perceptual Overlays to Enhance Operator Performance in Remote Environments (1992)
16. Ryden, F., Chizeck, H.J.: Forbidden-region virtual fixtures from streaming point clouds: remotely touching and protecting a beating heart. In: IEEE International Conference on Intelligent Robots and Systems, pp. 3308–3313 (2012)
17. Selvaggio, M., Chen, F., Gao, B., Notomista, G., Trapani, F., Caldwell, D.: Vision based virtual fixture generation for teleoperated robotic manipulation. In: 2016 International Conference on Advanced Robotics and Mechatronics, pp. 190–195 (2016)
18. Selvaggio, M., Notomista, G., Chen, F., Gao, B., Trapani, F., Caldwell, D.: Enhancing bilateral teleoperation using camera-based online virtual fixtures generation. In: IEEE/RSJ International Conference on Intelligent Robots and Systems (IROS), pp. 1483–1488 (2016)

Network-Aware Adaptive Sampling for Low Bitrate Telehaptic Communication

Vineet Gokhale[1][(✉)], Jayakrishnan Nair[2], Subhasis Chaudhuri[2], and Suhas Kakade[2]

[1] University of South Bohemia, České Budějovice, Czech Republic
vgokhale@prf.jcu.cz, vineet.goki@gmail.com
[2] Indian Institute of Technology Bombay, Mumbai, India

Abstract. While the adaptive sampling technique for kinesthetic signal transmission offers a phenomenal reduction in the time-average data rate, it does not guarantee a meaningful upper bound on the instantaneous rate, which can occasionally be comparable to the peak rate. This implies that for Quality of Service (QoS) compliance, a network bandwidth equal to the peak rate must be reserved apriori for the telehaptic stream at all times. On a shared network with unknown and time-varying cross-traffic, this is not always feasible. In order to address the intermittently high bandwidth demand as well as the network-obliviousness of adaptive sampling, we propose *NaPAS: Network-aware Packetization for Adaptive Sampling*. The idea is to intelligently merge multiple haptic samples generated by adaptive sampling in a packet, depending on the changing network conditions. This results in an *elastic* telehaptic traffic that can adapt to the available network bandwidth. Through qualitative and quantitative measures, we evaluate the performance of NaPAS and demonstrate that it outperforms standard adaptive sampling (SAS) in terms of maintaining the haptic perceptual quality and QoS compliance, while also being friendlier to the exogenous network cross-traffic.

Keywords: Telehaptic communication · Adaptive sampling · QoS
Shared network

1 Introduction

The possibility of transmitting touch signals (in addition to audio and video) over a network has unlocked the doors to a new realm of *telehaptic* applications, like telesurgery [1] and distributed touch therapy [3]. In order to perform such sensitive tasks in a seamless manner, strict Quality of Service (QoS) requirements, reported in Table 1, need to be satisfied [13]. It is to be noted that the presence of haptic modality makes the *teleoperation* extremely vulnerable to the irregularities of the communication network, viz., delay, jitter, and packet loss. Non-compliance to these QoS constraints can adversely affect the stability of

© Springer International Publishing AG, part of Springer Nature 2018
D. Prattichizzo et al. (Eds.): EuroHaptics 2018, LNCS 10894, pp. 660–672, 2018.
https://doi.org/10.1007/978-3-319-93399-3_56

the haptic control loop, albeit there exist control architectures, such as [16], that alleviate the effect to some extent.

In order to realize a QoS-compliant teleoperation, one typically needs to leverage an existing shared network (like the internet), since deploying dedicated networks solely for the purpose of teleoperation may be practically infeasible. However, ensuring telehaptic QoS compliance on a shared network is challenging, since the cross-traffic is both unknown as well as time-varying. Indeed, network congestion (overloading) can lead to high delays, jitter, and packet losses, often resulting in severe QoS violations. Moreover, certain networks tend to be resource constrained in nature; for instance, rapidly deployed adhoc networks for emergency operations and connections in rural areas. Therefore, the communication scheme in a teleoperation should be *network-aware* in nature, with the ability to relieve congestion by dynamically tuning the traffic rate to match the available network bandwidth in real time.

Table 1. QoS specifications to be satisfied for carrying out seamless teleoperation.

Media	Delay (ms)	Jitter (ms)	Loss (%)
Haptic	30	10	10
Audio	150	30	1
Video	400	30	1

The past two decades have witnessed rapid advancements in the design and development of communication techniques specifically for haptic-based teleoperation. Amongst them, the most widely accepted model is *adaptive sampling* – a human perception based compression scheme for haptic signals [6,11,15]. Adaptive sampling classifies a haptic sample as *perceptually significant* if the percentage change in its amplitude with respect to a certain reference exceeds a pre-defined threshold δ. The work in [11] demonstrated that transmission of only the perceptually significant samples leads to a substantial reduction in the telehaptic data rate of up to 90%, without hampering the human perception. It is worth remarking that the data rate of the adaptive sampling technique depends purely on the haptic signal profile; a fast varying signal results in a high data rate, and vice-versa. This makes the adaptive sampling scheme *network-oblivious* in nature.

It is important to note that the rate reduction of adaptive sampling is in a *time-average* sense. In Fig. 1a, we plot the instantaneous rate of the adaptive sampling scheme for a real haptic trace recorded during a haptic activity [2]. It can be seen that despite the low time-average rate (186 kbps in this case), the instantaneous rate exhibits rapid fluctuations, occasionally reaching the peak value of around 600 kbps.

As per the recommendations of the references [6,11,15], reserving an amount of network bandwidth equal to the time-average rate guarantees QoS compliance, and hence smooth teleoperation. On the contrary, we demonstrate in Fig. 1b that the above network provisioning strategy (reserving 186 kbps for telehaptic stream) results in severe QoS violations, particularly when the instantaneous rate surpasses the average rate; see, for example, the range [11000, 13000] ms. Such QoS violations cause impairment of human haptic perception, as we demonstrate through subjective experiments in Sect. 4.2. Hence, we conclude that despite guaranteeing low time-average rate, adaptive sampling scheme provides no meaningful economies from the standpoint of network bandwidth requirement, since for QoS-compliance the network should be provisioned for the peak telehaptic rate. Henceforth, we refer to the adaptive sampling scheme described above as *standard adaptive sampling* (SAS).

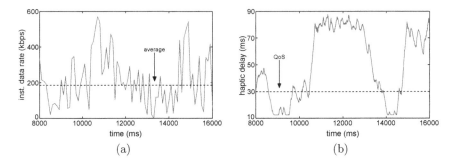

Fig. 1. Temporal evolution of (a) instantaneous data rate of SAS (b) haptic delay when the network is provisioned for the time-average data rate.

To summarize, SAS suffers two major limitations: (i) it is *network-oblivious*, and (ii) it lacks fine-grained control on the instantaneous transmission rate.

A recent work [9] attempts to address the aforementioned drawbacks of SAS through the design of *Dynamic Packetization Module (DPM)*. DPM is a lossless protocol that transmits every haptic sample, irrespective of its significance, in a *network-aware* manner. The idea is to merge k successive haptic samples into a single packet based on the changing network conditions. This packetization parameter k is dynamically tuned to match the instantaneous rate to the available network bandwidth. Note that a higher k corresponds to a lower transmission rate, due to a reduction in the packet header overhead.[1] The usage of k as the control lever enables DPM to generate steady traffic at multiple resolutions, where each resolution corresponds to a particular value of k, thereby offering a fine-grained control on the instantaneous rate. Note that DPM's data rate is insensitive to the haptic signal profile. Hence, DPM transmits even the perceptually insignificant samples (90%) leading to an improper utilization of the network resources.

---

[1] Given the high sampling rate of the haptic stream (typically 1 kHz), packet headers can account for upto 73% of the transmission rate on the forward channel when each haptic sample is packetized separately [9]. As a result, there is considerable room for data rate adaptation by varying the control parameter k (which determines the telehaptic packetization rate).

To summarize, SAS provides a significantly low average rate, compared to the peak rate, but is network-oblivious and lacks control on the instantaneous rate. On the other hand, DPM is network-aware and provides a fine-grained control on the instantaneous rate, but transmits unnecessary samples leading to a higher data rate. The question we ask in this paper is the following: Can we leverage the benefits of both SAS and DPM to obtain the best of both worlds?

In this paper, we propose NaPAS (Network-aware Packetization for Adaptive Sampling) for transmitting only the perceptually significant samples in a network-aware manner, characterized by a fine-grained control on the instantaneous rate. Like DPM, NaPAS responds to network congestion by aggressively cutting its transmission rate, thereby minimizing the chances of a QoS violation. Additionally, it compresses the generated haptic signal by transmitting only perceptually significant samples, thereby freeing up the network resources for other cross-traffic flows (as demonstrated in Sect. 4).

We conduct quantitative and qualitative assessments of our proposal through extensive simulations and bilateral telehaptic experiments, respectively. Our investigations reveal that NaPAS outperforms standard adaptive sampling in terms of telehaptic QoS compliance, and also in terms of preserving the quality of telehaptic interaction even under heavily congested network conditions. Further, we demonstrate that the dynamics of our technique are friendly to exogenous cross-traffic streams, more so than SAS and DPM.

2   Telehaptic Communication

In this section, we briefly explain the general framework of a point-to-point telehaptic communication framework, and then move to the detailed design of the proposed NaPAS framework.

2.1   Point-to-Point Framework

The point-to-point teleoperation system, shown in Fig. 2, consists of a human operator (OP) controlling the remote robotic manipulator known as the teleoperator (TOP). The OP transmits the current position and velocity commands on the forward channel. The TOP follows the trajectory of the OP through

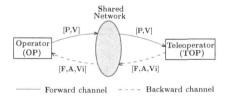

Fig. 2. Communication framework of a typical point-to-point teleoperation. Notations: [P, V]: [position, velocity], [F, A, Vi]: [force, audio, video].

execution of the received commands, and in response transmits the captured audio and video signals along with the force (haptic) feedback on the backward channel. This configuration is generally referred to as *two-channel position-force architecture* [12]. Note that the communication is inherently bidirectional and asymmetric in a teleoperation paradigm.

In the remainder of this section, we present the design details of the proposed communication framework; see Fig. 3. For the ease of presentation, we consider the standard haptic sampling rate of 1 kHz. In this work, we restrict our focus to rate control on the forward channel. On the backward channel, due to the presence of audio and video, the haptic data constitutes only a small portion of the overall payload. Hence, from the standpoint of data rate reduction, SAS on the backward channel is not as effective as it is on the forward channel. Accordingly, we perform standard DPM [9] on the backward channel.

2.2 Network Feedback

In order to accurately monitor the network under asymmetric conditions, we adopt the delay-based *network feedback* scheme proposed in [9]. The scheme in [9] exploits the bidirectional nature of the telehaptic communication for conveying to each transmitter the network delays on its channel by piggybacking this information on packets sent on the reverse channel. Specifically, the TOP piggybacks the end-to-end delays from the forward channel (d_{fwd}) on the backward channel packets, and the OP piggybacks the end-to-end delays from the backward channel on the forward channel packets. The OP extracts the piggybacked delay from the packet header to analyze the congestion state on the forward channel. Note that the end-to-end delays increase during congestion, and remain steady otherwise. Thus, if N successive, non-duplicate delay samples exhibit an increasing trend, then the OP infers that congestion is present in the forward channel.[2] In this case, a congestion trigger I_C is generated.

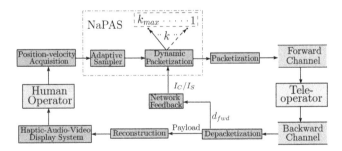

Fig. 3. Proposed communication framework for teleoperation featuring NaPAS on the forward channel. d_{fwd} denotes the forward channel delay that is piggybacked on the backward channel packets.

---

[2] The TOP transmits duplicate copies of a delay measurement if it transmits multiple packets in between adjacent receptions.

On the other hand, if N successive, non-duplicate delay samples exhibit a steady trend, then the OP infers that the forward channel is uncongested. In this case, a steady trigger I_S is generated. NaPAS performs rate adaptation based on these triggers, as described next.

2.3   NaPAS Rate Control

The goal of NaPAS is to transmit the perceptually significant samples with a fine-grained control on the instantaneous rate in a network-aware manner. As shown in Fig. 3, NaPAS subjects the perceptually significant haptic samples to a dynamic packetization process that results in an adaptive transmission rate.

The working principle of NaPAS is as follows: The time dimension is divided into continuous, non-overlapping blocks, each of length k-milliseconds, as shown in Fig. 4. Let the time interval $t \in [t_s, t_s + k)$ indicate the current block, where t_s and $t_s + k$ denote the time instants of the start and the end of the current block. The perceptually significant haptic samples, generated from adaptive sampling in the range $t \in [t_s, t_s + k)$ are merged into a single packet for transmission on the forward channel. Note that a packet can carry at most k haptic samples; see, for example, the second block in Fig. 4. No packet is generated if all the k samples in a block are perceptually insignificant; see, for example, the third block in Fig. 4. This is the primary departure from DPM, which essentially merges all haptic samples generated in a block, whether or not they are perceptually significant. Note that the parameter k allows for a tradeoff between packetization delay and transmission rate. Since haptic samples suffer a maximum packetization delay of $k - 1$ ms, an increase in k results in an overall increase in packetization delay. However, an increase in k also results in a lower packet rate, and consequently a lower data rate.

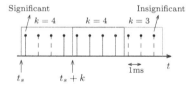

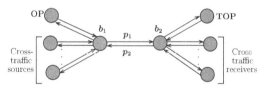

Fig. 4. Demonstration of the working principle of NaPAS based on division of time into blocks.

Fig. 5. Network topology used for the simulations. p_1 and p_2 - bottleneck links; b_1 and b_2 - intermediate nodes.

We perform rate control by using k as the control parameter based on the generated triggers. When the congestion trigger I_C is generated (indicating congestion), the update $k_{max} \leftarrow k$ is executed, where k_{max} denotes the maximum permissible value of k. This results in a drastic reduction in the instantaneous rate, facilitating the rapid draining of queues at the intermediate routers (which are either overflowing or fast filling). This minimizes the risk of QoS violations.

When the steady trigger I_S is generated (indicating an uncongested network), the framework executes the update $k - 1 \leftarrow k$, as long as $k > 1$. This results in a prudent increment in the instantaneous rate, seeking to avoid congestion while probing if the network has the necessary capacity to accommodate the rate increment. This gradual increase/aggressive decrease in transmission rate is in line with the classical additive increase/multiplicative decrease (AIMD) principle [4] in the congestion control literature. Note that when $k = 1$, NaPAS is equivalent to SAS. Hence, when the network is uncongested NaPAS reverts to SAS to minimize the packetization delay encountered by the significant samples. Note that during congestion, the data rate of NaPAS is at most equal to the data rate of DPM, since NaPAS transmits only perceptually significant samples while DPM transmits all samples.

At the TOP, the perceptually insignificant samples position-velocity samples are interpolated using the zero-order hold strategy. We choose $k_{max} = 4$, thereby restricting the maximum length of a block to 4 ms [9]. In our implementation, we set the parameter $N = 10$.

We conclude with a remark regarding the rendering of the received haptic signal at the TOP. Due to block processing, the TOP receives the latest (perceptually significant) haptic sample along with a few (upto $k_{max} - 1$) previous perceptually significant samples simultaneously. For reliable teleoperation, it is important to ensure that the TOP replicates the OP's movements as accurately as possible. Therefore, it is crucial to play-out all the received samples at the TOP sequentially, rather than render only the latest sample. This approach of transmitting/displaying a significant haptic sample even after the generation of more recent ones has also been advocated in the literature; see, for example, [5, 7].

3   Experimental Setup

In this section, we give a detailed description of the setups used for qualitative and quantitative evaluation of the proposed NaPAS framework.

3.1   Simulation Testbed

We perform quantitative evaluation using NS3 - a discrete event network simulator [14]. We simulate a single bottleneck dumbbell network topology, as shown in Fig. 5. We introduce cross-traffic sources on the forward channel. Hence, p_1 is the bottleneck link on the forward channel. We set the capacity of p_1 to 1500 kbps. The access links to the intermediate nodes b_1 and b_2 have high capacity. The propagation delay of each link is set to 4 ms. Hence, the end-to-end propagation (one-way) delay between OP and TOP is 12 ms. The details pertaining to the cross-traffic streams are reported in Sect. 4.

For our simulations, we use real haptic traces recorded during the telepottery task described in Sect. 3.2, and also from the trace repository of TU Munich [2]. We set the adaptive sampling threshold $\delta = 10\%$ as prescribed in [11], but can be tuned for an individual user. For brevity, we report the results corresponding to a single trace. However, we note that our findings remain consistent across different traces.

3.2 Subjective Evaluation

For qualitative evaluations, we use the telepottery setup in which the human subject manipulates a remote, virtual clay model through haptic and video feedback transmitted over a real network. It includes a network emulator tool for reproducing the effects of a shared network [9]. The task for the subject is to carve the clay model into a nice looking pot. Initially, the subject undergoes appropriate training involving a detailed explanation and hands-on demonstration of the telepottery task for familiarization with the experiments. The training is performed on a high bandwidth (100 Mbps) network to avoid the impact of network congestion. After the training, the subject is moved to a test setup where the bandwidth and one-way latency are set to 1500 kbps and 12 ms, respectively, as in simulations.

The testing phase consists of performing telepottery task twice: once with SAS, and once with NaPAS. On a scale of 5, the subjects grade the telepottery perception in each of the two test cases relative to the training phase based on three standard perceptual parameters: *transparency*, *smoothness*, and *overall experience* [9]. The subject provides a grade for each perceptual parameter in each test case relative to training experience based on the following grading scale: 5 - imperceptible; 4 - slight disturbance, but not annoying; 3 - slightly annoying; 2 - annoying; 1 - very annoying.

We performed the subjective evaluations with 20 human subjects (10 male and 10 female) belonging to the age group of 20 to 32 years, none suffering from any known neurophysiological disorders. Out of them, 3 were regular users of haptic devices and the rest were novices. Nevertheless, all subjects underwent meticulous training prior to the test experiments. The subjects provided informed consents prior to the experiments.

4   Experimental Results

In this section, we report the quantitative (Sect. 4.1) and qualitative (Sect. 4.2) performances of NaPAS, SAS, and DPM.

4.1   Simulation Results

We consider two classes of cross-traffic flows that are typically seen in a shared network: Constant Bitrate (CBR) cross-traffic (Sect. 4.1.1), and Transmission Control Protocol (TCP) cross-traffic (Sect. 4.1.2).

For a standard haptic sampling rate of 1 kHz, we get a forward channel peak rate of 688 kbps with a packet of size 86 bytes (including telehaptic payload and packet headers) transmitted every millisecond (see [9] for details). Through analysis, it can be shown that under heavily congested conditions, NaPAS can guarantee an upper bound of 316 kbps on the instantaneous data rate (this corresponds to $k = 4$) during congestion.

4.1.1   Constant Bitrate (CBR) Cross-Traffic

It is important to remark that in presence of CBR cross-traffic the performances of DPM and NaPAS are comparable. Hence, in this section we only
report the performances of SAS and NaPAS. We introduce a CBR cross-
traffic source with rate R_{cross} on the forward channel. For the test signal, we
observe that for $R_{cross} > 1250$ kbps the congestion level is beyond the control
of the proposed technique. Hence, we conduct the simulations over the range
$R_{cross} \in [0, 1250]$ kbps.

We begin by presenting the dynamics of k and the corresponding end-to-end
haptic delay measured at the TOP for NaPAS in Figs. 6 and 7, respectively.
For this experiment, we set $R_{cross} = 1200$ kbps starting at $t = 0$, so that the
telehaptic stream gets a bandwidth of 300 kbps. It can be seen that as the delay
increases due to congestion, NaPAS quickly switches to $k = 4$ resulting in an
effective congestion control, and thereby guaranteeing a strict QoS-compliance.
During intervals of steady delays, the OP reduces k in a step-wise manner. It
should be noted that the duration of the steady delay regions is not a constant.
For example, the steady delay region corresponding to $k = 4$ starting at $t =
1000$ ms is longer than that ending at $t = 800$ ms. This is an artifact of the
haptic signal profile; during periods when the rate of generation of perceptually
significant haptic samples is greater, the rate of packet transmissions on the
forward channel is also greater. This results in a greater reception rate of (non-
duplicate) delay measurements at the OP, in turn leading to faster updates in k.

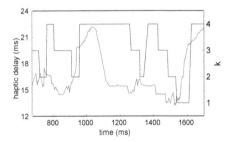

Fig. 6. Temporal evolution of end-to-end
haptic delay and the corresponding value
of k for $R_{cross} = 1200$ kbps.

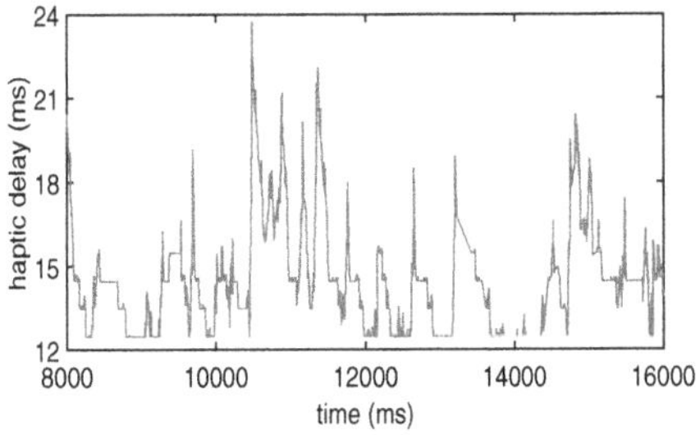

Fig. 7. Temporal evolution of end-
to-end haptic delay for NaPAS, with
$R_{cross} = 1200$ kbps.

Under the same cross-traffic setting, we compare the end-to-end haptic delays
resulting from SAS and NaPAS. Note that SAS has a much lower average data
rate (186 kbps) compared to the available bandwidth (300 kbps). However, due
to its network-obliviousness, the standard adaptive sampling scheme faces severe
violations of the haptic delay QoS conditions, comparable to Fig. 1b. This can
lead to perceptual artifacts that can cause significant degradation in the quality
of teleoperation (as demonstrated by the results of our subjective evaluations
in Sect. 4.2). On the other hand, due to the timely congestion detection and

control measures, NaPAS comfortably adheres to the delay QoS requirements of teleoperation, as shown in Fig. 7. The above observations demonstrate that from a network provisioning and QoS standpoint, it is essential to control the *instantaneous* data rate in a network-aware manner. We note that the haptic packet loss in the above experiment for both schemes is zero.

As per the standard definition, haptic jitter refers to the variation in the delay encountered by successive haptic samples. However, we note that for an adaptive sampling based communication, the haptic packets are generated irregularly in time. Thus, the standard definition of jitter does not apply, and so we do not report on haptic jitter in this paper.

Until now all our measurements were carried out in presence of a steady cross-traffic. We now vary R_{cross} over time to demonstrate the ability of NaPAS to adapt to changing network conditions. Specifically, we introduce a time-varying cross-traffic profile as shown below.

$$R_{cross} = \begin{cases} 700 \text{ kbps}, & \text{for } t \leq 10 \text{ s}, t > 12.5 \text{ s} \\ 1250 \text{ kbps}, & \text{for } 10 < t \leq 11.5 \text{ s} \\ 900 \text{ kbps}, & \text{for } 11.5 < t \leq 12.5 \text{ s} \end{cases}$$

In Fig. 8, we report the temporal variation of the instantaneous rates for SAS and NaPAS. While SAS is insensitive to the cross-traffic variations, the NaPAS scheme senses the level of congestion and tunes the instantaneous rate appropriately to below the available bandwidth. During heavy congestion ($R_{cross} = 1250$ kbps) NaPAS achieves peak congestion control, and when the network is uncongested ($R_{cross} = 700$ kbps) it reverts to SAS. Indeed, we note that NaPAS achieves a *network-aware haptic signal compression* that beats SAS. The maximum haptic delays in this experiment for SAS and NaPAS are measured as 85.19 ms and 29.42 ms, respectively. Note that NaPAS is able to ensure QoS compliance in spite of heavy cross-traffic ($R_{cross} = 1250$ kbps) during part of the experiment. For both schemes, haptic packet losses are measured to be zero in this experiment.

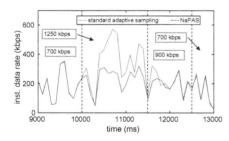

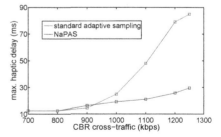

Fig. 8. Temporal evolution of the instantaneous data rate of SAS (red curve) and NaPAS (blue curve) against a time-varying cross-traffic. (Color figure online)

Fig. 9. Comparison of performances of SAS (red curve) and NaPAS (blue curve) in terms of maximum haptic delay over a wide range of R_{cross}. (Color figure online)

Finally, we report the variation of the maximum haptic delay (Fig. 9) for both techniques across the considered range of R_{cross}. When $R_{cross} < 800$ kbps, the network is uncongested and hence there is no notable difference in the performances of the two techniques. As R_{cross} increases, SAS continues to transmit packets in a network-oblivious manner. This causes extremely high end-to-end haptic delays, severely violating the QoS needs. On the other hand, the network-aware behavior of NaPAS ensures QoS compliance even under heavily congested network conditions. Further, the back-off behavior with increasing R_{cross} suggests that the proposed technique is friendly to CBR cross-traffic streams, which are themselves network-oblivious in nature. Once again, haptic packet losses are zero for both schemes under consideration.

4.1.2   Transmission Control Protocol (TCP) Cross-Traffic

We now turn to Transmission control protocol (TCP) cross-traffic. TCP is the dominant rate control protocol on the internet, employed by over 90% of all internet traffic [17]. Our goal is to analyze the performances of SAS, DPM, and NaPAS in presence of TCP, and get a sense of the improvement of NaPAS over the others. For our experiments, we consider TCP NewReno [8] which is the most widely deployed variant of TCP. In these experiments, we add a TCP source on the forward channel, and switch off the CBR cross-traffic source. We configure the queue size at b_1 to 2.7 kB as prescribed in [10].

The maximum haptic delays are measured to be 26.51 ms, 29.97 ms, and 29.95 ms for SAS, DPM, and NaPAS, respectively. Note that the dynamic packetization process in DPM and NaPAS results in a marginally higher haptic delay (around 3 ms) compared to SAS. However, it is worth remarking that all of the above schemes satisfy the haptic delay QoS conditions. Further, we note that the telehaptic stream suffers zero losses in all three cases.

Since the impact of TCP stream on telehaptic stream is comparable for the above three schemes, we move on to evaluating the impact of the haptic stream on the TCP cross-traffic stream. We consider the TCP throughput as the performance metric for this evaluation. The TCP throughput under SAS, DPM and NaPAS are measured to be 1160 kbps, 1114 kbps, and 1270 kbps, respectively. It can be observed that NaPAS yields significant improvement in TCP performance over both SAS (due to its lower peak transmission rate) and DPM (due to the signal compression obtained by transmitting only the perceptually significant samples). We conclude that NaPAS is friendlier to TCP cross-traffic than DPM and SAS.

4.2   Subjective Evaluation

We now report the qualitative evaluation of SAS and NaPAS in presence of $R_{cross} = 1180$ kbps. Note that for this value of R_{cross}, both DPM and NaPAS guarantee QoS compliance. Both these schemes transmit the perceptually significant samples in addition to employing the same congestion control scheme. Hence, from the standpoint of perception, we expect their behavior to be similar.

We validate this argument through our subjective evaluation. However, for the purpose of brevity, in this section we do not report the findings for DPM. Table 2 presents the mean opinion score (MOS) and the standard deviation (SD) for the subject grades. It can be seen that while SAS introduces significant perceptual degradation, NaPAS is able to preserve the perceptual quality of telepottery (in comparison with training) even under heavily congested network conditions.

Table 2. Mean opinion scores (MOS) and standard deviation (SD) of subject grades for the perceptual parameters corresponding to SAS and NaPAS.

	Transparency		Smoothness		Overall Exp.	
	MOS	SD	MOS	SD	MOS	SD
SAS	2.05	0.88	1.85	0.87	1.90	0.71
NaPAS	3.95	0.68	4.30	0.47	4.20	0.52

We perform paired t-test in order to statistically validate our findings. The results for the three perceptual parameters are as follows: (i) transparency - $t(19) = 7.29$, $p < 0.001$; (ii) smoothness - $t(19) = 10.43$, $p < 0.001$; (iii) overall experience - $t(19) = 10.50$, $p < 0.001$. This confirms that our findings are statistically significant, and therefore NaPAS consistently outperforms SAS under heavy CBR cross-traffic conditions in terms of preserving the perceptual quality of telepottery.

5   Conclusions

In this paper, we demonstrated that provisioning the network for time-average data rate given by SAS causes severe QoS violations. In order to overcome this drawback, we proposed NaPAS, a network-aware refinement of SAS for teleoperation in resource constrained, time-varying networks. We validated the proof-of-concept of NaPAS through simulations and subjective evaluations through a haptic-based telepottery activity. Our simulations revealed that the proposed technique outperforms SAS and DPM in terms of telehaptic QoS compliance, as well as friendliness to network cross-traffic. Through subjective evaluations we demonstrated that NaPAS outperforms SAS in preserving the perceptual quality of telepottery even under heavy cross-traffic scenarios.

Acknowledgment. The authors acknowledge support from a DST sponsored Indo-Korean grant.

References

1. Anderson, R., Spong, M.: Bilateral control of teleoperators with time delay. IEEE Trans. Autom. Control **34**(5), 494–501 (1989)
2. Bhardwaj, A., Cizmeci, B., Steinbach, E., Liu, Q., Eid, M., Araujo, J., El Saddik, A., Kundu, R., Liu, X., Holland, O., Luden, M., Oteafy, S., Prasad, V.: A candidate hardware and software reference setup for kinesthetic codec standardization. In: International Symposium on Haptic, Audio and Visual Environments and Games (HAVE) (2017)
3. Bonanni, L., Vaucelle, C., Lieberman, J., Zuckerman, O.: Taptap: a haptic wearable for asynchronous distributed touch therapy. In: CHI 2006 Extended Abstracts on Human Factors in Computing Systems, pp. 580–585. ACM (2006)
4. Chiu, D.M., Jain, R.: Analysis of the increase/decrease algorithms for congestion avoidance in computer networks. Comput. Netw. ISDN Syst. **17**(1), 1–14 (1989)
5. Cizmeci, B., Chaudhari, R., Xu, X., Alt, N., Steinbach, E.: A visual-haptic multiplexing scheme for teleoperation over constant-bitrate communication links. In: Auvray, M., Duriez, C. (eds.) EUROHAPTICS 2014. LNCS, vol. 8619, pp. 131–138. Springer, Heidelberg (2014). https://doi.org/10.1007/978-3-662-44196-1_17
6. Clarke, S., Schillhuber, G., Zaeh, M.F., Ulbrich, H.: Telepresence across delayed networks: a combined prediction and compression approach. In: IEEE International Workshop on Haptic Audio Visual Environments and their Applications, HAVE 2006, pp. 171–175. IEEE (2006)
7. Condoluci, M., Mahmoodi, T., Steinbach, E., Dohler, M.: Soft resource reservation for low-delayed teleoperation over mobile networks. IEEE Access (2017)
8. Floyd, S., Gurtov, A., Henderson, T.: The newreno modification to TCP's fast recovery algorithm (2004)
9. Gokhale, V., Nair, J., Chaudhuri, S.: Congestion control for network-aware telehaptic communication. ACM Trans. Multimedia Comput. Commun. Appl. (TOMM) **13**(2), 17 (2017)
10. Gokhale, V., Nair, J., Chaudhuri, S.: Teleoperation over a shared network: When does it work? In: International Symposium on Haptic, Audio and Visual Environments and Games (HAVE) (2017)
11. Hinterseer, P., Hirche, S., Chaudhuri, S., Steinbach, E., Buss, M.: Perception-based data reduction and transmission of haptic data in telepresence and teleaction systems. IEEE Trans. Signal Process. **56**(2), 588–597 (2008)
12. Lawrence, D.A.: Stability and transparency in bilateral teleoperation. IEEE Trans. Robot. Autom. **9**(5), 624–637 (1993)
13. Marshall, A., Yap, K.M., Yu, W.: Providing QoS for networked peers in distributed haptic virtual environments. Advances in Multimedia (2008)
14. ns3: The network simulator (2011). http://www.nsnam.org/
15. Sakr, N., Georganas, N.D., Zhao, J.: Human perception-based data reduction for haptic communication in Six-DoF telepresence systems. IEEE Trans. Instrum. Meas. **60**(11), 3534–3546 (2011)
16. Xu, X., Cizmeci, B., Schuwerk, C., Steinbach, E.: Haptic data reduction for time-delayed teleoperation using the time domain passivity approach. In: IEEE World Haptics Conference (WHC), pp. 512–518 (2015)
17. Yao, S., Xue, F., Mukherjee, B., Yoo, S.B., Dixit, S.: Electrical ingress buffering and traffic aggregation for optical packet switching and their effect on TCP-level performance in optical mesh networks. IEEE Commun. Mag. **40**(9), 66–72 (2002)

Congruent Visuo-Tactile Feedback Facilitates the Extension of Peripersonal Space

Ali Sengül[1(✉)], Michiel van Elk[2], Olaf Blanke[3], and Hannes Bleuler[3]

[1] Helbling Technik, Hohlstrasse, 614 8048 Zurich, Switzerland
ali.senguel@helbling.ch
[2] University of Amsterdam, Postbus, 15900 Amsterdam, Netherlands
m.vanElk@uva.nl
[3] Ecole Polytechnic Federal de Lausanne, 1015 Lausanne, Switzerland
{olaf.blanke,hannes.bleuler}@epfl.ch

Abstract. Effective tool use relies on the integration of multisensory signals related to one's body and the tool. It has been shown that active tool use results in an extension of peripersonal space, i.e., the space directly surrounding the human body. In the present studies we investigated whether the mere observation of a virtual tool that could be manipulated via a haptic robotic interface would also affect the perception of peripersonal space. Participants passively observed a tool being used (Study 1) and received simple visuotactile feedback related to the tool (Study 2). We assessed the extension of peripersonal space by using the cross-modal congruency task, which measures the interference of observed visual distractors presented at the tool on judgments about tactile stimuli presented to the fingers. We found that passive observation of tool use resulted in a crossmodal congruency effect for both crossed and uncrossed arm/tool use postures (Study 1). This effect was even more pronounced when participants were presented with simple visuo-tactile feedback during the observation phase (Study 2). These findings suggest that additional visuotactile feedback enhances the integration of the tools into the body schema. We discuss the relevance of these findings for the development of surgical robotics, virtual tool use and for motor rehabilitation.

Keywords: Extension of peripersonal space · Action observation
Haptic feedback · Multisensory integration · Rehabilitation technologies
Telepresence

1 Introduction

One of the unique characteristics of the human brain is its exceptional plasticity and its ability to reorganize itself. Recent findings showed that the body representation in the brain arises from the multisensory integration of vision, touch, proprioceptive and motor cues. This body representation is plastic and it can change over time. The rubber hand illusion is an illustration of this phenomenon, in which the conflicting interaction of vision and touch results in the feeling as if the rubber hands were real hands [2]. Another illustration comes from tool-use studies [3, 4], suggesting that the brain incorporates tools into the body representation. This claim originated from the study of Iriki et al.

© Springer International Publishing AG, part of Springer Nature 2018
D. Prattichizzo et al. (Eds.): EuroHaptics 2018, LNCS 10894, pp. 673–684, 2018.
https://doi.org/10.1007/978-3-319-93399-3_57

(1996) [5]. Some other studies of tool use with humans also showed the plasticity of the body representations measured by showing how visuo-tactile interactions are modulated or changed resulting in an extension of peripersonal space (space around the body) by tool use [6, 7, 21–23].

The extension of peripersonal space in humans is measured with the so-called cross-modal congruency effect (CCE). CCE experiments typically involve vibrators on the fingers and LEDs placed on tip of the tools; subjects are asked to make speeded elevation judgment (up vs down) of the vibrotactile stimulus while ignoring the any LED stimuli. CCE magnitude is calculated as the reaction time difference between incongruent conditions (light and vibration in opposite position (up vs. down)) and congruent conditions (light and vibration both either up or down) [6, 7]. The CCE has been used to study the mechanisms of tool-use and changes in the peripersonal space representations. Maravita et al. (2002) [7] used golf clubs as tools to study whether active tool-use could change multisensory representation of peripersonal space. They tested the interaction of visual stimuli presented at the end of the tools with simultaneous vibrotactile stimuli on the handle. They found that after active tool use visual stimuli and vibration stimuli on the same tool interacted more than when these two stimuli were presented at different tools, irrespective of whether the tools were held in a crossed or uncrossed posture. This finding indicates that visual information was remapped according to the actual position of the tool and this effect was interpreted as reflecting an extension of peripersonal space by active tool use.

Two possible mechanisms play a role in this process. 1: Learning by observing tool movement 2: realistic visuo-tactile feedback. Learning by observing movement can be explained by ideomotor theory. This theory suggests that observing the movements elicits 'motor representations' and could thereby facilitate motor learning. Could it be that observing movement can enhance the feeling that a virtual tool can remap the peripersonal space representation? Previous studies illustrated insights in the second mechanism plays a role in the integration of object in body schema. For instance, in the rubber hand illusion realistic visual-tactile feedback results in the feeling that the rubber hand is a part of one's body. Could it be that a similar manipulation can also enhance the feeling that a virtual tool is an extension of one's body? Hence, we use a cognitive neuroscience method (CCE) to study how (1) observing tool movement and (2) realistic visual-tactile feedback enhances the incorporation of the tools.

The ideomotor and simple visuo-tactile feedback mechanisms have crucial implications for the surgical robotics and rehabilitation. For instance, current surgical systems do not have force feedback and the role of force feedback was not shown from the concept of neurocognitive mechanisms. Additionally, the role of movement from the concepts of body representation is also has not been studied from the concept of body representation. This line of research has crucial implications for studying neurocognitive mechanism for the rehabilitation.

In this study, we performed two experiments to analyze the effect of tool use observation as well as providing realistic feedback on the multisensory representation of peripersonal space as measured by the CCE. To analyze the effect of observing tool movement on the peripersonal space mapping, in the first experiment, participants observed the movement of a virtual tool being crossed and uncrossed. In the second study, we tested whether simple feedback such as simultaneous vibrators and lights could result in a stronger extension of the peripersonal space. We expected an increased interference of visual distractors with the tactile stimuli connected to the hand by the tool for both uncrossed and crossed postures, thereby an increased remapping measured by CCE. We propose that studying how peripersonal space representation changes and how the extension of peripersonal space by observing tool use can be an objective assessment of the effect of VR and feedback with simple vibrations. It has been shown previously that active tool use remaps the peripersonal space of the user [21–23]. Recently the study form Costantini et al. (2011) illustrated that tool use observation has also similar effects [10]. The impact of tool use observation on the peripersonal representation was shown with a reach to grasp movements [10]. They performed experiment by using the spatial constraint of the object-related and showed that action observation remaps the peripersonal representations with the visual distance judgment task [10]. To date, there is no evidence of tool-use observation on the multisensory representation of the peripersonal space measured by CCE. The present study provides first step towards investigating the effectiveness of VR and multisensory stimulation techniques in rehabilitation using CCE.

2   Methods and Materials

2.1   Subjects

A total of 20 healthy right-handed participants took part in these experiments: Ten participants (3 female, ages 19–28, mean age (SE): 23.5 (2.5) years) in study 1 and ten participants (5 female, ages 19–29, mean age (SE) 23.1 (2.6) years) in study 2. All participants had normal or corrected to normal vision, no disorder of touch and had no history of neurological or psychiatric conditions. Each experiment took approximately 60 min per participant. The participants were informed about the general purpose of the research, were fully debriefed and were given the opportunity to ask questions and to comment on the research after the experiment. All subjects gave written informed consent and were compensated for their participation. The experimental procedure was approved by the local research ethics committee – La Commission d'éthique de la recherche Clinique de la Faculté de Biologie et de Médecine – at the University of Lausanne, Switzerland and was performed in accordance with the ethical standards laid down in the Declaration of Helsinki.

2.2   Materials and Apparatus

We employed a robotic system consisting of a bimanual haptic interface for the training of operations with the da Vinci surgery system (Mimic's dV-Trainer, Mimics Technologies Inc, Seatle see Fig. 1). The da Vinci system is a well-known surgical robotic system that is used for minimally invasive surgical procedures. The system has two lightweight grippers that enable transparent interactions with virtual reality making realistic bimanual manipulations possible. The participants were seated at a table and held two haptic interfaces, one in their left and one in their right hand. The index and thumb of both hands were positioned in the haptic device as shown in Fig. 1 and their movements and interactions with virtual objects were presented on a head mounted display (HMD, eMagin Z800 3DVisor, 1.44 megapixel resolution).

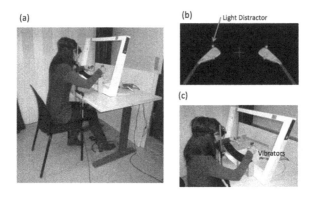

Fig. 1. (A) The experimental setup (the da Vinci Simulators) used in the current study. (B) Virtual tools in uncrossed posture: the small balls on the upper and lower part of the tools are the visual distractors. (C) Four vibrotactile target stimulators were attached to the participants' thumb and index fingers of the left and right arm. Participants responded to vibrotactile stimuli using the foot pedal.

An open source platform, CHAI 3D, and a set of C++ libraries were used for the modeling and for simulating the haptics, and for visualization of the virtual world. This platform supports several commercial haptic devices and it is possible to extend it to support new custom force feedback devices. We have extended this platform by adding the drivers and libraries of our custom force feedback device. Four vibrotactile target stimulators (Precision MicroDrive shaftless vibration motors, model 312-101, 3 V, 80 mA, 9000 rpm (150 Hz) 1.7 g with a diameter of 12 mm and a length of 3.4 mm) were attached to the participants' thumb and index fingers of the left and right arm. Foam and rubber padding was used to insulate the vibrotactile stimulators from the surrounding material, thus minimizing any conduction of vibrations through the haptic device itself. For each participant, these stimulators were tested to generate easily localizable and clearly perceptible sensations. Vibrotactile stimuli were driven by electrical signals generated by a desktop computer (Intel Core i7 CPU with 2.8 GHz, 3 GB or Ram, with NVIDIA GeForce 9800 GT Graphic Card). Two data acquisition cards (NI PCI-6014 and NI PCI 6052E) were used to read pedal responses and to drive vibrotactile stimulators. To minimize any unwanted reflections, the participants were seated in a dimly illuminated room enclosed by black curtains. Two additional vibrotactile target stimulators were attached to the participants' left and right arm in the second study to provide a vibrotactile feedback, see Fig. 2. To increase the association of the movement of the virtual tools during action observation with the handheld tools, two virtual balls were illuminated synchronously with the vibrotactile stimuli. The participants viewed two virtual-robotic tools through a head mounted display. The distance between the tools subtended approximately 35° of visual angle. Visual distractor stimuli subtended approximately 0.9° of visual angle, positioned at the upper and lower locations of tips of the virtual-robotic tools that had a visual angle of 6.4°. For the modeling, simulating the haptics, and visualization of the virtual world, CHAI 3D and set of C++ libraries were used. A virtual world with two virtual golf clubs was developed, see Fig. 1B.

(a) 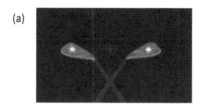   (b)

Fig. 2. (A) Snapshot of the virtual reality in Experiment 2: The big balls in the middle of the tools used to increase the association of the movement of the virtual tools during action observation. They were illuminated synchronously with the vibrotactile stimuli. (B) Additional two vibrotactile target stimulators were attached to the participants' left and right arm in the second study to provide a vibrotactile feedback.

A fixation cross was positioned at the vertical and horizontal mid-point of the corresponding four LEDs on the two tools. A chin rest system was used to prevent undesired movement of the head. To measure the participant's responses, two pedals were attached to the floor next to the participant's right foot. The pedal separation was adjusted to fit the participant's foot size. One of the pedals was placed under the heel and the other under the toe of the participant's right foot. The participant raised his toes to indicate that the vibrations were felt at the index finger or raised his heels to indicate that the vibrations were felt at the thumbs. White noise was presented over the headphones at an adequate level so that participants could not hear the vibrotactile stimulators or the operation of the other hardware during the experiments.

There were two blocks of 16 practice trials each, which were not analyzed and experiment started when the participant achieved an accuracy of more than 85%. For each experiment, a total of 480 experimental trials were given, divided into 15 blocks, with 240 trials for the straight tools and 240 trials for the crossed tools. Participants observed crossed or uncrossed the tools between every four trials in study 1 and received visuotactile feedback while observing tool crossing between every four trials in study 2. Each of the 16 conditions (4 visual distractors × 4 vibrotactile target locations) was presented 15 times (crossed or uncrossed), in a pseudo-randomized order determined by the computer.

2.3 Analysis

For the CCE analysis, trials with an incorrect response were discarded from the RT analysis but they were analyzed in the percentage error analysis. Trials with RTs larger than 1.500 ms and three standard deviations above and below the subject's mean RT were removed. Data from all trials that resulted in correct responses were analyzed by using a repeated-measures three-way analysis of variance (ANOVAs) on the mean values of RTs. The three factors in the ANOVA design were: Congruency (congruent/ incongruent), Side (same/different) and Tool posture (uncrossed/crossed). Paired t-tests were used for post-hoc comparisons on the CCEs. In addition, the inverse efficiency (IE) was calculated by dividing the reaction times by the accuracy of each condition to control effectively for any speed-accuracy trade off in the reaction time data [3].

3 Results

3.1 Study 1: Action Observation

Congruency effects derived from RT data from the first experiment are represented in Fig. 2 and Table 1. The ANOVA performed on RTs from Experiment 1 revealed a main effect of congruency (F (1, 9) = 13.21, p < 0.01) and a significant interaction between congruency and side (F (1, 9) = 7.30), p < .05) confirming that CCEs were significantly larger in the same side conditions compared to the different side conditions (t (9) = 2.70; p < .05). Crucially, we also found a three-way interaction between Congruency, Side and Tool Posture (F (1, 9) = 15.10, p < 0.01).

Table 1. Mean reaction times (RT) in milliseconds, percentage of errors (%) and inverse efficiency (IE) for Experiment 1.

Same side				
Tool posture		Congruent	Incongruent	Mean CCE
Crossed	RT	636.2(23.7)	671.0(30.8)	34.8(17.4)
	%	1.83(0.98)	6.34(1.68)	4.50(1.76)
	IE	648.7(25.0)	716.7(29.8)	68.0(24.6)
Uncrossed	RT	609.8(25.6)	688.6(27.1)	78.8(18.9)
	%	1.67(0.70)	8.18(1.90)	6.51(1.44)
	IE	620.2(25.7)	752.2(30.8)	132.0(26.3)
Different side				
Tool posture		Congruent	Incongruent	Mean CCE
Crossed	RT	628.1(21.5)	676.7(28.4)	48.6(14.3)
	%	3.50(1.10)	6.50(1.82)	3.00(1.49)
	IE	652.1(24.6)	725.1(30.2)	73.0(21.3)
Uncrossed	RT	639.1(27.7)	654.1(26.5)	15.0(8.3)
	%	3.67(0.70)	4.50(1.90)	0.83(0.90)
	IE	663.8(28.7)	685.2(26.8)	21.4(12.5)

To determine the driving factor of this three-way interaction, we performed post-hoc comparisons between same side CCE versus different side CCE for the RT measures for each tool posture. This analysis revealed that the CCE differed significantly between same side and different side for the uncrossed (t (9) = 3.64; p < 0.01) but not for the crossed condition (t(9) = 1.72; p = 0.12 NS) (see Fig. 3 and Table 1). As can be seen in Fig. 3, same side CCEs were larger than the different side CCEs only for the uncrossed condition but not for the crossed conditions.

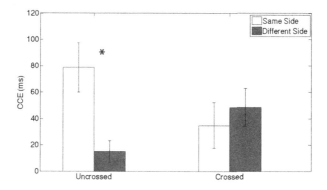

Fig. 3. Crossmodal congruency effect (CCE) with standard error in Experiment 1 White bars represent the condition in which visual stimuli were presented to the same visual hemifield with tactile stimuli, black bars represent trials in which the visual stimuli were presented to the different hemifield. The bars on the left side are for the uncrossed posture and bars on the right side are for the crossed posture.

The ANOVA on the error rates revealed a main effect of congruency (F (1, 9) = 10.52, p < 0.01), a significant interaction between congruency and side (F (1, 9) = 12.63), p < .01) and a three-way interaction between Congruency, Side and Tool Posture (F (1, 9) = 9.03, p < 0.05). The ANOVA on the IE data revealed a main effect of congruency (F (1, 9) = 15.33, p < 0.01), a significant interaction between congruency and side (F (1, 9) = 23.96), p < .01) and a three-way interaction between Congruency, Side and Tool Posture (F (1, 9) = 22.95, p < 0.01) (see Table 1). Thus, the analysis of the IE confirms the main findings from the analysis of Reaction Times and Error rates, indicating that the CCE side effect is modulated by the posture of the virtual tools (i.e. crossed or uncrossed). More importantly, this analysis provides further support that this effect cannot be accounted for by a speed-accuracy trade-off between the different experimental conditions.

3.2   Study 2: Action Observation with Vibrotactile Feedback

Reaction time data from the second experiment are represented in Fig. 4 and Table 2. The ANOVA performed on RTs from Experiment 2 revealed a main effect of tool posture (F (1, 9) = 7.55, p < 0.05) and a main effect of congruency (F (1, 9) = 85.77, p < 0.001). Crucially, we also found a three-way interaction between Congruency, Side and Tool Posture (F (1, 9) = 17.96, p < 0.01). Post-hoc comparisons between same side CCE versus different side CCE for the RT was performed to determine the driving factor of this three-way interaction. This analysis revealed that the CCE difference between same side and different side was significant for the uncrossed (t (9) = 2.75; p < 0.05) and for the crossed case (t(9) = 3.92; p < 0.01) (see Fig. 3 and Table 2). As inspection of Fig. 4 reveals the direction of these effects differed for uncrossed versus crossed conditions. In line with previous studies that used physical tools, for the uncrossed condition the same side CCEs were larger than the different side CCEs, whereas for the crossed condition the different side CCEs were larger than the same side CCEs. These data indicate that the additional visual-tactile feedback enhanced the incorporation of the virtual tools and resulted in an extension of peripersonal space, depending on the position of the tools.

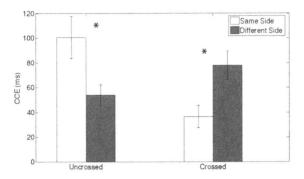

Fig. 4. Crossmodal congruency effect (CCE) with standard error in Experiment 2. White bars represent the condition in which visual stimuli were presented to the same visual hemifield with tactile stimuli, black bars represent trials in which the visual stimuli were presented to the different hemifield. The bars on the left side are for the uncrossed posture and on bars on the right side are for the crossed posture.

Table 2. Mean reaction times (RT) in milliseconds, percentage of errors (%) and inverse efficiency (IE) for Experiment 2.

Same side				
Tool posture		Congruent	Incongruent	Mean CCE
Crossed	RT	614.2(35.7)	650.8(37.2)	36.6(9.0)
	%	2.16 (1.24)	5.00 (2.76)	2.84 (1.97)
	IE	631.4(42.4)	695.5(55.9)	64.1(28.1)
Uncrossed	IE	573.0(32.5)	673.5(40.9)	100.5(17.0)
	%	1.17 (0.56)	5.15 (1.77)	3.98 (1.30)
	RT	580.8(34.8)	716.1(52.3)	135.3(4.5)
Different side				
Tool posture		Congruent	Incongruent	Mean CCE
Crossed	RT	594.1(36.7)	672.1(39.4)	78.0(5.9)
	%	1.66 (0.82)	4.14(1.03)	2.48(0.83)
	IE	605.9(40.1)	703.4(45.3)	97.5(13.0)
Uncrossed	RT	595.2(34.1)	649.3(40.9)	54.1(8.1)
	%	2.00(1.02)	4.17(2.21)	2.17(1.34)
	IE	609.7(39.0)	685.1(54.4)	75.4(21.1)

The ANOVA performed on error rates revealed a main effect of congruency (F (1, 9) = 7.58, p < 0.05). The ANOVA performed on the IE data revealed a main effect of congruency, (F (1, 9) = 38.71, p < 0.001) and a tendency for a three- way interaction between Congruency, Side and Tool Posture (F (1, 9) = 3.18, p = 0.10) (see Table 2). Thus, the ANOVA on the IE data confirms the main findings of the analysis of the RT and error data and provides further support that no speed-accuracy trade-off underlies the present results.

3.3 Between-Experiment Comparison

In experiment 1, we found a significant three-way interaction between Congruency, Side, and Tool posture, as expected. In experiment 2, this interaction was also significant. To directly investigate eventual differences between both experiments, we performed a between-experiments comparison, by using a 4-way ANOVA with Experiment as a between-participants variable. The 4-way ANOVA performed on RTs revealed a main effect of congruency (F (1, 18) = 61.89, p < 0.001), a significant interaction between side and congruency (F (1, 18) = 4.30), p < 0.05) and a three-way interaction between Congruency, Side and Tool Posture (F (1, 17) = 33.00, p < 0.001). The 4-way interaction was not significant (F (1, 18) = 0.12, p = 0.72 NS) suggesting a remapping according to tool posture for both action observation and action observation with additional visual-tactile feedback.

4   Discussion

In the present study, we investigated the remapping of the multisensory representation of the peripersonal space under action observation and vibrotactile feedback in virtual reality. At least two findings support the notion that action observation result in the remapping of the multisensory representation in peripersonal space with the vibrotactile feedback. First, our result showed that there was an interaction of vision and touch as reflected in the CCE for the action observation. Second, it was found that providing vibrotactile feedback during action observation increased the remapping of peripersonal space as reflected in a stronger CCE when visual stimuli appeared at a different side than the tactile vibration, at the tip of the tool that was held in the stimulated hand. Thereby these results extend previous tool use studies to the domain of rehabilitation and surgical robotics.

The extension of peripersonal space with tool use in healthy humans was studied with the CCE. The CCE was used as a measure to assess the interaction of vision and touch. Previous studies showed that active tool-use reversed the visual tactile integration, that is, visual distractors from the left visual field interfered more strongly with the tactile stimuli from the left hand (and vice versa for visual distractors presented at the right visual field) in the uncrossed condition and visual distractors from the left visual field interfered more strongly with tactile stimuli form the right hand (and vice versa for visual distractors presented at the right visual field) in the crossed condition. Thus, visual stimuli were primarily associated with the hand that was holding the tool rather than the spatial side at which the stimuli appeared. This finding suggests that tool use can alter multisensory representation of the peripersonal space, as reflected in a stronger CCE when visual stimuli appeared at a different side than the tactile vibration, at the tip of the tool that was held in the stimulated hand.

Together, the results of the current study showed that cognitive neuroscience measures can be used to investigate the effectiveness of multisensory stimulation techniques for the rehabilitation. This suggests that CCE measurements may be used as an objective assessment of multisensory stimulation techniques. Up to now, multisensory stimulation techniques in rehabilitation, especially in stroke patient rehabilitation was quantified by means of brain imaging techniques [12]. Intracellular recording with monkeys showed that there exist some neurons called mirror neurons in the premotor cortex that discharge with a motor task as well as observing the same action [13]. A similar mechanism has been shown for humans in the human primary motor cortex, for instance by Hari et al. 1998 [14]. It was also shown that these neurons are activated not only when performing a task or observing a movement but also with the anticipation of an upcoming event [15] hence in a later study by [16, 17] these neurons are related with associative learning and it was claimed that these neurons are plastic that can be modified with sensorimotor learning [18, 19]. Recent fMRI studies have shown that motor imagery also activates brain regions that are involved in movement such as the supplementary motor area and premotor area. In this study, we illustrated an easy and cost-effective neuroscience technique based on the extension of peripersonal space. This technique can give new insight about the analysis of the multisensory stimulation techniques in VR. VR has many benefits for the upper limb rehabilitation. The VR environment coupled with games and robotics allows customized, repetitive and effective rehabilitation for each user. VR application merged with motor imaginary and action observation used in fMRI studies and it illustrated the advantages of mental process in the evaluation of stroke patients [20].

In addition to the VR environment for training, providing feedback is also very effective in motor rehabilitation. To assess the effectiveness of providing simple tactile feedback, vibrotactile stimuli were provided in the second study. The result of the second study, obtained in a different subject sample, illustrated that providing simple vibrotactile stimuli resulted in a stronger change in the peripersonal representation as reflected in a complete remapping of visuo-tactile integration. In contrast to the results obtained in the first study, when the tool crossing was observed without any feedback, the CCEs for visuotactile stimuli presented at the same and different side were comparable in size. Thus, action observation without vibrotactile stimuli did not completely remap the peripersonal space representation. It did affect to some extent the representation of peripersonal space, as reflected in a significant 3-way interaction. The further analysis of this 3-way interaction revealed that the difference between the same and different side CCE differed between crossed and uncrossed postures. However, the same side CCE differed than the different side CCE only for the uncrossed tool posture but not for the crossed tool posture. Providing a simple vibrotactile feedback as in the study 2 resulted in also in a significant 3-way interaction. Further analysis revealed that the difference between the same and different side CCE differed between crossed and uncrossed postures. Additionally, the same side CCE differed than the different side CCE not only for the uncrossed tool posture but also for the crossed tool posture. Thus, this difference between the first study and second study illustrated the importance of having simple vibrotactile feedback.

The results of current study extend previous studies for several reasons. This is one of the first tool studies that illustrate the role of action observation and the role of simple vibrotactile feedback on the changes in the peripersonal representations measured by CCE. The findings of the current study could give new insights in the role of action observation and vibrotactile feedback in the multisensory techniques in rehabilitation. Additionally, these findings could also give new insights in the role of feedback in surgical robotics. For instance, it is a very challenging task to provide force feedback during surgical operations. Due to the size, price and sterilization, it is challenging to develop a force sensor for the surgical operations. Our results illustrated the importance of providing feedback with simple vibrators on the hand and light sources at the tip. They showed that having simple vibrators on the hand and light on the tip would help the robotic tools to be incorporated to a stronger extent. Thus, due to technical challenges, it is not possible to include force feedback, but having simple feedback with vibrators could be achieved, thereby possibly enhancing the effectiveness and realism of virtual tool interaction.

In sum, the current study presented two experiments on the multisensory integration through action observation with feedback. Our results showed that action observation changed the multisensory representation of the peripersonal space. This representation was changed further with providing a simple vibrotactile feedback. The results extend the previous studies on the cross-modal congruency effect (CCE) and tool use. This study establishes the link between cognitive neuroscience, virtual reality, rehabilitation and surgical robotics, thereby opening exciting new possibilities for neuroscience experimentation and assessment of several factors that could improve the effectiveness of the future rehabilitation and surgical systems.

References

1. Carpenter, W.B.: Royal Institution of Great Britain (1852)
2. Botvinick, M., Cohen, J.: Rubber hands 'feel' touch that eyes see. Nature **391**, 756 (1998)
3. Holmes, N.P.: Docs tool use extend peripersonal space? A review and re-analysis. Exp. Brain Res. **218**, 273 (2012)
4. Maravita, A., Iriki, A.: Tools for the body (schema). Trends Cogn. Sci **8**, 79 (2004)
5. Iriki, A., Tanaka, M., Iwamura, Y.: Coding of modified body schema during tool use by macaque postcentral neurones. NeuroReport **7**, 2325 (1996)
6. Holmes, N.P., Sanabria, D., Calvert, G.A., Spence, C.: Tool-use: Capturing multisensory spatial attention or extending multisensory peripersonal space? Cortex **43**, 469 (2007)
7. Maravita, A., Spence, C., Kennett, S., Driver, J.: Tool-use changes multimodal spatial interactions between vision and touch in normal humans. Cognition **83**, B25 (2002)
8. Bohil, C.J., Alicea, B., Biocca, F.A.: Virtual reality in neuroscience research and therapy. Nat. Rev. Neurosci. **12**, 752 (2011)
9. Saposnik, G., Levin, M.: Virtual reality in stroke rehabilitation: a meta-analysis and implications for clinicians. Stroke Journal Cerebral Circulation **42**, 1380 (2011)
10. Costantini, M., Ambrosini, E., Sinigaglia, C., Gallese, V.: Tool-use observation makes far objects ready-to-hand. Neuropsychologia **49**, 2658 (2011)

11. Shore, D.I., Barnes, M.E., Spence, C.: Temporal aspects of the visuotactile congruency effect. Neurosci. Lett. **392**, 96 (2006)
12. Johansson, B.B.: Multisensory stimulation in stroke rehabilitation. Front. Hum. Neurosci. **6**, 60 (2012)
13. Gallese, V., Fadiga, L., Fogassi, L., Rizzolatti, G.: Action recognition in the premotor cortex. Brain **119**(Pt 2), 593 (996)
14. Hari, R., et al.: Activation of human primary motor cortex during action observation: a neuromagnetic study. In: Proceedings of the National Academy of Sciences of the United States of America 95, 15061, 8 December 1998
15. Kilner, J.M., Vargas, C., Duval, S., Blakemore, S.J., Sirigu, A.: Motor activation prior to observation of a predicted movement. Nat. Neurosci. **7**, 1299 (2004)
16. James, J.M., Kilner, M., Jennifer, J.L., Marchant, L., Frith, C.D.: Relationship between activity in human primary motor cortex during action observation and the mirror neuron system. PloS one **4** (2009)
17. Heyes, C.: Where do mirror neurons come from? Neurosci. Biobehav. Rev. **34**, 575 (2010)
18. Ertelt, D., et al.: Action observation has a positive impact on rehabilitation of motor deficits after stroke. NeuroImage **36**(Suppl. 2), T164 (2007)
19. Celnik, P., Webster, B., Glasser, D.M., Cohen, L.G.: Effects of action observation on physical training after stroke. Stroke J. Cereb. Circ. **39**, 1814 (2008)
20. Beck, L., et al.: Evaluation of spatial processing in virtual reality using functional magnetic resonance imaging (FMRI). Cyberpsychology Behav. Soc. Network. **13**, 211 (2010)
21. Sengül, A., van Elk, M., Rognini, G., Aspell, J.E., Bleuler, H., Blanke, O.: Extending the body to virtual tools using a robotic surgical interface: evidence from the crossmodal congruency task. PloS one (2012)
22. Sengül, A., Rognini, G., van Elk, M., Aspell, J.E., Bleuler, H., Blanke, O.: Force feedback facilitates multisensory integration during robotic tool use. Exp. Brain Res. **227**, 497–507 (2013)
23. Sengül, A.: Cognitive neuroscience based design guidelines for surgical robotics, EPFL Ph.D. thesis No. 5669 (2013)

Harmonious Textures: The Perceptual Dimensions of Synthetic Sinusoidal Gratings

Corentin Bernard[1,2], Jocelyn Monnoyer[1,2], and Michaël Wiertlewski[2(✉)]

[1] PSA Peugeot Citroen, Paris, France
{corentin.bernard,jocelyn.monnoyer}@mpsa.com
[2] Aix Marseille Université, CNRS ISM, Marseille, France
michael.wiertlewski@univ-amu.fr

Abstract. Natural gratings explored by a finger generate vibratory patterns. These vibrations contain a wide range of frequencies, which include the fundamental spatial frequency of the grating and other (higher) harmonics. In this study, it was proposed to investigate how the fundamental and harmonic frequencies contribute to the perception of a virtual grating presented in the form of spatial pattern of friction force. Using multidimensional scaling methods, we established that the first overtone was the main characteristic used by the participants to identify gratings. When asked to rate the pleasantness to the touch, participants' preferences were for gratings with low spatial frequencies and low amplitudes. These results suggest new ways of creating meaningful, pleasant human-computer interactions in the context of surface-haptic displays.

Keywords: Surface haptic · Texture synthesis · Texture perception

1 Introduction

Clicks and detents are valuable features used to signal the progression of scrolling down a list or tuning a value. One example is the tactile feedback provided by an indexed volume knob, where the periodic mechanical events are used to precisely control the volume even in the absence of visual feedback. A sense of progression can be created while scrolling on a touchscreen by using force feedback [1] or vibrotactile stimulation [2] or by varying the finger-to-surface friction [3,4] while the user is exploring the surface.

Natural texture perception provides an interesting framework for creating virtual gratings that are intuitive, enjoyable and easily discriminable. Texture is often perceived via multiple physical quantities such as compliance, thermal conductivity and roughness [5]. The latter characteristic is thought to be one of the main factors contributing to the sensation of tactile texture [6]. Roughness is perceived partly via the changes in lateral force that a finger experiences while it is sliding over a surface [7]. Although the relationship between surface geometry

© Springer International Publishing AG, part of Springer Nature 2018
D. Prattichizzo et al. (Eds.): EuroHaptics 2018, LNCS 10894, pp. 685–695, 2018.
https://doi.org/10.1007/978-3-319-93399-3_58

and changes in the friction force is non-linear and stochastic [8,9], recording and replaying the spectra of these friction force profiles suffices to produce realistic impressions of the roughness [10]. It has been previously reported that the spatial spectra and the magnitude of the lateral force vibrations both contributed to participants' subjective assessment of texture, and low amplitude and high frequency textures were judged to be more pleasant [11].

Changes in the tangential forces can elicit realistic impressions of relief and texture [12] in subjects exploring a surface with a finger. In the case of virtual spatially-periodic gratings, roughness was found to be correlated with spatial period, modulation amplitude and the nominal friction level [7]. A study on the dimensionality of periodic texture has also shown that frequency is one of the key factors involved in the distinction of texture [13].

It has been found to be of interest to render virtual grating directly on a surface using variable friction approaches based on either ultrasonic levitation [14,15] or electro-adhesion [16]. To create sharp sensations, square waves have often been used although the falling and rising edges of the steps are perceived differently [17]. A more suitable approach was based on the fact that the friction force elicited by natural textures is composed of a spectrum of frequencies that can vary with time and space [18]. Even purely sinusoidal gratings generate a complex pattern in which fundamentals, harmonics and noise are superimposed [8].

In music, harmonics play a central role in the perception of notes, as well as being responsible for the timbre, which we use to discriminate between one instrument and another. The perception of their haptic counterpart is not well understood. For example it has recently been found that gratings composed of two spatial frequency components (between 2 and 6 mm^{-1}) can be perceptively matched to a single intermediate pure tone grating [19]. The aim of the present study was to determine how the fundamental frequency and subsequent harmonics contribute to our judgment and our ability to discriminate between artificial tactile textures simulated on an ultrasonic variable friction device in the same way as the harmonics affect our perception of musical notes. The results obtained here show that the overtone frequency and the strength of the signal are major factors involved in generating the impression of an artificial grating.

2   Experimental Procedure

2.1   Virtual Textures

The virtual gratings are rendered by varying the frictional force of the fingertip on a glass surface as a function of the coordinate of the finger using squeeze film levitation methods. Since changes in the friction force correspond to the user's hand motion, the periodic fluctuations are perceived as a spatially-distributed corrugated pattern. Textures were encoded along the medial-ulnar axis and defined as a 2000-point vector, where each 12-bit value represented the amplitude of the ultrasonic vibration, and hence the decrease in the friction

occurring at a specific point across the 50-mm width of the surface-haptic interface. The 0.25 mm spatial resolution of the gratings was sufficiently low to be
unnoticeable.

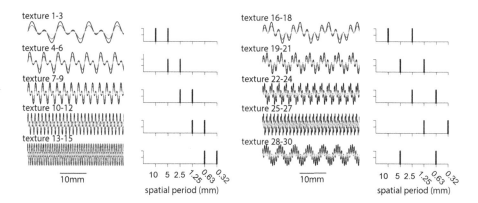

Fig. 1. The 30 spatially modulated periodic signals used in these experiments and their
respective spectra. Each spectrum encodes 3 gratings of different amplitudes.

Each of the gratings tested was generated by superimposing two harmonic
sinusoidal signals called a tone and an overtone. This waveform was selected
for its relative simplicity, easily producing a sharp, uncluttered sensation while
showing enough complexity to be able to create a large range of textures. Three
factors were varied to create the 30 signals illustrated in Fig. 1. First the spatial
period of the fundamental tone was made to vary between $\lambda =\{10, 5, 2.5, 1.25,$
and $0.625\}$ mm in order to simulate a wide range of spatial frequencies. The
overtone spatial period was either $n = \{2, 4$ or $8\}$ times smaller than the spatial
period of the fundamental. Samples with an overtone spatial period smaller than
0.317 mm were too fine to be simulated faithfully and were therefore discarded.
As can be seen from Fig. 1, the first five grating spectra were created with 2
successive frequencies ($\times 2$ ratio), while only four gratings had a x4 ratio and
one grating had a x8 ratio. The relative phase between the fundamental and
the overtone was set at 0. Since friction reduction phenomena can only affect
the magnitude of the lateral force that the fingertip experiences and not the
direction, the baseline friction of each signal was set at 50% of the total range of
friction forces that the device could produce. Lastly, the peak-to-peak amplitude
of AC part of the textural waveform was made to vary between 3 levels: $a = \{25\%,$
56% and 87%\} of the total dynamic frictional range.

2.2   Apparatus

The apparatus used here was based on squeeze-film levitation methods whereby
the friction of the fingertip touching a glass plate is controlled in real time.

The ultrasonic friction reduction device used in the present experiments was built on a rectangular plate $(60 \times 50 \times 2 \text{ mm}^3)$ actuated by 4 piezoelectric actuators bonded to the surface. The actuators excited a 5×0 mode at a frequency of 39 kHz with a maximum amplitude of 4 μm peak-to-peak at the anti-node. With this particular normal mode, users could explore the surface from left to right on an anti-node and therefore have a constant friction modulation power across the width of the interface. The friction coefficient could be varied from an initial value of 0.8 when the ultrasonic vibration was small to a minimum value of around 0.2 when the vibration was at its maximum strength.

The device was equipped with four semiconductor strain-gauge force sensors placed in each corner of the glass plate. These sensors measured the normal force and the position of the center of pressure exerted by the finger using the relative amplitude of the force measured by each sensor. A calibration procedure using a least-square regression ensures an accurate estimation of the position. Semiconductor strain-gauges and low-noise amplifier used in the design resulted to a position resolution of 0.25 mm at a rate of 2 kHz. The real-time loop measured the position of the finger, and sent the appropriate value stored in the signal vector to a digital-to-analog converter. The signal was then multiplied to the ultrasonic carrier, amplified and fed to the actuators. The amplitude-modulated signal thus created changes in the friction force when a fingertip was sliding over the plate.

2.3   Participants and Protocol

Thirty healthy volunteers, 6 women and 24 men, 4 left-handed and 26 right-handed, age ranging from 23 to 57 years (mean 35 years), participated in the study. They were naive to the aims of the study and had no previous experience with surface haptic devices. Participants sitting in front of the haptic surface were provided with a touchscreen interface for giving their answers. They could explore a single grating at a time on the haptic surface without any time or speed constraints. In order to ensure that they perceived a consistent signal, they were instructed to keep their finger movements to the median-ulnar axis, parallel to the nodal lines of the ultrasonic vibration pattern. They wore headphones to prevent them from using any auditory cues.

The experiments were conducted in two sessions. The first session involved a free-sorting procedure, in which participants were asked to place textures that felt similar in a group. Participants could select and move the textures on the touchscreen in front of them. Clicking on a texture would load it onto the haptic device. They were free to make as many groups as they wanted, but all the gratings had to be placed in one of the groups. In the second session, participants were presented with all the textures sequentially and asked to rate their pleasantness to the touch on a scale ranging from "not pleasant at all" to "very pleasant". The textures were presented in Williams Latin Square Order to prevent the occurrence of any position and succession effects.

3   Multidimensional Scaling Analysis

Participants made from 2 to 9 groups of gratings, with the majority choosing 3 or 4 groups, as shown in Fig. 2a. A similarity matrix was constructed from the groups. Whenever two gratings were placed in the same group, they scored one similarity point. This matrix was then transformed into a dissimilarity matrix by normalizing it to unity and subtracting it from 1, and the result was used as an input in the non-metric Multidimensional Scaling analysis (MDS).

The aim of the MDS algorithm was to place each grating in an N-dimensional space so that the distances between gratings, regarded here as perceptual differences, would show up as clearly as possible. Coordinates were then assigned to each grating in each of the N dimensions. Figure 2b shows the evolution of the fitting stress as a function of the number of dimensions chosen for the analysis. A model with a high number of dimensions captures more of the variability of the data, but at the expense of a less parsimonious description. The stress curve shows a knee in the case of a 2 dimensional model. The rest of the study was therefore performed using a 2 dimensional space.

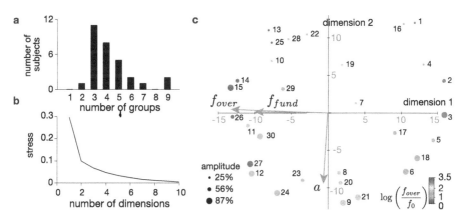

Fig. 2. a. Number of groups formed by the subjects during the free-sorting task. **b.** Multidimensional Scaling Stress depending on the number of dimensions. **c.** 2-dimensional perceptual space obtained with the MDS algorithm. Numbers refer to the name of the grating. Amplitude and overtone frequency are indicated by the size and color of each point respectively. The signal parameters f_{fund}, f_{over} and a are projected as arrows, with their size showing the goodness of fit.

Figure 2c shows the positions of the gratings in the 2-dimensional space. In this figure, the more perceptually similar two gratings are, the closer together they are placed. The first dimension is called the principal perceptual axis because it has a better discriminatory power.

In order to examine these dimensions more closely, we searched for models explaining the dimensions in terms of the 3 main construction parameters:

the amplitude and the two defining frequencies (the fundamental and overtone frequencies) using polynomial regressions. We noted that the regressions were more accurate when the frequencies were expressed as a logarithmic ratio to the first harmonic frequency $f_0 = 0.1$ mm^{-1} such as $\log(f/f_0)$. One possible reason why the logarithmic function performed better than the linear function is that spatial frequency judgments are made along a logarithmic scale [20].

3.1   First Dimension

The amplitude was almost invariant to change in the case of the first dimension (linear regression, $R^2 = 0.004$) but was affected by the frequency of the fundamental and that of the overtone. As shown in Fig. 2c, the amplitude a vector obtained was perpendicular to the first dimension, while the frequencies were almost colinear with the first dimension. Interestingly, linear regressions of the frequencies showed that the goodness of fit with the dimension of the frequency of the overtone ($R^2 = 0.92$) was greater than that of the frequency of the fundamental vibration ($R^2 = 0.69$). Higher polynomial orders did not significantly improve the fit.

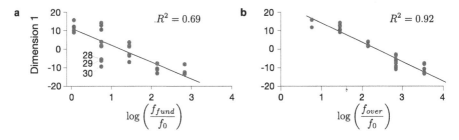

Fig. 3. Linear regression of dimension 1 coordinates of each grating with the frequency of their **(a)** fundamental and **(b)** overtone.

The data and the linear regression on the fundamental frequency and the overtone frequency are presented in Fig. 3. One of the reasons why a less than ideal regression was obtained with the frequency of the fundamental, is that three of the samples (Nos. 28, 29 and 30) were outliers. These samples were also those giving the highest ratio between the fundamental and the overtone, which suggests that the participants may have decided to classify the texture based on the height of the pitch rather than on the low frequency component. Since the principal perceptual axis is best explained by the overtone, it can be assumed that this axis mainly determined the perceptual quality of a texture, at least to a larger extent than the frequency of the fundamental and the amplitude of the signal Since the overtone had the higher frequency, this might also indicate that most efficient way of distinguishing between two friction-modulated haptic gratings consists in comparing the shortest spatial variations.

3.2   Second Dimension

Conversely to the first dimension, and in accordance with the Fig. 2c, the second dimension is invariant to both frequencies (linear regressions, both $R^2 < 0.001$). In contrast, it is well explained by the amplitude of the gratings (linear regression, $R^2 = 0.63$). The linear regression is shown in Fig. 4a. Figure 4b illustrates that even if the data are best explained by a linear relationship with the amplitude, it seems that the error between the regression and the data is weakly dependent on the frequency, without major differences between the frequency of the fundamental (quadratic regression, $R^2 = 0.17$) and frequency of the overtone (quadratic regression, $R^2 = 0.17$).

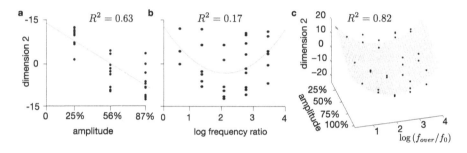

Fig. 4. Regressions of the second dimension coordinates of each grating depending on **(a)** the amplitude and **(b)** the overtone frequency. **(c)**. Mixed model in which the amplitude is combined with the overtone frequency to predict the dimension 2 data.

A multi-factor polynomial regression performed using a linear relationship on the amplitude and the square of the log of the overtone frequency, resulted in a better fit with the data ($R^2 = 0.79$) than the simple linear regression performed on the amplitude.

4   Subjective Ratings of Pleasantness

After completing the free sorting experiment, participants were asked to rate the pleasantness of each texture on a 7-points Likert-type scale ranging from "not at all pleasant" to "very pleasant". Each grating was therefore awarded 30 pleasantness scores ranging from 1 to 7.

Subjects' opinions as to which textures were more pleasant than the others were not always in agreement. A hierarchical clustering algorithm based on a principal component analysis was performed to place subjects in groups depending on their responses, as shown in the dendrogram presented Fig. 5a. The simplest method of segmentation consisted in separating 5 individuals giving unusual answers from the majority (25 participants). Based on these results, the group of 5 participants whose answers were significantly different from the others were classified as outliers.

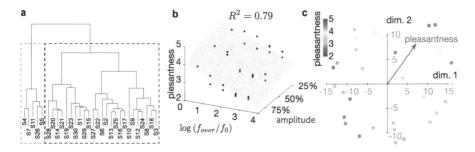

Fig. 5. (a). Dendrogram resulting from the hierarchical cluster analysis on subjects' clustering patterns. **(b)** Bilinear regression of pleasantness with respect to the overtone frequency and the amplitude in the case of each grating. **(c).** Results in terms of the pleasantness of textures in the 2 dimensional MDS space

Pleasantness scores were averaged in order to determine the correlations with the constitutional parameters of the grating. Pleasantness was found to be linearly correlated with the amplitude of the modulation (linear regression, $R^2 = 0.42$) and the frequencies. In line with previous findings, the correlations were greater with the overtone frequency (linear regression, $R^2 = 0.40$) than with the fundamental frequency (linear regression, $R^2 = 0.34$). This difference supports the hypothesis that higher frequencies were the main factor on which the participants' perception depended. Higher polynomials did not significantly improve the correlations. A bilinear model (bilinear regression, $R^2 = 0.82$) gave a satisfactory fit, see Fig. 5b. The fact that the most pleasant gratings in the opinion of the remaining 25 participants were those which had the lowest overtone frequencies and the lowest amplitudes suggests that subtle low-pitch textures are the most pleasant to the touch. The projection of the data onto the multi-dimensional space showed that the pleasantness rating is a vector that falls between the opposite frequencies and amplitude vectors, see Fig. 5c.

The same analysis performed on the 5 outliers yielded exactly the opposite results as far as the subjects' pleasantness judgments were concerned. The outliers preferred high-amplitude and high-frequency gratings, possibly because of their distinctive quality.

5   Discussion

Overall, the results obtained in this study show that the perception of two-tone periodic friction-modulated gratings depends mainly on the spatial frequencies, in line with previous findings on the perceptual effects of haptic icons presented in terms of force feedback [13], and that the frequency is a strong predictor of texture saliency. The textures tested in this study were composed of two superimposed harmonics with a frequency ratio ranging from 2 to 8. The gratings with the highest ratio between the frequency of the fundamental and that of the overtone (28, 29, 30) had a negative impact on the correlation between the fundamental frequency and the first dimension, but strengthened the correlation with the overtone frequency. This indicates that when two frequencies differ conspicuously, the higher frequency of the two provides the clearest distinctive cues. The prevalence of the overtone frequency is probably due to subjects having a more acute sensitivity to the high frequencies involved in the fast undulations [21]. A larger set of frequency ratios should now be tested in order to confirm whether the higher frequencies have the greatest effects on the perceptual quality of periodic textures. Also, because the dynamic of the friction force modulation is highly variable, future experiments will take advantage of finer control of the lateral forces provided by friction force feedback [22].

The results obtained on the second dimension show that the amplitude of the modulation was also a major factor in the perception of textural pleasantness. The amplitude of the modulation can be thought as the strength of the sensation. The correlation between the amplitude and the second dimension was not as straightforward as that observed between the frequency and the first dimension: the frequency content also affects the second dimension. In particular, the medium spatial frequencies (corresponding to spatial periods of 0.63 and 1.25 mm) required less amplitude than the high and low frequencies to be perceived as strongly as the latter. Since the subjects' typical speed of exploration was around 100 mm/s, this would correspond to temporal frequencies in the 80 to 160 Hz range, which are perceived at lower perceptual thresholds [23]. It is worth noting that in the present study, the finger velocity was unconstrained, so temporal signals produced could differ. However the perception of the textures is known to be invariant to exploration speed [24].

Mapping the signal parameters in two dimensions is a useful means of obtaining a set of textures which are easily distinguishable. However, the perceptual space alone does not tell us much about the subjective quality of each texture. The pleasantness ratings given by the participants certainly give an idea of how the frequency content and the amplitude contributed to the perceived quality of each texture. The majority of the participants (25 out of 30) preferred a low frequency content and a low amplitude, in line with the results obtained in previous studies in which participants were asked to judge the pleasantness of natural textures [11]. These findings should be taken into account in order to create enjoyable tactile interfaces. However, presenting subjects with an unpleasant grating (one with a high amplitude and a high spatial frequency) may also be a useful means of obtaining information such as the existence of an undesirable area or the limits of a setting.

6   Conclusion

In this study, participants were asked to form groups of similar textures, which were simulated by superimposing two sinusoidal waves with spatial frequencies differing by an integer multiple. The multidimensional analysis performed here showed that the frequency content, especially the overtone frequency, was the main descriptor used by the subjects, followed by the strength of the vibration.

The participants' pleasantness ratings showed that their preferred textures had a low frequency content and a low amplitude.

The results presented here should provide a useful basis for creating artificial sensations for mimicking the sensations which occur when tuning a indexed slider directly on a touchscreen. The spatial presentation generates salient distinguishable sensations that can be modulated on a pleasantness scale.

Acknowledgments. The authors would like to thank Vincent Roussarie, Sebastien Danjean, Emmanuelle Diaz, Rodolphe Houdas and Claire Lescure for the thoughtful comments on the experimental procedure. This work has been conducted in the framework of the Openlab PSA-AMU "Automotive Motion Lab". MW acknowledges support from ANR-16-CE33-0002-01.

References

1. Saga, S., Raskar, R.: Simultaneous geometry and texture display based on lateral force for touchscreen. In: World Haptics Conference (WHC), 2013, pp. 437–442. IEEE (2013)
2. Ternes, D., MacLean, K.E.: Designing large sets of haptic icons with rhythm. In: Ferre, M. (ed.) EuroHaptics 2008. LNCS, vol. 5024, pp. 199–208. Springer, Heidelberg (2008). https://doi.org/10.1007/978-3-540-69057-3_24
3. Lévesque, V., Oram, L., MacLean, K.: Exploring the design space of programmable friction for scrolling interactions. In: Haptics Symposium, pp. 23–30. IEEE (2012)
4. Casiez, G., Roussel, N., Vanbelleghem, R., Giraud, F.: Surfpad: riding towards targets on a squeeze film effect. In: Proceedings of the SIGCHI Conference on Human Factors in Computing Systems, pp. 2491–2500. ACM (2011)
5. Okamoto, S., Nagano, H., Yamada, Y.: Psychophysical dimensions of tactile perception of textures. IEEE Trans. Haptics **6**(1), 81–93 (2013)
6. Bergmann Tiest, W.M., Kappers, A.M.: Analysis of haptic perception of materials by multidimensional scaling and physical measurements of roughness and compressibility. Acta Psychol. **121**(1), 1–20 (2006)
7. Smith, A.M., Basile, G., Theriault-Groom, J., Fortier-Poisson, P., Campion, G., Hayward, V.: Roughness of simulated surfaces examined with a haptic tool: effects of spatial period, friction, and resistance amplitude. Exp. Brain Res. **202**(1), 33–43 (2010)
8. Wiertlewski, M., Hudin, C., Hayward, V.: On the $1/f$ noise and non-integer harmonic decay of the interaction of a finger sliding on flat and sinusoidal surfaces. In: World Haptics Conference, pp. 25–30. IEEE (2011)
9. Janko, M., Primerano, R., Visell, Y.: On frictional forces between the finger and a textured surface during active touch. IEEE Trans. Haptics **9**(2), 221–232 (2016)
10. Wiertlewski, M., Lozada, J., Hayward, V.: The spatial spectrum of tangential skin displacement can encode tactual texture. IEEE Trans. Rob. **27**(3), 461–472 (2011)
11. Klöcker, A., Wiertlewski, M., Théate, V., Hayward, V., Thonnard, J.L.: Physical factors influencing pleasant touch during tactile exploration. PLoS ONE **8**(11), e79085 (2013)
12. Minsky, M., Lederman, S.J.: Simulated haptic textures: Roughness. Proceedings of the ASME dynamic systems and control division. **58**, 421–426 (1996)
13. MacLean, K., Enriquez, M.: Perceptual design of haptic icons. In: Proceedings of EuroHaptics, pp. 351–363 (2003)

14. Meyer, D.J., Wiertlewski, M., Peshkin, M.A., Colgate, J.E.: Dynamics of ultrasonic and electrostatic friction modulation for rendering texture on haptic surfaces. In: Haptics Symposium, pp. 63–67. IEEE (2014)

15. Vezzoli, E., Sednaoui, T., Amberg, M., Giraud, F., Lemaire-Semail, B.: Texture rendering strategies with a high fidelity - capacitive visual-haptic friction control device. In: Bello, F., Kajimoto, H., Visell, Y. (eds.) EuroHaptics 2016. LNCS, vol. 9774, pp. 251–260. Springer, Cham (2016). https://doi.org/10.1007/978-3-319-42321-0_23

16. Shultz, C.D., Peshkin, M.A., Colgate, J.E.: Surface haptics via electroadhesion: expanding electrovibration with Johnsen and Rahbek. In: 2015 IEEE World Haptics Conference (WHC), pp. 57–62. IEEE (2015)

17. Saleem, M.K., Yilmaz, C., Basdogan, C.: Tactile perception of change in friction on an ultrasonically actuated glass surface. In: 2017 IEEE World Haptics Conference (WHC), pp. 495–500. IEEE (2017)

18. Meyer, D.J., Peshkin, M.A., Colgate, J.E.: Modeling and synthesis of tactile texture with spatial spectrograms for display on variable friction surfaces. In: 2015 IEEE World Haptics Conference (WHC), pp. 125–130. IEEE (2015)

19. Fenton Friesen, R., Klatzky, R.L., Peshkin, M.A., Colgate, J.E.: Single pitch perception of multi-frequency textures. In: Haptics Symposium. IEEE (2018, in press)

20. Nefs, H.T., Kappers, A.M., Koenderink, J.J.: Amplitude and spatial-period discrimination in sinusoidal gratings by dynamic touch. Perception **30**(10), 1263–1274 (2001)

21. Bolanowski Jr., S.J., Gescheider, G.A., Verrillo, R.T., Checkosky, C.M.: Four channels mediate the mechanical aspects of touch. J. Acoust. Soc. Am. **84**(5), 1680–1694 (1988)

22. Huloux, N., Monnoyer, J., Wiertlewski, M.: Overcoming the variability of fingertip friction with surface-haptic force-feedback. In: Prattichizzo, D., Shinoda, H., Tan, H.Z., Ruffaldi, E., Frisoli, A. (eds.) EuroHaptics 2018, vol. 10894. LNCS, pp. xx–yy. Springer, Heidelberg (2018)

23. Verrillo, R.T., Fraioli, A.J., Smith, R.L.: Sensation magnitude of vibrotactile stimuli. Attention Percept. Psychophysics **6**(6), 366–372 (1969)

24. Bochereau, S., Sinclair, S., Hayward, V.: Perceptual constancy in the reproduction of virtual tactile textures with surface displays. ACM Trans. Appl. Perception **15**(2), 1–12 (2018)

Haptic Logos: Insight into the Feasibility of Digital Haptic Branding

Muhammad Abdullah, Waseem Hassan, Ahsan Raza, and Seokhee Jeon[✉]

Department of Computer Science and Engineering,
Kyung Hee University, Yongin-si, Republic of Korea
{abdullah,waseem.h,ahsanraza,jeon}@khu.ac.kr

Abstract. Companies design brands to invoke distinct perceptions in customers about their products. Currently digital consumers experience the identity of a brand subconsciously through only visual and aural logos. However, the sense of touch is a valuable conduit for establishing strong connections. Although haptic properties (e.g. engrossing textures) are part of a brand's identity in the physical world, the digital world lacks this presence. In this paper we present the concept of creating haptic logos for brands that can be digitally distributed to consumers. To achieve this task, we utilize vibrotactile haptic feedback. Haptic logos for brands were created by varying frequency, waveform and temporal properties resulting in distinct vibration patterns. We conducted two user studies: (1) assignment of appropriate haptic logos to brands by participants, and (2) judgment of the logos based on user experience and emotional response. Based on these studies, the applicability of haptic logos has been discussed.

Keywords: Vibrotactile · Haptic icons · Digital haptic logos
Haptic branding

1 Introduction

Successful companies have created iconic brand identities that capture the user's imagination, providing a unique and pervasive emotional connection [2]. Iconic designs such as the Apple logo, McDonald's golden arches and Intel's unique jingle have helped them become recognizable. To distinguish themselves in a saturated market, companies associate sensory cues to promote their brand. Visual and aural modalities are most commonly used in sensory branding. Visual logos include the combination of colors associated with a brand or other visual aspects [19]. Audio logos involve the distinctive sound made by a brand product or audio jingles associated with a brand [25]. The sense of touch utilizes haptic properties such as textures, hardness and weight to convey the brand message. In the digital world artists and designers only utilize the visual and auditory stimuli for branding. If we can digitize haptic branding, it can add more creative options. Engaging multiple senses always result in a stronger impact and helps

© Springer International Publishing AG, part of Springer Nature 2018
D. Prattichizzo et al. (Eds.): EuroHaptics 2018, LNCS 10894, pp. 696–708, 2018.
https://doi.org/10.1007/978-3-319-93399-3_59

to retain a brand's message [2]. In this paper, we outline the concept of creating digital haptic logos for brands. We have chosen the vibrotactile modality, as it can transmit emotions [24] and is easily incorporated into existing devices.

Current research is enabling high quality vibrotactile haptics in mobile and wearable devices [7,14,21]. This modality was first developed as a means of information transfer by Tan et al. using a multi-finger tactile pad [22]. Short tactile stimuli presented through vibration which can portray meaningful information are called tactile icons. They were introduced by Brewster et al. [3]. As the main application of these icons was information transfer, Enriquez et al. tested if users were able to uniquely discriminate, identify, and recall different tactile icons [9]. Further research was conducted by Ternes et al. to increase the amount of distinguishable icons by including rhythm [23]. Since then research has been conducted into exploring the effects of different parameters such as amplitude, frequency, and duration on the emotional perception of these icons [24]. The main difference between previous research and our work is that tactile icons are usually used for transferring discrete data. The user learns them consciously and associates each one with certain objective information, e.g., directions for navigation [8] or warning signals [6]. Our research focuses on creating haptic logos that can be associated positively with the perceptual image of a brand.

The world of touch has been extensively explored from a marketing design perspective [2]. Contemporary branding strategies engage this sense by providing rich haptic stimuli to the somatosensory system. Haptic properties of a product such as machined textures, weight, and thermodynamics [10] can be manipulated, resulting in an artifact with affective properties [5]. Researchers have also conducted studies to assess the impact of haptic information on product evaluations [17]. They stated that for certain type of products, if consumers can't use active touch they are inclined to feel frustration and rate the product adversely. The impact of haptic branding on the endowment effect is discussed by Peck et al. in [18]. They report that physically touching an object can enhance our perceived sense of ownership. Recently the Immersion Corporation [1,13] is promoting TouchSense Ads that introduce vibrotactile haptic effects into video advertisement. Although they only provide simple cues e.g., adding basic vibration feedback to footsteps or when an object is hit, they are reporting a huge impact of haptics in advertisement. A marketing report by IPG Media Labs, MAGNA, and immersion [11] stated that the inclusion of vibrotactile sensations has increased brand favorability by 50%.

The main contribution of our research is the introduction of haptic based logos, a novel concept that can enhance the digital perception of an entity e.g. brands, companies etc. To investigate the idea we conducted two user experiments. Binary levels of six different parameters (waveform, frequency, envelope, decay, duration and amplitude) were used to create a set of 64 unique haptic logos. Four different test brands (soft drink, hardware, sports car and fabric) were designed. In the first user experiment the participants rated the association of each haptic logo to the different brands. The best rated logos were then used in the second experiment, where a new group of participants judged them based on their relevance and value to the test brand. We also provide an insight into how the emotional perceptions of the participants towards the test brands is changed after haptic logos are added. Finally based on the results of both user experiments, a comprehensive design guideline is provided that highlights which parameters to manipulate for a specific kind of brand.

The Soft Drink Company   The Hardware Company
        Cool & Refreshing   Strength & Reliability

The Sports Car Company   The Fabric Company
        Powerful & Fast   Comfort & Warmth

Fig. 1. The left side shows the experimental setup used for both the user studies. The Haptuator connected to the mobile phone is shown in the middle. The right side of the figure shows the collection of text logos (as seen by the participant) used for the test brands

2   User Studies

To validate the concept of haptic logos, two separate studies were carried out. In the first study, a variety of haptic stimuli, in the form of vibrotactile feedback, were produced and provided to participants. Furthermore, four different brands or companies were selected to be used in the study. The users were asked to rate the perceived associativity between the vibration patterns and a given visual logo of the selected brands. As a result of this study, three haptic logos which received the highest rating from the participants were shortlisted for every brand. These three logos were put to further testing in the next user study. The main focus of the second user study was to quantify the association of the haptic logos with the given brands, the emotional effect of the haptic logos, and the user response towards the haptic logos.

2.1   Experiment 1

Since the concept of using vibrotactile feedback as a haptic logo is new, it was required to check that what type of vibrations were acceptable by the users and if these vibrations could portray the identity of a brand to the user. Various kinds of vibrations patterns based on related research were used to find out the correct match for the myriad of brands that exist. In the current study, as a proof of concept, four everyday brands were considered. Users evaluated all the haptic logos (vibration patterns) against these four brands. As a result, the top three logos for each brand were selected for further testing.

Hardware Setup. Vibration feedback to the users was provided using a haptuator (Mark 2, Tactile labs TL002-09-A [12]) mounted on the back of a cell-phone. This haptuator is widely used in haptics research as its frequency response covers the most sensitive frequency range for humans. Signal to the haptuator was provided through a computer. Figure 1 shows the overall setup of the hardware.

Table 1. The six independent variables used to generate 64 distinct haptic logos. Each variable has two levels

Parameters	Levels	
Waveform	Sine	Sawtooth
Carrier Frequency F_c	100 Hz	300 Hz
Envelope Frequency F_e	4 Hz	32 Hz
Decay	On	Off
Duration	1.5 s	3 s
Amplitude	High	Low

Participants and Stimuli. A total of 15 participants took part in this experiment. They were paid for their participation. Five participants were females and ten were males. They had no prior knowledge about the design of the experiment or haptics in general. They reported no disabilities.

The main stimuli in this experiment were a set of 64 distinct vibrotactile patterns. A wide range of vibrotactile stimuli were created by varying six different parameters/independent variables, namely, the waveform [15], carrier frequency (F_c) [16], envelop frequency (F_e) [16], decay rate [4], duration [4], and amplitude [15]. All these parameters were varied on two levels, which were significantly different from one another, as shown in Table 1. These values were based on related research as cited with each parameter. Another approach for selecting the number of parameters and their levels could be to select fewer parameters and create a higher number of levels for each one of them, but as mentioned earlier, the main aim of the current study was to search and distill out the vibrotactile sensations suited for haptic branding or logos. Therefore, it was decided to widen our search radius so as to cover as wide a range of parameters as possible. For instance, if we vary all the parameters on three levels, the resulting number of vibration patterns would be 729, which is not feasible for such studies.

Furthermore, four characteristically distinct and easily relatable companies or brands were selected to which the haptic logos were to be assigned by the users.

These were *The Soft Drink Company, The Hardware Company, The Sports Car Company*, and *The Fabric Company*. Their visual logos can be seen in Fig. 1. The visual logos designed for these brands were text-based to keep them neutral and avoid bias due to visual design. These companies were selected because most people have a general perception about such companies, and therefore, assigning logos based on those perceptions would be natural. Furthermore, these perceptions were reinforced by providing the users with a general description of the product and services associated with the brands. For example the fabric company makes clothing while the hardware company makes power-tools etc.

Procedure. One user took part in the experiment at a time. The user was seated on a chair while holding the cell phone in hand. The haptuator was attached to the back of the cell phone. The users wore headphones playing white noise and were instructed not to touch the haptuator directly. All the visual logos were displayed together on a screen in front of the user. The 64 haptic logos were played one by one in a random order using Latin-squares. The participants scored each haptic logo four times i.e. once for each brand. The experimental setup can be seen in Fig. 1.

In this experiment the users were asked to rate the association of each of the 64 haptic logos against each of the four companies. The experiment was designed to get the perceived associativity without modulus. A haptic logo which was perceived to be related to a given company received a higher score, while the

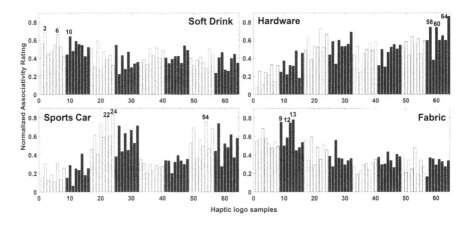

Fig. 2. The results from the associativity rating in experiment one. The independent variables repeat in the following manner: waveform - sine is 1–32, sawtooth is 33–64; F_c - repeats every 16 samples, 1–16 is 100 Hz and 17–32 is 300 Hz and so on; F_e - repeats every 8 samples, 1–8 is 4 Hz and 9–16 is 32 Hz and so on; Decay repeats every 4 samples, 1–4 is on, and 5–8 is off and so on; Duration repeats every two samples, 1–2 is 1.5 s and 3–4 is 3 s and so on; Amplitude repeats after every sample, 1 is low and 2 is high and so on. The color alternates every 8 samples to help in distinguishing the variables. The top three most associated logos for each brand are numerically highlighted

haptic logos which were perceived to be dissociated were assigned a score of zero. There was no upper limit on the associativity score, however, the users were asked to keep the rating scale consistent throughout the experiment. The users were given short breaks during experiment to avoid bias due to fatigue. On average the experiment took 60 min per participant.

Results. The associativity scores for all participants were averaged together after normalizing them from zero to one as shown in Fig. 2. It can be seen that there exist some haptic logos for each of the companies which received high associativity ratings. To find out the specific parameters which mattered the most for each of the brands, multi-way anova tests were carried out for all brands. Table 2 shows the results for the anova tests where some interesting trends can be seen.

In case of the soft drink company, the levels of waveform and carrier frequency showed statistically significantly different means (p-$value \leqslant 0.01$). This indicates that the users were able to judge the logos on the levels of these parameters easily. On the other hand, if we look at Fig. 2 (Soft Drink), the haptic logos with sine waveform, carrier frequency of 100 Hz, and high amplitude have received high scores. Thus it can be argued that the users associated the vibrations having sine wave and 100 Hz carrier frequency as the most associated with the soft drink brand. The nature of these logos can be described as slow (100 Hz carrier) and smoothly (sine wave) varying vibrations [16].

For the hardware company, waveform, carrier frequency, decay, and amplitude showed significantly different means (p-$value \leqslant 0.01$). Additionally, from Fig. 2 (Hardware) it is evident that the vibrations having sawtooth wave, 300 Hz carrier frequency, a positive decay, and high amplitude received higher association scores. All these parameters characterize a bumpy and abrupt (sawtooth), rapidly changing (300 Hz carrier) heavy (high amplitude) vibrations [15]. Such a choice of vibrations can be accredited to the general perception of a hardware company in users' minds, which usually is related to heavy machinery and tools.

Users readily associated the logos for sports car company using the carrier frequency and amplitude (p-$value \leqslant 0.01$). Furthermore, most of the highly rated vibrations for this company carried a carrier frequency of 300 Hz, a high amplitude, and a sine waveform [15, 16]. Such vibrations generally characterize smooth (sine wave) rapidly (300 Hz carrier) varying heavy (high amplitude) vibrations, such as usually exuded by a sports car.

The logos for fabric company were associated based on the waveform, carrier frequency, and amplitude of the vibrations. Figure 2 (Fabric) shows that the haptic logos with high association scores for the fabric company contained sine waveform, 100 Hz carrier frequency, and a low amplitude. Generally, fabrics carry a smooth and calm perception, and this characteristic is readily available in the smoothly varying (sine and 100 Hz carrier) and calming (low amplitude) vibrations which received high association scores for the fabric company [24].

The top three logos for each brand which received the highest associativity ratings were selected to be used in the second experiment. These logos were {2, 6, 10} for soft drink, {58, 60, 64} for hardware, {22, 24, 54} for sports car, and {9, 12, 13} for fabric.

Table 2. The result of multi-way anova analysis for the six independent variables against the four test brands. The p-values less then 0.01 are considered as significant. These are highlighted as bold face numbers

	Soft drink	Hardware	Sports Car	Fabric
Waveform	**0.004**	**0**	0.512	**0**
Carrier frequency	**0**	**0**	**0**	**0.0005**
Envelope frequency	0.233	0.029	0.504	0.63
Decay	0.553	**0.0001**	0.02	0.51
Duration	0.832	0.105	0.017	0.256
Amplitude	0.301	**0**	**0**	**0.006**

2.2   Experiment 2

The three best logos selected from the experiment 1 were put to further testing in this experiment. One of the main aims of this experiment was to evaluate the user's perception of the selected logos and check if they are appropriate from a design perspective. For this purpose the users evaluated their excitement, relevance, and the value added by the given logos to the associated brands. They also evaluated how annoying the logos felt. Another aspect of this study was to calculate the change in the emotional response of users due to the haptic logos. Based on these studies the best logos for the given brands were highlighted. The same hardware setup was used in this experiment also.

Participants and Stimuli. A new group of 15 participants, three females and 12 males, took part in this experiment. They were paid for their participation and reported no disabilities. The stimuli for this experiment were a set of 12 haptic logos, the best three for each brand.

Procedure. The physical setup used in the first experiment was used here. This experiment was divided into two parts. In the first part, the user was provided with a questionnaire comprising of four questions, which are generally asked in brand design studies to assess the quality of a logo [11]. The questions were to rate: the relevance of the logo, the value it added to the brand, their level of excitement, and how annoying it felt. The users answered the above questions for each of the three best logos. The process was repeated for all four test brands. The user response was recorded on a seven-point Likert scale. The users were also asked if they would like to experience haptic logos in case they became a part of mainstream designs. Lastly, they were asked to give candid attributes and comments about the associated haptic logos for each brand. These attributes and comments are considered at their relevant points in the discussion section.

In the second part, the users were asked to provide their emotional response to the given haptic logos. The emotional response was recorded on circumplex of affect which is also known as the valence-arousal (V-A) space [20], a two dimensional space with valence (x-axis) and arousal (y-axis) as the two independent axes. The main aim of this exercise was to examine the effect of haptic logos on the users' pre-conceived emotional perception about the brands. Initially, the users recorded their emotional response on the V-A space for the visual logos of a given test brand. Afterwards, the three best haptic logos for that brand were presented alongside the visual logos, and the users mapped them onto the same V-A space. This process was repeated for all four test brands.

Results. The scores assigned by the participants to the questionnaire answers were averaged out and these are shown in Fig. 3. Based on these scores, the top logo for each of the test brands is highlighted. In case of the soft drink logo 6 was assigned high scores in all questions. However, it was also rated as the most annoying logo. A logo is a representation of a companies perception and thus it should not be annoying. Therefore, logo 6 was discarded. The two other logos (Logo 2, 10) were rated almost equally by the participants across all the questions. Therefore, at this stage we selected both of them to be equally representative of the soft drink brand. Selecting the top logos for hardware (logo 60), fabric (logo 9), and sports car (logo 24) was straightforward as they were rated highly across all the questions by the users.

The emotional response for the 12 haptic logos and the visual logos for the four test brands is provided in Fig. 4. The emotional response for the visual logos of the test brands are located at different positions in the V-A space. This signifies that users had different pre-conceived notions about the given brands.

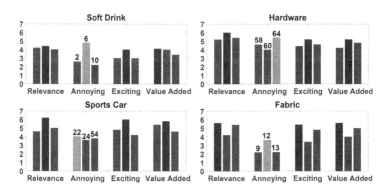

Fig. 3. The results obtained from the questionnaire in the second user experiment

Furthermore, it is also evident that the emotional response for all the best logos shifted positively with the inclusion of haptic logos.

The visual logo for soft drink is located in the high valence, low arousal region. The two best haptic logos for soft drink occupy different locations. The overall valence value is considerably decreased for logo 10. However, logo 2 maintains the valence value and enhances the arousal (more exciting) value considerably. Therefore, it was selected as the best logo for the soft drink brand. The initial perception about the hardware company based on the visual logo occupies a low negative arousal and low negative valence (sad) location in the V-A space. However, all three haptic logos shift the emotional response towards positive valence and high arousal. The emotional response for the visual logo of sports car already lied in the high arousal and high valence state. With the inclusion of the best haptic logo it moved higher on the arousal scale while maintaining its valence value. The visual logo for the fabric company is present in the low negative arousal and positive valence region. The inclusion of haptic logos shifted the emotional state of the users towards low arousal (calmness). The location of best logo is a combination of reasonable arousal and valence values which can represent a fabric brand.

When asked if the participants would like to experience the haptic logos again, twelve out of fifteen participants answered yes and showed high interest. The other three participants mentioned that the repeated logos were somewhat annoying.

3   Discussion

Based on observations from the first study, we can infer some guidelines for designing haptic logos so that they can be easily associated with specific brands. It is evident from Table 2 that Envelope Frequency (F_e), Decay, and Duration,

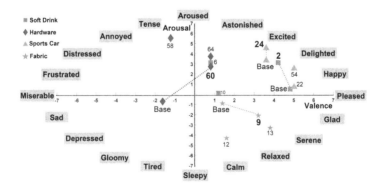

Fig. 4. The Valence-Arousal space showing the emotional rating of the top three logos for each brand. The base indicates visual logo (without haptic feedback) of the given test brands. The best logo for each brand is indicated in boldface numbers. The dotted lines indicate the shift in emotion after experiencing the best haptic logo for that given brand

did not have any clear effect, while the Carrier frequency (F_c), Waveform, and Amplitude parameters appears significant across all or most of the different brands, meaning that the users were easily able to discriminate and associate the different brands with haptic logos based on these parameters. The vibrations having F_c at 100 Hz significantly achieved high associativity ratings with the soft drink and fabric brand, while those having 300 Hz F_c were strongly associated with sports car and hardware brands. Such a behavior shows that the logos for former brands (and other such brands) can be considered as having a calming effect and the latter as more energetic.

Similarly, the waveform parameter appeared to be significant for three out of four brands. The fabric and soft drink brands are perceived to be relaxing and were readily related to the smoothly varying sine wave. The hardware brand which is perceived as harsh was more associated with the abruptly changing sawtooth wave. Some participants attributed the term "disruptive" to the logos associated with the hardware brand. For the sports car brand the effect of waveform was found insignificant. This can be attributed to the fact that each participant had a different perception about sport cars. Some people might relate to the relatively contained sine wave, while others may have preferred the more jarring sawtooth waveform. It can be inferred from the comments of two participants, as one thought that a good car is not "noisy and shaky" while the other mentioned "raw uncontrolled power".

Lastly, the amplitude parameter was also significant across three brands. As expected, the hardware and sports car brands were considered high power brands thus their haptic logos were predominantly high amplitude. On the other hand, fabric received low amplitude rating as it is perceived as a more serene brand. For the soft drink brand the amplitude parameter was rated as insignificant. The reason could be that soft drink provides a nice blend of energy and relaxation. This duality can also be found in the attributes assigned by the users to the soft drink logos, i.e., "relaxing", "fizzy", "popping", etc.

3.1 Design Guidelines

In the current study we tested four brands. We selected hardware and sports car as representatives from the high energy/power brands. To represent the other side of the spectrum we chose the soft drink and fabric brands. When designing logos for high power brands two major parameters, the F_c (around 300 Hz) and amplitude should be kept high. If we wish to increase this perception further, the sawtooth waveform should be specifically employed. The reason is that the sawtooth waveform, due to its abrupt changes, can be more readily associated with this perception. For brands such as fabric and soft drink the sine waveform and a low F_c (around 100 Hz) should be considered. In order to design logos for brands that can be associated to an even more relaxing/calming perception, the amplitude should be kept low.

For the decay parameter, results from the experiments did not establish any significance. However, a question in the second experiment asked the participants to rate how annoying each haptic logo felt. From Fig. 3 it was seen that three out of the four most annoying logos contained no decay factor. Generally, decay is considered an important aesthetic factor in visual and audio logo designs. In case of haptic logos this design parameter may also play a more vital role. Thus the inclusion of decay should be considered for designing pleasant logos.

In the field of haptics a duration of two seconds is considered effective for haptic icons. However, the duration values of 1.5 and 3 s were adopted from audio logo designs. This limit, according to the anova tests, did not cause any significant effect in our study. The reason could be that haptic icons are for information transfer while we are dealing with perceptual brand identities. Thus, a longer range of duration can be exploited for designing haptic logos.

The aim of this study is to provide high level guidelines for designing haptic logos. These generic guidelines can be manipulated to cover a wider range of brand identities. Brands such as extreme sports, motorcycles, fitness, and construction can emulate the guidelines provided for the sports car and hardware brands. Whereas, brands that wish to exude a calm and relaxed impression can follow the guidelines similar to those provided for fabric and soft drink brands. A few examples of such brands include I.T., perfumes, airlines, furniture, etc. Some brands (such as energy drink, or electronics) may want to utilize the space in between the given test brands. These can extrapolate the given guidelines to achieve their specific requirements. A number of options (rhythms, melody, etc.) still remain unexplored which can be used creatively by artists and designers to craft relevant digital haptic logos.

3.2   Limitation and Future Works

For this research we used an external actuator for providing the haptic logos. The frequency response of this actuator covers the most sensitive frequency region in the human vibrotactile perceptual spectrum. Although, it would be preferred to have such an actuator in off-the-shelf consumer devices, it may take some time for the current technology to catch up.

Another caveat is the relatively limited capacity of vibrotactile haptics as compared to audio and visual. Nevertheless, it still affords additional creative options and can add novelty to a brand. In the future, these logos may be able to utilize other haptic modalities when the technology matures sufficiently.

In the current study, we examined 64 haptic logos across six independent variables with binary levels against four test brands. For a more in depth research the independent variables, their levels, or the number of test brands can be increased.

4   Conclusion

In this research, we introduced the idea of haptic logos, where the identity of a brand can be associated with a digital haptic pattern. The result of two separate user studies provided us with a set of guidelines to design logos in accordance with the perceptual image of a brand. User perception and logo design values were also taken into consideration while providing the design guidelines. These studies showed that the addition of an associated haptic logo positively influences the emotional response of a user towards a given brand. This also proves that there is scope for the inclusion of haptic logos into mainstream branding design practices. The outcome of this research can play a major role in the world of digital design and will increase the creative options available to the design team. Inclusion of these logos will give a novel edge to early adopting brands. Most visual logos alone cannot completely define the brands' image in the digital domain and adding haptic logos can further clarify their perceptual identity.

Acknowledgments. This work was supported by the NRF of Korea through the Global Frontier R&D Program (2012M3A6A3056074) and by the MSIP through IITP (No. 2017-0-00179, HD Haptic Technology for Hyper Reality Contents).

References

1. Birnbaum, D.M., Grant, D., Ramstein, C., Ullrich, C.J.: Systems and methods for providing haptic effects (2017). US Patent 9,678,569
2. Biswas, D.: Sensory aspects of branding. The Routledge Companion to Contemporary Brand Management, p. 218 (2016)
3. Brewster, S., Brown, L.M.: Tactons: Structured tactile messages for non-visual information display. In: Proceedings of the Fifth Conference on Australasian User Interface - Volume 28, AUIC 2004, pp. 15–23. Australian Computer Society Inc., Darlinghurst (2004)
4. Bronner, K.: Jingle all the way? basics of audio branding. In: Audio Branding, pp. 76–89. Nomos Verlagsgesellschaft mbH & Co. KG (2008)
5. Carbon, C.C., Jakesch, M.: A model for haptic aesthetic processing and its implications for design. Proc. IEEE **101**(9), 2123–2133 (2013). https://doi.org/10.1109/JPROC.2012.2219831
6. Chun, J., Lee, I., Park, G., Seo, J., Choi, S., Han, S.H.: Efficacy of haptic blind spot warnings applied through a steering wheel or a seatbelt. Transp. Res. Part F Traffic Psychol. Behav. **21**(Suppl. C), 231–241 (2013). https://doi.org/10.1016/j.trf.2013.09.014
7. Dementyev, A., Kao, H.L.C., Choi, I., Ajilo, D., Xu, M., Paradiso, J.A., Schmandt, C., Follmer, S.: Rovables: miniature on-body robots as mobile wearables. In: Proceedings of the 29th Annual Symposium on User Interface Software and Technology, UIST 2016, pp. 111–120. ACM, New York (2016). https://doi.org/10.1145/2984511.2984531
8. Elliott, L.R., van Erp, J., Redden, E.S., Duistermaat, M.: Field-based validation of a tactile navigation device. IEEE Trans. Haptics **3**(2), 78–87 (2010). https://doi.org/10.1109/TOH.2010.3
9. Enriquez, M., MacLean, K.: The role of choice in longitudinal recall of meaningful tactile signals. In: 2008 Symposium on Haptic Interfaces for Virtual Environment and Teleoperator Systems, pp. 49–56 (2008). https://doi.org/10.1109/HAPTICS.2008.4479913
10. Klatzky, R.L., Lederman, S.J.: Touch. Handbook of Psychology (2003)
11. Labs, I.M.: Ads you can feel (2017). https://www.ipglab.com/wp-content/uploads/2017/01/Magna-IPGLab-Immersion-Ads-You-Can-Feel.pdf

12. Labs, T.: Haptuator mark ii (2017). http://tactilelabs.com/products/haptics/haptuator-mark-ii-v2/
13. Levesque, V., Zhu, W., Gervais, E., An, F., Lajeunesse, E., Maalouf, J.: Systems and methods for object manipulation with haptic feedback (2017). US Patent 9,600,076
14. Liu, Q., Tan, H.Z., Jiang, L., Zhang, Y.: Perceptual dimensionality of manual key clicks. In: 2018 IEEE Haptics Symposium (HAPTICS) (2018)
15. MacLean, K., Enriquez, M.: Perceptual design of haptic icons. In: Proceedings of EuroHaptics, pp. 351–363 (2003)
16. Park, G., Choi, S.: Perceptual space of amplitude-modulated vibrotactile stimuli. In: 2011 IEEE World Haptics Conference, pp. 59–64 (2011). https://doi.org/10.1109/WHC.2011.5945462
17. Peck, J., Childers, T.L.: To have and to hold: the influence of haptic information on product judgments. J. Mark. **67**(2), 35–48 (2003)
18. Peck, J., Shu, S.B.: The effect of mere touch on perceived ownership. J. Consum. Res. **36**(3), 434–447 (2009)
19. Raghubir, P.: Visual perception. In: Sensory Marketing: Research on the Sensuality of Products, pp. 201–215 (2010)
20. Ressel, J.: A circumplex model of affect. J. Pers. Soc. Psychol. **39**, 1161–78 (1980)
21. Strasnick, E., Yang, J., Tanner, K., Olwal, A., Follmer, S.: shiftio: reconfigurable tactile elements for dynamic affordances and mobile interaction. In: Proceedings of the 2017 CHI Conference on Human Factors in Computing Systems, CHI 2017, pp. 5075–5086. ACM, New York, (2017). https://doi.org/10.1145/3025453.3025988
22. Tan, H.Z., Durlach, N.I., Reed, C.M., Rabinowitz, W.M.: Information transmission with a multifinger tactual display. Percept. Psychophysics **61**(6), 993–1008 (1999). https://doi.org/10.3758/BF03207608
23. Ternes, D., MacLean, K.E.: Designing large sets of haptic icons with rhythm. In: Ferre, M. (ed.) EuroHaptics 2008. LNCS, vol. 5024, pp. 199–208. Springer, Heidelberg (2008). https://doi.org/10.1007/978-3-540-69057-3_24
24. Yoo, Y., Yoo, T., Kong, J., Choi, S.: Emotional responses of tactile icons: effects of amplitude, frequency, duration, and envelope. In: 2015 IEEE World Haptics Conference (WHC), pp. 235–240 (2015). https://doi.org/10.1109/WHC.2015.7177719
25. Yorkston, E., Menon, G.: A sound idea: phonetic effects of brand names on consumer judgments. J. Consum. Res. **31**(1), 43–51 (2004). https://doi.org/10.1086/383422

Erratum to: Human Guidance: Suggesting Walking Pace Under Manual and Cognitive Load

Tommaso Lisini Baldi, Gianluca Paolocci, and
Domenico Prattichizzo

Erratum to:
Chapter "Human Guidance: Suggesting Walking Pace Under Workload" in: D. Prattichizzo et al. (Eds.): *Haptics: Science, Technology, and Applications*, **LNCS 10894, https://doi.org/10.1007/978-3-319-93399-3_36**

The original version of this chapter contained an error in the title. The title has been changed from "Human Guidance: Suggesting Walking Pace Under Workload" to "Human Guidance: Suggesting Walking Pace Under Manual and Cognitive Load".

The updated online version of this chapter can be found at
https://doi.org/10.1007/978-3-319-93399-3_36

© Springer International Publishing AG, part of Springer Nature 2018
D. Prattichizzo et al. (Eds.): EuroHaptics 2018, LNCS 10894, p. E1, 2018.
https://doi.org/10.1007/978-3-319-93399-3_60

Author Index

Printed in the United States
By Bookmasters